GENERALSHIP
and the
ART OF THE ADMIRAL:

PERSPECTIVES ON CANADIAN
SENIOR MILITARY LEADERSHIP

GENERALSHIP
and the
ART OF THE ADMIRAL:

PERSPECTIVES ON CANADIAN
SENIOR MILITARY LEADERSHIP

Edited by
Bernd Horn and Stephen J. Harris

Vanwell Publishing Limited
St. Catharines, Ontario

DISCLAIMER

The opinions expressed are those of the authors and do not necessarily represent those of the Department of National Defence.

Copyright© 2001 by Bernd Horn and Stephen J. Harris. All rights reserved. No part of this publication may be reproduced, stored in a retrieval system, or transmitted in any form without written permission of the publisher.

Vanwell Publishing acknowledges the financial support of the Government of Canada through the Book Publishing Industry Development Program for our publishing activities.

Design: Linda Moroz-Irvine

Vanwell Publishing Limited
1 Northrup Crescent
P.O. Box 2131
St. Catharines, Ontario L2R 7S2

Printed in Canada

Canadian Cataloguing in Publication Data

Main entry under title:

Generalship and the art of the admiral : perspectives on Canadian senior military leadership

Includes bibliographical references and index.
ISBN 1-55125-056-X (bound)   ISBN 1-55125-060-8 (pbk)

1. Canada – Armed Forces – Officers. 2. Command of troops.
3. Generals – Canada. 4. Admirals – Canada. I. Horn, Bernd, 1959- .
II. Harris, Stephen John.

UB415.C3G46 2001   355.3'3'0971   C00-932958-7

TABLE OF CONTENTS

Foreword ix

Introduction xi

I Generalship and the Art of the Admiral, A Historic Perspective

Some Reflections on Generalship
through the Ages. 17
Hal Klepak

Canadian Officership: An Overview 37
Bill McAndrew

Canadian Generals in the Second World War:
Better Than Expected. 69
J.L. Granatstein

II The Nature of Higher Command

What is a Commander? 79
Ross Pigeau and Carol McCann

Distinguishing the Concepts of Command,
Leadership and Management. 105
Lieutenant-Colonel Peter Bradley

Military Command in Canada 121
Douglas L. Bland

Officership: A Personal Reflection. 137
General Maurice Baril

Leadership Challenges for the New Century:
A Personal Reflection 147
Lieutenant-General (retired) D.N. Kinsman

A Matter of Trust: Ethics and Self-Regulation
among Canadian Generals 155
Major-General K.G. Penney

Leadership in an Era of Change and Complexity 167
Lieutenant-General George E.C. Macdonald

Command Challenges in the 21st Century 189
Colonel H.J. Marsh

III Operations

A Perspective on Contemporary
Canadian Generalship: Operations in NATO. 213
Lieutenant-General (retired) J.K Dangerfield

The Naval Commander in Joint
Operations in the Gulf War 233
Rear-Admiral D.E. Miller

The Theatre Commander in Conflict Resolution 249
Lieutenant-General Roméo A. Dallaire

Modern Canadian Generalship in Conflict Resolution:
Kosovo as a Case Study. 275
Lieutenant-General R.R. Henault

Kosovo, The Military-Civilian Challenge
and the General's Role 291
Brigadier-General J.H.P.M. Caron

Stressors and Stress on Peacekeeping Operations:
Implications for Operational Level Commanders 301
Colonel Richard A. Hatton

Stress Casualties and the Role of the Commander 319
Terry Copp

IV Civil-Military Relations

The Politics of Defence Decisions
at Century's End. 341
Joel Sokolsky

The Political Skills of a Canadian
General Officer Corps 361
Desmond Morton

Let Canadians Decide. 373
Larry Gordon

The General / Admiral's Role in Public Affairs in
International Operational Theatres 383
Colonel (retired) Ralph Coleman

The Media as a Tool of the
Military Commander 399
Major-General (retired) Lewis W. MacKenzie

A Man (or Woman) for All Seasons:
What the Canadian Public Expects from
Canadian General Officers 409
David Bercuson

Public Expectations of the General Officer Corps. 423
General (retired) Ramsey Withers

V The Functional Roles of Generalship

Generalship and Defence Program Management 437
Major-General D.L. Dempster

The Flag and General Officer as a Resource Manager. . . . 465
Vice-Admiral Gary L. Garnett

Contemporary Canadian Generalship and the
Art of the Admiral: The Importance of Intellectualism
in the General Officer Corps. 481
Lieutenant-General (retired) Robert Morton

Intellectualism in the General Officer Corps 491
Brigadier-General (retired) W. Don Mcnamara

Strategic Thinking General / Flag Officers:
The Role of Education 507
Brigadier-General Ken C. Hague

The General as a Trainer. 521
Brigadier-General (retired) Ernest B. Beno

Index. 553

ACKNOWLEDGEMENTS

ANY PROJECT OF THIS MAGNITUDE owes its existence to a multitude of people. Initially, we wish to thank Lieutenant-General Romeo Dallaire and Brigadier-General Charles Lemieux for their support of the idea and its maturation into reality. Their prescience and zealous efforts at reforming the Canadian Officer Corps will surely be seen in the years to come as a defining moment in Canadian military history.

We would be remiss if we did not thank the wide array of contributors who took the time and effort to share their thoughts, experiences and ideas. A special thanks must also go to Lew West, Lieutenant-Colonel Mike Day and Lieutenant-Commander Kevin Johnston for their help and support. We would also be remiss if we did not acknowledge the invaluable contribution of Bernadette Power and Eric Tuttle for their efforts in assisting with the initial formatting of the book as well as helping out with the general administration of the project at large.

Although they are too numerous to mention individually, we would also like to thank collectively the staff of the Directorate of History and Heritage, the National Archives, the Royal Military College of Canada, and the Canadian Forces Photographic Unit Central Negative Library for their stellar cooperation and assistance.

Finally, we would like to thank Angela Dobler and her design team for adding the polish to the original manuscript.

FOREWORD

THIS BOOK, ON GENERALSHIP AND THE ART OF THE ADMIRAL, is a compendium of essays that articulate a uniquely Canadian outlook on this important yet often misunderstood subject. The term generalship, commonly used to refer also to the art of the admiral, is somewhat cryptic and indeterminate. Generals and flag officers are many things. They are commanders of armies and fleets, resource managers, executives and trainers to mention but a few. Clearly, they are an integral element of the leadership component of any society from which they are drawn and which they serve. Needless to say, it is difficult to conceptualize such a wide and diverse range of responsibilities and roles encapsulated into a single term such as generalship.

The renowned British military historian, John Keegan, captured the mystery of generalship in what he referred to as the "mask of command." He believed that commanders not only wear, but also carefully form and shape this mask to reflect the needs and expectations of those they lead in times of peace, crisis or war. This book is an effort to strip away that mask and describe the true essence of Canadian generalship.

The contributors to this volume represent both serving and retired officers, as well as leading academics and scholars in the subject area. I commend all for their contributions, particularly those serving officers who took the time to impart their wisdom. Too often those of us serving in the military are overcome with an impulse to focus exclusively on the daily crises that arise and forget that we have a responsibility to educate, inform and prepare both our internal constituencies as well as the general public. Serving and retired officers possess extensive experience, knowledge and skills. Some have been tested in war-zones and others in general operations at home and abroad. As with our predecessors, many of us have sat back and reviewed our past performances, particularly those rooted in conflict, but have been hesitant, if not negligent, in putting pen to paper in order to express what we learned and share it with those who will follow. Clearly, the thoughtful discourse on the profession of arms is critical for the wellbeing and growth of the military institution and the society it serves.

This book is a valuable source of information for those serving in the armed forces, as well as the general public who may be interested in military matters. It provides a thoughtful and provocative study of the issues of command at the senior-most levels. Simply put, it reveals the challenges and responsibilities of the Canadian General / Flag Officer Corps. To achieve this, the book has been divided into five components. The first affords a historical perspective of Canadian generalship. Part II explores the nature of higher command and reveals both the complexity and difficulties that general / flag officers face. These intricacies are fully exposed in Part III of the book dealing with actual operations from classical Cold War roles in NORAD and NATO, to the Gulf War of 1990 / 1991, and the more recent conflict resolution experience in the Balkans. Part IV delves into the crucial but complicated realm of civil military relations, and the book concludes with the functional roles of generalship. As a whole, the book pulls back the mask of command and furnishes a better understanding of the trials and tribulations of the nation's senior military leaders.

I cannot over-emphasize the significance of this book. The subject of Canadian generalship has for too long been cloaked in mystery and misunderstanding. It has been an enigma that has never been clearly articulated to the nation, let alone its service personnel. This book is but one more example of our ongoing initiatives at reform and transparency. I hope it instigates intellectual thought, reflection, and discussion on the full breadth of Canadian officership, specifically generalship. Duty demands that we open up our profession and nurture critical discourse to ensure the advancement of the Canadian profession of arms.

General J.G.M. Baril
Chief of the Defence Staff

INTRODUCTION

SELF-ANALYSIS IS ALWAYS DIFFICULT. The military, although not alone, is especially known for its conservatism, insularity and reluctance at self-scrutiny. In the late 1950s, author and journalist Pierre Berton wrote *The Comfortable Pew*, a critical examination of the Christian Church's complacency and self-satisfaction. In many ways, the Canadian Forces (CF) were in a similar position of self-satisfaction in the late 1980s. To be sure, there was grumbling about defence budgets that were too small, equipment that was getting old and, in comparison with the 'golden' years of the 1950s (when regular force strength, navy, army, and air force tipped 120,000, all ranks), establishments that left something to be desired.

Yet these years were still something of a 'comfortable' (or at least familiar) pew for the armed forces. You knew where you stood. Although there were signs of strain in the Warsaw Pact, the Cold War continued, and that gave the navy, army, and air force their main *raisons d'êtres*. 4 Brigade remained the army's jewel in the crown, and so long as there were Allied politicians like Helmut Schmidt around, eventually the need to maintain Canada's reputation in NATO would result in at least some new equipment. The NATO commitment sustained the navy too and, combined with NORAD, was the air force's main focus as well. Within the cyclical process of capital procurement and defence spending, at some point in every decade one of the elements was the winner—*Leopard* tanks were followed by CF18 fighter aircraft, and they were followed by patrol frigates. The CF could not claim to be up to date in every respect, but they could still be valued members of the team. And as members of the team, Canada happily left strategic and operational thought to others with more clout. We really didn't have to think for ourselves.

Peacekeeping was also a routine, especially for the army. Units rotated in and out of Cyprus and the Middle-East, taking their turn on various 'green lines' in what were generally predictable deployments. There were surprises from time to time, but nothing earth-shatteringly new, and for the most part the CF took pride (without thinking about it too much) in their reputation as the armed forces with the greatest peacekeeping experience and expertise in the world.

Then came the changes and the shocks. The end of the Cold War and the withdrawal of Canadian Forces from Europe demolished old strategic truths: Canada and the Canadian Forces were going to have to think for themselves about their place in the world. Decidedly non-traditional peacekeeping operations in the Balkans, Rwanda, and worst of all, Somalia produced incidents that equally demolished the old peacekeeping truths and, at the same time, raised questions about moral standards in the Canadian Forces. Further dramatic budget cuts followed, the Department of National Defence (DND) was re-engineered, the regular force grew smaller, and from the perspective of public opinion it seemed that Canadians had lost faith in their armed forces.

That had never happened before. The country may well have taken the armed forces for granted most of the time—and not very seriously most of the rest of the time, at least in peacetime—but never before had there been any indication of such a loss of faith. Initially, the reaction within the Department of National Defence and the Canadian Forces was to circle the wagons, but there were those who understood that the status quo had to change; that like the US Armed Forces after Vietnam, this was a time for professional renewal that went beyond mere organisational change. These individuals saw that there were real lessons to be learned from Somalia, the Balkans, and the Gulf War, and they realised that the way ahead required a fundamental rededication, if not reform, to their profession and to professionalism. They understood that this process required both looking back and looking forward, and that for thoroughgoing change to occur the general officer corps of the next few years had to be in the forefront of that transformation. For it was the generals who had the moral authority to translate written and spoken prescriptions (or hopes) into reality.

Warrior Chiefs: Perspectives on Canadian Military Leaders (Dundurn Press, 2001) and its companion volume, *Generalship and the Art of the Admiral: Perspectives on Canadian Senior Military Leadership* together form part of the process of rededication and reform to the longstanding values of the Canadian military profession by examining the experience of Canadian admirals and generals in war and in peace, with all their commonalities and differences—to help us understand where we have come from and what the Canadian military profession has been—and by looking at the present and the future, to help us better understand where we may be going and how we might arrive there.

In *Warrior Chiefs*, our intent was to commission articles on leaders from the past to discover the good (and sometimes not so good) elements of their experience, and to examine the different styles of leadership to determine their success and suitability in a given context. In *Generalship and the Art of the Admiral* our perspective is somewhat different. This book is divided into five thematic parts. Initially, we look into the past to provide an historic overview of Canadian officership and generalship, but in a very general way. Next, we investigate the nature of higher command. Terms such as leadership, command and generalship are often tossed about with a misplaced, if not misguided, confidence in common understanding of the words themselves. There is an apparent absolutism in their usage. However, these terms have as many definitions as there are those defining them. Moreover, the words are frequently misused and / or misconstrued. This part of the book is intended to address this issue, as well as others that impinge on higher command—specifically, such matters as ethics, self-regulation and coping with change.

The third section of the book explores actual operations and the lessons that can be derived therefrom. Essays by serving and former serving officers range from NORAD and NATO in the Cold War, to Rwanda and the Balkans in the tumultuous post Cold War period.

Next, the book boldly examines civil-military relations in the context of senior military leadership, an area that has not been well understood in the past. Finally, this volume ends with a look at the functional roles and responsibilities of the Canadian Forces generals and flag officers.

At one level we hope that these contributions will stimulate thought and debate about the future of the military profession in this country—not necessarily the specifics of defence policy but rather about what Canadian generalship actually means. It should not be construed as just another promotion with a higher pay scale, but rather entry into the senior leadership cadre of the nation with all the obligations and responsibilities that entails.

The attempt to spark this discourse, in full recognition of the divergence in opinion on many of the subjects broached in this book, is consciously made. We hope that it will be clear that unfettered discussion on these subjects cannot only be tolerated, but should be encouraged. Readers must understand that, without transparency on such issues—a readiness for unselfconscious self-examination—there is no foundation for critical debate, thus no opportunity for improvement and progression as an institution or officer corps. It is this critical debate that will take the armed forces successfully down the unpredictable roads that lie ahead. As Lieutenant-General (retired) R.A. Dallaire so succinctly stated, "never again in ignorance."

I

Generalship
and the
Art of the Admiral

A Historic Perspective

Some Reflections on Generalship Through the Ages

Hal Klepak

Dr. Hal Klepak is a Professor of History at the Royal Military College in Kingston, Ontario.

THERE IS SOMETHING VAGUELY PRETENTIOUS about an academic, even a historian, writing a perspective on generalship or the art of the admiral. While one may spend one's life studying war, or even higher military administration, and a specialist might even spend life studying generalship alone; one is unlikely to have "been there." However often one looks at the subject, one will not have experienced that combination of great danger, enormous responsibility, and need for quick and accurate analysis and decision which, according to both Jomini and Clausewitz, is at the very centre of generalship.

Both those keen students of war felt, however, that the study of military history was not only valuable but also essential for good generalship and even for understanding the art of command. Hence, despite the need for great modesty in approaching the subject, a historian may perhaps do so without too much of a blush on his cheek.

INTRODUCTION

The approach taken here is far from an entirely academic one. The editors of this work have asked for some reflections on the evolution of generalship and the art of the admiral over the ages. That is of course a tall order. What is attempted here is a look at what the ages tell us about generalship in the formal but often useful sense of the dictionary, followed by a quick look at what some major thinkers on the subject have said about the art, finishing off with the longest section, attempting to give some very brief idea of the actual evolution of generalship.

To undertake this last effort, the author will look at the origins of the centrepiece of the general and admiral's art—*strategy*—and see if tracing its key elements in relation to this art and its practitioners, can help us understand the evolution we are studying. In doing so, we will need to keep well to the fore the ancient Greek concept of the *strategos*—the general or admiral, and ideas of what he, and others before and after him, did over many millennia. We shall return to this question after looking at a definition or two, and several thoughts of the masters.

THE DICTIONARY

Dictionaries may be, as the old saw goes, the "great enemies of understanding," but they can also be terribly useful when coming up against a major subject of wide importance. And the *Concise Oxford Dictionary* gives us a fascinating definition for generalship: "office of a general; strategy, military skill; skilful management…" adding in an intriguing way "…tact, diplomacy." It says, in a rather unhelpful manner for our purposes, that the word "general" means "officer next below Field Marshal" and also "officer above rank of colonel," going on to say "commander of army; tactician, strategist."

The *Concise Oxford* is, of course, a British tome so it should not surprise us that "admiralship" is not entirely ignored as it is in some other volumes with pretensions to being real dictionaries. While a bit of work is needed to tease out the definition, it turns out to be "being (an admiral)… status, office, honour… tenure of office, skill (of an admiral)." And an admiral is "commander-in-chief of a country's navy, naval officer of highest rank, commander of fleet or squadron."

SOME WHO OUGHT TO KNOW

This gets us started, of course, but it is not entirely satisfying. It proves important then to go to those scholars (some of whom, unlike this academic, had the honour of holding the rank and exercising the skills of generals and admirals) who have studied the subject most closely. The list of such people is a long one, including some of the most important minds of all ages and regions of the world. For such is the importance of the art of war, the consequences for all of its being handled well or poorly, that it has been central to the evolution of most cultures.

Plato spends much of his time, especially in the *Republic*, discussing security affairs, although he does so with relatively little time spent on generals and their art. Machiavelli's *Art of War* as well as much else in his writing speaks more directly to our subject. So do not only specifically military thinkers like Sun-Tzu, Thucydides, Jomini, Clausewitz, Liddell-Hart, but also more general analysts such as Winston Churchill.

All agree that the choice of commander is of vital importance. Jomini says that if the prince does not have military skills, his most important duty will be the proper choice of a commander of his armies. In this he was following on thinking we see over two millennia earlier in China with Sun-Tzu. Frederick the Great speaks to the difficulty of finding or training a great general:

> To form a perfect general, the courage, fortitude and activity of Charles XII, the penetrating glance and policy of Marlborough, the vast plans and art of Eugene, the stratagems of Luxembourg, the wisdom, order and foresight of Montecuccoli, and the grand art, which Turenne possessed, of seizing the critical moment, should be united. Such a phoenix will with difficulty be engendered.[1]

Jomini gives us, in characteristic style, the successful general's necessary characteristics

> The most essential qualities for a general will always be as follows:— A high moral courage, capacity of great resolution; Secondly, A physical courage which takes no account of danger. His scientific or military acquirements are secondary to the above-mentioned characteristics, though if great they will be valuable auxiliaries…[he will] be perfectly grounded in the principles at the base of the art of war…[although not necessarily] a man of great erudition. A man who is gallant, just, firm, upright, capable of esteeming merit in others instead of being jealous of it, and skilful in making this merit conduce to his own glory, will always be a good general.[2]

Clausewitz takes us to the subject with characteristic thoroughness in *On War*. After reminding us that "war is the realm of danger" and that "therefore courage is the soldier's first requirement," he goes on to state that this courage is of two kinds—physical in the face of danger and moral in the need to accept responsibility.³ Following this with his famous analysis of war as the realm of physical exertion, suffering, and uncertainty; he concludes that therefore "sensitive and discriminating judgment is called for; a skilled intellect to scent out the truth."[4]

This leads him to his even more famous conclusion:

> If the mind is to emerge unscathed from this relentless struggle with the unforeseen, two qualities are indispensable: first, an intellect that, even in the darkest hour, retains some glimmerings of the inner light which leads to the truth; and second, the courage to follow this faint light wherever it may lead. The first of these qualities is described by the French term 'coup d'oeil'; the second is determination.[5]

He praises determination as a means of dispelling doubt, calls for a "strong rather than a brilliant mind" in the commander-in-chief, and considers presence of mind crucial as a result of the dominance of the unexpected in war. The successful senior commander must be quick-thinking in the face of danger, have a high degree of intuition, be a statesman without ceasing to be a general. In short, the commander needs:

> …a sense of unity and a power of judgment raised to a marvelous pitch of vision, which easily grasps and dismisses a thousand remote possibilities which an ordinary mind would labor to identify… blend of brains and temperament…the calm rather than the excitable head.[6]

The demands Jomini and Clausewitz suggest impinge on the work of a great commander are thus daunting indeed. The former raises a point of great importance in recent years. "It may well happen that after a long period of peace, there may not be a single general in Europe who has commanded in chief."[7] Under such circumstances of a long peace, who is in a position to decide who would be best as commander-in-chief? One thinks of the discussions in the United Kingdom as to who should command the task force sent to the Falklands in 1982.

There is little here which would surprise a Sun-Tzu or a Thucydides writing well over two millennia before, and in a context enormously different. Are then the requirements of successful generalship constant over time?

THE EVOLUTION OF GENERALSHIP

We can now return to the discussion of the actual evolution of generalship in the context of strategy, as suggested at the beginning of this chapter. Traditionally, and before modern or total war, strategy was often defined as "the management (or handling) of men and equipment up to the battlefield," tactics being "the management of men and equipment on the battlefield." Thus the general responsible for strategy would be in charge of getting the troops and equipment necessary for the battle's proper conduct to where the battle would take place, and this of course involved assembly, movement, the conduct of the campaign, and the like. Similarly, the admiral's strategy would be those efforts at preparation and planning, movements and operations that led to the naval battle where tactics would take over. In ancient Greece, of course, the strategos responsible for a land campaign at one time might be asked to conduct a naval campaign on the next occasion.

If one is to discuss the evolution of generalship, it is essential to keep in mind, as Martin van Creveld reminds us, that "command cannot be understood in isolation" and must be seen in its relation with technology, intelligence, arms, training, discipline, ethos of war, politics and a host of other factors.[8] The evolution of generalship takes place alongside the evolution of (and occasional revolutions in) technology, armaments and the prevailing ethos of war. The same is true for intelligence and politics. And while it is true that training and discipline do not evolve in the same way, it is nonetheless clear that the conditions for them vary enormously over time, place, and leadership conditions.

If we keep to our definition of strategy, however, we may be able to move some way towards an understanding of what this evolution has been about. Here we take as a given that generalship, and especially the art of the admiral, relate essentially to fighting at significant levels and with substantial planning, preparation, movement, combat complexity, and the like. Thus for our purposes we would not be speaking about tribal warfare, however interesting that might be for other elements of such a study.

The first written work of what can still be called the Western world is the *Iliad* of Homer, and it should not surprise us that it was about war, and included vast images and descriptions of leadership and leaders. But elements of tribal warfare abound. The invasion force attacking Troy is a hodgepodge affair which, while doubtless impressive to the besieged, was terribly divided, ill-disciplined, and held together by a thread. The confusion of chain of command, the divisions of city-state forces, the jealousies and petty intrigues among generals remind us of Napoleon's axiom *"un mauvais général vaut deux bons."* Mercifully for the Greeks, the taking of the city could be made to depend on a ruse.

Our impression of generalship at the time is one of petty bickering and self-importance combined with personal style and courage of a high order. Combat between the actual commanders appears to have been central to battles. This is far from command as we know it today or as it was to evolve in the ancient Mediterranean world in the centuries following the ten years' war for Troy.

Nonetheless, to take our idea of "to the battlefield" and "men and equipment," there clearly was an aristocratic and command function of getting the ships and men to Troy and then handling the tactics, such as they were, once they were there. Logistics may have consisted mostly of raiding neighbouring cities and villages, but this is hardly the story only of the early years of Greece, and can be said of some fighting in our own era as well.

The armies of the Greek city-states later on, especially from the fifth to the third centuries before Christ, look much more modern. A form of conscription, at least of the wealthy, produced small but competent armies with personnel that spent enormous periods of their lives under arms. While there was no formal method for training senior land and naval commanders (the strategos again), their election or appointment, with any number of exceptions, tended to be based on their success in previous campaigns, and thus presumably, at least much of the time, on skill in their craft.

The names of great commanders of this era have come down to us in significant numbers and call out to us for study from works such as Plutarch's. While tactics and equipment were still unimpressive in many senses, several individuals showed themselves to be good tacticians and even excellent strategists. Naval commanders showed great skill in a number of ancient Greek battles. And land commanders were obliged to get their troops to their destination and arrange at least some of the elements of their deployment in ways which would give their phalanx the best chance in the inevitable clash to come on the battlefield.

Towering above these commanders were and are of course, Alexander the Great and his father, Philip of Macedon. It would surely be fair to say that this combination built the army of men and equipment with which they would master first Greece and then most of the known world. Changing the weapons, tactics, deployment, arms, system of discipline, ethos, and structure first of the Macedonian and then the international army Philip and then Alexander commanded, the two added the essential ingredient of leadership of exceptional quality.

Their planning was long-term and detailed. Their intelligence was reasonably good. Their inspiration of their men and their mobilisation of the Macedonian state, then the Greek states, and finally so much of the known world, for their wars was a model for the future. Philip handed his son Alexander an army (and a state) moulded for war. Flexible, still centred on the heavy infantry phalanx but with all manner of auxiliaries providing it balance, Alexander's Macedonian, and then his international force, shattered everything important in its way along all the route to India. But prime responsibility for this rested with his leadership of this army. He was courageous, principled, always leading from the front, and knew his army and its potential like few leaders of a major force before or since. It is probably not too much to say that he became *a*, or even *the* model for most commanders since his day and there are surely few others who can compare with him.

Rome, as in so much else, took the ideas of the Greeks (its military system was in many senses from early days very like the Greek) and the Macedonians which they found to their liking and moulded them to suit their own needs. Roman generalship also emphasized planning, organisation, courage, discipline to an exceptional degree, and was based on an army of great prestige. Leadership remained remarkably personal here as elsewhere in the ancient world and this of course was to have its price in terms of civil wars as the Republic gave way to the Empire and the conscript force became more and more professional and non-Roman in make-up.

Be that as it may, Roman generals had a superb instrument early on, in their legions. And while the navy may have taken much more time to develop, and after Carthage's defeat may have never again dominated imperial thinking, even its development showed Rome's ability to improvise and overcome. And both services' equipment benefited from exposure to a vast part of the world, as well as incorporation of the advances of many other states. War engines and artillery developed as they were not again to do for many centuries afterwards.

These commanders had to command in wars as distant as Scotland and Persia and to move vast distances at rapid speed. Little wonder that their forces developed personal loyalties to them so far from Rome and so often forgotten by the metropolis. Successful commanders saved their soldiers' lives, brought them bounty or pay increases, and led them to victories (often the source for both).

With the fall of Rome, all of this evaporated. And while some modern scholarship has shown that our scorn for Medieval military issues and generalship is sometimes too extreme, when they are compared with the era before the fall of Rome or that arriving with the Renaissance and after, this reaction is not entirely unfounded.

Nonetheless, leadership in the Dark Ages and Medieval times could be exceptional even if many other elements of generalship seem to have tended to atrophy during this period. Except in the Carolingian wars and the Crusades, Western Europe was largely a sorry sight where military developments were concerned. Small states essentially cut off from the Roman heritage made war as best they could with few resources—financial, manpower, technological, or in other areas.

At the same time, they did produce leaders of great courage and individual fighting prowess who, on occasion, proved capable of higher military skills as well. But despite the fame of names such as William the Conqueror, Richard the Lion-Hearted, El Cid, and a host of others, that very reputation tends to emphasize a return to the almost Iliad-like importance of the individual commander. He, at the head of a few other men of war (knights now rather than the princes of Greece and Troy) and a host of lesser sorts, made war as best he could and was closely tied to principles of personal honour and glory shared by his ancient forebear.

The Renaissance was over time, of course, going to change all that. In military terms as well, there was "rebirth" with Europeans again able to see how the ancients made war. Machiavelli's famous *The Art of War* in 1521 studied in detail the armies of Rome at the height of its power (especially Vegetius' *De Re Militari*) to find the secrets of the ancestors' stupendous success story. The modern Western world began to put significant resources, especially money, into the hands of statesmen, first in Italy and then in the new national states. At first such money tended to go on the mercenaries so in vogue in European armies desperate for troops who actually knew their *métier*.

Machiavelli was only one of several thinkers who pointed out the obvious weaknesses of military forces whose profit margins only increased if wars continued indefinitely rather than were won immediately by one's own employer. Princes gradually saw the advantages of having armies at least dominated by soldiers genuinely loyal to them and their state. Modern nationalism may have been some way away still, but elements of it were increasingly visible and the cohesion of armies and navies was not only a result, but also a factor in the creation of such nationalisms.

Technology made enormous advances across the board but nowhere more dramatically than in armed forces. Artillery became cheaper and easier to make, less heavy and thus more manoeuvrable. Metallurgical advances also helped with cheaper and faster production of other arms, including firearms. Navigation steadily improved as did ship construction and design.

Generals and admirals thus began to have at their command military instruments on a scale not seen in the West since before the fall of Rome over a millennium before. And while military modernization was in many senses slow, it was relatively steady and stimulated by conflicts spurred by the founding of modern states and their competition for territory, power and influence. Aristocracies born in the Middle Ages expected to maintain, and to a great degree, did maintain their leadership in the military field, as they felt they had the duty, right, and honour to do.

Command went generally to those of high birth, and dynastic issues ensured that royal families as well were strikingly represented among the ranks of senior commanders. Too much was at stake for crowned heads to quickly relinquish military command to others. That would take longer and would only be completed long after professional militaries, or at least professional officer corps, became the rule. As late as the nineteenth century, Jomini could still claim that the best military leader would be a prince heading his own army and thus combining in one person both source and executor of national strategic thinking. Despite differing on many other issues, Clausewitz was not far from the same traditional analysis.

The Enlightenment brought further progress in the sense of small professional armies led by increasingly professional officers. European armies became more and more alike. Based on long-service soldiers, highly (and often ferociously) disciplined, with similar arms, training, and tactics, these armies depended more than those of many generations on the quality of their leadership. It is not surprising to find that generals, even those with no royal connections of note, came now to be more respected, more carefully chosen, more famous for their strategies, and probably better compensated for their victories.

If the Thirty Years' War of 1618–48 brought us some names such as Gustavus Adolphus and Wallenstein, the limited wars of the century and a half until 1792 brought us dozens of the likes of Eugene, Frederick, Marlborough, Montecuccoli, Peter the Great, Saxe, Turenne, and even Wolfe and Montcalm. The concepts of generalship and strategy were linked again and in more dramatic fashion than perhaps ever before. And if the Spanish Armada and other great sixteenth century naval campaigns brought us individual admirals' names like Barbarossa, Drake and Raleigh, true seamen all; by the eighteenth century there were literally dozens like Anson, Boscawen, Collingwood, Hawke, Howe, Jervis, Rodney, Tourville, and the young Nelson—recognisably *professional* naval officers, and admirals, to a man.

Armies were complex machines now, requiring massive logistics to keep them moving and fighting and doing so without living off the land, a practice unthinkable in this new kind of warfare. The enemy commander was a professional man of war in most cases, even if he still came from the ranks of the aristocracy. Planning became critical and wars of manoeuvre, aimed at cutting the enemy off from his supplies, required detailed preparation at all levels. Military academies were founded to ensure well-trained officers were available. And while the stakes in such limited wars were indeed usually limited, the costs of maintaining armies were high, and of losing them higher still. All elements pointed to more emphasis being placed on the general who would not only get his army to the battlefield but also lead it in the fight. Military administration became part of the stuff of generalship at a level rarely seen in the past.

Navies were also expensive and required even more specialisation. It took time and money to produce a qualified soldier capable of standing up to the rigours of campaign and especially the battlefield itself. But it took longer still, and more money still, to produce the sailor trained in the complex navigation and ship-working of the era. And at least for Britain, while its relatively small and inefficient army could lose a major battle but the kingdom survive and even prosper, the same could not be said of war at sea. Defeat at sea could spell almost instant disaster for the island state. This fact was not lost on the British—as Admiral Mahan makes so clear—except on rare, and always dangerous, occasions.[9] Professional admirals, that is commanders of formations of ships well schooled in their handling, were essential. Training and experience were vital for such a goal.

THE FRENCH REVOLUTION AND NAPOLEON

Then came Napoleon as if to remind us that all the training in the world does not make a great general. It can help. Military history can help too, giving as it does depth to the study of war that a general must undertake if he takes his job seriously. But they are not enough. For a great general to be *great*, there must be genius. Here again Jomini and Clausewitz are of one accord. And if their interest in him doubtless reflects their own era, their own "role in his downfall" as one might have said in the 1970s, and their own immediate personal and national concerns; generations of analysts and soldiers since them have agreed with their assessment of him as a "genius" and a "meteor" where the darkness of war is involved.

In ways reminiscent of Alexander, Napoleon took the army of his "father" (the Revolution rather than Philip of Macedon in this case) and transformed it through his own leadership and genius. The *levée en masse* had given Paris a vast supply of manpower, necessary in a Europe where nearly everyone was out to smash France. The Revolutionary government had shown itself to be a master of the use of propaganda, fiscal policy, foreign intrigue and invasion, and much else to provide that army with much of what it needed to make war against the rest of Europe—a sense of identity, ideological and nationalist motivation, numbers, funds, freedom to live off the land, and much else. But only a man of genius could transform that army into a fully victorious one.

Through an exceptional understanding and handling of the principles of war, and through a leadership style marked by trickery but mastery, Napoleon made the instrument he inherited from Revolutionary France his own. Tactics were designed to suit its strengths (élan, speed, numbers, ability to concentrate, relative lack of desertions, etc.) as well as its weaknesses (lack of discipline in younger conscripts, rejection by local populations, etc.). Strategies were sought which did the same.

The mass column was developed greatly from its revolutionary model. Artillery was added in quantities that took advantage of France's strengths in that field while aiding in reassuring the conscript that all was well on the battlefield. The cavalry arm was perfected. Foreign contingents were brought in often and with specialist forces retained by the Imperial Army for their advantages and the added flexibility they brought (the Polish Lancers are perhaps the best known example of this). Like Alexander's, the army became an international one not only through conquest (Belgians, Danes, Dutchmen, all manner of Germans and Italians, Spaniards, etc.) but also through the voluntary incorporation of units such as the Mamelukes or some Swiss regiments.

Little technical improvement was necessary or readily available. What was there was leadership and genius in the making of war. And that combination—army and leadership—gave France the most extraordinary series of victories it, or any other European state, had ever known, or was to know in the future. Even the early years of *blitzkrieg* offer no parallels.

Warfare after Napoleon was to be dominated by his shadow, despite his eventual defeat and exile. Jomini may have placed the emphasis on how to defeat his kind if it ever rose again. And Clausewitz may have exaggerated the speed with which his way of making war would become the norm. But both agreed that he was the phenomenon itself of a genius of war.

Future generals took him as their model just as the successors to Alexander remained fascinated by his figure for centuries, and for similar reasons. Each had moulded an army to suit himself and a strategy and tactics to suit that army.

With Napoleon's defeat, Europe returned in many senses to the military world it had known before the Revolution. Small professional armies again prevailed in a continent whose rulers had no intention of arming the masses again. Limited wars for limited objectives again became the rule with a tacit agreement that this was to be the case, a common feature of all foreign policies.

The United States Civil War (1861-65) and the Franco-Prussian War (1870-1) gave the lie, however, to hopes that limited conflicts would remain the rule. The stakes involved were, or became, so great in these wars that it proved impossible to retain them as limited affairs. Instead, both conflicts saw conscription return, mass armies deploy again, and the utter defeat of the enemy (as well as his humiliation) become standard practice. Mounting casualty figures made moderation of policy difficult (*démocratie oblige*) if not impossible, laying the groundwork for revanchism and hatred.

In addition, these wars both benefited from and stimulated the Industrial Revolution then in full swing, and many examples of industry and inventiveness turning their eye to war can be found, all making the killing of men more effective. Machine guns appeared as did rapid-fire (and now breech-loading) rifles and artillery. Railways carried men farther and more rapidly than could have been imagined before. The telegraph sent them orders instantly. And navies increasingly moved ships propelled by messy coal-produced steam rather than nature's wind, and wrapped in armour rather than the wooden walls of Athens (or indeed Britain). When added to the stakes of modern wars, these new inventions made total war more likely and more likely to be horrific.

Generalship and the art of the admiral had little choice but to respond to these challenges, like them or not. As a rule, generals did not like them. Admirals perhaps did so even less. This "revolution in military affairs" could simply not be denied. But it could be delayed by a combination of military conservatism and a return to smaller wars, this time largely colonial ones, in the years up to the First World War. And while some of these, such as the Boer War of 1899-1902 or the Russo-Japanese of 1904-5 could hardly be considered small, they were far away from Europe and seen as somehow not fully part and parcel of that continent's military affairs.

When machine guns, quick-firing artillery and rifles, and so much more of the modern panoply of war dominated the battlefields of those two conflicts, not to mention others in the colonies, headquarters in Europe took note. But they failed to fully incorporate what the long trench lines in North Asia or the dismally slow infantry advances of South Africa meant for the future of European warfare. Only the First World War, and to some extent preparations for its outbreak, forced dramatic change in military perceptions of strategy and tactics, and of the generalship required to apply them. In many fields, such as the role of the new aeroplane, other countries' senior officers joined their French colleagues in considering *tout ça c'est du sport*.

Navies tended to trade sail for coal very slowly as they did wood for armour. The Nelson tradition of the great sea combat leading to decisive victory remained strong despite the long-standing and less dramatic demands of *Pax Britannica*. Army commanders reduced the role of the bayonet, élan, and the professional soldier himself with great reluctance, wincing at the idea of mass armies, machines, the decline of the horse, and so much else.

The world war ended most of that. Four years and more of slaughter and the crippling of Europe in so many ways made commanders adjust when least they wished to do so. The war remade war. By the end of it air forces were bombing civilian targets as nearly a matter of course, unrestricted submarine warfare had shattered many of the most sacred of naval and maritime traditions, and army casualty rates (especially among officers) had bludgeoned the social and political structure of European civilization.

Generals handled millions of men across hundreds and even thousands of kilometres of distance and fronts. War dragged on in the trenches of the Western Front or the relatively free movement of the Eastern, but in all cases machines began to demand their part in conflict. The aircraft, the tank, and the submarine were merely the most dramatic of these. It could be said that such was the horror and endlessness of trench warfare that from now on generals and other strategic thinkers would aim to bypass it or overcome it through original ideas. Advance through wire, machine gun fire, rapid artillery fire, and the rest seemed impossible.

The attempts to break out were novel. Giulio Douhet, one general, would propose air power as the way out. Concentrate the national defence in the air, with bombardment of the enemy's capability to make war as his "centre of gravity" and hence your target, and you will not have to face the trenches the next time. Guderian, another general, argued that the solution was still on the land. One should strike not to destroy the enemy physically but rather to confuse, terrorise, paralyse him. This required armoured forces that could produce speed, surprise, and shock effect. The tank had shown the way forward. Even the admirals of defeated navies, and some victorious ones, could argue for a new way. If the Royal Navy ruled the surface of the seas, go below them and strike at the enemy through his merchant marine with the submarine. Starve him of the sinews of war or even starve him *tout court*.

The stakes of war were now so high that the pressure was on generals and admirals as rarely before in recent centuries. For modern war was no longer dynastic and was certainly not "limited." The stakes were now to be survival itself; as powers, as nations, as economies, and as ideological systems. And science was to be put to work to achieve victory as never before, largely because these stakes were so high. "Communist" ideas like income tax could be justified by the need to make war and survive. Bringing women into the labour force, whatever the social costs, could be justified in the same way, as could the abandonment of civilized traditions in war which, while often shunted aside, had still served to limit its horrors to some extent in the past. Little wonder then that nuclear weapons would be born in the next war as would the mass bombing of cities, even more unrestricted submarine warfare (and not just by Germany), and much else.

Generals in the Second World War were often of a very different breed from their First World War predecessors. They had usually served in the trenches themselves and had resented the staff officers at the rear perhaps even more than the rank and file. They wanted to be seen to be forward with the troops, approachable, and open to new ideas. Armoured formations belied the traditional breakdown of units into infantry, cavalry and artillery. Amphibious operations became commonplace, if far from easy, at least for the Allies. Navy-army-air cooperation was simply a must for victory. Generals as low as brigadiers were now truly brigadier-generals, having more "general forces" under their command than was usually the case in the past. Reflected already in World War One, this became virtually the rule in World War Two.

At the same time, coalition warfare also became the rule, at least for the Allies. While the Axis powers' ability to coordinate their efforts must be viewed as abysmal, the Allies, facing Germany, could afford no such luxury. Much as they disliked it, the British and the Americans would have to work together. It was not true that the problematical V-1 was the "ideal US weapon," killing, as it did, Nazis on departure and Limies on arrival. The British Commonwealth could not win the war without the United States, and the latter power, for all its strength, could not, at least at affordable cost, do so without Britain. And both would have to accept that the Soviet Union was an essential ally in the war, whatever their thoughts about "long spoons" when dealing with that enigmatic power.

Generals and admirals would have to get used to working, not only with one another, but with foreign counterparts. This seemed easier for the navy perhaps because, as the quip goes, in the end all navies are British. But even then it was hardly a walk in the park. For the army, it was difficult indeed. The difficulties of Patton and Montgomery are merely part of the intricate story of Anglo-American general officers' mutual distrust during the war.

Be that as it may, in large part they managed. The alliance with the Soviets held, perhaps because it simply had to. Anglo-American bickering remained just that and that central pillar of the alliance against Hitler finally worked remarkably well when compared with so much else in the history of coalition warfare. This must in part be credited to generals in both countries who saw the need for a joint approach even if they did not do so happily.

Thus we had in the Second World War, at least at senior ranks, a more political general than in recent years. But even here it would be easy to exaggerate.

Coalition warfare builds political sensitivity in generals if success is to be achieved. And coalition warfare is actually the norm in the West, even if it is not traditionally seen as such by the United States.

Since the war, the US has had to face this fact in its dealings with the world, although it has done so in its own way. The US came out of the Second World War as the undisputed power on the world scene. It is now clear to what extent the USSR was a superpower *par courtoisie* even though this remark requires *nuance*. It may not have been in the league with the US but it did from early on have nuclear weapons.

Nonetheless, since 1945 the US has been obliged, outside its own hemisphere at least, to frequently engage in coalition warfare. Indeed, such war-making became the norm. Only the Vietnam War, again with *nuance*, was different. The Korean War was a US-led United Nations coalition affair.

More recently, both the Persian Gulf War of 1991 and the more recent conflict over Kossovo were coalition wars. Indeed, even in the Americas, the US has shown a strong preference for Organisation of American States or other multinational collaboration (and legitimization) for its military actions in the hemisphere, in the Dominican Republic in 1965, Grenada in 1983, Panama in 1989, and Haiti in 1995. And while this has not always been forthcoming or very impressive, the felt need was there in Washington.

Even the Vietnam War was fought with a major ally in Saigon itself, not to mention the eventual contingents of troops sent by Australia, New Zealand, Korea, etc. What has been different is the extent to which such coalition warfare really placed restraints on the US ability to decide policy and act virtually alone and hence the need for its generals and admirals to work in a truly international coalition context or merely in one hoping to appear as such to the world at large. This has of course varied from war to war but it must be said that there has been a tendency for the conflicts to be conducted in more of an *imperial* than a true coalition tradition.

The reverse of this coin is that other countries' generals and admirals have been obliged to become more coalition-minded (a cynic would say colonial-minded) since their own abilities to conduct other kinds of wars have waned. None of what still might be called the great powers has fought a *major* war by itself for many decades. Suez was a coalition affair, although a limited one, in 1956. Otherwise, the British and French, with the notable, and totally surprising, exception of the Falklands War of 1982, have been in the business of coalition wars exclusively since the Boer War in one case, and the Franco-Prussian in the other. Otherwise, their wars have all been essentially colonial. The

Russians have been involved in basically "near-home" conflicts for many years and have not fought anyone alone since (take your pick) either the war with Poland during the USSR's own civil war, or the Russo-Japanese War. And China has not fought anyone entirely alone since facing various European powers (and Japan) in the nineteenth century.

Thus generals and admirals of lesser states than the US have long been accustomed to coalition warfare and the need to be politically sensitive at the inter-state level. The armed forces of the British dominions may indeed have had the most experience in the sense that they had, long before losing that status and coming into the US-dominated world, been accustomed to alliance warfare as part of the British Empire and then Commonwealth. Generals and admirals from these countries had always had to ponder wider imperial considerations when thinking about national defence. Political issues were always close to hand. And while this is doubtless true of all such officers, those from the dominions would have had such thinking all too clear from early on in their careers. Experience with peacekeeping operations in more recent decades can only have heightened this long-term experience, especially for armed forces such as those of Canada.

Politics are hardly the only element increasingly impinging on the military senior officer's normal duties. For technology has not stood still since the Second World War; neither has social change. Armed forces personnel are no longer the same as those faced by generals and admirals only a few short decades ago. And the technology they handle has been subject to the speeding up of the revolution which began almost two centuries ago, and this to such an extent that now one speaks of another "revolution in military affairs."

To take the social side first, Western armed forces are in some senses almost unrecognisable when compared with their traditional counterparts. In most of our countries, women have taken on all manner of roles in military affairs, many of which would have been literally unthinkable thirty years ago. Sexual preference matters which would have been thought central still at that time are no longer an issue in any NATO country with the exception of the United States and even there things are doubtless soon to come into line with the rest of the West. The rights of personnel have come to dominate questions of their duties with grievance procedures overwhelmed in many countries. Expectations of serving members of armed forces are higher than at any time in history.

At the same time there is a steady return to professional forces after the long years of Clausewitzian "mass." Quality rather than quantity is again the byword in most Western and many other countries not only as a result of the reduced threat accompanying victory in the Cold War but also because increasingly sophisticated tactics, equipment and weaponry seem to call for full-time career personnel to work them. All NATO countries have at least considered the consequences of all-professional forces. The traditionally well-disposed countries of Canada and the United Kingdom were first joined by the United States as the Vietnam War ended, and then after the Cold War by a number of others. Even France, with its most powerful *levée en masse* tradition, is joining the trend. Thus in many countries generals, and to a lesser extent admirals, accustomed to conscript forces, are returning to their earlier traditions, which they have not experienced for what is often centuries. Long-service personnel produce other kinds of demands from senior officers, and of course many advantages as well.

Links between these issues and technology do not stop with those related to professional forces. Equipment and weapons are becoming more sophisticated at a dizzying pace and nowhere is this more evident than in elements related to command and control. Generals and admirals must assess a greater amount and complexity of information than their predecessors could ever have imagined. And while this obviously has its positive side, it also has the negative one of potentially overwhelming the commander and his ability to digest such information and act on it. A brigade commander now not only has infantry, armour and artillery but also signals, engineers, air assets, complex service battalions, and more. His ability to call on still other elements is vast. Senior headquarters', and heads of governments' ability to call on him seem equally great.

It seems just as true that modern armed forces appear to move, at least during peacetime, through masses of paperwork. The cry is worldwide that one is becoming overwhelmed by bureaucracy, that initiative is being held back, that commanders spend more time on minor administrative issues than they do on the major matters of their profession. Actually, the complaint is an old one going back probably to the organization of modern armies during the late Renaissance and Enlightenment, and seemingly to Rome itself. But there can be little doubt that the modern age, its accounting practices, and the sheer complexities of armed forces and the jobs they have to do, have burdened commanders with greater administrative responsibilities than at any time before. Successful commanders have learned to organize their own, and their staffs' time, with care so as to avoid going under in the face of this problem.

WHAT DOES THIS HISTORICAL PERSPECTIVE GIVE US?

Military history, and especially the study of military leadership, is an extraordinary field. It deals with the life and death of nations and many other political groupings, as well as their struggles to defend themselves or attack others. It is important as a result of the subject matter itself, and of the vital nature of the job of getting it right in wartime. Generalship is at the heart of it. It is essential that generals understand just how important their job is, as has been said by virtually all great analysts of war since Sun Tzu himself.

A historical perspective on generalship shows us a number of things about the art of war and its application at the highest level. Generalship is about command and the administration that allows command to prosper in combat. It is about responsibility of the utmost importance to the state and its wellbeing. It is about loyalty. And it is about flexibility.

The last of these deserves some further comment. As we have quickly reviewed definitions, then the perceptions of experts, and finally the brief overview of actual experience of generalship, we have seen that command at the highest level has changed greatly over time. And those changes have not even been linear. Generalship has had to react to often rapidly-changing technologies, political circumstances at home and abroad, social evolution and revolution, and military contexts of often bewildering complexity.

Flexibility, tempered by knowledge, in this context must be a mark of successful generalship. It must not lead to soft thinking but it must guide the general or admiral to, in modern terms, not fight change but rather manage it. The modern senior commander must be able to leap, as in the past, from peace to war, but now must also be able to fit into all manner of grey situations short of the latter but far from the former. He has never been so easily reached by politicians anxious for an easy answer or a quick solution to a complex problem. His own military superiors have access to him with a speed and facility never known before. All this can be unnerving, to say the least. Only a flexible mind can hope to face such challenges and not lose control.

As we have seen, however, flexibility has been the mark of successful generals in the past as well and should not surprise us as being central today. Alexander and Napoleon knew they had to mould and re-mould their armies to meet the changing circumstances they faced with grim regularity. Nelson knew that turning a blind eye to superiors' orders was on occasion necessary in the ever-changing conditions of battle. And some air commanders knew that a shift from terror bombing of cities in the Second World War to targets more central to German industrial production was vital in bringing about a speedy end to the war.

Flexibility then has always been a trademark of a successful general or admiral. The difference today may well be that such flexibility tends to be needed more often, and with greater speed, than in the past, and seems to be as required in peacetime as in time of war.

In addition, a final word should be said about courage. In Lord Moran's exquisite little book *The Anatomy of Courage*, he reminds us of much of what Clausewitz and of course others have said about this quality in the past.[10] The general and admiral of today is often farther from physical danger than ever in history. He is more likely to be surrounded by whirring machines and racing aides-de-camp than to be directing personally a campaign with his troops about him. The chances that he will be shot at are slim indeed. Thus his courage is less often of the heroic stamp to which films and books have made us accustomed, and which is part and parcel of military history.[11]

Instead, his courage is of a different kind, the sort that involves the constant doing of one's duty and the equally constant acceptance of responsibility. This often unremarked-upon courage which has the general showing unquestioned loyalty down the chain of command as well as up it, which has him take the difficult decision when needed and not always the one that is easier for him, and the one which has those higher headquarters (and politicians) being told what they must hear rather than what they want to hear about difficult situations. The days of distance and poor communications making these problems easier are long behind us. Instead, no modern commander can fail to recognise the daily nature of the requirement for this sort of courage.

CONCLUSIONS

The key qualities of good generalship may well have varied somewhat over the centuries and even among the continents. Many principles of effective command at the highest level, however, have not changed very much after all, as we have seen. The principles of war remain remarkably steady as do the principles of command, even if the latter may be more difficult to put into a few phrases or words.

Generalship has asked for the greatest commitment from those who have wished to exercise it well. It has required deep study of the military profession, military history, current tactics and strategy, the nature of soldiers and sailors and now airmen, politics and much else. It has required an instinct for self-sacrifice, often a good measure of personal ambition (although this we like less to talk about), learning from one's experience, and a host of other qualities and traits.

It still requires all of these, and more. The modern member of the armed forces does not give his loyalty easily. He or she is sceptical to a degree that with reason worries many observers. Probably better educated than any of his or her predecessors throughout the ages, such people expect to be well led, have their lives valued, and their professionalism appreciated. It is simply silly to suggest that these personnel are easy to command. They are anything but. However, once they give their confidence to a commander, their service can be second to none and produce exceptional results.

The threats to good generalship are everywhere. Small-minded politicians unknowing or uncaring about defence constitute the bane of existence of dedicated generals. One's seniors may value their careers too much and the truth too little. Bureaucratic battles may obscure those that really matter. Loyalty *up* may be only too visible while its counterpart *down* may seem nearly non-existent. Advancement may appear to have little to do with merit. But none of this is new, only appearing in perhaps occasionally different forms today.

Such threats must be overcome, as in the past. And the battle is not of one day but of every day in the life of a commander, at whatever his level although to varying degrees.

Military history, and history itself, teaches us that the effective general or admiral is a leader in the full sense of the word. He can get people to do things they would not normally be willing to do, and to do them well, and he does this at the highest level of the state's activities—those ensuring its survival. In this era as in the past this is not easy. It is doubtless becoming harder in some senses, but easier in others. Knowledge and love of the profession of arms and its practitioners, added to flexibility, and mixed with courage would seem to have been the best recipe for success in the past. There is reason to suspect it still is.

NOTES

1. Jay Luvaas, *Frederick the Great on the Art of War* (New York: The Free Press, 1966), 360.
2. Antoine de Jomini, *The Art of War* (New York: Lippincott, 1862), 55-6.
3. Carl von Clausewitz, *On War*, edited by Michael Howard and Peter Paret (Princeton: Princeton University Press, 1976), 101.
4. Idem.
5. Ibid, 102.
6. Ibid, 111-112.
7. Jomini, 54-5.
8. Martin van Creveld, *Command in War* (Cambridge, Massachusetts: Harvard University Press, 1985), 261.
9. Alfred Tahyer Mahan, *The Influence of Seapower upon History* (New York: Sagamore, 1957), 43-59.
10. Lord Moran, *The Anatomy of Courage* (London: Constable), 1946.
11. See John Keegan, *The Mask of Command* (London: Jonathan Cape, 1987), 9-11.

Canadian Officership: An Overview

Bill McAndrew

Dr. Bill McAndrew is a retired Military Historian from the DND Directorate of History and Heritage.

INTRODUCTION

> *The general must know how to get his men their rations and every other kind of stores needed for war. He must have imagination to originate plans, practical sense and energy to carry them through. He must be observant, untiring, shrewd; kindly and cruel; simple and crafty; a watchman and a robber; lavish and miserly; generous and stingy; rash and conservative. All these and many other qualities, natural and acquired, he must have. He should also, as a matter of course, know his tactics; for a disorderly mob is no more an army than a heap of building materials is a house.*
>
> Socrates

Beneath that self-effacing, laid back cover Canadian soldiers I knew had a toughness I never sensed in talking to American servicemen of any war. Also if they had any demons lurking within about killing Germans they have kept it well hidden from me. I have always been uncomfortable, if not downright suspicious, of the "John Wayne, Top Gun" American style, or dare I call it "macho" style? Don't tell me how tough you are; show me out there where the shells are falling that you have the right stuff.

Cameron Highlanders of Ottawa, 1942-46
Corporal Dixon Raymond, US citizen

DESPITE MARKED VARIATIONS IN TECHNIQUES of soldiering over the centuries, in vastly different societies, armies have shared certain general conceptions about their officers. In return for special privileges and conditions of service, an officer has been expected to accept and exercise special, sometimes exceptional, duties and responsibilities. For their responsible execution he/she is held accountable. Implicitly, at least, an officer is assumed to be a leader; to have whatever it is that persuades others to follow. Ideally one will display qualities of character like honesty, integrity, moral courage, responsibility, loyalty up and down, determination, steadfastness, among others. Officers reflect the societies that make them, and Canadians have participated in the age-old attempts to reconcile the contradictions of Socrates' ideal general, and produce officers fit to command the soldiers Corporal Raymond describes.

THE FIRST 300 YEARS

The first officers in Canada, members of French Imperial regiments sent to colonize North America, were representative of those in seventeenth and eighteenth-century European armies that evolved from roving mercenary bands, that themselves had emerged from feudal, knightly crusades. Change was gradual but, as Michael Howard has written:

> By the eighteenth century European wars were being conducted by professional armed forces of a kind with which we would be familiar today. Their officers were not primarily members of a warrior caste fighting from a concept of honour or of feudal obligation; nor were they contractors doing a job for anyone who could pay them. They were servants of the state who were guaranteed regular employment, regular wages, and career prospects and who dedicated themselves to the service of the state, or rather of their "country" (to use a more emotive term) come peace, come war. It was only with

the development of these full-time professionals that it became possible to draw any clear distinction between the "military" and the "civilian" elements in society.[1]

With some exceptions, French officers came from the minor nobility, defined by birth and property. Unsurprisingly, New France mirrored that image. Within decades Canadians were being chosen "from families of Canadian gentlemen" to raise militia companies in their communities. In time, the sons of landowners and social leaders evolved into a colonial military élite. In 1683, all officers were French. Within a decade one-quarter were Canadian-born, and a generation later three-quarters were Canadian. The pattern was extended after the Conquest when British regular regiments replaced their French counterparts. British units were supplemented, gradually and not always enthusiastically, by community-based militias officered by those in the colonial gentry with the right political connections. Class and property distinctions more than military merit determined place in the militia hierarchy.[2]

The withdrawal of British regiments, the creation of a small permanent force, and the founding of the Royal Military College in the late nineteenth century nudged Canada's military towards professionalism, but it was hesitant at best. In what has been a staple theme in Canadian affairs, there was precious little social and political support for a substantial military establishment that spent a good deal of money for no apparent purpose. After all, the mythology proclaimed it had been an enthusiastic and untrained militia that defended the country from the Americans in 1812, stymied two western rebellions, and helped defend the Empire in South Africa at the end of the century. It was generally assumed, especially by themselves, that colonial gentlemen, officers by inclination and social position, were natural leaders requiring little specific preparation for military life and war. Military command was simply an extension of their community leadership.

Formal standards of officership at the beginning of the twentieth century were prescribed in *King's Regulations and Orders for the Canadian Militia* issued in 1910 (revised in 1926). Its general injunctions are not unlike those in effect at the end of the century. An officer was "at all times responsible for the maintenance of good order and the rules and discipline of the service; he is to afford the utmost aid and support to the C.O. It is his duty to notice, repress and instantly report, any negligence whether the offenders do or do not belong to his particular unit." Commanding officers had the responsibility "not only to enforce by command, but to encourage by example the energetic discharge of duty." Officers had to observe high standards of personal behaviour: "by advice and by timely intervention, endeavour to promote a good understanding and to prevent disputes." Tendencies towards gambling, drinking, practical joking "or extravagance, were to be discouraged." They were to "maintain at all times that courtesy towards each other which is calculated to perpetuate friendly and social relations between them and create an 'esprit de corps.'" Commanding officers were also to "impress upon all under [their] command the propriety of courtesy in intercourse with all ranks and classes of society, and should particularly caution them to pay deference and respect to civil authorities."

THE FIRST WORLD WAR: A HIGHLAND CALL TO ARMS

These were the standards of conduct, responsibilities, and behaviour expected of officers at the onset of the First World War—that momentous collision between attitudes and brutal technological realities that challenged all peacetime assumptions. Its nature was hardly foreseen when, in 1914, the Minister of Militia, Sam Hughes, issued a "highland call to arms" to anyone who wished to join up for the grand crusade.[3] A South African war veteran and the country's foremost militiaman, Hughes held the tiny Permanent Force in great contempt. Its officers, mere "bar-room loafers" with no better prospects, failed to live up to their professional and personal standards, and he had convinced himself that any good Canadian could serve well, either as soldier or officer, without undue preparation. Hughes personally chose the officers for the first two contingents sent overseas. Standards for most were confined to compatibility with the Minister's views and a correct political allegiance. Only nine of forty-four senior appointments were permanent officers and almost half of combatant officers had not even the most modest qualifications for their jobs.

The principal requirement of an officer in the Canadian Expeditionary Force (CEF) was not unlike that of ancient times[4]—sacrificial courage—and selection criteria were sketchy at best. An individual had to be eighteen years of age; be at least five feet four inches tall with a chest measurement of thirty-three inches; have a militia commission and the approval of a militia commanding officer. It helped materially if he had influential family, social, and political connections. For infantry officers, attendance at a training establishment for one month qualified as a lieutenant, two months made a captain, and three a major. Artillery and engineer officers required more. Most of the officers were middle-class individuals from settled parts rather than frontiersmen of popular image. One study of western Canadian battalions found among a sample of 369 officers that 100 had backgrounds in commerce; 87 in the professions; 72 from finance; 22 from trades; 26 were students; 20 were farmers. Just 3 had previous military connections of some sort. More than one-third was British born, and another third were from Ontario. Professionalism and military knowledge were not required. They could easily learn soldiering, and officering, on the job. Some did, creditably; others did not, and lost an untold number of their soldiers' lives.[5]

Once deployed in France the Canadian Expeditionary Force found an additional source of officers in its own ranks. Soldiers were selected and sent to newly formed officer training schools, but selection remained personal and random. Family and social background counted as much or more than merit—a colonial equivalent to having the proper accent. In any case, selection to officer status was a mixed blessing that some declined. In a military culture not far removed in values from those prevalent in eighteenth century Europe an officer was expected to lead, and die, by example in order to motivate his soldiers to do likewise. This presented singular challenges at a time when traditional, almost feudal attitudes encountered the reality of modern, technological, bureaucratic warfare. War meant the doctrine of the offensive: but against machine guns, barbed wire, and in-depth trench systems. For his expected sacrifice, an officer's life was incontestably less arduous than a soldier's. He ate better, lived better, and did less physical labour. His quarterly ten days' British leave contrasted with his soldiers' ten annual days.

Did they perform their part of the exchange well? Some did, others did not. Desmond Morton and Stephen Harris, the historians who have looked most closely at the matter, concluded that officers were not the strongest element in the CEF. Anecdotal evidence suggests that soldiers respected officers who were courageous, considerate, honest, humane, responsible, had some military skill, and displayed a measure of common sense. Above all, soldiers wanted no part of an officer who foolishly exposed them to unnecessary hazards.[6] An indeterminate number met those standards. Morton's conclusion: "Men in the ranks seem to have accepted officers as inevitable. They admired an officer's courage and unselfishness, resented his privileges, remembered injustices, and saluted only when it was unavoidable."[7]

THE SECOND WORLD WAR: TO SCIENCE FROM THE MAGIC EYE

The Second World War was a watershed in the process of officer selection, when military forces attempted to find more or less objective means to identify those individuals who might make effective officers. As in other countries, the sheer magnitude of the Canadian problem of finding and training officers for three services grown from a few hundred to several hundred thousand in a few years demanded new approaches. The social sciences volunteered to find a way. Psychologists had introduced personnel selection techniques, in an attempt to rationalize manpower policy, when the United States rapidly raised an army for Great War service in 1917.[8] Afterwards, the civil sector, looking for ways to increase industrial production and business efficiency, adopted many of the testing procedures pioneered during the war. In Germany, the inter-war Wehrmacht applied their own version of psychological selection as did, after 1939, the Canadian, British and American armies.[9] The aim was to replace traditional methods, based on social status and subjective judgements of personal traits and appearance, with an objective methodology based on measurable criteria—to replace eyeball assessments with scientific method.[10]

The evolution of procedures to select Second World War RCAF aircrews well illustrates the transition from subjective bias to what observers thought or hoped would be objective standards. Initially, selection followed traditional paths: interviews to assess physical health, education, mechanical aptitude, and learning potential. A high incidence of training failures, with their attendant expense, led personnel administrators to look for more efficient and effective ways, specifically, a means to measure an individual's aptitude for acquiring flying skills. The Link trainer and a battery of suggestive psychological tests eventually provided an apparently satisfactory alternative. At least the trainee failure rate dropped. Accepting only the most promising candidates seems to have raised the efficiency of the training system, but it also probably discarded some, possibly many, potentially capable flyers who did not make it through the initial assessments. Standards for any manning program, of course, are dictated by supply and demand.[11]

The selection system concerned itself with technical aptitude for flying an airplane, not with the more abstruse matter of officership, where scientific method met entrenched traditional attitudes. In the British Commonwealth Air Training Plan, which employed the flying selection process, the RCAF and RAF differed over which of the aircrew graduates should be made officers. The RAF insisted on commissioning only those graduates who met pre-war traditional standards of an officer and gentleman; that is, standards of class, school, and social position. These, clearly, were open to widely different prejudices that were continually debated between the two flying services. The RCAF eventually set its own standards and commissioned more flyers than did the RAF, but trainees were left to a random, ill-defined process whereby one graduate became an officer while another equally proficient flyer was made an NCO. Scientific methodology seeking technical proficiency met the magic eye. They differed over who was entitled to be an officer. Just what attributes that officer was expected to display, who was to define them, not to say how and why, remained vague.[12]

The Canadian Army also looked to science for help in devising more objective ways for selecting its officers.[13] Personnel administrators had little choice given the scope of the problem. Between 1939 and 1946, the army granted 42,528 commissions. In a relatively few years selection decisions passed incrementally from senior serving officers relying on their experience, with its inherent personal bias, to Army Examiners, or Personnel Selection Officers, who relied on largely untested psychological criteria that categorized personalities. Psychologists reckoned that in a short discussion they could identify eleven of sixteen key personality traits that identified a potentially successful officer. These included: robustness, adventurousness, convictions, moral character, magnetism, self-confidence, articulateness, reserve, discretion, and freedom from annoying traits. Even assuming that the criteria might somehow measurably predict training success, let alone combat behaviour, (after all, annoying traits might be helpful if they annoyed an enemy) accurately assessing these characteristics in a short interview demanded superhuman intelligence and character, qualities that were as rare among Army Examiners as elsewhere. Essentially, individuals continued to render judgements on other individuals, but now they were based on supposedly scientific criteria rather than intuition based on experience.

The search for a psychological breathalyzer that would identify the worthy and reject the incapable, and the transition from traditional subjective assessments of an individual's essential worth, character, and potential to a quasi-scientific one, was not dramatic. Over time, the system was continuously modified and remained a work in progress to the end of the war and beyond as administrators tried to locate a workable weighting of the relative merits of factors like personality traits, education, learning potential, physical appearance, military experience, and training success.[14]

The army's selection problem differed from that of the air force in at least two respects. While the air force could focus its search on technical and physical aptitude for flying, the army's task was more complex. For one, it had to find officers for a much wider range of tasks, both combatant and non-combatant, and it was not at all clear that the same officer-like characteristics applied to both. Would an effective infantry officer display the same characteristics as an efficient administrator, or static engineer, or staff officer?[15] More vital to the army's needs was leadership; especially in a combat milieu where an individual—an officer—was expected to be able to persuade others to risk mutilation and death to accomplish a mission of which they might be only dimly aware. What was it that motivated soldiers to risk their lives? What made one individual a leader and another a follower? Why was it that an individual led in one situation but not in another? Was leadership a matter of individual character, however defined, or was it determined by the situation? Could leadership be taught, or was it embedded in an individual's inheritance? Were there ways to identify actual and potential leaders?[16]

The questions were as old as Homer, and the search for answers as circuitous as that for a Holy Grail. They remain as elusive. Both in Canada and overseas, psychologists, commanders, trainers, and others all searched for appropriate criteria that would accurately identify actual and potential leadership qualities. One major advance occurred in Britain. Usual selection criteria attempted primarily to detect negative qualities. There was no means of assessing positive leadership capabilities, actual or potential. "It was at this point," Shelford Bidwell has written, "that Major W.R. Bion made his insufficiently celebrated contribution (probably as important to the country's war effort as the 25-pounder gun or the Bailey bridge). What was required, in the absence of evidence of behaviour under fire or in active operations, was a situation of strain involving leadership of a small group." Bion devised the "Leaderless Group Test." This free-form exercise gave small groups a field task, like moving a large object across a defile, for which there was no real solution, but which afforded training officers and psychologists an opportunity to observe the leadership dynamics which evolved naturally within the group. Some led, others followed; some assisted, others obstructed; some took part, others kept aloof; some led in one situation and followed in another. The scheme, along with peer assessments, offered fresh insights on leadership because, in Bidwell's words, "even a pennyworth of exact observation is worth any amount of metaphysical speculation, social prejudice and folklore." For the British Army, particularly, it helped displace an old school tie selection system with one based on merit.[17]

In the midst of the systemic changes underway, General H.D.G. Crerar, then commanding I Canadian Corps, felt constrained to define what an officer was, what his responsibilities were, and what was expected of him, particularly in the exercise of leadership. With his *Oxford Concise* at hand, Crerar wrote that an officer, "means a person holding authority." Authority, in turn, was the "right to enforce obedience," and it was "derived from being appointed to a position of responsibility and possessing the ability to fulfil its obligations." In his usual formal bureaucratic way, he distinguished the role of an army officer as different from that of an airforce officer. An air force officer's effectiveness was measured by his individual rather than command skills. In contrast, army officers required an aura of leadership that embraced

> special qualities historically demonstrated after long years of experience. Perhaps the more outstanding of these are ready acceptance by the individual of responsibilities which convince others of his ability to carry them out. In the latter connection is associated the special and general knowledge requisite for the purpose. Moral strength, determination and physical fitness are highly necessary....[There were] no invidious distinctions between Officers who are Commissioned and those who are not. The character and qualities of a leader are necessary in Officers of all grades. The highest responsibility of an Officer in the Army, whether Non-Commissioned, Warrant, or Commissioned is effectively to lead and command his men in battle. Consequential responsibilities are the continuous and thorough training of all under his command, in their military duties, as individuals and as a team, the efficient administration of that command, and the inculcation in it of high discipline and morale....[There were] important differences in both the nature and scope of the responsibilities which are allotted to those grades. Higher qualifications, more particularly in respect to education and general knowledge, are essential in the commissioned ranks.[18]

In the meritocracy he envisioned, Crerar thought promotion was open to all.[19] In earlier eras when officers came from moneyed classes they alone could afford education, but with the advent of public schooling education was now available to anyone. Consequently, "Given the required characteristics of a leader, and good education, progression from Corporal to Colonel, or higher is a matter which largely lies in the hands of the individual concerned."[20]

Perhaps it is surprising that General Crerar felt it necessary to define officership in the midst of the war. It was probably due to the massive expansion of the officer corps. Did he get the officers he wanted? We don't really know. Too many variables intervene in assessing an individual's performance at different command levels, too many measuring sticks: success in battle, or success at least cost in lives, or something else? There is no precise means of evaluating and comparing to what extent officers, specifically, contributed to or detracted from the combat effectiveness of their units. Nor is there is a realistic way to gauge the effectiveness of social science as officer selector in the Second World

War. There was no alternate system with which to compare it. While the newer quasi-scientific selection procedures may have reduced failure rates in aircrew training, they do not seem to have been capable of identifying individuals who made the best combat pilots. Nor is it clear that they were more accurate in identifying which candidates made the best infantry combat leaders, or artillery observers, or tank commanders, or staff officers, or Brigadiers.

Colonel Charles Stacey, the official army historian, concluded that at his best the Canadian regimental officer "had no superior. He worked to make himself master of his craft, which usually was not his profession; he watched over his men's welfare and led them bravely and intelligently in battle." The problem was, he thought, that there were not enough of them, and that the army

> suffered from possessing a proportion of regimental officers whose attitude towards training was casual and haphazard rather than urgent and scientific. Analysis of the operations in Normandy seems to support this opinion....There still remained that proportion of officers who were not fully competent for their appointments, and whose inadequacy appeared in action and sometimes had serious consequences.[21]

It is not at all evident why Stacey stopped his critical assessment at the regimental officer level. It was the responsibility of senior officers to supervise training and correct faults.[22]

Possibly the major defect in the evolving selection process was its incapacity to distinguish between an officer's effectiveness in training and his performance in combat. The Personnel Selection history concluded that those rejected displayed several characteristics: an inability to think and act decisively, lack of intellectual ability; lack of maturity; lack of motivation; and lack of stability. But given the questionable nature of the tests themselves, and the tenuous nature of the screening procedures, we do not know how many of those rejected by the selection process would have performed adequately in battle. Consequently, it is not at all clear that the scientific methods adopted were any better than the more traditional magic eyes they were meant to replace. The elusive qualities of character remained elusive, as did the sources of the vital and intangible factors of determination, commitment, motivation and morale that underlay effective performance.[23]

Not long after demobilization reduced the wartime military forces to their familiar denuded state, Army Headquarters formed a committee, in 1947, to consider ways to find, train, and employ officers most efficiently in the post-war years. This was an era, before the solidification of Cold War premises and policies, that in many ways resembles the current one. Then, like now, there was no readily discernible enemy. That made it difficult to project in any generally acceptable social and political context what kind of military forces might be desirable or feasible. Planners had little guidance, and only the most prescient among them might have foreseen the drastically changed military circumstances that occurred soon after, when the Korean War and the semi-permanent commitment of troops to NATO propelled all three services into unprecedented peacetime expansion. Gazing into an implacable future is always a tenuous exercise. Planners had to make speculative assumptions about the future: whether technological and other changes were quantitative or qualitative; whether historical precedents applied and, if so, which were the most relevant. They had to speculate about what sort of officers would be best suited to cope with the uncertainty and change facing them. The questions would have sounded familiar to their planning predecessors; also to their successors who face strikingly similar problems and options. Threads of continuity link past, present, and future.

At that time the planners concluded that they had to arrange a structure equally useful in peace and war. That was a paradox: a "Jekyll-and-Hyde" organization highly efficient and competitive in wartime but which, in peacetime, was essentially non-competitive and inefficient:

> In consequence, it is subject to fluctuations in size, composition, personnel and functions. Thus, despite its long existence, its store of experience is not of that coherent kind typical of most other organizations. It is not only difficult for the Army to profit by decades of experience but to be certain that the lessons of past experience are of any great efficiency in current practice. A peacetime army, then, is in this dilemma: its only real proofs of efficiency are historical; its reliance on successful practices learned in the past may or may not be conducive to its future efficiency; yet it cannot afford to await the competition of actual warfare to prove itself efficient or inefficient.[24]

The types of officers needed to man such an organization depended upon the roles it was given. An operational army had to organize and train like one. Therefore: "Mobility, flexibility, tactical mastery of the arms, knowledge of the strategy of all arms and skilful man-management would be paramount in the training and employment of officers—with intrinsic excellence in the particular job being a desirable but by no means essential consideration." If, however, the army's primary task was to mobilize a fighting force when one was needed, "that is knowing how to procure, process, assemble and employ a civilian army," then the army would have to train and employ specialists in military organization, administration, manning, education, and planning. Alternatively, there might be a third role, that of "routinely processing, storing, revising and replacing the civilian components of a fighting force." If so, the training and employment of officers might then be highly intensive and specialized; as a body they would not be unlike the management and faculty of a university where instruction and collateral study and research were pursued within loosely joined 'departments' representative of all aspects of military science.[25]

If, the planners advised, the army had to prepare for all three roles it was absolutely necessary to clarify its paramount function and assign priorities for the others in descending order.

In an ideal world, the numbers and types of officers an institution needed would flow naturally from an unequivocal definition of national interests. A force structure might then be fashioned to achieve and maintain those interests, and individuals found and trained to fit the parts: round pegs for round holes. Instead, the real world invariably intercedes. The 1947 personnel planners were overtaken by rapidly evolving international and domestic change. Recruitment for Korea and NATO reverted back to the precedents of 1899, 1914, and 1939: an ungainly scramble for bodies to fill immediate recruiting quotas. Veterans, militia officers, and university cadets, selected for the most part by the traditional magic eye, composed most officer establishments. For the longer term, the Royal Military College had reopened in 1948, and schemes to recruit officers through subsidized university training programs proved to be one of the most fruitful sources of future senior commanders.[26] As well, officer candidate schools were formed in 1951 to give short-service commissions to serving soldiers and airmen, and high school direct entry candidates.

In large measure the military's golden age of the 1950s and 1960s echoed Second World War experience: in operational doctrine, training, values, and the ways officers were identified and judged. Social scientists, in the United States in particular, refined their research programs, and their theories, on the basis of data accumulated during the war and extrapolated them.[27] Adapted selection techniques, for instance, peer assessments and leader/follower group exercises juggled the balance of science and the magic eye, but with little better assurance of their predictive accuracy or dependability. A retired senior officer and Director of Military Training at that time who was responsible for the results, recalled that he had to be cautious not to overstate the veracity of the procedures. At one of his briefings a sceptical Major-General J.M. Rockingham remarked that he had failed his own initial leadership assessment. Fortunately this mishap had not prevented "Rocky" from maturing into one of the army's outstanding combat leaders of the war.[28]

Rapid expansion required a lot of new officers, quickly. Most, especially those given quick short-service commissions, had to be instructed about what it meant to be an officer, and possibly a gentleman. Major-General Howard Graham, soon to be the Army Chief of the General Staff, spoke to the graduates of one of the first officer candidate school courses about what was expected of them. He told them that the mark of an officer consisted "of two elements: knowing what the standards are and having the strength of character to live by them." He impressed upon them the weight of responsibility they were assuming with their commissioning scrolls. While civilians might violate their own professional standards at personal cost, an officer's responsibility went much further. "For the officer, the consequences go beyond the personal to affect the reputation of the Army and the welfare of the country. An officer's conduct can affect the lives of many soldiers, the outcome of battles, and sometimes may even determine the future security of Canada." They were expected to give unlimited, selfless service. Success, he told them, "will be directly proportionate to the loyalty, effort and enthusiasm that you put into it."[29]

Such injunctions were heady stuff for a brand-new second lieutenant, unsure of either the standards or his own capacity for maintaining them.[30] Clearly, he also had to be acculturated in the mores and traditions of service life. One means of instruction for the young officer was a series of well-received articles, published in the *Canadian Army Journal*, which expanded on General Graham's generalities with more specific advice. They provide a revealing snapshot of the prevalent values and expectations of the times.

The articles, written by a senior serving officer and pre-war RMC graduate, were styled as letters from a father passing on timeless verities of soldiering to his son, a recent OCS graduate.[31] Expanding on the metaphor of the regiment as family, the first and most important demand on the new officer was his total personal commitment. His was not just a job or profession, but the "mother of professions." This meant that an officer had to have an ideal of service to country that embraced an unlimited commitment of time and self because his professional and personal lives were dedicated to that higher ideal. His loyalty went upwards to his superiors and down to his men, whom he had to know and respect as individuals, while caring for all aspects of their welfare. He had to accept the responsibility of enforcing discipline with intelligence and humanity but without favour. He had to make himself professionally competent and pass on his knowledge to his soldiers, and display the humility to admit error.

Besides these attributes of character, much of the advice dwelt on personal behaviour. Father took pains to impress upon his son that he was now an integral part of an organic living tradition with threads woven through the centuries, back even to Knightly times. In their 1950s guise, the young officer had to pay proper deference to his superiors, not hesitating to ask for their advice; be carefully respectful of the sergeants' mess; and avoid trying to be pals with the men under his command: fair, firm, and friendly, but not too friendly. He had to learn to handle drink, money, and relations with women. The last included not marrying before he had had time to become an effective officer: "You will be torn by two loves and as a young officer you can't afford two, a wife and a unit."

Manners were an aspect of personal behaviour that, if not already ingrained, had to be learned, because they were in the tradition of being a proper officer.[32] After the democratization of wartime, which had ingrained the principle that rather than social position it was "the man himself who counts," a code of manners appropriate for peacetime service was still evolving. Yet some traditions remained important: father advised son that it was courteous to call on at least the senior officers in garrison, and that he should take pains to repay any hospitality shown him in being invited to the homes of his married colleagues.[33]

The articles also spoke of an officer's relations with civilians between whom, surprisingly so soon after the war, there seems to have been considerable misunderstanding. Like Sam Hughes, many civilians thought that an officer was in the job simply for what he could get: "free rations, free housing, clothing, medical service....[and was one] who could not otherwise earn a fair living." Officers had to change those attitudes by being a model of selfless service. Without that ideal, father advised son, "you can never be more than a drone and deserving of the civilian sneer."[34]

No doubt, as is invariably the case, the colonel's advice to his subaltern son was breached as much as observed. But it represented an ideal to be aimed for, romantic yet useful, and written in readily comprehensible language. The advice would have been familiar before the Great War. After all, some material conditions had not changed that much in the interlude: a subaltern's pay of five dollars a day in 1951 was the same as it had been half a century earlier. Nor had the values of officership been drastically modified from then, or even much earlier. The advice is uncannily similar to that offered in a memoir written in 1760 by an OLD OFFICER, that he called *CAUTIONS and ADVICE to OFFICERS: particularly SUBALTERNS*. Like his successor two centuries later, the OLD OFFICER emphasized an officer's unlimited commitment to service: "You are no longer to look upon yourself as the Master of your own Time. It is now the Publics: and your Sovereign, your General, and your Superior Officers have the absolute Disposal of it." In almost identical terms he also advised that an officer's primary concern was, or should be, the men under his command. He must treat the soldiers in his charge as he would have his superiors treat him; enforce discipline impartially and without insult; treat soldiers as men not slaves because all were servants of the same sovereign; gain their confidence and obedience with fairness not fear; be honest and never give promises that he could not keep.[35]

Traditional principles, or maxims, or axioms, of officership and leadership from the 1750s were familiar two centuries later. Values of service, selflessness, integrity, loyalty, moral courage, honesty, responsibility, accountability, among others, were ideals to be reached for if not always gained.[36] To what extent the ideals have lingered in the half-century since is a matter of some speculation.[37] Two related topics illustrate a clash of values and attitudes that has intruded on a search for the next generation of leaders and commanders: leadership and management, and educational means and ends.

VALUES—LEADERS AND MANAGERS

Leadership is of the spirit, compounded of personality and vision—its practice is an art. Management is of the mind, more a matter of accurate calculation, statistics, methods, timetables, and routine—its practice is a science. Managers are necessary; leaders are essential.

Field Marshal Sir William Slim

For people the two terms arouse two distinct psychological sensations: management invoking visions of controlling, dominating, arranging, containing, demeaning and reducing; while on the other hand, leadership inspires feelings of team building, motivating, inspiring, freeing, growing, advancing, energy releasing, but above all trust and confidence.

Commandant Michael Murphy

Managers loaded soldiers onto landing craft for Normandy. Leaders led them off.

Concepts of leadership and management coexist, but uneasily. Inconvenient and awkward contradictions are brushed aside. Traditional concepts of officership and relatively recent management practices have contradictory norms. Governments, armies, and societies in general have not been notably successful in harmonizing them. They may be essentially irreconcilable. Consider their fundamental differences. One is concerned with individual goals, the other with group achievements. One is concerned with end results, bottom lines and the premises of economic analysis; the other with the complex human dynamics of persuading individuals to do things that rationally they would not ordinarily do. One is concerned with "managing individual persons on the one hand and mass manpower on the other,"[38] the other with the region in between. One is oriented to atomistic individualistic values: the other to organic, collectivist ones. One applies organizational rationality, and is unconcerned with intangibles like motivation and morale that cannot be measured and quantified: the other is inherently dependent upon the emotions that affect the intangibles.[39] One assumes that material rewards will produce desired behaviour: the other is concerned with job satisfaction through achievement. One is preoccupied with tidy organizational charts: the other with the human realities that give life and meaning to the charts. One is concerned with efficiency: the other with effectiveness. One assumes that theory shapes reality: the other that the sum of realities forms theory.[40] One relies on impersonal systems to which individuals are expected to conform: the other prefers that individuals arrange systems that best serve their group goals. One is a workplace: the other a community.[41] Regimental fiefdoms look back to traditional values that produced real or imagined tribal glories: but they function within uncomprehending bureaucratic structures with quite different goals and operating assumptions. Professional standards frequently clash with institutional goals.[42]

An illustration of a conflict between managerial efficiency and military effectiveness occurred in the Canadian Army in Britain in 1942. Wide-scale personnel selection on a base of untested and unproven psychological assumptions created unforeseen sociological problems in the overseas army. Allocation non-policies at the beginning of the war had scattered talent randomly: too many cooks were driving trucks and too many drivers were cooking. Psychologists persuaded personnel administrators that they could rationalize the allocation of manpower by properly fitting pegs to holes. The army's efficiency would automatically increase. Consequently army examiners combed field units in the UK with a battery of tests that they assumed would identify potential tradesmen. Those so identified were then posted for specialist training. Units, losing some of their best men and the group cohesion they had developed and fostered, were left to fill the gaps as best they might. General Crerar, 1 Corps Commander, protested. An army, he wrote, required more of itself as an institution that mere rational efficiency. If an army traveled on its stomach, it was also powered by emotions that could not be calculated and measured.[43] In terms that echo universally, he wrote in the summer of 1943 that Canadian Military Headquarters, was:

> making the fundamental error of judging 'efficiency...required towards winning the war' by the technical efficiency of an administrative system. I say that this is a fundamental error because, whether we like it or not, the average man is not a 'scientific animal' and he reacts more importantly to emotions than to logic. No administrative system which fails to take this situation into full account will produce successful military results. The same observation applies to a unit. If the officers and men which it comprises, are imbued with mutual regard and confidence, and a desire to maintain at the highest level the reputation of the regiment in which they are proud to serve, then that unit will most certainly do what is 'required towards winning the war,' whether or not it produces the desired answers to certain administrative questions....
> [From] the point of view of general fighting efficiency, I believe that it would be wise to accept a relaxation in the ideal policy of 'employing every individual in that capacity for which he is best suited by reason of his physical and mental capacity, his training and natural aptitude,' in order that the human ambitions of individuals to serve in the capacity which satisfies them most, and in the unit to which they are attracted for sentimental and other reasons, may be largely met.[44]

General Crerar's observation that institutional efficiency does not necessarily produce unit effectiveness is universally relevant. As one informed observer of the process has commented: "There is no law that social reality must conform to the theories of social scientists." To which one can only add, Amen.[45]

Leadership and management do share at least one notable characteristic. Each is a means to an end and not an end in itself.[46] Leaders can lead in any direction.[47] Hitler was a remarkable leader who mesmerized German society and led it to a catastrophic end. Managers can manage in whatever direction. The Holocaust was a remarkable managerial achievement. Ordinary bureaucrats displaying the "banality of evil" rounded up individuals, arranged train schedules, ordered gas, and activated gas chambers according to an intricate management plan: means to an unspeakable end.

A modern officer has little choice but to try to be both a leader and a manager, or a leader of managers. But there is a price paid.[48] One British officer has described the schizophrenia of "Warrior and Worrier."[49] There is a need, another has remarked, to find "leaders who know how to manage and not leaders who see themselves as managers."[50] It might help the search for solutions if the differences were frankly accepted. But, rather than acknowledging their divergence, one observer has noted, social science research "has aggregated leadership, management, and a variety of other processes, and attempted to address them collectively under the general rubric of 'command,' which has a nice military ring to it."[51] It would help, also, to reject, or at least seriously question, the common assumption that officers are merely business executives in uniform, the more senior of them CEOs. The two professions may share common characteristics, but ends and purposes are not among them. One has a bottom line and limited liability: the other has unlimited liability with a profit and loss statement reckoned in soldiers' lives. The difference is fundamental.[52]

EDUCATIONAL MEANS AND ENDS

The Officer Corps will be highly educated, flexible in thought and action, capable of dealing with ambiguity and uncertainty, innovative, proactive, comfortable with a technological and information-rich environment and committed to a philosophy of life-long learning.

Officership in the 21st Century[53]

The prime requisites for a successful Staff Officer were cheerfulness and accuracy. [I would] much rather have a cheerful nit-witted bloke who performed his duties with a smile, than a quiet, surly extremely clever bastard.

Lieutenant-Colonel George Kitching, GSO 1, 1st Division.[54]

Students who used to read the classics now study executive management, and where they once learned how Caesar addressed his men, or Napoleon tweaked his grenadiers' earlobes when he was pleased with them, they now absorb graphs and mathematical formulae that are supposed to guarantee magic results. It is a sort of acupuncture of the mind: if you put the needle in here, the object will respond by doing whatever it is supposed to do.

James Stokesbury

There was considerable soul-searching in the postwar years about the role and place of education for military officers. Much of the debate was in the context of determining the fate of the Royal Military College (RMC). Closed during the war, the College reopened in 1948 only after the RMC Club mustered sufficient political muscle to overcome the view that officers could be found more economically in civilian universities. Then an internal service debate ensued over whether RMC should be primarily a military training institution or an educational one; and, in either case, what the proper balance of teaching in science, technology, or the arts should be.[55]

A generation ago, in the 1970s, participants in a symposium held at the Royal Military College possibly had an ideal officer in mind similar to the one currently sought when they exchanged views about educating the officers needed by the end of the twentieth century.[56] Many of their concerns will be familiar today, at the end of that century. Like now, it was an era fraught with uncertainty. Widespread social and technological changes were underway. Looming over all was the incomprehensible spectre of nuclear war. Consequently, one speaker noted:

> Disciplined, motivated, young men, capable of independent decisions, will be needed more than ever before.... These men will be required for the problems of a quarter of a century of uneasy peace punctuated by periodic crises, by international blackmail, by internal disturbance, by subversion, terrorism, and even guerilla warfare.... The officers of tomorrow must also have the necessary technical knowledge to cope with weapon development that is now so rapid that it cannot be forecast for much more than five years in advance. They must also have a thorough general education to be able to understand the complex social and international problems that provoke crises, and they must be able to deploy force without permitting it to escalate to a nuclear exchange between great powers. By the end of a quarter of a century the world will almost certainly be a very different place in ways that we cannot now conceive and for which we find it hard to prepare. The nation-state may have been considerably altered. To plan for half a century ahead is unthinkable.[57]

Speakers raised a wide range of specific issues, explicitly and implicitly, none of which was new and all of which remain relevant. How to distinguish between training and education? How to stimulate students to think critically: that is, to be aware of and critically evaluate the premises and assumptions underlying any proposition? How was it possible to encourage and sustain critical thinking in an institution based on hierarchical obedience? What to teach: what balance of arts, science, and technology? When to teach it: at what rank level and what stage in an officer's career?[58] At what level should an officer be given a broad education: at the beginning, in mid-career after a period of service experience, or on reaching senior levels of command with broader and deeper perspective?[59] How to structure a continuing educational system in which officers might acquire professional training without overwhelming the broad education they needed to exercise balanced judgement when they reached senior command levels?[60] Was it possible to educate for judgement?[61]

The topics are universal and essential, if unanswerable.[62] More questions might well be added. What military roles will be demanded of officers a generation hence? Will they function in a peacetime bureaucracy, in a peacekeeping constabulary, or in combat? How best to identify, select and train individuals for each or all those roles? Are generalists or specialists more suitable? Which is more relevant to leadership and command: brawn or brains, physical courage or technical skill?[63] Who will be more effective: the technocrat or the snake-eater, the ordinary person or the trained killer?[64] Are the qualities required in an officer functioning in the traditional Canadian top-down way of war, the same as those needed for a mission-command doctrine requiring delegation of authority, creative thinking, and individual initiative?[65] Is it possible to grow tropical plants in the tundra?[66] While it is a straightforward matter to train an officer to be professionally competent, how can one be educated to be honest, morally courageous, determined loyal, and humane: from a book or a model?

Education by itself, of course, is no panacea for solving fundamental human dilemmas. Education may contribute to ethical behaviour and constructive judgement but will not ensure it. The historical record is littered with educated fools, charlatans, and tyrants; and with illiterate wisdom. That said, especially in an era of rampant change, when it is impossible to foresee accurately even the near-term future, specialized training must surely be guided by a broad liberal education that can provide breadth, depth, and context to any individual's necessarily constricted existence. It is well to keep in mind Sir John Hackett's caution that officers must realize "only a person of liberal mind is entitled to exercise coercion over others in a society of free men."[67]

CONCLUSION

If you want a new idea, read an old book.
The two great dilemmas likely to be encountered in the practice of military leadership lie in reconciling the inflexible pursuit of the aim with infinite flexibility in reaching it; and firm control of strong-minded subordinates with the ability to accept unpalatable advice.[68]

Now, as well, officers have to direct twenty-first century technology with minus twenty-first century bodies that bleed and minds that break. Human capacities are finite.[69] It might help if an effective way was found to tap into the immense potential of creative energy that is available in the institution's uniformed ranks. That is not easy in a hierarchical, top-down institution, but a few specific topics may be raised in conclusion.

Revolution or evolution. Corporate, institutional memory seldom outlasts the posting cycle. This is particularly the case in the era of the so-called Revolution in Military Affairs (RMA), whose technological presumptions focus on the future rather than the human factors that have influenced and defined officership over the ages. Curiously, technological fixes march alongside a ritual rhetorical obeisance to the aphorism that the moral is to the physical as three is to one. Yet the essential questions about what makes a good officer being asked today echo those that have been asked over the centuries. Do the old standards and values apply, or have they been left in a technological backwater? It is impossible to say, in the midst of it, in this or any other era, if on-going change is qualitative or quantitative.[70] Historians still debate whether military innovations in the sixteenth century, or in the Napoleonic regime, were revolutionary or evolutionary. It is rarely clear whether and which historical precedents apply. Nor is it now. But the present is distinctly cloudy, and the future highly speculative. The past is all we have to go on. The right questions asked of it can inform the present:

> Studying the past may be a matter of marginal utility only, but the past is us and it is on the past alone that all decision making is inevitably based. If systemic study of the past is taken away, only personal experience, hearsay, and intuition remain. Military history may be an inadequate tool for commanders to rely on, but a better one has yet to be designed.[71]

On the assumption that there are few new problems in human affairs, only old ones endlessly recycled, it may help to look back in order to see ahead.[72]

Historical continuities. It is ironic that the twentieth century began with new weapons and the communications technology to coordinate the delivery of vast quantities of high explosives in a battle of attrition; and is ending similarly, with newer technology to deliver vaster quantities of explosives in other attritional battles. Officers who arrange, manage, and direct their delivery face the same fundamental questions, even if dressed in different language, as their predecessors at the Medak Pocket, Kapyong, Caen, Vimy Ridge, Waterloo, Breitenfeld, Cannae, or Troy. It may offer some comfort to acknowledge the threads of continuity that connect today's concerns with identical ones in the past. The current search is hardly new, nor does the past reveal a golden age of Canadian officership. Gaps between the ideal and reality have always existed, and always will.[73] Each generation assumes its milieu to be unique. No easy solution beckons, there is no quick fix. Societies and armies have been groping for the questions, let alone answers, forever.

Leadership theory and practice. After the Second World War the combination of Cold War dynamics, technology, military professionalism, and academic specialization produced libraries of ever more closely focused studies of the psychology and sociology of officers and their soldiers.[74] New terminology, like transactional and transformational leadership, has evolved to describe older intuitive essentials of character and behaviour but without clarifying them. While there is considerably more information available, and possibly more knowledge, there is questionably more insight, and certainly no more wisdom. Moreover, it is considerably more difficult to apply theory than simply know it. A recent commentator has suggested, wisely, that:

> Leadership principles and lists of traits and descriptions of required situational behaviours will continue to flood the market, even though the basics of leadership that derive from timeless human needs and aspirations changed little in all of recorded history. While studies and the deductions therefrom will shed light, our challenge is to move into the 21st century with a good record of practice, not just a solid platform of theory.[75]

Civil-military. Canadian military forces have never had a comfortable relationship with civilian society. Other than the militia, military forces have been located apart from general society, its enclaves located far from population centres. Its wars have been fought abroad and society has experienced them only at second-hand. The practice of burying Canadian bodies abroad rather than in Canadian communities has masked the human costs. Universal military service, conscription, has been a severely divisive, not unifying, force as it has not been in other countries. Demographic change may exacerbate an already wide gap.[76]

Motivation and Morale. Fundamental social change raises the question of motivation and morale, the basic sustaining forces of military operations. Machiavelli was the first modern commentator to suggest the vital importance of the two when he observed that an indigenous militia was needed because mercenaries were unreliable; and that a country's defence required individuals motivated by something beyond personal gain. Frederick the Great's soldiers were motivated by, besides the gauntlet, loyalty to church, king, and country. Napoleon put a nation in arms as he transformed France. Soldiers on both sides of the US Civil War cited a higher cause guiding their sacrifice, as did those who fought on all sides in earlier twentieth century wars. In the modern era notions of "my country right or wrong" gave way for a generation to "my alliance right or wrong." In the current void, self-interest, pay, loot, hard times, and the promise of adventure will move some, but it may be doubted that self-preoccupation in a consumer society will have the same power to motivate individuals to extraordinary sacrifice as in the past.

Values and culture. The matter of conflicting value systems is possibly the most troublesome currently. Rampant technological change, major demographic shifts, narrow intellectual specialization, ideological fundamentalism, social and economic transformation, have all caused uncertainties, not just in military institutions but in all sectors of society. The balance of personal and social assumptions that frames attitudes and values has clearly changed in the past generation. A society with greed, self-interest, self-absorbed individualism, and systemic bureaucratic unaccountability as its principal, if not exclusive, values differs dramatically from a traditional military culture.[77] Military culture faces a dilemma functioning in a society with contrary values. Absorbing them transforms its very nature. Yet it cannot deviate from them too sharply. Creating a separate, distinct system of norms could transform it into a Praetorian Guard.[78] Catch-23.

Individuals and Institutions. At the centre of the search is the human factor. Human physiology and psychology have not changed for 30,000 or more years. In that time humans have behaved admirably and atrociously. There is little indication that the human condition has changed in the interval, or will in the future. It is exceedingly unlikely that this or the coming generation of officers will shed the golden chains of human nature and be smarter, more capable, more honest, or less venal than their predecessors.[79] Some officers will behave well and others badly, because they are human beings. Voltaire's Candide nicely illustrates the point. "Do you think," said Candide "that men have always massacred each other as they do today, always been liars, cheats, faithbreakers, ingrates, brigands, weaklings, rovers, cowards, enviers, gluttons, drunkards, misers, self-seekers, carnivores, calumniators, debauchers, fanatics, hypocrites and fools?" "Do you think," said Martin, "that sparrow hawks have always eaten pigeons when they find any?"[80]

Hawks still eat pigeons and humans behave as humans. It follows that it is an institution's responsibility to enhance appropriate individual behaviour by rewarding the good and sanctioning the bad. Voltaire informs. Candide and Martin were curious on arriving in Portsmouth to find a crowd "gazing intently at a rather stout man who was kneeling blindfold on the deck of one of the naval ships. Four soldiers, posted opposite this man, each fired three shots into his skull, as calmly as you please, and the assembled multitude then dispersed, thoroughly satisfied." The man, it turned out, was an admiral, accused of cowardice and sentenced for dereliction of his duty. Candide asked what it all meant. "In this country," was the reply, "it is considered a good thing to kill an admiral from time to time so as to encourage the others."[81]

Accountability. A slightly less extreme, institutional reaction to misadventure might help close the current obvious gap between desired and actual behaviour. Although of little comfort, the military's inadequacy reflects that in institutions generally. Common threads link three major recent examples: the Krever enquiry into blood contamination; the Westray enquiry into a mine explosion; and the Somalia enquiry into operational dysfunction. All revealed a systemic disinclination or institutional incapacity to fix responsibility and firmly establish accountability.[82]

Choosing historical precedents is a very tenuous exercise. At the beginning of the new century events may well be driving societies back to much earlier historical periods; reverting to the medieval age of mercenaries as sovereign states fragment, and a perceived need for armed interventions passes to corporate entities with no inherent ties to particular nation-states. Globalism and corporatism are fundamentally altering state relationships that have become commonplace in the last two centuries, and this will surely affect the nature of national responses to crises. In Michael Howard's telling comment, "wars are not discrete entities but the expressions of state policy. As states change their nature, so will their policy change, and so will their wars."[83]

APPENDIX A

Following is a summary of what one Canadian Army militia battalion in the Second World War thought about officership and leadership from the perspective of "What a follower seeks in a leader." *(Canadian Army Training Memorandum,* No. 30, September 1943)

1. He wants to follow a leader who is not afraid...not afraid of his position, not afraid of his own boss, not afraid of a tough job, not afraid of the people who work for him, not afraid of honest mistakes—either theirs or his.
2. He wants a leader who believes his work is important, and all those who are in it with him.
3. He wants a leader who gets a kick out of his work and helps his followers to get a kick out of theirs.
4. He wants a leader who gets a kick out of seeing a man do what that man thought he would never be able to do.
5. He wants a leader who will fight for him until hell freezes over, if the

leader believes him to be in the right.
6. He wants a leader who will tell him what's what when he knows darn well it's coming to him, and a leader who will do it without losing his temper.
7. He wants a leader who recognizes him as a person, regardless of his experience, school or training, and regardless of his religion, race, station in life or the lodge he belongs to.
8. He wants a leader who knows most of the answers, but who will admit if he doesn't know, and go get the answer.
9. He wants a leader who is predictable—that is, one he can depend upon to be the same all the time.
10. He wants a leader he can't put anything over on but who is human enough to look the other way when he occasionally makes an ass of himself.
11. He wants a leader who he knows understands him, to whom he is not afraid to go when he has been a fool, when he's ashamed, when he's about washed up, or when he's proud and happy.
12. He wants a leader he can get to when he really needs him and can get away from when he's through with him.
13. He wants a leader who can show him how to do a job without showing off or showing him up.
14. He wants a leader who will give him a chance to try something hard he has never done.
15. He wants a leader who he believes sincerely wants him to succeed and who will be proud of him when he does.
16. He wants a leader who respects his pride and never corrects him in the presence of others or gossips about him.
17. He wants a leader with the authority to promote, demote, or let him go, as he knows he deserves.

NOTES

1. Michael Howard, *War in European History* (London: Oxford University Press, 1976), 54.
2. René Chartrand, *Canadian Military Heritage, Volume I, 1000-1754* (Montréal: Art Global, 1993); and *Volume II, 1755-1871* (Montréal: Art Global, 1995).
3. On selecting soldiers, the followers, John Prebble wrote of eighteenth-century Britain, "In return for a solemn oath that he was a Protestant, that he had no rupture, was not troubled by fits, and was in no way disabled by a lameness not immediately apparent, he acquired the privilege of translating diplomacy into death. For this he received sixpence a day and the contempt of most of his officers.... He stood on a no-man's land outside the law, its victim and its guardian. When called upon to support it during civil riots he risked death by shooting if he refused, and trial for murder by the civil power if he obeyed. The whip, the nine-tailed cat

with knots of precise size kept him in order.... from the minimum of twenty-five strokes to the maximum of three thousand." In *Culloden* (London: Seeker and Warburg, 1961), 20-21.

4. "In Homeric times the art of command had a beautiful simplicity (as no doubt in early Rome, too) which is not to denigrate it. A chieftain was expected, above all, to march at the head of his men, seeking the opportunity for a model and decisive duel in full view of his troops. He was the protagonist, the spearhead of his army. His position required that he prove the might of his arm and pay with his life, if necessary. That was how he demonstrated to both gods and men his aptitude for command." Yvon Garlan, *War in the Ancient World: A Social History* (London: Chatto and Windus, 1975), 145.

5. Desmond Morton, *When Your Number's Up: the Canadian Soldier in the First World War* (Toronto: Random House, 1993).

6. See for example, R.H. Roy (ed), *The Journal of Private Fraser, 1914-1918; Canadian Expeditionary Force* (Victoria: Sono Nis Press, 1985); and Will Bird, *Ghosts Have Warm Hands* (Toronto: Clarke Irwin, 1968).

7. Morton; Stephen Harris, *Canadian Brass* (Toronto: University of Toronto Press, 1988).

8. The exercise was not notably successful. See Stephen Jay Gould, *The Mismeasure of Man* (New York: Norton, 1981).

9. See Williamson Murray, *German Military Effectiveness* (Baltimore: Nautical Publishing Co, 1992), especially chapter eight.

10. See Geoffrey Hayes, "The Development of the Canadian Army Officer Corps, 1939-1945," paper presented to the Canadian Historical Association, 1990.

11. Allan English, *The Cream of the Crop: Canadian Aircrew, 1939-1945* (Montréal: McGill-Queen's University Press, 1996).

12. On the debate over commissioning see W.A.B. Douglas, *The Creation of a National Air Force* (Toronto: University of Toronto Press, 1986).

13. The navy's experience in selecting and training its officers is analyzed by Bill Glover in his thesis, "Officer Training and the Quest for Operational Efficiency in the Royal Canadian Navy, 1939-45."

14. In reflecting on their wartime experience the historian of the personnel selection service noted a difference in motivation in individuals from that of WWI. In 1914-18 more than half of recruits had been European born and had a more direct connection with that war. In 1939-45 most recruits were Canadian born, and their "motivation for fighting was not, therefore, stimulated by any traditional or deep-rooted national emotions but had to arise out of a coldly rational philosophy. Furthermore, in marked contrast with the spirit of enterprise characteristic of an age of migration , expansion and economic development, the young officers of this war had grown to maturity during an economic depression and its aftermath. Caution, prudence and security had been held up before them as worthy motives....[this] was not an atmosphere for kindling leadership....It may be impossible for them to acquire that essential attribute of a military leader, the impulse of the thrust to kill." Carver, "Personnel Selection." The impulse to kill, the author may have added, in socially sanctioned fashion. Siegfried Sassoon noted the vital significance of timing in his poem "Decorated." "I watched a jostling mob that surged and yelled/ And fought along the street to see their man/ Was it some drunken bully that they held/ For justice – some poor thief who snatched and ran?/ I asked a grinning news-boy, 'What's the fun?'/ 'The begger did for five of 'em!' said he/ 'But if he killed them why's he let off free?'/ I queried – 'Most chaps swing for murdering one'/ He screamed with joy; and told me what he'd done-/ 'It's Corporal Stubbs, the Birmingham V.C.!'

15. "Roman soldiers promoted through the ranks to Centurion were chosen for their judgement and self-control, and an ability to 'keep cool' in an emergency. Daredevils were not what was wanted." Michael Grant, *The Army of the Caesars* (London, 1974, xxxiii-xxxiv).

16. The questions are not dissimilar to other puzzling aspects of human behaviour; such as what is

it that causes an individual to act as a hero in the morning and a coward in the afternoon. Some of the nuances are discussed in Terry Copp and Bill McAndrew, *Battle Exhaustion: Soldiers and Psychiatrists in the Canadian Army, 1939-1945* (Montréal: McGill-Queen's University Press, 1990).

17. Shelford Bidwell, *Modern Warfare: A Study of Men, Weapons and Theories* (London: Allen Lane, 1973). For a personal description of how the selection process evolved see Brigadier F.H. Vinden, "The Introduction of the War Office Selection Boards in the British Army: A Personal Recollection," in Brian Bond and Ian Roy (eds) *War and Society 2* (London: Croom Helm, 1979), 119-128.

18. Quoted in Hayes.

19. Oliver Cromwell democratized officer selection in his New Army of the seventeenth century. In both the infantry and cavalry officers were chosen from the ranks: "I had rather have a plain, russet-coated captain that knows what he fights for and loves what he knows, than what you call 'a gentleman' and is nothing else." Education was one factor, religious zeal an even more important one: "If you choose godly, honest men to be captains of horse, honest men will follow them." See C.H. Firth, *Oliver Cromwell and the Rule of the Puritans in England* (London, 1901), 91-92: and Firth, *Cromwell's Army*, (London, 1905), 40-41. All this was reversed at the Restoration.

20. Hayes.

21. C.P. Stacey, *The Victory Campaign* (Ottawa: Queen's Printer, 1960), 275. It was an old refrain. Wellington wrote from Portugal of his officers: "We may gain the greatest victories but we shall do no good until we shall so far alter our system as to force the officers of the junior ranks to perform their duty and shall have some mode of punishing them for their neglect....Nobody ever thinks of obeying an order; and all the regulations...of the War Office and all the orders of the Army...are so much waste paper." Cited in John Keegan, *The Mask of Command* (New York: Viking, 1987), 129.

22. The turnover of divisional and brigade commanders was high. From the landings in Sicily in July 1943 until the end of operations in 1945 the five divisions had 14 commanders. The 16 brigades had 42 commanders. Some were replaced for being ineffective. On the inadequacy of higher commanders see John English, *The Canadian Army and the Normandy Campaign: a Study of Failure in High Command* (New York: Praeger, 1991).

23. The unpublished personnel selection history is Major H.S.M. Carver, "Personnel Selection in the Canadian Army: a Descriptive Study, 1945." An intractable problem was disposing of officers who became battle exhaustion casualties. If an officer acknowledged that he was less than an exemplary combat officer he was disgraced; if he failed to acknowledge that reality he was a menace to his troops.

24. "Army Officer Development," DHH, 113.3(D1).

25. Ibid.

26. A retired senior general officer recalled recently that in the late 1970s he attended an NDHQ meeting at which ten of the twelve generals present had entered service through the Canadian Officer Training Corps. All had had earlier experience in military cadet corps. Personal communication.

27. The major works were the multi-volume studies by E. Ginzberg, et al, *The Ineffective Soldier* and *The Lost Divisions* (New York: Columbia University Press, 1959); and S. Stouffer, *The American Soldier* (Princeton: Princeton University Press, 1949).

28. Personal communication. Equally fortunate, B.M. Hoffmeister, while he was a company commander, recovered from a psychological episode that manifested itself as a conversion hysteria, to become the army's most outstanding divisional commander. There is something to be said for an inefficient personnel system that missed sidetracking his military career.

29. *Canadian Army Journal,* 1952 (CAJ).

30. As a graduate of one of these early OCS courses, at the tender age of eighteen years, the author can attest to that.
31. The author was Colonel A.G. Chubb, then Director of Armour.
32. It seems extraordinary but in 1944, with the Red Army crashing in from the east and Allied forces closing from the west, the Waffen SS officers' training school at Bad Tolz reserved part of its curriculum for teaching social behaviour. The segment on Social Form included injunctions against singing in the Mess, and in putting "your hand on the decollete of the lady during dancing." R. Shulze Kossens, *Militarischer Fuhrernachwuchs der Waffen-SS: Die Junkerschulen* (Osnabruk: Munin Verlag GMBH, 1982).
33. Little mention was made in the articles to professional development. There may have been a lingering sentiment that education was best avoided. As comment on a much earlier era noted, "There was often a feeling that book-learning might dilute the physical courage and qualities of leadership which were really essential to young officers, and that it was hard to reconcile with the noble status that most of them enjoyed." M.S. Anderson, *War and Society in Europe of the Old Regime, 1618-1789*, (Montréal: McGill-Queen's University Press, 1998), 178. Other than noble status not much seems to have changed; a similar attitude towards education has persisted to the current era.
34. The articles were published in successive volumes of the CAJ in 1952-54.
35. Ibid.
36. See Martin Cook, "Moral Foundations of Military Service," *Parameters*, Spring, 2000, 117-129.
37. The British Army has recently found it necessary to give instruction in values to counter "a mercenary and self-interested" attitude to soldiering that has supplanted the traditional "vocational" approach that relied on "selflessness and trust." "New recruits had no understanding of values such as loyalty, respect, courage and commitment." *The Electronic Telegraph*, 28 February 2000.
38. Quoted in David Segal, "Leadership and Management: Organization Theory," in James Buck and Lawrence Korb (eds.), *Military Leadership*, (London: Sage, 1981), 41-69.
39. Institutional dichotomies are evident, of course, in almost all sectors of society. An obvious one is the reflex of hospital administrators to fire nurses because they cannot quantify compassion.
40. In military matters, the points of view reflect differences in the arguments presented by Jomini and Clausewitz in their assessments of Napoleon's military achievements. Jomini concluded that Napoleon discovered the theories of universal principles and laws of war and applied them. Clausewitz concluded that Napoleon responded to real conditions and invented theory.
41. It may have been simpler in medieval times to reconcile society's conflicting values. The warrior monks of the Order of the Templars combined the essential elements of the religious order and chivalric order, the two ruling categories of human society. "Imperiling their own bodies in the struggle for Christ while remaining strictly obedient to monastic discipline, submitting without hesitation or resistance, possessing nothing of their own, never touching women, denying themselves any form of boastful speech, gambling, and any useless embellishments." Georges Duby, *William Marshal: the Flower of Chivalry* (New York: Pantheon Books, 1985), 13.
42. Any daily newspaper cites instances of value clash: whether scientists pressed to compromise their research, or journalists pressed to compromise their objectivity, all in the cause of institutional goals that differ from their professional values.
43. The British soldier and writer J.F.C. Fuller made the same point when he wrote of "soul stirrers" and "mind awakeners" and cited Ardant du Picq who wrote in the nineteenth century that "The soldier is governed through his heart and not by his head." "The Application of Recent Developments in Mechanics and Other Scientific Knowledge to Preparation and Training for Future War on Land." See Lieutenant-Colonel Russell Glenn, "Earning the Thanks of Harry and Jack," *RUSI Journal* (February, 1997), 49-53.

44. Crerar to Commands, NA, RG 24, vol 10771.
45. David Segal, "Leadership and Management: Organization Theory" in James Buck and Lawrence Korb (eds), *Military Leadership* (London: Sage Pubs 1981), 63. Driven as they are by notions of replacing people with technology in the name of alleged efficiency, many government and corporate managerial practices seem so out of touch with the realities they supposedly oversee that they border on the psychotic.
46. The same may be said of science and technology. Science may at some point cure cancer; it can also be made to cause it.
47. An opposite view, that leadership in itself is intrinsically good, must be acknowledged. See James Toner, "Leadership, Community, and Virtue," *Joint Forces Quarterly*, Spring, 1996, 98-103.
48. There seems little doubt that the problem of defining the modern military officer in Canada was complicated by unification. The attempt at unity set three quite distinct service traditions of leadership and discipline warring for space in the bosom of a single green jacket. See, for example, Lieutenant-General G.G. Simonds, "Commentary and Observations," in Hector Massey (ed.), *The Canadian Military: A Profile*, (Toronto: Copp Clark, 1972), 267-290. Purple staffs may mask differences but have hardly reconciled them.
49. Brigadier A.G. Denaro, "Warrior or Worrier: Is the British Army Producing the Right Man to Command its Troops on Operations?" *RUSI Journal*, June, 1955, 37-42.
50. Comdt Michael C. Murphy, "Leadership, Management and Change," *An Cosantoir Review*, 1995, 93-100.
51. Segal, "Leadership and Management."
52. For a manager's critique of modern management practices see Henry Mintzberg, *The Rise and Fall of Strategic Planning: Reconceiving Roles for Planning, Plans, and Planners* (NY: the Free Press, 1994). See also Patricia Picher, *Artists, Craftsmen, and Technocrats* (Montréal, 1994).
53. *Canadian Officership in the 21st Century: OPD 2020, Statement of Operational Requirements.* The officer envisaged in the Statement of Requirement for the next generation has the physical attributes of a Rambo, the intellect of a Stephen Hawking, the command presence of an Alexander, and the moral authority of Christ. It is a contemporary statement of an eternal ideal, one that may be glimpsed if not actually grasped.
54. Major-General D. Spry also commented on the attributes of a staff officer. "(i) All staff officers must be cheerful no matter what the course of the battle. Glumness is contagious and its rot may spread. (ii) They must be polite; sharpness of speech, even when caused by worry and over-work, will not be tolerated. (iii) No staff officer may refuse a request. If in his judgement it seems reasonable, he can grant it, but he cannot say no without first referring the matter to the GOC or to the GSO1." NA, RG 24, vol 17506.
55. See Richard A. Preston, *To Serve Canada: A History of the Royal Military College Since the Second World War* (Ottawa: University of Ottawa Press, 1991).
56. The timing of the symposium was possibly not unconnected with the painful process going on at the same time as the US Army searched for its institutional soul after its Vietnam debacle. See Roger Spiller, "In the Shadow of the Dragon: Doctrine and the US Army After Vietnam," *RUSI Journal*, December, 1997, 41-54.
57. Richard Preston, "Training the Officers of the Next Quarter of a Century," in *Signum* (August, 1976), 153-169. The officer corps they were considering is the one now in senior command of the CF. Readers will judge for themselves how well the military educators succeeded.
58. One speaker commented that, "If education for that non-Newtonian world with which officers must deal at the top is to be possible, the military colleges must look beyond current alarums. Unless officers are educated by the time they are commissioned, the demands of technological and professional specialization will make it harder for them to educate themselves before they reach posts which will demand critical, imaginative and comprehensive intelli-

gence." Theodore Ropp, "The Military Officer and his Education in the next Quarter of a Century," Ibid.
59. As, for example, is the practice in the Israeli Defence Forces.
60. One officer pointed out that, "after unification for the Canadian Armed Forces was authorized in 1966, a board of officers developed a sequential system, from initial qualification at a military college, through technical environmental training, a junior staff course, an intermediate staff course for land officers, an environmental senior command and staff course, and an advanced military studies course [now combined with the preceding course] to a final national security course (NDC). Quoted in ibid. The reference was likely to the comprehensive report on military education prepared by Major General Roger Rowley that, unfortunately, was cherry-picked to oblivion rather than implemented.
61. "The demands on his moral courage, integrity and other personal leadership characteristics become all the greater as an officer advances in rank and responsibility." Murphy, "Leadership, Management and Change."
62. The subject of a prize-winning essay in the *RUSI Journal* of April 1914 was "How can moral qualities best be developed during the preparation of the officer and the man for the duties each will carry out in war." Cited in Glenn, "Earning the Thanks of Harry and Jack."
63. It is an old contest. In ancient times an officer's duty was clear and unequivocal: to fight in front of his soldiers and win or die. But even then individual combats gave way to formed bodies of troops and the commander's role changed. Individual physical prowess was no longer enough to influence the actions of soldiers who were out of the commander's immediate sight. A commander had to use his brain and develop the skills needed to organize and place his soldiers for battle. This inherently raised the question of "whether the foremost quality of a general is bravery, as was thought in ancient times, or reflection which may enable the weaker to triumph over the stronger." Garlan, *War in the Ancient World*, 146.
64. In 1941-42 the British Army experimented at battle schools to teach hate and aggression and thereby produce better killers. It was not notably successful as "the sole result was to disgust the trainees or – a more typical British reaction – to arouse their sense of ridicule. Some of the less intelligent and less stable in character became seriously disturbed. It is doubtful in any case if the 'killer' type is ever required in armies; but if he were he would not be produced by such methods. Killers are not howling maniacs, but psychopaths with cold personalities devoid of hatred and affection alike.... It is the man trained to recognize the dangers of the battlefield, understand his own fears without surrendering to them and equipped with the skills he must have to carry out his task, who can endure the prolonged stress of modern war." Shelford Bidwell, *Modern Warfare*.
65. Another aspect of doctrine, and the type of officer needed to implement it, is the continual oscillation between theories of attrition, requiring managers, and manoeuvre, requiring officers possessing an approximation of Clausewitz's coup d'oeil. Continuities echo.
66. Canadian infantry battalions displayed imaginative initiative in the Second World War, when allowed. Above battalion level a certain rigidity set in when staffs delivered set plans for units to implement. See Bill McAndrew, "Fire or Movement: Canadian Tactical Doctrine, Sicily, 1943," *Military Affairs*, 1987; and Bill McAndrew, "Operational Art and the Canadian Army's Way of War," B.J.C. McKercher and Michael Hennessy (eds), *The Operational Art* (Westport Conn: Praeger, 1996), 87-102. A similar top-down process is evident currently when abundant initiative and creative energy at the unit level is smothered if not extinguished when otherwise intelligent and skilled individuals are plugged into an over structured managerial system at NDHQ.
67. Sir John Hackett, *The Profession of Arms*, (London: London Times Publishing, 1963), 58.
68. Bidwell, *Modern Warfare*.
69. Emerging studies of recent operations in Kosovo offer a ready example; in this case, of human limitations in evaluating masses of data made available by technological means, and making

effective judgements about it. "Information superiority allowed NATO to know almost everything about the battlefield, but NATO analysts did not always understand everything they thought they knew." Timothy Thomas, "Kosovo and the Current Myth of Information Superiority," *Parameters* (Spring, 2000) 13-29.

70. Realities of the battlefield sometimes impinge on the certainties of technological premises. In Sicily in 1943 units often found that mules were more helpful than their new vehicles, and that semaphore communicated when their radios would not.

71. Martin Van Creveld, *Command in War* (Cambridge: Harvard University Press, 1985), 15. Even the most advanced computer war games are based on someone's historical experience.

72. Policy and decision makers in all sectors could profit from absorbing the insights in Richard Neustadt and Ernest May, *Thinking in Time: The Uses of History for Decision Makers* (New York: the Free Press, 1986).

73. Any undergraduate senses the gap between the ideal and reality on carrying a book on Plato into the Registrar's office.

74. Unfortunately, much of it is published in very specialized journals and written in incomprehensible jargon that obfuscates more than it clarifies.

75. Walter F. Ulmer, Jr., "Military Leadership into the 21st Century: Another 'Bridge Too Far'?" *Parameters* (Spring, 1998), 4-25. Having difficulty in applying known theories is common to other activities, for example, dieting and getting fit. Beyond theories, it takes constant diligence and self-discipline to lose weight and get fit, as well as exercise leadership.

76. A recent study in the United States examines the growing gap between military and civilian societies in that country. See Peter Feaver and Richard Kohn, "Project on the Gap Between the Military and Civilian Society," Triangle Institute for Security Studies.

77. Of course most individuals, including officers, have elements of both selfishness and selflessness in their make-up. Charles DeGaulle noted that: "Every man of action has a strong dose of egotism, pride, hardness, and cunning. But all those things will be forgiven him, indeed they will be regarded as high qualities, if he can make of them the means to achieve great ends." Quoted in James Stokesbury, "Leadership as an Art," in Buck and Korb, loc cit. Problems arise when means become ends.

78. Some American officers have looked into that murky future. See the imaginative paper by Charles Dunlap, "The Origins of the American Military Coup of 2012," in *Parameters* (Winter, 1992-93), 2-20.

79. Instances of officers betraying their responsibilities to their men have not been uncommon. The following is a soldier's petition of January 1660 complaining of officers' actions: "Did not most of those officers... purchase your debentures (the price of blood) from two shillings to a noble in the pound to enrich themselves and perpetuate your slavery? And through their cruelty many of our fellow soldiers, who were wounded in battle and made unserviceable, with wives and children starved in the streets for want of bread, while they lorded over you tyrant like. Now examine yourselves whether when you have demanded your pay, you were not had before Court martials and hanged to all your shames, while they robbed you and the Commonwealth of your dues." From "Truth seeks no Corners; or advice from a non-interested soldier to his loving fellow-soldiers that were under Fleetwood and Lambert, 1660." Quoted in C.H. Firth, *Cromwell's Army: A History of the English Soldier During the Civil Wars, the Commonwealth and the Protectorate* (London: Methuen, 1902), 207. John Prebble documents other instances of untoward behaviour in *Mutiny: Highland Regiments in Revolt, 1743-1804* (London: Penguin, 1977). Highlanders also mutinied in Italy in 1944 for not dissimilar reasons, that is, when commitments made to them were betrayed.

80. Voltaire, (trans. Donald M. Frame) *Candide, Zadig and Selected Stories* (Bloomington Indiana: Indiana University Press, 1966), 64. The passage is also cited in another context in Alex Danchev, "Liddell Hart and the Indirect Approach," *The Journal of Military History* (April, 1999), 313-337.

81. *Candide,* 75-76.
82. Institutional defenders and their critics in all three instances shared common premises, that is, to preserve the institution. They differed on means, the former citing the bad-apple case and the latter systemic faults. Another example is the difficulty in defining acceptable and unacceptable individual behaviour in police forces in order to preserve the institution's professional integrity.
83. In *War in European Society,* 70. See Thomas Adams, "The New Mercenaries and the Privatization of Conflict," *Parameters* (Summer, 1999), 103-116.

Canadian Generals in the Second World War: Better than Expected

J.L. Granatstein

> *Dr. J.L. Granatstein was the Director and CEO of the Canadian War Museum from 1998-2000, and taught at York University. He has written extensively on the history of the army and was a commissioner on the Special Commission on the Restructuring of the Reserves and an adviser to Defence Minister Young.*

IF, AS PEOPLE SAY, NATIONS GET THE LEADERS THEY DESERVE, Canada's army in the Second World War disproves that rule. The sixty-eight officers[1] who held ranks of major-general or higher were far better on the whole than the nation had any right to expect. For a country that had underfunded its tiny Permanent Force (PF) and its larger but almost wholly untrained Non Permanent Active Militia (NPAM) for two decades before the war, for a nation that initially had few of the weapons required for training or battle, for an officer corps that was, with very few exceptions, completely backward in its thinking, Canada's army proved to be surprisingly well-led during the war.

With the Permanent Force having only four hundred and fifty officers in September 1939 and with many too old for service in the field or physically unfit, the PF's effective cadre was only about two hundred and fifty strong. In this number, however, were substantial numbers of graduates from the Royal Military College (RMC) and, more important, most of the sixty-three Canadians who had attended the British Army Staff College. These were the routes to high command.

The Militia had approximately five thousand officers in its fifty thousand all ranks; again many were Great War veterans too old for service in the field. Most RMC graduates went to the Militia, and the Militia Staff Course (MSC), run by PF officers each year for the NPAM, had trained hundreds of officers for staff work and command posts—after a fashion. The MSC, however, was not the equivalent of Staff College; certainly the PF did not consider it as such.

Nonetheless, the army's commanders came from these PF and Militia officers, with most of the highest ranks going to those who had staff training or eventually proved themselves in battle. What was different in 1939 was that the Permanent Force, anxious not to repeat the events of 1914 when Militia minister Sam Hughes had bypassed it to place Militia officers into the key positions, intended to ensure that the regulars kept control.

The Permanent Force was successful in doing so, as the key posts in Ottawa and overseas initially and through most of the war were held by regular officers. The Chiefs of the General Staff were all PF officers, for example. In September 1939, Major-General Andrew G.L. McNaughton, the former Chief of the General Staff, was placed on active service to command the 1st Canadian Infantry Division. McNaughton filled the key command and staff posts with those officers he knew well, most being permanent force officers. He would eventually ascend to command of the Canadian Corps and then of First Canadian Army in 1942.

But the PF did not always get its way. The 2nd Division had its commander plucked off the shelf of retired officers in April 1940. Major-General Victor Odlum of Vancouver had excellent political connections with the Liberal government of Mackenzie King, connections strong enough to override the fact that he was sixty years of age and had not even been in the Militia since 1925.[2] The post of General Officer Commanding (GOC) of 3rd Canadian Infantry Division similarly went to another militiaman, Major-General Basil Price of Montréal. Such appointments were inevitable. For political reasons (and, frankly, because PF officers were not widely admired across the land), the NPAM had to receive its share of positions.

In truth, the Militia and the Permanent Force were not totally dissimilar, as both were almost wholly amateur organizations. Moreover, McNaughton proved no good judge of commanders, and even if he had been, there were very few senior officers of competence for him to choose from in the first years of war. As a consequence of underfunding and lack of training, while Canada had many men who had been brave officers in 1918, it completely lacked leaders who could competently command divisions, brigades or even battalions in the new kind of war that the Nazis unleashed against the democracies in 1939-40. The Simonds, Fosters, Sprys, Hoffmeisters and Mathews were all too junior for senior posts—Spry, a successful division commander in 1944, was a lieutenant in 1939, for example—and there literally was no one to turn to except the old sweats of the earlier war. Few nations were in any different a condition and certainly not the British on whom Canada's army modelled itself.

In fact, the British had a major impact on the Canadian generals of the early war years. Like their pukka role models, the Canadians often affected the mustaches, the swagger sticks, the stiff upper lips, the round bellies, the clipped accents, and relied on the best of British luck. They were just as ineffective, too, especially in the eyes of competent British commanders like the Chief of the Imperial General Staff (CIGS), General Alanbrooke, and Lieutenant-General Bernard Montgomery. To read the Alanbrooke diaries or Montgomery's personal letters when Canadian senior officers were discussed is to be embarrassed. McNaughton was a tinkerer with engines, not a commander or a trainer,[3] they thought. Basil Price of the 3rd Division should go back to his Montréal dairy, Montgomery wrote, "where his knowledge of the milk industry will help on the national war effort."[4] There were others who felt the lash of Monty's scorn—Militia Generals Ganong and Potts, and PF General and Victoria Cross winner George Pearkes, for example, all of whom would be sent home on Montgomery's say-so before he went off to command the Eighth Army in the Middle East. The British officer's phrasing was often cruel, unnecessarily so, but it was right enough. What Montgomery did not quite realize was that there was no one better, no one. The Canadian troops' good fortune was that Monty seized control of their training and imposed his tough standards instead of the generally lax rein exercised by McNaughton and his appointees. As a result, all the division GOCs from the first three years of war lost their posts because of their age or incompetence; eventually, so too did McNaughton and one of his corps commanders. When the Canadians went into action, almost all their commanders except for Generals H.D.G. Crerar and E.L.M. Burns would be younger men who had not fought in the Great War.

The best Canadian officers developed in action and, as the army did not fight a sustained operation until mid-1943, this progress was slow to come. The Japanese assault on Hong Kong in December 1941 produced nothing except casualties because the entire force was killed or captured. The raid on Dieppe in August 1942 was a failure that ruined reputations. Major-General J.H. Roberts, GOC of 2nd Canadian Division, had been thought to be one of the best Canadian senior officers by Montgomery,[5] but he became the scapegoat for the disaster.

In July 1943, Major-General Guy Simonds took the 1st Canadian Infantry Division into action for the first time in Sicily and, though only a major in 1939, and the beneficiary of the sacking of his superiors (and the death of Major-General Salmon who had been picked to command the Sicily operation), he and his troops proved themselves in action. One of the very few Canadian officers who had paid close attention to his profession in the prewar years, one of the handful who could engage in discussions on tactics and strategy, in operations Simonds showed an ability to innovate and to learn. He used his infantry, armour, and artillery together with increasing confidence and skill, and he got on well with Montgomery, then commanding the Eighth Army in Sicily. The testy British general thought Simonds the only Canadian commander of first rank ability, a view shared then and since by American observers and by most Canadian ones too.

The difficulty was that Simonds was a cold fish, tightly controlled and tightly wound. He generated his own plans and, however brilliant they were, they were perhaps too complicated for what was essentially a civilian army to execute well. His subordinates admired him, but they did not especially like him or his style in Orders Groups where he laid down the law and brooked no discussion. As Major-General Chris Vokes put it in his own inimitable style, his RMC classmate was "the finest Canadian general we ever had," but as "a leader of men" he wasn't worth "a pinch of coonshit."[6]

The same thing might be said of Simonds' antagonist in the one good prewar debate on an operational level engaged in by Canadian officers. In 1938, Lieutenant-Colonel E.L.M. Burns, a Signals Officer, wrote an article in the *Canadian Defence Quarterly* on armoured warfare, a piece that drew a spirited reply from then Captain Simonds.[7] This was argument at a high level between Canadian officers who had scarcely seen a modern tank or anything more than an understrength brigade of militia in the field. Instead, they argued as the divisional and corps commanders they would be five years hence.

Unfortunately Burns proved less effective than Simonds in operations. He briefly led the 5th Canadian Armoured Division in Italy and, when Lieutenant-General Harry Crerar was called back to England to take over First Canadian Army from the just-sacked McNaughton, Burns succeeded him at I Canadian Corps. A brilliant man, a genuine military intellectual, but a colder fish even than Simonds, "Smiler" Burns proved unable to get on with his division commanders or his British superiors. Although his corps broke the Hitler and Gothic Lines, Vokes at 1st Canadian Division and Major-General Bert Hoffmeister at the 5th Canadian Armoured could not abide Burns' abruptness, and they developed a deep mistrust of his ability. Burns had fallen into difficulty with the Eighth Army commander when the pursuit after the Hitler Line was botched by traffic jams (by no means wholly caused by Canadian errors), and he was rescued from dismissal only by Crerar's intervention. After the Gothic Line, Burns' superiors at Eighth Army and his subordinates at I Canadian Corps united to oust him. General Vokes put it bluntly, telling a confidant that he and Hoffmeister and their key staff officers were prepared to resign if necessary: "In spite of no able direction we have continued to bear the cross for an individual who lacks one iota of personality, appreciation of effort or the first goddam thing in the application of book learning to what is practical in war & what isn't."[8] Crerar tried but proved unable to save his friend a second time, and Burns would end the war in rear area positions.

The coldness that afflicted Burns and Simonds was not limited to them. Harry Crerar, the man who led First Canadian Army through the campaign in Northwest Europe, was very similar in make-up to his two subordinates. Crerar and Burns were close friends; Crerar and Simonds were not, and as corps commander in Italy Crerar actually tried to argue that Simonds was mentally disturbed.[9] Prior to this, in Britain, Crerar had showed outward loyalty to his old friend and superior McNaughton but had consistently undercut him with the Canadian High Commissioner, Vincent Massey, and Alanbrooke, the CIGS, another old friend from the Great War Canadian Corps and interwar service. Crerar "poured his heart out to me as regards his worries," Alanbrooke wrote in his diary. "He is very unhappy about Andy MacNaughton [sic]."[10]

Whatever his ambitions and his jealousies, Crerar was a competent army commander and a more than competent national commander. There can be no doubt, however, that he lacked the tactical genius of Simonds. Commanding 21st Army Group in the fall of 1944, Montgomery and Crerar clashed bitterly, Montgomery clearly seeing Crerar as an amateur forced upon him by the Canadian government. When Crerar fell ill and Simonds replaced him in command of First Canadian Army, Monty was delighted; when Crerar recovered and returned to his post, the Field Marshal was far from pleased.[11] Nonetheless, Crerar directed First Canadian Army in the battle to cross the Rhine and then to liberate the Netherlands. That a Canadian officer could competently lead an army in the field, with British, American, Polish, and other nationalities serving happily under his command, was quite literally a miracle considering where the Canadian Army had been five years earlier.

Equally miraculous was the profusion of competent and much better than competent officers who emerged from the crucible of battle. An officer like Dan Spry, a lieutenant in the Royal Canadian Regiment in 1939, rose to command his regiment in Italy, then quickly earned a brigade. When division commanders failed to meet the test in Normandy (there were several who failed), Spry was promoted again, capping an extraordinary rise of six ranks in five years. Nonetheless, Simonds had to relieve him in 1945.

Spry was a regular force officer, like Harry Foster, Chris Vokes, and Charles Foulkes, other successful senior officers. But, even more remarkable were the NPAM officers who won similarly rapid promotions in the meritocracy that was the army overseas. Bruce Mathews, an artilleryman from Toronto with the best of political connections, was accomplished enough by 1943 to serve Simonds as his Commander Royal Artillery in Sicily. Simonds soon brought Mathews to England to head II Canadian Corps' artillery, a post that in Normandy completed his education in all-arms cooperation. In the fall of 1944, Simonds promoted him once more and gave him the hard-luck 2nd Canadian Infantry Division which he led successfully until V-E Day. No intellectual, Mathews was careful and competent, a commander who cared for his troops, tried to minimize casualties, and who was not awed by his responsibilities. In effect, Bruce Mathews had become a professional soldier during six years of war, an officer who mastered his craft under the stress of wartime.

The same could be said of Bert Hoffmeister, arguably the greatest commander Canada produced during the Second World War. A major in Vancouver's Seaforth Highlanders in 1939, Hoffmeister had none of the social advantages Mathews did. What he did have was a powerful but quiet charisma, the courage of a lion, a desire to learn, and the conviction that it was his task to bring his men home safely. In England in January 1941, Hoffmeister's concern that he knew too little of war to do this, too little of tactics to face the *Wehrmacht* in action, led to a nervous breakdown and the eventual re-building of his personality by an army psychiatrist. Extraordinarily, Hoffmeister was not sacked despite his crack-up, and he subsequently proved himself at Staff College and in command of his regiment. In Sicily, he proved himself in action, always leading from the front and sending his Seaforths into battle with armoured and artillery support in textbook attacks. Quickly promoted to brigade command, Hoffmeister bore the brunt of the Ortona battle in December 1943, and a few months later, he took command of 5th Canadian Armoured Division.

Because he had so recently been commanding an infantry battalion, Hoffmeister knew what men could—and could not—do under fire, and he translated this knowledge into his command style. Indeed, he made his division into the only Canadian one with a distinctive personality—Hoffy's Mighty Maroon Machine—and he led it superbly. It was Hoffmeister who, seizing an opportunity, cracked the Gothic Line, and it was Hoffmeister whose division drove the Nazis out of eastern and northern Holland after I Canadian Corps rejoined First Canadian Army. His reward was command of the Canadian Army's Pacific Force, the division assigned to work with the Americans in the invasion of Japan. That a Militia officer could get such a position was a sign of Hoffmeister's worth—and of how far the Canadian Army had come over six years.

In Ottawa and at the Military Districts in Canada, the older generals and the officers who had been sent back from overseas, tended to gather. Their task was training and administration—and dealing with the politicians. In general, the trainers did better than the Chiefs of the General Staff who dealt with the Minister of National Defence and the Prime Minister. Colonel J.L. Ralston, the Minister from 1940-44 did not get on well with Crerar, for example, finding him hyper-ambitious, too cautious, too cold. He did get on well with Lieutenant-General Kenneth Stuart, but Stuart eventually took the fall for the failures to train enough infantry reinforcements to keep the army overseas up to strength. Only Lieutenant-General J.C. Murchie, Stuart's successor, survived unscathed, even though the so-called "generals' revolt" took place on his watch. When the government dawdled on sending home defence conscripts overseas in November 1944, to meet a need for infantry, District Commanders and other senior officers signed a memorandum that might have been read as a threat to resign. Certainly Mackenzie King took it that way. Instead of acting against the officers, however, the Prime Minister staged a sudden reversal of course on conscription in mid-November and decided to send 16,000 home defence conscripts overseas. No officers were disciplined. The CGS too survived.

That suggested that, during a war, the military had genuine power. The generals had failed to win their case for conscription from 1940 to November 1944, but when the First Canadian Army was *in extremis*, when the press and politicians were in full cry, the generals' "revolt" tipped the scales. The military had come a long distance.

But not too far in some important ways. Canada was only a provider of troops, and neither the government nor its senior commanders had a role in strategic decision-making; indeed, no such role was ever sought. Canada's was a colonial army, essentially resembling the British Army in thinking and appearance and serving where Britain wished. The United States assumed more importance for Canada with the Permanent Joint Board on Defence's creation in August 1940, but despite closer relations with the US Army, the British influence remained completely dominant throughout the war. It is certainly fair to say that neither a distinctive Canadian strategical or tactical doctrine developed during the war, even though the army generated five divisions, two corps, and an army headquarters.

Perhaps that was too much to expect. Canada has not developed its own strategic thinking in the fifty-five years since the end of the Second World War. We still remain only a generator of troops, and there is scarcely a glimmer of a Canadian strategic doctrine. More than six decades after the Burns-Simonds debate in the *Canadian Defence Quarterly*, those articles remain the high point of thinking about war by Canadians.

NOTES

1. There is a list of these officers in J.L. Granatstein, *The Generals: The Canadian Army's Senior Commanders in the Second World War* (Toronto: Stoddart, 1993), Appx A, 269-71.
2. Ibid, 34.
3. See ibid, 70.
4. Imperial War Museum, Trumball Warren Papers, Montgomery to Warren, 1 June 1942.
5. National Archives, H.D.G. Crerar Papers, vol. 8, 958C.009(D182), Montgomery's "Beaver III, Notes on Commanders," 25 Apr 1942.
6. Tony Foster Papers (Halifax, NS), Foster interview with Vokes, 5 Apr 84.
7. Burns, "A Division that Can Attack," *Canadian Defence Quarterly (CDQ)*, XV, April 1938; Simonds, "An Army that Can Attack—A Division that Can Defend," *CDQ*, July 1938. There were subsequent replies from both in October 1938 and January 1939.
8. National Archives, M.H.S. Penhale Papers, vol. 1, Vokes to Penhale, 2 November 1944.
9. John A. English, *The Canadian Army and the Normandy Campaign: A Study of Failure in High Command* (New York: Preaeger, 1991), 186.
10. Alanbrooke Papers, Liddell Hart Library, University of London, "Notes on my Life," file 3/A/IX, 18 Jun 43.
11. Granatstein, 113.

II

The Nature
of
Higher Command

What is a Commander?[1]

Ross Pigeau
& Carol McCann

Dr. Ross Pigeau and Carol McCann are DND defence scientists at the Defence and Civil Institute of Environmental Medicine in Toronto, Ontario.

A perfect general, like Plato's republic, is a figment of the imagination.
Frederick the Great in his Instructions for Generals[2]

INTRODUCTION

WHEN SCIENTISTS STUDY A NEW AREA they usually begin by defining its key concepts and delineating its known characteristics. Without this most basic of first steps, scientists run the risk of studying phenomena that do not belong to the class of behaviour they wish to investigate. To the military community, however, such abstract ruminations often seem unimportant, even irrelevant. After all, it is the military that have the difficult task of finding concrete solutions to real world problems. But as we have argued elsewhere,[3] the issue of definition can affect a military organization and ultimately, its operations. For example, Command and Control (C^2) has been hampered by imprecise and often circular definitions that have done little to guide military doctrine, policy, training and procurement.[4] Therefore in scientific parlance, although it is necessary for a concept to have *face* or *external* validity—that is, the concept must at least make sense to the people most affected by it—it must also have *construct* validity—that is, it must make sense within a larger theoretical framework.[5] In previous work we have attempted to develop such a framework for Command and Control: first, by dissecting the concepts and listing their unique characteristics,[6] and then by devising new definitions that are internally consistent and yield researchable hypotheses.[7] In this chapter we will use our new definitions of Command and Control to answer the apparently straightforward question "What is a commander? We say "apparently straightforward" because the term "commander" has historically been a remarkably illusive concept to define. The discussion arising from our new definition will then allow us to explore such questions as: What is the relationship between commander authority and responsibility? Do commanders' competencies change as they acquire rank, seniority and experience? What difference is there, if any, between a leader and a commander?

THE PROBLEM

When you ask military personnel the question "Who is your commander?", the answer will undoubtedly be clear and precise. The question is trivial because the hierarchical nature of most militaries actually specifies the chain of command, making the path to authority unambiguous. However, if you ask *"What is a commander?"*, their answers will be much more equivocal. They will struggle with imprecise and vague descriptions that, in the end, are circular or beg the question: e.g., "A commander is the next person up in the chain of command;" or "A commander is someone who commands;" or "A commander is someone who leads;" etc. Yet, from a military perspective, the question "What is a commander?" has serious operational and organizational implications. As the role and function of modern militaries broaden and change (e.g., to accommodate peace support, conflict resolution, humanitarian relief, etc), commanders, as well as their subordinates, will need to be effective across a spectrum of operational contexts. If the answer to the question "What is a commander?" is unclear, then the role and function of the commander will be unclear also, leading to confusion, frustration and (quite possibly) danger. Considering that a military is a nation's most forceful means for expressing its policies and ideology, and that commanders are often charged with executing these policies, it behooves us to be clear and unambiguous as to what a commander actually is.

There is a tendency to answer the question "What is a commander?" by pointing to a successful commander and saying that commanders in general are people who should display the same kinds of social skills, personality traits and cognitive styles as that person. This has been a strategy that many writers have adopted.[8] A collated list of the "good" commander characteristics named by these authors is quite large (see Figure 1). Indeed, the list could have been longer, but at over ninety items it contains more commander qualities than any single individual could be expected to possess.[9] Being researchers, we could have run a study where military personnel would rate the importance of each item to command effectiveness and then conducted a factor analysis on the results, hoping to distil unique principle components of commandership.[10] In the end, however, the results would still leave our main question unanswered. After all,

able	dynamic	inventive	ruthless
accountable	eloquent	judgement	self-confident
action-oriented	empowering	knowledgeable	self-controlled
adaptable	energetic	leadership	self-improving
alert to moral issues	expert	loyal	selfless
analytical	fit	management	self-reflective
can anticipate	flexible	mature	self-sacrificing
articulate	force of character	moderate	sincere
assured	good humoured	moral courage	smart
audacious	heroic	not shy	spirited
brave	honest	obstinate	steady
competent	honour	organizational skill	tough
competitive	imaginative	perceptive	trusted
considerate	industrious	perseverant	trustworthy
cool-headed	influential	personal integrity	undaunted
courageous	initiative	physical courage	unflappable
creative	innovative	practical	valourous
decisive	inspirational	professional	virtuous
dependable	inspiring	resilient	will
determined	integrity	resolute	will power
diligent	intelligent	respectful	willing to take risk
dutiful	intuitive	responsible	wise
			zealous

Figure 1: Compilation of terms used to characterize good commanders

describing the human traits necessary to be a successful commander presupposes knowledge or familiarity with the concept of commander (good or bad) to begin with. And although we do not doubt that many in the military profession know implicitly what a commander is—that is, they can recognize a good or bad commander when they see one—it is precisely the *explicit* definition of the concept that is at issue. Listing commander traits is, at best, only a comparative activity—i.e., it may distinguish among types of commanders (strong versus weak, etc), but it leaves moot the issue of what a commander really is.

For instance, there have been great commanders in history, just as there have been poor ones. But by far, most commanders have been simply competent—that is, they have performed their duties adequately for the circumstances. According to the trait approach, the list of human traits describing adequate commanders must, in principle, be different from that of successful (or unsuccessful) commanders. But is it not possible that there have been adequate commanders in history who have shared the same set of traits as their more successful counterparts but who were less successful because of extenuating circumstances—for example, political climate, resources limitations, personnel differences and adversary competence? Describing "commander" only in terms of the traits of the fortunate few who have excelled in their positions assumes that the pressures, circumstances and difficulties affecting commanders are constant. Even worse, there is a tendency to judge those who had not attained greatness as somehow deficient in their personal traits and skills, when this, in fact, may not be the case.

So what, exactly, is a commander? To answer this question, it is first necessary to expose a false assumption: that when discussing the concept of a commander, one is invariably discussing only a person. This error is understandable since whenever one is asked to give an example of a great (or bad) commander, it is a specific individual (in history) that is recalled. A commander, however, is not simply a person. A commander is also a position—a position with known duties and functions that exists within a larger military and national bureaucracy. Sooner or later this position must, of course, be *filled* by a person with the appropriate skills and competencies for realising the *potential* of the position, but it is not sufficient to define "commander" solely in terms of the qualities and traits of people who have, in the past, filled the position itself.

We suggest that a definition of commander should be divorced from any (ideal) individual who may have commanded in the past. It should be anchored in a conceptual framework that, first, fully describes the super-ordinate concept of Command. Only then can a concept of command*er* be derived and delineated. Lastly, the confusion over commander-as-person versus commander-as-position has led to confusion in other areas as well—for example, that of equating commander with leader. As we will see, a commander is a superset concept that includes, but cannot be reduced to, a leader. In fact, the commander position provides the context for leadership to emerge.

USING THE COMPETENCY, AUTHORITY AND RESPONSIBILITY STRUCTURE

The proper context for describing the concept of commander should, not surprisingly, be found within Command and Control. Our previous explorations of the concepts of Command and of Control have yielded insights into the dynamics and the relationship of the two concepts.[11] We will use these insights as a base for addressing the question "What is a commander?"

From our past explorations of C^2 we have concluded that Command is a uniquely human behaviour, one that is manifested through the structures and processes of Control.[12] In principle, Command is a behaviour that any military person—regardless of rank—can demonstrate as long as 1) he or she is being creative, and 2) this creativity is in the service of the mission. As a creative act, Command is the realization of human potential from which military power and effectiveness is derived. We argue that the position of commander is a military's attempt to harness this Command potential, to give it stability and fiduciary power, to formalize its structure by situating it within a *chain of command*, and to maximize the probability of its expression when it is operationally necessary to do so. Ironically, the commander position is one way that a military imposes control on the expression of Command: although all individuals within a military can, in principle, exhibit Command behaviour, the position of commander is where such behaviour, by decree, is encouraged and ultimately expected. Therefore, a tension exists between the necessity for creative Command and the necessity to control Command creativity. This tension is implicit in much of the commander, manager and leadership literature.

Our definition of commander will be derived using the CAR structure, a structure we developed to delineate the factors that comprise Command. The CAR Structure[13] is an abstract three-dimensional space formed by the axes of Competency, Authority and Responsibility (CAR). The three axes (or dimensions) define a volume of space within which any Command capability—and, by extension, commander capability—can be located.

The Three Dimensions of Command

The CAR structure was originally developed to deal with the powerful implication from our new definition of Command: that all ranks, from the most junior to the most senior, are capable of expressing Command; that Command is a capacity inherent in humans.[14] If this conclusion is true, then what distinguishes Command capability among different individuals? How does Command for the general officer differ from that for the private? We propose that the three dimensions of Competency, Authority and Responsibility (CAR) are sufficient for making these distinctions.

Competency

Command requires skills and abilities so that missions can be accomplished successfully. These abilities fall into the following four general classes of competencies: physical, intellectual, emotional and interpersonal.

For most militaries, *physical competency* is the most prerequisite of abilities, one that is mandatory for any operational task, from conducting a ground reconnaissance, to loading a weapon, to flying an aircraft. Physical competency is not limited to physical strength, however; it also involves sophisticated sensory motor skills, good health, agility, and endurance. Although much technological development has been devoted to extending physical competency in humans—e.g., weapons, night vision goggles, G-suits, etc—militaries still place great importance on personal physical fitness.

The second skill set, *intellectual competency*, is critical for planning missions, monitoring the situation, for reasoning, making inferences, visualizing the problem space, assessing risks and making judgements. Above all, since no two missions will ever be the same, intellectual competency must include creativity, flexibility and a willingness to learn.

The importance of physical and intellectual competency for Command is well acknowledged. Most militaries institute physical and intellectual aptitude testing at recruitment and follow this with extensive physical and intellectual development during basic training and then subsequently in specialist courses and staff colleges. Indeed, militaries expend significant resources to ensure that their personnel have the requisite physical and intellectual competencies to accomplish the mission. Interestingly, much less effort is expended in developing the two other competencies—emotional and interpersonal—though they are equally important for command.

Missions (especially Operations Other Than War) can be ill-defined, operationally uncertain, resource scarce, and involve high risk to humans. Military deployment in theatre is often very stressful for those deployed as well as being disruptive to family life. Military members inevitably suffer a range of taxing negative emotions: guilt, anxiety, anger, frustration, boredom, grief, and depression.[15] Command under these conditions requires significant *emotional compe-*

tency, a competency strongly associated with resilience, hardiness and the ability to cope under stress. Command demands a degree of emotional "toughness" to accept the potentially dire consequences of operational decisions. The ability to keep an overall emotional balance and perspective on the situation is critical, as is the ability to maintain a sense of humour.

Finally, *interpersonal competency* is essential in a military organization for interacting effectively with one's subordinates, peers, superiors, the media and other government organizations. Rarely are directives or orders sufficient to rally human will and spirit. The development of trust, respect and effective teamwork requires articulateness, empathy, perceptiveness and social understanding on the part of the individual in command.

The physical, intellectual, emotional and interpersonal are classes of competencies that play a part in Command capability. The issue of whether an individual actually possesses the requisite amount, type and distribution of competencies needed to excel in a particular commander position is, for now, immaterial.[16] We have described this dimension of the CAR structure to describe the broad set of competencies necessary for commandership.

Authority

Authority, the second dimension of Command, refers to Command's domain of influence. It is the degree to which a commander is empowered to act, the scope of this power and the resources available for enacting his or her will. We distinguish between the Command authority that is assigned from external sources and that which an individual earns by virtue of personal credibility—that is, between *legal authority* and *personal authority*.

Legal authority[17] is the power to act as assigned by a formal agency outside the military, typically a government. Legal authority, as expressed explicitly in law, assigns commanders resources and personnel for accomplishing the mission. Furthermore, the legal authority assigned to a nation's military goes well beyond that of any other private or government organisation. Militaries have the authority to enforce obedience among their members[18] and, more importantly, militaries can knowingly place these members in harm's way if the operational needs of the mission demand it. These unique powers, formally assigned to militaries, are key in distinguishing *commander* positions from the *managerial* positions found in any large corporation (this is discussed in more detail later in the chapter).

Personal authority is that authority given informally to an individual by peers and subordinates. Unlike legal authority, which is made explicit through legal documentation, personal authority is held tacitly. It is earned over time through reputation, experience, strength of character and personal example.

Personal authority cannot be formally designated, nor can it be enshrined in rules and regulations. It emerges when an individual possesses the combination of competencies that yields leadership behaviour. The distinction between legal and personal authority is critical for understanding the differing requirements that managing and leading have for a commander.

Responsibility

The third dimension of Command is responsibility. This dimension addresses the degree to which an individual accepts the legal and moral liability commensurate with Command. As with authority, there are two components to responsibility, one externally imposed, and the other internally generated. The first, called *extrinsic responsibility*, involves the obligation for public accountability. For example, the assignment of legal authority is usually accompanied by a formal expectation by superiors that one will be held accountable for resources assigned. Since superiors (by definition) have greater legal authority than the individual being empowered, extrinsic responsibility implies (in this case) accountability *up* the chain of command. It implies a behavioural contract between the individual and his or her superiors. We must emphasize, however, that although legal authority implies accountability, extrinsic responsibility is not synonymous with accountability. Rather, extrinsic responsibility taps a person's *willingness* to be held accountable for resources—that is, their willingness to take responsibility for the legal authority that comes with the commander position. So although it is possible for a superior to explicitly delineate (e.g., to list in written form) what the subordinate is expected to be accountable for, until this accountability is accepted, extrinsic responsibility is not in place.

Extrinsic responsibility is also associated with personal authority. Personal authority is earned from peers and subordinates who, through implicit acts of trust and commitment, empower the individual with informal authority—an authority often associated with leadership. Personal authority comes at a price, however. Subordinates and peers (the followers) expect that the individual (the leader) will behave in a manner consistent with their trust and not treat their loyalty frivolously. Personal authority, therefore, implies accountability *down* to those who are the source of the empowerment.

Extrinsic responsibility is the degree to which an individual feels accountable both up to superiors and down to followers. As such, it should be correlated with the amount of legal authority assigned and personal authority achieved and it should act as a guarantee or commitment on the part of the individual to dispense power responsibly. History has shown, however, that authority and extrinsic responsibility are not always correlated—sometimes there is an unwillingness to be held accountable for authority given. When this happens, the potential for abusing authority becomes great.

Intrinsic responsibility, the second component of responsibility, is the degree of self-generated obligation that one feels towards the military mission. It is a function of the resolve and motivation that an individual brings to a problem—the amount of ownership taken and the amount of commitment expressed. Intrinsic responsibility is associated with the concepts of honour, loyalty and duty, those timeless qualities linked to military ethos. Of all the components in the dimensions of Command, intrinsic responsibility is the most fundamental. Without it, very little could be accomplished. It is the source of all motivation, effort and commitment. Indeed, it is the source of the very *will* that our definition asserts is essential for Command. Intrinsic responsibility will be affected by such factors as whether military personnel are conscripted or allowed to volunteer, whether civilians support the role of military in society, and whether the military organization itself is perceived to be upholding the values deemed important by its own members.

When we first developed the CAR structure, we presented it to a number of military officers, either in lecture format or in focus groups,[19] to determine whether CAR adequately encompassed the full range of military Command (both good and bad). The overwhelming response from these officers was positive, with CAR being evaluated as a good conceptual structure for discussing Command in a systematic way. The few negative comments centered on the criticism that CAR oversimplified the "art" or "mystique" of Command. Although the officers who made these comments could not actually articulate where CAR fell short in its description, they were quite adamant that "something" was missing. We are sympathetic to their concerns, for Command is a remarkably textured and complex phenomenon, but unless we succumb to Wittgenstein's dictum that "One must be silent about that which one cannot speak,"[20] we must begin somewhere, and CAR is a beginning that has both face and construct validity. We should add, however, that we do give a nod to the mystique of Command when we propose later in this chapter that commanders are not deliberately made, but rather emerge.

The Command Capability Space

We have asserted that the command capability of a commander is due as much to the characteristics inherent in the position as it is due to the qualities of the person filling the position. CAR allows us to map out the entire space of command capability as well as situate a commander within this space. As Figure 2 illustrates, each of the CAR dimensions describe one axis of an abstract three-dimensional space. To better understand the implications of this space for command, first imagine a horizontal slice of this space taken at some arbitrary level of competency (see Figure 3). This slice is a planar surface describing only the responsibility and authority dimensions (i.e., for the moment it ignores the competency dimension). For the discussion that follows, we have arbitrarily divided the resulting surface into quadrants representing high and low values for each axis (see the right-hand side of Figure 3).

When there is high authority (both legal and personal) and there is acceptance of responsibility associated with this degree of authority (both extrinsic and intrinsic) this is Maximal (balanced) Command. In this situation, the military organization can be assured that the authority assigned (and earned) will be treated responsibly in accordance with stated intentions, implied military values and general societal expectations. Balanced command is the desired state because responsi-

Figure 2: The Command Capability Space

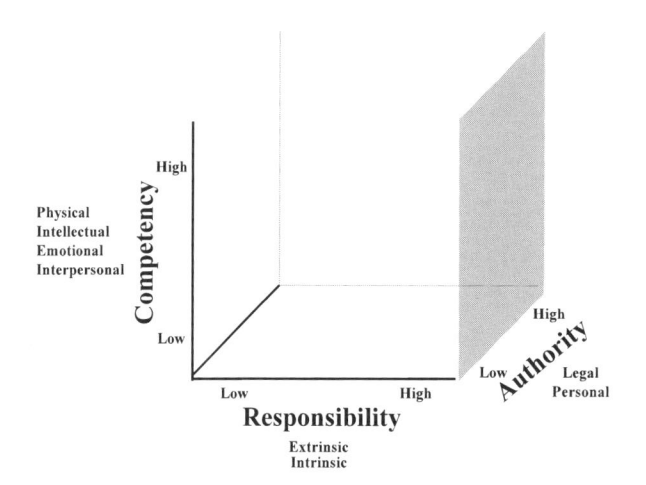

Figure 3: The Relationship Between Authority and Responsibility in the CAR Structure—Holding Competency Fixed.

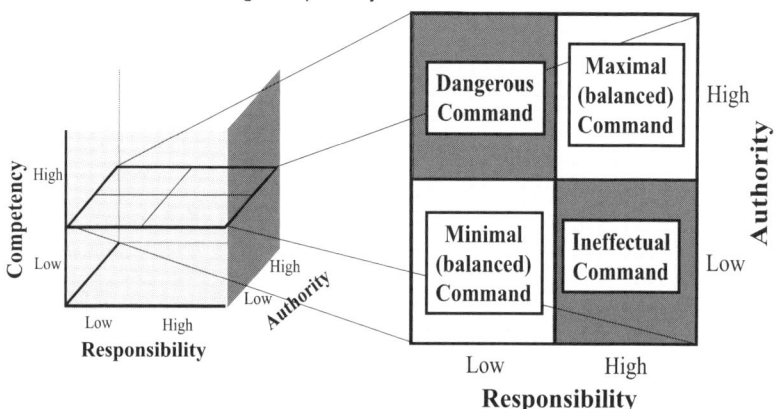

bility is the only mechanism by which militaries can guarantee that their extreme power will be exercised safely and appropriately.

There are cases, however, when there is an acceptance of high levels of responsibility without commensurately high levels of authority being given. This condition results in Ineffectual Command: although responsibility has been taken, power over resources has not been assigned or no clear mandate to act is authorised. For example, the experiences of military commanders like Lieutenant-General Dallaire[21] in Rwanda or Colonel P.L.E.M. Everts in Srebrenica[22] provide examples of the frustration and perceived ineffectuality of command that can occur in peace support operations, despite the extremely high levels of intrinsic responsibility that both of these individuals brought to these missions.[23] Ineffectual Command undermines the very purpose of a military. Without authority, a commander is powerless to properly accomplish the mission, yet can feel responsible for not having done so. Without sufficient authority, commanders are seriously compromised in their missions, and worse, the individuals filling the commander positions are at a tremendous psychological disadvantage.

When little authority is assigned to (or earned by) an individual and he or she has little expectation of being held accountable for actions, Minimal (balanced) Command results. The levels of authority and responsibility are indeed in balance, but little scope for initiating change is expected or granted. Command capability, therefore, is minimal.[24]

Finally, the fourth quadrant in Figure 3 represents the potential for abuse of command and is called Dangerous Command. It results when significant authority has been assigned (or earned) but the individual has not been willing to accept responsibility for the proper use of this power. There have been many examples of abuse of command in history (e.g., Hitler, Eichmann, certain American officers at My Lai in Vietnam)[25] and it is an outcome that most nations and their militaries try to avoid by invoking and enforcing judicial powers of punishment.

Yet abuse of authority is only one example of dangerous command. This quadrant also represents the potential outcome from automating command capability. As technology becomes more sophisticated and the need for greater speed and accuracy more pressing, "empowering" automated systems to make very fast defensive and offensive actions seems to be an attractive solution. However, two potentially negative outcomes for command are possible should this option be invoked. First, empowering automated systems pushes command into the Dangerous Command quadrant because such systems are incapable of accepting responsibility for their actions (i.e., they have the authority but not the responsibility). Second, since the human commanders in this situation will still be expected to accept responsibility for the actions of automated systems (but now have less authority) they will find themselves situated in the Ineffectual Command quadrant.[26] According to the CAR structure, militaries must carefully consider the repercussions of empowering automated systems.

Having discussed the four quadrants of the authority-responsibility surface, we are now in a position to reintegrate the competency dimension and to hypothesize the desired relationship among the three dimensions. Figure 4 illustrates three slices of the authority-responsibility surface for three different levels of competency (low, medium and high). The dot-filled ellipses located in each authority-responsibility surface represent the preferred commander capability areas. When competency is low, as is usually the case for an entry-level military member, the level of authority for a position given to such a member should also be low, as should the expected level of responsibility. Too much authority and responsibility would overwhelm an individual who has not, as yet, attained the level of competency (physical, intellectual, emotional and interpersonal) necessary for the position. And from the organizational perspective, it is risky to assign authority to someone who does not have adequate competency to wield it. Conversely if competency is high, too little authority and responsibility will induce boredom, low motivation and professional dissatisfaction.[27] Notice that the ellipses (i.e., the preferred command regions) in Figure 4 move diagonally across the authority-responsibility surface as competency increases. Also notice that regardless of the level of competency, the off-diagonals of the authority-responsibility surface should be avoided (i.e., Dangerous Command and Ineffectual Command). We assert, then, that the level of competency should match, or be well balanced with, levels of authority and responsibility. A large imbalance in any one of the dimensions will lead to compromised command

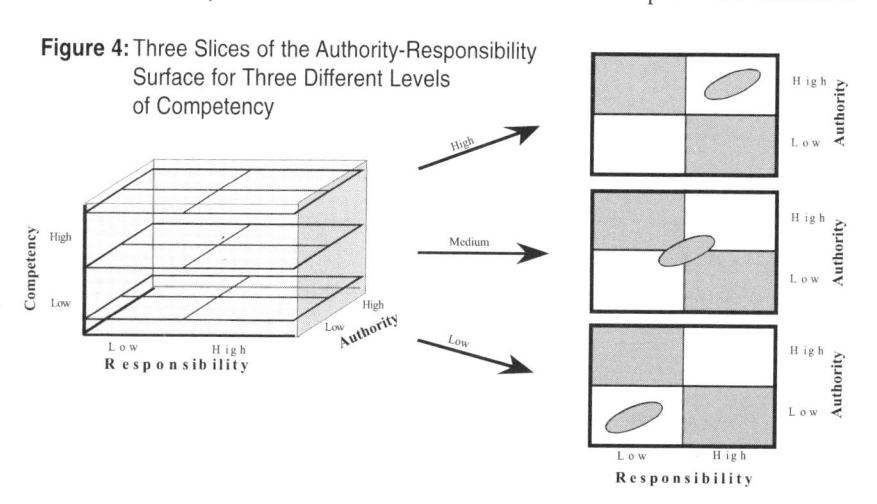

Figure 4: Three Slices of the Authority-Responsibility Surface for Three Different Levels of Competency

capability. The importance of balanced Command capability is addressed more extensively in "Clarifying the Concepts of Control and Command," by McCann & Pigeau.[28]

Finally, if the ellipses in Figure 4 are plotted successively for each increasing level of competency, a diagonal volume of space emerges that represents the ideal (or preferred) combination of competency, authority and responsibility. This Balanced Command Envelope (BCE) is the region of the command capability space (see Figure 5) within which military organizations should ensure that all of their members lie, throughout their careers. It is the region where competency, authority and responsibility are most in balance. It is the region that best protects militaries from dangerous or ineffectual command, and it is the region where motivation and initiative are maximized while the likelihood of poor performance and fear of failure are minimized. Although being (slightly) outside the BCE can sometimes have positive benefits—e.g., an acting position may motivate an individual to acquire greater levels of competency, thereby re-establishing the CAR balance—extreme outliers typically induce negative command conditions.[29]

Figure 5: The Balanced Command Envelope

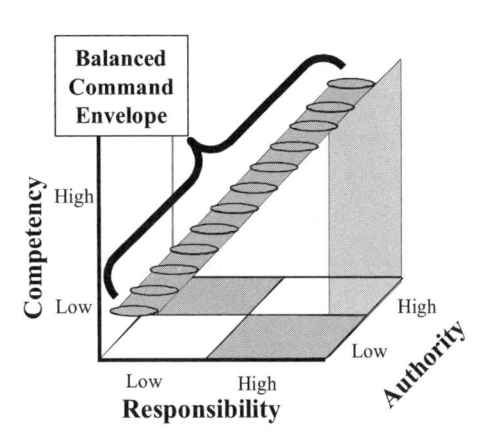

The BCE offers a rich conceptual framework for exploring military organizational structure, the role of tradition in military life, selection and training approaches, even promotion practices. But the remainder of this paper will concentrate on how it contributes to answering our primary question: "What is a commander?"

COMMANDER DEFINED

We are, at last, in a position to answer this question. Consistent with the discussion thus far, we define a commander as a *position/person combination lying on the balanced command envelope with special powers to 1) enforce discipline and 2) put military members in harm's way.*

There are three important components to this definition. First, a commander is a manifest combination of both an official position within a military organization and a person filling that position. Second, this position/person combination must lie on the balanced command envelope to ensure safe and effectual command. Third, a commander must be able to use the unique powers that governments assign to their militaries. If any of these three components is compromised, then the designation "commander" is compromised also.

The position/person

Legal authority specifies the actual position of commander within a military. A military organization consists of a set of hierarchically structured positions of legal empowerment, each with their own specific functions, duties and resources. Ideally, each of these positions should be distinct without overlapping authorities or reporting structures, and their terms of reference should be clear. Without clear lines of authority and function (e.g., chain of command), militaries run the risk of not sufficiently delineating unambiguous paths of accountability. Recall that balanced command requires commensurate levels of authority and responsibility (for any equivalent level of competency). Yet, legal authority by itself—remember we are speaking here only of *positions* in an organizational structure—cannot guarantee that responsibility for authority will be accepted by the individuals who eventually fill these positions. The best that it can do is to be precise in its expectations for accountability. This is why militaries have their own judicial systems: they provide an explicit mechanism for judging obligation to help ensure that legal authority is not abused.

As we said, legal authority specifies the position of commander. Along with this position comes resources, and it is the extrinsic responsibility of the person filling this position that these resources be properly managed. Hence, one of the roles of the commander is to be a *manager*—someone who controls the proper use of equipment, supplies and people to accomplish the mission. A manager produces order and consistency, identifies problems, interprets situations, makes decisions and judiciously applies resources.[30] In organizations that are as complex as militaries, with their critical national and international mandates, to be a manager is no trivial task. It requires considerable physical, intellectual, emotional and interpersonal competencies. It requires that the manager bring intrinsic responsibility to the position (i.e., the motivation to do well) and that he or she also accepts the extrinsic responsibility of being held accountable to superiors for accomplishing the mission and for using resources efficiently.

The CAR structure, however, identifies two types of authority—legal and personal. A manager who has legal authority but who has earned little or no personal authority is left exercising rigid and inflexible command based largely on enforcing explicit rules and regulations (see the lower right-hand quadrant of Figure 6).

This situation occurs when managers fail to realise that people are a unique resource. Unlike tanks or planes or ships, people must be *willing* to follow directives. They must *want* to accomplish the mission. People are a special resource who have their own intrinsic responsibility and, as such, can display a phenomenal amount of resolve, commitment and loyalty (e.g., duty above and beyond the call). The surest method for a commander to harness the commitment of personnel is to earn their trust and respect, i.e., to develop personal authority. This difference between legal and personal authority is critical. Legal authority is power for manipulating resources while personal authority is power to influence motivation. With both, effective and influential command is possible (upper right-hand quadrant in Figure 6).

In the discussion so far we have been very careful in our use of terms. We have used the word *manager* to describe that aspect of being a commander specifically associated with legal authority—i.e., properly *managing* resources. When discussing that aspect of being a commander associated with personal authority, however, we will use the term *leader*. Military leadership is usually defined as the ability to influence others to accomplish some (usually the leader's) task.[31] But "influencing others" is simply another way of saying that leaders must motivate their followers—i.e., leaders must somehow make followers *willing* (even *eager*) to perform the task. Whether this is accomplished through charismatic, transformational or transactional styles of leadership is, for the moment, inconsequential. The point is that followers endow leaders with personal authority, which leaders can then use to influence motivation (responsibly) for accomplishing tasks.

Figure 6: The Relationship Between Legal and Personal Authority

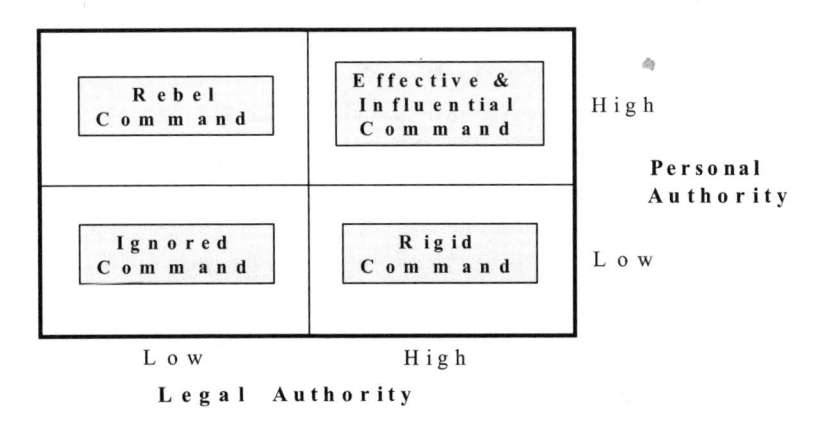

Rebel Command	Effective & Influential Command	High
Ignored Command	Rigid Command	Low
Low	High	Personal Authority

Legal Authority

Managers manage resources. Leaders lead people. Our CAR structure distinguishes between the two and we assert that that they should not be confused. Managing and leading, as separate capabilities, are direct consequences of the two types of authority contained within CAR. Consequently, it is possible to lead with little or no legal authority.[32] Some individuals, for example, are capable of gaining personal authority well in excess of the legal authority they possess. If they take commensurate responsibility, such people may feel more accountable to their followers than to the organization itself. This situation could lead to a form of "rebel" command (upper left-hand quadrant of Figure 6) where the values of the group (i.e., leader plus followers) supersede the values of the organization. Professor Winslow describes the negative impact of such a situation in a peacekeeping deployment by the Canadian Airborne Regiment into Somalia.[33]

Finally, if individuals have neither legal nor personal authority, but attempt to tell others what to do anyway, they will probably be ignored (lower left-hand quadrant in Figure 6). Although people like this might strongly desire to invoke change within the military organization (i.e., may possess strong intrinsic responsibility), they will be continually frustrated at their inability to influence change.

The purpose of this section was to argue that being a commander requires a combination of person and position. Emphasizing only the traits and characteristics of an individual without situating these traits and characteristics within the context of a position, ignores a key facet of being an effective commander. It is the continuous interplay between the two that is important. It follows, therefore, that the traits and characteristics of a *strategic* commander may be different from those of an *operational* commander and different still from a *tactical* commander. Undoubtedly, there will be some commonalities among the three—they are all humans who think, and feel—but the differences may outweigh the similarities. CAR is consistent with these differences, and to some extent predicts them, as discussed in the next section.

The Balanced Command Envelope

The second key element in our definition of a commander is that the position/person must lie on the Balanced Command Envelope (BCE). As we saw in the section dealing with the Command Capability Space, levels of competency, authority and responsibility must be commensurate to ensure balanced command capability. In most militaries, strategic, operational and tactical commanders have different levels of legal authority as reflected by their rank in the military hierarchy. Strategic commanders have the most authority over resources and people, operational commanders possess intermediate levels of authority and tactical commanders have less authority. If we assume that the commanders at each level must lie within the BCE, then it follows that each must also possess different levels of competency and responsibility (see Figure 7). Furthermore, it would be unreasonable to assume that the same combination of competencies (i.e., physical, intellectual, emotional and interpersonal) would express themselves equally for each level of command capability. An obvious example is physical strength and endurance—a competency less necessary at the strategic level than at the tactical. Another example is intellectual ability. The tactical commander deals in short time-frames (minutes and hours) and must make decisions quickly based on vast amounts of information that can change or degrade quickly. The operational commander must function in moderately long time-frames (days and weeks), which can place considerable loads on long-term memory and require extensive planning skills. The strategic commander must be able to think in months (and years) and must be capable of making abstract decisions based on breadth of knowledge and wise forethought. Similarly, emotional competency will vary with burden of responsibility and interpersonal competency will depend upon the number and range of individuals with whom a commander must interact. The point is that the CAR structure is not inconsistent with the notion that different *combinations* of competencies will be associated with different levels of military authority and responsibility.

Figure 7: Commanders at Different Levels of Competency, Authority and Responsibility

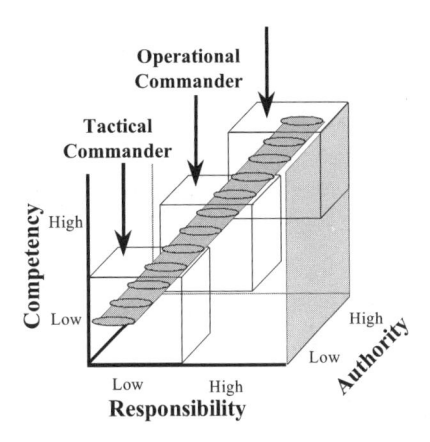

Earlier, we argued that being a commander meant being both a manager of resources and a leader of people. Neither by itself was sufficient to produce effective and influential command (upper right-hand quadrant in Figure 6). Furthermore, the competencies necessary for managing resources are different from those for leading people.[34] Add to this the fact that strategic, operational and tactical commanders must possess different competencies to function effectively, then this implies that there are many different combinations of competencies or talents required for being commanders. Now consider that recent theories of talent development suggest that talent potential is dependent on the expression of many different traits, but more important, it is also dependent on the multiplicative (rather than on the additive) effect of these traits.[35] Thus there can be a very great number of combinations of traits that will produce exactly the same behavioural talent—that is, a large combination of different commander traits can produce the same level of commander competency. More significantly, the multiplicative law also predicts that there are many more combinations of traits that will yield mediocre or poor commanders than will yield talented commanders. Simonton's work suggests that predicting overall command competency on the basis of traits is very difficult.

Finally, the entire argument thus far has ignored the crucial fact that commanders must operate in drastically different environments: land versus sea versus air, in garrison, during war, peace support, disaster relief, drug interdiction, surveillance, etc. It is unreasonable to expect that the optimum commander during times of peace necessarily should also be the optimum commander during times of conflict. The skills and temperament required for each may be quite different as pointed out long ago by Hamilton in his book.[36] Indeed, there are many cases in history where great commanders in one domain were mediocre or even poor commanders in another (e.g., Winston Churchill and Douglas MacArthur).[37]

A commander is a complex combination of competencies, authorities and responsibilities that must be balanced appropriately to suit the given level and situation of command. We maintain, therefore, that the search for ideal commander traits—traits that are predictive of command performance—is doomed to failure.

Before we move on to the third aspect of our definition of commander, "special powers," we will address a potential criticism of our position. "I understand," a concerned reader may argue, "that the search for an all encompassing set of ideal traits capable of covering the full range of the balanced command envelope may not be possible, but certainly there must exist a limited number of latent traits that, if identified early and properly nurtured, would nonetheless maximize the probability of attaining talented strategic, operational and tactical commanders. After all, if this is not possible then what chance does a military, or any large organization for that matter, have for producing competent commanders?" Since militaries, by and large, *have* been successful in producing competent commanders, this is a valid criticism. However, because militaries have been successful at producing competent commanders does not mean 1) that these commanders would have been competent for all military domains and situations, or 2) that these commanders *therefore* would have shared a common set of traits (latent or otherwise).

We suggest that the reason for the military's success may have as much to do with the law of large numbers and a form of Darwinian emergence, than it does with any single strategy put in place by militaries to select and then to train commanders. Just as recent theories of creativity,[38] brain development[39] and self-organizing systems[40] postulate that complex behaviour emerges spontaneously through the interaction of large numbers of separate units, we postulate that commandership similarly emerges as a result of the interaction of large numbers of units—in this case, from the large pool of military recruits. This does not mean that the process of creating good commanders is random, nor does it mean that selection and training are superfluous. It does mean, however, that commandership must be viewed as an emergent outcome of the entire military experience, from recruitment to retirement, an experience that draws in military culture, values, disciplinary and reward practices, traditions, force size, operation type and frequency, organizational structure, political stability, clarity of mandate, etc—in short, a dynamic confluence of many factors. Individual traits do play a role in shaping a commander but, in the end, they may account for only a small proportion of the variance.[41] Space limitations prohibit us from expanding this idea further, but a non-linear dynamical systems approach to commander development is a promising avenue for research (see Guastello for how emergent leadership can be described using a dovetail catastrophe).[42]

Special Powers

The third key component of our definition of commander is the notion of the special power to enforce discipline and to put military members in harm's way. Although these powers are aspects of the legal authority formally conferred to the position of commander (and as such could have been discussed earlier), these powers have such wide-ranging implications for commandership that they must be discussed separately.

Militaries are a nation's sanctioned method for exerting lethal force and this "...unique status inevitably leads to a large number and variety of laws designed not only to control the armed forces but also to assist in ensuring that the values of broader society are maintained within the social fabric of the military."[43] The power to (legally) enforce discipline and to (legally) place members in harm's way effectively distinguishes the military from every other segment or in society.[44] Were it not for these two special powers, military commanders would be no different from executives or managers in any large civilian corporation. The military's organization and traditions, as well as its standard operating procedures and rules of engagement, are direct and indirect consequences of these two special powers.

Our definition implies that not everyone in the military is given these powers, otherwise every military member would be a commander (which is not the case). For example, the very fact of being assigned a senior military position may give an individual the right to influence policy and expend considerable funds, but it will not mean that this individual *automatically* has the powers of a commander. While such individuals can certainly perform important tasks, and have duties equivalent to directors or managers in civilian organizations (and they should lie on the Balanced Command Envelope to perform these duties effectively), they are not commanders. The position does not confer on them the legal authority to enforce discipline or put people into harm's way. Therefore, just as a military's extreme power is unique in the society, a commander's power is unique in the military. Commanders are the concentrated repository of a nation's potential to violently express its will. This is why commanders must lie on the BCE—to ensure that their powers of command will neither be abused nor made ineffectual, and to ensure that the individual filling the position is competent enough to accomplish the mission.

Two types of commanders are implied by our definition: Type I and Type II commanders. Type I commanders have the power to enforce discipline but do not have, at that moment, the legal authority to place members in harm's way. This may occur when a commander is in charge of a training unit or is tasked to maintain its readiness, either at home or abroad, but is not actually taking part in an operation. Type II commanders have both powers and are on active duty during officially sanctioned operations. It is the Type II commander that provides the *raison d'être* for a military's status as a unique organization. If a nation never required or allowed its people to die for their country (or its interests) then there would never be a need for Type II commanders. There would then be no need for Type I commanders either, since special laws to enforce discipline are necessary only if extreme circumstances are anticipated. Without Type II authority militaries would simply be large police forces and, like police forces, could operate quite adequately under civil law.

Another implication of our definition is that a person occupying a commander position ceases to be a commander (regardless of his/her competency) when the position is vacated or the status of the position changes. For example, without an officially designated operation, Type II commanders default to Type I commanders—i.e., they may have the power to enforce discipline, to prepare and to train subordinates for future operations, but they cannot legally put these subordinates in harm's way. This is a direct consequence of the tight coupling between position and legal authority. Another consequence is that the special powers of Type I and II commanders are only as immutable as the whim of the governments who legislate the legal authority associated with these positions in the first place. For instance, Lieutenant-General Romeo Dallaire describes the difficult circumstances he faced as a commander of a multinational force during the genocide in Rwanda (italics added):

> I then made the further decision to extract the future prime minister, Faustin Twagiramungu… from his encircled home and bring him to my headquarters. The extremists heard about this intercession and began verbal and military attacks on both my headquarters and me. I therefore *asked* the contingents in my headquarters to defend the headquarters and the Prime Minister designate. Was I authorized to order the contingents to do so? At that point, UNAMIR [United Nations Mission for Rwanda] *no longer had a mandate.* Would my troops have fought to defend the headquarters at the risk of being wiped out? What were their own national orders at that point in time?… Ultimately, why should they have risked their lives to follow a Canadian or other foreign general [the vast majority of troops within UNAMIR were not Canadian] when their own nation was not at risk, their government *did not want casualties,* and our chances of success were minimal?[45]

Essentially, Dallaire is questioning whether he had, at that moment, the powers of a Type II (and perhaps even a Type I) commander. Notice that he felt he needed to ask, rather than to order, the contingents to defend the headquarters. Without a UNAMIR mandate, he effectively no longer had legal authority. Prime Minister Designate Twagiramungu's life, therefore, was saved both by Dallaire's personal (not legal) authority and by the intrinsic responsibility his troops felt for trying to stop the slaughter. Without a mandate, without legal authority, Dallaire was vulnerable to disciplinary action from the UN as well as from Canada. Unfortunately, even when Dallaire did have an official mandate to operate in Rwanda and could operate as a Type II commander, the loss of ten Belgian soldiers under his command precipitated an outcry that lead to an official Belgian inquiry (at which Dallaire then needed to testify). So being a multinational commander, especially under politically complex and sensitive circumstances, can be a very transient, elusive and precarious occupation.[46]

There are also times when a designated commander may not be *allowed* to exercise Type II authority. Modern society with its immediate media coverage has little tolerance for casualties when no direct threat to national security exists. Therefore commanders of peace support operations experience tremendous pressure from their political masters to incur "zero casualties." Under these circumstances, should a commander's priorities change from "the time-honoured military ethos of 'my mission, my personnel, myself' to 'my personnel, my mission, myself'?"[47] Would this not render powerless a commander's Type II authority, then bringing the whole reason for military involvement into question?

These examples of changing commander status—i.e., going from Type II to Type I, either inadvertently or due to political intervention—imply that commanders may find themselves on the edge (if not totally outside) of the Balanced Command Envelope. According to our definition, lying outside the BCE compromises command capability. Therefore, Dallaire's command in Rwanda was less effectual than perhaps would have been suggested by his high levels of competency and responsibility because circumstances pushed Lieutenant-General Romeo Dallaire from the upper right-hand quadrant of Figure 3 (Maximal Balanced Command) into the lower right-hand quadrant (Ineffectual Command). As we have already mentioned, it was his personal authority that allowed him to be as successful as he was. However without legal authority, carrying out the responsibilities of a commander becomes a frustrating and extremely stressful affair—as Dallaire can personally attest.

Lastly, since the two special powers that Type II commanders wield embody the very reason militaries have a unique status in society, it follows that Type II commander positions will be highly coveted. And for those who have successfully mastered the challenges of commandership—by exercising well-honed competencies and accepting grave responsibilities—it can be an exhilarating and fulfilling experience. What happens then when Type II commanders move to staff positions, as often happens—positions that may not have even Type I authority? We predict that such a move would be psychologically stressful and that the loss of concentrated power will push the individual outside the Balanced Command Envelope. How the military organization now responds to this imbalance will determine this individual's command capability for the future.

CONCLUSION

It is our contention that the world's militaries exist to help resolve extreme human conflict,[48] conflict that reflects the complexity of human society in general and human psychology in particular. It is the commander who is pivotal in military intervention in these complex conflicts. Defining commander as a *position/person combination ideally lying on the balanced command envelope with special powers to 1) enforce discipline and 2) put military members in harm's way* encapsulates the key aspects of commandership, while at the same time giving full due to the complexity of the concept.

Command is the uniquely human activity of creatively expressing will, but one that can be expressed only through the structures and processes of control.[49] A commander, as a manifestation of Command, is a human who works within a defined military position with assigned authorities (i.e., control structures) to achieve mission objectives. It is through the commander position that Command energy and capability is most obviously legitimised and channelled. It is the means by which militaries can, on the one hand, encourage creative Command, and on the other, control Command creativity. Marrying position and person is an important condition for adequately defining "commander."

Equally important is to chart the domain of influence that impacts this marriage. We believe that competency, authority and responsibility (CAR) specify three dimensions of influence that, when combined, define a Command capability space within which all potential commander types (e.g., dangerous, ineffectual, over-competent, balanced, etc) reside. Furthermore, competency, authority and responsibility must be balanced, as represented by the Balanced Command Envelope, for effective commandership to take place. Militaries must ensure that their commanders—throughout their missions and indeed throughout their careers—stay within the BCE.

Neither the position/person combination nor the requirement for balance across the CAR dimensions restricts our definition to militaries. Our distinctions between manager and leader, as well as our discussion of the dangers of lying outside the BCE are as pertinent for the private and public sectors as they are for militaries. The characteristic that distinguishes commanders from executives or directors or department heads is the right (and responsibility) to exercise the unique powers that only militaries are allowed to wield. Thus our definition of commander explicitly mentions the special powers for enforcing discipline and for putting military members in harm's way because, without these qualifiers, any executive from any civilian could call him- or herself a commander. It is our view that commanders exist only in militaries (with the exception of the few political leaders in charge of the militaries themselves).

But neither is everyone in the military a commander. We defined *Command* to include anyone who creatively expresses his or her will to accomplish the mission, but we defined *commander* more restrictively. Both Type I and Type II commanders possess powers that set them apart, even within their own militaries. Therefore, militaries should be selective as to who is assigned these special powers, because they supersede the individual rights and freedoms that most democratic societies guarantee to their citizens.

Finally, the special powers in our definition are meant to specify the *executive* legal authority of commanders, not just their *potential* legal authority. If designated commanders are not allowed to execute their powers then they are, in effect, no longer commanders (even though they may still be called such). As we have seen in the case of Dallaire in Rwanda, this diminishing of commander capability may be an inevitable consequence of the complex social, cultural and political circumstances of peace support operations.

We believe that our new definition of commander has face validity—i.e., it makes sense to the people most affected by it—and it has construct validity—i.e., it is consistent with our general theoretical development of command and control. Our next task is to assess its empirical validity. We invite the scientific community, both within the civilian and within the military sectors, to generate hypotheses and conduct studies on our concepts. Our aim is to develop an internally consistent and scientifically supported theory of command and control, one that will provide a common and useful new language and framework for all militaries.

NOTES

1. A shorter version of this chapter has been published as "What is a Military Commander?" in the proceedings of the Workshop on the Human in Command in Peace Support Operations 2000, Breda, The Netherlands: Royal Military Academy.
2. John Hackett, *The Profession of Arms* (London: Sidgwick & Jacobs, 1983), 220.
3. R. Pigeau & C. McCann, "Redefining Command and Control," in *The Human in Command*, eds. R. Pigeau and C. McCann, (New York: Kluwer Academic/Plenum Publishers, 2000), 163-184.
4. G. D. Foster, "Contemporary C2 theory and research: The failed quest for a philosophy of command," *Defense Analysis, 4*(3), 1988, 201-228.
5. There are of course other types of validity such as concurrent and empirical validity, but these are usually developed after external and construct validity have been established.
6. R. Pigeau, & C. McCann, "Putting 'Command' back into Command and Control," *Proceedings of the Command and Control Conference,* (Ottawa, ON: Canadian Defence Preparedness Association, September 26, 1995)
7. Pigeau and McCann, "Redefining Command Control,"163-184; C. McCann & R. Pigeau, "Clarifying the Concepts of *Control* and of *Command*," *Proceedings of Command and Control Research and Technology Symposium,* Vol. 1 (Washington, DC: CCRP, Dept. of Defense, 1999), 475-490.
8. For example S.L.A. Marshall, *Men Against Fire* (Alexandria, VA: Byrrd Enterprises, Inc. 1947); I. Hamilton, *The Commander* (London: Hollis & Carter, 1957); B.W. Tuchman, "Generalship," *Parameters,* 1972; W. Slim, "Higher Command in War," *Military Review,* 1990; and R.R. Crabbe, "The Nature of Command," in *The Human in Command,* eds. C. McCann & R. Pigeau (New York: Kluwer Academic / Plenum Publishers, 2000).
9. In compiling this list we made no attempt to eliminate redundancies (e.g., brave/courageous, smart/intelligent) or resolve apparent contradictions (e.g., ruthless/selfless, flexible/obstinate) among the items. We assumed the authors used these specific words knowingly to infuse their descriptions with nuance and meaning.
10. There have been numerous studies attempting to find the key predictors of effective leadership using multivariate techniques— for example, see R.D. Mann, "A review of the relationship

between personality and performance in small groups," *Psychological Bulletin, 56,* 1959, 241-270;, R. G. Lord, C.L. DeVader & G. M. Alliger, "A meta-analysis of the relation between personality traits and leadership perceptions: An application of validity generalization procedures," *Journal of Applied Psychology, 71,* 1986, 402-410; and R. M. Stogdill, *Handbook of Leadership: A Survey of Theory and Research* (New York, NY: Free Press, 1974).

11. C. McCann, & R. Pigeau, "Clarifying the Concepts of *Control* and of *Command*," Vol. 1, 475-490; R. Pigeau, & C. McCann, "The Human in Command: A Brief Introduction," in *The Human in Command,* eds. C. McCann & R. Pigeau (New York: Kluwer Academic / Plenum Publishers, 2000), 1-8.

12. We have defined Command as *the creative expression of human will necessary to accomplish the mission* and Control as *those structures and processes devised by Command to manage risk* (C. McCann & R. Pigeau, 1999).

13. Pigeau and McCann, "Clarifying the Concepts of *Control* and *Command*."

14. This is not to say, however, that every member in a military will be encouraged or even choose to express Command. Often it is perfectly appropriate to follow well-established procedures and guidelines without needing to invent new solutions to old problems

15. R. A. Lane, "The Fog of War: A Personal Experience of Leadership," in *The Human in Command,* eds. C. McCann & R. Pigeau (New York: Kluwer Academic / Plenum Publishers, 2000), 51-64; and M. Thompson and M. Gignac, "Adaptation to Peace Support Operations—The experience of Canadian Forces Augmentees," Paper presented at the Human in Command Workshop and Symposium, 5-8 June 2000, Breda, Netherlands.

16. This point is important, otherwise we risk making the same mistake that we have accused other authors of making— i.e., of trying to identify *ideal* commander traits.

17. Also referred to as positional authority in P. G. Northouse, *Leadership: Theory and Practice* (London: Sage Publications, 1997).

18. In Canada, this authority is referred to as "powers of punishment."

19. The lectures addressed approximately two hundred and fifty individuals from captains to generals, while the focus groups included about fifty Majors and Lieutenant-Colonels.

20. L. Wittgenstein, *Tractatus Logico-Philosophicus* (New York: Humanities Press, 1961). Translated by D.F. Pears & B.F. McGuinness.

21. R. A. Dallaire, "Command Experiences in Rwanda," in *The Human in Command,* eds. C. McCann & R. Pigeau (New York: Kluwer Academic / Plenum Publishers, 2000), 29-50.

22. P. L. E. M. Everts, "Command and Control in Stressful Conditions," in *The Human in Command,* eds. C. McCann & R. Pigeau (New York: Kluwer Academic / Plenum Publishers, 2000), 65-82.

23. Lieutenant-General Romeo Dallaire commanded the United Nations Assistance Mission for Rwanda (UNAMIR) in 1993/94. Colonel P.E.L.M. Everts commanded Dutchbat 2 (the second of three infantry battalions provided as peacekeeping units within the United Nations Protection Force [UNPROFOR] in the former Yugoslavia). Both commanders were limited by their mandates (or lack thereof) in the actions that they could take in alleviating humanitarian disasters in peace support operations. It was a tribute to their personal command capability (as well as the commitment of their personnel) that they were as successful as they were.

24. However, this quadrant could represent a military's pool for potential future commanders (e.g., junior officers).

25. N. Dixon, *On the Psychology of Military Incompetence* (London: Random House, 1976).

26. Although the commander usually has veto powers over such automated systems, this so-called "command by negation" philosophy, is undesirable because it reduces command to a re-active rather than a pro-active function.

27. M. D. Capstick, "Command and Leadership in Other People's Wars," in *The Human in Command*, eds. C. McCann & R. Pigeau (New York: Kluwer Academic / Plenum Publishers, 2000), 83-92.
28. McCann and Pigeau, "Clarifying the Concepts of *Control* and of *Command*," Vol. 1, 475-490.
29. Ibid.
30. J.P. Kotter, "What leaders really do," *Harvard Business Review*, May-June 1990, 103-111.
31. S.H. Hays and W.T. Thomas, *Taking Command: The Art and Science of Military Leadership* (Harrisburg, PA: Stackpole Books, 1967).
32. G. de Souza and H.J. Klein, "Emergent leadership in the group goal-setting process," *Small Group Research*, 26(4), 1986, 475-496; and R. M. Sorrentino & N. Field, "Emergent leadership over time: The functional value of positive motivation," *Journal of Personality and Social Psychology*, 50(6), 1986, 1091-1099.
33. D. Winslow, "Misplaced Loyalties: Military Culture and the Breakdown of Discipline in Two Peace Operations," in *The Human in Command*, eds. C. McCann & R. Pigeau (New York: Kluwer Academic / Plenum Publishers, 2000), 293-310.
34. J .Hackett, *The Profession of Arms* (London: Sidgwick & Jackson, 1983); and J.P. Kotter, "What leaders really do," *Harvard Business Review*, May-June 1990, 103-111.
35. D. K. Simonton, "Defining and finding talent: Data and a multiplicative model," *Behavioral and Brain Sciences*, 21, 1999, 424-425; and D. K. Simonton, "Talent and its development: A emergenic and epigenetic model," *Psychological Review*, 106 (3), 435-457.
36. I. Hamilton, *The Commander* (London: Hollis & Carter, 1957).
37. B. Bond, *Fallen Stars: Eleven Studies of Twentieth Century Military Disasters* (London: Brassey's, 1991).
38. D. T. Lykken, M. McGue, A. T. J. Tellegen & Bouchard, "Emergencies: Genetic traits that may not run in families," *American Psychologist*, 47, 1992, 1565-1577; and D.K. Simonton, *Origins of genius: Darwinian perspectives on creativity* (New York: Oxford University Press, 1999).
39. G. M. Endelman, *Bright Air, Brilliant Fire: On the Matter of Mind* (New York: BasicBooks, 1992).
40. S. Kaufmann, *At Home in the Universe* (Oxford: Oxford University Press, 1995).
41. For example, "less than 10% of the variance in leadership can be accounted for using intelligence as the predictor." D. K. Simonton, "Intelligence and personal influence in groups: Four nonlinear models," *Psychological Review*, 92(4), 1985, 532-547.
42. S. J. Guastello, "Self-organization in leadership emergence," *Nonlinear Dynamics, Psychology and Life Sciences*, 2(4), 1998.
43. Judge Advocate General, *Military Justice at the Summary Trial Level* (Ottawa: Office of the Judge Advocate General, Department of National Defence, 1999).
44. Although there are many high-risk non-military organizations in society whose members may risk death (e.g., police, fire-fighters, etc), these individuals cannot be *ordered* to place themselves in mortal jeopardy. Furthermore, these individuals are bound only by civil law, whereas military members are bound by civil and military law.
45. Dallaire, "Command Experiences in Rwanda," 29-50, in *The Human in Command*, eds, C. McCann and R. Pigeau, (New York: Kluwer Academic/Plenum Publishers, 2000). Italics added by authors.
46. T.D. Young, *Multinational land formations and NATO: Reforming practices and structure* (Carlisle Barracks, PA: Strategic Studies Institute, U.S. Army War College, 1997).
47. Dallaire, "Command Experiences in Rwanda," 29-50.
48. Pigeau and McCann, "Redefining Command and Control,"163-184.
49. McCann and Pigeau, "Clarifying the Concepts of *Control* and of *Command*," 475-490.

Distinguishing the Concepts of Command, Leadership and Management

Lieutenant-Colonel Peter Bradley

Lieutenant-Colonel, Dr. Peter Bradley is a serving CF officer who is presently the Head of the Military Leadership and Psychology department at the Royal Military College of Canada.

INTRODUCTION

THE TERMS COMMAND, LEADERSHIP, AND MANAGEMENT are often confused in the Canadian Forces (CF). This chapter will provide some clarity on what is meant by each term. The central arguments are: (a) leadership and management are different, and (b) leadership and management are properly conceived as subsets of command. In this way, a commander exercises command by alternatively leading and managing. Therefore, there are no command behaviours that cannot be classified as either leadership or management behaviours.

This chapter will begin with an examination of CF doctrine on command, leadership and management to highlight how these three concepts are defined and related. This will be followed by reference to other works to show how leadership and management have been differentiated by writers outside the CF. Next, a classification of command behaviours will be presented showing which are leadership behaviours and which are management. The chapter will conclude with some implications for leadership training for aspiring commanders and some thoughts on leadership and management at the general officer level.

CF DOCTRINE ON COMMAND

In CF doctrine, the term "command" is used in two ways. When used as a noun, it refers to "the lawful authority which a superior exerts over his subordinates in the Services by virtue of his rank and appointment."[1] When used as verb, it refers to the actions associated with command. In this regard, B-GL-300-003/FP-00, *Command* states that "command ... embraces both management activities ... and leadership ...."[2] Thus, there are two aspects of command—the authority vested in the commander and the command actions that the commander takes to exercise this authority. This chapter will focus exclusively on the action of command, specifically the behaviours commanders engage in as they exercise their command.

The central argument of this chapter is that command behaviour is properly conceptualized as comprising leadership and management. B-GL-300-003/FP-00, *Command* does say that command involves both management and leadership, but the publication is not always clear in distinguishing between these two subordinate concepts. For example, command is described in Chapter 1 as "identifying what needs to be done and why .... management [as] allocating resources to achieve it and leadership [as] getting subordinates to achieve it."[3] Certainly, leadership and management are distinct but this description does not adequately capture the difference between the two concepts. In the same chapter, the publication states that "military command encompasses the art of decision-making, motivating and directing all ranks into action to accomplish missions,"[4] but, as will be shown later, decision-making is a management behaviour and both motivating and directing are leadership behaviours. A simpler way of displaying the relations among leadership, management, and command is displayed in Figure 1 where the action of command is conceptualized as involving simply management and leadership behaviours.

From this model, it follows that all command behaviours that a commander will engage in can be classified as either management or leadership behaviours. The ratio of leadership to management behaviours will vary depending

Figure 1:

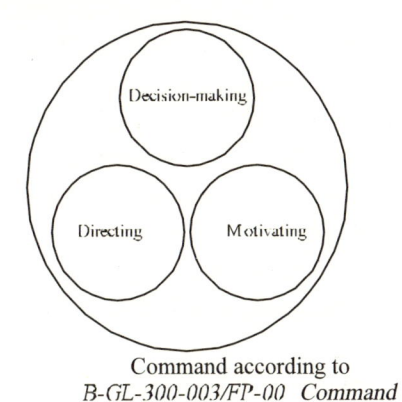

Command according to
B-GL-300-003/FP-00 *Command*   A more parsimonious view of command

on the characteristics of the commander or situational factors. Some commanders will be more inclined to leadership and exhibit more leadership behaviours whereas others may be more comfortable with a managerial style of command and exhibit more management behaviours. Different situations will also call for a different mix of leadership and management behaviours from the commander and proficient commanders will be able to provide either leadership or management behaviours as the situation and followers warrant.

The concept of control is often associated with command. B-GL-300-003/FP-00 *Command* stresses that control is the means by which commanders exercise their authority and the method by which decisions are implemented. Both of these are management functions; therefore, a more economical way of conceptualizing command is to say that it involves both leadership and management.

CF DOCTRINE ON LEADERSHIP

There is some confusion in the CF on what constitutes leadership. Most of this confusion is due to two factors: (a) CF leadership doctrine is based on an inadequate definition of leadership; and (b) much of what is presented in CF courses as leadership training is actually training in management practices, so that graduates of these courses naturally confuse the two concepts. The problems with the CF doctrinal definition of leadership are of primary interest in this chapter. There are two main problems: an inadequate definition and the assumption that leadership is an art.

Canadian Forces Publication (CFP), A-PD-131-002/PT-001, *Leadership, Volume 2: The Professional Officer,* promulgated on 31 July 1973, states that "leadership is the art of influencing human behaviour in order to accomplish a mission in the manner desired by the leader."[5] This definition of leadership is repeated in CFP A-PD-131-002/PT-001, *Leadership, Volume 2: The Professional Officer*, also promulgated on 31 July 1973 and CFP B-GL-318-015/PT-001, *Leadership in Land Combat, Volume 15: Military Training*, which was published fifteen years later on 4 July 1988. From this definition it is not clear how the commander can or cannot influence followers. For example, the use of coercion to secure follower compliance is within the scope of this definition, even though most professional officers would say that coercion is not leadership.

In 1973, the Chief of the Defence Staff at that time, General Jacques Dextraze, defined leadership as "the art of influencing others to do willingly what is required in order to achieve an aim or goal" in a paper that was widely distributed throughout the CF. This definition represents a marked departure from the CF doctrine described above, even though all were originally published about the same time—the early 1970s. Nowhere in the CF doctrinal definition presented earlier is there a requirement for the followers to respond willingly. By Dextraze's definition, a leader's use of force in securing follower compliance is not leadership. The 1973 CF definition, on the other hand, seems to allow for coercive measures in "influencing human behaviour in order to accomplish a mission in the manner desired by the leader,"[6] even though coercive measures are not actively promoted.

The Dextraze definition of leadership appears later in CFP B-GL-300-003/FP-00, *Command*, a Land Force publication promulgated on 21 July 1996, where it is stated that "Leadership, essentially, is the art of influencing others to do willingly what is required in order to achieve an aim or goal."[7] Thus, it would appear that the army's conceptual definition of leadership has changed over the years from one of an influence relationship in which the leader could use whatever means necessary to secure follower compliance to a more persuasive, influence relationship that would result in willing followership. This parallels the societal shift in Canada over the past three decades from a society of compliant followers who deferred to leaders because they were in charge towards a society of more autonomous followers who need to be persuaded and inspired before falling in step with any leader.[8]

Another problem with the CF definition of leadership is in classifying it as an art. What exactly does this mean? Well, *The Concise Oxford Dictionary* (1990) defines art as a "human creative skill" suggesting that one requires a certain talent in order to be able to successfully exercise leadership and that the practice of leadership is a creative enterprise. Both of these implications are consistent with the CF practice of devoting considerable resources each year to the task of selecting officer candidates with the right stuff. On the other hand, they are not consistent with the CF practice of devoting larger amounts of resources each year to training our leaders so that they can become more proficient. The waters become even more murky when we compare the CF definition of leadership, where leadership is classified as an art, with the CF definition of management, where management is classified as a science. Does this mean that there are certain principles and theorems that are applicable to management, but not to leadership? Does this mean that management can be taught, but leadership cannot?

CF DOCTRINE ON MANAGEMENT

CFP 131(1) defines management as "the science of employing men and materiel in the economical and effective accomplishment of the mission." Implicit in this definition is the understanding that management can be taught for it is a science with fundamental laws and precepts.

CFP B-GL-300-003/FP-00, *Command*, 21 July 1996, defines management as "the use of a range of techniques to enhance the planning, organization and execution of operations, logistics, administration and procurement"[10] and then, more succinctly states that "management is primarily about the allocation and control of resources (human, material, and financial) to achieve objectives."[11]

The two definitions of management are quite similar. Management is goal-directed and involves control. Implicit in both definitions is the requirement for the manager, the agent dispensing the management, to engage in activities like problem-solving, budgeting, allocating, directing, measuring, and supervising. Thus, management is a rational exercise that is deliberate, mechanical, and efficient.

LEADERSHIP AND MANAGEMENT LITERATURE OUTSIDE THE CF

Confusing leadership and management is not unique to the CF. It occurs in the business and academic communities as well. The business community abounds with courses and programs in leadership and leader development. A close look at many of these programs reveals that much of the curriculum is actually focused on management activities like budgeting, planning, and the like. In the academic community, "confusing leadership and management and treating the words as if they were synonymous have a long and illustrious history in leadership studies."[12] There are some scholars who do distinguish between leadership and management[13] and it is the work of this group that is of greatest relevance to our present discussion.

Before examining this literature in detail, we need to recognize that most of this work is based solely on the experience and opinions of the authors; there is little or no data to support their positions. On the positive side, however, there is remarkable similarity in the positions taken by the various writers.

Although the focus of this chapter is on the extent to which leadership behaviours are different from management behaviours, Zaleznik published a much cited article in which he argued that managers and leaders were essentially different types of people.[14] Summarized in Table 1, an examination of Zaleznik's types shows that leadership is focused on innovation, ideas and change, whereas management is concerned with coordination, control and maintaining the status quo.

Table 1

Leaders...	**Managers...**
Adopt active attitudes toward goals, shaping ideas instead of responding to them	Adopt impersonal, passive attitudes toward goals
Leaders develop fresh approaches to problems	Managers act to limit choices
Leaders create excitement in their work	Managers view work as an enabling process involving people and ideas interacting to establish strategies and make decisions
Leaders work from high-risk positions and are temperamentally disposed to seek out risk	Managers negotiate and bargain on the one hand and use rewards and punishment on the other.
Concerned with ideas, leaders relate with people in more intuitive and empathic ways	Managers relate to people according to the role they play in a sequence of events or in a decision-making process
Leaders see their role as profoundly altering human, economic and political relationships	Managers see themselves as conservators and regulators of an existing order with which they identify

A. Zaleznik, "Managers and leaders: Are they different?" *Harvard Business Review,* May-June, 1977, 67-78.

Katz and Kahn declare that "every act of influence on a matter of organizational relevance is in some degree an act of leadership."[15] They do not provide a corresponding definition of management, but may be comparing leadership with management when they say "we consider the essence of organizational leadership to be influential increment over and above mechanical compliance with routine directives of the organization."[16] Thus, leadership is influence that results in behaviour that transcends basic job requirements, according to Katz and Kahn.

Kotter argues that "leadership and management are two distinctive and complementary courses of action" with each having its "own function and characteristic activities."[17] Kotter views management as a control function aimed at "coping with complexity" and leadership as an innovative function aimed at "coping with change."[18] Thus, management is about bringing order and consistency to organizational practices and leadership is about making adaptive changes to ensure that the organization remains viable. The major activities that Kotter associates with leadership and management are listed in Table 2.

Table 2

Leadership is about...	Management is about...
Setting a direction	Planning and budgeting
Aligning people	Organizing and staffing
Motivating people	Controlling and problem solving

J. P. Kotter, "What leaders really do?" *Harvard Business Review*, May-June, 1990, 103-111.

Rost distinguishes between leadership and management by describing leadership as an influence relationship and management as an authority relationship. In addition, he maintains that management operates top-down from manager to subordinate, whereas leadership is multi-directional. That is, subordinates can influence (and therein lead) their superiors just as supervisors can lead subordinates. Moreover, he declares that leadership is aimed at producing change, whereas management is aimed at coordinating activities for the purposes of producing and/or selling goods and services. Rost's distinction between management and leadership is summarized in Table 3.

Table 3

Leadership is an influence relationship in which the influence is multidirectional and noncoercive.	Management is an authority relationship.
Leaders and followers are involved in this relationship.	The people in this relationship include at least one manager and one subordinate.
Leaders and followers intend (i.e., desire) real (i.e., substantive) changes.	The manager(s) and subordinate(s) coordinate their activities.
Leaders and followers develop mutual purposes.	The manager(s) and subordinate(s) produce and sell particular goods and/or services.

Adapted from J.C. Rost, *Leadership for the Twenty-first Century* (Westport, Connecticut: Praeger, 1993).

Bennis and Nanus see leadership as influence and vision, whereas management is associated with authority and efficiency. They contend that:

> to manage means to bring about, to accomplish, to have charge of or responsibility for, to conduct. Leading is influencing, guiding in direction, course, action, opinion. The distinction is crucial. Managers are people who do things right and leaders are people who do the right thing. The difference may be summarized as activities of vision and judgement—effectiveness—versus activities of mastering routines—efficiency.[19]

Table 4

Leaders tend to ...	Managers tend to ...
Stress relationships with others, values, commitment—the emotional and spiritual aspects of the organization.	Stress organization, coordination, and control of resources (e.g., plant, equipment, and people).
Create and articulate a vision of what the organisation could achieve in the long run.	Focus on the achievement of short-term objectives and goals.
Move the organization in new directions—being unsatisfied with the status quo.	Concentrate on maximizing results from existing functions and systems.
Empower people to act on their own to achieve objectives.	Insist that people check with him/her on every detail before they act.
Favour taking risks and making changes.	Fear uncertainty and act cautiously.
Generate a feeling of meaning in work—its value and importance.	Enforce fulfillment of agreements and contracts for work.
Frequently think strategically.	Seldom think strategically.
Have an insatiable passion to continuously develop themselves—eager to learn.	Tend not to push themselves to learn new things.

Reprinted with permission from F.A. Manske Jr., *Secrets of effective leadership: A practical guide to success* (3rd ed) (Columbia, Tennessee: Leadership Education and Development, Inc., 1999).

Manske describes leadership as comprising "two key dimensions: (a) creating a vision for the future and (b) inspiring people to make the vision reality."[20] Similar to Kotter, Manske views management as focusing on control, optimizing existing systems, and maintaining the status quo. Table 4 summarizes his view of leadership and management.

The common theme that runs through the writings of these authors who have attempted to distinguish between leadership and management is that leadership is generally seen as an influence process that energizes followers and management is a control process aimed at bringing coordination and efficiency to people and organizations. In this way leadership is widely seen as inspirational and management is seen as rational.

OTHER ISSUES ON LEADERSHIP AND MANAGEMENT

Before leaving our discussion of how leadership and management differ there are two issues that warrant examination. First, is the occasionally heard view that the difference between leadership and management is that leaders lead people and managers manage things. Second is the tendency to value leadership over management.

In the military, one occasionally hears the opinion that leadership deals with people and management deals with equipment and materiel. McDermott has examined this perspective and correctly dismissed it as "essentially misleading and, possibly, even dangerous."[22] In fact, commanders do manage followers. Standard operating procedures, operations orders, and reporting procedures, to name a few, are all tools that commanders use to manage their forces.

Linked with the concept of leaders leading followers and managers managing things is the implicit value we place on leadership and management when we make such a statement. What officer would want to be considered a good manager after hearing that leaders lead followers and managers manage things? The tendency to elevate leadership while under-valuing management is not unique to the military. Rost examined the tendency of some of the leadership literature of the 1980s to denigrate management and ennoble leadership and found it misinformed.

> First of all, the universal human experience, at least in the western world in the last few centuries, is that people do like to be managed—as long as management is not equated with dictatorship. If you want to find out how much people love management, try these simple strategies:
>
> • Deliver the payroll checks late.
> • Decrease the supplies people need to do their job.
> • Stop any utility service people need to live and work.[23]

Having examined how leadership and management are conceptualized in the CF and having seen how writers outside the CF have distinguished between leadership and management, let us now turn our attention to leadership. This next section shows that some of the confusion with leadership is due to the many ways the term can be used and the many definitions we have for the term.

LEADERSHIP—WHAT IS IT?

Part of the confusion we have in discussing leadership is that the term is often used in three different ways, "as the attribute of a position, as the characteristic of a person and as a category of behaviour."[24] First, we can talk about a position like that of commanding officer as a leadership position. Using the term in this way we accord the incumbent of such a position the label of leader whether he/she actually exhibits any leadership or not. According to Holloman, "the major shortcoming of this assumption is its failure to distinguish clearly between the static position of headship and the dynamic process of leadership." Simply holding high office or a position of authority does not mean the office holder is a leader. Gibb takes an even stronger position; " The leader's authority is spontaneously accorded him by his fellow group members, the followers. The authority of the head derives from some extra-group power which he has over members of the group, who cannot meaningfully be called his followers."[26]

Second, we can say that someone is a leader because they have demonstrated leadership ability in a particular position, but in doing so we fail to consider that leadership does not operate in a vacuum. Without followers there is no leadership. Furthermore, leaders operate in an environment. Hence, talking about leadership as an ability is somewhat problematic, for the leader who is successful in one environment with a certain type of followers may be entirely ineffective in a different situation with different followers. Military history has many examples of commanders who were successful leaders in the field, but failed when they were moved into more politically-charged, bureaucratic positions.

Third, we can talk about leadership as action—the action of influencing others. An interesting aspect of this use of the term is that there must be followers in order for leadership to exist. In fact, leadership is actually determined by the followers, for if leadership consists of influencing others, the results of the leader's influence will be manifested in the followers. Conversely, if there is no change in the followers, in their actions, their attitudes, their morale, their beliefs, there has been no influence, and hence, no leadership.

Another factor contributing to the confusion around the term leadership is the large number of definitions that have been developed for the concept. In his review of leadership research conducted in the twentieth century, Rost "analyzed 221 definitions of leadership ... found in 587 books, book chapters and journal articles."[27] How are we to make sense out of a concept with so many definitions? Yukl provides some clarification in this matter with his observation that "most definitions of leadership reflect the assumption that it involves a process whereby intentional influence is exerted by one person over other people to guide, structure, and facilitate activities and relationships in a group or organization."[28] Yukl's position is consistent with the way the concept of leadership is often viewed in the military—leadership as influence, as guidance, as providing structure that is goal-directed.

Another confusing issue in defining leadership is the extent to which coercion is permissible. Military history has many examples of commanders who have taken forceful measures to move subordinates toward a desired outcome. Were these actions leadership behaviours? Many would say no. In fact, a number of writers have stated that an essential requirement of leadership is that the influence tactics must be noncoercive.[29] According to Rost, "if the behaviours are coercive, the relationship becomes one of authority or power,"[30] therefore, the behaviours are properly classified as management, not leadership behaviours. Of course, there will be occasions when commanders must employ their coercive power. The point is that, according to a growing number of writers such as Gibb, Rost, Kanungo & Mendonca, this is not leadership. In fact, using coercion may not even be good management. To be effective, it must be employed infrequently and only on small groups of followers. Perhaps this explains why Katz and Kahn noted a general decline in the use of coercion by authority figures over the past two centuries.

TRANSFORMATIONAL LEADERSHIP

One of the more appealing conceptualizations of leadership in recent years has been the development of transformational leadership. Originally conceived by Burns in 1978[31] and later refined by Bass,[32] transformational leadership has begun to emerge in CF discourse, as witnessed by the following quote from the Department of National Defence's *Strategic Vision 2020*: "With transformational leadership and coherent management, we will build upon our proud heritage in pursuit of clear strategic objectives."[33]

According to Bass, transformational leadership is to be distinguished from transactional leadership. A transactional leadership relationship between leader and follower is based on social and economic exchange. The leader identifies goals and objectives, standards of performance, and monitors followers to ensure satisfactory performance. Followers work to achieve the unit mission in turn for rewards from the leader. Thus, transactional leadership is a quid pro quo relationship, based on extrinsic motivation—you scratch my back and I will scratch yours. In short, transactional leadership is more like management than leadership.

Transformational leadership, on the other hand, relies more on the intrinsic motivation of the followers. Transformational leadership has a strong moral component as transformational leaders connect with their followers on an emotional level that is not evident in transactional leadership. Transformational leaders raise the level of follower awareness about the importance of certain objectives. They present followers with a compelling vision and motivate them to transcend their own interests for the sake of the unit. In this way, transformational leadership is about influence and change, concepts which are at the root of leadership.

There are four classes of transformational leadership behaviours, referred to as the factors of transformational leadership. Each of these is summarized below.

Called *idealized influence*, the first transformational factor is sometimes referred to as Charisma. This factor consists of behaviours in which the leader acts as a role model, cultivating faith, trust and respect in followers. This factor is probably the cornerstone of transformational leadership, for without the example of a strong role model who imbues trust and loyalty into followers, the other factors of transformational leadership will not take root.

Inspirational motivation refers to those behaviours in which the transformational leader communicates a vision of a desired future state with fluency and confidence, sets high standards and convinces individuals that they can achieve beyond their expectations. In this way, the transformational leader exhorts followers to transcend themselves.

The transformational factor of *intellectual stimulation* represents those actions in which the leader promotes the development of future leaders, challenging subordinates to think for themselves and to think about old problems in innovative ways. In this way, the leader creates an atmosphere that encourages creative thinking, careful reasoning, and methodical problem-solving instead of acting on unsupported opinions.

Individualized consideration refers to those transformational leadership behaviours that focus on the relationship between the leader and each follower, placing special emphasis on paying personal attention to followers. Transformational leaders who are strong on this factor treat each follower individually, investing time for one-on-one communication, coaching and advising them, and recognizing subordinates' achievements.

CLASSIFYING COMMAND BEHAVIOURS AS LEADERSHIP OR MANAGEMENT

Building on the parsimonious model of command presented in Figure 1, let us now turn to the task of classifying those activities that commanders traditionally perform as either management or leadership behaviours (See Table 5). Although this distinction is made in an effort to provide clarity on the concepts of leadership and management, it is recognized that some of the behaviours may not fall entirely under only one category. Take, for example, the behaviour of decision-making. Based on earlier discussion, decision-making is a management behaviour. However, a commander who makes a thoughtful, timely, sensible decision in a particular circumstance can, in the course of making this decision in such a manner, also serve as a role model for followers, inspire followers, and convince followers of the competence of the commander and the importance of the mission. Thus, even while engaged in what was seemingly a management behaviour, the personal influence of the commander transformed this behaviour into a leadership event.

Table 5

Leadership behaviours	Management behaviours
Visioning—developing and communicating the vision (Bass, 1996), developing and communicating commander's intent	Planning and budgeting (Kotter, 1990), business planning, allocating forces and resources
Motivating (inspiring) people (Kotter, 1990)	Organizing and staffing (Kotter, 1990)
Influencing change in people, organizations (Rost, 1993)	Controlling and problem solving (Kotter, 1990)
Setting an example, acting as a role model (Bass, 1996)	Producing goods, providing services (Rost, 1993)
Engender faith, trust, respect (Bass, 1996)	Supervising
Subordinates identify with leader (Bass, 1996)	Decision making
Convince individuals they can perform beyond their expectations (Bass, 1996)	Monitoring activities
Develop subordinates, challenge them to think for themselves, help them think about problems in innovative ways (Bass, 1996)	Controlling
Provide support to followers (Bass, 1996)	Coordinating
Coach and advise followers (Bass, 1996)	Administering
Recognize followers' achievements (Bass, 1996)	Analyzing, conducting estimates

TEACHING LEADERSHIP AND MANAGEMENT IN THE CF

Based on the foregoing distinction between leadership and management, it appears that much of the content in formal leadership courses in the CF is actually management training. As described earlier, behaviours that serve to outline procedures (whether tactical or administrative), impose order, control, coordination, discipline and such are properly classed as management behaviours. Activities like visioning, motivating, counseling, coaching, influencing, role modeling and persuading are leadership behaviours, but our officers and NCOs receive little formal training in these areas. Instead, many of these skills are acquired informally through practical experience and by observing the successes and failures of others.

It seems clear then that CF leadership training needs to be examined to ensure that our officers and NCOs learn as much about influencing the actions of subordinates as they do about controlling subordinates. A good place to start this examination is with a review of leadership doctrine. As pointed out by Hammond, CF leadership doctrine has not kept pace with developments in this area.[34]

LEADERSHIP, MANAGEMENT AND COMMAND AT THE EXECUTIVE LEVEL

CF doctrine in leadership and management makes no distinction between organizational levels. Thus, one might assume that the leadership definition presented in CFP A-PD-131-001/PT-001, *Leadership, Volume 1: Junior Leaders Manual* applies equally to sergeants, captains and generals. However, Canadian war fighting doctrine makes distinctions between levels of command—tactical, operational, and strategic. This distinction reflects the increase in scope and complexity of the commander's job as one moves from the tactical level to the higher levels. The leadership behaviours that are required to influence soldiers, sailors or air personnel at the tactical level and the management behaviours required to control and coordinate their actions at this level are different than the leadership and management behaviours required at the higher levels. Certainly, there will be some commonality across these three levels, but there are important differences as well. With respect to commonality across levels of command, all commanders need to set the example and serve as a role model if they are to influence (i.e., lead) subordinates. As for differences across levels, leadership at the general officer level is about influencing units, organizations and events whereas leadership at the tactical level is about influencing individuals.

The leadership action of visioning—that is, developing a vision and communicating this vision in a compelling manner—is more important to successful general officer leadership than it is to junior officer leadership. Inspiring and motivating followers is important at both levels, but it is more difficult to achieve at the executive level, because of the number of layers of command between the generals and the rank and file. Captains and majors can use direct, face-to-face influence behaviours in motivating subordinates. General officers have less opportunity to relate directly with the lower ranks. Therefore, they "must take into account the various organizational filters, the communication leakages, and misinterpretations, sometimes deliberate, of desired policy, goals and priorities."[35] As a result, generals often must use different leadership behaviours than the junior or middle grade officer when motivating followers.

Command at the general officer level may involve more management behaviours than leadership behaviours. This is not always the case, for Field Marshall Slim's 1952 address to the US Army Command and General Staff College[36] includes a healthy mix of leadership and management tips for aspiring commanders. However, the size of the force under command and the complexity of challenges that must be faced by generals, requires they devote a lot of effort to what are largely management behaviours—analyzing situations, organizing forces to respond to various threats, allocating resources, assigning missions, and the like. Because the influence of the general officers must travel through multiple hierarchical levels, a lot of emphasis needs to be placed on control (i.e., management) measures like policy statements, administrative instructions, and operations orders.

CONCLUSION

The fundamental message of this chapter is remarkably simple. Command involves both leadership and management. Both are distinct processes that need to be employed by all commanders. Leadership has personal, moral, and emotional dimensions. Leadership involves a form of influence in which the follower freely submits to the will of the leader. In this way, leaders transform followers. Management has rational, mechanical, and economic dimensions. Management involves the control and coordination of people and resources based on a relationship that is formal and authoritative.

In his discussion of officership in the US air force, McDermott suggests that "management is the mind, and leadership the heart of officership" and they are "as two arms of a single body,"[37] the body being officership. These metaphors can be applied to command as well. The commander who relies more on one arm than the other is limited in the types of situations that can be successfully handled. A highly capable and motivated force may need mostly good management to succeed, whereas a force with less commitment to the mission will require more leadership from the commander.

NOTES

1. Canadian Forces Publication: A-PD-131-002/PT-001/art 202, 1, 2-1, *Leadership, Volume 2: The Professional Officer*, 31 July 1973.
2. Canadian Forces Publication: B-GL-300-003/FP-00, *Command,* 21 July 1996, 1-7, 1-8.
3. Ibid, 1-7, 1-8.
4. Ibid, 1-4.
5. Canadian Forces Publication: A-PD-131-001/PT-001/ art 401, para 1.a., 4-1, *Leadership, Volume 1: The Junior Leaders Manual,* 31 July 1973.
6. Ibid, art 401, para 1.a., 4-1.
7. Canadian Forces Publication: B-GL-300-003/FP-00, *Command,* 21 Jul 1996.
8. P.C. Newman, *The Canadian Revolution: From Deference to Defiance* (Toronto: Viking, 1995).
9. *The Junior Leaders Manual,* art 401, para 1.a., 4-1.

10. *Command*, 59.
11. Ibid, 1-7.
12. J.C. Rost, *Leadership for the Twenty-first Century* (Westport, Connecticut: 1993), 129.
13. D. Katz, & R.L. Kahn, *The Social Psychology of Organizations*, 2nd ed. (New York: Wiley, 1978. Original published in 1966); J. P. Kotter, "What leaders really do?" *Harvard Business Review*, May-June, 1990, 103-111 and J.C. Rost, *Leadership for the Twenty-first Century* (Westport, Connecticut: Praeger, 1993).
14. A. Zaleznik, "Managers and Leaders: Are They Different?" *Harvard Business Review*, May-June, 1977, 67-78.
15. Katz and Kahn, 527.
16. Ibid, 528.
17. J. P. Kotter, "What leaders really do?" *Harvard Business Review*, May-June, 1990, 26.
18. Ibid, 27.
19. W. Bennis, & B. Nanus, "Leaders: Strategies for Taking Charge," 2nd ed. (New York: Harper Business, 1997), 20.
20. F.A. Manske, Jr., *Secrets of Effective Leadership: A Practical Guide to Success*, 3rd ed. (Columbia, Tennessee: Leadership Education and Development, Inc., 1999), 3.
21. Major J. McDermott, "Leadership and Management: a Balanced Model of Officership," *Air University Review*, 1983, 34, 55-63 and Colonel D. M. Malone, *Small Unit Leadership, A Commonsense Approach* (Novato, CA: Presidio Press, 1983).
22. McDermott, 55.
23. Rost, 141-142.
24. Katz and Kahn, 527.
25. C.R. Holloman, "Leadership and Headship: There is a Difference." In W.E. Rosenbach and R.L. Taylor, eds., *Contemporary Issues in Leadership* (Boulder CO: Westview Press, 1984). Originally published in *Personnel Administration*, Vol. 31, July-August 1968, 109.
26. C.A. Gibb, "Leadership." In G. Lindzey, ed., *Handbook of Social Psychology* (Reading, MA: Addison-Wesley, 1954), 882.
27. Rost, 44.
28. G. Yukl, *Leadership in Organizations*, 4th ed. (Upper Saddle River, N.J: Prentice Hall, 1998), 3.
29. Gibb, "Leadership"; Rost; and R.N. Kanungo & M. Mendonca, *Ethical Dimensions of Leadership* (Thousand Oaks, CA: Sage Publications, 1996).
30. Rost, 105.
31. J.M. Burns, *Leadership* (New York: Harper and Row, 1978).
32. B. M. Bass, *Leadership and Performance Beyond Expectations* (New York: The Free Press, 1985); and B. M. Bass, *Transformational Leadership: Industrial, Military and Educational Impact* (Mahwah, New Jersey: Lawrence Erlbaum Associates, 1996).
33. Department of National Defence, *Shaping the Future of the Canadian Forces: A Strategy for 2020* (Ottawa: National Defence Headquarters, 1999).
34. Major J.W. Hammond, "First Things First: Improving Canadian Military Leadership," *Canadian Defence Quarterly*, Vol. 27, 1998, 6-11.
35. W.E. Turcotte, "Leadership Versus Management," in R.L. Taylor and W.E. Rosenbach, eds., *Military Leadership: In Pursuit of Excellence*, (Boulder CO: Westview Press, 1984), 107. Originally published in *The Washington Quarterly, A Review of Strategic and International Issues*, Winter 1983, Vol 6, 107.
36. Field Marshall Sir W. Slim, "Higher Command in War," *Military Review*, Vol. 70, 1990, 10-21.
37. McDermott, 61.

Military Command in Canada

Douglas L. Bland

Dr. Douglas Bland is the Chair of the Defence Management Studies Program at Queens University in Kingston, Ontario.

A CANADIAN WAY IN WARFARE

MILITARY COMMAND HAS SEVERAL FACES. It might appear as a romantic notion—leading warriors in combat against frightful odds. At other times, command is about conducting a great enterprise, harmonizing others in various activities towards a concerted aim. Command is also organization and cannot escape the interweaving of resources, people, and information in organization. Command is essentially about deciding, making choices from (usually) imperfect information about what is to be done. Though normally related to warfare, command is also exercised in peacetime and beyond the sound of gunfire. Indeed, "high command" is mostly divorced from its romantic face, replaced by the officer/manager "responsible to create forces, to support combat forces, and to employ combat forces."[1]

Of course, military command may display shades of all these faces from time to time. But no matter which image predominates, one idea is clearly evident in liberal democratic societies and that is that military command must not be separated from the society it serves. In one sense commanders, acting through the authority of their most senior leaders, have no choice but to follow the directions of the civil authority—civilians elected to parliament. In another sense, commanders who wander away from social norms, no matter the reason, soon discover in critical times that decisions taken without regard for "the facts of national life" are groundless and impotent.[2]

The decisions and the actions of soldiers and politicians begin at home. Military command is sets of decisions that reflect what people and leaders think about such things as national interests, national security, rules of warfare, allies, armed forces and society, and civil-military relations. Often people's thoughts are shaped by what they think has gone before, by explanations of national experiences and by national myths.

All societies include people who hold diverse views on the state and the place of warfare in its history and future. Insofar as groups of people hold to similar views and act on their beliefs, we can identify "interest groups" wed to certain national policies. Moreover, when beliefs about military affairs become embedded in significant segments of society or when particular interest groups wield power and influence, we can construct predictable patterns of national behaviour concerning defence and foreign policies, reactions to crisis, and responses to allies, among other things.

A national way in warfare is an expression of a national behaviour. It is evident primarily in the role of armed forces in society, the place of military officers in the national decision making process, the use of force in national and international relations, in ceremonies and symbols, including national military history, and in the allocation of national resources to military purposes. For officers, the national way in warfare is often demonstrated in how high command is controlled and exercised. Although the facts of national life may change from time to time—defence expenditures may vary, for example—officers cannot escape the consequences for command imposed on them by the national way in warfare.

Military command in Canada since 1945 has been greatly influenced by several recurring facts of national life. Canadian politicians hold consistently to a few notions about Canada's national defence. Although different parties may declare different policies, their actual policies—those they enact and support when they are in power—are similar. This natural policy has been especially evident since about 1949 if only because national defence policy was highlighted for so long by the Cold War.

The framework is composed of a few critical ideas concerning threats, international relationships and responsibilities, and the role of military professionals in the national policy process. Few prime ministers (and they are the politicians who matter in this discussion) in this century have worried much about military threats to Canada. For most prime ministers, the greatest threat to national defence came from involvement in other people's quarrels meaning, generally, those engaging the British Empire and later those generated by the superpowers. Second, politicians, and some senior officers too, came to understand that national defence meant the avoidance of war and spent national resources to this end. In effect, Canada has never had obvious "war aims" other than to avoid international commitments. Partner to this idea is the important notion that even if Canada were threatened and attacked, someone else would save the nation.

Finally, many politicians, like most Canadians at the turn of the century, assume that Canada has no national interests that can be achieved through the use of Canadian military power, at least outside Canada. Despite Canada's actual military history, the general conclusion is that Canada never has and never will have much need for armed forces, except, perhaps, to shape the world in Canada's image.[3] Even where armed forces are useful, the guiding assumption is that they will be used peacefully and, therefore, need not be extensively equipped for warlike operations. No matter the rhetoric, an important contradiction runs through this political framework. Canada needs armed forces and employs them in combat from time to time within "a realist paradigm" to advance national interests and influence.

The influence of these political assumptions, though present throughout Canada's history, has varied as other determinants changed. For example, Prime Minister Mackenzie King struggled mightily to keep Canada out of the Second World War and, once in, to minimize Canada's fighting commitments, but he was overpowered by popular sentiment and allied pressures. Between 1994 and 1999, the Canadian government tried to follow a "collective security" agenda based on support for the UN, but found itself wrapped up in old "collective defence" strategies fighting alongside traditional allies in the Balkans. New factors, such as the apparent "revolution in military affairs" and a world order built around unpredictable "coalitions of the willing" are changing the methods, if not the nature, of military command. Officers in Canada, therefore, must cope with a national way in warfare characterized by political indifference, disharmony between policy and objectives, an uncertain commitment horizon, a national skepticism (largely founded on a national myth) about the utility of Canada as a military actor, and a growing complexity of technologies and international politics.

Officers, too, have their own view of history and of the world and Canada's place in it. Canadian officers today are haunted by the unpreparedness of the armed services before both world wars and especially by the lack of government attention to the military in the inter-war period. Mackenzie King's government is held up as an example of what can befall the nation when civilian leaders fail to heed military advice. If only, so the argument goes, the government had begun in the early 1930s to prepare the armed forces for war outside Canada, war might have been averted or the armed services might have been fully prepared to fight and win in 1939. The sin of unpreparedness in 1939, is the penalty of political neglect and it is paraded before every government that ignores the opinions of their military advisers.

Today, the unpreparedness legend is closely entangled with what can be called the world war assumption. Officers, perhaps blinded by their view of history, seem unable to see any other possibilities. They tend to assume that a state prepared for global warfare is effectively prepared for any conflict. It is a dangerous assumption and can unnecessarily dislocate national defence planning. "Proper soldiering" is a recurring military notion centred on the romantic idea that warfare can be conducted according to military ideals, uncluttered by political interference, rules and laws, and civil interests.

On the other hand, Canadian officers, partly because they come from a minor state and obviously benefit from the ideas and experiences of officers from larger armed forces, and partly from choice, expect to be under someone else's command. Finally, the most persistent and deep-seated idea in the minds of Canadian Forces officers is that a tri-service organization of the Canadian Forces based on the army, navy, and air force is the preferred structure for the armed forces. This preference rests on the questionable assumption that equally strong (or "balanced") navy/army/air forces are, in all situations and in all times, good for national defence.

Each of these beliefs more or less fractures the bonds between Canada's armed forces and society. They have often caused significant civil-military relations problems for governments, for instance, during the Hellyer and Trudeau periods. However, the chief characteristic of civil-military relations in Canada is mutual inattention—politicians are uninformed and ignorant of military matters and officers assume this is a natural state of affairs.

PATTERNS OF COMMAND

The history of command or "generalship" in Canada is, not surprisingly, dotted with successes and failures. Officers have lead various elements of Canada's armed forces to fame in the First and Second World War, in Korea, and in the early days of UN peacekeeping operations. Perhaps less obvious, but critically important to these efforts, were the officers who planned for and built credible forces out of next to nothing—again during the great wars and Korea, but less well noticed during the early 1950s when Canada made a major effort to remobilize national defence.

Between 1950 and 1959, senior officers in the much maligned pre-Hellyer days, built a force from about 30,000 persons to over 120,000 regular sailors, soldiers and airmen, fought a war in Korea, deployed large units to NATO, organized NORAD and its forces, conducted and commanded the UN's first large peacekeeping mission (in the Middle East in 1956), managed well enough an unprecedented expanding defence budget and constructed a vast national infrastructure to support the "force-in-being." This other aspect of command was an enormous feat of planning, organizing, management, and military leadership. Just how important it was is illustrated by Lester Pearson's Nobel Prize for peace, an award that was due to the high-quality armed forces those senior officers had assembled and made ready to undertake a most unusual mission, nearly independent of any foreign assistance.

Successful command, however, is never assured by what has gone before. Traditions and examples help officers situate the present, but command can fail for many reasons. Not all failures of command are blameworthy events. Commanders can fail because the enemy is better prepared or more numerous, because their superior's plan is defective (Hong Kong and Dieppe), because support is wanting, or because Mars is unkind. Negligent failure, on the other hand, as in the 1993 Somalia deployment, results, as the term implies, whenever officers "failed in their duty as commanders."[4] One lesson from Canadian commanders is that the exercise of command is never entirely in the hands of a commander and is always linked to Canadian society, the state of the armed forces, and to fate. Another lesson is that this fact notwithstanding, successful command demands great intelligence, creative imagination, discipline, and moral courage coupled to an irrepressible urge to take the right and proper command decision without regard for rewards or punishments.

Understanding Canadian command is complicated by the differences imposed on officers by circumstances, historical periods, missions, political leadership, and the "facts of national life" as they are played out over time.

Grading command, except for certain notable successes and failures, is also problematic for these reasons but also because history presents us with so many examples and categories of command. Yet some attempt to bring order to this history is warranted, if only to help direct younger commanders.

Canadian officers have held command (beyond the routine demands of garrison duty) in one or more of four main categories: colonial, allied, UN, and national command. Colonial command, or rather command of forces within a colonial context or operation (Boer War, early First World War) was characterized by near total subordination to the Imperial Majesty and Her agents. While the period and history have many interesting things to say about the early evolution of command in Canada, they are well known and not especially germane to this brief chapter. Allied command refers to the command of Canadian forces in war and peace exercised within an allied context, generally from 1921 to the present. But unlike the colonial experience, commanders were (and are) responsible to a Canadian civil authority and the chain of accountability for the armed services and the Canadian Forces flowed from the field to Canadian governments. United Nations command obviously refers to command of Canadian and others nations' forces by Canadian officers within a UN mandated operation. National command is command exercised over Canadian units solely within a Canadian context according to Canadian laws and political direction.

Each of these categories of command have their own characteristics, although they might overlap to some degree—as in the case of conditional allied command delegated from overriding national command. Measuring, or even describing, command experiences in the armed services and the Canadian Forces is thus further complicated by the various situations in which command has been exercised over the years. Therefore, a somewhat arbitrary formula is necessary to overcome (to a degree) the uniqueness of each type of command experience if useful general comments are to be made from them.

Each category of command will be assessed from six perspectives—fidelity, interdependence of strategies, relation to national military doctrines, command competencies, complexities of command, and demands for national political judgement on the part of commanders. In each case, the purpose of this style of analysis is to consider the demands on commanders and to relate the category of command to Canadian sensitivities. Perhaps such formal assessments might yield guides for future officer education or at least an awareness of the problems of command in a world of multiple and different commitments.

Fidelity is defined as an individual sense of faithfulness to obligations, duties, or institutions. Clearly, in armed forces, as in many other lifetime pursuits, individuals become attached to certain concepts, manners, and traditions. Indeed, much of early military training is intended to instill "core values" in recruits so as to condition their behaviour. Officers, including senior officers, are likewise accustomed by training, experience and education to certain ways of thinking and acting and their decisions are predictably influenced by these factors. Many ideas and modes of behaviour are embedded in military institutions and account for the differences between, for instance, the navy and the army. More precisely, ideas embedded in institutions can significantly prejudice (for better or worse) the decisions officers take in any situation. In some cases, fidelity to embedded ideas may prevent officers from thinking beyond prescribed or accepted ways and might even propel them into conflicts with the civil authority in some situations.

Strategy—sets of decisions about ends and means—is a critical component of national defence policy and command at any level. Yet in Canada a *national conceived strategy* is a rare item.[5] That is not to say that Canada has not had strategies of a sort, but they have almost always been dependent in essence on decisions taken elsewhere, in NATO for example. Much of Canada's post-Second World War strategy was simply a "strategy of commitments" so poorly defined as to become a major source of political and military disagreement. The lack of strategic independence in Canada prompted many commanders to identify their professional responsibilities and institutional interests with strategies written outside Canada and that tendency, at times, places officers in conflict with their military superiors and political authorities.

Canadian military doctrine, somewhat like strategy, has been overpowered by foreign and allied ideas. While some might argue that this is a logical outcome of alliances, doctrinal dependence has influenced the exercise of command in Canada in several ways. Perhaps the most significant effect has been on military thought in Canada. If officers never have to devise a national doctrine, then this principal military responsibility to society is sure to atrophy. However, the types of command situations Canadian officers encounter have an effect on military doctrine as well. Obviously, commanding forces in NORAD produces demands for doctrine different from what one could expect from UN experiences. In a perverse way, the development of a national military doctrine of command is defeated by too many command experiences.

Command experience and what one might draw from it is often modified by the complexity (or lack of complexity) of the command. Each category of command has, generally, a degree of complexity that shapes commanders, conditions their decisions, and promotes their future consideration of command. An officer who in his/her early years encounters difficult choices and ambiguous situations and manages to exercise command successfully is likely to be comfortable in demanding situations at higher rank *in similar circumstances*. On the other hand, officers who earned their spurs in easy assignments might find it difficult to lead major units and formations. In the same sense, officers wholly trained in an allied environment in NATO might find it difficult to apply that experience to UN command.

What do general officers need to know to command Canadian units and formations? In some regards, the answer is a noncommital, "it depends on the situation." If officers could be sure they would only command one type of unit in one type of environment, then it would be rather easy to train and educate them for this duty. But Canadian officers, generally, can over a career expect to command national and international units in more than one category. Thus, what an officer needs to know is problematic. Moreover, what officers know about command as an activity is mostly derived from their own command experiences. To understand what officers need to know is related to understanding what one learns in the various types of command situations.

Finally, high command, at least, requires political judgement. That is not to say that officers should learn to think from partisan political norms. Rather, it suggests that because military objectives emerge from and are mingled with political objectives, senior officers need to understand their place as commanders who are also advisers to governments. They also need to know how to shape command decisions to meet the civil authority's political objectives without undue risk to their missions and subordinates. Some categories of command magnify these requirements and some experiences enhance an officer's capability to function in these overlapping roles.

ALLIED COMMAND

During the Second World War most Canadian commanders worked within a super-nation command structure in which they were a barely identifiable entity. After the formation of NATO's military establishment and alliance system of command, Canadian commanders became independent actors, at least according to NATO principles and norms. But the enormity of the NATO experience and its longevity tended to produce Canadian officers whose fidelity rested with the alliance and not necessarily with Canadian governments. Command in NATO, whether on land, at sea, or in the air, was always predicated on an alliance strategy and an alliance doctrine. There were very compelling military reasons why the major determinants of commands should be harmonized on an alliance-wide basis, but those reasons sometimes clashed with national imperatives. It was for this reason that the alliance purposefully limited its authority over national units to something less than "full command." But because Canadian political leaders paid little attention to national defence arrangements—in fact, ministers often encouraged integrated approaches—Canadian commanders tended to believe that they owed allegiance to the alliance first and Canadian governments second.

Few command appointments at any rank involved such a wide array of military complexities. The political scenario was layered in historic, ideological, and bitter hostilities not just between the contending pacts, but also within the alliance itself. The battle space, to use a modern jargon, stretched from North America across Europe and Russia and beyond to the Pacific Ocean. Vast, complicated armed forces stood face-to-face, mated in a type of strategic dance. The range (in every sense of the word) of weapons available to commanders seemed unlimited and commanders required extensive training in tactics and methods to understand how best to employ them. Officers who successfully commanded NATO-based forces could credibly claim that they had achieved the summit of modern military command.

Senior command in this demanding environment appeared to carry with it, so some officers thought, a prestige that not only invited them into national security decision making, but led some to believe that anyone without this experience was not fit to offer any advice at all.[6] Whatever the truth of this assertion, command in NATO tended to exaggerate alliance interests in national planning, a consequence that at times derailed coherent planning from national interests. The belief that what officers thought was good for NATO was also good for Canada moved General Gerry Theriault to observe that the officer corps at times "[had] great difficulty differentiating between its own institutional interests and aspirations and the real interests of the state, viewing both as coincident when, in fact, they are often very different."[7]

In a Cold War world where every day seemed a copy of the previous day, officers needed to learn just enough to do their bit before an unchanging background. The Cold War passed from year to year in an unending political stalemate, and defence policy followed suit. Officers literally grew up and progressed from junior to senior command often merely repeating at each level the routine they had experienced many times before. Predictability was the essential characteristic of a military situation where troops were assembled ready to react swiftly to surprises. This enduring deployment rarely promoted new ideas or those who broke with established truths. There were few rewards for strategic thinkers simply because strategy was padlocked by international bureaucracy. Canadian commanders simply needed to know how the Canadian Forces functioned within the alliance, not how to move the armed forces, let alone the alliance, in any new direction.

Command in the alliance made few demands on Canadian commanders as political advisers. The stability in NATO's military routine was largely mirrored in political fora and in the alliance's bloated bureaucracy. Canadian defence policy from about 1957 to 1989 concerned mostly getting by with just enough resources to make a credible contribution to the alliance, credible that is in the eyes of Canadian political leaders. Officers, including service chiefs and then the chiefs of the defence staff, were rarely asked for their strategic opinion on any major national issue. Though they might be involved in some particular decision, such as purchasing a major weapons system, they were not often invited to speak to cabinets or the prime ministers about Canada's national defence strategy. Command in the alliance context demanded little from Canadian commanders in the way of political judgement or intercourse and they appreciated that relationship.

Canadian command in alliances whether in NATO or in NORAD produced different outcomes, some beneficial and some less so. Officers experienced many opportunities to command large sophisticated army, naval and air force units and formations, they shared in the development of multinational plans and procedures, and contributed to the overall success of western alliances as deterrent forces. "Growing up allied,"[8] however, tended to separate the Canadian Forces from Canadian society, to undermine the necessary links between military leaders and political authorities, and, ironically, inhibited the evolution of a truly professional officer corps in Canada. This later result is illustrated in the weakness of command leadership in the development of a national military interest and competencies in strategic and doctrinal thinking about warfare and national defence. So long as the alliances were robust and active, then this weakness was not critical. However, as the alliances faded and new challenges faced Canada, the lack of command intellect became increasingly evident and worrying.[9]

COMMAND IN THE UNITED NATIONS

Canadian officers have commanded Canadian Forces units and international formations under the flag of the UN since the institution's very first days.

Indeed, Canadians like General E.L.M. Burns, provided the UN with competent commanders and may have set the standard for command in this unique international effort. Canadian officers continue to provide senior commanders for UN operations in various parts of the world and others support UN missions as leaders on UN staffs and as senior advisers.

United Nations command is different from allied command in a number of ways. It is detached in a sense from the usual "national interest" paradigm and matches Canadians with partners from many nations not traditionally associated with the defence of Canada. Working within UN mandates exposes officers to unusual procedures and norms not taught in Canadian Forces staff colleges. In UN operations everything is "on-the-job-training." Finally, UN duty separates officers from national command mechanisms and obliges them to find their own ways and to command international units without the support of law-based rules of command and obedience.

Although few officers have been attached to the UN in the same manner as officers have grown up in NATO and NORAD formations and regions, some officers have developed a certain fidelity to the UN as a peacekeeper. These officers, and they are not all commanders by any means, have come to accept the oddities of UN command and operations and they are expert in making weak mandates effective. They have as well come to see their duty to the UN as a clear duty to Canada. Where many officers might dismiss UN operations as "a sideshow," especially when compared to the large mainline deployments to Europe and the Atlantic theatres of NATO, officers with long experience on peacekeeping missions respond that they are where the real action is happening. For this and other reasons, many officers repeatedly seek UN duty and some senior officers strive for UN command. These long-service mercenaries of the UN wars are truly a unique class of officers and commanders.

The UN has no strategy, nor much that would pass for military doctrine. Rather, the UN begins operations, especially since 1989, from a philosophical base which is often antithetical to "the military way." Each mission is planned around certain basic factors, but the institution has no set of decisions about ends and means simply because the UN has no ends or means independent of the member states. Officers, including commanders with long experience on peacekeeping operations, have invented UN strategy and operational doctrine piecemeal as individual missions come and go.

Command in these circumstances demands a certain persuasive nature, an ability to guide followers to decisions rather than order them to their duties. The lack of strategy and standing procedures that follow from strategy and the seeming inability to invent one, frustrates some commanders, but it has had another negative influence. Senior officers, convinced that ad hoc methods are the UN way in warfare, have simply abandoned any attempt to learn from command in the UN. That is to say, they have made little effort to record UN doctrine or to invent a UN system of command. Unfortunately, when larger numbers of Canadian Forces personnel have been called to UN duty or near-UN duty, there is no available body of knowledge, despite Canada's many years in the field and the service there of dozens of commanders.

Although few UN missions ever approach the *potential* complexity of planned NATO or NORAD operations, actual UN operations have always had a complexity of their own. Today, UN operations, rolled over into "Operations Other Than War" (OOTW), have many of the characteristics of classic warfare and many unique complexities besides. Throughout UN history, command of mandated operations was complicated by the lack of doctrine, standing procedures, agreed rules and norms for staff work, logistical standards to guide support and so on. Furthermore, UN missions often brought to the field oddly paired units that commanders had to stitch together into operational formations. Negotiation, not command in the usual military sense, is the order of the day. Command in these circumstances demands special abilities and temperament and many Canadian officers excelled in command as team-building.

Until very recently, most Canadian Forces officers believed that training for general war was sufficient training for UN duty. Moreover, they believed that a typical general staff course provided an adequate background for senior command in any armed force, including UN missions. These notions stood for many years mainly because they were never tested rigorously. In Cyprus, for instance, operations after the first few months became routine and success depended on the skill and discipline of non-commissioned officers more than on the commanding skills of officers. In more complex situations, as in Somalia in 1993, a supposedly highly trained unit and its commanding officers and some other officers failed in their duties primarily because they were not trained for the special circumstances of UN-type command and operations.

Since the abortive Somalia mission and in response to experiences in the Balkans and elsewhere, officers have acknowledged that UN operations and some OOTW require both general military training and specific-to-mission training. Senior officers, as well, are beginning to understand the importance of education to operations and to command. The history of Canadian command under the UN, however, contributed little to this evolution and may have retarded it in fact. The main lessons carried by commanders from year to year and mission to mission was that effective command was possible if one simply followed the past, until, of course, that lesson was disproved by a new future.

Political interaction with peacekeeping in Canada hardly extends beyond rhetoric. Observers have complained that Canadians have always been content just "to lend troops" to international organizations and expect them to be well cared for and efficient in their duties without valid national political oversight. Canadians deploy units for peace operations, but do not employ them. Commanding officers and commanders have been left alone, accountable only to the UN system and usually without any decent support for even routine matters. It is the skill of commanders that made most operations a credit to Canada.

Yet officers who have commanded significant Canadian Forces operations under the UN have been neglectful in some cases as advisers to governments and protectors of members of the Canadian Forces. Their political judgement seemed corrupted by the assumption that Canadians could always get by, no matter the stress this attitude might have placed on the Canadian Forces in fact. Many officers, now more than before, recall the limited and in some cases dangerous state of UN operations. However, few officers ever publicly denounced the failure of the UN to properly organize, support, or direct deployed forces until events began to tarnish their reputations. Some commanders of experience seemed oblivious to their responsibility to Canada to alert political leaders or to question their decisions until they had left military service. But under the democratic code of civil-military relations senior officers are expected to clearly state the military consequences that might result from faulty political decision making and it is a failure of command not to do so. Too often, Canadian officers who have commanded UN missions and units have not exercised this duty of command explicitly and forcefully enough.

United Nations command provided Canadian officers with significant command experiences in the early years of peacekeeping and in the days since the end of the Cold War. In the meantime, command assumed a complacency that in some instances produced a lethargic response to serious questions and impending danger. Unfortunately, that legacy was played out in the Balkans, Somalia, Zaire, and Rwanda and in Ottawa and the UN headquarters, discrediting the Canadian Forces and the reputation of some Canadian officers as commanders.

NATIONAL COMMAND

Command at the national level, "the higher direction of national armed forces," has been a sometimes thing in Canada. Generally, command in the sense of directing forces to national ends, has been entirely absent in favour of command as building, supporting, and deploying forces. The prevalent assumption in Canada, especially throughout the Cold War period, was that the Canadian Forces would operate in the field and at sea as part of some other allied formations and under some type of allied or foreign command. The role of national headquarters and senior Canadian officers, therefore, was one of support and administration. National Defence Headquarters and Canadian Forces doctrines of command were built around these assumptions and there are still military and public service advocates for them, even in 2000.

National command involves the direction of national forces according to the principles, laws, and interest of Canadians and it is not something that can be passed to foreign leaders. NATO rules expressly proscribe its commanders from exercising "full or national command" over any units assigned to the alliance. Whether Canadian officers believe that they have little control when they have national command is beside the point, for national command always resides with Canadian officers, principally the Chief of the Defence Staff.

The problem is that the assumption of inevitable foreign command only holds until it is subjected to a harsh test and then it falls apart. Such was the case during the Cuban missile crisis.[10] Prime Minister John Diefenbaker was particularly uninterested in military affairs until the crisis arrived and then he was most interested in exercising through Canadian offices the control and direction of the Canadian Forces. When he and other politicians realized that their control of national policy had been all but passed on by Canadian officers to Allied officers they moved to correct the situation. This was the genesis of Paul Hellyer and unification of the armed forces. Nevertheless, the pattern was repeated in the Gulf War and it was at the root of the Somalia failure. Recent reforms in defence organization have been made to address this problem but it persists, at least in some debates on defence arrangements and procedures.

The weakness of national command in Canada accounts in large part for the lack of strategic thinking and doctrinal development in defence policy. It accounts as well for the absence of conceptual curiosity in the officer corps—if Canada is always to act under someone else's direction and strategy, why waste time thinking about an alternative situation?

Few officers seem aware of the complexity entailed in the idea and the fact of national command. At a minimalist level, national command requires officers under the Chief of the Defence Staff to arrange military forces, provide systems for their support, raise, train and equip military units, and deploy forces into operations at home and abroad. Command demands also the careful interaction of the Canadian Forces with government agencies and departments, the coordination of policies and plans and the marshaling of advice to government. At a maximalist level, national command demands all these things and the active supervision of Canadian Forces in operations. Where no concept of national command exists, as through most of the 1970s and 1980s, then no leadership in any of these issues can emerge. In other words, command fails.

What are officers to do in the absence of informed political direction of the armed forces—when the civil authority vacates its duty? What they ought not do is superimpose themselves on the political process nor invent a system of command that assumes away the civil authority for all times. Rather, senior officers ought to develop a system of national command commensurate with the facts of national life and robust enough to adjust to changing circumstances and crises.

COMMAND IN CANADA

The evolution of a truly national concept and system of command in Canada has been retarded by a colonial past, a liberal democratic aversion to armed forces, political neglect, and institutional preferences within the Canadian Forces and the tri-service attitudes of certain senior officers. However, the Canadian Forces cannot continue in this way now that the colonial and allied eras have passed. Command is important not merely because effective command often wins wars, but because national command is the instrument that connects the Canadian Forces to the government and the government to the Canadian Forces. Whenever it is weak or distorted, then national defence may be imperiled.

A truly national, even nationalistic command, engenders strong ties, bonds of fidelity between the armed forces and society. Officers who believe that Canada ought to act independently in international affairs, must also believe that Canadian officers should help governments develop coherent national strategies and doctrines for this purpose. Otherwise, governments may come to assume that Canadian Forces officers only speak for allied and foreign interests and are thereby untrustworthy as military advisers. On the other hand, if Canadian officers show no interest or competence in strategic issues, then who can blame governments for going to other sources of advice?

Command at any level is a complex social, military, technical, and intellectual activity. It is a changeable activity also, though it is grounded in certain fundamental ideas proven in history. Officers should be trained in these fundamentals of command, but they must be educated to think of other possibilities if they are to adapt to emerging emergencies. Command is essentially a creative endeavour and inspiration always springs from fertile intellectual ground.

Command cannot be separated from politics and organization. The first provides the direction, the objectives of command, and the latter provides the instrument for moving declarations into actions. National command cannot be separated from the facts of national life. Inevitably, Canadian Forces commanders will be raised from Canadian society and they will command the armed forces according to Canadian social norms, Canadian laws, and Canadians' sense of the just use of force in international relations. For too many years some officers believed that they could escape this relationship, perhaps because politicians were not watching. But if military command in Canada is to mature beyond the simple direction of soldiers, sailors, and airmen, then officers must find their place in the social and political fabric of an ever-evolving Canadian society.

NOTES

1. Henry Eccles, *Military Concepts and Philosophy* (New Jersey: Rutgers University Press, 1965), 257.
2. The term is attributed to Brooke Claxton, see Douglas Bland, *Chiefs of Defence: Government And The Unified Command of The Canadian Armed Forces.* (Toronto: Canadian Institute of Strategic Studies, 1995), 46.
3. See for example, Lloyd Axworthy, "Canada and Human Security: The Need For Leadership," *International Journal,* Vol 2, Spring 1997.
4. The term is one of the conclusions reached by the "Somalia Inquiry" in regards to several senior commanders of the Canadian Forces. See, *Canada, Dishonoured Legacy: The Lessons of the Somalia Affair,* Report of the Commission of Inquiry into the Deployment of the Canadian Forces to Somalia, (Ottawa: Minister of Public Works, 1997).
5. Bland, *Chiefs of Defence,* 211-260.
6. For a particularly strident criticism on the fitness of Canadian politicians see, J.V. Brock, *Memoirs of a Sailor: The Thunder and the Sunshine.* (Toronto: McClelland & Stewart, 1983).
7. General Gerry Theriault, "Democratic Civil-Military Relations: A Canadian View," in *The Military In Modern Democratic Society.* (Toronto: Canadian Institute of Strategic Studies, November, 1996), 10.
8. See Jame Eayrs, *In Defence of Canada: Growing Up Allied,* Volume IV (Toronto: University of Toronto Press, 1972).
9. Preston, Adrian, "The Profession of Arms in Postwar Canada, 1945-1970," *World Politics,* 23 January 1971, 189-214; and Bland, *Chiefs of Defence.*
10. Peter Haydon, *The 1962 Cuban Missile Crisis: Canadian Involvement Reconsidered* (Toronto: Canadian Institute of Strategic Studies, 1993).

Officership: A Personal Reflection

General Maurice Baril

General Maurice Baril is the current CF Chief of the Defence Staff.

THE END OF THE COLD WAR in the late 1980s and early 1990s marked the beginning of significant change for the Canadian Forces (CF). The demise of the Soviet Union and the Warsaw Pact created momentous geopolitical ramifications. The post Cold War period no longer enjoyed the stability shaped by two diametrically opposed superpowers armed with massive nuclear arsenals. The result for Canada was that the CF was increasingly involved in new forms of peace support operations as a member of coalitions or alliances. In the past decade the Forces have deployed on more complex and more dangerous missions than they had during the entire Cold War. In short, the world has become a much more unstable place.

Concurrently with these geopolitical changes were other dramatic challenges that have also impacted on the Canadian Forces. In North America and Western Europe the industrial age has been overtaken by the information age. This in turn has fuelled a revolution in military affairs, which has forced the Canadian Forces to redefine its whole approach to the conduct of military operations.

THE CHALLENGE

To be a leader during these turbulent and rapidly changing times has been an enormous challenge to us all. The Canadian Forces and the Department of National Defence (DND), like many other Canadian institutions, have not always been quick to anticipate and react to these new transitions. Although some of our slowness to change was because of prevailing institutional attitudes and cultures, much of the trouble was due to the unparalleled operational tempo. One thing we have learned is that we can no longer be simply reactive. Maintenance of the *status quo* cannot be tolerated. As leaders we must ensure we are proactive and forward-looking.

This requirement is clearly evident when one looks at the number of emerging trends that are clearly apparent in the security environment. These are:

A revolution in operations. Peace support operations have gone from classic peacekeeping to missions where there is no peace to keep. This has been complicated by the fact that these operations take place in the context of civil war. We have had to help in the post-conflict nation-building process, and to provide a secure environment for this process to take place. These types of operations seem likely to continue for the foreseeable future. This will require the leaders of the Canadian Forces to continue developing the specialized skills needed to meet these complex operational challenges.

A greater emphasis on resource management. Commanders today, and in the future, are facing unprecedented levels of accountability and transparency. More importantly, human resources are acknowledged as, by far, the most valuable asset of the Canadian Forces. For an organization like ours, which could not exist without the dedication of its people, the best possible management of our soldiers, sailors and air force personnel will be a critical requirement for the leaders of tomorrow.

A reflection of the trends in Canadian society at large. Canada is a distinctly pluralist country. In addition, the younger generations coming up tend to be highly individualistic, questioning of authority, and better educated. The challenge here is twofold. First, to reconcile the pluralist-individualist voice that has become a hallmark of our society with operational imperatives and the chain of command. Second, to reflect the fundamental values of Canadian society. Although we can be proud of our distinctive military ethos and our institutional values, often described as being of a much higher level than society at large, we must be aware that any group that moves too far from its parent society risks isolating itself. Clearly then, the danger would be the emergence of an entity that becomes a closed society unto itself; one that would become very intolerant of others who do not fit the high standards of acceptance to the group.

A revolution in information. The information age is upon us and the widely accepted revolution in military affairs will continue to have a profound impact on all aspects of military affairs. The necessary relationship between the officer and the ensemble of hardware, software, analytical frameworks and cognitive processes that together make up the information technology world is particularly relevant. These tools will become a virtual extension of an individual's intellectual persona.[1] Being able to operate in the information revolution will be a critical requirement of officership.

The effective functioning of the Canadian Forces in this changed environment of the twenty-first century will require superior leaders with high professional standards capable of successfully fulfilling the missions and tasks that the government will assign the Forces. Our officers must have a clear, well-articulated sense of military purpose based on the concept of the unlimited liability that puts service to the nation before self, and a readiness to apply and manage lethal force in the execution of government policy. To this end, the Forces must be better linked to the government and the people of Canada through a relationship based on a common understanding, mutual trust, shared values and collective purpose. Finally, the impact of the ongoing information revolution will intensify and will alter organizations, operations, training and education in ways not yet clear. For this reason our officers must be given the knowledge and skill sets that will enable them to function effectively in this dynamic and challenging environment.

PREVIOUS APPROACH

Our approach over the last twenty-five years has focused almost exclusively on the practical side. In the area of officer education for example, there was little opportunity or encouragement for officers to undertake academic study. It was generally accepted that to take time out for post graduate work was detrimental to your career. In 1996, as Commander of the Army, I tried to change that trend. I actually took the top two Lieutenant-Colonels on the merit list and sent them off for post-graduate education.

My motive was to pass a visible signal to all. This is not to say that academic qualifications equate with leadership. But, rather that officership ability can only improve with education and as such, it is career enhancing, not debilitating. In short, I challenged the common belief that experience gained in the course of assignments and promotions was in itself sufficient to create skilled and accomplished leaders. This is clearly not so. There is another dimension for maintaining the skills of military leaders. Undeniably, the 1990s represented the first strong test of the contemporary CF Officer Corps and we found that part of it was broken. Experience in and of itself was not enough.

With this in mind, both today and in the future, we will see that the dimension of *knowledge renewal* or *continuous learning* will be critical. Within the Canadian Forces we have understood its importance for some time. It is interesting to note that in 1947 Brooke Claxton, then the Minister of National Defence, stated that "the role of the officers in modern war can only be properly discharged if they have education and standing in the community comparable to that of any of the professions…" Nonetheless, we tended only to focus our efforts on the renewal of our technical skills.

If we want to be sure, in this era of globalisation and the knowledge-based economy, that our young officers coming up are ready to take the reins in the future, we must throw ourselves into their intellectual development now to create leaders who are intellectually rigorous, and multi-disciplined. Officers of all ranks will be continuously faced with risk and ambiguity, especially in the types of operations the Canadian Forces can expect into the twenty-first century. Training *per se* is necessary but not sufficient to deal with these situations. Education prepares individuals for those unknowns.

FUTURE REQUIREMENTS

Even though we are perceived by our allies as being an extremely competent and professional military, we cannot rest on these laurels. Rather, we must measure our success by the Canadian public. Their perception and beliefs in regard to our worth and effectiveness is of great importance. After all, *our duty is to serve this country*. We must never forget that Canadians are very demanding of their armed forces. They judge us according to the standards derived from the values that our society holds dear. The ethics and moral values to which we subscribe must be the reflection of the values and principles held by Canadian society as a whole. In fact, good old honesty is still the basis of our society. This therefore must be accorded pride of place in the pantheon of values that constitute the military ethos of the Canadian Forces. In addition, as for society as a whole, tolerance, openness, justice and respect for the law must be completely integrated in our leadership model. Only then will we be able to succeed. The Canadian public will not accept anything else.

We have a duty to inform Canadians on questions of defence to a level far beyond what was previously demanded of us and what we have historically provided. Just as our elected representatives are being called upon to be more transparent and more responsive to public participation in the decision-making process, so too do we have an obligation to ensure that they are adequately informed on all aspects of their Canadian Forces.

Events in the 1990s have demonstrated that leaders must become specialists in crisis management, military operations and resource managers. We need a balance of competencies between the profession of arms and program management, between regimental spirit and the corporate ethos, between risk and getting the job done. We must establish clearly where we are in this balance and where we must go. As mentioned earlier, to be satisfied with the *status quo* is unacceptable. We cannot be found wanting by the Canadian public again.

In acknowledging the need for change, we must not forget that we did in fact have many successes in meeting the challenges of the past decade. The myriad of CF activities during that time—including aid to the civil power, assistance in domestic natural disasters, humanitarian operations, and peace enforcement in the Balkans—demonstrated the dedication and skill of our personnel. Nonetheless, we must ensure that we address the core leadership issues of the future environment. These are:

- character;
- agile and flexible leadership;
- the ability to evolve as well as to master conceptual complexity;
- the ability to sustain life-long learning;
- the need for skills in complex conflict resolution and negotiations;
- inter-cultural awareness;
- linguistic and cultural sensibility;
- new approaches to decision-making and team building in the future; and
- leading in an information-rich environment.

These concerns cannot be addressed exclusively with an experiential approach. We must invest significantly and press the development of the "grey ware" in our officer corps. This is particularly true for the junior officers who are in the front lines of operations, leading under complex mandates and rules of engagement that lead to moral, ethical and fundamental value-based mastery of emotions and resolution of dilemmas, and being observed by the nation, at every step, in the accomplishment of their duties.

There are three key concepts, which I believe are fundamental to the kind of officership that we will need to see the Canadian Forces successfully through the next decade and beyond. Although not new, they must be re-emphasized and updated to ensure they remain relevant to the times. These critical concepts of Canadian officership are:

- Professionalism;
- Leadership; and
- Strategic Thinking.

PROFESSIONALISM

The profession of arms is fundamental to officership. To be professional by definition implies the mastery of a certain body of knowledge. In our years in the service, we have made ourselves expert in this profession through long hours of study and many years of practical, operational experience. As professionals, we are characterized by specific attributes.

- Our officer corps must be guided by a code of ethics and moral values. This code is the very foundation of our profession. Perhaps more than any other occupation, we are bound and guided by the values of patriotism, respect, honour, loyalty, and above all, to self-sacrifice and service on behalf of our fellow Canadians. Too often, however, an objective assessment of the state of the officer corps as a whole might conclude that all were *saying* the right thing but not all were *acting* the right way.
- A true professional must be constantly evolving and adapting to reflect and respond to the changing world. In the military, we are only too aware of this constant need to adapt to emerging circumstance.
- A true professional is motivated by a will to serve, to achieve excellence for the sake of others. I believe one of the challenges we are facing as we revitalize our officer corps is to put this quality into practice. As leaders, we cannot be afraid to take risks in the interests of doing what is right, even if it may seem to jeopardize our personal careers.
- The mastery of a certain body of knowledge is another characteristic of professionalism. Military knowledge in particular is unique for the

breadth of disciplines it covers. A true knowledge of the military art requires a strong foundation in history, politics, international relations, communications, and the sciences. Those who do not possess this disciplined knowledge cannot succeed as military commanders. It is just such a life-long commitment to learning and education that separates amateurs from professionals, managers from leaders.

LEADERSHIP

The next fundamental component of officership is leadership. But, what exactly is leadership? General Dextraze, a former Chief of the Defence Staff who served for an unprecedented five years in that position in the late 1970s, believed "leadership is the art of influencing others to do willingly what is required in order to achieve an aim or goal."[2]

But, what makes a good leader? Leadership is an intensely personal attribute that must be developed according to each individual's strengths, style and personality. A true leader spends his whole life learning and developing his skills. In my attempt to provide able leadership within the Canadian Forces, I have personally turned to the examples of our former CF leaders and my own experience. This has led me to believe that there are certain qualities that are fundamental to strong leadership.

The first is that leadership is not merely a mechanical process of control. Because a leader works with that infinitely complex entity called a human being, he must be an artist, not a mechanic. The everyday dealings of our officers involve by far the most valuable asset of the Canadian Forces—people. As we know, people are infinitely complex, influenced by the subtlest nuances of environment and emotion. That is why, as leaders, we must rely on something other than simple process to provide the guidance our personnel require to do their job effectively.

To assist us there are several timeless traits fundamental to good leadership:

- *Loyalty* is the foundation upon which a relationship of trust and respect is built. It is a two-way street, both upwards to our superiors and through them to the government and the country and downwards to our subordinates. It is not always easy to reconcile these two aspects of loyalty and it is often difficult to keep a proper balance between the two in the face of conflicting demands. As a battle-tried former CDS noted, "any commander who has ever ordered troops into battle must certainly have paused to reflect, or should have, on the need to risk lives for a higher cause."[3]

- *Integrity*, the refusal to deceive others in any way regardless of the circumstance, is also indispensable in building trust and respect. As leaders we make decisions. We must hold ourselves accountable for the consequences of our decisions, good and bad. In so doing, the sacred trust that leadership represents will be preserved and strengthened.
- *Knowledge* makes us effective. Without such competence we cannot command the respect necessary. "You must never stop learning," commented General Dextraze, "sound, knowledgeable leadership makes the difference, and the necessary knowledge can only come through hard work. Do not be under the impression that, as your career progresses, the piece of grey matter in your head will grow in size proportionate to the loftiness of your rank. This just doesn't happen." A blunt statement, but one with which I agree completely. It is a sound observation and provides a good model. Quite simply, this means I have high expectations both of myself and of those with whom I share the leadership of the Canadian Forces.
- *Courage* in wartime usually involves physical bravery. In peacetime the moral courage to speak up against what one honestly believes to be wrong is the hallmark. Both types of courage have their own inherent risks.[4]

It is often difficult to improve on what our previous senior leaders have given us in terms of a better understanding of what leadership means. General Norman Schwartzkopf, in an interview with David Frost defined leadership as a combination of character and competence. Leadership for me means standing up for one's values, making decisions based on the best information available and on one's best judgement, taking the necessary action and accepting responsibility for those decisions and actions.

STRATEGIC THINKING

The final component of officership is strategic thinking. The Canadian Forces have always recognized the value of a strong educational foundation. But in the past we have been guilty of focusing our efforts too narrowly on junior officers. As a result, the senior officers of the Canadian Forces have too often been left to their own devices or forced to rely on "on-the-job" experiences in their various appointments to prepare them for their senior duties. When you consider the new and complex responsibilities officers assume in higher command this expectation to "learn as you go" is inadequate and unfair.

OFFICERSHIP: A PERSONAL REFLECTION

If there is one quality that distinguishes the leadership of a senior officer as compared with a junior officer, it is the strategic element. Their roles up to now have been, appropriately, more focused on the tactical activities and operations that confront the Canadian Forces on a day-to-day basis. This must change. Our most senior officers will spend less time at the "coal-face" monitoring day-to-day events and dealing with the latest crisis of the moment. These roles must be delegated, with decision-making decentralized so that the most senior officers are freed to focus on the longer-term decisions that are required to provide a strategic vision for the Canadian Forces for the future. This implies a form of leadership that incorporates a strategic leadership and vision that I would call *Generalship*. It is not about developing intricate plans to preserve or maintain the *status quo*. Strategic vision is ultimately about aligning means—where we will be in terms of structure and resources—with ends—where we need to go in the future. It relates where you are to where you want to be. Generalship brings together the two concepts of strategic thinking and leadership. It is about reacting to the forces of change at the same time as new mechanisms for addressing the future are created. The focus must be more than management alone. The focus of our vision is the future. Strategic vision combined with strong leadership is required if the CF is to successfully meet the challenges of the future. We must create and articulate a vision that is understood and embraced by all the men and women serving in the Canadian Forces and the Department of National Defence.

This is one reason that makes ongoing officer education and professional development so important. The Canadian Forces exist in a world that demands the highest levels of effectiveness, efficiency, flexibility, dedication and vision. No one can accurately forecast the future. Therefore, we cannot train or educate our personnel with specific skills to meet the requirement of 2020 with any precision. But, we can prepare them intellectually to be able to cope and deal with ambiguity and complexity. While training furnishes predictable responses to predictable situations, education enables a reasoned response to an unpredictable situation—in other words, disciplined and critical thinking in the face of the unknown and the unknowable.

The theme of education continues to emerge in this chapter. It is no coincidence. As early as 1969, in a report by Major-General Roger Rowley[5] the vital importance of ongoing officer professional development was clearly enunciated. One of the keystones of this development, even thirty years ago, was ongoing formal military education. Most recently, the 1997 Report to the Prime Minister[6] repeatedly underlined the need to strengthen the professional development of the officers of the Canadian Forces. So how is it that we did nothing for thirty years? The answer may be simple ignorance of the requirement. Nonetheless, there is no sense in trying to apportion blame. We must now focus on correcting the deficiencies of our past. Our ultimate goal must be to better prepare our officer corps to face the challenges today and in the future.

MY VISION

In the introduction to the Rowley report of 1969 on officer professional development, the Chief of the Defence Staff at the time, General Jean Victor Allard said, "it matters little whether the Forces have their present manpower strength and financial budget, or half of them, or double them; without a properly educated, effectively trained professional officer corps the Forces would, in the future, be doomed at best to mediocrity, and at the worst, to disaster."[7]

Wise words from the past, which we would all do well to heed. For my part I am deeply committed to ensuring that the Canadian Forces have the leadership they need to successfully confront the challenges of the future with confidence. To do so, my personal goal is to ensure that the officers of the CF receive the development and support necessary, particularly in the area of officer professional development, including military education. It is our duty. Our legacy will be the Canadian Officer Corps of the future. As such, we will share their successes, as well as their failures.

NOTES

1. Department of National Defence, *Canadian Officership in the 21st Century - OPD 2020 Statement of Operational Requirement* (Draft), January 2000, 7-8.
2. General J.A. Dextraze, "The Art of Leadership," *Canadian Forces Personnel Newsletter*, June 1973.
3. Ibid.
4. The fundamental traits given are derived from General Dextraze's paper given at note 2.
5. Department of National Defence, *The Report On The Officer Development Board* (Rowley Report), Ottawa, March 1969, v.
6. Department of National Defence, *The Report to the Prime Minister on the Leadership and Management of the CAF*, Ottawa, 25 March, 1997.
7. Rowley Report, iv.

Leadership Challenges for the New Century: A Personal Reflection

Lieutenant-General (retired) D.N. Kinsman

Lieutenant-General D.N. Kinsman retired from the CF in the summer of 2000. His last appointment was Chief of the Air Staff.

MUCH WAS MADE DURING THE FINAL YEARS OF THE 1990s concerning the arrival of the year 2000. In particular, the crossover into a new century and a new millennium precipitated more than the normal amount of speculation on what type of world we were moving into and what challenges might confront us during the next century. As with any new year, we were moved to look back over our shoulders to review the past and attempt to link that past with the present to the future. Of course, in a practical sense, there is absolutely nothing unique about moving into the year 2000. However, it has provided a more obvious milestone in time at which to reflect.

Let us begin, then, with a bit of retrospection because it is essential, after all, to know and have analyzed the lessons and experiences of the past before preparing for the future. Any review of the 1990s from a Canadian Forces (CF) or leadership perspective quickly reveals a decade of unforeseen change, challenge and crisis. By the late 1980s, Canadians had enjoyed nearly four decades of continuous peace. The reality of the Cold War had created, in a military and economic sense, a relative sense of stability or status quo. Few of the assumptions upon which the Canadian military based its thinking and activity had been seriously challenged during that timeframe. Indeed, a White Paper in 1986 seemed only to reinforce the validity of what the CF was doing and how it was doing it.

What happened next within an international, economic and legislative context has been, and will continue to be, the subject of much analysis, learned and otherwise. Practically speaking, however, the relatively stable world those of us who were generals and admirals at the time had grown up in disappeared within a few short years, only to be replaced by remarkably different and frequently changing dynamics and assumptions. Whereas we had previously planned to a relatively stable strategic threat assessment, we were now dealing with much more unpredictable operational planning assumptions including speaking to and assisting those who were the former "enemy." Whereas we had represented a country whose economic status since the Second World War had been unquestioned, we were called upon to do our part, both as citizens and leaders of the CF, to help Canada back from the brink of economic calamity. Whereas we had previously conducted the affairs of the military in relative isolation from, and for reasons not well understood by, the majority of the Canadian public, we were now being scrutinized and challenged for explanations from every quarter of society and in virtually every area of endeavor. Whereas we had assumed our men and women in uniform were largely prepared to do what was asked of them without requiring any explanation for the "why," we were forced to the realization that "Because I told you to!" no longer served the purpose adequately in most circumstances. Whereas we had assumed that being prepared to fight an all-out war would automatically prepare us for any military activity short of war, we soon found that the more interventionist style of peacekeeping/peacemaking in which we found ourselves involved presented a whole new set of problems for which we simply were not well prepared.

LEADERSHIP CHALLENGES FOR THE NEW CENTURY: A PERSONAL REFLECTION

Much has been written about the CF in the 1990s and much remains to be said. Surely, however, history will reflect fundamental reforms to this institution which, had they not been undertaken, would probably have resulted in the collapse of the CF as we know it. At the very least, the organization would have had its ability to apply military governance and regulation from within diminished or eliminated. Were it not for those changes, the renewed esteem Canadians have for their military would not have been possible. Nor would the CF have benefited in a more tangible sense from increases to their funding levels as provided for in the federal budgets of 1999 and 2000. Allies would not have continued to press for our assistance in operations, nor would they have continued to make frequent visits to determine in what manner they might benefit from our experiences and the many transformations we have effected.

In a written personal message to the CF in 1973, General Dextraze, then Chief of the Defence Staff, wrote on the Art of Leadership. He stated that "...the basic principles of leadership and man management are both timeless and universal." He went on to say "Leadership ... is an art rather than a science" and that the leader "... must be an artist, not a mechanic." The decade of the 1990s put the General's thesis to a severe test. History will reflect that leadership at all levels was under excruciating pressure during this period of time but that, with some notable exceptions, it was essentially sound. There is no other way to explain the many distinguished successes realized by our military throughout this period while placing in context the obvious failures. That does not mean that a fundamental overhaul of much of the military leadership's thinking or methodologies was not in order. It was, and that transformation continues to take place. What then should the generals and admirals, as well as the other levels of leadership in the CF, retain from these experiences to ensure the strongest possible institution and profession for the future?

Nearly thirty-seven years of military service, with five separate opportunities to command, have repeatedly underscored for me the wisdom of the observations of General Dextraze cited above. The elements of leadership are indeed, for all intents and purposes, "timeless and universal." What has changed, however, is the context in which those elements must be applied in the future if we are to conform to expectations of those who serve the institution and those who are served by it. Therefore, the general and flag officer of today and the future must be able to retain those characteristics of leadership that are enduring and apply them through diverse and changing media to an audience, internal and external, that expects a full and ongoing understanding of how our military functions.

The principles of individual rights and freedoms, rights to privacy and the expectation of transparency in the actions of organizations and individuals are elements of today's Canadian society that have placed demands for change on traditional military leadership styles and concepts. Leadership styles that were "acceptable" and "effective" up until only a few short years ago are no longer considered to be such. The CF is still working its way through the transformation demanded in this regard. This will be one of the foremost challenges of leadership in the forthcoming years; the changes that have been achieved or undertaken are not an aberration. There is no going back to "the way it was." Of that there can be no doubt nor can there be any lack of resolve to ensure the full and enduring incorporation of these changes. In the early years of this century, there may well be a tendency to return to old habits. Tomorrow's leaders must resist that temptation at all costs for it would inevitably result in unacceptable consequences and this institution cannot afford, or perhaps ever withstand, a crisis similar to that of the mid-1990s.

The question of decisiveness is at the heart of this transformation in leadership approach or style. The traditional view of a decisive leader is of one who, by whatever means, has collected all of the factors and knowledge upon which to base a decision and makes those decisions rapidly, forcefully and with unwavering conviction. A style that includes reflection, collaboration and willingness to admit uncertainty on occasion has traditionally been seen as weak or inferior, even if it produced a better solution in the end. Which of these approaches will be valid in the future? As always, there is no single answer or style that responds to all requirements. Unilateral decision making and forceful presentation will always have a role to play. However, given the trend towards transparency and inclusiveness, I would conclude the "John Wayne" style should be used only in special circumstances and not as the norm. Some might contend that such an inclusive or collaborative approach undermines confidence and that subordinates will be less likely to follow such a "wishy-washy" leader. I would counter that leaders who, under normal circumstances, are willing to showcase their vision and logic, subsequently incorporating the good ideas of others, will nurture a level of trust and confidence within their superiors, peers and subordinates that will encourage unqualified support in those circumstances where rapid decisions and action are called for.

To strengthen my thesis, I suggest one has to look no further than the type of individuals we now seek to attract, train and retain within the CF. We require much more by way of personal qualifications in those we wish to recruit today. We demand much more of them intellectually in their training, in their day-to-day responsibilities and in the way we expect them to conform with and, indeed, exemplify the best of Canadian values and morality. How then could we possibly expect such highly qualified people not to wish to play a more active role in the factors and decisions that affect their day-to-day lives?

A critical area in which I sense the leadership transformation is not yet complete is that of change, the manner in which it is sought out, the manner in which it is embraced and the manner in which it is communicated. I have already made the point that the last four decades were not ones in which rapid and fundamental systemic changes were required, especially when compared to the last five years of the 1990s. A good friend confided in me recently that while he was a senior officer in the CF, his sense of loyalty to the troops centered largely on trying to reduce the impact of change on his subordinates, meaning that he tried to defend his organization from most change, particularly if it involved any form of reduction. After retirement, he became a senior executive in industry where his perspectives changed significantly and rapidly. He now believes that the effective leader detects where change is required and acts quickly, not to save jobs or infrastructure or equipment or to protect people from change but rather to make sure mitigating measures are in place to protect them from unnecessary ill effects and to get on with it quickly and decisively for the wellbeing of the organization.

One of the fundamental principles articulated by the Department and the CF in the strategic guidance document, *Shaping the Future of Canadian Defence: A Strategy for 2020*, is that of "Continuous Improvement." Very few would not want to belong to an organization that is constantly striving to be better in all respects. Yet, implicit with that principle is the requirement for "Continuous Change," for there can be no improvement on the status quo if there is not change. Most humans do not embrace change naturally and certainly most military organizations have traditionally not been advocates of sweeping change except, perhaps, in the area of technology as it applies to equipment. There remains a great tendency to do as my friend admits to having done, to avoid change completely or, if confronted with it to take the slow route instead of acting swiftly but with compassion. All effective leaders in the future, at every level of rank, will have to overcome the natural tendency to expend energy on the protection of the status quo and embrace the importance of seeking and being a champion of change where the requirement exists.

Having foreseen the requirement for and initiated a change, how will the challenge of effective communication be met? In a world where technology plays an increasingly pervasive role, where face-to-face contact is increasingly supplanted by other means of communication, and where the pace of life tends to modify the ways in which we interact, we must be careful not to forget the fundamentals of human behavior. We have evolved as social creatures and the importance of our interactions will not change nearly as rapidly as the technology that surrounds us. I sense we have incorrectly assumed that mass media communications such as CANFORGEN messages, e-mail, web sites, pamphlets and the like are effective means of conveying messages of fundamental importance. Leadership in this new century must not forget, and indeed must reinforce, the critical importance played by in-person communication. I am not suggesting that only the senior leadership can effect that personal communication; that would not be realistic. Traditionally, we have been reliant upon supervisors at all levels to ensure their people knew what was happening and why. I postulate that the wholesale changes of the last decade have diminished the basic understanding of many fundamental issues to the point that the traditional communication function performed by the chain of command has frequently been disabled. Reestablishment of an understanding of the issues within the full length of the chain of command must be a priority if the negative emotional effects of the change agenda are to be minimized.

Although I was invited by the Chief of the Defence Staff (CDS) to offer my perspectives on "The Role of the General—Preparing the Air Force for the Next Century," you will note that I have offered nothing specific to air power in the foregoing thoughts. That is because the elements of excellence in leadership, which must be the dominant characteristic of any general or flag officer, are common to excellent leaders at all levels, in all colours of uniform, and, indeed, in every dimension of human endeavour. Certainly, one could describe circumstances in the air force which differ from those in other environments. Furthermore, we all recognize the varying "cultures" which form the mosaic of the profession of arms. That aside, those fundamental characteristics of excellent leadership that have marked notable generals and admirals of the past are the same characteristics that distinguish effective leaders of today and will be those that identify leaders of note in the future.

In his 1973 paper, General Dextraze cited the four qualities that were, in his opinion, the most essential ingredients of successful leadership. As I retire from this wonderful institution, I will avail myself of this final opportunity in uniform to briefly state the three qualities I have aimed for personally and which I admire most in others. They are: *be fair, be consistent and be human.* These would, of course, apply to all levels of leadership but I think it is the last quality that requires the most attention by general and flag officers. Not that they are any less human than those at other levels of leadership but rather that they have to overcome a popular perception that they care little about individuals who work at lower levels within the organization. They must also contend with the reality that their duties and relative isolation from the field, with the exception of the relatively few commanders at general/flag rank, don't afford them frequent opportunities to dispel that perception, except within their immediate entourage. In the context of an increasingly pluralistic society with an expectation of more inclusive workplace mechanisms, such isolation, perceived or real, can do nothing but undermine faith and confidence. As mentioned earlier, technological solutions to communication do nothing to assist in this regard. Therefore, generals and flag officers of the future will have to be particularly attentive to maintaining a level of personal contact that ensures such myths remain localized or are dispelled completely.

If the 1990s taught us nothing else, it should be that we as individuals and as an institution must constantly revalidate the fundamental principles upon which we are based and then renew our commitment to and employment of those principles. Our failures have invariably been associated with blind adherence to traditional methodologies or beliefs which, in retrospect, did not have a solid foundation or for which modifications were in order. On the other hand, where we have ensured the principles were sound and have acted upon them, we have prevailed and, indeed, strengthened our institution. Generals and flag officers of the new century will find their greatest challenge to be one of determining which principles are enduring and should not be changed, those which have been enduring but need to be modified to respond to the exigencies of a changing military/society/world and those which are no longer relevant. This has always been the hallmark activity of an excellent general or admiral. However, such determinations will have to be made more frequently and more rapidly in this new century than was the case for the majority of the last. Of all the requirements of our military leaders, this will be the most demanding and critical of their professional obligations and the one for which they will have to be meticulously groomed and prepared.

A Matter of Trust: Ethics and Self-Regulation Among Canadian Generals

Major-General K. G. Penney

Major-General K.G. Penney is the current Department of National Defence Chief of Review Services.

IN RECENT YEARS, societal attitudes towards traditional models of authority have been all but overturned. In western culture especially, reacting against longstanding and sometimes tragic abuses, society now routinely subjects the words and deeds of its leaders, politicians, lawyers, doctors and priests to new depths of scrutiny.

The military is not immune to such distrust of authority. In a society that insists the public and private lives of its leaders be characterized by pure and unimpeachable behaviour, senior military officers who in any way take advantage of their positions risk the skepticism, even cynicism, of their subordinates.

Will soldiering go the way of doctoring? In the future, might troops ordered into battle log onto the Internet for a second opinion before taking up arms? Unlikely. But these questions, which may at first seem frivolous, underscore the reality that now more than ever effective leadership is dependent on respect and achieved by example. Ethical behaviour, then, is the fundamental requirement of every person entrusted with command. For general officers, carrying out their duties in the most visible of all rank groups, the expectation of accountability may be the greatest.

The issues of ethics and accountability have recently taken on heightened importance because of the nature of military missions, and the context in which military decisions at every level are made. Colonel Paul Maillet, Director of Defence Ethics for the Canadian Forces, recently joined an international conference in England at the Royal Military Academy, Sandhurst, to examine the complex issues surrounding the question of accountability in a modern context. He concluded that:

> If these issues are combined with the various revolutions sweeping the military and society, there is no doubt that the military will never be the same again. The technological revolution requiring high levels of education and knowledge, the social revolution which demands a rights-based military force that reflects societal values such as gender, diversity, respect, human rights, and the transparency revolution with its all-seeing and instantaneous media are all transforming military accountability.[1]

Amid these revolutions, and in the emerging context-sensitive realm of global military intervention, it is not just our roles and expectations of behaviour that are changing. As Colonel Maillet points out, it is a new paradigm in which our very definition of military victory must be overturned. In the future, a legitimate claim of victory might be the achievement of a break in the cycle of violence that hopefully creates a reluctance by the belligerents to return to armed conflict and instead provides them the opportunity to rebuild the social structure.

We live in an age of deployed operations, long-term missions in foreign circumstances where moral decisions are made moment-by-moment by troops on the line. Ours is an age when the corporal on patrol is a *strategic* soldier, visible to the world. Whether face-to-face with a native warrior in full view of the media, plucking landmines from a farmer's field in a nation ravaged by civil strife, or patrolling a border where today's victims may well be tomorrow's oppressors, our soldiers more than ever are thinking men and women called upon to base their actions not only on *rules* but also on *values*.

THE NEW TRUST EQUATION

In Canada the following values are embraced: fairness, decency, collaborative spirit, respect for the individual and passion for peace. In the forces, we also embrace the four traditional military values of courage, duty, discipline and honour. But how does one motivate and enable soldiers in peacekeeping operations to affirm these values on each and every watch? In deployed operations, the situation may be understood and the mission clear enough, but the execution of that mission can instantly place any on-duty soldier, sailor or airperson into a gray zone where ethical obligations may be in conflict.

Consider the pressures. Often, in these situations, there is no threat to our homeland. The local populace may resent our presence. And the local government may not even support the intervention. Finally, the long-revered dictum of "the mission before the men" may be reversed, as the loss of a single Canadian life in peacetime may be considered unacceptable. In these conditions, the trust equation takes on a whole new balance. Self-knowledge, self-determination and ultimately self-regulation provide direction as important as any formal order.

For Canadians, trust of and insistence on self-regulation by our military flows logically from our national character. We are a people who prize order and civil obedience highly. Our own disbelief at the behaviour of some members of the Canadian Forces (CF) in Somalia was soon matched by a national shame. The subsequent disbandment of the Airborne Regiment in the wake of the controversy seemed reasonable and fitting to most Canadians, even if some military personnel privately dismissed the decision as unwarranted and politically motivated. The sensibility of Canadians had been offended beyond all tolerance. The trust equation had been betrayed, even though by all accounts our military mission in Somalia had been fulfilled. I believe strongly that it is this very sensibility that makes Canadians such valuable collaborators for peace on the world stage.

When I first took up the post of Chief Review Services, our branch was investigating a senior officer suspected of activities that might require what is called "administrative recovery." This term refers to an intervention by which someone receiving undue financial benefits must return some portion of the funds. I was informed by the investigators that their probing suggested more than mere administrative error might be at play. They considered that, should they continue their search, they would likely uncover evidence that the officer's actions had been clearly selfish and inappropriate. Given that the officer in question was a senior general, they were uncertain whether I, a general officer new to the branch, would wish to pursue the evidence.

As a fellow general, I had the power to encourage, discourage or limit the investigation. I could not, of course. The notion of denying an investigation that might possibly uncover real wrongdoing, and therefore a breach of trust, was unacceptable. I required them to press on. They did, and subsequently discovered that the officer had made a number of claims for compensation that were clearly inappropriate. I found out some months later, that our finding was not really a discovery. As it turned out, the troops under his command had been aware of the issue long before the matter surfaced, and could not understand why the leadership had not acted sooner.

Their challenge, as mine, was an ethical issue rooted in traditional military notions of privilege of rank. The unspoken acknowledgement was that the higher your rank, the more you can get away with. Cynical though it may be, this adage is based on experience.

When I was a lieutenant, I was surprised to discover that a powerful base commander I encountered suffered from a severe drinking problem. All the classically codependent systems were in place; everyone knew about the problem, superiors, peers and subordinates, but no one talked about it, except in hushed conversations in private places. No one dared raise the issue.

We all knew this was wrong; the situation had already caused an erosion of trust. And sadly, the question for the troops was not whether this man could act competently: they already knew that answer. The real issue was how such behaviour could be overlooked, and therefore sanctioned in a senior officer when it would not be tolerated in anyone else. Such inequality seemed unthinkable on a training base where future leaders were being groomed. The irony and the hypocrisy did not go unnoticed.

Neither was this situation an isolated example of unfair rule. Under the mantle of rank and authority, undue entitlements have been claimed through history, even recent history. It was rare that a base construction officer was not confronted by married-quarter renovation requests from senior officers (and sometimes their spouses) who had been led to believe that preferential treatment at the expense of the Crown was to be counted among the privileges of rank. For base engineers struggling to ensure at least minimally acceptable housing standards for service personnel living in quarters, such requests were difficult to stomach.

The general who falsified his claims, the base commander who abused his authority while in an alcoholic haze, and the officers who insisted that military resources be used to renew their décor may have believed that no one discussed, or perhaps even noticed, the inappropriateness of what they were asking of those around them. They were wrong. In every case where an abuse is perpetrated, an injustice committed, or an unfair advantage gained, everyone knows and everyone talks. The Canadian military is small and quietly vocal. There are few secrets and none where unfair privilege is concerned. But notoriety is not the greatest risk. It is the inevitable and disastrous destruction of trust that results from such abuses. Those who wander outside ethical limits, even innocently, risk the cynicism of all those of equal and lower rank. For generals, the faith of the entire military is therefore at stake. The trust equation is easily upset and extremely difficult to restore.

ASSESSING LEGITIMATE ENTITLEMENT

A long-held leadership adage in the military states "Don't expect those around you to undertake any task you would be unwilling to undertake yourself." The corollary is equally relevant: don't take anything for yourself that you would be unwilling to give your colleagues in arms.

In Canada, in a military whose landscape is changing as quickly as that of any other social institution, our generals have a difficult task in assessing what entitlements or benefits they fairly need to do their jobs. Increased scrutiny, the spectre of past courts martial, and the enlightened sensibility of generals in a highly educated force have made the acceptance of even the most legitimate benefit of rank a difficult choice.

Many generals have become overly cautious about their rights and entitlements as senior officers. I know. I get the calls. Flying business class is a telling example. Like other executives, generals are required to travel frequently and are expected upon arrival to make coherent presentations of complex material. They are in accordance with Treasury Board policy, under certain conditions clearly entitled to fly business class. Some of our generals, however, unwilling to be perceived as taking more than they deserve, choose to fly economy regardless of the entitlement.

Similar awkward moments arise with increasing inter-departmental and inter-sectoral collaboration. If invited to dinner, may a general accept? If asked to include a game of golf during a round of business meetings with our allies, may a general oblige without compromising or being seen to take advantage of the unique status a flag officer enjoys?

REGULATION VERSUS SELF-REGULATION

A number of mechanisms can be put in place to answer those kinds of questions. In the US military, a compendium of rules is available to officers who can look up almost any situation and read what is and what is not permissible. This kind of directory of rules has a certain appeal: it is always good to know where you stand, but rules themselves can only apply to known or probable situations.

In living memory, the military's affection for rulemaking moved from legendary to notorious. When I joined, everyone knew the drill; if someone screwed up, someone else wrote a rule so it would not happen again. Those rules were not always insightful, but they were preventative and thus acknowledged as valid. The inevitable result, of course, was that the sheer preponderance of rules often hindered the kind of inspired leadership that can make a military effective.

In time, our forces, like so many bureaucracies, found themselves mired in administration, spending small fortunes to avoid misuse of petty cash. An audit conducted in the early nineties, for instance, found that the Department of National Defence and the Canadian Forces were spending $2 million each year on hospitality. Meanwhile the complex administrative structures put in place to oversee that hospitality budget were costing the Canadian taxpayer close to $1 million each year. The insistence on ethical certainty had created an additional expense that was difficult to comprehend.

In the modern day, in our flattened, devolved structural model of the military, less bureaucracy and fewer rules are the necessary conditions for the effectiveness of the forces. In such an environment, self-regulation in matters of ethics is the only assurance of trust.

The option of self-regulation for generals is far more than an avoidance of an external scrutiny or formal investigation. It is a modus operandi with profound downstream benefits. Fortunately, in the development of a self-regulation model for generals, I believe Canada is leading.

Important developments in our understanding of military ethical issues span almost a decade. In that time, there has been a heightened focus on the values operating within the Department of National Defence and the Canadian Forces, and a growing awareness of the ethical obligations that arise from those values. In 1993, management principles for the Defence Team were a priority. In 1996, ethical principles and obligations were drafted and endorsed. In 1997, a statement defining military ethos was discussed in the minister's report to the prime minister. That statement affirmed that an ethos is not simply a collection of values, but indeed the community of people who hold those values, and the behaviours that spring from them. In part, that statement reads:

> Canada has never been a military power, primarily because Canadians are not a militaristic society. Canadians admire duty, courage, discipline and honour, but we cherish fairness, decency, respect and compassion above all. Perhaps that is why we value civic virtue and civilian accomplishment over military heroism. Canadians are not aggressors; we are collaborators. Thus, when the Canadian Forces take action, we do so in concert with the forces of other countries. For their part, our allies in other nations have long respected and celebrated our diligent and unrelenting pursuit of peace.
>
> This quest for peace is Canada's great cause and sets out the obligation and the accountability that the Canadian Forces have to the people of our nation. It emphasizes the importance of the unwritten contract which exists between Forces members and the Canadian people: We, the Canadian people, will trust and support you, the Canadian Forces, only if we can see that you deserve our support.[2]

Management principles, ethical obligations, and an ethos statement: together these documents trace the growth of our collegial understanding of the values which must underpin all military activity in the new century. They also reflect an unprecedented level of dialogue and collaboration which, I believe, has not yet been undertaken anywhere else in the world.

Instrumental to this work was the active participation of Canadian generals in the development and endorsement of the value-based statements that shaped the documents. Canada is fortunate in this regard for, as a unified force, the Canadian military has enjoyed a cross-service dialogue since the 1960s when unification condensed our administrative structure. As a result, the art of the general and the art of the admiral can be discussed knowledgeably and fruitfully in a single room by the same people.

As Canadian generals came together to discuss the values on which military action should be based, we also undertook a deeper dialogue about the ethical issues they face as a unique group with a unique set of challenges and responsibilities. We recognized that generalship carries its own liabilities; the very traits that enable one to survive and succeed in flag rank can complicate self-assessment and self-discipline. Just as genius and madness are considered to exist on the same continuum, the general's qualities of ambition, success, determination, persistence and high self-esteem are not necessarily far removed from egocentricity.

Caution must be exercised; when egoism prevents an individual from accepting someone else's point of view or admitting errors, personal interest may overshadow one's ability to properly address the best interests of the community. The influence and the perils of ego also take on greater importance at higher levels in the chain of command where power increases and external controls decrease. The fractured proverb "Power is delightful; absolute power is absolutely delightful," reminds those in command not to indulge indiscriminately in the liberties that they have been given.

COUNTLESS NEW CHALLENGES—FOUR NEW TOOLS

How then can members of the general officer cadre self-regulate with relation to Canadian Forces values and obligations? I suggest that there are four critical interventions that can make self-regulation an effective assurance of ethical standards.

The first is *the selection process*. We know that the selection of candidates for promotion to flag rank is strongly influenced by those officers already serving as generals. In many ways, the members of the cadre shape the criteria for selection itself, then participate on promotion and selection boards where their personal and professional opinions about the suitability of any officer to general rank are considered. As the military evolves, these boards must evaluate a candidate's stewardship of the Canadian Forces: both performance and potential must be assessed not only for one's ability to get the job done, but also for the degree to which one's methodology reflects the values and ethics of the military community itself. Demonstrating respect and dignity for all, openness and dialogue, and the practice of rigorous self-assessment must be qualities sought in any selection-board deliberations.

The second tool is *the case study*, by which generals can discuss a wide variety of practical scenarios and reflect on the values that would shape a senior officer's decision when faced with a similar situation. In May of 1998, I extended an invitation to all general officers of the Canadian Forces to gather at the Royal Military College to explore the ethical dimensions of generalship. Case studies were a key component of the discussion, with participants encouraged to submit ethical dilemmas for debate. Fourteen general officers were able to participate directly and many others, who for operational reasons could not attend, submitted typical dilemmas, then registered their subsequent opinions electronically. The consensus of the officers who participated in the dialogue was that it had great practical benefit; hope was widely expressed that such case-study discussion would continue, and it has.

Since that first forum, three more formal discussions on matters of ethics and generalship have been mounted. At one of them, the question of entitlements came up for debate; generals sought to assure themselves that any entitlements given flag officers be clearly justified and utterly transparent. Notwithstanding the unselfish focus, even those discussions were undertaken with some reservation. I hope that in the not-too-distant future, entitlements may surface again as a worthy topic for open dialogue, for there are certainly small benefits that can rightly be claimed, and can reduce, even in a small way, the burden of senior command. Moreover, they may serve to heighten the effect of that command, as in the case of what the British forces refer to as gardening leave, that critical reflective time away from daily routine that senior officers are given before they take on a new strategic command.

The third tool of self-regulation is *peer support*. It is not lonely at the top if one is supported by other people at that same level. Canadian generals have repeatedly expressed their desire to develop a more regular consultation with each other. Electronic communication makes such support far more accessible, and allows our generals to provide collegial support on issues and problems as they emerge. That support becomes more necessary, and therefore valuable, as issues become more complex.

The fourth tool is *networking*, looking outward and also valuing the experience of others outside the military community. Networking is a strategy long prized in the private sector and is now gradually being acknowledged in the military as a means of gaining access to new and enlightened opinion about the challenges and strategies of generalship.

Taken together, these four tools offer a powerful portfolio of supports for our generals, who have expressed considerable enthusiasm in the early practical outcomes of their collaboration. One such outcome is an initiative of the generals by which regular communiqués are distributed throughout the cadre, articulating the issues and insights probed in the now-regular sessions that generals attend to discuss ethical matters. These communiqués have addressed ethical risks, general officer entitlements, gifts and hospitality, peer support and self-regulation itself. These documents have been well received for both providing focused advice on an issue and soliciting additional feedback and debate.

BACK TO THE BASICS

It will interest readers to know that, from the first session on, generals participating in ethical discussions have sought to better understand their fundamental obligations as generals before concerning themselves with how they might execute their duties. A statement proclaiming the responsibilities of the rank of general was developed over a period of two years and recently endorsed. At the time of writing, elements of that statement are awaiting final approval as the wording for a general officers' scroll, to be presented upon investiture to flag rank. The wording of the scroll is a ringing affirmation of the unique responsibilities our generals shoulder when they accept their promotion:

We do by these presents constitute and appoint you a general officer of the Canadian Forces, willing and requiring you forthwith to take upon you the charge and command of this rank;

We do will and require you accordingly to assume the unique and strategic obligations for the defence of Canada, the security of Canadians, the stewardship of the Canadian Forces, and the education, training, discipline and welfare of all those serving under you; and

We do further will and require you in fulfilling your duties to demonstrate excellence in leadership and the profession of arms, to promote and sustain faithfully the military ethos and to be a constant and exemplary advocate of Canadian values. And in so doing, you shall act at all times in a manner, which reflects the utmost integrity, loyalty and courage, bringing honour to Canada and the Canadian Forces.[3]

Once their mandate is known, generals must determine the expectations that emerge from this mandate. Clearly, the first expectation relates to leadership; that generals must actively set the example, living and advocating the values that Canadians hold high. It is therefore their duty to lead the dialogue on ethical issues as much as to foster innovation, initiative and trust. Indeed, general officers are responsible for creating that atmosphere of trust both within the Defence Team and within Canadian society.

As members of the larger society, generals must fully embrace what can be called the nature of our times, the expectation by Canadians of transparency and social responsibility in all dealings on behalf of the public. To do so they must actively engage in Canadian issues and support Canadian values, while demonstrating an ethic of care, a profound respect for the dignity of all, including subordinates, minorities, and those who become disabled or are casualties of service.

Lastly, general officers have an obligation to support their peers and contribute to a climate of fraternity, candour, trust and collegiality. Such a climate depends on the practice of self-regulation for its health. To grow as a community, to flourish in self and professional development, generals must open themselves to the candid critique of their peers in a spirit of openness and desire for self-improvement.

THE UNACCEPTABLE ALTERNATIVE

Canadian military officers have been trained and are increasingly able to apply their knowledge, experience, values and conscience to determine the best way to carry out their military duties. Today's generals will help shape and propel this introspective tradition, leading by example *and* by decree, making values-based decisions in every aspect of their work. Judgment is key. Unlike our US counterparts, we have no ethics manual declaring behaviours that are permitted or prohibited. There is, however, a growing resource of shared opinion on matters of ethics that can inform and support a general's decision-making process.

The argument for self-regulation in no way discounts the value of external intervention. We have professional review boards. We have an expert national investigative service. We have ministerial inquiries. And we have annual reports of the auditor general. We have the most to gain, however, by policing ourselves first. If outside agencies are called in, or sent in, we have already failed as a cadre of generals.

We must adhere scrupulously to our values and demonstrate to the Canadian public that we take our obligations of stewardship, leadership and discipline as overriding priorities in our professional and personal lives alike.

We must make it clear to new generals that unethical behaviour, no matter how subtle, no matter how private, is intolerable because its impact on the morale and effectiveness of the military is devastating.

We must assure our serving generals that, while the path of value-based leadership is challenging and an endless pursuit there is ample support from those on the same route.

Finally, we must regain and hold the trust of the personnel who serve under us, and inspire them by our example and by our deliberate and persistent transformation of the military to one of respect, fairness, dignity and honesty.

If we cannot self-regulate, Canada will react swiftly and unambiguously, as our nation did following Somalia. We have a duty to ourselves, to our personnel and to our country to regulate our own actions. The alternative is not acceptable.[4]

NOTES

1. Colonel Paul Maillet, *Ethics and the Expeditionary Era: The Ethical Challenges of the New Roles and Tasks of the Armed Forces.* Rapportage Report, NDHQ 20 January 2000.
2. Honourable M. Young, P.C. Douglas, M.P., *Ethos and Values in the Canadian Forces,* (Précis) NDHQ 25 March 1997.
3. Text of proposed General Officers' Scroll. NDHQ 01 January 2000.
4. I dedicate this article to my two oldest sons, both of whom serve in the military. As junior officers, they know how important it is to lead by example, and they continually encourage me to strive for respect and dignity for all personnel. K. G. Penney.

Leadership in an Era of Change and Complexity

Lieutenant-General George E.C. Macdonald

Lieutenant-General George E.C. Macdonald is the Deputy Commander in Chief of North American Aerospace Defense Command at Peterson Air Force Base, Colorado.

The times in which we live...are full of restlessness, uncertainty and change....The social and economic uncertainties and changes, which affect Canada as they do the world and the general deterioration in the discipline of family life, which is one of the misfortunes of our times, press with particular intensity on the lives of our young men.
—Mainguy Report, 1949.[1]

EXERCISING GOOD LEADERSHIP during a period of change and complexity is a challenge from which the Canadian Forces (CF) is certainly not exempt. When taken in the context of rapidly accelerating technological developments, changing individual expectations, transition to a knowledge or information society, and ever-present resource constraints, leadership in the future will continue to demand the best of our most talented people. It is not good enough to rest on our military laurels by simply applying the principles of leadership in the traditional way. We in the CF must demonstrate the flexibility and mental agility to competently address the myriad of changes that are upon us. We need to make sure that we measure up to these changes by recognizing them and adapting our leadership approach to ensure that we are as effective as possible. One thing that is certain through these adjustments is that uncertainty, change and complexity are here to stay.

This chapter will discuss the long-term challenges and opportunities that this environment of discontinuous change presents to the senior leadership of the future CF. It will address the nature of the change, the fundamental issues upon which all leaders, but especially the General Officer Corps, must focus and the adjustments we all need to make if we are to maintain the viability and resilience of the CF. We may not be able to predict the future with any certainty, but we can posture ourselves and our thinking to address the vast array of uncertainties and complexities that face us.

OUR ROOTS

We have many longstanding leadership norms which we, and other military forces, have developed over centuries. There is no doubt that it is important to be professionally competent, to lead by example, to be able to make sound and timely decisions and to communicate effectively. These principles are the motherhood embedded in every leadership manual and professional development course. We have been well served by their common sense and have found that the ideas have stood the test of time.

But have these principles really kept up with the times? Have we really anticipated the appropriate evolution of application of these principles in the twenty-first century? Have we really done a vigorous re-examination of our leadership style to ensure that it is relevant for the future? I submit that the answer to these questions is decidedly tilted towards the negative, and that we need to reconsider our leadership approach in an era of unparalleled and perpetual change and uncertainty.

We have not always been successful in addressing the demands, precipitated by dramatic change, placed on us. During the Cold War the CF and other armed forces in the Western world drew considerable comfort and stability from the fact that the enemy was clearly recognized as such. It was a relatively simple affair to determine the military capability needed to address the threat and the Canadian public generally accepted the expenditure of resources on the CF as a necessity. While our contribution to NATO decreased over the years, the military approach to dealing with the former Soviet Union remained consistent. Leaders were leaders in the traditional military style and were able to exercise their command and leadership in a fairly predictable environment.

The end of the Cold War caught us flat-footed. In fact, it took us three or four years to begin to meaningfully react to the significant changes which were underway. Valuing the time-proven practices of the past, we had a particularly difficult period of adjustment to a multi-polar world and the public demand for a peace dividend. I believe that we did not fully appreciate the profound changes that were to occur through the 1990s until they were well underway. The leaders of the day should not be blamed for their lack of prescience—they were doing their best to address the challenges of the Gulf War and a then-unprecedented number of personnel deployed on peacekeeping and peacemaking missions. It was clearly an era of being asked to do more with less, and it simply took us some time to catch up to the reality of the situation. It is not surprising that circumstances precipitated a focus on operations, to make certain that resources were expended appropriately for our primary mission. Only after the tempo decreased was there time and energy to step back and consider the "how" as well as the "what."

One of those realities was a decreasing defence budget and the need to downsize personnel. It was decided in late 1994, to mount a major effort to address this, along with a number of related issues. The Management Command and Control Reengineering Team (MCCRT) was formed and empowered with a mandate to manage personnel reductions and reduce the headquarters structure of the CF commensurately. The primary guidance for the MCCRT was contained in the *1994 White Paper*. Additional direction from senior management included a mandated fifty percent reduction in resources devoted to headquarters, the relocation of environmental commanders to Ottawa to become Environmental Chiefs of Staff, and the elimination of the command and some other subordinate headquarters. Further guidance identified process reengineering as the means to achieve these dramatic reductions.

The MCCRT's work was based on what was known as Vision 97 (for the year it was to be realized) which included four pillars or components. These were reengineering of headquarters processes themselves, creation of a new headquarters structure, integration of the information environment, and transformation to a new culture. The breadth of this activity soon permeated almost every aspect of DND activity at the operational and strategic levels. In addition to dealing with the identified processes of the organization, teams were formed to address defence policy development, resource management, business planning, performance measurement, delegation of authority, alternate service delivery, information management strategy, accommodation needs, administrative support, communications needs, and cultural evolution. The work of the MCCRT was focussed on keeping the various and diversified balls in the air with the ultimate goal of achieving Vision 97. The Team accomplished some dramatic change in its thirty months of existence and many of the concepts and initiatives continue on, in principle if not in name.

There was a multitude of lessons learned during this period of radical adjustment, many of which have also been experienced by other organizations. With the overwhelming impetus to live within shrinking resources, the department had to implement some major changes in a relatively short time. Throughout, the MCCRT often found itself having to adjust the approach to effecting change. Uncharted territory was encountered almost daily. The ability to deal with and manage ambiguity became a necessary skill of those involved. There was a need to balance radical vision with reality and pragmatism. Although many, many specific lessons were assimilated into ongoing work, some, which were supported by the senior leadership, achieved mixed results due to the enthusiasm and conviction with which they were applied. An example was a frustrating inability to identify specific tasks that we would *stop* doing, despite unanimity at the highest level that we could not continue to do everything that had been done before. Overall, there were many successes, but there were also many rocky periods which exercised everyone involved—over a period of two years, the Defence Management Committee spent more meeting time on change-related issues than on all others combined.

From all of this, one absolute became utterly clear. The commitment and alignment of the senior leadership was critical to effecting change throughout the organization. For all the success stories, there is no doubt that the work could have been even more dramatic, effective and long lasting. When leaders agreed on a specific course of action, understood the corporate and personal consequences, bought into making it happen, and empowered the troops to get on with it, success was virtually assured. However, if there was a difference of opinion in the full nature or scope of the problem, ambiguity in exactly which course of action had been chosen, or lack of acceptance-in-depth of the implications of the solution, mediocre results were almost automatic. Throughout, the importance of effective leadership during an era of change and complexity was repeatedly demonstrated.

Coincidentally, during this period of transition, the CF has been the brunt of much critical media attention which has tended to overshadow some of the

> **Reengineering Lessons Learned**
>
> **Senior Leadership Alignment is Critical**
> **Sources of Non-alignment**
> - Understanding of the realities are not shared
> - Alignment is at the first order of implications only -- no commitment "in depth"
> - Not agreed on the magnitude and scope of change
> - Fundamental differences exist in philosophies and principles -- leaders come from different backgrounds and experiences
> - Failure to confront personal implications and the need for change
>
> 12/14/99   Management, Command and Control Reengineering Team   7
>
> (James Champy 1995 In Reengineering Revisited, an MCCRT Briefing, Department of National Defence, May 13, 1997).

very significant achievements in effecting change and in conducting operations. The reality of having successfully responded to a number of very demanding taskings, domestic and international, has been faithfully documented, but with less lasting effect than some of the negative press. For those who are members of the cohort described as the "high brass" it is difficult to be objective when reading an article that is critical of the leadership of the CF—but we must. Michel Drapeau, one of the stalwart critics of the leadership has opined "I believe that the case for reform can never be truly articulated by its [the Canadian military] officer corps, for the simple reason that in Canada and elsewhere, institutions do not reform themselves without a great amount of external pressure being brought to bear. There are simply too many 'old boys'."[2] We are not alone. In the US, for example, a *Washington Times* article includes "At the top levels of leadership, careerism now prevails over professionalism. Indicative of the shift has been the unwillingness of uniformed leaders to stand against policies that damage readiness."[3] It takes a strong and well-centered leadership to objectively recognize and deal with truths that may be lurking in criticism such as this.

At the same time, this type of criticism must also be balanced with other perceptions. The reality is that Canadian citizens are supportive of the CF and what we do. In recent polling (by Pollara in November 1999 for example), we have confirmed and reconfirmed that the average citizen is predisposed to support the need for the CF and national defence in general. The challenge for the leadership is not to emotionally succumb to harsh criticism, nor to adopt a false sense of well-being from positive indications. There are valid points contained in critical reports which we should incorporate into our thinking. They should be balanced with the changes we know we must introduce, or continue. We should never assume that the status quo is acceptable.

Guidance from the top leadership is clear in this regard. The Minister of National Defence (MND) confirmed "I believe that Canadians are not well served by an unbalanced assessment of the department's efforts. It is important to understand that these changes are part of a much larger, longterm effort to effect cultural change in this organization. I am fully engaged and committed to this reform effort, as is the military and civilian leadership of the department."[4] The Deputy Minister (DM) and the Chief of the Defence Staff (CDS) in a joint message included internal reform as one of their five priorities:

> A lot more progress has to be made in implementing the various reform initiatives that emerged from last year's (1998) Minister's Report to the Prime Minister and other commissions and inquiries. This is going to need a lot of attention, energy and resources. More importantly the reforms must be accompanied by "cultural change" in the Department and the Forces.[5]

Everyone in the CF—not just the General Officer Corps—needs to contribute to effect these change initiatives. Lasting change will only be effective and responsive to our needs if it enjoys the intellectual support and commitment from all members of the defence team. And, as indicated by our three most senior leaders this change has to be embedded into our culture.

The Essence of Change

> *There is no more delicate matter to take in hand, more dangerous to conduct, or more doubtful in its success, than to take the lead in the introduction of a new order of things. For he who innovates will have for his enemies all those who are well off under the existing order of things and only lukewarm supporters in those who might be better off under the new.*
>
> —Machiavelli, 1531

Throughout the experiences of the 1990s it has become increasingly clear that the stability experienced during the Cold War is gone. We live in a period where change is precipitated by new technology, changing defence needs, personnel demographics, new threats, and regional conflicts that we never imagined. We are really not, therefore, in an "era" of change, but in a continuum of discontinuous change. We should not anticipate that predictability and stability are achievable in the future—the evidence all suggests that this will certainly not be the case. The plethora of demands on military forces and the need to function in the information age are together enough to guarantee continual change for the foreseeable future. We need to embrace and deal with the demands of change if we are going to maintain our relevance as the military force for Canada. The bottom line is that, as leaders, we must evolve or wither into mediocrity.

> The Forces must learn to adapt much more quickly to change, and to do so in a way that will support and enhance the fundamental elements of military professionalism…The Forces must be pro-active, aware of trends and the need for adapting military professional fundamentals, and be ready to present cogent and believable arguments for or against the adoption of changes that would impact the fundamental elements of military professionalism. Being blind-sided is a sign of lack of professionalism.[6]

All leaders need to recognize the reality and the paradoxes of continuous change and learn to live with them. The requirement to deal with uncertainty, increasing complexity and a diversity of new demands must become commonplace in the skills-set of the future leader. Leaders need to pay careful attention to the effect of change on the people in the organization, focussing on how to help individuals and groups deal with it, and how to exploit the opportunities that conflict and change present. After all, the organization is the people.

> What leaders need to do is to ensure the acceptance of change by subordinates. The acceptance of change is best attained by the demonstration of a personal commitment to the change by the leaders: the provision of education on the value which the change provides to individual members and the military as a whole; and the enforcement of the policy should individual members become too resistant to the changes. The existence of change should be primarily seen as a leadership challenge, rather than a threat.[7]

Leaders must recognize that change is not viewed the same by everyone. For most, "change is neither sought after nor welcomed. It is disruptive and intrusive. It upsets the balance"[8] Perhaps the most daunting challenge for leaders is to provide the strategic focus, or context, of change. Individuals need to be infused with a sense of meaning and helped to understand the linkage between their efforts and the change being undertaken throughout the organization. After all, the human resources of the organization are the focus and perpetrators of change. Senior leadership—all leadership—needs to nurture and cultivate the incentives to ensure that a rhythm of meaningful change continues to take place. This is no small challenge and demands that CF leaders be able to think out-of-the-box and be willing to try new and different approaches to leadership, without abandoning the fundamental principles that have served the CF well in the past.

The determinants of leadership skills for successfully dealing with change are not surprising. Leaders must be prepared to cope with ambiguities and paradox. At first glance, this may seem contradictory in a military context where we always try to seek the best information and intelligence for any undertaking. In reality, however, military operations often call upon us to make choices and decisions without complete information or a total appreciation of the consequences, or under circumstances of conflicting information or goals. We need to further develop these skills at all levels and use them in implementing strategies as well as the conduct of operations. Leaders need to work hard at being interpersonally and interculturally competent. With a reduced personnel force structure, and one which is more diverse from a gender and cultural perspective, leaders should hone their networking and personal skills to ensure that every single member of the organization is fully engaged in contributing to the mission. We also need to emphasize a sense of selflessness. Leaders need to be "imbued with a mission bigger than themselves, bigger than any one individual."[9] And of course leaders must be accountable for their performance—the principles under which they operate (such as those expressed in our *Statement of Defence Ethics*) must be transparent. If we can leverage these types of skills, we can tune our traditional leadership approach to meet the demands of the future.[10]

Leaders in the CF should also be prepared to learn from non-traditional sources. Many military members have difficulty accepting that some of the lessons learned in the private sector can be of benefit to the CF. While we must always apply new ideas in a military context, there is a wealth of information available to exploit. Peter Drucker, perhaps the best known author on management, writes:

> There are, of course, differences in management between organizations—mission defines strategy, after all, and strategy defines structure. But the differences between managing a chain of retail stores and managing a Roman Catholic diocese are amazingly fewer than either retail executives or bishops realize…The differences are mainly in application rather than in principles…[and] apply to only about 10% of your work. This 10% is determined by the organization's specific mission, its specific culture, its specific history and its specific vocabulary. The rest is pretty much interchangeable.[11]

We have to learn wherever we can. The average Canadian associates much more readily with civilian concerns—we in the military should not hesitate to learn from the corporate world. If we are truly going to stay abreast of change, and respond professionally to fulfil Canada's defence needs, we must be prepared to be flexible, open to new ideas and always willing to learn.

LEADING AND COMMANDING IN AN ERA OF CHANGE
Mission, Vision and Values

How many members of the CF can recite our mission and vision? Do the words "ring" true with everyone? They certainly seem to enunciate the right kind of approach for the CF, but do they serve to really motivate the individual? To be "real" and meaningful directives, everyone at every level in the organization needs to be able to clearly associate with the formal statements in order to uphold and support them in their daily military life. The mission and vision are only words if they are not lived by those meant to fulfill them.

- The **mission** of DND and the CF is to defend Canada and Canadian interests and values while contributing to international peace and security.
- Our **vision** is to be a highly professional Defence Team, fully capable of executing our mission and viewed with pride by Canadians.

What are the values of the organization? Are they being practised by everyone every day? The overall values with which our organization is generally associated are good ones and are relevant to all of us, but they need to be more fully enunciated. Work coordinated by the MCCRT proposed four core values for the Defence Team: *professionalism, loyalty, integrity,* and *mutual respect.*[12] It is not critical that we each share explicitly the same interpretation of what each one means. Most everyone would accept that professionalism, loyalty and integrity are fundamental to the military and our mission in life. Professionalism can also be interpreted to include the concept of unlimited liability for CF members, that is, service even at the risk of one's life, when necessary. Similarly, integrity has wide application, to include honesty, trustworthiness, and ethical behaviour. The one established value that might not be readily identified with is mutual respect. However, if we are to operate together as a team and as sub-teams, we must unfailingly adhere to practising mutual respect. This applies to each other, Canadians at large, our allies, civilians encountered on peacekeeping missions, and prisoners of war—everyone. This does not mean that we have to agree with another's point of view, nor do we have to condone their actions, but it is only professional and appropriate that we stay on the high road in our dealings with others, not only while in uniform and while at work, but in everything that we do.

Other values identified for the CF are "love of country, courage, loyalty, submission to discipline, duty, honour and the call to put service before self" (DND, *Serving Canada and the World, Values and Ethos*, undated). We also acknowledge the things Canadians value—"security, human rights, the rule of law and democracy."[13] Moreover, our ethics program has carefully enunciated ethical principles and obligations which purport to be values as well, although the actual word is not contained in the *Statement of Defence Ethics*.[14] "The Defence Ethics Program is a values-based program that fosters the shared values we possess in common in our society."[15] While there is some lack of definition on the "official" values of the CF, the themes prevail as ones that we intrinsically hold dear as Canadians and as military members. We need to be more specific in identifying, and identifying with, our values for everyone's benefit. That is, we need to be clearer in our expression of our values by adopting short, precise, easy-to-remember terms with which everyone can associate.

> New values cannot be instilled through a crash program, nor should existing belief systems be chucked or subverted without careful consideration of the effect on the relationship between the organization and its members. In fact, the goal for most companies should be to build on the strengths and modify the limitations of the existing set of values, not to make radical changes in values."[16]

"Identifying, communicating, and shaping organizational values is more difficult than articulating a strategic vision because it relies less on analysis and logic and more on emotion and intuition."[17] Nevertheless, heartfelt recognition of the mission, vision and values has to become commonplace. Every member of the CF should be able to find a way to associate with them in their daily work. For example, when managing conflict in an interpersonal relationship, an approach showing respect should prevail. This must become ingrained in our culture.

Familiarization with values (and ethical principles and obligations for that matter) should begin the day one joins the CF because the values we uphold reflect the very essence of what we stand for. If we can model our behaviour on universally applied principles, we can achieve a level of identification with our mission and our reason for being that cannot be otherwise realized. We need to attain a level of comfort with our values so that we would not hesitate, for example, to explain our work to our children—and grandchildren—in terms of our values. We need to be able to uphold and be accountable for key decisions based on our values and principles. Our values should be so fundamental that we would apply them even if we were not being compensated for being in the

CF. They should be the ones we honour even when we retire. They should stand the test of time—will they still be valid fifty years from now?[18]

> On Being a Marine.
>
> I recently attended a formal dinner commemorating the 224th Anniversary of the founding of the U.S. Marine Corps. As part of the pre-dinner ceremony, a video commissioned for the anniversary by the Commandant of the Marine Corps was shown. It included clips of personal interviews with members of the Marine Corps, past and present, old and young, combat veterans and inexperienced. The common thread through each interview was a spontaneous recognition that the Marine Corps was more important than the individual. Each member (and they consider themselves Marines even long after retirement) expressed in his or her own way how they felt loyal to the Corps and how they revered the ideals of the organization. One of the prevailing concerns was the importance of their personal conduct and individual behaviour living up to the ideals of the Corps.

Leadership is critical in interpreting, promoting and reinforcing values. The extent and intensity of this responsibility increases as one rises in rank, and becoming a General/Flag Officer serves to accentuate the significance of this responsibility. Not only do leadership responsibilities increase, they become more visible. Being a model, internal and external to the organization, is a real and important part of a general's role. Accordingly, the example that is set—fairness in dealing with people, demeanor in crises, competence, respect and compassion, willingness to listen, and decisiveness—is pivotal to the effectiveness of that individual. Throughout, a member of the CF must always recognize the responsibilities and restrictions explicit and implicit in assuming the military as a profession. While these apply at any rank, the significance of adhering to a high standard (one which is higher than that expected in society at large) is greater at higher rank levels. Senior officers are, and should be, expected to live up to an impeccable standard—and one which may vary with time. Approaches to performing our mission and the leadership role we assume change with rank, maturity and circumstance—but our values are always there to guide us.

Evolving Our Approach Towards Our Human Resources

Much of our reengineering and change work in the past has had a heavy emphasis on the structure and processes of the organization. For the most part, this was forced on us by the need to downsize and to adjust the "tooth-to-tail ratio." Throughout, we have eliminated some layers in the organization with significant cultural resistance. After all, militaries typically have hierarchical structures—and these structures work well in operations and during periods of conflict. We all understand the responsibilities and accountabilities that rest at the various levels of the structure and the need to ensure that command and control is exercised appropriately using the chain of command. There are contemporary pressures on hierarchical structures, however, that we must recognize and deal with. We must include in our thinking the need to strike a balance between the vertical and horizontal tensions in the CF. There is no one right organization, nor one that is absolute in all cases. The organization "is a tool for making people productive in working together. As such, a given organizational structure fits certain tasks in certain conditions and at certain times."[19] There are situations where the leader must have absolute (hierarchical) authority, where there is no time for meetings or arguments; everyone must do their part to ensure the best possible chance of making it through the crisis. "But what is the right organization to handle crisis is not the right organization for all tasks. Sometimes the team approach is the right answer."[20]

There are other pressures on our organizational structure. The downsizing of personnel, in addition to making the organization small, also makes it shallower. Where there once was a team of four or five people to fulfil a role, we may now be reduced to one or two experts. In reducing the size of the bureaucracy, we need to empower these experts and learn to trust their knowledge; we simply don't have the resources and the structural depth to provide checks and balances to the extent that we have in the past. We have some wonderful opportunities to capitalize on the capabilities of individuals, and their contribution to the team. For whatever reason—a deadline, the inconvenience, or logistics—we often miss these opportunities. "Insightful top managers recognize that it is impossible for them to have all of the answers, and are willing to learn along with others."[21] We can all learn from others in the organization, but we have to make the effort, imbed our culture, and communicate, communicate, communicate.

Indeed, one of the most significant cultural issues for the CF relates to our willingness to communicate more widely and exploit horizontal networking where it is appropriate. Some leaders see this as a threat to the core structure of any military force, but we must embrace the advantages, all the while maintaining the integrity of an appropriate hierarchical structure. "The difficult stuff, centers on the different nature of human interaction in a networked organization, as opposed to a hierarchical one… learning to relate horizontally as well as hierarchically is our hardest organizational issue."[22] With the trend for all organizations to become "electronically flattened," and the technology we now have for the exchange of information, we have the ability to cut across vertical barriers. It can be a powerful organizational tool if used sensibly and with flexibility of approach.

The other component of structural evolution relates to the people themselves. We all recognize the generational differences that exist, between the general officers and new recruits, for example. There is clearly a need for members new to the CF to receive the appropriate indoctrination and training, to include cultural issues. There is also a very real requirement, however, for the leadership to recognize the differences in outlook of these young people compared to previous generations. For example, younger people tend to see employment in a company in transactional terms. "They hope to learn something, and they trust the company will gain something as well, but it's a very impersonal, rational connection—worlds away from the emotional attachment we see with older subjects."[23] The CF is not a company, and we should not even suggest that the relationship between the organization and its members is simply economic. However, the generally lower level of permanency and the different time horizon of younger people is something we clearly need to take into account. We need to ensure that we respect their personal goals, all the while imbuing them with those of the organization. This is indeed a matter of survival, for we need qualified, motivated young people in the CF at a time when the demographic resource pool is decreasing. They need to be attracted to the organization for the adventure, the travel, the unique opportunities, and the desire to serve Canada.

The leadership of the Canadian Forces has to recognize these individual needs—and to ensure that its members "get" something in return for their services. The right individuals need to be kept in the CF because we need and value their long-term contribution and respect their expertise and input, all the while demanding their obedience and loyalty to the larger mission. We should also recognize that there are some who can offer positive contributions in the shorter term, but should then move on to something else.

Each of these contributions needs to be encouraged and recognized. It is no small challenge to motivate individuals in the myriad of circumstances and pressures extant for the CF. "In the end, every individual extracts the most basic sense of purpose from the personal fulfillment he or she derives from being part of an organization...an organization must bring its big ideas and bold initiatives down to a personal level."[24] After all, "Leaders are people who can make other people feel good about themselves. People simply want their talents and efforts to be acknowledged. There is a deep human yearning to make a difference."[25] Throughout, communications are key.

All leaders recognize that effective communications are critical. The time spent in town halls, management sessions and retreats is very valuable and appreciated, but the half-life of the results is often much shorter than expected. Experience has shown that it is only after we take the time and truly make the effort to listen to each other that the channels of communication really take root. There must also be buy-in to the message at all levels of the organization. The most eloquent and heartfelt message by the CDS is vastly diminished in the mind of a subordinate if his boss or his boss's boss doesn't actively support it. We have seen example after example of dashed enthusiasm because of a lack of alignment or understanding. Some of it is by bent of ignorance but some is blatant resistance. If we don't get everyone pulling his or her oar in the same direction, the best we can hope for is to simply muddle through. Fundamentally, we all need to become better at "reminding people of what's important."[26]

> It was Military Day at Cheshire High School, Cheshire, Connecticut, and the military service representatives were attempting to recruit students into their respective branches. The junior and senior boys assembled in the school auditorium with faculty members observing from the rear of the room… The Air Force recruiter got up to explain the advantages of joining the United States Air Force. He was greeted with catcalls and whistles from the young high schoolers… The Army recruiter received the same treatment, as did the Navy recruiter. The Marine recruiter, a seasoned gunnery sergeant, rose and glared at the assembled students. 'There is no one here worthy of being a United States Marine,' he growled. 'I deplore the fact that the faculty in the back of the room would let the students carry on like this. There isn't anybody here I want in my Marine Corps.' When he sat down, several eager students swarmed around his table.
>
> (Peter C. Lemon, Beyond the Medal: a journey from their hearts to yours. (Golden, Colorado: Fulcrum Publishing), 1997, 27).

We also need to work to exploit the technological advances that have been made to communicate key messages. What is the point of distributing breaking news of key developments by hard-copy message, readily available to a limited audience, if we could put the information on the DND intranet for all to see? While we must be careful not to overload the individual with information not directly useful to him or her, we should seize the opportunity to use the technology available to communicate the views of the CDS on a topical issue, for example. This would increase transparency, and help those in the organization understand the principles and rationale behind decisions taken or not taken.

Proactive internal communication can quickly put the record straight for everyone, and give CF members a sense of belonging and involvement. In the words of the CDS and DM on communications:

> We need to continue to improve. Our efforts to become more open and transparent as an institution have been necessary and will be pursued. A better job has to be done on internal communications as well so that all of our personnel are kept better informed about issues that matter to them...we know there is a problem and we know we can do better.[27]

In May 1996, the MCCRT hosted a week-long Leadership Forum for 75 military and civilian personnel from all across Canada. We discussed the mission of the CF and DND, the values, and the ways in which we could make improvements. Although from various backgrounds and levels in the organization, everyone was given the opportunity to contribute from their particular perspective. At the end of an intense, emotional week, comments made were along the lines of: "working as a team, we can make a difference"; "this has been the best weeks of my career"; "before I came, I didn't really believe my views would be listened to"; "I was considering leaving DND, now I'm staying."

Much of the benefit of communicating is simply the fact that we do it. The information passed may not be particularly new or revealing, but the fact that the effort was made to ensure that it was available is critical. Equally critical is the need to ensure that meaningful, two-way communication occurs. Leaders at all levels must, and must be seen to, solicit and value the inputs of their subordinates and peers. The fundamental desire of every individual to be "plugged into" the organization as a valued member simply cannot be underestimated. This is particularly valid during periods of acute transition where the lack of information (and the concomitant perception that there is no concern for the individual) can debilitate the productivity of the team dramatically.

This critical aspect of our culture relates also to the management of conflict. Through reforms such as the provision of an ombudsman, the streamlining of the grievance process, and higher awareness of harassment issues, we are becoming more effective in exploring options and addressing the resolution of issues where the individual is in conflict. The ability to address these concerns is an important extension of fundamental, basic communication, because conflict is often the result of the lack of appropriate communication. The need to professionally deal with issues of legitimate conflict goes right to the root of one of our core values—respect for the individual. We need to become even more adept at surfacing the concerns of stakeholders for any particular issue so that a mature and meaningful resolution can be achieved. Overall, we can use conflict as an opportunity to explore options and bring about change.

Also related to communication, and the value to which we hold the members of the organization, is the way in which we recognize the individual's contribution. Our culture is predominantly one of problem-solving and making improvements to the way we do things. We do not often stop to reflect upon our accomplishments and to recognize the members of the team who have made a contribution. It is important to make an effort to ensure that individuals and teams know that they are genuinely appreciated, even if through some simple mechanism such as being singled out at a gathering of peers. While more substantial recognition is always appreciated, and should also be pursued vigorously for deserving cases, the simplest and most readily available forms of acknowledgement can go a long way to bolstering the spirit, visibility and commitment of a person or team.

SUSTAINING AN EFFECTIVE ORGANIZATIONAL CULTURE

The problem with culture is that it is hard to deal with—difficult to define and tough to address in a characteristically military manner. Many even argue that we should not even discuss "culture," that it is too "soft" a concept for a military organization. The reality is that there is no traditional framework to follow and we feel awkward talking about our feelings and values, especially in the military. The macho thing sometimes is to avoid things cultural as irrelevant. We argue that the terminology does not apply to us. We accentuate our uniqueness and our internal differences (civilian, army, navy and air force) instead of capitalizing on our similarities. By the same token, even the hardest cases will admit to the value and importance of a military ethos. We all need to recognize the importance of culture and deal with it by promoting some aspects and changing others.

We certainly do not have to overhaul our culture, but we need to understand it in order to evolve it and to deal effectively with change. Fundamental to this understanding is the recognition of impediments to essential cultural evolution. For example, people become resigned to certain limitations because they are not encouraged (or are discouraged) to explore the possibilities. We need to expand our horizons so that individuals feel free to work to their true potential.

Others may feel that their identity is threatened. They may have successfully contributed to the organization for years—change threatens the source of their professional validity. They may not intellectually resist the change, but they do not know where it is leading them. They may not understand or embrace the vision. We need to give everyone a sense of identity and a reason to be proud of their contribution to achieving the mission.

For many, new ideas are generally viewed with skepticism and free-ranging discussion is limited, or even discouraged. Personal priorities during a period of change are often on a different page. Competing priorities and "stovepipe issues" cause people to be restrained or to withdraw from meaningful discussion of real problems. Trust and mutual respect may never attain the level necessary for everyone to speak freely, without fear of retribution or negative consequences. Many refrain from offering their views at all to avoid going out on a limb. They need to be able to draw upon some fundamentals.

Under these circumstances, a powerful, and common, vision of the future can open up many new possibilities. It can sanction and foster discussion and can encourage inquiry into how it can best be implemented. It can give people a rope to grab onto as they let go of the traditional lifeline of the status quo. This can only work if the vision means something to everyone in the organization and motivates individuals. A vision has to provide a reason to come to work in the morning. Furthermore, individuals need to be able to break the vision down into meaningful conceptual parcels to personalize it. The challenging work is not formulating the vision in the first place, but rather developing and implementing the strategy and initiatives to make it real. "The challenge to leaders is to create a culture of change, a relaxed work environment where people's ideas are listened to, where there are rewards for contributions…and where trust is earned through full and frank communication."[28]

LEADERSHIP AND CHANGE—CONCEPTS FOR THE FUTURE

> [Leaders of successful companies] share a surprisingly consistent philosophy. First, they place less emphasis on following a clear strategic plan than on building a rich engaging corporate purpose. Next, they focus less on formal structural design and more on effective management processes. Finally, they are less concerned with controlling employee's behaviour than with developing their capabilities and broadening their perspectives. In sum, they have moved beyond the old doctrine of strategy, structure, and systems to a softer, more organic model built on the development of purpose, process and people.[29]

The bottom line of much of the discussion on leadership during an era of change and complexity is that all organizations need to be able to adjust to evolving circumstances, pressures and trends. The requirement for organizational agility should not be underestimated. Pascale, Millemann and Gioja, in describing this agility, identify it as "what an organization is being over time" rather than what it is "doing at any particular moment...Agility is an ongoing institutional capacity for change; it is a capacity more profound, and more profoundly important, than any given change initiative that may be under way."[30] We in the Canadian Forces need to inspire appropriate organizational agility as a cultural strength. In fact, being agile is critical to being a learning organization. Being agile is being able to seize opportunities to learn and exploit them effectively. In the US Army, former Chief of Staff, General Gordon Sullivan, developed the "After Action Report" to a much higher plane by making it a superlative opportunity to learn. He encouraged immediate, meaningful, straight-talking assessments of operational and administrative situations so that everyone learned the lessons and instigated improvements right on the spot.[31] In his view, we need to catch up with the future by challenging ourselves to be agile and to anticipate the demands of tomorrow. General Sullivan refers to our traditional approach as "making the past perfect" where we are always behind and always responding to yesterday's problems.[32]

If we the leadership in the CF expect to be relevant, we need to anticipate future needs and implement changes that are understood, accepted, and appropriately consistent with the priorities of other organizations with whom we relate. However, at the same time, we need to recognize that we are the military in Canada and that there are procedural and structural practices unique to a military force that must be maintained and respected. Adapting to the future while respecting the essential elements of our organization and history is a challenge for all of us. Without an appropriate balance, we lose focus on our reason for being; but without a sharp eye on the future, we will lose relevance in today's complex and uncertain world.

The key to leadership in a continuum of change is to create the context for success. In addition to providing resources and empowering individuals and teams to carry out their duties, it is important to ensure that the environment is open and trusting and that they have room to grow and explore new ideas. On one hand, this involves breaking away from strict adherence to a hierarchical structure. Within reasonable limits, individuals should feel free to network up, down, and across the organization to do their work and to innovate. If people learn to explore beyond their own immediate area of responsibility, they begin to make linkages between what they are doing and what others are doing, all in the name of fulfilling our mission. New concepts and ways of enhancing the mission or its execution can begin to evolve if participants are encouraged to engage and feel that they can do so without being threatened.

This demands a more open approach than that normally experienced in military activities. The synergy of effectively functioning as one large team can really only work in a conducive environment. To create and maintain that kind of environment, the leadership must promote trust, openness and fairness throughout the organization.[33] Members of the CF and DND need to feel free to share information, collaborate on new concepts, and learn together in the process.

In the past we have, by necessity, often focused on the process and the structure of the CF. We now need to go further. In a recent study on corporate renewal, it was found that the most successful companies "focused their attention beyond the conventional concern about restructuring the hierarchy and reengineering its processes, and devoted most of their attention to the more subtle, demanding task of changing individual attitudes, assumptions, and behaviours."[34] We, the leadership of the CF, can realize the benefits of this kind of approach and adapt it appropriately to our military circumstances. If we could truly motivate every individual to spread their wings and then challenge them to fully apply their skills and knowledge to the CF mission, we would be well on the way to a more effective and relevant organization. But that should not be the extent of our aspirations. "The role of leaders at all levels is to demonstrate to people that they are capable of achieving more than they think they can achieve and that they should never be satisfied with where they are now."[35] As stated by Bartlett and Goshal, we should evolve to focusing more on purpose and people.[36] After all, our real goal is to achieve a purpose and it is the people of the organization, the members of the CF and DND, who can be empowered to fulfil that purpose. We should not become slaves to the more concrete aspects of military roles—we should encourage everyone to step back every once in a while and consider how we are accomplishing our purpose. This is not just something for the senior leadership, but for everyone in a learning organization.

To encourage learning and maintain agility in an organization, all members have to truly engage in the challenges and the future of that organization—to identify with its roles and mission. That is, we all have to be engaged as "meaningful contributors (not just doers) in the principal challenges of the organization."[37] Additionally, the leader needs to "lead from a different place," that is the leader needs to place himself in a zone of discomfort where conflict is accepted, ambiguity is tolerated and urgency is the norm.[38] Rather than seeking control and feeling a need to have all the answers, the leader acts as an information sharer, communicator and clearinghouse.[39] Leaders in the CF should make the effort to find this "different place," that is, to be open to non-traditional approaches to building a committed and respected Canadian Forces.

I have no doubt that the new organizations will be less easy places than they have been. They will certainly be less predictable, less measurable, less amenable to the traditional disciplines. But we cannot reject the future just because it is uncomfortable. What we have to do is find a way to understand it so that we can make the new organizations work for us.[40]

Indeed, the future can be uncomfortable. Our military culture has encouraged us to "perfect the past" and to build on our experiences in a carefully measured way to ensure that we minimize the risk of failure and the human consequences with which that failure may be associated. We should not abandon that philosophy and seize upon all of the new corporate trends and practices simply to make ourselves the most efficient, well-managed organization in Canada. If we did that, we would certainly lose the thread of what it means to be a military organization. By the same token, we need to exploit new concepts that are relevant to leading and managing a military organization in the uncertainty of the twenty-first century. We can model our values and what they mean to us in our daily lives. We can provide the people of the organization with the training, information and resources they need to excel. We can motivate and challenge individuals and teams to achieve levels of accomplishment beyond what they thought possible. We can encourage everyone to exercise leadership in their own right, respecting what they bring to the larger team—a team which should be seen as a "community of leaders." And we can communicate across the organization, carefully listening to ideas and inputs in order to make the organization resilient, effective and forward leaning. If we do all these things, all the while keeping our eye on our principal role in life, to defend Canada and Canadian interests and values, we can surely evolve to an organization of the future.

NOTES

1. "Report on Certain 'Incidents' Which Occurred on Board H.M.C. Ships *Athabaskan*, *Crescent* and *Magnificent* and on Other Matters Concerning the Royal Canadian Navy,". *The Mainguy Report* (October, 1949), 7.
2. Michel W. Drapeau, "Reforming Canada's Military: A Leading Critic of the Defence Department Offers his Prescription for Renewal," *The Ottawa Citizen*, (2 November, 1999), A19.
3. Robert Maginnis, "Up Against the Military Culture," *The Washington Times* (23 October 1999), 17.

4. Arthur Eggleton, "In defence of change: Arthur Eggleton, the Minister of National Defence, says major reform is under way in his department and the Canadian Forces. Give it a chance, he pleads," *The Ottawa Citizen* (3 November 1999), A19.
5. General Maurice Baril and James Judd, "A Message from the Deputy Minister and the Chief of the Defence Staff," Department of National Defence insert to *Maple Leaf* magazine.
6. Richard Evraire, "The Canadian Military Profession: A Question of Credibility" *On Track*, Conference of Defence Associations Institute, Vol 3, No. 3 (November 1998), 6-7 and 13.
7. Office of the Judge Advocate General, *Military Justice at the Summary Trial Level*, Department of National Defence (8 July 1999).
8. Paul Strebel, "Why Do Employees Resist Change?" *Harvard Business Review* (May-June 1996), 86-92.
9. C.K. Prahalad, "Preparing for Leadership" in *Leading Beyond the Walls*, eds, Frances Hesselbein, Marshall Goldsmith, and Iain Somerville (San Francisco: Jossey-Bass Publishers, 1999), 34.
10. Ibid.
11. Peter F. Drucker, "Management's New Paradigms," *Forbes* (October 5, 1999), 152-176.
12. *Management, Command and Control Reengineering Team Historical Report*. Department of National Defence (June 1997), 20.
13. General Maurice Baril, "From the Chief of the Defence Staff—Our Proud Heritage Shapes Our Commitment to the Future," Department of National Defence, Director General Public Affairs, 1998, 1.
14. Chief of Review Services, *Defence Ethics Program Implementation Handbook*, Department of National Defence, Fourth Edition (5 February 1998), Section 1.3.
15. Major Denis Beauchamp, *The Canadian Defence Ethics Program and the "Corporate Model": Canadian Military Prefers Values-Based Program to Compliance-Based Program*, Department of National Defence (February 1997), 19a, 71 and 4.
16. C. Bartlett, and S. Ghoshal, "Changing the Role of Top Management: Beyond Strategy to Purpose," *Harvard Business Review* (November-December 1994), 85.
17. Ibid, 84.
18. J.C. Collins and J. I. Porras, "Building Your Company's Vision," *Harvard Business Review*, (September-October 1996), 68.
19. Drucker, 158.
20. Ibid, 158.
21. Duane R. Ireland, and Michael A. Hitt, "Achieving and Maintaining Strategic Competitiveness in the 21ST Century: The Role of Strategic Leadership," *Academy of Management Executive* Vol. 13, No. 1, 1999, 43-57.
22. Jim Manzi, "CEO Thought Summit," *Sloan Management Review* (Spring 1995), 14.
23. Creative Services Department, "Job Loyalty Isn't Completely Dead – It's Just Taken a Different Course" (Special Advertising Feature), *Denver Post* (21 November, 1999), 1.
24. Bartlett and Ghoshal, 86.
25. General Rick Findley, "The 'P' in Air Power – People," Speech to the Air Power Conference (29 July 1997), 3.
26. Warren Bennis, "The End of Leadership: Exemplary Leadership is Impossible Without Full Inclusion, Initiatives, and Cooperation of Followers," *Organizational Dynamics* (Summer, 1999), 78.

27. Baril and Judd, 2.
28. Lawrence A. Bossidy, "Mastering Change," Allied Signal Inc. Public Affairs Department, (July 1, 1993), 8.
29. Bartlett and Ghoshal, 80.
30. Richard Pascale, Mark Millemann, and Linda Gioja, *Organizational Agility, The 21ST Century CEO, Senior Executive Insights for Now and the Future*, CSC Index, 1996, 5.
31. Lloyd Baird, Phil Holland, and Sandra Deacon, "Learning from Action: Imbedding More Learning into the Performance Fast Enough to Make a Difference," *Organizational Dynamics*, New York (Spring, 1999), 1.
32. Ibid, 1.
33. Bartlett and Ghoshal, 93.
34. Ibid, 4.
35. Ireland and Hitt, 47.
36. Barlett and Ghoshal, 80.
37. Richard Pascale, Mark Millemann, and Linda Gioja, *Organizational Agility, The 21ST Century CEO, Senior Executive Insights for Now and the Future*, CSC Index, 1996, 131.
38. Ibid, 131.
39. Ibid.
40. C. Handy, "Unimagined Futures" in F. Hesselbein, M. Goldsmith & R. Beckhard (eds.), *The Organization of the Future* (San Francisco, Jossey-Bass 1997), 383.

Command Challenges in the Twenty-First Century

Colonel H.J. Marsh

Colonel Howard Marsh is the current CF Land Forces Command Inspector.

INTRODUCTION

COMMAND IS ASSIGNED; COMMAND IS PRACTICED. Command has an authoritative aspect prescribed by regulations and a human side exercised by the incumbent—leadership. As both are well covered by other authors this chapter will examine command challenges from the situational context. What is the current situation? What lessons can be learned from present circumstances and what do these foretell?

Sir Michael Howard, the military historian, concludes that flexibility of mind and organization is essential to the survival of military organizations in peace and war.[1] However my examination of strategic decision-making in the last two decades raises the suspicion that the Canadian Forces in general, and the army in particular, is lacking in both flexibility of mind and organization. Should past behaviour continue then the future of the military organization in Canada is not assured. Establishing a culture that rewards flexibility of mind and organization is one of the great challenges facing commanders in the twenty-first century.

The first part of this chapter examines current difficulties and concludes that officer selection and development are the likely barriers to timely transformation. The second part explores future determinants that are likely to overwhelm those currently being groomed for strategic-management[2] (command) twenty years hence. Perhaps I am unduly pessimistic but I believe that circa 2020 the army could be strategically managed by other means.[3] I have resisted offering a solution. Future command challenges are unlikely to be solved by the inhabitants of the present military culture.

PART 1: THE COMMAND LEGACY

I've seen the enemy and he is us.

-Pogo

A short twenty years ago I graduated from the Canadian Forces Command and Staff College.

Although one could argue that much has happened in the last two decades an equally compelling argument can be made that the military culture and traditions have preserved the past, preventing change. In fact the air force resurrected the past by renaming Canadian Forces bases in memory of Second World War Air Wings. Our collective tendency to fight yesterday's battles with today's technology has kept the last two decades of innovation harnessed to doctrine.[4] The artillery still has guns. Armour has the tank. The infantry have the assault rifle. Bullets are more accurate but they are still bullets. Today's Total Force structure of 2000 is still in the shadow of 1930s decisions. (The sixty remaining infantry battalions trace their heritage to the inter-war six-division structure).[5] Although the Regular Force component has increased and decreased in size during the last fifty years the current brigade group structure is not far removed from that stipulated in the 27 June 1946 Order-in-Council.[6] Likewise officer education is still patterned on the post First World War, Oxford-Cambridge syndicate approach to learning. Unlike a high-tech company that flourishes and vanishes in five years the military has the enduring qualities of longevity and institutional inertia. Positively viewed, inertia keeps things going. Negatively viewed, inertia prevents rapid adaptation.

The existence of a ministerial committee to monitor change[7] is a clear indictment that external pressures or events are required to bring about institutional modification. An inability to change is not new to militaries but in times when rapid adaptation is critical to success, even survival, a nation cannot afford a slow-to-change military culture.[8] The Canadian military's, especially the army's, reaction to the first decades of the Information Age is not encouraging. This externally mandated change, precipitated largely by advances in telecommunications has either been resisted, misapplied or wrongly embraced to such an extent that the "rank and file" believe that senior leaders have proven that they cannot navigate the organization into the future.[9]

INFORMATION MANAGEMENT

Marshall McLuhan, the communication theorist of the 1950s and 1960s, identified that the linking of electronic information would guide society into an Information Age and globalization.[10] The technology to prove McLuhan's theories first appeared in the early 1970s and became self-evident in the early 1990s when the ARPA Net became the Internet.[11] The Information Age is at least thirty years old. Yet, since its published announcement, the necessary elements to achieve an Information Age military in Canada have withered.

Shortly after integration (1968) the army eliminated brigade intelligence platoons. In the 1980s CF surveillance sites were automated. These people reducing decisions saved money but were instrumental in endangering the very classifications that analyze information. Shortly after the announcement of the Tactical Command Control Communications System (TCCCS) contract (1988) the Chief of Land Doctrine and Operation (CLDO) eliminated the army's strategic-level information management directorate, Directorate Land Communications Information Systems (DLCIS). The concomitant decision (1989) to separate the information management components of TCCCS from the communication system ensured that communication technology and information technologies would advance on disparate paths. In the same year (1989) the army's Land Force Command Control Information System (LF CCIS) Acquisition and R&D team at Defence Research Establish Valcartier (DREV)[13] was disbanded.

In the 1980s Information Management and Information Technology (IM/IT) acquisition mirrored that of the Miscellaneous Requirement (MR) acquisition process, i.e. off-the-shelf purchase to meet an immediate demand without due consideration of integration with other management systems. (The MR process of buying individual items of soldiers' clothing ceased in 1995 and was replaced by an integrated process—Clothe the Soldier Project.) A decade of buying-to-need created a "stove-piped" patchwork of systems that at its pinnacle (1998) produced a mosaic of one hundred and fourteen information management systems.[14] The elimination (1993) of Engineering Physics and Engineering Management programmes at RMC further weakened the CF's capacity to generate system integration and information management expertise.

The IM/IT situation was further worsened in mid 1990 by MCCRT (Management Command and Control Review Team). The nineteen sub-committees of MCCRT attempted to corral earlier IM/IT processes and identify cultural weaknesses in the organization. The Culture Committee recommended that it be eliminated as no cultural biases were identified.[15] Without the benefit of a data flow and system decision-making analysis the other MCCRT teams procured what they thought would be best.

As a consequence PeopleSoft, the human resource IM/IT system, reflects data flows of USA mid-size corporations, FMAS (Financial Management and Accounting System) is a derivative of financial management practices in the German automotive industry and MINCON (Supply System) is based on the manner in which Australians control their inventory. Although each system may be the best in the world DND/CF now has the daunting task of integrating European, USA and Australian software protocols and aligning them to DND/CF management processes.

The Canadian military is not well positioned for the fourth decade of the Information Age. IM/IT skills and corporate knowledge are dwindling rapidly, the ability to regenerate this expertise is difficult if not impossible and the few remaining information engineers are likely to exhaust their energies on the integration of legacy IM/IT systems. The resources required to achieve data fusion and knowledge-based decision-making for the army and air force are unlikely to be available this decade.[16] This IM/IT legacy is linked to decisions from the same époque that mixed management philosophies and muddled military virtues with commercial values.

Management Philosophies

Books have been written on organizations and management philosophies. Henry Mintzberg, a Canadian, and Annie Cornet, a Belgian, best describe the Canadian military management dilemma.[17]

In the last decade DND/CF has attempted to evolve from a functional (bureaucratic) organization with vertical control mechanisms to a process based organization with devolved authority. The IM/IT systems installed in the 1990s reflect the management philosophy of devolved decision-making and automated process. However militaries unlike private sector corporations are charged with the sanctioned application of lethal force on behalf of the state. As a result DND/CF has a hybrid system of devolved, functional processes controlled by highest, centralized authority. For the control of the application of lethal force central control is essential. Control of lethal force is a basic tenet of sovereignty under international law.

It goes seriously wrong when those sacred vertical control means are used to achieve objectives other than that of controlling authorized lethal force. Military and civilian staffs quickly learn that the vertical controls are the most responsive in implementing decisions and abuse the inherent upward loyalty of leadership. Examples are legion.

The pettiest that I experienced was being compelled by MND direction to serve only Québec maple syrup at CFB Suffield, Alberta in 1991. A more recent example of process interference by central authority is the public affairs interference in the Recruiting Group. In this case a well-researched recruit advertising campaign was thwarted because the recruiting poster themes appealed to aspirant's expectations (challenge, skill, employment) and not those of central control (A Force for Change).[18] The office responsible for the devolved recruiting process failed to meet the recruit quotas. Neither the owner of the devolved process or those who exercised central control were held accountable largely because neither knew the outcome. (There is no commonly shared IM/IT database for recruiting and recruit advertising).

A darker corollary of mixing devolved process management within a functional organization with central control mechanisms has been brewing for sometime—selective obedience. If the vertical controls are being used for purposes other than the control of lethal force, and if those directives run counter to military virtues then is not the leader honour bound to ignore the direction? What does a project director do when told by a central agency to acquire equipment that maximizes departmental objectives but puts soldiers at risk? What does a course officer do when a centrally produced training timetable allocates no administrative time? (A course without course administration periods requires less training days therefore it is more efficient!) However the local support unit that used to supply goods to the training unit has been "centralized" for efficiencies at another base one hundred and fifty kilometres from the training unit. Impossible tasks require selective obedience. Selective obedience now governs a significant portion of military life; it is euphemistically referred to as "local initiative."

The hybrid management philosophy—devolved authority with centralized control— combined with the unconnected IM/IT systems has rendered some soldiers' lives Byzantine.[19] A lack of confidence in the military's ability to quickly rectify soldiers' daily frustrations has created a plethora of alternate "voice" mechanisms (1-800 CALL CDS,[20] Ombudsman, Conflict Resolution Centres, Harassment Coordinator, Quality Of Life Information Form [QOLIF], etc).

Negotiating change poorly, not appreciating the impact of Information Age technologies and being seduced by the siren call of management gurus is understandable, but we should not have traded the military ethos for a commercial ethos.

Commercial or Military Ethos?

The practice of inappropriately mixing the management of resources with the leadership of souls has been well documented. When the management of lethal force is based on commercial values history records that contractual arrangements with mercenaries do not guarantee loyalty or security. Conversely when military leadership is not constrained by market realities a nation's wealth can be misappropriated. Jane Jacobs advocates that management based on commercial values, and military leadership based on a "guardian" ethos must be equally strong and always in tension to ensure the wellbeing of a nation.[21]

Now that senior commanders' performances are to be rewarded by the attainment of management objectives it would appear that DND/CF is well on the road to leadership based on commercial values and not military virtues.[22] Military leadership based on monetary reward was so feared by our ancestors that guardians of society were required to shun trading. An officer (knight) could not serve in his nation's military unless he was four generations removed from commerce (occupation by contract).[23] Reducing loyalty to a monetary arrangement meant he who had the most gold bought the most loyalty. For this reason past guardians of society (militaries) were required to live a virtue-based ethos that required them to shun commercial valued practices.

In the Canadian military the gulf between the commercial and guardian ethos has just about disappeared at the strategic-management level. The practice of obtaining military services through contract is about to be visited upon tactical level units on operations.[24] The Royal Military College of Canada has long wrestled with this conundrum. Free education in return for indentured service is marketed to prospective clients. The client is restrained by a commercial contract while being taught the military virtues of the vocation. It is little wonder that the resolution of ethical issues dominate college leadership.[25]

What is taught and what is lived come from disparate ethos: guardian and commercial. Blending commercial values with military virtues is likely to bankrupt the military purse or the military ethos or both.[26]

Commercial values are being mixed with military virtues to the confusion of all and the detriment of the military institution. Should trends continue history warns that monetary rewards rarely buy loyalty in the face of adversity. People in combat do not respond to best business practices; military leadership is the art of motivation and inspiration. A military functions on two planes: the physical and moral. Management of physical assets is essential; leadership of moral assets is essential. The commercial and guardian (military) ethos must be co-equal.

The strategic management of the army has not adapted well to the Information Age, has not well understood management theory, misapplied organizational philosophies and is in the process of losing the military ethos. Can strategic-management redeem itself?

A caveat: The negative impact of the foregoing has been anticipated by some. As a result since 1996 steps have been taken to re-establish strategic level IM/IT in the army, establish a doctrine and training centre, repatriate technical staff training, and develop a future focus. The question still remains. Why did we wait so long? Can the current strategic-management ride future waves of change?

Officer Selection in the Information Age

What is in our collective psyche that has created such a legacy for future commanders? Some would blame politicians; others would blame the lack of financial resources and societal trends. I share, to some extent, Dr. Norman Dixon's thesis that the fault lies with the social psychology of military organizations and the personalities of military commanders.[27] Personality plus culture produces behaviour and our behaviour has not been stellar.

The army culture that culls personality develops dominant behaviour. Dominant behaviour is a weakness in rapidly changing environments especially at the strategic level of decision making.[28] The regimental system, the pedagogy of staff colleges and the personality that excels at tactical command all negatively contribute to the selection of strategic-level commanders. A proper defence of this statement requires a doctoral length dissertation. Five short paragraphs outline my suspicions.

The army functions on a regimental system. The regiment instills a military ethos, comradeship, and cares for its soldiers. It does this well. However, by default, the regiments have been assigned the task of selecting future strategic-management. This is an institutional weakness. The regiment selects its best leaders on how well the officer functions at the tactical level. Excellent tactical leaders are most likely to have the Myers Briggs[29] personality type ISTJ (Introverted, Sensor, Thinker, and Judge).[30] This person excels at rapid decision-making by eliminating extraneous information through introverted thinking. This person is often selected to command the unit. The majority of generals (strategic-managers) are chosen from those who have commanded a tactical unit well. Unfortunately at the strategic level of decision making introversion—seeking for the answer from internal resources or past experiences (gut feel decision-making)—is unlikely to produce an innovative solution to a new situation. Of the Myers Briggs sixteen personality types the ISTJ personality is the strongest at resisting change. They excel at maintaining the status quo and populate stable bureaucracies like the public service.

The ENTJ (Extroverted, Intuitive, Thinker, Judge) personality type—an extroversion thinker—excels in strategic decision-making and gravitates to CEO positions in the private sector. I perceive that the ENTJ personality types often depart the military at junior rank because of their inherent difficulty of applying drills. To an ENTJ a drill is a theory to be critiqued. ENTJ thrives on newness and a changing environment. Lessons by rote encumber the ENTJ and they normally perform below their ISTJ peers in school and in the regiment. The military institution would function better if those naturally inclined to tactical leadership lead units while those suited for the strategic environment shaped the institution's future. Likewise the other fourteen Myers-Briggs personality types would bring excellence to the military if they were employed in those positions where they naturally excel.

The Industrial Age approach to leadership selection and development—mass production from the same mould—should cease and be replaced by the Information Age approach—tailor made for the requirement. Is strategic-management capable of transforming a selection process that would no longer replicate them? How much longer can an institution survive in the Information Age with an Industrial Age succession methodology?

The Regimental Culture in the Information Age

Information Age concepts of command demand integration of knowledge and effort within coherent structures. Words such as "seamless" and "three-dimensional battlespace" describe future doctrinal concepts, but the various branches and regiments function more like Scottish clans and labour unions. The army is far removed from being a coherent structure. Why are infantry Pioneers not trained at field engineer schools? Why are infantry mortarmen not trained by the indirect fire experts (Artillery)? Why do these sub-classifications exist? The reasons are rooted in historical experience and defended by traditions forged in combat. Structural barriers should be challenged as the army negotiates its entry into the Information Age. At present the regimental system creates artificial barriers that contribute to the army's difficulties in achieving coherency and flexibility of organization.

While the army contemplates knowledge-based units (ISTAR units[31]) at the tactical level the Canadian Navy practices operational-level data fusion daily at MARLANT HQ, Halifax. Why is the navy so far ahead of the other environments? The manner in which the navy organizes for battle, classifies its officers and selects commanders could be the reason. Perhaps the navy's two predominate classifications (MARS, MARE) approach to professional development permits the advancement of multi-personalities and a greater spectrum of talent.

Should the army reduce its classification system to four? *Sense; Act; Shield, and Sustain,* are four future doctrinal concepts that could provide the bases for new army officer classifications. Perhaps one hat badge *à la* the US Marine Corps with one entry plan is best to achieve coherency of effort and eliminate artificial barriers. Multiple classifications prevent the army's best talent from realizing their full potential with the concomitant degradation in the institution's performance.

Professional Development

The present staff college approach to officer education is based on the British Staff College (Camberley) syndicate model which in turn is borrowed from the late nineteenth century Oxford-Cambridge pedagogy of omniscience. At the turn of the century a syndicate discussion at the university level functioned on omniscience—the premise that the collective knowledge in the syndicate encompassed all known on that subject. A topic under examination could be introduced, analyzed and concluded within the syndicate discussion. This style of teaching served mankind well while Newtonian physics reigned (prior to the First World War); it serves less well when knowledge doubles every two years. Syndicate based learning is a dangerous pedagogy when the syndicate is dominated by ISTJ personalities who have just been rewarded by their regiment for tactical excellence. An introverted ISTJ thinker headed for strategic command should not be taught in an omniscience teaching environment. A personality that has the natural tendency to look to his experiences for answers should be taught in a pedagogical environment that forces external exploration.

The command challenge of moving from Industrial Age practices designed for mass production and conformity to Information Age practices where classifications and pedagogy serve to develop individual talent and identify the best persons for a multitude of disparate leadership roles may prove to be too difficult for the military. An attempt in 1996 to "modernize" army staff college education resulted in more of the same.

Summary

The CF is trying to embark on a revolution in military affairs caused by a technological cornucopia but the transformation is being impeded by the military culture. Time is running out; perhaps it has run out. The current crop of tactically competent junior officers has already been culled and is being prepared for 2020 command. They are unlikely to have the natural personalities and behavioural traits to readily negotiate future change and address the legacy backlog. Future trends examined in Part 2 are likely to demand greater transformational leadership while simultaneously emerging technologies could expose genetic and behavioural weaknesses.

Will the informed taxpayer tolerate inflexibility and inadequacy in its military circa 2020?

PART 2: FUTURE CHALLENGES

The future ain't what it used to be.
        -Yogi Berra

Introduction

The next twenty years portend unprecedented innovation that will seriously challenge not only the military, but also all extant institutions. The Information Age has just begun. Only highly adaptable, visionary-led organizations will survive. The present military culture produces insufficient, highly adaptable visionaries. As the military is currently not an "employer-of-choice" for highly adaptable visionary persons the Canadian military is likely to continue to play catch-up for the next two decades. Getting on top of the innovation wave may prove impossible but wallowing in the trough is probably not acceptable.

The Nature of DND/CF Change

It has been my observation that significant change in DND/CF takes about a decade to implement. The personnel downsizing in response to a demand for a peace dividend at the end of the Cold War (1989) was realized in 1999. The impacts of Defence Economic Review (1994) are still reverberating throughout the environments. The operation to support imbalance has yet to be adjusted but is projected to be stable by the middle of this decade (2000s).

Likewise DND/CF tends to adopt best commercial practice from the previous decade. Most of DND/CF management practices implemented in the 1990s were borrowed from private sector practices of the 1980s.[33] The direction taken by successful private sector companies in the 1990s is likely to be mimicked by DND/CF in the 2000s. The massive downsizing by General Electric in the 1980s left that corporation with a "spiritual crisis." A dispassionate survivor mentality existed. The CEO, Jack Welsh, embarked on a "spiritual revitalization" program in the 1990s designed to shift managers and workers to a human-value-based organization.[34] DND/CF is starting to acknowledge the "spiritual" cost of the 1990s downsizing and is attempting to promote human values through Quality of Life initiatives.

The time-lag between commercial application and defence implementation of information management and information technology (IM/IT) is shorter (about five years), but considering the legacy difficulties with IM/IT, it will probably take another five years (2005) to achieve best 1995 private-sector, integrated IM/IT practices.

Should DND/CF maintain the traditional time-lag trend—ten years to copy, another ten years to implement—then what the private sector is researching now ("spiritual credo," 360-degree assessment, holographic management, brain-computer interface, etc.) should be fully implemented in the military by 2020. This is not encouraging. As the rate of innovation is accelerating the military runs the risk of falling further behind.

The Nature of Innovation

The yearly rate of worldwide patent application is fifty times greater than that of a hundred years ago.[35] Faster and more efficient tools accelerate research and development. The quantity of innovation in the next twenty years is likely to exceed all that discovered in the twentieth century. From a technological perspective the year 2100 is only twenty years away. Time is not what it used to be.

As promising as the foregoing may appear technological change is still constrained. For the next twenty years technology is unlikely to exceed the limits of modern theoretical physics. Negative energy, warp drives, and travel faster-than-light may be possible at sub-atomic scales but not at macro-scales until the energy of entire galaxies can be harnessed.[36] Thirdly, technology advances according to market need.[37]

The biggest investors in research as a percentage of gross sales are the drug industry (11%), second at 9% is the telecommunications sector, the least researched is the energy sector at less than 1%.[38] Of the $20 trillion(US) developed world economy approximately five percent, or $1000 billion(US), is invested in research and development. As this amount exceeds the Canadian GDP and the USA defence budget it is likely that most innovation will occur in the commercial sector on non-Canadian soil. The Canadian public sector to which the Canadian military belongs will not be able to legislate problems away nor contain innovation that is harmful to Canada.

From a military perspective the technologies most likely to affect the institution are those bred from the union of electrons and photons and the bonding of nanotechnology and synthetic DNA. Most of the action will occur at microscopic scales—protein size to sub-atomic particles. The tools that reformulate molecules are likely to give governments a huge policy challenge. Simply put, Information Age technologies should bring greater empowerment, freedom, and choice to the affluent as well as the disenfranchised. Governance will become more challenging, as the individual becomes less dependent on community, more self-contained, and more powerful.

The Microprocessor

Annual production of microprocessors now exceeds the earth's population.[39] This trillion-dollar industry fuels telecommunications, computing and is about to become ubiquitous. The R&D effort behind this industry will ensure that microprocessors performance, (or their replacement optoelectric circuits or its replacement molecular DNA circuitry), evolve geometrically. By 2020 the common PC will be at least a million times more capable or a million times smaller.[40] The Internet by 2020 should be passing data at gigabyte/second rates to households as compared to current kilobyte/second rates.[41] For the average household a million-fold increase in microprocessing when multiplied by a million-fold increase in data flow rates will revolutionize most practices. E-surgery is achievable![42] Most specialized expertise will be either on-line or portable. The army is a collective of specialties that are about to be distributed and shared.

Photons and Electrons

Ever since the acceptance of the *Big Bang* creation theory astrophysicists have theorized that light begets matter. Theoretical physicists have long been challenged with the nature of light. In most conditions light takes on the characteristics of waves and is a frequency, but light can also behave like clusters of sub-atomic particles that have mass. In 1997 a team of particle physicists at the University of Syracuse demonstrated that light at very high energy levels could be forced to produce electrons. Electrons have mass. Converting light to matter has since been replicated in other high-energy laboratories.[43]

The relationship of photons to electrons can be expressed as an equation; science has proven it. Now technology must produce a marketable product—the optoelectric circuit. A circuit that can readily convert electrons to photons to electrons would, over night, accelerate computer-processing speeds from bips (billion) to tips (1000 billion).[44] Equally such a device would revolutionize solar energy conversion, stealth technologies, clothing apparel (dial-a-colour) and quantum encryption to list but a few sectors. As such a device would be the genesis of a trillion-dollar industry it is likely to happen sooner than later.

Camouflage materials that are chameleon-like, or better, permit one to hide in the non-visible frequencies of the Electro-magnet spectrum will be available to the wealthiest. Security forces will have to be similarly equipped and purchase counter technologies. Having the resources to buy this commercially available technology in the next twenty years is the real challenge. Fighting "phantom forces" has always distressed soldiers.

Planning capital acquisitions years in advance will be very difficult, if not impossible. The accelerating rate of innovation is likely to cause more immediate deficiencies and force the CF to have two streams of capital acquisition: deliberate and immediate. Immediate is not Miscellaneous Requirements (MR).

Nanotechnology and Synthetic DNA

Nanotechnology, the engineering of molecules and molecular-sized machines, atom by atom is more than a decade old (1988). IBM (Zurich) is probably still at the leading edge of this technology but there are many strong competitors.[45] The technology is proven but the current tools for this engineering are expensive and cumbersome. However that is about to change. Coherent mass amplifiers, referred to as Bosers,[46] (1997) and laser light "tweezers"[47] (1999) will accelerate the production of pure materials and molecular machines. The computer industry is already experimenting with microchips of molecular thickness with pure atomic structures.[48] On a more practical application, reformulated hydrocarbon fuel is now available.

Reformulation of hydrocarbons and proton-electron membranes (fuel cells) will dramatically change the energy distribution and transportation sectors of our economy. The abundantly available natural gas (CH_4, methane) when reformulated to $2H_2$ and passed through a fuel cell offers electricity to the home owner sixty percent more efficiently than Ontario Hydro without the by-product carbon dioxide.[50] The automobile industry has promised fuel cell cars for 2004. As the likely fuel-of-choice for the automotive fuel cell is either ethanol (ethyl alcohol) or methanol (methyl alcohol) it will be interesting to watch the competition between the Alberta Oil Patch and Eastern Ontario's corn-belt. Which energy sector will produce the most methanol, genetically modified corn or reformulated hydrocarbons?

One of Canada's energy producing sectors will have to transform this decade. Will customers remain loyal to Ontario Hydro and help pay down their $32 billion debt or buy natural gas (methane) powered fuel cells for home electrical production?

Early in 2000 the University of Texas announced the creation of a 100,000 DNA pair synthetic life form. A bacterium designed from a genetic blueprint and made from chemicals is unsettling. Should genetic engineering evolve as rapidly as computing, billion DNA pair synthetic life forms (mammals) could be a reality by 2020. As the technology that links DNA protein to electronic microprocessing already exists, synthetic life forms with inbreeded electronics are an eventuality. Swarms of synthetic "hornets" with generic transponders, surveillance suites and toxins would revolutionize fighting in built-up areas, but this is an old doctrine. "And the Lord your God will send hornets to drive out the few survivors still hiding from you." (Deuteronomy 7:20, NLT version.)

A more benign and possibly a more enhancing form of the DNA-microprocessor meld is brain-computer interfacing. My generation (1960) was not permitted pocket calculators during university examinations. Will my grandchildren be permitted brain-computer interfacing assistance during exams? Why would one need to go to school if portable microprocessors, a million times more capable, and possibly a million times smaller, interfaced with the brain from the earlobe dock? Academia and teacher's unions would no longer meter education. Everyone from mediocre to brilliant, rich and poor could have their own portable tutor. Capturing experiences and wisdom in electronic format should be the professional development priority for the next two decades.

Other Important Factors

Global warming is not going away soon. The Industrial Age legacy of billions of tons of carbon dioxide and a general abuse of the environment will be with us well into the twenty-first century. As it is human nature not to react until either pocketbook or conscience is affected anticipate deferral of this problem until the world's major coastal cities are forced to move to higher ground. By 2020 science should have very accurate global climate models. The question of whether polar-ice melt floats on top of the Gulf Stream will be answered. European and North American climates should be foretold decades in advance. Predictions that land masses above the forty-fifth parallel (Canada, Russia) will warm at four times the global rate will be proven true or false.[51]

As a nation with one of the longest ocean shorelines Canada may have to adapt to climate changes on three fronts: Atlantic; Arctic, and Pacific. Sovereignty issues related to the Canadian archipelago could no longer be ignored should climate change permit transit of the Northwest Passage. Adapting to global climate change could be as financially burdensome as the national debt. Meanwhile south of the border our major ally and trading partner might be redefining national security.

The US Commission on National Security 21ST Century is to comprehensively review the national security environment, processes and organizations.[52] This committee co-sponsored by the President and United States Congress is likely to cause modification to the USA National Security Act of 1947. The continuation of the 1947 defence structures of the US Navy, US Army US Air Force and Marines is being questioned. The emergence of new threats, resolving inter-service rivalries, addressing strategic command and force readiness issues will probably require the United States to create new security structures and command relationships. Current Canadian structures, likewise, will not be immune to changes adopted by the ally with whom we wish to remain interoperable.

Michael Ignateiff in his book, *A Warrior's Honour*, underscores that nations rarely react unless their conscience is pricked or their pocketbook threatened.[53] The national moral sense of right and wrong in the early 1940s produced a military expression that consumed half of the nation's gross domestic product and uniformed a million persons. Today a daily stream of international injustice fed by the media to a graying population evokes a lesser response. National conscience evolves in concert with demographics and culture. Although the pollster Michael Adams warns his readers not to conclude too much from demographic surveys, his latest book, *Sex in the Snow*, a compilation of over eighty surveys of Canadian attitudes by region and age, leads me to deduce that future Canadian societies are likely to be more isolationist and less intrusive in international affairs.[54]

Attitudes, albeit important, are but one aspect of demographics; the other—quantity—presents a significant employment and taxable income challenge. Those born in the post Second World War years exceed those born in the 1990s by a wide margin. Circa 2011 new retirees are likely to exceed new graduates; competition for replacement workers should be fierce.[55] Maintenance of the Canadian social "safety-net" while making interest payments on the national debt is likely to further limit Canada's options and to contribute to a collective withdrawal from the international scene.

The Canadian economy has inertia all of its own. Spendthrift of previous decades has left Canada (all levels of government) with a public debt that requires $77 billion(CDN) in annual interest payments. When public debt is added to that of personal indebtedness the population of Canada has a liability estimated at over $2 trillion(CDN). Debt acts like a gigantic millstone around the proverbial neck of the Canadian economy. The debt will encumber Canadians for decades. However a large debt like a large flywheel does provide stability. The country is unlikely to find the extra resources to finance expensive new initiatives, such as a fleet of nuclear-powered Class 10 polar-icebreakers for archipelago patrol.

A Scenario

The preceding collection of future trends requires a harmonized scenario to better portray the likely impacts and give the reader a better appreciation of where DND/CF might be twenty years hence. At the risk of being ridiculed, (future-scenario-based planning is the weakest type), the following possible events by decade are my guess of what could transpire. You be the judge.

2000-2010

Legacy issues, dispirited personnel and an accelerating Information Age economy place the military on uncontrolled downsizing.

A shortage of IM/IT personnel forces a major rationalization of command support with the concomitant reduction in headquarters. All environments will be forced to share and form joint regional headquarters.

In order to stabilize attrition remuneration becomes commercially competitive. Competent people truly become the most valuable asset and the capital program is not realized. The new USA Security Act revolutionizes national security. Anticipate the unusual. Hacker and counter-hacker brigades, genetic and quanta warfare units with Electro-magnetic spectrum warriors could augment the USA military. Doctrines of swarming and warfare by automaton could guide USA doctrine. Much of the extant USA Regular Force capabilities could migrate to the Reserves, including precision strike and manoeuvre warfare.

Canada conducts a defence review.

2010-2020

Advances in education along with the realization that soldiers are in ever-shorter supply forces the wholesale contracting of professional development and training to the private sector or an ally or both. Closure of CFRETS, CFCSC, RMC, etc. is likely.

CF moves to USA-like hybrid force structure based on the Canadian version of swarming doctrines and automaton. The talent to command these new capabilities is problematic. Command support and a majority of staff functions are contracted to a Canadian bioscience, optoelectronics consortium.

With the realization that training, possibly doctrine, and command support are no longer germane to the CF and that most of Canada's military capability is interoperable with the USA public discussion of amalgamating the two nations' armed forces is initiated.

Genetic examination proves that the majority of military leadership is inadequate for strategic-management in the Information Age, but this is also endemic throughout the public service and government. With the assistance of computer assisted virtual environments and quantum computing the nation strives to achieve consensus on new models of governance while an interim committee administers the nation.

All three dossiers—a MARS officer, a Combat Arms officer, and a pilot—submitted for the position of CDS in 2020 are rejected. The position is contracted to a former USAF Colonel with dual citizenship. Excerpts from her résumé read:

> Genetic behaviour and personality traits suited for strategic-management.
>
> Mensa level intellect. Dual undergraduate degrees in DNA computing and quantum mechanics. Has a Master degree in holographic management. Commanded first USAF Automaton Squadron.
> Decorated for tenacity and adaptability in the Indo-Asian cyber war. Wrote "swarming" doctrines as a training and doctrine staff officer. Project Manager of Neural-Holographic Command and Management Project.[57]

Conclusion

Technological innovation has become the source of a country's economic, military and political power. The triumvirate of innovation, wealth and power is emerging as the new authority of the Information Age. Some hold that a globalized economy, fueled by technical innovation, could become a more powerful force for peace than defence spending.[58] Be that as it may technological innovation is still the crucible from which the instruments to do well or to do evil emerge. World peace is not likely; national security is still required.

As the rate of innovation is accelerating it is highly unlikely that legacy security practices will prove adequate. However, flexibility of mind and organization still remain as the critical assets of national security.

Since the start of the Information Age the Canadian military has demonstrated an inability to transform. A culture that rewards introverted thinking and guards ossified organizations is unlikely to keep pace. Those slated for command in 2020 have already been tainted by the previous century's military culture and are unlikely to be the transformational commanders of 2020. This is the command challenge.

In Quantum physics to observe is to alter; may the same be true with us.

NOTES

1. Sir Michael Howard's full statement on future conflict is, "We cannot predict the exact nature of future conflict. In a conflict everyone starts wrong, the advantage goes to the side which can most quickly adjust itself to the new and unfamiliar environment and learn from its mistakes. It is this flexibility in mind and organization that needs above all to be developed in peacetime."
2. The majority of senior military commanders in the CF perform as strategic-managers. Canada's last strategic level commander was probably Lieutenant-General Arthur Currie. He evolved doctrines and had national command over a long campaign. Since the First World War most Canadian senior commanders were operational-level military leaders within allied formations. The civilian strategic management role as described by Macintosh (Queens University) has strong parallels to the NDHQ culture.
3. At the end of apartheid in South Africa the challenges facing the nation's military were assessed as being so great that the government contracted the RAND Corporation to integrate the nation's military factions and to develop new strategic management. Other means could include civilian or allied trusteeship.
4. Colonel Howard Marsh, "Emerging Technology and Military Affairs," Royal Military College of Canada 1998, a paper presented at and to be published by the University of Laval Strategic Institute.
5. The Total Force army of the year 2000 has 51 Primary Reserve infantry battalions and 9 Regular Force infantry battalions. A Canadian mechanized infantry division is established with 9 infantry battalions. From an infantry unit perspective there exists adequate resources to generate 6 to7 infantry divisions. Between the First and Second World War General McNaughton, the CGS was able to marshal the political support to reduce the militia from a 15-division structure to six divisions. The legacy of the decision endures to today. During the Second World War the army deployed a seven-division force with an additional two home guard divisions. For more details see the Harris Report. Steve Harris, PhD., DND Directorate of History, "Militia Reform: A Paper Presented to LFCHQ 30 March 1995."
6. Maloney, Sean A. PhD, "An Identifiable Cult: The Evolution of Combat Development in the Canadian Army 1946-1965," Directorate of Land Strategic Concepts Report 9905, DND Publication, Kingston, Canada, (August 1999), 2.

7. Minister's Monitoring Committee On Change In The Department Of National Defence And The Canadian Forces, Chaired by John A. Fraser, established October 14, 1997. Four reports: March 1998, November 1998, July 1999, December 1999[Final Report] 222 Queen Street, Suite 701, Ottawa. The committee was established to monitor progress on 339 decisions that originated from six externally contracted reviews.
8. President Lincoln removed most of the union generals from command because they were unable to adapt to doctrinal change as a result of the introduction of the rifled barrel.
9. The Phillips (1997) Survey of military members reported that only 17% assessed that senior leadership could lead the organization out of its present challenges.
10. Marshall McLuhan Foundation, www.icgc.com/mcluhan.
11. Janie Fouke, editor, Trudy E. Bell, and Dave Dooling, authors, *Engineering Tomorrow: Today's Technology Experts Envision the Next Century* (Piscataway, NJ: IEEE Press, 1999), 308pp. See first chapter by Vinton C. Cerf, "A Short History of the Internet."
12. Tactical Command Control Communications System is a billion-dollar project to provide secure, digitized communications for the army.
13. Defence Research Establish Valcartier at that time was a leader in land forces CCIS. Most of the military and civilian team members have since migrated to the private sector. Fortunately some can still be hired.
14. Interview with Director Land Information Requirements, 1996-1998.
15. The author was Director Land Requirements at that time, 1994-1996 and personally knew the chairman of the MCCRT Culture Committee.
16. The navy is in a much better position. In the 1980s the navy effectively digitized their entire command and control through PMO TRUMP and PMO CPF. During the 1990s all their MARS officers were "raised" in a digitized command environment. The navy is now functioning at the operational level of command with data fusion technology and doctrine. Due to the navy's approach to officer classification the navy "owns" two-thirds of all CF IT/IM trained officers.
17. Cornet, Annie, chargée de cours adjoint à l' École d'Administration des Affaires de l'Université de Liège en Belgique, *Dix ans de réingénierie des processus d'affaires:qu'avons-nous appris?* Gestion, volume 24, numéro 3, (automne 1999).
18. Colonel H. Marsh, Land Force Command Inspector, "Review of Gender Integration: Recruit Centre to Unit," (29 January 1999), A-2/4.
19. Tonight's homework is posted on http.www, but I don't have access to a computer. In the event of a medical emergency call 1-888 before proceeding to the hospital. Military clothing is required tomorrow; military clothing is only available from Area Support Unit next week!
20. 1-800-CALL CDS is not an actual phone number but the term used by soldiers cynical of the plethora of 1-800 phone numbers in the CF and the CDS letter of June 1996 when the CDS offered an open invitation to write directly to him.
21. Jane Jacobs, *Systems of Survival: A Dialogue on the Moral Foundations of Commerce and Politics* (New York: Random House, 1992), 236.
22. CFP 300, *Canada's Army* lists the military virtues as: truth; duty; loyalty; sacrifice; trust; competence; initiative; good example, and ability to inspire.
23. Jane Jacobs, chapter six, *Trading, Taking, and Monstrous Hybrids*, 93-112.
24. In the fall of 2000 due to a shortage of qualified military personnel the National Support Unit of MND SE (Balkans) was to be partially manned by Alternate Service Delivery (ASD). This creates a leadership challenge for the tactical commander. How does one motivate per-

sons in the same unit who are receiving widely disparate remuneration under differing obligations of service?

25. See RMC Survey of 1998 graduating class. Author was Acting Commandant RMC in 1997. Recent (2000) Interview with Deputy Cadets revealed an ongoing difficulty with cadets' practice of military ethos.

26. Major H. Bondy, *Canadian Forces Compensation and Benefits Fundamental Principles And Strategic Policy Vision,* 5000-1(CAT2) 28 June 1999. (Held by Director General Compensation and Benefits.) In addition to offering compensation models for vocational and occupational approaches to military employment the Annexes reveal that the CF has been aware of this issue since the early 1980s and despite many assessments the CF strategic-management has long ignored the ethos-compensation issue.

27. Norman F. Dixon, PhD, *On the Psychology of Military Incompetence.* (London: Hazell Watson & Viney Limited, 1976).

28. DiSC Behavioural analysis reveals that dominant leaders fear challenge whereas information specialists fear non-acceptance of ideas. These non-compatible behavioural traits may partially explain the IM/IT challenge in DND/CF. See www.tamcoinic.com/discins.html for Role Behaviour Analysis. 1998 TAMCO, Training and Management Consultants.

29. Otto Kroeger, and Janet M. Thuesen. *Type Talk,* (New York: Bantam Doubleday Dell Publishing Group Inc), ISBN 0-385-29828-59. Profiles all sixteen personality types. Myers Briggs Personality Type on the Web, www.mbtypeguide.com/Type/types.html for an application of the sixteen acronyms to famous personalities. Enter "Myers Briggs" on any search engine for on-line personality indicator tests.

30. Myers Briggs, Doctors of Sociology. United States Army War College (USAWC) conducts annual personality screening of course candidates using the Myers Briggs personality selection process. Approximately 65% of US Army officers recommended for attendance are ISTJ personalities. In the sixteen categories of Myers Briggs, if a normal distribution of personality types were present, the quantity of ISTJ should have been no more than 16%.

31. ISTAR: Information Surveillance Target Acquisition Reconnaissance.

32. The conceptual Canadian Army of the future is built on the five doctrinal constructs of Command, Sense, Act, Shield and Sustain. The Canadian Navy functions, for the most part, on two officer classifications: MARS and MARE. Officers in these classifications are required to have a secondary skill much like the US Army officer.

33. Norman B. Macintosh, *Management Accounting and Control Systems: An Organizational and Behavioural Approach* (Toronto: Wiley & Sons, 1994), 281.

34. Ibid, 71.

35. The year 1990 was celebrated with 5,000 registrations at the USA patent office. In 1999 IBM alone registered over 3,500 patents. My estimate is conservative. North American patent registrations now exceed 5,000,000. Math theorem registrations number more than 100,000 annually. Calculating innovation based on patents is difficult as companies register the same invention in several countries.

36. *Scientific American,* January 2000.

37. Arno A. Penzia, AT&T Bell Laboratories, IEEE *Spectrum* January 2000.

38. IEEE *Spectrum, The Journal of the Electrical, Electronics Engineer,* November 1999.

39. Production of microprocessors for 2000 is estimated to exceed 8 billion. Earth's population is estimated at 6 billion.

40. Microprocessing is likely to evolve through four stages: electronic based; electron-photon based; molecular DNA, and quantum computing. Interference by sub-atomic particles is the quantum computer's Achilles' heel.
41. The majority of proposed Internet 2 architectures offer gigabyte/second performance. Nortel's OS 182 servers perform at 10 gigabyte/second now.
42. As implausible as this may seem most of the technologies exist now. Microscopic surgery by remote control (up to five metres distance) is practised in operating rooms. Lucent Medical Systems (Washington) sell personal catheter locators and applicators that are far more precise than those placed by a doctor. Within ten years all of the above is likely to be a thousand times smaller and available at distances up to five kilometres from medical "servers." As devices shrink and become smaller than nerves it should be possible to conduct surgery without anaesthetic. The patient could watch his own surgical procedure at home and record it in his personal medical history.
43. But only those with a tetrawatt laser. A tetrawatt laser is a million times more powerful than a megawatt laser.
44. One bip (billion instructions per second) is a measure of microprocessor performance. The Sony Play Station performs at 6 bips. A tetra instructions per second (tip) processor would be a thousand times faster. A mip (million) was the 1980 standard of performance.
45. My latest search on the Internet revealed 167 laboratories and universities researching nanotechnology, but most search engines only find 15-30% of all listings on any one subject. The number of like-minded competitors is probably closer to 500.
46. Drs. Einstein and Boser co-theorized "coherent mass" as a distillate at absolute zero in the 1920s.
47. Atoms gravitate towards bright light.(More photons have a greater gravitational attraction than less photons of light.) As the centre of a laser light beam is brighter than the circumference a very narrow beam of laser light serves well in holding and moving atoms.
48. IEEE *Spectrum*, October 1999.
49. The Ballard 900 series of fuel cells is designed to do this and is available to Japanese homeowners in 2000. With a $32 billion electrical distribution debt the province of Ontario and Ontario Hydro have no incentive to embrace this technology.
50. A parallel hydrocarbon reformulater and fuel cell has been developed by the University of Pennsylvania (March 2000). This cubic-inch-sized device converts hydrocarbon fuels into electricity with by-products of pure water and carbon dioxide.
51. Northern landmasses when snow-covered reflect sunlight. Without a snow covering the land absorbs heat. Thermodynamically the landmass can be modelled according to "black-body" radiation models. The ratio of heat absorption between white and brown is significant. Recently (March 2000) in the Ottawa valley record high temperatures were broken by margins of 10 degrees centigrade, due to this phenomenon of no reflective snow cover.
52. US Commission on National Security/21ST Century—Hart-Rudman Commission. Visit http//www.nssg.gov/ to read full mandate, reports and schedules. Recommendations are due circa 2002 for next United States President.
53. Michael Ignatieff, *The Warrior's Honour: Ethnic War and The Modern Conscience*. (Toronto: Penguin Books, 1999), 207.
54. Michael Adams, President of Environics, *Sex in the Snow: Canadian Social Values at the End of the Millennium* (Toronto: Viking Penguin, 1997), 220.

55. Sherry Cooper, *The Cooper Files: A Practical Guide to Your Financial Future.* (Toronto: Key Porter Books, 1999), 375. See page 102 for Canadian and United States birth rates 1920 to 1999.
56. Canadian 1996 Consensus table.
57. Neural-Holographic command does not yet exist. The word "neural" expresses the capability to understand the meaning of data flowing through junctions. The word "holographic" captures the inherent nature of a hologram to replicate the whole image from the smallest fragment of the image. Such a command or management system would, in theory, explain local events, describe the total situation and be infinitely redundant.
58. IEEE *Spectrum* January 2000, "Views of the Future."

III

OPERATIONS

A Perspective on Contemporary Canadian Generalship Operations in NATO

Lieutenant-General (retired) J.K. Dangerfield

Lieutenant-General (retired) J. K. Dangerfield served for 38 years in the Canadian Forces retiring in April 1995. He served for 15 years in Europe with NATO forces.

I have seen good colonels become very bad generals. Very few officers study the grand detail and so, if they arrive at the command of armies, they are totally perplexed. From their ignorance of how to do what they ought, they merely do what they know, often with disastrous results.

-Marshall Saxe

INTRODUCTION

I HAVE OFTEN MAINTAINED that there are two areas where I thought Canadian senior officers (at least army officers) were badly prepared for the responsibilities of senior appointments—the study of Operational Art and the intricacies of the political/military interface. Obviously the two are regularly linked. Operational Art is something often talked about but seldom understood and, in my opinion, even less frequently practiced by Canadian senior officers. It is worth a book onto itself. The intricacies of the political/military interface are experienced only by a few, and in an international sense by even fewer. I spent over fifteen years in Europe in NATO and perhaps I am one of these latter officers. Accordingly, I offer this chapter in the hope that it might help our profession.

I need to state some disclaimers. The highest level of command that I achieved was in NATO—at the divisional level. I can only discuss the issues of *senior command* from the division and corps level and as a staff officer at Army Group and NATO Headquarters level observing the senior commanders. My most educational experiences were at NATO HQ but I left there in the summer of 1994. A lot has happened since then—expanded member nations and a different view of NATO by France.

With a broad topic, such as "Operations in NATO," one must be selective and I will concentrate on a more narrow viewpoint—political/military interfaces in an alliance or coalition. These political/military interfaces are, in my opinion, *the* most important factor in operations at the operational and strategic levels. It is also the component for which our formal training least prepares us. I therefore ask readers to forgive my "return to basics" approach. I do that deliberately and make no apology if I am insulting. It is based on my experience that few senior Canadian officers (of my day) knew of the intricacies of NATO at the various levels. At the end, I shall try to draw some conclusions from my NATO Alliance experience with an aim of assisting to prepare officers for senior appointments in this type of environment. To do so I must make some recommendations in a national context.

POLITICAL/MILITARY INTERFACE
Canadian Context

I could not find mention of "political/military interface" in any of the current Canadian doctrinal publications in my possession. Perhaps that is significant. Broken down in a simplistic form, there is obviously some sort of intercourse between today's Canadian political leaders and the senior Canadian

Forces officers. In the late 1970s and early 1980s there was also a formal process with the production of a strategic assessment and a follow-on combat development process. Critics will say that the process was theoretical and seldom practiced. Nevertheless, there was an attempt to articulate the interrelated concepts of national purpose, national interest, national goals or objectives, national strategy (which should include national military strategy), and military strategy. The strategic assessment was closely entwined with the government's White Paper. It was the attempt to develop a military strategy to help achieve the national strategic ends desired. Force structure and operational planning are the two key follow-ons, but so are doctrine, training, and equipment.

I believe most Canadian officers understand that the military object of war must be subordinated to the political object. However, some great strategic thinkers (Moltke in particular) took the political/military interface to mean that the military should be free from political restraints in the conduct of military operations. I suppose that there are many American Vietnam War veterans who share that view. However, the Canadian contemporary experience more probably follows the theory that was espoused by Edward Mead Earle (a US Naval War College instructor) as early as 1949. He explained that under modern conditions military questions are so interwoven with economic, political, social, and technological phenomena that it is doubtful if one can speak of a purely military strategy—politics and strategy have become inseparable. Can there be any doubt that is the present Canadian experience? Otherwise, how could one explain that the Canadian Forces in 2000 are operating from a White Paper that is dated 1994? Worse, the politicians of 2000 are stating that the White Paper is still valid. From my viewpoint there is very little correlation with the political decisions of the late 1990s and 2000 with the "strategy" that is contained in the *1994 White Paper*.

NATO Context

For the purpose of this chapter I shall concentrate on the strategic and operational levels and narrow the definition of "political/military" interface to mean the interactive process whereby:

> the political body sets political objectives and enunciates political guidance which may or may not include military constraints; the military develops options to support those objectives and in particular outlines the resources required; the political body selects an option (and by doing so agrees to provide the resources);and the military develops an operational plan.

The key element of my definition is that it is a dialogue—a two-way flow of guidance. I will use the North Atlantic Council as my political body and NATO's Military Committee, the International Military Staff and SACEUR as "the military."

LEVELS

This chapter is organized in matrix fashion to illustrate how these factors come into play at the political, strategic, operational, and tactical levels for both alliance and coalition operations. Before proceeding, it is important, as well as doctrinally correct, to differentiate between alliance operations and coalition operations (even those coalition operations undertaken by the NATO Alliance). Canadian Forces Publication (CFP) 300(3), *The Canadian Army*, defines these as follows:

- Alliance: the result of formal agreements between two or more nations for broad, long-term objectives; and
- Coalition: an ad hoc agreement between two or more nations for a common action (inferred by me to be temporary).

Initially, as a primer, I shall describe the conditions that are at play in NATO when one is considering my narrow definition of the political/military interface. In theory, NATO divides its headquarters to reflect the level of responsibility.

NATO'S POLITICAL LEVEL

At this level consultation takes place, diplomacy is practiced, economic, political and military advice is rendered, options are weighed, political decisions are taken and political guidance for implementation is formulated. There are two principal political organs of NATO. The first is the North Atlantic Council (NAC) with all member nations represented. It can meet at head of state or government, foreign minister, or head of delegation (Ambassador) level. The second is the Defence Planning Committee (DPC). France chose not to be represented on this committee when it withdrew from the military structure of NATO. This committee can meet at head of government, defence minister, or head of delegation level. Both are chaired by the Secretary General as a non-voting member. The chairman of the Military Committee sits as an advisor on both the NAC and the DPC. (The Nuclear Planning Group is also a major committee, but is not considered further in this chapter).

Committees of NATO, with very few exceptions, operate on consensus with *all* nations unanimously agreeing to proposals. In essence, every nation has veto powers. At the senior political level (NAC and DPC) consensus is sought through consultations, and the good offices of the Secretary General. Frequently, and more recently, consensus has been difficult to achieve. This has been caused by the deeper and deeper involvement of NATO in non-traditional roles and missions such as programs with the Central and Eastern European countries, and in peacekeeping operations. Both these examples are highly political with nations often having opposing views. Another complication was the unique situation of France who declared that she wished to be fully involved in any NATO peacekeeping considerations. NATO, of course, conducts its peacekeeping planning using NATO's integrated military structure and chain of command—neither of which had French representation other than liaison. Hence many innovative changes had to be made to long-standing procedures and precedents. Nations had to adjust their modus operandi to accommodate the fact that NAC was frequently doing what would normally be DPC business.

Another significant factor at NATO's political level is the interaction of the "circles within circles" which come to play in situations such as those in the early days of the Bosnia Herzegovina conflict. Here, there were NATO nations who were on the UN Security Council and NATO nations who were not. There were some Troop Contributing Nations (TCN) and some nations who were not represented in UNPROFOR. There were nations of the "contact group" and those not in the group. Strangely, there were even some nations who were not contributing troops in the group while some nations who were contributing troops, including Canada, were not in the "contact group." This led to at least two situations in the political decision-making process. It was not axiomatic that a nation that supported a specific resolution in the UN would render the same degree of support in the implementation of that resolution by a regional organization, such as NATO, and vice versa. The use of air power in support of UNPROFOR is an example. Second, the consensus rule and the "circles within circles" can mean that a resolution is of the lowest common denominator and noticeably less than specific. Both these present challenges at the next level down—the strategic level.

NATO'S STRATEGIC LEVEL

It is this level where the political and military interface, particularly in crisis management and defence planning. The key here is that it truly must be an interface where political imperatives are clearly enunciated but, at the same time, taking due consideration of the military implications of those imperatives. The politicians direct; the military advises. Political guidance is then

translated into military directives by a military staff. The principal activities at this level include:
- Interfacing the organization with the nations and other world and regional organizations;
- Developing long-range strategic concepts and plans;
- Force planning, force proposals, organizational structure and long-term defence planning;
- Crisis management to include the provision of command, control and information capabilities;
- Preparing assessments and studies, and operational contingency planning; and
- Transferring political direction and guidance into operational guidance (and in some cases operational plans) for use by subordinate headquarters.

The Military Committee is the highest military authority in the Alliance and has these main responsibilities:
- Providing the NAC and DPC with international military advice and recommendations;
- Conveying NAC and DPC decisions to those responsible for their implementation; and
- Providing executive over-watch of the integrated military structure and, in particular, its execution of political decisions.

The Military Committee (MC) operates on the basis of consensus and is composed of the Chiefs of Defence (CHODs) of the nations who make up NATO's integrated military structure and a senior representative from Iceland (which has no military). The Chairman (CMC) is an ex-CHOD, appointed by the CHODs for a three-year secondment and is a non-voting member of the committee. As previously mentioned, the CMC attends all NAC and DPC meetings and, providing he has consensus, represents the views of the national CHODs in those forums. The CHODs are permanently represented by Military Representatives (Milreps) who are senior general/flag officers accredited to their national delegation for a normal period of three years and whose role varies from nation to nation. Some receive their instructions *solely* from their CHOD, others receive them from their ministry of defence, yet others receive inter-departmentally coordinated instructions. Some are fully integrated into their national delegation; some are quite separate. Thus it is possible, but rare, for a nation to vote one way in the MC and vote another in the NAC (in essence a CHOD being overruled by his political masters).

The stresses and strains at the political level that come into play when NATO considers peace-keeping ("circles within circles") are also quite naturally applicable in the MC. Also, understandably, nations with troops on the ground in places like Bosnia and Kosovo tend to have specific and focused military viewpoints and cannot abide with generalities where lack of clarity puts those troops at risk. Consensus building under these circumstances is hard work.

The two staffs of NATO headquarters—civilian and military—operate somewhat differently. The civilian International Staff (IS) operates through their Assistant Secretaries General to the Secretary General and is therefore able to offer assessments and recommendations that are uninhibited by national positions and, indeed, may not even be known to the nations. The International Military Staff (IMS) on the other hand has no executive authority unless specifically given that authority by the MC. It operates directly to the CMC and the MC, and any formal recommendations or assessments passed on to the political organs of the organization must first have the consensus blessing of the MC before they are transmitted.

The Operational Level

This is the level where the military directives are translated into coherent, complete, military operational plans. The senior level of the military chain possess all the resources needed to implement the political decision and is the focal point where responsibility and resources must match. In the NATO context it is also the level where national inputs begin to lose influence in favour of organizational (and multi-national) imperatives and procedures.

In NATO this level is manifested in the headquarters of the two Major NATO Commanders (MNCs)—Supreme Allied Commander in Europe (SACEUR) and Supreme Allied Commander Atlantic (SACLANT), who command the integrated military structure. While there are national liaison missions attached to both headquarters, the staff of the headquarters operates on an international basis similar to the IMS at NATO HQ. Both MNCs attend high level NAC and DPC meetings and are permanently represented on most NATO committees including the MC.

The MNCs are the highest level of command (the MC at NATO HQ is a committee and the highest collective military authority, but it does not command). The MNCs are individuals who have been appointed to command the troops placed at their disposal by the nations. This command relationship is predetermined in most instances and may be graduated. ("Full command," as one would expect, covers all aspects of operations and administration. It exists only in national services):

Operational Command: the NATO commander is given command of the national troops and may assign missions or tasks to individual components of those troops. In other words he may "break up" national contingents, assigning geographically and functionally different tasks to sub-components. This level of delegation is common for long-standing contingency plans.

Operational Control: is assigned for a given mission (limited by function, time or location) but the NATO commander may not assign tasks to sub-components of national contingents. A task is given to the national commander who may use all, or a portion, of his troops. Normally the national commander is responsible for logistics. This level is common for less clearly defined contingencies where the nations wish to maintain more control. It became the norm for coalition operations.

An unofficial variation that is sometimes used is *Under Operational Command (or Control) except for....* Nations may put restrictions on the degree of delegation it gives to NATO commanders by using the "except for" clause when normal procedures do not satisfy their concerns. Examples could be deployments or redeployments, cross border movements, etc.

In any military organization unity of command is a principle that is ignored at great risk. Simply stated there has to be one person, and one person only, in charge. In NATO this is the MNCs or their subordinate commanders (MSCs). Once a nation has agreed to the mission and assigned forces at the political level of NATO, it rescinds its control of those forces to a NATO commander and the international integrated chain of command. Of course a nation can still influence the destiny of its forces at the political and strategic levels, but it is implicit that they will not interfere with operational decisions at the operational and tactical levels, a principle more and more broken in recent years.

The Tactical Level

This is a "field" headquarters responsible for implementing the operational plan or a proportion of it. It is normally small, mobile and more concerned with operations than politics. In the past it was mainly a single nation entity (exceptions being formations like ACE Mobile Force or Standing Naval Forces) but more recently there has emerged more and more multi-national formations with international headquarters commanding them, e.g. ACE Rapid Reaction Corps (ARRC).

Some Personal Experiences

I will start at the tactical/alliance level and move up to the political and strategic/coalition level. Conscious of the senior command aspect of the chapter I shall be concentrating on this latter level.

As a young officer I had little idea of the political/strategic influences that were at play in the 1960s. All I was concerned about was the "enemy"—the Russian Front that was going to attack across the Hanover Plain on its way to the Atlantic. My day was occupied making sure that my sub-unit was as technically and tactically proficient as possible. However, one incident comes to mind when considering political/military interfaces.

I was commanding an independent armoured reconnaissance squadron in Northern Germany in the late 1960s. I was doing so when the Canadian Brigade was in its heyday—about 6700 soldiers, full combat arms units, nuclear firepower, and well plugged into the British Army on the Rhine. We had a clear and very important mission with most of the tools necessary to do it. Then, in 1969, came Prime Minister Pierre Trudeau's indication that Canada would pull out of Europe. Although this decision was later recanted it was followed by the completely arbitrary decision to chop the Brigade from 6700 to 2800 soldiers and to move it south to collocate it with the air force in Lahr. The decision was taken at the national political level but its ramifications were felt by NATO at every level and by the Canadian soldier at the tactical level. There was no consultation done in good faith. The military could not put the decision into a context of national goals and objectives. I can still recall the Brigade Commander, Brigadier Jim Gardner, standing in front of his commanding officers at a loss for an explanation. As the good soldier that he was, he got on with trying to make it happen. He gave each of us a figure and told us to design our units to match that figure. Mine was eighty-eight. I was to take my reconnaissance squadron of over three hundred and redesign it so that it could be manned by eighty-eight soldiers. We had no idea what our role and missions were; not even where we were to be committed and how we were to be supported. Many books have been written on this period and I have read most of them. To this day I think that this was the best (or worst) example of a lack of a clear political objective having to be translated into a military objective and plan. I am sure that even Mitchell Sharp (then Minister of External Affairs) and Leo Cadieux (Minister of

Defence) would agree with me. There was a political decision—period. In short, there was no political/military interface. What a disaster! It took years to get some sense of military order.

Although bordering on the operational level as much as the tactical level my next example illustrates the dilemma the Trudeau decision caused. It occurred a decade after that decision when I was commanding 4 CMBG in the mid 1980s. The brigade was assigned the role of Central Army Group Reserve. In a military sense this was nonsense. The Army Group consisted of two American corps and two German corps. To think that a tiny brigade (now at 3200 soldiers) was a suitable reserve for the Army Group would earn an "F" grade for any staff college student. The truth of the matter was that the 1st French Army was the reserve but this had political problems. The idea that French forces would come under command of a NATO commander was not one that would be politically popular (see below). So the Canadian contribution took up the political slack. Militarily it made little sense. Politically it brought the Canadian flag to the Army Group table rather than to a German or American division commander's table. While there were military advantages to the arrangement, particularly in training with both allies, it was very difficult for any brigade commander to make a tactical plan to be an Army Group reserve. The only reason that it was possible to work out any plan at all was because of the complete understanding of the Canadian political situation by the American Army Group Commander, the American VII Corps commander and the German II Corps commander. These officers never pushed (as they had every military right to) to have the brigade come under operational command of one of their divisions. Instead they cooperated as best they could in accommodating the Canadian contribution of an under-strength and badly logistically supported demi-brigade. From an army point of view it was all that was on the ground and they knew that it was better than the first Trudeau alternative. There was some truth to the "hostage" theory.

I left command of the brigade to assume the appointment of Chief of Staff (Operations) at Central Army Group in 1986. It was here that I began my real education in political/military interface in an international context and at the operational level. I was instructed in the political and military intricacies of the different strategies of mobile defence and forward defence. I was schooled (by SACEUR, General Bernard Rogers) in the strategy that a modest increase to the NATO budget would permit a shift from early use of nuclear weapons to a conventional force sufficiently strong to deter aggression without threatening the use of nuclear weapons. Also, there were many examples of NATO/national interfaces with the Americans and the Germans. However, the main effort was with the French.

Recall that the French were not in NATO's integrated military structure and would not put their forces under command of NATO. Yet they understood that the best defence of France started at the West German/East German and West German/Czechoslovakia borders. Their military planners were in a dilemma. How could they integrate their plans with those of NATO if they were not part of the planning process? Indeed, II French Corps was, in large measure, stationed in Germany. How could they plan to be involved in operations in Germany if those operations were not coordinated with NATO?

Operational planning for Central Army Group was my prime responsibility. I felt comfortable and well prepared to do it with the Americans, Germans, and Canadians. In fact, it was easy. However, we had to find mechanisms to interface with the French military planners without creating the political impression that we were militarily committing France. The solution was dozens of liaison officers and a number of "cooperation committees." In the main these were meetings of multi-national planners from NATO and French planners, alternating venues between Heidelberg and Strasbourg. Occasionally they became "summits" with Commander Central Army Group and Commander 1st French Army. The outcome was a number of corps and army-sized counter-attack operational plans being produced that may not have been perfect but they were workable. Any difficulties always centered on two politically charged issues—command, and transfer of authority (TOA). The highest level of command that the French would agree to was Operational Control. This meant that NATO commanders could not integrate French forces into other forces. This became a difficulty with such elements as artillery, intelligence and reconnaissance, which need to be integrated laterally and in depth. Transfer of authority is describing the conditions that need to be met before a previously specified command authority is transferred from a supporting command (the French) to a supported command (the Army Group). This was relatively clear from a military point of view (e.g. a line on the map that the enemy reaches or the committing of a specific force) but it was always very difficult to get French political approval to those conditions.

I learned a lot during these days, particularly on the art of compromise. I believe I can say that at any given time period I would be spending about forty percent of my time dealing with the American, German and Canadian plans (i.e. integrated military NATO) and sixty percent of my time dealing with the French issues. To a lesser degree this repeated itself in my next example.

I consider myself to be at NATO Headquarters during a most dramatic and exciting time. When I arrived in the spring of 1991, even though the wall had come down, NATO was still immersed in the General Defence Plans mentality. The Gulf War had just ended. A few weeks after arrival I was representing the CMC at the NAC that was discussing the Alliance position on the kidnapping and coup that overthrew Mikhail Gorbachev. A few weeks after that the NAC approved a brand new strategic concept which "extended the hand of friendship to the East." In December, at the first exploratory meeting of an expanded NAC the Soviet Ambassador announced that he no longer represented the Soviet Union because the Union had, literally minutes before, ceased to exist. I spoke to a group of Russian officers at a symposium on peacekeeping in Moscow in 1992. I headed the military representation of NATO's first visit to the United Nations Headquarters. Under my supervision the IMS prepared the greatest number of NATO level operation orders and contingency plans that NATO had ever considered up to that point. Later, I shall use some of these experiences to illustrate the difficulties of the political/military interface.

Three significant events occur in this time frame. They are:
- the Partnership for Peace initiatives;
- the expanded role of NATO to include peacekeeping; and
- the emerging appeal for a European Defence and Security Identity.

When the Alliance decided to take advantage of the changing geo-strategic situation and approved the Alliance Strategic Concept in Rome in 1991, it was a turning point for the alliance in many important ways. Arguably, the most important and far-reaching part of the Strategic Concept was the decision to give tangible effect to the Alliance's willingness to "extend the hand of friendship" to the countries of Central and Eastern Europe. It did this by creating another political body, the North Atlantic Cooperation Council (NAC C), with membership open to non-NATO nations. Nothing was ever tabled at these meetings which required a vote. It would have been impossible to get consensus given the differences of opinion between some of the members (such as Belarus and Estonia versus Russia). However, it was a good forum for exploring the issues of European security and enlargement.

It soon became obvious that the military side of this cooperation could move more quickly than the political. The Military Committee developed its own MC Cooperation and met with CHODs of the eastern nations. Seeing this, the SACEUR of the day, General John Shalikashvili came up with a formula that was presented by his defence minister at the DPC in Travemunde in 1993. It was called Partnership for Peace (PfP). This allowed cooperation between NATO and non-NATO members in such things as exercises, seminars, etc. It caught on like wildfire, soon east and west were visiting each other like crazy. I lost my boss, the chairman of the Military Committee, for about six months because he was visiting Romania, Hungary, the then Czechoslovakia, etc. Almost on a daily basis I was involved with a visiting military delegation from some eastern country. Dozens of nations signed up for PfP, including Russia. Many of them assigned permanent liaison officers to NATO HQ and to the Partnership Coordination Cell at SHAPE. This had a significant impact on the next event, the expansion of NATO into peacekeeping operations.

At Oslo in June 1992, Alliance foreign ministers agreed to add peacekeeping to NATO's task. I can tell you that this was a surprise to most military in the HQ because we did not believe that France would agree. This agreement caused the staff to enter a flurry of activity on developing SOPs to carry out this task. The major concern was command and control. There were three almost mutually exclusive positions on the table. The American position that American troops would operate only under NATO Command (and therefore under an American SACEUR). The French position was that they wanted to be part of NATO's expanded peacekeeping role but would not operate within NATO's integrated military structure (namely not under SACEUR). The United Nations position at the time was that all operations in conjunction with UN (such as UNPROFOR) had to come under UN command. Here was a classic case of the military being told to get on with developing policy and procedures for an initiative developed by the Council at ministerial level but thwarted at every turn by individual nations at ambassadorial and military representative level.

The third development was initiated at the December 1991 meeting of the European Council at Maastrich when the European nations agreed to develop a separate European Security and Defence Identity. This manifested itself with a resurrected Western European Union complete with its own form of military staff and advice. Thus, we had many nations with their NATO ambassador and military representative double-hatted to also serve on WEU councils. A very confused Canada and United States tried to understand how this was going to work.

My dealings with France continued in Brussels. France was a member of NAC (which is foreign ministry driven) but not of DPC (which is defence ministry driven). Even though many peacekeeping issues are defence related, France would not allow them to be discussed in DPC. Thus, DPC (in permanent session) never really met after the summer of 1992 for quite some time. Instead NAC took this on. (Nowadays, to get around this dilemma NAC sometimes meets at defence minister level!)

France was only an observer in the MC. Yet she declared that when peacekeeping was being discussed she was to be considered a "full member." France wanted to become involved in the nitty gritty of military planning for peacekeeping but could not do so because she was not a member of the integrated military staff and thus not represented (other than liaison) on the IMS or at SHAPE. She wanted to create a new committee which would discuss military matters and to create an add-on headquarters at SHAPE which would look after peacekeeping and PfP matters.

France did not want NATO's integrated military structure to be used to control peacekeeping operations. Instead she wished the NAC (advised by the Military Committee) to directly control the "field" headquarters which would be *supported* by NATO's integrated military structure but not *commanded* by it.

Let me give a few personal anecdotes to illustrate these issues. By the late spring of 1991, NATO had a well-honed crisis management policy and procedure. Years of Cold War exercises such as WINTEX had perfected the politico-military interface so that the chain from capitals to NAC to the MC to the MNCs was well practiced in dealing with reporting and direction. Indeed in a real life situation like the summer 1991 overthrow of Gorbachev, I believe NATO activated its intelligence organization and began a series of events that tied the political to the military fairly well. Things began to change in June 1992, when the NATO foreign ministers agreed that the Alliance might offer itself to the Organization for Security and Cooperation in Europe (the OSCE) for peacekeeping missions on a case by case basis.

For the next twelve months, while Bosnia was discussed, NATO had to evolve its relationship with the UN. Obviously the missions of UNPROFOR and NATO would be fundamentally different. Inwardly the Alliance still wrestled with the concept of whether the Alliance would ever be involved with out-of-area operations under a UN mandate. Except for Bosnia itself acting as the catalyst, NATO might still be in this debate because of the conflicting positions of its members. Not the least of these were the US, who was not keen to send ground troops and France, who believed that the UN should handle it (recall that the UN commander in Bosnia was French). Also recall that Greece was watching closely what was happening in bordering Macedonia and concerned about Turkish involvement in any troop contributions. In the end, however, the

Security Council, in its resolutions, provided the legal justification and "political guidance" for NATO's performance. The Alliance, as a military instrument, contributed actively to the implementation of UN decisions. But this was not easy! In my time there were over fifty UN Resolutions calling on NATO to do such things as enforce an arms embargo, an economic embargo, a ban on military flights, the protection of UN personnel, the protection of "safe areas," the monitoring of heavy weapons, and to conduct contingency planning for the implementation of a UN peace plan for Bosnia. The real trick for NATO's military leadership was to try to achieve political clarity from the UN resolutions, which, frequently, were deliberately vague.

In the early days, France forbade any military contact between the UN and NATO. After repeated pleas by the CMC the NAC finally allowed a small delegation to visit UN HQ to discuss how the two organizations could cooperate. I headed the military side of this delegation. We got a polite but not overly warm reception from the UN. When I got back and reported through the CMC to the NAC, France agreed to a *case by case* basis of contact with the UN. In other words if we were developing an operation plan and needed information, we were supposed to first ask the NAC what we wanted and then they would authorize me to conduct liaison on that specific subject, and *only* that subject. Obviously this was not workable, if for no other reason than the time delays. The less than satisfactory solution came in two forms. The first was informal liaison (which could therefore not be quoted—a type of "off the record"). The second was a convoluted and backward way of getting approval. Based in large measure on the informal liaison results, the staff would include such and such in the draft operation plan. We would circulate the draft to the nations via the military representatives, and get feedback. In most cases the nations would clear their comments with their capitals, who, in turn cleared them with New York. Hence, we got our information either by not receiving a reaction or by giving us alternate wording. This was not a great way of doing business but it was how the initial military guidance to the MNC for Operations Sharp Guard (the naval blockade) and Deny Flight (the aerial blockade) were sorted out.

France was also the major player in developing relations with the Western European Union and first coined the phrase that NATO should have "separable but not separate" military structures and resources. There was (and I believe there still is) tension between the two organizations because the split of responsibilities allowed duplication. Operation Sharp Guard is a case in point. When the UN decided to blockade Serbia, NATO set up a small naval force under

SACEUR and COMAFSOUTH to carry this out. The WEU wanted to do the same thing but did not have any resources (other than French resources) to do it with. Believe it or not we ended up with a very convoluted political/military interface where *both* the NAC and the WEU *as separate bodies* gave political direction to a new *joint* NATO/WEU body—the "Military Committee Adriatic." This body was for all intents and purposes the NATO MC with the addition of a few WEU military representatives (notably France). It was supported by both the NATO military staff and the WEU military staff. It gave direction to SACEUR and COMAFSOUTH who in turn organized two naval forces, one NATO and one WEU! So we ended up with two naval forces in the Aegean Sea reporting to two different political bodies (but who were largely the same individuals). The naval forces swapped location every two weeks between the north and the south so that, I assume, one could not say that they had a more important role than the other. The whole thing was a military hybrid born out of EDSI imperatives.

Rules of Engagement are where the "rubber meets the road." It is here that absolute clarity must be achieved in the political direction to the military. Soldiers', sailors' and airmen's lives are at stake. In an international coalition environment it is also the area where it is most difficult to get clarity. Each nation has its own agenda and national interests. Remembering that all Council members have a veto power, the use of air power in defence of safe havens in Bosnia is a good illustration of the difficulties encountered. Everyone, including the NAC, had difficulty understanding the UN resolution on safe havens. Even after listening to hours of debate on the subject in the NAC, I still do not understand what the political objective to this concept was. In addition, while trying to draft military guidance for the concept, I always stumbled when it came to the issue of command. Every military educational system stresses the need for unity of command, one person responsible. That did not politically work during this debate between UN advocates and NATO advocates. UN was not going to put its troops under command of a NATO commander. A new phrase, "Unity of Effort" was coined and eventually the infamous "dual key" trigger mechanism (where both UN and NATO must agree to strike a target) was the compromise. For those who had troops on the ground UN veto power of an air strike seemed logical. For those providing the air power it was a problem. This lack of collective political will long delayed an effective coercive measure from encouraging the belligerents to negotiate.

Development of collective political will is the key to action. The more risk involved the more difficult it is to achieve. Remember the situation then. The

Bush administration found itself in an election campaign that continued to refer to the Bosnia issue as a European problem. The EC was not able to transfer the European Security and Defense Identity theory into practice. None of the Europeans, except France, were willing to contribute significant numbers of troops. The UN was largely ineffective, limiting itself to humanitarian relief. Strangely enough, all the UN resolutions concerning Bosnia were under Chapter VII—meaning they did not require the belligerent's agreement. But these resolutions were seldom accompanied by either the correct rules of engagement or the will to use force. After the Sarajevo marketplace bombing in February 1994, the "safe area" concept was produced. However, the will to exploit these initiatives was decidedly lacking. The dual key proved totally impractical. Indeed, limited use of NATO air power invariably led to UN hostages. The fall of Srebrenica was the low point.

I drew two key conclusions from my NATO experience. They are not revelations but, I am afraid, they are frequently ignored. They are:

1. *Political Direction*: A mission may not necessarily be successful merely because it is clearly enunciated, but it cannot be overemphasized that the mission is doomed without such clarity. Regardless of the difficulty of achieving consensus, the mission statement (in whatever format—resolution, declaration, proclamation, manifest, communication, etc.) must be unambiguous and unequivocal. Striving for this clarity will also provide cement to the political will. It goes without saying that the mission must be achievable and this infers (but sometimes slighted) solid military advice before the final political decision is taken.

2. *Political / Military Interface*: Rarely will the political direction be in a format that is readily transferable to the military as operational guidance. A mechanism is needed to provide the two-way dialogue necessary to draft this guidance. Similarly a body such as the NAC, usually made up of diplomats representing politicians, is not a good organization to exercise control over all the details of a military operation. However the NAC using the MC is a relationship that works well. It is important to note that the MC is a body operating outside of the international staffs but (on behalf of the NAC) it is able to task them and receive support from them.

NATO's first peace implementation force in Bosnia Herzegovina—IFOR—has undoubtedly been a turning point for NATO. Operation Joint Endeavour was a new, extremely important and challenging mission for NATO, an operation of firsts. It was the first ground-force operation in Alliance history. It was the first ever deployment out of area. It was the first time Allies have been joined by non-NATO nations in a peacekeeping mission. It was an operation that was quite unthinkable when I joined NATO HQ. Fifty-five thousand soldiers, sailors, airmen and civilians from all sixteen NATO nations, plus sixteen other nations including twelve PfP partners took part in the operation. The principal military tasks of separating the armed forces of the former warring factions and creating a stable environment have been, for the most part, achieved—particularly now with SFOR. I attribute this to a robust force, and the delegation of the decision to use force to "the senior soldier present." The operations in the Balkans, from my perspective, are going as well as can be expected. I believe that we shall be involved for a long while but do believe that they are making a difference and are accomplishing the political objective.

So the biggest gold nugget that I took away from my time at NATO is this—it behooves the military senior officer to be fully involved in the overall process (not just purely military operations). He or she must have knowledge of the world geo-political issues and use that knowledge to reach consensus in the alliance or coalition. The political objective must be influenced by what is militarily achievable. Once chosen, the political objective and resulting military mission have specific military capability requirements. Every effort must be made to ensure these requirements are not jeopardized by artificial, politically induced babble.

Political/military interface is at the strategic level (and in the case of coalition operations, at the operational level). NATO has a process—Strategic Assessment, Risk Assessment, Strategic Concept, Capability Planning Guidance, Defence Planning Questionnaire, etc. Recommending changes to that process is beyond the scope of this chapter. However, nationally, Canada can learn from this process and certainly improve its situation. There are two aspects we should look at, designing and implementing a process, and education.

Some will say that Canada has a process to develop a military strategy. I do not think so. Some will say the end result of the process is contained in the Departmental document *Shaping the Future of Canadian Defence: A Strategy for 2020*. I am sure this document is useful; however, it falls short of what I am advocating. The signatories state that the conclusions have flowed from a rigorous assessment of Canada's current strategic environment, from a review of the current defence mandate and missions, and a review of current geopolitical, technological and military trends. No doubt there are reams of background documents to this paper but the paper itself is only twelve pages long. There is one short page on the emerging strategic environment. Brevity and conciseness are admirable but, in this case, it is at the expense of clear explanations. There is reference to the *1994 White Paper* but there is no indication (other than the very general ones referring to the Defence Mission) that the principles in that document still apply (e.g. "multi-purpose, combat capable forces," "able to fight alongside the best against the best," "multi lateral operations," etc.).

One is looking for answers to some basic questions in *Strategy 2020*. What are the force structure imperatives? Why? What are the roles of the Reserves? What vulnerabilities and risk are we prepared to accept and what are the ones we cannot accept? What is our reinforcement policy? What is our mobilization policy? What is our reaction to global trends, such as EDSI? The list goes on.

There are four "five-year targets" in *Strategy 2020* that encourage me:

> Enhance the collective strategic decision-making ability of the senior leadership team.

> Define the long term strategy in five year increments, and review and update them periodically.

> Undertake joint planning with Other Government Departments, where appropriate, to achieve synergies and efficiency.

> Support a coordinated approach to national security strategy.

The key points in *Strategy 2020* need to be transferred into an integrated process at intra-governmental level. The requirements posed must somehow be translated into strategic *decisions* that will impact on today's budget decisions. Without such impact, long-range planning becomes an interesting, but largely sterile, exercise.

The second part of my proposal is to prepare the senior leadership *before* they become senior leaders, by education. Without question there is a requirement for field and senior officers to study the geo-political situations of our areas of interest. In addition, we need to study what we are going to do with that knowledge. In my day the strategic assessment process was taught at every level from staff college onward. Today, I am told senior leadership courses such as the National Security Studies Course do examine a strategic assessment process. I marvel that they are able to do so in the absence of intra-governmental approved inputs. Without a process that contains these elements the student would be forced to do so in a theoretical environment, or by studying how our allies do it.

In the final analysis there are two fundamental and competing approaches to the development of a mid-range military strategy and its supporting force structure and tasks. In the first the finance minister, in Cabinet, allocates a share of Canada's budget to defence (often after all the domestic and foreign programs are funded), and the minister and chief of defence are expected to "make do." The second approach (which I have never seen implemented in Canada but occasionally did see implemented in NATO) requires a confirmation of interests and a declaration of goals and objectives. A strategy would be developed to achieve those goals and a military strategy (with its force structure) would be created to implement it.

Unfortunately, budgets continue to dominate objectives and strategies. I acknowledge that professional military officers must demonstrate the mastery of their profession in the real world. However, a military strategy developed through the interest, objectives, strategy approach is the only way I know of that one can convincingly explain the logic of what we in the military are doing.

In the absence of such an approach we tend to flounder.

The Naval Commander in Joint Operations in The Gulf War

Rear-Admiral D.E. Miller

Rear-Admiral D.E. Miller is the current Chief of Staff SACLANT in Norfolk, Virginia.

IN AUGUST 1990, Her Majesty's Canadian Ships *Protecteur, Athabaskan* and *Terra Nova* sailed from Halifax to the Arabian Gulf in what became known to the sailors as the "Persian Excursion." Being in the right place, at the right time, with the right people was key to the success of Canada's contribution to the Gulf War. Following Operation Friction (as it was termed) the numerous anecdotes to describe the leadership challenges and events during the war determined the requirement for a written record. The Chief of the Defence Staff, General John de Chastelain, met the ships in Dubai following the war. He considered that the naval job given Canada was both significant and worth recording. The result was *The Persian Excursion*, published by the Canadian Institute for Security Studies and the Pearson Peacekeeping Centre Press. The chapter headings used in that book describe those command type issues, which are useful for this chapter.

There are three parts, therefore, to this chapter: a few words about each of the chapters in *The Persian Excursion* from an operational naval commander's perspective; a couple of anecdotes from the book and their application to recent operations; and, an updated reprint of the lessons learned during Operation Friction and Canada's naval contribution to a joint operation—the forerunner of the way we do business as a navy today.

PART I: THE PERSIAN EXCURSION

Chapter 1: "This is what they've paid me for, mum."

The title of this chapter came from a direct quote by then Lieutenant-Commander Jim Hayes when told he was off to war and had to console his mother! At the time there was a survey done by some polling company, which indicated twenty-five percent of the Forces people would refuse to go to a war in 1990. How wrong they were. There were so many volunteers to actually join the ships off to the Gulf that we had to be very selective.

This chapter details how we selected the right people with the right experience to be comfortable in the most demanding of operations—war. There is always a requirement in any operation to ensure that those in the leadership positions have both the right training and the right experience to handle the job. If these two criteria are not there then risk management becomes much more challenging. Doing something about this before an operation is essential!

Chapter 2: "Making Do With What You Have"

The Naval Dockyard in Halifax went on a refitting frenzy not seen since the Second World War. Luckily the navy was about to receive brand-new frigates which were contracted and under construction. Making do with what we had or rather what we could get our hands on was a fundamental criteria. The thirty-year-old ships were fitted with the very latest anti-missile systems obtained directly from the factory but destined previously to the new ship construction yard. Prior to any operational mission the commander must ask what else can be obtained in equipment, training or people to ensure the survivability and combat capability of the men and women who put their lives on the line. This is a duty and a unique responsibility.

Chapter 3: "With a Little Help From Our Friends"

One can always learn from those who went before. We obtained the post deployment reports from both the UK and US operations in the Arabian Gulf during the "Tanker War" and the UK Armilla Patrols. We had action teams in Halifax to pass on these lessons or to buy specific pieces of equipment for arrival in a 55°C environment. The air-conditioning plants in the ships were fully reconditioned for instance.

En route we took advantage of several NATO nations who helped us with services and training to prepare us fully for any eventuality. We pre-ran every scenario we could think of including all-out war in our Fleet School and Warfare Centre in Halifax before we left. Each watch from each ship went through this training. We knew how best to use each ship, the Task Group and our sailors for everything from boarding uncooperative merchant ships to firing missiles. Asking the "what if this happens" questions prior to any mission is essential. Knowing from your allies what those situations could be and asking for their help is also critical.

Chapter 4: "SCUDS, Sand and Sea Snakes"

What an apt description of the unreal world the ships entered. In fact any mission sails into the unknown. Nailing down what is known is essential.

SCUD missile launches by Iraq against its neighbours presented unique challenges. The ships needed to know when these ballistic missiles were fired, what trajectory they were on, and hence figure out the intended target. On several occasions these missiles headed towards Bahrain where our national joint commander was based with his staff. The ships had to react quickly to divert towards their rescue with a complete plan to do so if required. North American Air Defence Command provided immediate notice and trajectory. This was critical given one SCUD flew within one nautical mile of the ships!

Sand was the operating environment ashore. The occasional sand storm meant that even at sea the ship's air intakes had to be protected. We used foam inserts obtained from Canadian Tire stores before sailing (one of those very useful tips from our allies).

Sea snakes would bathe on the surface during hot calm sea days. Their bite is ten times more venomous than a rattlesnake's. They are called "two steppers"—if bitten you have two steps to live. We kept anti-venom aboard for morale purposes—our divers occasionally had to clear sea snakes alive and dead from the seawater intakes. Proper protection required—you bet! Knowing the environment and planning for it is critical.

Chapter 5: "We're a Canadian Group Here!"

We learned some lessons from the Second World War: ensure you make an identifiably Canadian significant contribution. The grid we set up to organize the Combat Logistic Force (some sixty ships at times) used the provinces of Canada down one side and numbers down the other. A US supply ship would request Alberta 5 for instance. Everyone knew Canadians were running this aspect of the operation!

More importantly, however, the Task Group remained intact and in overall control of this multinational combat logistic force. Sticking together for both mutual support, security and as a collective identifiable Canadian group was critical to success. The Canadian ships and helicopters conducted twenty-five percent of all the sanction challenges in the Gulf with only three percent of the multinational force assets. Canadians work tirelessly when faced with a mission and are noticed if they stick together rather than split up.

Chapter 6: "Reach Out and Touch Someone"

Reliable and secure communications were the key to information, knowledge and proper responses. Both long-range strategic and short-range tactical communications provided a tremendous challenge. As always our naval communicators and technicians had thought ahead, reacted and subsequently found that the ships had the best set-up of all the allies.

The link (data transfer) systems aboard provided a full picture of everything that could or would move in the Gulf. At one point there were two hundred and nineteen allied ships alone being tracked. Many of them did not have the equipment or capability to receive this information. Of all the allies Canada was best equipped to coordinate the logistics force.

The challenge will be to maintain this capability in the future. Canada aptly demonstrated keeping current in this regard when in 1999, both *Athabaskan* (updated from 1990) and *Iroquois* became flagships for NATO's immediate reaction force, Standing Naval Force Atlantic. As higher data rates and super computers increase in quantity and quality it will be essential to be transparently connected with our US counterparts.

Chapter 7: "Okay he wants the missiles—Take Off."

Any joint operation takes an enormous amount of cooperation. An upgraded solid state Sea Sparrow Anti-Aircraft Missile had been developed, trialed and available for *Athabaskan*. The timing, however, couldn't have been worse (or better depending on your perspective). The missiles had a fifty percent better range and would in fact be a huge improvement for our air defence in a war zone. They were available 10 January 1991, and every indication would have the UN Security Resolution to allow force to be used by the coalition in effect 15 January. Could we afford to take a chance on a new missile change so close to possible coalition hostilities? Could we afford not to?

Every commander in a mission has to ensure that all possible measures are taken to provide the best combat capability for both the mission and protection of the troops/sailors. Hence the phone call to headquarters in Halifax to the Chief of Operations, whom I could hear in the background instructing his staff (on the phone to CFB Trenton where the missiles were loaded in a Hercules aircraft which would or would not take off depending on my decision): "Okay he wants the missiles—take off." The missiles arrived 11 January, loaded aboard and successfully trialed in the following three days enabling *Athabaskan* to take charge as Command Ship on 15 January. Around midnight that evening the coalition fired at Iraq. Timing, cooperation, jointness, faith in sailors all came together incredibly well.

Chapter 8: "Good Day Captain. This is Canadian Warship ..."

Sometimes as a military dealing with civilians (non-DND) we tend to be terse, job-like, no-nonsense disciplinarians. A little more personable approach can reap enormous benefits. During joint operations with twenty-two navies serving in the Gulf, sending correspondence to other nations in their own language encouraged incredible cooperation. For instance, one example was the commander sending instructions on Combat Logistic Force operations to the Italians in Italian. Ensuring an Italian speaker in our Canadian ship did the talking by voice communications at sea to the Italian warships encouraged a sense of cooperation one could feel. Think about it. It's not just the two official NATO languages, which have become prominent in multinational coalitions.

We had our junior sailors practice being nice to merchant ship captains we wished to stop to search during the operation—hence Good Day/Evening Captain as a start. It works!

Chapter 9: "You're going to be busy."

Not only will any crisis be busy, but then it will get busier! Sailors and staff routinely worked twenty-hour days, months in a row. You cannot buy or pay for that kind of loyalty. It comes from the basic values of the profession.

The Canadian ships stayed together as an identifiable Task Group and in fact made a significant recognizable Canadian contribution. We were subsequently volunteered to take charge of the Combat Logistic Force. If the ships had been split up there would have been no requirement for the Task Group Commander or his staff. Taking on an enormous task was far better than returning home and hence continuing our contribution when the allies used force.

Pacing oneself mentally, physically and recognizing the requirement to sustain the effort with people, resources and equipment should be a principle of war despite the fact "you're going to be busy."

Chapter 10: "You guys need me here!"

In the navy the most junior sailor becomes Captain for the day for the ship's Christmas. This signifies to all that the youngest most junior sailor on board is as important to the ship's survival as the Captain.

Over the eight-month deployment there were a total of five people repatriated for what I would call a real emergency—near death of spouse, etc. This was truly a remarkably small number. On one occasion I had to personally convince a sailor to return home as his wife's life was medically in danger and still his response was "but you guys need me here." I explained that we indeed could cover his specialty, that his family at home was more important, that we understood and that he must return home and that I was ordering him to do so. He replied with "All right, but if it all works out I reserve the right to return." I agreed. He left. His wife came through the crisis and was fine. Two months later he came back to the Gulf! Gotta love sailors and their commitment to both their families!

Chapter 11: The Second Front—The Media

Paying or not paying close attention to all aspects of the media can make or break a campaign even if it is operationally successful. Interview every reporter who joins your command in an operational mission to do a story. Canadian lives cannot be subjected to danger because of a naive media news report. There is a fine line here of being distracted by the Second Front and being able to concentrate on the mission. If you as commander cannot deal with the media personally then make sure you pick a combat operator as a trusted agent who does. You will be able to affect your mission positively if you deal with the media up front, honestly and with a cooperative attitude even when you might not like what they print.

Chapter 12: The Day the War Ended—We Think!

Sea or land mines do not care if the war is over. When in the special duty zone remember it is just that—no time to let the guard down, not even to relax—you must leave the zone to do that! At the end of the Gulf War *Athabaskan* was a couple of miles off Kuwait City, under an acrid oil-burning cloud, partway through a sea minefield where a few weeks before a US ship had been severely damaged by a mine. It was not the time to celebrate that hostilities had ended, but rather a somber reminder that all is not over until you are home. When faced with such a challenge the mind tends to remember every detail. Try talking to veterans and you will get the impression that the events they experienced in the First or Second World War happened minutes ago, not years.

Such is the requirement to be forever "ready aye ready." The navy fosters this out of hard-learned lessons.

PART II: ANECDOTES

"Laundry and Morale" as they say in the Navy—It's the Thought that Counts

As with soldiers and sailors everywhere, keeping morale high over a lengthy deployment depends on regular contact with the people back home. Delivery of the mail was therefore given a high priority.

> You could feel the electricity in the air when the mail was due, and I made sure that we had a helicopter ready to go immediately to pick up the sacks. In fact, I was too quick to send the helicopter in to meet the aircraft the first time we had mail arriving.

The problem is there's bags of mail and they all have to be sorted along with the other supplies that came in on the flight. The supply techs had to figure out what went to which ship, and where each ship was, and then get it ready to go.

To have a helicopter sitting on the tarmac, burning fuel while they're unloading the cargo, was putting a lot of pressure on them. So I got a call from the commander of the Logistics Detachment. He said, "You know, really doing it fast, it takes us about three hours to get this stuff sorted out. So how about scheduling your aircraft four hours after the arrival?" So that's what we did. And when that helicopter arrived on board, there was no shortage of volunteers to unload it, sort the mail and distribute it. Within ten minutes the letters, care packages, and parcels would be all through the ship, and people would be whistling and cheerful. Then there would be a hush over the whole ship while they all read their mail.

> The sailors on watch in the ops room, however, would be tensed up because they wanted to read their mail, but they couldn't. So they devised a routine where they would relieve each other in the jobs that they were doing. They'd take a proper turnover, they'd keep their eyes down, looking at what was going on, and then someone would relieve them, within the watch on a 10-15 minute basis. So, if you were the

standby, you'd read your mail as fast as you could read it, and then whip in to relieve the next fellow. You had to do it that way. Mail meant everything.[1]

The Sea Kings were the key to a successful mail delivery system. The aircrew and technicians who maintained those hardworking machines became quite attached to them. In fact, that attachment was fostered by an idea launched by Lieutenant-Colonel McWha. He suggested that the technicians give each of the five aircraft a nickname prompted by the machine's personality. The first one to be named was aircraft 417. Because of its reliability and the way it always seemed to be hovering around during major operations, it was called "Big Bird" after the famous Sesame Street character who also seems to be constantly hanging around. Master-Corporal Pat "Rat" McCafferty, the resident artist, painted a picture of the character on the side of the Sea King. He designed other appropriate pictures for the other aircraft as they were named. "Hormuz Harry" had a goofy-looking camel, "Chicken Hawk" had an ugly, mean-looking little bird, "Lucky Louie" had a big, grinning, sharp-clawed, well-fanged, fat cat, and "The Persian Pig" was adorned with a silly, clumsy-looking pig.[2]

SPECIAL DATES WERE REMEMBERED. EVEN HALLOWEEN.

> Howard Dill of Windsor, Nova Scotia, who grows the world's biggest pumpkins, and who had just watched the local TV station broadcast a message from a sailor who suggested a pumpkin or two might remind them of home, called the Admiral and said, "Admiral I've got a 350 pound pumpkin here and I want to send it to those guys out in the Gulf." So they crated up this huge pumpkin along with a lot of little pumpkins, trucked them out to a Hercules aircraft, and sent them to Bahrain. I was in *Protecteur* with Captain Doug McClean at the time the crate arrived. We watched it craned on board and opened by the crew.
>
> The ship's cooks carved a beautiful design on the pumpkin—two maple leaves for the eyes—even carving 'Halloween' into the mouth—and while we were admiring it, the ship's air officer came up to me and said, "You know, sir, what we should do is fly that pumpkin around the Arabian Gulf for Halloween!"
>
> I looked at him and said, "If you think I'm going to authorize a pumpkin flight in the middle of the Arabian Gulf with 90 missile-firing ships out there, you've got to be crazy!"

He looked a little dejected, so I asked him, "Do you have a training flight to do tonight?" that night being Halloween night.

He shook his head, "No, sir, I don't have one scheduled tonight."

Doug McClean kicked him and said, "Of course you've got a training flight!"

The officer, not picking up the hint, continued to protest. "No, I don't." ... Then the penny dropped. "Well, I guess we could always do some crew training."

I said, "Well, if you've got training to do, I'll authorize a training flight for tonight and if you happen to have a 350-pound pumpkin in the rear end of that aircraft with the cargo door open, all lit up, and it flies around, that's okay."

So that's what we did. The pumpkin was put in the back and lit up with chemlights. And I sent more messages about that pumpkin to the ships to make sure it didn't get shot down than I did for just about any other flight we made.

So the Great Pumpkin flew around the ships in the central Gulf on Halloween night, and I got messages from our allies that went mostly like this: "You Canadians are crazy. You were crazy in the First World War, you were crazy in the Second World War, you're still crazy, and don't ever change."

There were other "crazy" moments.

When the media joined us in the Suez Canal, they did interviews with the ships' companies for the express purpose of showing them on local television so that the sailors could send a message back to their families to tell them they were doing okay. One sailor got in front of the camera and said he was okay, he was a little bored, and that he missed things back home like Greco pizza. He hadn't had a pizza as good as Greco for some time. The next thing you know, Greco Pizza was sending out the components of 1400 pizzas—dough, toppings, and cheese—complete with boxes decorated with a picture of a yellow ribbon. So we were able to have Greco pizza night in the middle of the Gulf. You could call down from the bridge for a pizza "all dressed" and the joke was, because it had taken more than 30 minutes to get there—it had taken more like 30 days from Halifax—it was free!

PART III: LESSONS FROM NAVAL OPERATIONS DURING GULF WAR 1990-1991

The Gulf War was one of many firsts for the Canadian Navy:

It was the first time Canadian ships, designed for anti-submarine warfare, sailed with the sophisticated Phalanx Close-In Weapon System for air defence.

It was the first time the Harpoon missile system was fitted in a Canadian ship and certified for use by Canadian operators.

It was the first time that many of the electronic sensors, including the Canadian Electronic Warfare System, were ever tested under operational conditions.

It was the first time a Canadian supply ship, HMCS *Protecteur*, was used operationally as a "destroyer" and as an alternate command ship.

It was the first time that the navy had employed Canadian Forces women in a combat zone.

It was the first time that the navy used the army to provide air defence on board ship.

It was the first time Canadians had been put in charge of a multi-national logistics force.

It was the first time since the Korean War that a Canadian ship, HMCS *Athabaskan*, sailed through a mined area in a combat zone.

It was the first time that the navy relied on satellite communications to provide real-time contact with commanders back home and at sea.

And, finally, it was the first time that Canada used a tri-service joint system of command, putting into the operational theatre a representative of the Chief of the Defence Staff to command a national effort.

Not only did the navy rise to meet these challenges, but it succeeded beyond all expectations. The result will be long lasting. Sending three ships and their helicopters to participate in the allied action against Iraq provided an opportunity to use skills and equipment that for nearly 40 years, the navy had only exercised under peacetime conditions. From this initiation into the operational side of modern warfare sprang a number of key lessons which continue to serve as the basis for shaping Canada's future navy.

When you're needed, you go with what you have.

When the order came to deploy to the Gulf, the navy was awaiting delivery of its new City class patrol frigates and modernized Tribal class destroyers. These ships, equipped with anti-submarine warfare systems, area air defence systems, and point defence systems, as well as helicopters for over-the-horizon reconnaissance and tracking, give the navy a true general purpose capability. In 1990, however, the navy had to make do.

> *We once again learned that for any wartime venture you go with what you have, or more aptly, with what you can lay your hands on at the time. While we sailed in ships over 30 years old, we did manage to divert the latest in anti-missile defence systems to the ships in a dockyard fitting spree not seen since the Second World War. We found ourselves in the fortunate state of having equipment versions more modern than any aboard the US ships despite the ages of our hulls.*[3]

Luck was on the navy's side in at least one area: in 1990, there were no submarines in the Arabian Gulf. Consequently, the Canadian ships and aircraft did not need most of their anti-submarine warfare equipment. By removing some of those systems, Maritime Command and Maritime Air Group had more room to fit air defence and mine detection systems. It is unlikely that the navy will be so lucky in future. More than forty countries, in all regions of the world, now possess submarines. Even the Arabian Gulf is not immune from this proliferation. In the few years since the Gulf War, Iran has taken steps to acquire at least three submarines. Thus, in future multinational operations, Canadian ships will likely need their anti-submarine warfare capability.

The navy will also need to keep its other defensive equipment up-to-date because old threats never entirely disappear. Iraq's nuclear and chemical weapons capability may have been destroyed after the war, but Baghdad is already attempting to rebuild. Other countries are also interested in acquiring these weapons of mass destruction. For those that can't afford a nuclear research program, there are always the cheap and plentiful chemical weapons—often referred to as the poor man's nuclear bomb.

Such a threat means the Canadian Forces must maintain a nuclear-biological-chemical (NBC) defensive capability. In the navy that means having ships that are able to close up and maintain a contaminant-free environment for extended periods of time. And for both the navy and Maritime Air Group, it means supplying NBC defence suits and masks to the officers and crews, as well as providing realistic training opportunities.

The Arabian Gulf operations proved once again that sea control remains a key naval role, both at home and abroad. Sea control—the ability to control who uses an area of ocean—is the basis of most of Canada's maritime activities and requires a surface, sub-surface, and air capability. In the Gulf, the allies used their aircraft and ships to prevent the Iraqis from bringing in supplies, exporting goods, and attacking the coalition ships. An anti-sub-surface capability was not needed because, as previously mentioned, no one in the region had any submarines.

Off the Canadian coasts, sea control remains a prime naval function. Using ships, submarines, aircraft and electronic sensors, the navy is able to keep abreast of what is going on in Canadian-claimed waters. By having multi-capable ships and aircraft, it is able to help enforce Canadian laws and protect Canadian interests. Without that naval ability to control its ocean areas, Canadian sovereignty would be infringed.

Ships that are able to exercise sea control, to sail in self-supporting task groups, and to defend themselves in a modern war, are also of further benefit: they can be used as floating command centres for land operations in hostile territory. The navy provided just such a service to the army in Somalia, offering *Preserver's* facilities for command, control and communications, and providing armed Sea King helicopters for reconnaissance and support to the ground troops.

At the base of all of this, however, lies one key factor: the navy must not lose its combat skills, because when needed, they are needed quickly and there will be no time to reacquire those that have been lost. Allowing, for example, its blue water anti-submarine warfare abilities to wither in order to concentrate on a coastal protection role, would leave the navy with limited options in an international crisis. As General John de Chastelain told a parliamentary committee:

> ... even if you have a small force that is combat capable, and that maintains all the capabilities of structure, organization, equipment, doctrine and policy, you have the capability to expand on it. If you do away with that capability, you do not have the capability to put it back quickly. If we can be certain of our future and certain of the threat that this country may face or this country's allies may face, in which they would wish us to play a role, then we can be less concerned about combat capability. If we cannot be that certain, then I suggest we must be very careful in doing away with it.[4]

It is important to have self-supporting task groups.

Navies rarely send one ship to participate in an exercise or operation.

Rather, a country will send a task group or task force made up of varying numbers of ships. By taking this approach during the Arabian Gulf War, Canada was able to make a distinctive national contribution to the allied effort.

A key component of the Canadian Task Group was the supply ship *Protecteur*. She provided the fuel, food, spare parts and other supplies necessary to keep *Athabaskan* and *Terra Nova*, as well as five Sea King helicopters, operational during the extended deployment.

> *Our Canadian-invented one-stop-shop replenishment ship again was more valuable than gold. By modifying Protecteur to have an operational and alternate command capability, as well as self-defence capabilities, she provided triple worth. She was used as a replenishment ship in the Central Gulf—the only one for the first couple of months—and as a "destroyer" for challenging shipping during the interdiction phase. Finally, and even more valuable, she was the maintenance supporter vessel for air operations.*

Without a Canadian supply ship as part of the mission, the destroyers would have had to rely on the allies for fuel and other consumables, and the Sea Kings would not have attained the high flying rate that they did. By using the maintenance facilities on board *Protecteur*, the technicians kept the helicopters flying. Lieutenant-Colonel Larry McWha, the Task Group Air Commander, stated it "showed what you could achieve at sea if you had the right mix of qualifications and the right kind of tools." By having the shop trades—the machinists and metalsmiths—right on hand, "there was no delay while waiting for the right person and equipment; you could fix things immediately instead of having to nurse them along while waiting." This capability was perhaps best demonstrated by having periodic inspections done at sea—the first time ever. McWha says it "changed our way of looking at inspections; putting aircraft on the line so that there's more time available for flight operations rather than sitting in a hangar waiting for a scheduled maintenance."

The importance of having operational Auxiliary-Oiler-Replenishment (AOR) ships cannot be overestimated. Former Commander of Maritime Command, then Vice-Admiral John Anderson, underlined the AOR's importance when he noted the limitations which would face the navy if it carried through on plans to pay-off HMCS *Provider*. He said without a replacement the navy will have to hope that it won't be caught in a time of crisis with its two remaining supply ships in dry dock for repairs, scheduled or otherwise. If that were to happen, one option would be to "do nothing." He said, "Where you might have been asked to take on a task, [you would have to say] 'No, I can do it in six months when I have a tanker back but I can't do it now'." If a crisis erupts, however, and Canada is asked to help out, the first choice would be to work with allies. Another option would be to adapt operations to fit the circumstances, but as Anderson said, "clearly, it limits your ability."[5]

Alliance ties and exercises are an essential proving ground for multinational operations.

If ever there was a need to prove that NATO provides an irreplaceable service to international security, look no further than the Arabian Gulf War. For many years NATO has been a proving ground for multinational operations. The allied training and procedures, with their emphasis on interoperability, served as the base upon which the eighteen navies in the Gulf—not all of them NATO members—conducted their successful operation.

Canada's allied ties also proved immensely useful during the Task Group's training en route to the Gulf.

> *Our Western allies were of incredible help. The British provided their Fleet Readiness and Air Defence Unit (FRADU) resources for operational work-ups outside Gibraltar—everything from full missile attacks on the ships to identifying surprise press aircraft. The French provided their Exocet missile simulator aircraft for several valuable hours of anti-ship missile training off Toulon. In Djibouti, the French Admiral operating in the Indian Ocean gave a full briefing for the ships' captains concerning special Gulf operating requirements. The Italians provided the NATO degaussing range in Augusta to calibrate the ships' anti-mine capabilities. The Americans provided invaluable assistance prior to departure by summarizing their lessons for us from years of operations in the Gulf, including the tanker war. Finally, all of the navies in the Gulf provided training in situ which will provide a base for future multinational operations.*

One of the reasons that Canadians were given a key role in the naval war against Iraq was that the ships' communications equipment allowed them to communicate with all of the allies. This flexibility was no accident.

> *Over the years we have consciously sought to have our equipment compatible with that of the United States. This proved invaluable given that the communications, cryptographic, and weapons systems need a common basis for both operations and maintenance. When we were getting ready for the Gulf, we added some British equipment, knowing that they would be major players in the crisis. Some countries, with only national-*

type communications equipment were hamstrung during the war given that they could not receive the complete range of information available.

And finally, the most important lesson of all:

Good People are the Navy's Most Valuable Asset

The ships were jury rigged with a mix of old and new equipment and the crews given a short burst of intensive training for their new role. By any measure, the odds were stacked against the Task Group's success. But added to the mixture was another "first," that in another organization, another country, could have sunk the mission before it even got started. By an extraordinary coincidence, all three ships going to the Gulf had new commanding officers.

Captain Doug McClean, Commanding Officer of *Protecteur*, had never commanded an auxiliary oiler replenishment vessel before. He took command on July 7, straight from his work at NATO headquarters for the Supreme Allied Commander Atlantic (SACLANT) in Virginia Beach, Norfolk. His Executive Officer, Commander Frank Scherber, was a submariner who suddenly found himself on the surface of the sea aboard the largest vessel in the Canadian Navy. Commander John Pickford, who had previously been the Executive Officer of *Protecteur*, had taken over command of *Athabaskan* just that summer, and hadn't yet taken the ship to sea before being told he was taking her to a war zone. Commander Stu Andrews took command of *Terra Nova* that summer after serving as Executive Officer of *Athabaskan*. Finally, not only did the ships all have new commanding officers, but so did the squadron—Miller was brand-new to his job.

That the naval task group was able to acquit itself so well, given all the odds against it, was due to the quality of the navy's people and their training. Miller is enthusiastic in his praise. He stated that "the ships' companies were incredible: well-educated, tremendous initiators and great thinkers. Individually the people were ingenious, collectively they rank with the best in the world."

Protecteur's Captain Doug McClean is of the same opinion. He says every day somebody would come up with a good idea, everyone from the ship's officers to young leading seamen. McClean stated that the young men and women on board the ships were:

...intelligent young people who, because of the training system we have in our Navy, were given the opportunity to think; they weren't just robots. They didn't learn by rote. All of our training meant 'let's leave a little room for a person to think.' And if I hadn't had that we'd have never got it right, because there's no way I or just my officers could come up with all the solutions, all the things undone that we had to fix.

That attitude and enthusiasm provided McClean with the trust and confidence needed to do the job of using a supply ship in both its intended role and in the role of a destroyer/escort. He recalled:

When we pulled into the Gulf I felt that my ship was about 85 percent combat ready, in terms of being able to fight the ship to the best ability of the systems that we had. We busted our butts to get there and were then down to fine-tuning. We were still finding out a few little wrinkles about some of the weapons systems, slightly better ways to maneuver the ship perhaps, and some of the young guys were still being trained up. By the time the first patrol was over, I'm sure we were 100 percent, and we maintained that for the rest of the time I was there.

What was true aboard *Protecteur*, was also true aboard *Athabaskan* and *Terra Nova*. The men and women who sailed in the Task Group learned quickly, adapted easily, and worked unselfishly.

The sailors we had in the Gulf did a remarkable job of keeping old equipment running. The old ship HMCS Terra Nova—*boiler driven, 45 degrees Celsius in the engine room. They kept that going almost without a hitch. She was out of commission, I think, for a day maybe, on a small engineering item. And that is just remarkable pioneer stamina of Canadians and I wouldn't want to change that. That's the way we are.*

NOTES

1. All block quotes in Part 2 indicate personal anecdotes.
2. My thanks go to Lieutenant-Colonel Larry McWha for his descriptions of these characters.
3. Italics are my anecdotes from the Gulf.
4. Special Joint Committee on Canada's Defence Policy, Minutes Issue No. 1 (March 16, 1994), 25.
5. "Aging supply ships weaken navy's support capability" by Parker Robinson, in *Halifax Chronicle Herald* (July 14, 1992), A1. The navy has since decided that *Provider*, the oldest of the three replenishment ships, will continue in service for a few more years.

The Theatre Commander in Conflict Resolution[1]

Lieutenant-General (retired) Roméo A. Dallaire

Lieutenant-General (retired) Roméo A. Dallaire retired from the Canadian Forces in April 2000 after 36 years of service. His last position was that of Special Advisor to the CDS on Officer Professional Development.

INTRODUCTION

WE CANADIANS POSSESS A MASTERY of technology, a strong work ethic, a regard for individual rights, and perhaps an uncommon sense of altruism. These qualities are reflected in our military commitments, which, in the last few years, have been oriented toward peace support operations rather than toward traditional warfighting. The lessons we have learned and the skills we have acquired during the past decade will prove crucial in solving the complex military problems of the future. I believe that Canada's recent experiences in military operations are likely to be the norm for the decades to come.

Accordingly, by reviewing my experiences as Commander of the United Nations Assistance Mission for Rwanda in 1993/94, as well as discussing some of the lessons learned from my experience with conflict resolution in that mission, I hope to identify some of the skills that I feel are important for success in these often very complex circumstances. Mine is fundamentally a Canadian perspective, given by a senior officer from a Western middle-power nation that has recently advanced its own global security, political and economic interests in the context of peace support operations. There is a real sense of leadership desire by the government and the nation to open a whole new era of conflict resolution doctrine. This is a challenge that must both be studied and prepared for by the senior military leadership of the Canadian Armed Forces (CAF).

BACKGROUND

In October 1993, the United Nations sent a lightly armed peacekeeping force to Rwanda to assist in implementing peace accords between the Rwandan government (controlled by Hutus, the country's largest ethnic group) and the Rwandan Patriotic Front, commonly known as the RPF (chiefly ethnic Tutsis who had fled the country after the Hutus overthrew them in the 1960s). The peacekeeping force, the United Nations Mission for Rwanda, (UNAMIR) was comprised of 2,500 troops. As per normal Chapter VI rules[2], they were forbidden to use force except in self-defence. This, however, was not fully reflected in my Rules of Engagement (ROE) as the use of force in situations of crimes against humanity was added by myself. The actual peace accords, signed after a two-year civil war, were meant to end hostilities that were rooted in longstanding political and ethnic tensions. But Hutu extremists resisted the power-sharing arrangements.

Fatefully, on 6 April 1994, the presidents of Rwanda and neighbouring Burundi were killed when their plane was shot down. This event set off a 100-day tidal wave of violence that saw the civil war resume while behind the lines, government extremist forces massacred more than 800,000 Tutsis and moderate Hutus, including the acting prime minister and ten of the Belgian soldiers UNAMIR assigned to protect her. Belgium, a key UNAMIR contributor, promptly withdrew its forces. Two weeks after the Belgian soldiers were killed, the UN Security Council cut UNAMIR back to two hundred and seventy troops, with no change in its mandate.[3] One account succinctly captured the resulting dilemma: "Some UN camps shelter civilians, but most of the UN peacekeeping forces ... [can only] stand by while the slaughter goes on. They are forbidden to intervene, as this would breach their 'monitoring' mandate."[4] Not until 17 May 1994, amid a growing international outcry, did the UN finally agree to send 5,500 troops (UNAMIR II) to Rwanda. But disputes over costs, participation and support from the powerful nations delayed the troops' deployment. On 22 June 1994, the UN Security Council authorized France to deploy 2,500 troops (Operation Turquoise) to Rwanda as an interim peacekeeping force, under Chapter VII with a two-month UN mandate.

The war ended on 18 July 1994. "The RPF took control of a country ravaged by war and genocide.[5] Up to 800,000 had been murdered, in excess of 500,000 were injured physically and another 2 million or so [both Tutsi and Hutu] had fled. Another million or so were displaced internally"[6] and it is impossible to determine how many suffered deep psychological injury. In sum, this casualty list represents a substantial proportion of the country's population, which was an estimated 7.9 million before the war. Even after the hostilities ended, the return of the displaced persons and the "repatriation of these refugees [were] marred by periodic outbursts of violence"[7] that continued well into 1995. UNAMIR II took over the original mission. It also took on the responsibility of the protection zone created by Operation Turquoise once the French forces left on 22 August. The mission itself continued until 8 March 1996.

In November 1994, the UN Security Council set up the International Criminal Tribunal for Rwanda (ICTR), which meets in Arusha, Tanzania, to prosecute those responsible for the genocide. Trials are ongoing.[8]

In May 1998, UN Secretary-General Kofi Annan apologized to Rwanda's parliament, saying that "[t]he world must deeply repent this failure. ... Now we know that what we did was not nearly enough.... [I]n their hour of need, the world failed the people of Rwanda."[9] In the eyes of too many leaders in the world, the guilt will end with the final tribunal results. Unfortunately, 800,000 black Africans will become even more lost in time than the Armenian genocide. Undeniably, this reflects my own pessimistic assessment of the self-interest that will always remain in the forefront of Western nations.

THE NATURE OF CONFLICT RESOLUTION OPERATIONS

In conflict resolution, troops are typically deployed in a theatre of operations (for example, into Rwanda) as part of an international coalition. They operate under a complex mandate with demanding milestones, together with multidisciplinary partners (for example, political groups, humanitarian organizations, police, and organizations dedicated to rebuilding the area's infrastructure), and under continuous media scrutiny. If coalition soldiers are not intimately familiar with the demanding rules of engagement (ROEs) and have virtually no inventory of non-lethal weapons to control their use of force, they are doomed to mishandle ambiguous tactical-level actions and possibly jeopardize the success of the entire mission.

In this type of operation, many factors can conspire to compromise a commander's ability to make correct decisions. I have already mentioned the impact of complex and too often confusing ROEs on the average soldier. The problem worsens if field commanders also experience confusion in interpreting these rules. Because of the numerous levels of responsibility and accountability commanders must shoulder in the field, confusion breeds caution; hence these commanders inevitably perform at a margin of safety well below the mandated level of use of force. This phenomenon spreads until the whole coalition operates well below the level of force necessary to accomplish the mission. Add to this the ever-present media analysis of each military decision and the equally ever-present concern of national governments and populaces over casualties, it is not surprising to find coalitions performing at much lower effectiveness than the actual forces deployed. It can get so bad that the mission itself becomes a secondary priority to "ensuring the security of our troops." The end result is that these pressures undermine the commander's ability to determine the best operational method for accomplishing the job.

CLASSIC WARFARE SKILLS ARE NOT ENOUGH

The conventional wisdom—widespread among most militaries—is that training for war is more difficult than training for operations other than war or for conflict resolution. I believe the opposite to be true. The skills required for peace support operations demand a much broader range and depth of knowledge—and a much richer set of experiences—than those acquired in conventional warfighting training programs. Militaries must ensure that their personnel also develop linguistic, cultural, and analytic skills that are unique to peace support operations —skills that are not currently taught in military education and training programs.

In 1990, Canada's armed forces were tasked to provide aid to the civil power when a provincial government was unable to handle an insurrection by Aboriginal Canadians in Oka and near Montréal, Québec. Two key aspects of this operation made it unique. First, it was deemed crucial that no martyrs be made of the individuals involved in the insurrection. Second, as a result of this decision, it was ordered that in the event of a violent confrontation, our troops would take the first casualty—before any response with weapons could be made. In other words, we were sending troops in harm's way, and we were deliberately eliminating the most fundamental component of any rule of engagement, namely, that self-defence is a sufficient reason for a response with lethal weapons. Although I did not realize it at the time, this event was a significant portent of the future.

Next came the 1991 Gulf War, an event that I contend was an anomaly in the post Cold War era, just as future conflict scenarios involving classic warfighting will most likely be exceptions. Although there may be similar crises in the next ten to twenty years, conflict resolution, not warfighting, will be the main context for the employment of our forces. Armed forces will always need to maintain and develop warfighting skills in order to respond to national security problems, and such responses could include offshore allied and coalition operations. But if, as I believe, the majority of military operations in the next couple of decades involve conflict resolution, then a serious disconnect exists between our current training and educational approaches, even as they are more and more based on the philosophy of the revolution in military affairs (RMA) and the human skills necessary for successfully executing conflict resolution operations. I believe that we need in the immediate instance to realign and broaden the education of the Canadian officer corps to more closely reflect a fundamental balance of competencies of the type and complexity that, realistically, we will end up facing. Although the skill sets of classic warfighting, along with the credibility they provide, will certainly remain essential and fundamental for all militaries, they will serve only as the necessary starting point for mastery of the more complex dimensions of conflict resolution. Warfighting skills and equipment mastery alone are simply not enough to meet the Canadian demands of its military operations.

Martin Van Creveld in his book *The Transformation of War* (1991) provides a convenient starting point for pondering a new doctrine for conflict resolution operations in which many modern militaries are now becoming involved. Van Creveld argues that in certain countries, the nation-state structure; that is, the triumvirate of the nation, the people, and the armed forces, is only partly formed. Africa represents one region where many nation-states have not yet really matured and where, for example, the government is not responsible to the people.[10] As a result, either by interest, or due to pressures emanating from the globalization of bureaucracies from progressive non-governmental organizations (NGOs), militaries will undoubtedly find themselves embroiled in the trauma of these African nations as they adjust to the democratic processes that usually entail significant new philosophies of power sharing and respect of the individual.[11] The breakdown in Rwanda is a particularly brutal example of political trauma resulting from ineffective power sharing and ethnic frictions. We can expect that similar scenarios are likely to recur in the future.

The Rwandan crisis represents a catastrophic failure by the international community, who were unwilling to deploy even a small component of their enormous collective diplomatic and military power to contain the situation. Unfortunately, Rwanda was incontestable proof that self-interest—not human rights—remains the dominant criterion determining the involvement of world powers in such crises. The March 1994 US Presidential Decision Directive 25,[12] published barely three weeks before the genocide has rendered the above criteria official policy in the world's most powerful nation. As a consequence, independent middle powers and countries that are committed to human rights, such as Canada, may find themselves increasingly involved in these new types of conflict resolution situations, although they may lack the resources needed to achieve success, combined with an ever increasing unwillingness to tolerate military casualties. My experience in Rwanda has convinced me that we must expand our skills beyond those of classic warfighting, including a whole new lexicon of action verbs if the government continues to send the Canadian Forces into these types of situations.

CULTURAL AWARENESS

In Rwanda I quickly found that my initial view of the country was biased by history and by naive preconceptions. To me, much of Africa was the domain of missionaries and non-government organizations (NGOs) and it had been the victim of ruthless resource extraction by colonial powers. But as I discovered, the quality of the political leadership in Rwanda (as well as in many other African nations) was very high. Since the numerous revolutions against colonial rule that occurred during the late 1950s and early 1960s, many of the country's leaders had been educated in North American and European institutions. The astuteness of the political and military leaders of the belligerent groups in Rwanda was quite evident in the way they counteracted Operation Turquoise, a UN Chapter VII coalition of French-led forces, many of whom were also participants in my Chapter VI mission. Operation Turquoise attempted to maintain a protection zone against the Tutsi-led rebel forces of the Rwandan Patriotic Front (RPF) and to protect nearly two million displaced Hutus. As the Chapter VI[13] UNAMIR Force Commander, I negotiated the separation and monitored, with my small force, the line between General Paul Kagame's rebel forces (RPF) and the forces of Operation Turquoise, which included Jaguar jets, helicopter gunships, heavy mortars, armoured personnel carriers (APCs) and 2,500 special forces troops. There were a number of confrontational situations during Operation Turquoise's two-month stay in Rwanda, including two occasions when the rebels beat the French, in the field, capturing over twenty

French soldiers. These incidents demonstrated that the best Western equipment and training do not necessarily lead to success. As General Kagame so shrewdly and ruthlessly pointed out, "Kigali [the Rwandan capital] can handle more body bags than Paris can." Many factors besides raw military power can influence success in complex conflict resolution situations: power sharing amongst the élites, protection of the moderate elements, cultural pre-conditionings and societal sensitivities are among the most influential. As an example, the enormous influence of the radio in a largely illiterate agrarian nation such as Rwanda, was appreciated far too late.

Experience with peace support operations in remote nations suggests that military leaders need additional cultural (such as anthropology, social science, philosophy) and linguistic skills. For example, the local translators usually are (or are perceived to be) biased toward one faction or another either voluntarily or through coercion. But this does raise a dilemma. Should we expect our officers to master all the common international languages (like Spanish), let alone languages as rare as Kinyarwanda? In Canada, simply implementing national bilingualism continues to pose challenges long after the policy was originally mandated. But militaries cannot gain nor keep the initiative essential for mission success if they are unaware of the cultural nuances and the subtle messages that are being passed around them with impunity by the ex-belligerents. The solution is to provide either a broadly educated (specifically in the humanities) officer corps that is linguistically adept or build a special group of civilian/military experts in such matters. Of the two, the former option is less risky to failure and more flexible. The eventual size of the CAF and the limitations on the defence budget may well determine which of these options is feasible, practicable or realistic.

RISK, MANDATE AND MORAL AMBIGUITY

Issues of risk, mandate, and moral ambiguity were even prevalent during the UNAMIR mission. For example, after Juvénal Habyarimana, the Rwandan president, was killed on April 6, 1994, the only legal authority left in the country was the coalition Prime Minister, Agathe Uwiliyingimana. She was considered key to preventing the country from sliding into civil war. It was essential that she be protected and moved to a radio station under UNAMIR escort so that she could speak to her people. By that time our specific Chapter VI mandate was over, so what was to be UNAMIR's official role in this situation? War was imminent: both sides were ready to renew the fighting, and ceasefire violations had escalated both in Kigali and in the demilitarized zone (DMZ). Twelve hours later, the Rwandans did indeed go to war, and the killing of civilians gained momentum. Technically, we could have simply packed up and left.

From the start I decided to protect the Prime Minister by sending in my best troops, the Belgian contingent. This decision was fraught with moral and ethical dilemmas. What justification did I have for risking soldier's lives to protect the Prime Minister, as our formal mandate was not applicable anymore? I hoped to prevent open war and the mass killings of an ethnic minority, but was I overstepping the limit of my mandate? Tragically, by midmorning on 7 April, the extremists had captured and killed the coalition prime minister and her husband. In addition, ten of the Belgian peacekeepers who had been guarding her were massacred after being disarmed and tortured by the extremists. By 1600 hours that day, negotiations had broken down and civil war had begun in earnest. In fact, the murder of all the Tutsi and moderate Hutu political and judicial leaders accelerated. In the end, was my decision to try to protect the Prime Minister the right decision? Though the attempt was unsuccessful, was it at least morally correct? It remains my firm conviction that my decision to protect the Prime Minister in the pursuit of peaceful resolution of this crisis was absolutely correct. The loss of those ten Belgian heroes and the plunge of this small over-populated nation into four months of civil war and resultant genocide, at the cost of millions of Rwandans dead, injured, displaced and refugeed, remains the horrific legacy of my failure to achieve my mission.

At that point I made the decision to extract the future prime minister, Faustin Twagiramungu (who had been designated by an August 1993 peace accord to fill this position), from his encircled home and bring him to my headquarters. The extremists heard about this intercession and began verbal and military attacks on both my headquarters and me. I therefore asked the contingents in my headquarters to defend the headquarters and the prime minister designate. Was I authorized to order the contingents to do so? UNAMIR no longer had a mandate. Would my troops have fought to defend the headquarters at the risk of being wiped out? What were their own national orders at that point in time? What arguments could I have offered to persuade them to stand their ground and fight should they have wavered? Ultimately, why should they risk their lives to follow a Canadian or any other foreign general[14] when their own nation was not at risk, their government did not want casualties, and our chances on the ground of success were minimal?

In the end, some contingents were withdrawn and others belatedly replaced them. After six days of sporadic mortar and artillery attacks and attempts by the belligerents to overrun the headquarters we removed the prime minister designate from the country by subterfuge, and the rebel forces overwhelmed the extremists in our area. However, in the face of such crimes against humanity, should commanders continue to put their troops' lives at risk from a sense of moral duty, or should they cease operations, protect themselves, and withdraw because they no longer have a mandate? Such conflicting mandate and moral situations presented themselves several times a day throughout Rwanda at all levels of command.

Thirteen days later, after the presidential plane crash of 6 April 1984, on the ground as both the civil war and the slaughter gained momentum, I was ordered to withdraw all forces. I refused to comply with this order. We had about 30,000 Rwandans from both sides under our protection. Our departure would have guaranteed their death, as had already happened at one site when a military contingent, without orders but under national direction, retreated and left nearly 4,000 Rwandans to their fate. We found about 2,000 bodies a few weeks later. The UN headquarters accepted my offer to keep a reduced complement of approximately 450 troops and withdraw the rest. The 1,300 French and Belgian forces that had been evacuating white Europeans and certain Rwandans had by then withdrawn, together with the UN Belgian contingent. My tattered and logistically depleted force knew that no reinforcements or supplies would be forthcoming. And throughout it all, we received no formal mandate. I called our situation the "counter crimes against humanity operation," and my soldiers believed in that mission. Although a number of them became casualties over the months to follow, they pursued the mission with tireless courage. Clearly, no national government would have deserted their troops in the manner we were deserted by the world community in Rwanda.

These types of dilemmas will continue to confront commanders in conflict resolution situations, particularly when risk assessment is required.

How far should a commander go in negotiating with a belligerent leader (one with blood on his hands from the morning's slaughter) to save a couple of thousand people, when the commander knows that this same belligerent is killing others by tens of thousands?

How far should a commander risk the lives of his or her own international troops in order to save a few people when the belligerents are slaughtering thousands of others?

A more informed and open debate on risk assessment is essential. Canada's armed forces are being committed to theatres of operation where no direct threat to Canada exists. Indeed, I would suggest that Canadians are frequently unaware that their forces are even deployed on such operations. How can commanders in such situations reasonably balance the risks in an operation? Lacking a direct threat to their country's national security, should their priorities change from the time-honoured military ethos of "my mission, my personnel, myself" to "my personnel, my mission, myself"? In my opinion, we have entered a dangerous and delicate period with respect to conflict resolution; one which deserves early examination by all participants in UN operations. This is a situation that we ignore at our peril.

Commanders must be aware that their decisions will be influenced by such factors as national politics and international relations, factors that could well seem quite distant from the situation on the ground at the moment. International agencies and NGOs will lobby and act independently of the military plan and without consultation or, at best, with only a cursory acknowledgment of military help. Commanders therefore have to balance many paradoxical questions. How many casualties will the different national contingents in a multinational operation absorb before actually pulling out? What will inspire troops to commit themselves to enormous personal risks when they know that other nations will withdraw after (or even before) they take casualties? Should commanders spare the lives of their troops and possibly sacrifice the mission, but then face their nation's and possibly the world's moral acrimony? Or should they commit their troops to achieving the mission using the classic casualty assessment techniques for success? To help them make such decisions do commanders need a whole new set of rules, equations, and doctrine for conflict resolution situations?

INCURRING CASUALTIES

The political impact of incurring casualties in conflict resolution is guaranteed to be an overriding factor in a commander's decision making. As General Kagame understood, the Western world cannot cope with casualties. This explains why the United States pulled out of Somalia in October 1993 (six months before the events that precipitated the genocide in Rwanda) with eighteen killed and seventy-two injured, and why the Belgians decided to pull out of Rwanda within a few days of having lost ten soldiers. I found it ironic that in the latter part of the war in Rwanda, when American NGOs were all over the countryside, there was no US military presence in Rwanda itself,[15] other than a few hundred US military police and technicians securing the immediate perimeter of the Kigali airfield and assisting in the unloading of NGO personnel and supplies as part of the humanitarian airlift. Furthermore, the troops that were there were under absolute orders to take no casualties.

As a final example, I faced a situation where one contingent possessed the capability to provide UNAMIR with a supply of water—water that was urgently needed, because hundreds of the displaced persons under our protection were dying of thirst every day. But this particular contingent was officially forbidden to assist us, no matter how many people were dying, because of the grave concern about suffering casualties.

This overriding concern for the avoidance of casualties will have continuing implications for the employment of our armed forces in conflict resolution operations where contributing nations are not at risk and where they have no other self-interest. It will affect simple, routine tactical decisions, such as whether or not to escort a convoy, and it will inevitably raise difficult moral questions and operational dilemmas. It will limit the commander's options in any given situation and could well place unnecessary lives at risk.

AMBIGUITY FOSTERS UNCERTAINTY

Within the glossary of classic warfare there is an array of familiar action verbs such as *attack, defend,* or *destroy*. These, however, cannot be found in conflict resolution mandates. Instead, readers will encounter vague and ambiguous verbs like *monitor, assist, create,* and *investigate*. The broad spectrum of interpretation that such verbs elicit often makes it difficult for commanders to decide what and/or how much to do. After all, today's commanders have been trained in the very specific sets of actions associated with doctrine based on warfighting. Furthermore, in conflict resolution, the nuances of an agreement and the complex wording of mandates carry enormous political implications— implications that military organizations are not trained to handle, especially when they concern the delicate balance of power between rival factions in scenarios where the agreements between the factions have not been formalized. I maintain that commanders who insist on clear mandates and unambiguous decision processes should not be involved in conflict resolution, because the challenges they will face will be too complex and subtle to be explicitly addressed through simple short-term tactical objectives and readily identifiable milestones. For example, the mandate given to the military force in Rwanda did not address all aspects of the peace agreement signed by the belligerent parties. Thus, commanders and their troops were placed in a position of having to execute a mandate that the belligerent parties themselves were not fully committed to supporting due to the perception by the belligerents of shortfalls in the mandate. This situation created uncertainty and suspicion, leading to lengthy debates and frustrating meetings that inevitably watered down the original objectives and eventually undermined the peace agreement. Ultimately, this state of affairs provided an opportunity for the more cunning of the belligerents to seize the initiative and gain a temporary upper hand. Effective command under such conditions requires a leader who is able not only to maintain the intent of the mission but also to keep in view the full breadth of the peace agreement, all the while dealing with extremely uncertain and fluid circumstances.

MORAL AND ETHICAL DILEMMAS

As important as these specific examples are in conveying the complexity of conflict resolution, they can only begin to illustrate the scope and depth of the moral and ethical dilemmas awaiting commanders in the field, at all levels, during such operations. When a platoon commander is restricted to the Chapter VI rules of engagement, what should that officer say to his or her troops as they work their way into a village where the inhabitants have been slaughtered, where women and children have been literally hacked to pieces, but some are still alive and screaming for help? Does the platoon commander order the soldiers to help the survivors when thirty percent of the population is known to have AIDS, and the platoon personnel lack the gloves and other safety equipment needed to protect them from infection? Moreover, what happens when soldiers see a woman carrying a child on her back, in the midst of a killing spree by extremist groups, hacking to death another woman who is also carrying a child on her back? Do the soldiers open fire? On whom? What are the moral implications if they stand by and do not try to stop the killing?

In such nightmarish circumstances, what possible guidance or preparation can be given to soldiers and their leaders? Are Western beliefs and values even relevant in such extreme situations? Have Western militaries put those beliefs and values to the test in leadership training programs, and are their officers and noncommissioned members (NCMs) ready for these complex and horrific challenges? Are we really thinking about these issues and spending time developing doctrine, solutions, and practices that support personnel legally, morally, and ethically? Or are we simply counting on existing training and hoping for the best? In Rwanda, there was so much room for interpretation, so much pressure to stay within boundaries, so much difficulty in getting even a mandate from the UN Security Council, that I often based my course of action on my own assessment of what various contingent commanders could handle, with or without their nations' approval.

Such are the moral dilemmas of command in conflict resolution. None of the contingents either anticipated or were prepared for a scenario like the one we faced in Rwanda. I therefore believe that my experiences and those of other military leaders during the past decade of world disorder must be rigorously analyzed and studied to extract the lessons to be learned for future commanders in the field. These issues are far too important and too complex to be discussed, debated, and resolved only as troops are about to deploy. Education, development, and training in these demanding subjects must begin the moment a potential leader enters one of our institutions. We cannot let future leaders be commissioned without far more depth and breadth of knowledge concerning the multidisciplined arena they will face, under the nation's scrutiny, on graduation. The luxury of a four- or five-year apprenticeship phase is over. Young officers and even NCMs are thrust into these operational theatres within months of leaving our colleges and training establishments.

ACCOUNTABILITY

Within the first few days of the renewed violence in Rwanda, that is, the killings that began after President Habyarimana's death on April 6, 1994, it appeared painfully obvious to me that the world community was uninterested in resolving the situation there. Countries that had contributed troops began to recall their forces, fearing casualties and responding to diplomatic pressure from the Belgian government. Yet moral accountability in conflict resolution in the post Cold War era goes well beyond the lives of the military troops involved. In Rwanda, if we too had withdrawn outright when ordered to, not only would we have been abandoning to their certain death thousands of innocent men, women, and children who had been under our protection, but we would have had to live with having morally failed to *try* to avoid a catastrophe or at least try to save some of the moderate leaders on both sides in the process. History would have been warranted in painting us as the force with no clear mandate that withdrew for fear of casualties just when hundreds of thousands of people were being slaughtered. The United Nations, the contributing nations, and I myself could justifiably have been held accountable for cowardliness and a complete lack of moral fibre.

Unfortunately, such a concept of accountability has yet to be adequately discussed, debated, and resolved within the international community, let alone within the United Nations. Indeed, the debate so far has been limited to lawyers' discussions regarding whether it is legal to intervene in the sovereignty of failing nation-states and whether anyone has the authority to capture and prosecute the perpetrators of these terrible crimes. And sadly, when scapegoats are sought in order to defuse political problems, sometimes it is those in uniform—individuals who live by the doctrine of unlimited liability—who become those scapegoats, despite the fact that it is they who have just been the target of the belligerents.

Accountability for actions taken by armed forces during conflict resolution operations is increasingly being demanded at both the national and international levels. For Rwanda, as well as for the former Yugoslavia, international tribunals have been convened to investigate violations of the laws of armed conflict and crimes against humanity (for the Rwanda tribunal, see ICTR, 1999, and United Nations, 1999; for the tribunal dealing with the former Yugoslavia, see United

Nations, 1997). I have already testified once at the International Criminal Tribunal for Rwanda (ongoing in Arusha, Tanzania, since November 1995), and I expect to return there sometime this year (2000). Other senior commanders will no doubt find themselves drawn, as I have been, into these international legal investigations—investigations that question them about events, actions, and decisions that were far from clear-cut, having taken place in a context much broader and more complex than that of classic warfighting.

Military leaders are certainly accountable to their own governments for their actions, but are they also accountable to the United Nations or to international tribunals? What should a nation's policy be on allowing its military commanders to testify before a UN commissioner or participating in international tribunals? Many commanders would feel morally compelled to participate in such inquiries, but would their governments agree? After all, commanders who testify could well find themselves in the difficult position of giving testimony that embarrasses their own government.

From the perspective of accountability, the position of the Red Cross regarding the International Criminal Tribunal for Rwanda (ICTR) and the International Criminal Tribunal for the Former Yugoslavia (ICTY) is an interesting one. During the first three weeks of the genocide in Rwanda, the International Committee of the Red Cross (ICRC) was the only international agency in the country, except for the media and UNAMIR. The ICRC lost fifty-six nationals who had been negotiating for the safe passage of casualties during assaults on hospitals. Yet when asked to testify at the ICTR, the ICRC refused, arguing that to do so would jeopardize the perception of its impartiality in future world hot spots! Should military personnel similarly not testify before such bodies, since militaries must also be perceived as neutral and impartial participants for future conflict resolution operations?

I believe that accountability extends much further than the strategic level: it reaches down to the everyday tactical level as well. For example, what are the options for Chapter VI field commanders when belligerent units surrender to their supposedly neutral and nonbelligerent force (such as a UN force)? Do those who surrender become prisoners of war, even though the UN force is not actually at war with them? Does the commander hand them over to the other belligerents, who may mistreat or even kill them? And if the commander does turn them over, will he or she be held accountable for the rival force's subsequent actions? Finally, what should the ICRC's role be in such situations? When an entire battalion and their families (nearly 2,000 people) surrendered to a UNAMIR company in Rwanda, it took some time to clarify the status of both UNAMIR and the battalion, as well as the ICRC's role. Are the UN commander's forces compelled to protect those who have surrendered? How far should the UN commander go in defending them, given that UN forces comprise various contributing nations that may have quite different views on the issue? Finally, the faction leaders in many failing states are ruthless extremists who act solely according to their personal aims and may not recognize international law. How can a UN commander be sure that the belligerents will feel bound by the Geneva Convention and behave accordingly? (The killing of the Belgian soldiers who were captured within the first twenty-four hours of the war in Rwanda proved that at least one group of belligerents did not feel constrained by international law.)[16] Such situations raise whole new dimensions of accountability and responsibility on which commanders and senior officers have not traditionally devoted much thought.

MILITARY COHESION

In contrast to former UN peacekeeping missions, which tended to be static in nature, today's international crises demand that UN involvement be dynamic, time-sensitive, and flexible. But the nature of the United Nations rarely permits such a response. For example, the day before I landed in Kigali, Burundi (the country to the immediate south of Rwanda) experienced a coup d'état. Within days, over 300,000 Burundi refugees had arrived in the south of Rwanda, an area originally assessed as requiring limited UNAMIR attention due to the presence of moderates and a secure border between the nations. But the lack of attention and/or concern of the international community to this human crisis and UNAMIR's very limited resource base made it impossible for me to react quickly to this new situation, to take the initiative, or to bring about an atmosphere of security in southern Rwanda, let alone in Burundi.

Several procedural factors reduce the speed of the organization's response. The UN procedure for defining mission requirements, mandates, and funding mechanisms is complex and drawn-out; lengthy procedural and administrative delays are also common. Add to that the often slow decision-making processes involving extensive negotiations between the United Nations and the countries that are potential contributors to the military effort, and the result is that by the time forces are deployed, the mission and the resources may be out of sync with the actual situation in the field.

These delays create serious difficulties for commanders who are trying to establish an effective operational plan and a cohesive military coalition. Establishing military cohesion is further complicated by the enormous variance in training among member nations' militaries, along with differences in equipment availability and quality, and in the sustainability of the entire effort. The commander may appear to have an adequate number of troops, but if more than half of them do not meet minimum standards or do not have the requisite mobility and sustainability, then the commander is seriously limited in employing them. Imagine building a headquarters using staff who don't speak the same language and don't even have the same operating procedures! Although some UNAMIR participants—for example, the Dutch and the Ghanaians—had extensive experience in peace support operations and were real assets, others were there simply to gain on-the-job training, as one contingent's chief of staff explained to me. Another complicating factor in forming a functional force for peace operations is the fact that some participating nations may have terrible human rights problems of their own and therefore represent less-than-adequate role models. Lastly, in some cases a coalition's participating nations have previously been enemies in their own region of the world—and especially when adversarial sentiments linger from a time when one nation was a colony of another. Such situations make the task of establishing unit cohesion extremely delicate. Not only is it difficult for commanders to create and maintain a cohesive force under such circumstances, but the belligerents may well try to take advantage of the resulting lack of a common standard and commitment. They may play some components of the UN force off against others, and they may gain more freedom to act by taking advantage of the components of the UN force that have not had sufficient preparation and training.

A UNIFIED APPROACH

Conflict resolution requires a unified approach, with comprehensive coordination encompassing all plans—security, humanitarian, economic, and political—in ways that prove mutually supportive. Without a single overarching mission plan, it is difficult to seize and maintain the initiative as a crisis develops. It is even more difficult if the crisis is full-blown.

Often military forces are on the ground and ready to go, but the humanitarian operation is stalled because the needs have not been fully assessed, funding is not yet in place, or more coordination is required. Meanwhile, the political situation may be fluctuating or even may have stagnated. If we continue to be so disjointed in articulating, implementing, and coordinating these different plans, failures will continue to occur, precious resources will be wasted, and credibility will disappear.

Achieving an integrated conflict resolution plan is not a trivial task. Simply coordinating the many NGOs that may be involved presents a significant challenge—there were one hundred and sixty-nine NGOs in Rwanda! Some of these were very small, with lots of heart but little or no capability. Often they quickly became liabilities. Others were quite large, with extensive capabilities, but their actions were frequently governed as much by their media image (and the need to get resources for the next crisis) as by their humanity—sometimes seriously jeopardizing success in the current operation.[17]

The military and the NGOs have different aims and missions, and these can often be at odds. In 1994, NGOs were working behind the lines of one Rwandan belligerent group. Not surprisingly, these belligerents started using the fuel, medical supplies, and food that the NGOs had brought in for the displaced persons. Despite the fact that during the first months of the war, UNAMIR had no official jurisdiction over the activities of these NGOs (UNAMIR provided only security), the opposing belligerents immediately accused us of aiding and abetting their enemy. They did not understand the operational ethos of these NGOs—namely, to offer unconditional assistance that was unconnected to military intervention. Instead, they perceived the situation solely as evidence of favouritism on UNAMIR's part. Incidents like these complicated the political and military dimensions of the UNAMIR mission. How can commanders in conflict resolution situations work with NGOs to achieve both the military mission and the NGOs' missions, yet still appear consistent—and, more important, impartial—to the belligerents?

Our credibility was further undermined by the often rigid and narrow interpretation of the mandate by our higher headquarters—especially considering the actual situation on the ground. We were often ordered to pull out far too soon, without enough time to implement proper support strategies or to develop sound solutions that would be agreed to by all sides. Under these conditions, commanders and political decision-makers can find themselves implementing completely unachievable pullout solutions based on impossible milestones. Belligerents, particularly the extremist elements, may easily see through these supposed solutions. They may consequently use covert tactics and underground operations to preserve their power among the local populace—chiefly by sustaining people's fear levels. Eventually, the donor countries lose patience and withdraw, leaving the belligerents as strong as ever. I am adamant that conflict resolution must not be attempted unless we are willing to address all the dimensions of a problem (that is, its political, humanitarian, security, and economic factors) and to do so over the long term—for decades if necessary. Unless we are willing to make long-term commitments, we must not deploy troops under the pressure of media-driven hype. We must not risk the lives of our personnel in poorly conceived, guilt-driven humanitarian operations that are predominantly vehicles for political posturing by corrupt leaders who, in the end, have only a superficial concern for the real situation.

If you are in the business of conflict resolution, you must expect to be in it for the long haul. If you are not prepared for this type of commitment, then stay out—and learn to live with your individual and collective consciences.

TRUST

I believe that we in the military have developed a dysfunctional syndrome whereby too many of our leaders retreat to their offices during a crisis in order to answer phone calls from higher headquarters or write reports to "cover all the bases." Many times in UNAMIR, I observed officers from various nations who, when the shelling began, went inside and started writing plans and reports rather than gathering the information personally and controlling the situation directly by their presence. A perception exists that when trouble occurs, someone higher in the chain of command should be told immediately. This is both wrong and unnecessary. But how do you cure this insidious disease—a condition all too common among those who have experienced only garrison duty? Commanders at all levels should take it for granted that in conflict resolution situations their superiors are getting updates from CNN and the other media right in their offices! Details on the situation should be provided only after the crisis has been addressed or when support from higher command is truly required. In my opinion, the rear headquarters is the last place for leaders during a local crisis. They should be well forward, where they can quickly assess the situation and make informed decisions. I spent the bulk of my first four to five days in Rwanda in either the Hutu or the Tutsi military headquarters instead of my own. Only through his or her presence can a commander's force of will and determination steer the situation in the desired direction.

Senior officers must create an atmosphere that clearly demonstrates their confidence that their subordinates will undertake the proper and competent actions. Until officers can project this confidence—a cornerstone of effective leadership—personnel at all levels will be looking over their shoulders during conflict resolution operations and lapsing into inaction. Should this happen, the mission is doomed to fail.

DISCIPLINE AND OPERATIONAL STRESS

In Rwanda, significant numbers of officers and NCOs were unable to handle the pressures of the UNAMIR operational theatre, particularly during the civil war and genocide—and most particularly when deprived of water, food, and sleep and when casualties were being taken. Certain officers, for example, retreated to the safety of relief aircraft during an attack, leaving their troops under fire on the tarmac. Some NCOs withheld food and water from their soldiers. Other officers kept medication for their personal use. The pressures of the Rwandan operation turned it, for some, into an exercise in self-preservation. Discipline in their units broke down very rapidly. One such contingent actually refused to open the gates of its compound to allow another contingent to take refuge within. Trapped in an attempt to escape militia numbering in the thousands, the cornered contingent was forced to climb over the compound wall under fire. Fortunately, the contingent suffered only limited injuries in the process.

Military units that have not had the opportunity to gain self-discipline through participating in demanding and realistic peacetime exercises cannot be expected to meet the stringent disciplinary requirements of actual operations. I believe that haughty, image-obsessed, abusive leaders who demand unquestioning, instantaneous obedience from subordinates in garrison produce self-protective, survival-oriented units that disintegrate—losing their ability to function in their military roles or even secure their own welfare—within hours of a conflict's start. Only by applying day-to-day discipline considerately and according to sage standards can commanders keep units and their individuals focused, confident, committed, altruistic, and brave in operations. It is too late to expect discipline in-theatre if the troops have not learned it before deployment.

Not surprisingly, post-traumatic stress disorder (PTSD) casualties are becoming more prevalent in conflict resolution. Even if troops were thoroughly trained in and well prepared for these types of operations, many would have trouble coping with the outright horrors often faced in operational theatres. But as I have argued in this chapter, today's militaries are *not* thoroughly trained in, nor well prepared for conflict resolution operations that are often characterized by ambiguous orders. Not surprisingly, these problems produce extremely high stress levels. Commanders must be able to recognize in their subordinates any potentially dangerous responses to this stress. In Rwanda, UNAMIR personnel wore helmets and flak jackets when our headquarters was being shelled. One lieutenant-colonel suddenly began coming to my twice-daily Orders Group fully dressed for battle. The first time he appeared this way, he seemed to be functioning normally, so I did not react. At that evening's gathering, he again turned up with everything on: however, he still seemed rational, albeit worried and faint of voice. But by the next morning, he was obviously no longer functioning. He was the sheer embodiment of fear—bordering on terror—and he was infecting many of those surrounding him. People became scared just looking at him. As a result, I sent him to his room under escort and evacuated him from the operational theatre on the next flight. Although this action might seem precipitous, it was completely necessary for the well-being of both the individual and the contingent as a whole.

When military personnel succumb so spectacularly to stress, they must be removed immediately from active duty. Some, given a short break—even just a couple of days with good food, clean sheets, a wash, plenty of sleep, and an absence of risk—will recuperate and be able to return. Others become outright PTSD casualties and cannot return. Given that possibility, commanders must instill in their subordinates the knowledge that PTSD is an *injury* and that those who succumb to it are casualties and should not be considered inferior soldiers.

Commanders have a duty to be ruthless, yet fair in assessing their troops' effectiveness under stressful conditions. In addition, commanders also have the difficult task of recognizing when they themselves lose their objectivity, their patience, their ability to focus, their nerve, and most importantly, their sense of humour. After all, commanders are no more immune to stress than their subordinates. Recognizing that fact is all the more critical, because when a commander becomes debilitated, the risks to the mission and to subordinates are so much greater.

I believe that militaries must re-examine their whole rest-and-recuperation (R&R) policy in operational theatres. A single two-week recuperation period in a six-month operation may not be the best solution, since it can jeopardize cohesion and increase stress on the remainder of the team. Whatever new approaches are devised, they must be flexible enough to allow commanders to respond to the stresses and strains of each operation and cater to the fluctuating demands on the troops. Commanders must be able to pull soldiers out, let them vent their frustration under controlled conditions, and then bring them back, according to the mission's tempo, nature, and demands. The traditional R&R formulas (those based on the shorter tour lengths of the "good old days")—along with their mythology of boozing and having a "good time"—are destructive rather than recuperative. They reflect a very poor assessment of the nature and consequences of the stresses that soldiers experience in today's operational theatres.

As I have already intimated, revamped recuperation procedures must reflect a reconsideration of the use of alcohol. Allowing soldiers to use alcohol as a means of relaxation in-theatre is a surefire way of contributing to loss of instinctive judgment, slowing the ability to react, and ultimately increasing the number of casualties. More than fifty percent of Canadian casualties in operations over the past decade have been directly attributable to in-theatre alcohol consumption. I have come to the conclusion that there is no room at all for alcohol in the new generation of operational theatres, since hostile fire can come from any direction, at any time, where belligerents—especially extremists—operate without regard for the neutrality of your force. A soldier who is fatigued, lonely, and stressed, and who yet must react instantaneously and with sound judgment based on experience and skill, is less likely to make the right decision after drinking. Even a single drink dulls a person's abilities under physically and mentally demanding conditions. Militaries cannot afford any slackening of reflexes in the fluid, totally unpredictable scenarios of conflict resolution. Any compromise of a soldier's professional reactions is unacceptable under circumstances where hazardous situations can arise at any time without warning. During conflict resolution operations, soldiers are *always* on the "front line."

SOPHISTICATED TECHNOLOGY VERSUS THIRD WORLD STRATEGIES

Ironically, even when Western armed forces have a clear technical advantage (for example, in computer and weapon systems), operations like the one in Rwanda continue to present challenges. Historically, Western armed forces have equipped and trained themselves to fight adversaries that have technological competencies similar to their own, in classic warfare scenarios. This fascination with technology, along with the assumption that such technology provides superiority, has lulled Western militaries into a form of complacency, preventing them from arriving at simpler solutions to major operational problems.

For example, in Rwanda, the most sophisticated technology used by the general population was the ordinary public radio. Since eighty-five percent of the population was illiterate, the radio dominated life, particularly in the country's outlying villages. Rwanda functioned not through its road systems, televisions, or newspapers, but through its radio stations. Everyone had a radio. Even people in refugee camps found ways of getting batteries to run radios. The radio was, if not the voice of God, then certainly the voice of authority, with a status that made it a powerful tool for disseminating information, misinformation, and propaganda, as well as for overall control of the masses. For instance, military forces encountered a radio station run by extremists who were explicitly inciting people to kill, but had no way of jamming it (let alone of understanding what was being said). Such situations illustrate the military's failure to really comprehend the cultural dimensions of the problem in-theatre. And I am not talking about collecting sophisticated intelligence data here—but simply about getting readily available information from an ordinary radio broadcast!

The UN mission in Rwanda did not at first realize the importance of this communication method, much less appreciate its widespread influence and impact on the population. How that factor escaped us will always remain a mystery to me. And when we did finally realize the radio's importance—particularly that it was the nation's dominant instrument of hate propaganda—what happened? We were told to retreat to a safe position and that we could not stop those hateful, slaughter-inciting broadcasts because to do so would have encroached on Rwanda's sovereignty! This clumsy, outdated view of international law—that is, the idea that nations must not interfere with other sovereign nations' internal affairs—remains the Western world's single most common excuse for nonintervention. Yet the world's nations should realize that the Geneva Conventions *do* allow them to intervene for humanitarian reasons in situations where national sovereignty might previously have been an obstacle.[18] I believe that the United Nations can gain the moral and physical force to be genuinely effective in conflict resolution only if its participant nations put advancing global humanism ahead of blindly respecting the supremacy of national sovereignty.

In the end, we could not deploy a radio station to counter the propaganda in Rwanda. As a result, we failed miserably in our objectives and were left to witness daily escalations in the slaughter.

What advantage, then, does technological superiority provide in such situations? In Rwanda, it merely encouraged a dangerous arrogance toward the belligerents, a tendency to view them—inaccurately—as unsophisticated and insignificant. This attitude served us poorly. Moreover, our supposed technological superiority was marginalized anyway by political decisions—first, not to support the mission, and eventually, to pull out.

Moreover, whatever the Rwandans lacked in technology, they more than made up for in numbers. Furthermore, they had full confidence in their abilities to confront, and fight if necessary, white professional soldiers. Nonetheless, a single platoon of militia with machetes, grenades, and old rifles should pose little threat to a section of well-trained Western soldiers—*if* those soldiers understand the rules of engagement regarding the use of force, and if their leaders are ready to act on those ROEs. But in Rwanda, the belligerents never came in platoon size. They came by the hundreds and by the thousands. Their military was able to maintain such large numbers by drawing on the country's disaffected youth and capitalizing on the ethnic animosities. In a country where chaos reigns, displaced people are easily recruited. How then, does a peacekeeping force handle hundreds and thousands of belligerents (female as well as male), many of whom are intoxicated on narcotics and alcohol, and are easily incited to violence by their leaders' emotional appeals to ethnic, tribal, and religious identity? How do you handle that kind of volume and scale of threat? How many do you need to kill before they will stop? What conventional Western warfighting methods apply in such situations? What clause in the mandate handles such dilemmas, even in a Chapter VII mission? Have our rules of engagement matured to the point of guiding the answers to such moral and ethical questions?

COMMUNICATION AND THE MEDIA

All of these moral dilemmas, operational uncertainties, political sensitivities, and coordination issues happen under the close scrutiny of the media. I would argue that a productive way of looking at this unavoidable reality is to view the media as a new and positive instrument for communication. One of the responsibilities of command is to communicate mission objectives to the troops, to their families, to a nation's population, to the international community, and to organizations such as the United Nations and NATO (the North Atlantic Treaty Organization). Communication can happen directly between commanders and their troops, but it can also happen indirectly—through the media. The media also offer excellent ways to gather intelligence, to help assess the belligerents' intentions in zones that your mission cannot get into, and to get your side of the story out to the world. Putting the drama of a conflict on the world stage can actually help resolve a crisis by spurring international participation.

Some may consider it unethical to use the media to influence world leaders. I do not, particularly when those leaders show a tendency toward indifference. When world leaders deliberately abandoned the Rwandans to their plight, relegating my force to an impotent witness to the third genocide of the twentieth century,[19] only the media remained with us. In some ways, the media made the difference. To them go well-deserved accolades for courage, determination, and a sense of global social conscience. Force commanders should therefore regard the media as an asset, not as an impediment, to the mission. In modern military operations, the media should be embraced as an essential tool for mission success, albeit one that should be employed with caution and respect. Commanders who play "coy" with the media or try to conceal information from them risk undermining their own command. If the media in Rwanda had felt that I was being anything but honest with them, they would have turned on me with a vengeance; their reporting would have focused on UN ineptness rather than on the human tragedy. Minimally, such a negative media image would have affected the morale of my force. But it would also almost certainly have changed the belligerents' perception of our force, thereby putting the whole mission at risk, including the safety of the 30,000 or so Rwandans under our protection.

Communicating with the media, then, is a crucial aspect of postmodern command, an integral part of the many ways that commanders can influence their troops, their opponents, and their overall situation. Consequently, commanders should not relegate these activities to expert public affairs staff alone. Commanders must therefore become comfortable with having cameras and microphones thrust in their faces, often at the most sensitive of times, and they must be able to project confident resolve and professionalism without hesitation under those trying conditions.

Communication also involves more than words alone. In addition to words (for example, in the form of orders to the troops or statements to the media), commanders also communicate through their eyes, their face, their tears, their tone of voice, and their body language. And an effective commander uses all these channels to convey to the troops a complete willingness to risk his or her own life where necessary. Effective commanders present their orders personally, stand behind them, and are there in person to see the results. This point was reinforced for me in Rwanda. Initially, I gave my staff only the mission statement and intent for the first operations order, which the staff then wrote. But we took casualties with that first operation. After that, I would not let my staff write the orders. I wrote the next dozen or so myself, with staff input and I personally presented those orders to the troops at as many levels as I could manage. Each time, I told them that they were going to be in harm's way, and urged them to show courage, pluck, and determination. I also made clear to them our limited ability to get them to safety should they be injured or captured. And when they returned from those dangerous missions, I was there to cry with them over the loss of comrades. This is not the job of staff officers; neither is it the job of subordinate commanders alone. It is the responsibility of the most senior commander. The troops had to realize that I was also suffering when people under my command were injured or lost—that we would cry together, then collectively wipe the tears from our eyes and go back out again and again.

CONCLUSION

As military operations over the past decade have shown, the world has entered an era of complex, multidimensional missions in which forces are being committed much more frequently than during the Cold War. These deployments typically occur in cultural contexts for which militaries have not traditionally been prepared—largely because such operations have been shunned by some services and downplayed by others as being unworthy of and inappropriate for warfighting forces. This perception existed throughout the Cold War and has persisted even during this past decade of conflict resolution operations. I disagree with the adage "Peacekeeping dulls the warfighting spirit."

Officers and NCMs in conflict resolution operations need a spectrum of knowledge and skills that go well beyond merely understanding how the rules of engagement restrict the use of force. In contrast to classic warfare, conflict resolution is fraught with uncertainty and ambiguity, and further complicated by fear of casualties and by national self-interest and security agendas. The sheer number of multidisciplinary agencies that must interact in conflict resolution, even at the lowest tactical levels, requires a structured and evolving body of knowledge and skills to facilitate understanding and effective cooperation throughout the mission. Our continued inability or even outright refusal to appreciate the scope and complexity of—and the necessity for innovative doctrines to guide—conflict resolution missions has cost innocent lives, resulted in unnecessary casualties, wasted enormous resources, and ensured that no real lasting success has been achieved in many troubled areas for the last decade. We can no longer take an *ad hoc* approach to these operations, nor can we expect that sophisticated warfighting alliances and coalitions like NATO will be the solution. Consequently, for a middle power like Canada, it will become critical to develop adaptable resilient, task-oriented forces that are capable of successfully undertaking the full spectrum of potential operations.

I firmly believe that conflict resolution operations must be studied formally by our officer corps. Militaries must find the correct balance between providing the training, equipment priorities, and force structures required for classic RMA-type warfighting, as well as the much broader multidisciplinary competencies that leaders require to be able to develop innovative solutions and methods for conflict resolution. The officer corps needs a broader-based education, with increased emphasis on the social sciences in particular. Furthermore, conflict resolution operations will demand that military doctrine be modified, upgraded, or even created outright, and that changes be made in leadership training, stress management policies, and possibly even organizational structures. Unless we achieve this new balance of competencies, we will fail to meet our nations' expectations in ninety percent of the operations that we will be called upon to perform. If this fundamental change is not made, casualty levels will increase (with psychological injuries increasing the most); resource demands will never be met; military advice to democratic governments will not be accepted as credible; and trust in military leadership will erode. The challenge is before us. We must leave behind the security of familiar doctrines and accepted classic theories of warfare. We must pro-actively develop our leadership and force structures to enable us to execute the full spectrum of missions and tasks anticipated now and in the future.

NOTES

1. This chapter is largely based on Lieutenant-General Dallaire's presentation to the NATO RTO Workshop in the Human in Command, June 1998. His presentation paper titled "Command Experiences in Rwanda," was published in Carol McCann and Ross Pigeau, eds., *The Human in Command: Exploring the Modern Military Experience* (New York: Kluwer Academic / Plenum Publishing 2000).

2. Chapter VI of the UN Charter (Pacific Settlement of Disputes). In the event of a dispute between states, under this chapter, belligerents are called upon by the UN to seek a resolution through negotiation, mediation, arbitration, or other peaceful means. Chapter VII (Threats to the Peace) allows for the use of force by the UN to maintain or restore international peace and security.
3. Human Rights Watch (HRW) "The Genocide," in *Leave None to Tell the Story: Genocide in Rwanda*, 1999.
4. "100 Days of Slaughter: A Chronology of US/UN Actions," in *Frontline: The Triumph of Evil*, 1999, on line, http://www.pbs.org/wgbh/pages/frontline/shows/evil/etc/slaughter.html.
5. A. Destexhe, *Rwanda and Genocide in the Twentieth Century* (New York: New York University Press, 1995); and G. Prunier, *The Rwanda Crisis* (New York: Columbia University Press, 1995).
6. Republic of Rwanda, *Background Notes on Countries of the World*, March 1998, on-line, http://www.britannica.com/bcom/magazine/article/0,5744,212598,00.html.
7. "Rwanda" in *Encyclopedia Britannica*, 1999, on-line, http://www.britannica.com/bcom/eb/article/1/0,5716,66201+5,00.html.
8. For details see the International Criminal Tribunal for Rwanda (ICTR), 1999, on-line, http://www.ictr.org; and *International Criminal Tribunal for Rwanda* and United Nations, *Verdicts on the Crime of Genocide by the International Criminal Tribunal for Rwanda*, 1998.
9. "100 Days of Slaughter."
10. In such cases, advocating non-involvement on the basis of sovereignty becomes spurious, since the nations in question are *not* in fact sovereign in the sense of having a government that is determined by and responsible to the people.
11. The same may well prove true for large portions of Asia and South America.
12. Published only weeks before the commencement of the genocide and civil war in Rwanda, PDD 25 essentially formalized the decision-making process to be used by the US president in authorizing the use of US forces or other US involvement in various humanitarian or conflict resolution crises. The overriding criterion for involvement specified in the PDD is the degree of US self-interest in the conflict.
13. Chapter VI operations require the consent of the parties and usually limit the use of force to self-defence. By contrast, Chapter VII operations authorize the full use of force necessary to accomplish the mandate, as was the case, for example, in the Korean Conflict, the Gulf War and the Somalia Mission.
14. The vast majority of troops within UNAMIR were not Canadian.
15. The US deployed 2,500 troops in late July 1994, only after the civil war and most of the slaughter was over. 2,200 of those troops were located in the neighbouring countries of Uganda and Zaire (now the Democratic Republic of the Congo), not in Rwanda.
16. "Rwanda: A Historical Chronology," in *Frontline: Valentina's Nightmare*, 1999, on-line, http://www.pbs.org/wgbh/pages/frontline/shows/rwanda/etc/cron.html.
17. The extensive aid provided to 1.5 million persons in Goma, (in Zaire) in contrast to the much lower—and at times virtually nonexistent—levels of aid for so many of the millions of Rwandans who were displaced internally is an example.
18. M. Gee, "Rules of war are getting awkward," *Globe and Mail* (12 August, 1999), A18.
19. Destexhe.

Modern Canadian Generalship in Conflict Resolution: Kosovo as a Case Study

Lieutenant-General R.R. Henault

Lieutenant-General R.R. Henault is the current CF Deputy Chief of the Defence Staff.

INTRODUCTION

THE STARK REALITY OF THE POST COLD WAR environment within which the Canadian Forces (CF) and Department of National Defence (DND) currently operate presents some unique challenges for our military and its leadership. While some had expected that peace would break out everywhere in those heady times following the collapse of the Iron Curtain, the reality of the global situation is very different. Canada remains in a challenging, unpredictable and inherently more dangerous security environment than the situation experienced during the Cold War. In a world where there is an absence of superpower polarity, we now face the challenges of intra-state breakdown and regional conflict ignited by a variety of causes, some of which include ethnic differences, economic collapse, and environmental disaster.

Even though this new threat is very real, it is much more difficult to define than during the relatively predictable Cold War years. This phenomenon has had a dramatic influence on defence funding, and not only affected Canada, but also most countries in the developed world as they try to adjust to the new threats. In this climate, defence alliances and partnerships have become even more important, as it is likely that any future conflicts will be responded to with joint and combined forces, and in multinational coalitions. At the same time, we are living in the Information Age where the Internet and the media are making the world a very small place, figuratively speaking. Technology is increasing at an astounding rate, rapidly making existing weapons systems obsolete and challenging militaries to buy-in to the new technologies to remain relevant, despite shrinking defence budgets. All these factors have resulted in what many refer to as the Revolution in Military Affairs, or RMA, where precision munitions, interoperability and rapid global deployability have become key to military success.

To survive this "revolution" and position the CF/DND to be relevant and viable in the future, strong leadership, both political and military, is essential. Leaders in the CF/DND must not only be aware of the changing landscape of global defence, but must also position the institution to be able to take advantage of the Information Age and evolving technologies. They must also take full advantage of the lessons learned from the conflicts in which the CF has participated since the end of the Cold War, including the Gulf War, the conflict in Bosnia, and the Kosovo crisis. However, they cannot blindly use these as a template for future conflict, as the future is much more difficult to predict than ever. It is therefore essential to remain flexible and responsive, and seek to become as interoperable as well as rapidly and globally deployable as possible.

AIM

The aim of this chapter is to review the role of the modern general at the strategic level of operations in the CF/DND, in this new and evolving environment, using the experience gained from the recent Canadian military involvement in the Kosovo Air Campaign as a backdrop.

BACKGROUND

In the new global "disorder" of the post Cold War era, the CF/DND has been deployed into the Persian Gulf, the former Yugoslavia, Somalia, Rwanda, Haiti, East Timor and Kosovo. In addition, the 1990s saw two of the largest domestic deployments of military personnel in recent history—for the Ice

Storm and the Manitoba Floods. Compared to the relative stability of predictable rotations into operations such as Cyprus, that spanned over four decades, and "career managed" man-for-man rotations into NATO and other UN missions, the pressures and challenges of the New World Order have presented the CF/DND with some of the most challenging operational situations that it has faced since the Korean War.

To understand the dynamics in NDHQ during this challenging period, it is important to distinguish between the role of the Force Generators and the Force Employer. The three Environmental Commanders for the army, navy and air force, as well as some of the other group principals, act as the main Force Generators for the CF/DND and, as such, are responsible for ensuring that their respective personnel are properly trained and equipped to carry out their assigned missions. The Deputy Chief of the Defence Staff (DCDS) on the other hand, acts mainly as the Force Employer, on behalf of the Chief of the Defence Staff (CDS), and is responsible for assigning and commanding, at the strategic level, the necessary forces to conduct deployed operations for international missions and major domestic contingencies. Obviously, the past decade has been a significant challenge for both Force Generators and the Force Employer as the CF/DND was required to deploy more often and with more personnel at the same time as the overall personnel numbers were decreasing. In addition, throughout this period, the DCDS has been preparing to assume additional Force Generator responsibilities.

It is in this highly charged and challenging period that the Kosovo crisis emerged. It is useful to note that during the lead-in to the Kosovo Air Campaign, the CF had a variety of missions operating in the region. Besides the major contingent in Bosnia, there were Canadians flying daily missions as part of the multinational (AWACS) Airborne Warning and Control System crews operating out of Geilenkirchen, Germany, and six CF-18 fighter aircraft already stationed in Aviano, Italy. The number of CF-18 aircraft eventually increased to eighteen during the conflict. The CF also had a number of observers in Kosovo operating under the Organization for Security and Co-operation in Europe (OSCE) as members of the Kosovo Verification Mission (KVM). There was also a contingent of engineers and support personnel operating in Macedonia to support the French extraction force. Later in the conflict, the navy was represented as part of (STANAVFORLANT) Standing Naval Force Atlantic, which was incidentally being commanded by a Canadian. Back at home, the CF/DND contributed significantly to the reception, housing and care of some 5000 Kosovar refugees. Finally, numerous staff officers worked in multinational headquarters throughout Italy and the Balkans, including those in Vicenza, Italy, Macedonia and Albania.

Thus, it is quite clear that Canada has been dedicated to helping resolve the situation in the Balkans right from the outset. It is also important to recognize the benefit that was later gained from having these forces on the ground throughout the region.

STRATEGIC PLANNING

At the strategic level, the challenges and resultant stresses on the leadership were evident in this rapidly evolving environment, in which it was necessary to adapt significantly in order to continue to effectively operate and successfully accomplish missions that were both multiple and complex. Indeed, with the Kosovo crisis, the performance of the Canadian Joint Staff, or J-Staff as it is more commonly known, provides a good example of the evolving demands that are now placed on the military and civilian leadership in NDHQ in the New World environment.

The requirement for a joint staff was conceived out of the difficulties encountered during Operation (OP) Bandit, the aborted operation to evacuate civilians from Haiti at the end of 1987. OP Bandit was to be a joint operation, involving mainly a naval force, an onboard infantry company and some airlift for evacuation and resupply. Problems were encountered in the planning and co-ordination for the operation to the point where the decision was made to abort the plan. In 1988, as a result of these difficulties, a study was conducted to assess NDHQ's capacity to function in emergencies and war. This study began a process of reform that continues to this day. Over the past decade, beginning with the domestic crisis in Oka and during the Persian Gulf War, the J-Staff has continued to evolve to the point where it is now fully capable of planning and co-ordinating joint and combined operations in complex operational environments.

By the time that conflict in Kosovo appeared likely, the J-Staff had already proven itself capable of rapidly planning and co-ordinating operations, and the Force Employment Planning Process (FEPP) had been in place and tested on numerous occasions. The FEPP, which had also seen many iterations over the years, has evolved into a logical, tested and effective system for planning operations, from the most basic to the most complex. It is important to note that this process is both respected and adhered to by the staff, and certainly the preparations for all aspects of the Kosovo operations were no exception.

One very important recognition that fell out of the Kosovo crisis involved the Environmental Chiefs of Staff (ECS). The utility and wisdom of having embedded the Environmental Commanders and their supporting staffs in NDHQ was again validated. Accurate, timely and informed environmental input continues to be readily available for the planning and execution process and has proved its worth for every operation that has been undertaken since the ECSs' arrival, especially the Kosovo crisis.

Another major reason that Canada was able to successfully plan, deploy and execute the mission in Kosovo can be attributed to Canada's long-established and proven working experience within NATO. Countless exercises, an established common doctrine, equipment and procedural interoperability, and a familiar multinational working relationship at all levels enabled the J-Staff to effectively plan and co-ordinate the operation. Years of working in a NATO/CANUS framework have paid off in terms of interoperability with our allies, especially the US, and have clearly proven the necessity of continuing this training in the future. In addition, as alluded to earlier, our experience in the Balkans, including Bosnia, Aviano and STANAVFORLANT, as well as the other smaller missions leading up the Kosovo crisis, prepared us well for the events to come.

Despite the successful evolution of the J-Staff and FEPP, and the integration of the ECSs into NDHQ, it would be misleading to give the impression that there were no problems during the various phases of Kosovo operations. Although the pace of operations leading into the Kosovo Air Campaign had been high, the intensity of the Air Campaign initially took the staff by surprise. In many ways, the staff lacked the depth in trained manpower to ramp up and sustain full 24/7 operations. In addition to the operational responsibilities, practically everyone underestimated the media and political scrutiny that would arise and the demand across the staff was at times overwhelming. However, after some initial growing pains and staffing adjustments, appropriate fixes were put in place and things ran relatively smoothly throughout the Campaign.

One of the other challenges for the J-Staff during the planning and execution phases of the operation involved the National Defence Operations Centre (NDOC). Due to shortcomings in the NDOC facilities that negatively affected strategic command and control during the Ice Storm of 1998, a major project had been put in place to upgrade the facility before the potential problems associated with the Millennium Bug arrived. The timing could not have been worse for the Kosovo crisis. However, with the flexibility and ingenuity of the staff, temporary facilities were established until the new National Defence Command Centre (NDCC) opened just before the end of the Air Campaign. With this new state-of-the-art facility, the CF/DND is in a much better position to provide the command and control required for modern military operations.

The other issue that did not become a problem, but certainly had the potential of being a limiting factor, was personnel sustainment in the J-Staff. Although the operation had become very smooth by the end of the Air Campaign, the stamina of some of the key positions was being challenged by the sustained pace of the operation. It must be remembered that problems in the rest of the world did not stop during the Kosovo crisis and the CF/DND was involved in over twenty other missions worldwide at the same time. It is extremely important to keep this factor in mind when planning for future high-intensity operations. As Kosovo proved, never assume that a conflict will be short—plan for the worst.

MEDIA RELATIONS

As alluded to earlier, the one thing that was probably underestimated the most and caught everyone by surprise was the effect that information requirements would have on the day-to-day activity in NDHQ. There is no doubt that today the concept of a global village is reality. No one group plays a bigger part in that reality than our modern media. With an abundance of twenty-four-hour news channels trying to fill their airtime by capturing every conceivable "happening" for the digestion of a starving public, the demand for information during an event like the Kosovo crisis is practically insatiable. This was initially experienced during the Gulf War, where for the first time in history, a large-scale conflict was turned into a global spectator sport, of sorts. Almost ten years later in Kosovo, the technological enhancements in the broadcast arena, including the Internet, combined with the public's increased thirst for news, resulted in an even higher level of media interest.

To try and meet the media demand, DND set up daily news conferences. The goal from the outset was to be honest, credible and transparent with the media, and through them with the public, and to provide answers to all their questions to clearly show what the CF were doing in Kosovo. After all, this was a great opportunity to demonstrate to Canadians what their military is capable of doing and to shed a positive light on the CF. In the end, these news conferences proved very successful, but a lot of valuable lessons were learned along the way.

The first lesson involved the selection of the spokesperson. It was critical that the seniority of the spokesperson be commensurate with the significance of the event, in order to develop and maintain credibility with the media. In addition, the spokesperson had to have the appropriate specialty background. For example, for an event like the Air Campaign, it was essential to appoint a very senior officer with aircrew background who was involved in the operational planning. Fortunately, in this instance, both the DCDS and COS J3 just happened to be pilots, so the decision to assign them to the task was relatively straightforward. In addition, the selective participation of both the Minister and the CDS worked very well when major announcements were necessary. Although using DCDS and COS J3 as the main media spokesmen worked well because they were both intimately involved in the Kosovo operation, the challenge of juggling these media responsibilities with all the other responsibilities associated with these demanding positions started to become increasingly difficult. In any future undertaking of this nature, consideration should be given to having either more qualified spokespersons to help share the burden, or, perhaps, to dedicate an appropriate senior officer solely to the spokesperson duty.

The other major lesson was appreciating the time and effort it took to prepare for the daily media event. Although the media conference itself only took from thirty minutes to an hour, the behind-the-scenes effort to prepare for it was considerable. This preparation included ensuring that our message was consistent with NATO and our allies. This is where technology can both help you and work against you. It helped because the spokespersons and staff were able to watch both the British and NATO media briefings each day before the combined CF/DND/ Department of Foreign Affairs and International Trade (DFAIT) brief, as a result of the time zone difference. On the other hand, the extensive media coverage and accessibility allowed everyone around the world to hear all accounts and to compare notes, thus the need to maintain consistency, especially in light of the importance of keeping what was sometimes a fragile multi-national alliance united.

It was also important to ensure that there was a consistent message from across the government of Canada. For this reason, it proved critical to have a senior dedicated spokesperson from DFAIT to participate in the daily briefing and respond to the policy and political questions. During the operation that brought Kosovo refugees to Canada, senior officials from Citizenship and Immigration Canada (CIC), the Red Cross, Health Canada and others also assisted with the briefings and question and answer periods where necessary. Again, credibility with the media can be lost very quickly and is subsequently difficult to re-establish; therefore, providing knowledgeable spokespeople at the appropriate level was one of the success stories of this campaign and one of the main lessons that needs to be remembered for the future.

Another major challenge was the ethical dilemma of trying to balance the media's, and thus the public's, right to know against operational security. An example was the decision not to reveal the identities of the pilots and support personnel involved in the conflict. This was based on experience gained during the Gulf War, where it was revealed that families of participants were sometimes harassed back in Canada. It was also decided to keep target descriptions very general. These decisions were not easy because of the pressure, perceived or otherwise, from the media and the public to put a human face on a story and the ever-present criticism of military secrecy and non-transparency. However, operational security and force protection were paramount, and ultimately the media accepted those decisions when the reasons for withholding operational and personal information were clearly spelled out.

It is safe to say that after some growing pains, DND's media campaign during the Kosovo crisis was a success. The considerable efforts put towards providing consistent, timely and accurate information to the public, through the media, was critical in maintaining public support and building public confidence. The positive media exposure contributed significantly to enhancing the public image of the institution. In fact, the success of these press conferences led to the establishment of regular press conferences, even after the end of the main events in Kosovo, to report on relevant military issues. This positive interaction between the military and the public is necessary and beneficial, and is a positive by-product of the Information Age and the changing expectations of Canadian society. It also fully supports the current CF/DND Outreach program.

POLITICAL FACTORS

Any military officer will acknowledge that the military is really just an extension of government policy and, as such, it is critical that strategic military leaders be sensitive to the political realities of today and respect the political process.

In a situation like Kosovo, with the constant glare of the international media and the near-zero tolerance for casualties, our political members obviously had a close interest in the activities of the military. As a result, there was a constant demand for information from Members of Parliament (MPs), in addition to that already being given to the media. This translated into, at the height of the Air Campaign, twice-weekly briefings to a combined parliamentary (SCONDVA/SCOFAIT) Standing Committee on National Defence and Veterans Affairs/Standing Committee on Foreign Affairs and International Trade. In addition, there were requests to brief Senate sub-committees and senior MPs, not to mention regular briefings to the minister of national defence. Again, as with the media briefs, it was important to have the right level of representation to brief these distinguished individuals. For this reason, it fell upon DCDS and COS J3 again to do the honours. Although they were certainly the best qualified for the job, it resulted in yet another demand on an already over-crowded schedule.

The lesson here is to expect considerable political interest in high-profile events such as the Kosovo crisis and be prepared to dedicate the necessary time and energy to meet the needs of the MPs and parliamentary committees. It is also important to remember that, like the media, MPs act as a conduit to the public. Maintaining their support is not only a responsibility, but also pays dividends in garnering the support of the Canadian public at large.

ETHICAL ISSUES

Throughout the operations in Kosovo, several ethical issues had to be addressed. They are a reflection of the challenges of the New World Order, and those that the senior political and military leadership need to be prepared to face. Probably the most overriding ethical dilemma involved the ethics of intervention versus the rights of sovereignty. Interestingly, Kosovo was just the most recent example of a deficiency that has existed since the end of the Cold War. This deficiency lies in the fact that under international law, the ethical principles which guide response to international crises are themselves somewhat contradictory—protection of sovereignty versus international responsibility and the right to intervene. What has brought this deficiency to a head is that the post Cold War world has been characterized by a proliferation of ethnic struggles, disintegration of states, manmade and natural disasters, and the prevalence of the international media to record it all. The combination of pressures to do something to respond to the horrors of genocide and ethnic cleansing, waves of refugees, and starving masses has been unprecedented.

As a result, the post Cold War era has required a modification to the original standard for non-intervention, where the only exception used to be genocide. Now the international community has added the following to the "justness of the cause" criteria: ethnic cleansing, massive abuse/suffering, and refugees creating instability to neighbouring states. So, in the case of Kosovo, when President Milosevic started expelling the ethnic Albanians from their homeland and committing alleged atrocities, the international community had just cause to intervene on humanitarian grounds. Therefore, the government of Canada made the decision to intervene and was fully prepared to be accountable for the consequences.

Although the basis for Canada and NATO's intervention was sound, the unique circumstances surrounding the Air Campaign led to some challenging questions regarding the military personnel involved in the conflict. Issues such as the status of CF personnel if shot down and captured and the legal ramifications of collateral damage had to be addressed. These issues provide more examples of how things have changed with respect to military operations in the past decade, and how important it is for military leaders to be flexible and responsive to the situation as it unfolds. Experience based on past successes no longer provides a guarantee for success in the future.

Of course, one of the oldest ethical responsibilities of a military commander is to ensure that the assigned personnel are prepared to carry out the mission. Although it is always a political decision to send a soldier, sailor or air person into harm's way, senior military leaders share in the responsibility of ensuring that deployed forces have a clear mandate, have the right equipment to do the job, are properly trained for the mission, and have the basic amenities and support to live and work. All of these prerequisites were met in respect to the Kosovo crisis. As stated previously, the CF's varied presence and experience in the Balkans helped reassure leaders that CF personnel were ready to participate. The prominent role of CF pilots, their CF-18 aircraft and Precision Guided Munitions (PGMs), and excellent work by the support personnel was a testament to the training they received. Funding was made available to ensure the appropriate support was provided to the deployed forces, and, as important, arrangements were made to support the families who remained back in Canada. Care of your personnel is paramount and one of the basic responsibilities of any commander, at any level.

LEGAL ISSUES

Because of the circumstances that led up to the Kosovo Air Campaign, combined with the need to minimize collateral damage, lawyers, military and otherwise, had a prominent role to play during the Kosovo crisis. One of the major accomplishments for the CF during this campaign was the creation of a national targeting policy that established a process by which targets assigned to CF pilots were reviewed and validated. This process was essential to ensure that the CF demonstrated due diligence in the acceptance of NATO assigned targets. Among other things, this process included both a legal and moral evaluation of each and every target, where a military lawyer would assess the target in terms of the Geneva Conventions governing the Laws of War. It would be confirmed that the target was a justifiable military objective and that its value outweighed the potential costs of collateral damage. This litmus test was done by NATO before the targets were assigned, and, for targets assigned to Canada, it was also repeated by a Canadian legal officer, and the chain of command, where necessary, to ensure that it met Canadian legal and moral standards. If it did not meet the Canadian standards, then the Task Force Commander was given the authority to refuse the target, with the full support of the chain of command.

Another important legal and moral aspect of operations is the Rules of Engagement (ROE) that are assigned to the participating forces. The ROE process has come a long way in the past ten years, to the point where ROE development and authorization is a mature and well-structured process. This was particularly important during the Kosovo crisis, where the overwhelming sensitivity to collateral damage required very clear and strict ROE. Fortunately, combined with the extensive targeting review, the assigned ROE proved very successful for the CF. This was really a tribute to the discipline and training of the Canadian aircrew who flew the missions over Kosovo and fully respected and applied the assigned ROE. If at any time during an actual bombing attack the pilot was either uncertain about the target itself, or if he was concerned about the potential of collateral damage, he was under very clear instructions to abort his mission and to bring the bombs back. This, in fact, happened on many missions.

With the ongoing changes in the Laws of Armed Conflict, and the varying situations under which the CF is being asked to deploy and operate, the military lawyer is becoming one of the commander's most important advisors. Therefore, the requirement to carefully review, and build into an operational plan, the legal considerations and consequences pertaining to a specific mission cannot be overstated.

THE IMPACT OF TECHNOLOGY

Over the centuries, increases in technology have arguably been the biggest single factor in shaping the way military force is applied. With the rate of technological change ever increasing, it is no surprise that it was technology that ultimately determined how the operations during the Kosovo conflict were executed. The impact of stealth technology and PGMs on the battlefield is obvious, but perhaps even more telling is the impact that these advances have had on the expectations of the public. The Gulf War, now reinforced by the Kosovo Air Campaign, has forever changed the public's perception of armed conflict. The expectation now is for "surgical" air strikes on military targets with no friendly or civilian casualties. Obviously, for those familiar with conflict, even with the latest technologies, this is almost an impossible task. But, nevertheless, it is an expectation that is very real and one that will influence the way armed conflicts unfold in the future.

Given that technology will significantly influence how future battles are fought, it stands to reason that the participation of any nation will be contingent on its ability to provide equipment and personnel with the requisite technology and expertise to allow it to fight in the expected manner. This was clearly the case in Kosovo where a number of nations could not participate in the bombing missions because of a lack of a PGM capability in their aircraft. Canada, having learned from its experience in the Gulf War, took the initiative to achieve a PGM capability for its CF-18 aircraft in the mid 1990s. The results of this were clear, as the CF was a full and capable participant in the bombing campaign right from the outset.

Having a PGM capability in Kosovo is really just one example of the importance of enhancing interoperability with our allies. The trend in modern conflict is moving increasingly towards more joint and combined operations, as part of multinational coalitions. As a result, the weapons, equipment and tactics used during any campaign will not only be determined by the expectations of the public, but also by the level of technology of the lead nation. Unquestionably, the United States is leading the way in technological development, and the challenge for the rest of the allies, including Canada, is to try and keep up.

The advancement of technology in this Information Age has also given rise to weapons and threats that do not fit the traditional mould. As a result, doctrine that can take advantage of these new weapons and defend against them must be developed. A prime example of one of these new weapons/threats is information. With the global domination of the media and the Internet, control of information may become the most powerful tool of all. In the war of the future, there will be greater emphasis put on psychological aspects such as information operations, where each side will try to create the desired attitudes, beliefs or perceptions.

Kosovo showed that Canada and the CF/DND are able to participate and hold their own in a modern conflict. However, it also confirmed that this level of confidence is perishable and there is a constant need to upgrade equipment to incorporate the latest technology and ensure that the CF remains viable and relevant. This is why the CF/DND is pursuing numerous capital equipment and upgrade programs for its key weapon systems.

COMMAND AND CONTROL

When speaking of the role of a commander in a military operation, there is no more important topic than command and control. Of course, the role of a strategic commander overseeing a deployed operation differs greatly from that of the operational commander on the ground. Simply put, the most important rule of command and control for a strategic commander is to let his operational commanders command. In other words, it is critical to have complete confidence in deployed commanders and to trust their judgement implicitly. This confidence and trust not only comes from recognizing the deployed commander's training and experience, but by properly preparing him/her before deployment.

For example, in the context of Kosovo, the task force commander for the Air Campaign was provided with very clear terms of reference and a statement of the CDS's Intent. In addition, as discussed previously, the Rules of Engagement (ROE) were well understood and adhered to by all pilots and a comprehensive targeting process was put in place. With this guidance, the mandate of the operational commander was clear and set the foundation of the command and control relationship. At the strategic level, the job of the DCDS was to put the process in place, not to second-guess the results of its use. For example, if the commander had serious concerns over an assigned target, the DCDS and his staff were there to assist in his decision-making on the acceptance or refusal of a target. If all the pilots returned from a mission with all their bombs because they could not identify their targets, the results were not criticized. In summary, to use a sports analogy, it is important to give operational commanders the rules of the game and let them play it.

While letting the operational commander run the show, it is imperative that the strategic commander be not only supportive, but also accessible to provide guidance or authority when required, and to be responsive when the requests come in. An example of this accessibility and responsiveness during the Kosovo crisis occurred when the commander of Task Force Aviano requested permission from NDHQ to switch from PGMs to "dumb" bombs due to local weather conditions. Although this was not as easy a decision as one might think, due to the prevailing climate with respect to collateral damage, it took a mere thirty minutes to approve the request, with the necessary limitations, and transmit it back to the commander. Similar responsiveness and flexibility were demonstrated when there was a requirement mid-way through the Air Campaign to upgrade the PGMs from 500-lb to 2,000-lb bombs.

As alluded to earlier, another important role of the strategic commander and the J-Staff was to assist the commander on the ground by allowing him to concentrate on his mission, by acting as the intermediary as much as possible for the significant number of political and media responsibilities in Canada.

Finally, although a "hands-off" approach may be what the operational commander requires to carry out his responsibilities, it is imperative that the strategic commander have the means and tools available to remain current on the intelligence and operational situation on the ground. Although a lot of information can be shared among allies in a coalition operation, as was the case for the Kosovo campaign, a secure joint command and control communication system is essential. Although the JC2IS system currently used by the CF/DND proved to be adequate for the type of campaign that was undertaken in Kosovo, especially with the support of our allies, it is clear that improvements will be required for future operations. This is why the CF/DND is now pursuing a CF Command System that will expand the capability of the JC2IS to make it more joint and bring us to our goal of a "Common Operating Picture" for commanders. As mentioned previously, the upgrades to the NDCC were also a step in the right direction to help accommodate the technology that is required for the strategic commander to maintain command and control.

THE WAY AHEAD

It is clear in many ways that the role of the strategic commander has changed considerably since the end of the Cold War. In order to try and predict what role the strategic commander will have in future warfare, it is necessary to try and foresee what the future holds in terms of global security. In this vein, it is relevant to ask, "Was Kosovo an aberration, or did it provide a glimpse of what future conflict will look like?" Although no one can accurately predict the future, there are a few things that can be said with some certainty about future conflicts. It is clear that the capability for rapid global deployment of combat-capable forces, operating within an alliance or coalition framework, will be essential. Being compatible and able to effectively interoperate with these diverse forces will be an absolute necessity. Joint and combined operations will be the norm.

Technology will continue to make the world a smaller place. Real-time intelligence and more capable and smarter weapons systems will enable the decisive delivery and concentration of combat power. But improvements in intelligence and weaponry are a double-edged sword, as they not only result in high expectations in the eyes of the public, but also force any potential adversary to resort to unconventional, or asymmetric, means to try to even the odds. Characteristics of these asymmetric strategies can include: using complex terrain, camouflaged dispersion of equipment, trying to break the will of the coalition by protracting the conflict, trying to de-legitimize the coalition's actions, playing on the coalition's aversion to casualties or trying to manipulate their "victim" status. Obviously, Kosovo can be characterized as an asymmetric-type conflict. It is probable that Canada, and other coalition partners, will be faced with some, or all, of these characteristics in future conflicts, and it is important that they prepare for this eventuality.

Finally, the unique characteristics of the type of conflicts that will predominate in the future, when combined with the demands of the international media, will continue to result in unprecedented scrutiny of any military action. As a result, ethical and legal considerations will remain much more at the forefront in future conflicts than in previous history. In addition, multinational coalitions will result in all participating nations having to continue to face both the ethical challenges of dealing with other nations and the political challenges of finding consensus among many partners and agendas.

In conclusion, it is probably safe to say that the battlefield of the future will look a lot more like Kosovo than anything that was expected during the Cold War. Therefore, it will be the responsibility of all allied nations, including Canada, to assimilate the lessons learned during the Kosovo crisis and continue to prepare for the unexpected, as it is this uncertainty that may best characterize this post Cold War period.

CONCLUSION

As we enter the twenty-first century, from the perspective of the strategic commander, the Kosovo crisis provides an excellent insight into the type of conflict that might be expected in the future. Although the characteristics required to successfully command at the strategic level are much the same as for previous commanders throughout history, this post Cold War era has revealed a number of other qualities that will become more and more essential as this unpredictable period progresses.

It is often said that a commander is only as good as the people around him, and this certainly holds true at the strategic level in the CF/DND. This applies right from the operational commanders who lead deployed forces on difficult missions around the world, to the members of the J-Staff in NDHQ who provide the staffing "horsepower" and advice to the commander. Providing these people with the right training, experience and mandate to complete their mission, and then letting them get on with the job, is key to the success of any future operation.

Strategic commanders need to be technologically literate, as the rapid evolution of technology is affecting all aspects of the way that we operate, from the complex systems used to maintain strategic command and control, to what the soldier, sailor and air person uses to fight on the ground. Ethical and legal considerations will challenge future commanders as never before and they must be prepared for them. The highly charged media environment will also continue to provide both challenges and opportunities. Finally, it is necessary for strategic leaders to maintain close and informed links with the Canadian political and civil processes, as well as Canada's international alliances, as it is these processes that provide the CF/DND with its legitimacy and support.

Lastly, and perhaps most importantly, strategic commanders need to be open-minded, flexible and able to think "outside the box." Although their previous experience will be critical to their future decision-making, it cannot be allowed to interfere with continuous change and the innovative thought processes that will be essential to meet the challenges of this uncertain future.

Kosovo, The Military-Civilian Challenge and the General's Role

Brigadier-General J.H.P.M Caron

Brigadier-General J.H.P.M. Caron is the current Commander of Land Force Québec Area.

INTRODUCTION

FROM 29 NOVEMBER TO 1 JUNE 1999, I was deployed in the Balkans as the Assistant Chief of Staff (COS), of the Kosovo Verification Mission (KVM) of the Organization for Security and Cooperation in Europe (OSCE). This unprecedented and challenging mission revealed numerous important lessons in the realm of military-civilian affairs in a conflict resolution scenario. However, to fully understand the complexities of the General's role in this setting, it is important to first provide a short historical context of the situation in Kosovo at the time that KVM was established, as well as a brief synopsis of its creation from the agreement between the Former Republic of Yugoslavia (FRY) and the OSCE on 16 October 1998, through its evacuation to the Former Yugoslav Republic of Macedonia (FYROM) on March 20 1999, to its final termination on 9 June 1999.

HISTORICAL CONTEXT

One of the basic rules of the Balkans is to expect the unexpected. Because the cancer that killed Yugoslavia began in Kosovo in 1989, it was reasonable to expect that if there was to be a war, it would begin in Kosovo. This expectation proved false. The Albanians had fought the Serbs at least four times in the twentieth century, so the Albanian decision not to fight in the early 1990s was born not of passivity but of shrewd logic. With the demise of communism, the Democratic League of Kosovo led by Ibrahim Rugova dominated Albanian Kosovo. With the 1991 war in Croatia and the Bosnian conflict the following year, the respective leaders, President Tudjman and President Izetbegovic, implored Rugova to open a southern front. He rejected their plea. Rugova was a pacifist, and the vast majority of Kosovo Albanians heartily supported this sentiment. They were horrified by the ethnic cleansing campaigns which accompanied the Serb seizure, first of one-third of Croatia, and then almost seventy percent of Bosnia, particularly the expulsion of Croats and then Bosniacs from areas which fell under Serb control. Nonetheless, Rugova did not give up on the idea of independence. He felt this was inevitable since there were so few Serbs left in Kosovo. However, he also considered talk of an uprising at that time as irresponsible.

In August 1995 disaster struck the Serbs. First, the Croats drove them out of the Krajina, then they lost much of western Bosnia. Bombed by NATO, they agreed to go to Dayton to talk peace. There, an agreement was reached over the fate of Bosnia. In addition, Milosevic agreed to hand back Eastern Slavonia to the Croats. Western leaders breathed a sigh of relief with the mistaken impression that the Balkan wars were over.

In Kosovo, the effect of the Dayton Peace Accord was traumatic. Soon after its signing, European Union (EC) nations rewarded Milosevic by recognising his new Federal Republic of Yugoslavia, which comprised of Serbia, Montenegro and Kosovo. Suddenly, Kosovo Albanians realised that passive resistance had failed as a strategy. They were not to be rewarded. Not surprisingly, they felt themselves penalised for eschewing violence.

For years there had been warnings of the catastrophe that might follow once the Kosovars became disillusioned with non-violence. By 1997, the *Levizja Popullore e Kosoves*, (LPK), or Popular Movement for Kosovo (a group of radicals formed in 1982 calling for insurrection) suddenly took on a more menacing look. In late 1992, the LPK played a leading role in establishing a fledging guerrilla group, the *Ushtria Clirimtare e Kosoves* (UCK) also know as the Kosovo Liberation Army (KLA). Their activities were marginal until 1997. This changed when on 28 February 1998, the Serbs decided to arrest a local brigand named Adem Jashari who was associated with the KLA. A week later Jashari's extended family of some eighty members were dead. Rage spread like wildfire across Kosovo. As a result, a small movement that had been making preparations for a long-term guerrilla war suddenly found itself swept up by a full popular uprising.

The result at first was successful. However, in July 1998, the Serbs launched a sustained counter-offensive. They reaped their revenge, burning villages and driving out the Kosovar Albanians. In October, NATO, concerned that a quarter of a million people who were now homeless and camped in the countryside would soon freeze to death, threatened Belgrade with air strikes. Backed by NATO's warning, Richard Holbrooke, the architect of the Dayton Peace Accord, negotiated a new agreement on 16 October with Milosevic. It envisaged an evacuation of Serbian forces, the introduction of civilian "verifiers" from the OSCE and the beginning of dialogue.[1]

THE KOSOVO VERIFICATION MISSION AND THE ORGANIZATION FOR SECURITY AND COOPERATION IN EUROPE

The OSCE established the KVM on 25 October 1998. It had a two-part mandate. One element was military in nature, namely, supervising a cease-fire and monitoring the reduction of Serb forces. The other component was of a more humanitarian dimension. It included monitoring of human rights issues, co-ordination of humanitarian aid, preparation of elections and the training of local police. The KVM was an unprecedented mission for the OSCE for two reasons; first its size—2000 international "verifiers"—and second for its de facto peacekeeping operations.

It is important to note that the OSCE had a formal agreement with only one party—the Serb authorities. There was no such agreement with the Kosovo Albanian authorities or the KLA. The essence of the mandate were demands made by the Contact Group (US, UK, France, Germany, Russia and later Italy) to end the repression of the civilian population, establish the withdrawal of Serb special police, ensure the return of refugees and foster co-operation with the International Criminal Tribunal.

THE KOSOVO VERIFICATION MISSION

The KVM was responsible for undertaking these tasks. KVM was an unarmed civilian mission; all members were dressed in civilian attire. Our security was assured, in theory, by the FRY authorities. The KVM was composed of approximately one quarter serving military members with the remaining individuals possessing skills in human rights, governance, policies, elections and humanitarian disciplines. Fifty-five different countries belong to the OSCE. The KVM had representatives from thirty-six of them. There was a tremendous pressure from the international community to get the mission on the ground quickly. A planning group was put together in Vienna in late October 1998, under the leadership of the Head of Mission, Ambassador William Walker, an American career diplomat who had recently led the UNTAES mission in Eastern Slavonia. The first members reached Kosovo in mid-November.

Initially, the mission grew slowly, however the rate increased by January 1999. By mid-month the mission's strength was approximately twelve hundred international members from about thirty countries; twenty-five percent were women, and fifteen hundred were locally employed personnel. The headquarters was composed of six functionally based departments. The senior person in each one of the departments was a representative of one of the Contact Group countries. In addition, one of the department heads originated from Norway, to represent the Chairman of the OSCE, who was Norwegian. All civilians were senior diplomats and the two military members were major generals. The Executive Committee was composed of these senior members and had executive power over the field portions of the mission, the five Regional Centres (RC) and the Induction Centre (KVMIC).

The KVM had some initial success as a negotiator of local cease-fires and exchanges of prisoners. But with time the level of violence kept increasing. Furthermore, we were unable to prevent the massacre of approximately forty Albanian Kosovars on 15 January 1999. Once again, this event galvanised the international community. The antagonists met at Rambouillet, France, at the behest of the Contact Group to find a solution. Two rounds of negotiations failed. As a result, the KVM evacuated Kosovo on 20 March and NATO began its bombing campaign against Serbia four days later. In early June 1999, the KVM was replaced by the United Mission in Kosovo (UNMIK) which was another OSCE mission.

THE STRATEGIC LEVEL OF COMMAND

The mission demonstrated a clear need for effective civil-military relations in peacekeeping operations. Without proper co-operation, these missions are unlikely to achieve their goals. The OSCE secretariat had limited experience in mounting large and multidisciplinary operations such as the KVM. In this case the mission conception, planning and implementation were poor. Under the pressure of time and international expectations, the actions that launched the operations lacked unity and co-ordination. The composition of the reconnaissance group in theatre changed continuously. While a number of timely actions were taken by the planning group in Vienna, the production of a strategic campaign plan did not occur. One of the military's greatest strengths is its planning and co-ordination abilities. It is critical that military leaders convince their civilian colleagues of the value and necessity of detailed planning before initiating operations.

The command and control arrangements were also inadequate for the size and complexity of the KVM. The internal organization of the OSCE did not facilitate co-ordination. The interplay between the Chairman-in-Office, the Permanent Council of the OSCE, and the Secretariat of the OSCE was ambiguous. As may be expected, national interests assumed an overwhelming importance. It was quite obvious that the Head of Mission and his deputies from the Contact Group countries received direction from their capitals. In some events it was quite clear that we were pursuing the objective of a particular national foreign policy and not OSCE objectives. This often led to uncoordinated or improvised action and created an unacceptable level of tension in the mission. In international actions such as this, clear lines of political authority and accountability must be established and respected.

The decision-makers or leaders at the strategic level must also improve co-ordination of all other actors in the theatre. In this case, the European Union (EU), some countries of the Contact Group, and others had observation missions on the ground since August 1999, as part of the Kosovo Observation Diplomatic Mission (KDOM). On many occasions the actions of these entities on the ground were at cross-purposes with the KVM. Some countries of the Contact Group, at the OSCE Permanent Council, could not ensure that the actions of their nationals on the ground were co-ordinated, or at the very least, did not interfere with the KVM initiatives.

Clearly, these tensions will always take place in these types of operations. What needs to be done, however, is to minimize their impact. In addition, the political authority must be made aware of the consequences of their decisions and be convinced of the early participation of the military in the planning process. Our permanent delegation to these international organizations can be extremely useful in these circumstances. Timely advice to our ambassador can be very useful in his discussions with his colleagues. We also need to deal with the different personalities at play. All this requires diplomacy, empathy and patience. The credibility of the military is demonstrated by recognizing the leadership of the civilian political authority and by providing advice in a tone and method that does not undermine this leadership. The civilian authority must be made to understand the advice provided and the risks involved.

THE OPERATIONAL LEVEL

The Kosovo operational theatre was one of moderate risk. The main threat to the mission members was being caught in the crossfire of the antagonists. This happened on a number of occasions. In addition the oppression and intimidation by the Serbians was high and caused some serious stress among some of the members.

At the operational level a distinct clash of cultures occured in the field between military personnel and civilians on such issues as command and control difficulties and the differing attitudes towards the media and human rights issues. Most military members have little experience of working with civilians or in a civilian mission. Not surprisingly most of the members, primarily officers, had difficulties adjusting to this environment and to the civilian mission which had human rights and humanitarian assistance mandates. There is, as the American political scientist Samuel Huntington noted, a tension between an institutionally conservative military and a more liberal society.[2] A critique of the British Army describes it as an institution that looks forward technologically, but backwards socially.[3]

As a result, the situation on the ground was tense. Facing an oppressive regime which was clearly breaching the peace agreement, but having very little means of enforcement, left many military frustrated. Added to this was the tension within the mission itself. The largest overwhelming civilian component of the mission wanted to focus primarily on the human dimension of the task. Unfortunately, they were unfamiliar with previous lessons.[4] "Another important lesson which can be derived from the experience of the UN in the former Yugoslavia," commented General Sir Michael Rose, "is the need for a coherent campaign plan which can ensure the necessary high level of coordination that is required between political momentum, security action and the humanitarian aid delivery mission."[5]

There was also an absence at the operational level of a campaign plan that established priorities and focused the mission's efforts. It left the deputies with parochial attitudes and working only towards their own particular area of interest and not for the benefit of the mission as a whole. This had a very disruptive impact on the overall mission. Further exacerbating the problem was the fact that we were simultaneously trying to establish the mission and conduct operations. Similar to the strategic level, the military members must attempt to convince their civilian colleagues of the value and necessity of planning, unity of effort and co-ordinated actions. This is best done as leading by example. In these circumstances what is needed is a spirit of compromise, a good listening capability, patience and perseverance. If the civilian authority has limited experience with the military, there will be initially a need to build trust. The military member will need to demonstrate that he or she is a team player and fully understands the multidisciplinary aspect of the mandate. In our case some senior military officers did not know the difference between a humanitarian action and a human rights initiative. This did not simplify the situation. In these types of missions if the military agenda is overly emphasized by the military, schisms can be created that can jeopardize the complete mission. The only times when the military should show no compromise is when the safety and security of mission members are at risk. In any other case they should demonstrate flexibility. The military members should also become cognizant of all "human dimension" tasks and have a basic understanding of their particular requirements.

The military mind, accustomed to a rigid operational structure, can find civilians haphazard and undisciplined. Working with a multinational, multidisciplinary mission with a large civilian component can be a new and difficult experience. Senior officers, particularly those without service in a national level headquarters, can be uncomfortable working with and for civilians. On many occasions, Ambassador Walker remarked to me that the only problem with his mission was that the military personnel could not accept that the KVM was a civilian operation, and adjust accordingly. This was a graphic military example of the need to demonstrate professionalism and ingenuity.

The gender question also exacerbated the cultural gap between civilians and the military. Good portions of the "human dimension" members were women. That component of the mission had a perception that the "human dimension" issues were given a lower priority than the verification tasks. This perception further complicated the execution of the mandate by creating tension and misunderstandings. A good portion of the human dimension members had much more experience than the military in these types of operations and felt unappreciated and both misused and under-employed. The military type had difficulty accepting and appreciating the wealth of skills their civilian cohorts possessed. Another difference between the two groups was that the mindset of the civilians was based on a longer time frame. Most military personnel were geared for only a six-month tour. To overcome these differences the military member must attempt to review and understand the mandate from a non-military perspective. This may mean that the military member must use different methods to achieve the aim. He or she must constantly remind himself or herself that it is not a military operation, or that in some cases the human dimension of the mandate is as important, if not more so than the military component. Personnel must also demonstrate empathy. They must be sensitive, understanding and appreciate the feelings, attitudes and abilities of others.

However, a number of the civilian members also showed an inability to adjust to the military perspective. For example, they had difficulty adopting the discipline required in this high-risk environment. It took a lot of persuasion and diplomacy to have them accept the requirement for a recall system and the need to rehearse an evacuation plan. Civilian members must be reminded and in some cases trained to appreciate the threat involved. This can be done by their military colleagues.

Language was another source of tension. With members from thirty-six different countries we could not expect that all would be fluent in English. Certain sensitivity was necessary, but there should be no compromise when the security of members is involved. In other circumstances, however, patience must be used. Even as tough as the OSCE standard is, namely that all members should be fluent in English, the reality was quite different. This often led to misunderstandings and embarrassing situations that could be a risk to security, particularly over radio networks. Military members should always avoid using jargon or abbreviations that would not be understood by all.

The military personnel must not expect that the staff/bureaucracy will be as efficient as his or her national system. It may be quite different from any typical military organization, as was the case for the KVM. Here we must let our civilian colleagues benefit from our efficiency and our mission oriented processes. If done in a diplomatic and humble way, our advice and methods will be readily accepted. Unless the senior military member surrounds himself or herself with members from his or her own nationality, which is not recommended, we need to be ready to accept a lower standard than what we would demand in our own system. As a result, the military member may have to delegate less and accomplish tasks that in our national system would be done by more junior officers.

CONCLUSION

It seems that the international community was in a reactive mode in dealing with the break-up of Yugoslavia. The crisis in Kosovo was no different; improvisation and a feeling of crisis appeared to cause the creation of the KVM. This led to hurried but ill-conceived actions that plagued the mission for the duration of its short life. Political authorities must find a way to balance the need for quick response and the requirement for well-conceived execution. Sound planning will bring dividends throughout the life of any mission. The KVM could have benefitted from more in-depth planning at the strategic and operational level. Senior military officers need to find ways to pass on to the political authorities their knowledge and experience in this realm. The KVM was in a sense a first, a peacekeeping operation with a multidisciplinary mandate conducted by a civilian mission, in a less than benign environment. This brought added pressure to military-civilian relations. Leaders, both military and civilian, must demonstrate cohesiveness and team work in such operations. More often the military members will be better skilled to deal with the situation because of their training and experience. However, they must perform their duties with patience and a sense of compromise and empathy so as not to undermine the civilian authority. They must fully understand the mandate, in particular the aspect that they may have less experience in areas such as human dimension tasks. The only situation where they should not compromise is when the security and safety of mission members are at risk. The civilians may demonstrate an aversion for the military mindset, which creates the imperative for military personnel to build trust and confidence and demonstrate team spirit.

This will not be easy and frustration will occur. However, the success of the mission depends on effective civil-military relations. The civilian nature of the KVM probably complicated matters for the military senior officers more than in other peacekeeping missions. Nevertheless, my observations are probably also appropriate for the more conventional peacekeeping missions. All this is to say it is important that we stop re-learning the same lessons from operation to operation.

NOTES

1. For an excellent summary and analysis of the current crisis in Kosovo see Paul Garde, "Missile Intelligent et Chausse-pied Rouillé," in *Politique Internationale*, No 84 Summer 1999, 11-64.
2. Samuel Huntington, "Democracy and Armed Forces: Reforming Civil-Military Relations" in *Journal of Democracy*, Vol. 6, No.4 October 1995, 9-17.

3. Joyce Eric, *Arms and the Man: Renewing the Armed Services* (London: Fabian Society, 1997).
4. For a very enlightening discussion of the tension in these types of operations see Donna Winslow, *Military Culture in Complex Cultural Encounters* (Ottawa University, 1999).
5. Michael Rose, "Military Aspects of Peacekeeping," in Wolfgang Bierman and Martin Vadset, *UN Peacekeeping in Trouble: Lessons Learned from the Former Yugoslavia* (Ashgate Publishing Ltd, 1998).

Stressors and Stresses on Peacekeeping Operations: Implications for Operational Level Commanders

Colonel Richard A. Hatton

Colonel Rick Hatton is a serving CF officer. He is currently the Chief of Staff of Land Forces Atlantic Area.

INTRODUCTION

"COMMAND AT THE HIGHEST LEVELS involves ultimate responsibility for a military force, which includes the consequences of military action in the civilian, political and social spheres. ...To be effective, a commander at the strategic and operational levels requires a wide range of qualities and skills in addition to strictly military expertise."[1] Canadian Forces (CF) doctrine includes the human dimension in its definition of command as "the exercise of the authority vested in an individual for the direction, co-ordination and control of military forces"[2] as well as in its emphasis on the human component as the most important component of command. Even operational level commanders must cultivate the human element to inspire and direct the activity of their commands.

The subject of stress in combat and its effects on individual combatants and small units has long been studied and the supporting literature is abundant. Considerably less research has focussed on stress-related issues facing the senior commander and, until very recently, relatively little has been written about stress experienced in peacekeeping operations. These particular aspects are neither well understood nor adequately addressed in the Canadian Forces. The changing nature of peacekeeping has given rise to the need to understand the nature of stressors inherent in those types of operations and of their consequences for individual health and organizational effectiveness.

This chapter examines how the stressors and stresses inherent in contemporary peacekeeping operations impact on operational-level commanders and on the effectiveness of personnel and organizations under their command. The chapter will briefly introduce the nature of stressors and stresses experienced in military operations and the impacts on individuals and organizations. It will then consider the nature of contemporary peacekeeping operations, highlighting those aspects that could contribute to a particular context of "chronic peacekeeping stressors." Considerations of chronic or contextual stressors on peacekeeping operations will reflect the personal experiences of the author's service with the United Nations Protection Force (UNPROFOR) in Bosnia, as well as the emerging literature reporting on this and other recent UN missions, primarily in the Former Yugoslavia. The discussion will relate how those chronic stressors on peacekeeping operations, sometimes combined with traumatic stressors, produce stresses which some experts have recently called "Peacekeeping Stress." These stresses potentially affect the quality of the commander's decision-making and personal relationships with subordinates as well as jeopardise his own and his soldiers' health and effectiveness. Considerations for operational-level commanders relating to stressors and stresses on peacekeeping operations will be discussed. Recommended measures that a commander can take to mitigate the harmful influence of some of his mission's chronic stressors will also be provided.

STRESSORS AND STRESSES ON MILITARY OPERATIONS

Stressors may be defined most simply as sources of stress. A stressor is a relatively objective characteristic of the environment that can be verified outside of the individual's experience. There is no single agreed definition of stress. However, one authoritative source is Glynis Breakwell and Keith Spacie's practical description of stress:

> ...as occurring when an individual is faced with demands that he or she finds impossible to satisfy. The demands can call for physical action, mental analysis or emotional reactions. The essential defining

characteristic is that the individual must feel incapable of satisfying the demands made.[3]

Stress is a highly subjective phenomenon and reactions can vary widely. Strain is viewed as the individual's psychological, physiological or emotional reaction to the stress. Symptoms vary, but they are generally interpreted to include cognitive deficits, emotional disturbance, physical illness and behavioural disturbance. The pattern of symptoms is determined by the nature of the source of the stress, the history and nature of the individual and the context in which stress is experienced.[4]

Although the measurement of stress is complex, the abundant research concerning stress symptoms points out that stress impairs the social, psychological and physical functioning of the individual. People experiencing stress are more likely to report psychological changes such as irritability and anxiety at work and at home, more frequent technical mistakes and errors in judgement. As stress seems to weaken the auto-immune system, stressed individuals are more susceptible to disease. Long-term physical effects of stress include chronic diseases such as high blood pressure, heart disease, diabetes and asthma attacks. There is evidence that continued stress is associated with changes in behaviour such as increased substance abuse, usually alcoholism, and can lead to increased likelihood of marital breakdown and suicide.[5] Organizational outcomes of stress can include job dissatisfaction, job turnover or turnover intentions and degradation of job performance.[6]

Various moderators[7] have been considered by researchers to affect the relationship between stressors, stress appraisal and subsequent stress reaction. Moderators of stress that are frequently cited in the literature are work group (or unit) cohesion, confidence in unit leadership and social support.[8]

> Work group cohesion has been posited as providing an inoculating effect from combat/traumatic stressors...such that individuals working in cohesive units experience less deleterious effects as a consequence of exposure to traumatic stressors. The moderating effect may be attributable to either the increased confidence in the abilities of peers and leaders or the provision of social support by other work group members.[9]

In a study of Israeli Army units, the noted Israeli military psychologist, Reuven Gal, has associated high confidence in leaders with better unit performance and fewer adverse effects of stress reactions.[10] In his survey of returning CF peacekeepers, K.M. Farley from the CF Personnel Applied Research Unit reported that confidence in unit leadership and group cohesion significantly predicted decreased stress reactions.[11]

In the identification of stressors as sources of stress, most analyses distinguish between stressors associated with the individual, those generated by the employing organization and those which are external to the organization. As part of a recent study for the British Army, Glynis Breakwell and Keith Spacie conducted over one hundred interviews with army officers who experienced high or moderate intensity operations, mostly in the Gulf War or in Bosnia with UNPROFOR or IFOR. Their study developed a practical "Typology of Stressors," divided into four principal types: Organizational; Physical; Interpersonal and Psychological. The resulting list of stressors is summarized in Figure 1.

Many researchers have distinguished between chronic, acute and catastrophic stressors. Chronic stressors have been defined as having no specific time onset; they may be frequent or ongoing in occurrence and may vary in intensity. Acute stressors have a specific time of onset, occur very infrequently and are of high intensity. Examples of acute stressors include getting fired from a job or being involved in a shooting incident. Catastrophic events share many of the same characteristics, but involve more significant threat to life to a larger group and/or prolonged suffering.[12] Considerable research has been conducted concerning individuals' reactions to traumatic events. Various labels have been given to the nature of traumatic stressors, such as combat stress, critical incident stress and rescue stress. Traumatic stressors may be either acute or catastrophic.

There is increasing recognition that peacekeeping may incorporate significant exposure to traumatic events, including combat-like conditions such as exposure to direct attack from small arms, rocket, mortar or artillery fire, contact with land mines, witnessing the death or injury of others and handling of wounded or dead bodies.[13] The phenomenon has been given various and nearly synonymous labels such as "Peacekeeper Stress,"[14] "Peacekeeping Stress,"[15] UN Role Stress,"[16] and "UN Soldiers' Stress Syndrome."[17] This chapter will use the term Peacekeeping Stress. In addition to the acknowledgement of exposure to traumatic events, there is also increasing recognition that other more chronic or contextual stressors are associated with peacekeeping operations. In their study of peacekeeping stress, Lamerson and Kelloway suggest that "peacekeeping is characterised by the occurrence of acute and/or catastrophic stressors in an environment replete with chronic stressors" and they suggest that both traumatic and chronic stressors play an important role in the development of peacekeeping stress.[18]

With a view to considering implications for senior commanders, the nature of these chronic "peacekeeping" stressors will be examined further. Before this will be done, however, it would be useful to consider how the nature of peacekeeping operations has changed in recent years.

Figure 1—Breakwell's and Spacie's Typology of Stressors[19]

Organizational	Physical	Interpersonal	Psychological
Organizational culture cross cultural contacts working between/across organizations mission drift public interest/concern training deficits multiple roles command arrangements rules of engagement political intervention managing change communication systems inequity in recognition stereotypes inter-unit rivalry propaganda organizational arrangements	climatic conditions workload fatigue sleep loss physical conditions exercise regime dietary restrictions equipment functionality equipment availability physical danger	relationships with superiors (respect) relationships with peers (mutuality) relationships with subordinates (discipline) team dynamics separation from family/isolation loss/injury of comrades dealing with multiple fatalities relationship with opponents relationship with civilians negotiations non-operational life post-operational life	lack of knowledge or skill memory limitations capacity to delegate fear of failure/reputations ambition physical fear reaction to the Media moral repugnance

THE CHANGING NATURE OF PEACEKEEPING OPERATIONS

The relaxation of East-West tensions in the late 1980s and early 1990s, removed many of the political obstacles that had previously limited the scope of peacekeeping. As a result, the number of UN peacekeeping missions and the number of personnel deployed expanded significantly during those years. Peacekeeping tasks extended well beyond the traditional monitoring of cease-fires, to include such complex undertakings as implementing comprehensive peace settlements, monitoring elections and facilitating the delivery of humanitarian aid. Significantly, whereas peacekeeping forces were previously deployed into areas of inter-state conflict, they increasingly became involved in more complex intra-state conflicts. The new generation of peacekeeping operations began to involve a wider group of participants to include military forces, police, civilian monitors and non-governmental organizations (NGOs). Previous "traditional" peacekeeping operations had tended to be established under Chapter VI of the UN Charter and usually adhered to the peacekeeping principles of consent of the parties, impartiality and use of force only in self-defence. New generation peacekeeping operations could be established under Chapter VI or VII of the Charter and often did not benefit from full consent of the parties and at times mandated, and used, force beyond self-defence.[20]

A number of these new UN missions experienced considerable difficulty; some were clearly failures. A full examination of the reasons for these failures is well outside of the scope of this chapter.[21] Significant criticisms have been heaped on the UN, member states, the media and others, with plenty of blame for all to share. Examples include poor UN leadership, unclear mission command and control, inadequate or conflicting UN mandates, unrealistic and unreasonable political and public expectations, mission creep, inappropriate rules of engagement, absence of strategic vision, deficiencies in campaign planning, failure of the Security Council to deal decisively with emerging crises, failure of member states to provide adequate forces, and media distortion of events.

The changing nature of peacekeeping has required broader definitions to encompass the various types of operations. Use of the more comprehensive term "peace support operations" has come into fashion. There are five forms of peace support operations: preventive diplomacy, peacemaking, peacekeeping, peace enforcement and post-conflict peace-building.[22] Preventive diplomacy is "action to prevent disputes from arising between parties, to prevent existing disputes from escalating into conflicts and to limit the spread of the latter when they do occur." Peacemaking is "action to bring hostile parties to agreement, essentially through such peaceful means as those foreseen in Chapter VI of the UN Charter." According to the United Nations, peacekeeping is "the deployment of a United Nations presence in the field, hitherto with the consent of all the parties concerned, normally involving United Nations military and/or police personnel and frequently civilians as well."[23] The term peace enforcement is defined as "operations carried out to restore peace between belligerent parties who do not all consent to intervention and who may be engaged in combat activities."[24] Post-conflict peace-building is "action to identify and support structures which will tend to strengthen and solidify peace in order to avoid a relapse into conflict."[25]

Although there are a number of similarities between peacekeeping and peace enforcement operations, the terms clearly are not interchangeable. This chapter will focus on peacekeeping operations, although many of the observations and considerations it will make could apply as well to peace enforcement operations.

Since 1994, the number of UN peacekeeping missions and the number of UN troops deployed have declined dramatically. This is largely a result of the unwillingness or inability of the UN Security Council to respond effectively to intra-state conflicts, the reduction of the ability to respond due to the UN financial crisis, the onset of "donor fatigue" in many member nations and the failure to make substantial progress on UN structural reform. As the UN scaled back on its own involvement in peacekeeping, it has encouraged, or at least allowed, NATO, regional organizations or "coalitions of the willing" under Chapter VII of the Charter to undertake multi-national peacekeeping and peace enforcement operations.[26]

Despite the decline in UN-led peacekeeping operations, a number of missions were conducted or are presently underway,[27] including some very risky new UN missions in Africa. Canadian foreign and defence policies remain committed to multilateral security and the resolution of conflicts by peaceful means. Based on history and present policies, the CF can clearly expect to continue to be called upon to contribute personnel to peacekeeping operations, whether they be UN-led or NATO-led. CF personnel can expect to participate in peacekeeping operations and senior CF officers will continue to be in high demand for employment in some very challenging senior command or staff positions.

STRESSORS AND STRESSES ON CONTEMPORARY PEACEKEEPING OPERATIONS

As previously mentioned, Lamerson and Kelloway proposed that both traumatic and contextual stressors play an important role in the development of peacekeeping stress. In their transactional model, they propose that "contemporary peacekeeping deployments are characterised as comprising exposure to traumatic stressors in a context of chronic stressors."[28]

Whereas peacekeeping missions have always contained the potential for danger, more recent peacekeeping missions are much more dangerous than previous "traditional" missions.[29] Combat-like situations and other traumatic events have resulted in thousands of UN peacekeeping soldiers being subjected to traumatic stress.[30] Studies of emergency services personnel show that previous exposure to traumatic events may heighten individual reactions[31] and Israeli Army studies show that the effects of repeated exposure to traumatic events are cumulative[32]. If these reactions apply to contemporary peacekeeping operations, there are significant consequences to consider for CF personnel serving in the types of trades and units which can reasonably expect to deploy frequently on peacekeeping missions.

Peacekeeping missions have been known for a long time, at least anecdotally, to be characterized by chronic or contextual stressors. As stated previously, chronic stressors, as distinct from traumatic stressors, have been defined as having no specific time onset, occurring either frequently or on a relatively ongoing or unchanging basis. They may vary in intensity.[33] Examples of chronic stressors on peacekeeping operations will be explored later in the chapter. In contemporary peacekeeping missions, not only have traumatic stressors become more acute and more frequent, but chronic stressors have also become more pervasive and disruptive. This has significant implications for commanders and for armed forces frequently cycling units through such operations.

Reuven Gal has studied stress experienced by soldiers on UN peacekeeping operations in Lebanon, Golan, Sinai and the Former Yugoslavia and by Israeli soldiers who were deployed on internal security operations in the West Bank and Gaza.[34] While Gal notes that the ultimate stress faced by soldiers is that experienced in combat, he has concluded that peacekeeping stress exists, and has classified peacekeeping stress into four categories: Situation Stress; Professional Stress; Organizational Stress and Moral Stress. Gal's stressed peacekeeper is typified by the soldier who is deployed to a strange land, exposed to people with foreign cultures in a conflict he or she does not understand. He notes that the peacekeeper sometimes faces hostility and life-threatening hazards, is often called upon to carry out tasks for which he has not been trained, may be presented with moral dilemmas that challenge his beliefs and comprehension and is frequently required to respond to situations in a restrained manner, under-utilising his professional combat skills. He observes that such a peacekeeper can suffer a crisis in self-confidence and professional pride and, due to the nature of the organization of peacekeeping forces, might be deprived of the sense of patriotism, unit cohesion, camaraderie and the familiar leadership that would normally sustain him in such situations.

Lamerson and Kelloway contend that in peacekeeping operations chronic stressors contribute to individual stress reactions, in addition to the contribution exerted by exposure to traumatic events.[35] They assert that Role Conflict, Role Ambiguity and Role Overload have significant impacts as contextual stressors. Both intra-role conflict (experiencing incompatible demands within a given role) and inter-role conflict (experiencing incompatible demands from two or more conflicting roles) have long been identified in organizational research as stressors. Role conflict features highly in the recent literature commenting on the nature of contemporary peacekeeping missions. For example, peacekeepers in Bosnia with UNPROFOR, individually and collectively, experienced significant role conflict between the stated mission (humanitarian assistance), public and media expectations and self-preservation. Role conflicts were also apparent between the stated UN mission (facilitate humanitarian assistance) and the Western public/media-expected mission (defend and promote the Bosnian-Muslims, deter the Bosnian-Serbs). With unclear or conflicting mandates, hostile and unfamiliar situations, unsuitable rules of engagement and inadequate training and preparation, role ambiguity can be a significant stressor in peacekeeping operations. Role overload is another frequently studied stressor that exists in peacekeeping operations. This is experienced at all levels—the over-tasked individual, the over-extended unit, the force whose roles have had to expand, sometimes very dramatically, to suit the vagaries of "mission creep" with no increase in resources or reduction of other tasks. Lamerson contends that UN peacekeepers may experience a particular type of role stress—called UN Role Stress—when they fundamentally disagree with the premises or official UN policies of the peacekeeping deployment.[36]

Other contextual stressors noted by Lamerson and Kelloway include marital or family stressors. Researchers in surveys of personal stress on peacekeeping duties have frequently cited spouse or family separation, lack of family contact, worries over family problems and inability to assist families as significant concerns.[37]

In considering how different stressors interact, Lamerson and Kelloway consider that:

> The simultaneous experience of combat and contextual [chronic] stressors has multiplicative rather than additive effects. That is, individuals experiencing a large number of chronic stressors may be particularly vulnerable to exposure to traumatic stressors. Conversely, the experience of being fired on, or seeing friends wounded may heighten the effects of role or marital stressors. This suggestion is consistent with a vulnerability hypothesis, suggesting that personal and environmental factors may make individuals more susceptible to the effects of traumatic stressors.[38]

Breakwell and Spacie considered the key stressors evident on recent military operations to be divided into four principle types: Organizational, Physical, Interpersonal and Psychological. In the light of the foregoing discussion of stressors and stresses and the brief examination of the emerging literature relating to "Peacekeeping Stress," Breakwell's and Spacie's Typology of Stressors (Figure 1) would seem to be a practical and flexible framework within which to consider the nature of stressors on contemporary peacekeeping operations.[39] Of the four types of stressors noted, the operational-level commander on peacekeeping operations is more affected by, and is better able to mitigate, organizational, interpersonal and psychological stressors. Physical stressors, which are more immediate and localised, are largely in the purview of the tactical-level commander.

ORGANIZATIONAL STRESSORS

Chronic stressors relating to organizational considerations have clearly been present in recent UN missions such as UNPROFOR. The literature is replete with references to the lack of strategic vision, inadequate and conflicting mandates, faulty mission premises, flaws in UN organization and command relationships, inadequate rules of engagement, flawed and unenforceable peace agreements, role conflict/ambiguity/overload, mission drift, *ad hoc* headquarters and unit organizational arrangements, and incompetent UN financial and administration arrangements. The UN is attempting to reform, but progress is slow. Recent management changes and staff reductions in the UN Directorate of Peacekeeping Operations (DPKO) have significantly diminished its effectiveness. The cessation, at the insistence of envious non-aligned nations, of the practice of developed member countries providing professional military officers to augment UN DPKO planning staff on a *gratis* basis, has stripped that organization of its talent. As a result, the UN is becoming less able to plan for and cope with future complex peacekeeping operations.

Other chronic stressors that have been evident on peacekeeping operations include national conflicts between participant commanders and staffs, political interference or meddling from member states and both direct and indirect pursuit of nations' or private organizations' particular agendas. The author observed the detrimental effects of these elements on force cohesion and mission effectiveness in UNPROFOR in 1995, to the immense frustration of numerous participants, both military and civilian.

The conflict between the organizational culture of military services and the UN can generate stresses on peacekeeping operations. Personnel from Western military cultures frequently expect that there will be clear-cut military solutions to operational problems. Pressures arise when this expectation is unsatisfied and problems cannot be resolved by military means, or solutions are partial or compromises. Western military officers and soldiers tend to be accustomed to relatively rigid hierarchical structures. They are less comfortable with the looser structures and imprecise direction of the UN.

Officers who fail to recognise this constraint upon their efficacy harbour unrealistic expectations of themselves and of their potential impact. This can result in the experience of subjective stress. Furthermore, military organizational structure implicitly, and often explicitly, rejects the reality of stress as more than an excuse for inadequate performance... To the extent that this representation of stress is dominant, it acts as a form of stressor in itself for those who face significant pressures.[40]

Military operations have always involved cross-cultural contacts with enemies, local populations and allies, but this contact has become much closer and more pervasive in the multi-national forces and headquarters of peacekeeping missions. Organizations like NATO have the advantage of similar military cultures, experiences of working together and standardised doctrine and staff procedures. The UN has no such advantage. Commanders and staff with markedly different organizational styles, command ethos, degrees of openness, reliability and professionalism are required to work closely together. This introduces unpredictability, challenging expectations and assumptions, diminishing control, and results in stress.[41]

Contemporary peacekeeping operations tend to be very complex and increasingly multi-dimensional. In addition to traditional military components, recent UN peacekeeping missions typically include significant political, police, electoral, human rights, humanitarian and developmental dimensions and components. This introduces a level of complexity in working relationships, decision-making and resourcing in situations which often lack an adequate structure for command, control and co-ordination. The resulting conflicts and delays in arriving at decisions and effective solutions to problems can lead to significant pressure on both military and civilian participants.

Problems for senior commanders arise when there are doubts about the central purpose of the mission and when they lack the resources, authority or contributing nations' support to satisfy new demands. "Mission creep" or "mission drift" occurs when agencies become drawn into activities that are not core to the original mission. This situation has occurred with military forces on several complex UN peacekeeping operations, certainly in the missions in the Former Yugoslavia, and especially UNPROFOR. Inadequate or unclear Security Council resolutions and mandates often fail to provide sufficient guidance to adapt to changing situations. Humanitarian organizations, national publics or the media may introduce new expectations, either suddenly or gradually, which contribute to increased demands. Such uncertainties generate self-doubt and act as sources of stress. Well-meaning military officers, in search of more substantial missions or perhaps enhanced personal credit with civil organizations, can unwittingly contribute to the process.

The public and the media, especially in Western countries, increasingly subject military operations and senior officers to intense scrutiny. This can place operational-level commanders under enormous stress. The case of the operation in Somalia is perhaps most apparent and most painful to the CF. Commanders can feel, sometimes for good reason, that public concerns are misplaced or that media reports may be exaggerated, biased or simply not factual. They may believe that the public does not appreciate or respect the efforts and risks that they and their soldiers take. They may feel helpless to correct media or public misperceptions and intensely frustrated at the failure or unwillingness of higher authorities to help them. They may believe that the bias of media reporting places them and their soldiers at greater risk.

The effects of role conflict, role ambiguity and role overload, previously discussed, are clearly evident and are significant chronic stressors for commanders and troops on contemporary peacekeeping operations.

Political interference with force commanders or national contingent commanders can significantly undermine military authority, priorities and practices, placing commanders under considerable stress. Political pressures can arise as politicians may have different (and variable) perceptions of aims, priorities and events. Furthermore, the diversity and pervasiveness of international media and "instant reporting" of situations, factual or otherwise, may diminish the perception of military authority and credibility and interfere with the chain of command and communication processes.

Unity of command poses a greater challenge in composite or *ad hoc* formations, units and headquarters. Yet these are the types of organizational arrangements that have become increasingly the norm on peacekeeping operations. Even established units must often be reinforced by individuals or sub-units to deploy on operations. Such organizations may, at least initially, lack coherence and stability and are potentially more difficult to control than formed units who normally work and train together. This situation could not only result in increased stress for commanders and troops, but might actually suppress the mitigating influences of unit cohesion and confidence in leaders as stress moderators.

In the preceding paragraphs, it has been argued that organizational stressors that are often present on peacekeeping operations can result in stresses that could have both individual and group impacts. These stresses can be detrimental to personal health, can diminish the effectiveness of individual commanders and soldiers and could affect entire organizations.

INTERPERSONAL STRESSORS

"Poor command relationships are potentially the single greatest source of stress. A commander needs to engender trust and confidence. If these are not present, the relationship with subordinates will become a source of friction and stress. Achieving trust and confidence is ... extraordinarily difficult."[42] This is true in established field units in national armies and is even more evident in *ad hoc* or multinational headquarters and units typical of peacekeeping operations.

It is difficult to establish strong peer group relationships and effective team-building in such organizations.

Because of the increasingly multi-dimensional character of contemporary peacekeeping operations, senior military commanders must co-operate with civilian officials, representing the political authority, police, humanitarian or human rights organizations and development agencies. The military commander might be either equivalent in status or subordinate to a Special Representative of the UN Secretary General or another official. He might not be adequately prepared to deal with these complex and sometimes unclear inter-personal situations, which may severely tax both his patience and abilities.

The influence of separation from spouse, family and friends has been discussed previously. Commanders can also feel isolated, not only physically but also psychologically, through the nature of multi-national peacekeeping operations and the power and onerous responsibilities of their position. The sense of loneliness in command is a pressure in itself and magnifies the impact of other pressures.

The nature of contemporary peace support operations frequently brings senior UN commanders into direct contact with members of belligerent or opposing forces (military commanders, warlords, political or faction leaders). This contact may be informal or it may be through more formalised negotiations, consultations or joint commissions. The standards of professionalism, honesty and civilised behaviour demonstrated by these opposing leaders may often be highly disappointing to professional Western military officers. This can introduce stressors associated with unpredictability and even a sense of hopelessness.

PSYCHOLOGICAL STRESSORS

Commanders who believe they lack knowledge of either the operational situation or of the job that they have to perform are more likely to feel (under) pressure. This effectively means that poor briefing and poor training will be likely to precipitate stress. Genuine skill or knowledge deficits interact in complex ways to compound the negative impact of other stressors. They impair competency, retard decision-making and undermine confidence....The commander must be aware that the deficit exists for it to have maximum ill effect.[43]

Memory, including long and short-term retrieval capacity, varies widely amongst individuals. Increasingly complex peacekeeping operations place a high premium on a good memory in a commander. According to Breakwell and Spacie, baseline memory abilities will be degraded by sustained operations, lack of sleep, work overload, and poor working conditions. These conditions have certainly existed for senior officers serving in peacekeeping operations such as

UNPROFOR. "Commanders who recognize that they are not performing at their normal level can find these memory problems act as prime stressors."[44]

If a commander believes his staff or subordinates do not trust him or if he feels he cannot trust them, these are potent psychological factors that can put enormous pressure on a senior commander. On contemporary peacekeeping operations, the perceived inability of some subordinates to perform to the commander's expectations, especially in a complex and multi-dimensional environment, may inhibit the commander's capacity to delegate. Standards in training, military culture and professional abilities and personal competence can and do vary widely in the military forces of different contributing countries on peacekeeping operations.

Finally, many senior officers have experienced extreme moral repugnance when faced with horrific situations in the types of intra-state conflicts which have been associated with recent UN peacekeeping operations in the Former Yugoslavia, Rwanda and Somalia. Such situations have included the wholesale slaughter or abuse of innocents, including women and children, ethnic cleansing, murder of officials or peacekeepers, starvation and random acts of senseless violence. Despite a sense of professionalism that may sustain some officers, revulsion from the experience of these acts may, at a deep level, act as a stressor.[45]

CONSIDERATIONS FOR THE OPERATIONAL-LEVEL COMMANDER

In the view of the author, Peacekeeping Stress is real and its impact is potentially significant both in terms of individual health and organizational effectiveness.

The ability of the operational-level commander to personally deal with traumatic stressors and stresses may be somewhat limited. The immediate and localized nature of traumatic stressors put them largely in the purview of the tactical level, although the senior commander should at least be supportive of efforts, such as personal coping strategies and interventions available to subordinate commanders and units. Furthermore, the commander should do what he can to reinforce, at the tactical level, the well-established positive influences of unit cohesion and confidence in leadership in moderating the effects of traumatic stress.

Contemporary peacekeeping operations are replete with chronic or contextual stressors. This paper has discussed the nature of some of these stressors and examined how they act to cause stresses which can diminish individual health and organizational effectiveness. The operational-level commander is, in fact, the best able to understand and deal with these chronic stressors. This is because of the authority and status of his high command position, his direct relationship with the higher-level political authorities, his working association with other mission dimensions and agencies (e.g. political, police, humanitarian, human rights, electoral), his personal contacts with the most senior levels of belligerent forces (e.g. military commanders, political leaders) and finally his personal experience. Tactical-level commanders and organizations are limited in their abilities to influence these aspects and the operational-level commander should consider them to be part of the human dimension of his own command responsibilities.

Some researchers have recently studied the nature of chronic stressors on operations and have offered useful ways to categorise and study them. Breakwell's and Spacie's "Typology of Stressors"[46] in relation to contemporary peacekeeping operations is both valid and practical. CF officers preparing for senior command or staff positions on peacekeeping operations would also be well advised to read Breakwell's and Spacie's pamphlet *Pressures Facing Commanders* and keep it at hand. Such a typology is not a template to predict and resolve stress-related problems, but a prudent commander could use it as a tool in considering which stressors will have the greatest effect on him and his mission, and thereby help him determine where he should concentrate his efforts.

The nature of organizational and interpersonal stressors in particular, as described by Breakwell and Spacie and expanded upon in this chapter, seem to relate to the operational-level commander, both in terms of effects on him and his ability to affect them. Examples of areas in which the operational-level commander could involve himself more to reduce the impact of chronic stressors include clarification of strategic/operational guidance, role clarification and rationalisation, mission creep, organizational arrangements, cross-cultural conflicts, cross-organizational communication, rules of engagement and media/public relations. Other areas such as political interference and institutional competence will be more problematic issues to deal with.

Finally, the operational-level commander must understand that he is not immune to stressors on operations. He must recognize the stressors that impact on him and learn to identify symptoms of stress in himself. As discussed previously, this is frequently a problem in military organizational cultures that consider stress to be more associated with failure or an excuse for poor performance, than a genuine medical condition. For the sake of his own health and effectiveness, the commander needs to be prepared to employ personal coping strategies and informal support to deal with stress.

The CF has an excellent stress management program that includes effective preventive briefings and debriefings as well as critical incident stress counselling. Some of Canada's research in this area has been "world class" and Canada has been instrumental in helping the United Nations recognize the problem and adopt a stress management program.[47] But many senior officers are either unaware of, or shun, stress management programs which are available in the CF. Personnel deploying with formed CF units are generally being adequately handled, but many members who are deployed as individuals are not.[48] Better vigilance is required on the part of the CF as an institution, and on the part of senior officers themselves, to ensure that appropriate stress management programs are made available to all individuals and that follow-up action is taken.

The Canadian Forces do not appear currently to have a good appreciation of the extent to which stress is affecting its senior officers. Some of these officers have experienced horrendous situations as commanders or senior staff on peacekeeping operations, and have simply returned back to other high pressure duties in Canada, without ever being properly debriefed or treated. Clearly, the Canadian Forces need to conduct a comprehensive and scientifically-based analysis to determine the scope of this problem.

CONCLUSION

Much has been written concerning the subject of combat stress and its effects on both individuals and organizations. Until recently, very little research has focussed on stress-related issues facing the senior commander and even less has been written about stress experienced in peacekeeping operations. This may be due, in part, to the relatively benign nature of "traditional" UN peacekeeping operations during the Cold War. Since the early 1990s, however, the dramatically changing nature of peacekeeping has given rise to a growing body of research which points to the existence of a phenomenon which some call Peacekeeping Stress.

Recent research has pointed out the existence of a number of chronic situations or aspects of the operational environment that may form a context of stressors experienced by personnel serving on contemporary peacekeeping operations. These chronic stressors may, separately or together, result in stress that can degrade the health and performance of individuals and organizations. Furthermore, because of the changing nature of the types of conflict situations (intra-state, ethnic hatred, less consent, more violence) in which contemporary peacekeeping operations have been employed, traumatic stressors have also been increasingly present, compared with previous and more traditional missions. In studying how these stressors interact, some researchers have suggested that "contemporary peacekeeping deployments are best characterized as comprising exposure to traumatic stressors in a context of chronic stressors."[49] Some of these same researchers have also suggested that the simultaneous experience of traumatic and chronic stressors may have multiplicative rather than additive effects.

This has significant impacts for the armed forces of countries such as Canada, since it appears that Canadian foreign and defence policies remain committed to participation in multi-lateral peacekeeping missions. Senior commanders need to understand the nature of stressors inherent in peacekeeping operations and of their consequences.

A review of the nature of chronic stressors on peacekeeping operations suggests that a number of them may be influenced by the operational-level commander, by virtue of his special position. A prudent commander who understands the nature of stressors and stresses and their impacts on individuals (including himself) and organizations, should use the full measure of his authority, personal skill and experience to reduce the harmful nature of stressors which are contextual to his mission.

NOTES

1. Canadian Forces Publication (CFP), *B-GL-300-003/FP-000 Command* (Ottawa: National Defence Headquarters, Land Force, 1996), 6.
2. CFP, *Command*, 4.
3. Glynis Breakwell and Keith Spacie, *Pressures Facing Commanders* (Camberley UK: The Strategic and Combat Studies Institute, 1997), 4.
4. Ibid, 4-5.
5. Ibid, 5-6.
6. C.D. Lamerson and E.K. Kelloway, "Towards a Model of Peacekeeping Stress: Traumatic and Contextual Influences," *Canadian Psychology*, Vol 37(4) (Canadian Psychological Association: 1996), 257-258.
7. A moderator is a variable that affects the relationship between two or more other variables.
8. K.M. Farley, "Stress in Military Operations" Working Paper 95-2 (Willowdale ON: Canadian Forces Personnel Applied Research Unit, 1995). Also see various researchers cited in Lamerson and Kelloway 256.
9. Lamerson and Kelloway 256.
10. Reuven Gal, *A Portrait of the Israeli Soldier* (New York: Greenwood, 1986).
11. Farley, 9.
12. Lamerson and Kelloway, 253.
13. Lamerson and Kelloway's own research and other works they cited were based on Canadian Forces personnel engaged in UN peacekeeping operations in the Former Yugoslavia, 253-254.
14. Reuven Gal, "Le Stress du soldat de paix," *Les champs de mars* (Paris: Center d'étude en science sociales de la Defense (Paris: 1996)), Aut/hiver 175-184.
15. Lamerson and Kelloway.
16. C.D. Lamerson, "Peacekeeping Stress: Testing a Model of Organizational and Personal Outcomes" Unpublished Doctoral Dissertation (University of Guelph: 1995).
17. L. Weisaeth, *Preventive Intervention*, paper presented at the North Atlantic Treaty Organization Conference (1994). See also Lamerson and Kelloway.
18. Lamerson and Kelloway, 253.
19. For a detailed explanation of the nature of these stressors see Breakwell and Spacie, 8-27.
20. Elinor Sloan and Tony Kellet, "Trends in International Peacekeeping" Policy Briefing (Ottawa: National Defence Headquarters, April 1998), 2-5.
21. A number of books, articles and papers have been written, many based on personal experiences, regarding the difficulties and failures of the UN missions in Bosnia, Rwanda and Somalia. Various articles from different perspectives are in Wolfgang Biermann and Martin Vadset, Eds. *UN*

Peacekeeping in Trouble: Lessons Learned from the Former Yugoslavia (Aldershot UK: Ashgate Publishing Ltd, 1998). See also L. MacKenzie, *Peacekeeper: The Road to Sarajevo* (Toronto: Harper Collins, 1993).
22. Sloan and Kellett, 6.
23. Boutros Boutros-Ghali, *An Agenda for Peace* (New York: United Nations, 1992).
24. British Army Field Manual, Vol 5, *Operations Other Than War* (1994).
25. Boutros Boutros-Ghali, *Agenda for Peace.*
26. NATO led IFOR and leads the current SFOR mission in Bosnia and KFOR in Kosovo. Examples of regional organizations include the CIS in Tajikistan and the Economic Community of West African States (ECOWAS) in Sierra Leone. Examples of "coalitions of the willing" include the Italian-led operation in Albania and the aborted Canadian-led operation intended for the former Zaire.
27. Examples include UNTAES in Croatia, MINUGUA in Guatemala, UNOMIL in Liberia, MINURCA in the Central African Republic and a series of missions in Haiti.
28. Lamerson and Kelloway, 252.
29. Perhaps the best example of the relatively safe "traditional" mission for the CF was UNFICYP in Cyprus, in effect since 1964.
30. Sten Martini, "Peacekeepers Facing Horrors of Civil War-like Conflict: Danish Lessons Learned in Preparing and Taking Care of Soldiers" Wolfgang Biermann and Martin Vadset, CDS.,. *UN Peacekeeping in Trouble: Lessons Learned from the Former Yugoslavia* (Aldershot UK: Ashgate Publishing Ltd, 1998).
31. D.W. Corneil, "Prevalence of Post Traumatic Stress Disorders in a Metropolitan Fire Department" Unpublished Doctoral Dissertation (Johns Hopkins University: 1993) Cited in Lamerson and Kelloway, 254.
32. Z. Solomon, *Combat Stress Reactions: The Enduring Toll of War* (New York: Plenium Press, 1993). Cited in Lamerson and Kelloway, 254.
33. Lamerson and Kelloway, 253.
34. Reuven Gal, "Le stress du soldat de paix," 173-184. Although the Israeli security operations in the occupied territories are not strictly speaking peacekeeping operations, many of the military situations are comparable in relation to the experience of stressors and stress.
35. Lamerson and Kelloway, 254-256.
36. C.D. Lamerson, "Peacekeeping Stress: Testing a Model of Personal and Organizational Outcomes" Unpublished Doctoral Dissertation. (University of Guelph, Ont: 1995). See also Farley, 24.
37. F.C. Pinch "Lessons Learned from Canadian Peacekeeping Experiences: A Human Resource Perspective" (Dartmouth NS: 1994). See also Farley 20.
38. Lamerson and Kelloway, 256.
39. In the author's opinion, Breakwell and Spacie's concise pamphlet *Pressures Facing Commanders* should be studied carefully and kept close at hand by all officers who command or expect to command military operations, including peacekeeping.
40. Ibid, 10.
41. Ibid, 11.
42. Ibid, 20.
43. Ibid, 24-25. They also state that the commander who is unaware of his knowledge or skill inadequacies may never experience the stress normally associated with them, even though performance may be poor.
44. Ibid, 25.
45. Ibid, 27.
46. Ibid, 9.
47. The UN published its own program in a note by the Secretary-General, entitled "Human Resources Management: Respect for the Privileges and Immunities of Officials of the United Nations and the Specialized Agencies and Related Organizations – Stress Management" A/C.5/49/56 (New York: UN General Assembly, 16 Feb 1995).
48. These include senior officers commanding UN missions, officers filling HQ staff positions, UN Military Observers and some individual augmentees.
49. Lamerson and Kelloway, 252.

Stress Casualties and the Role of the Commander

Terry Copp

Terry Copp is a Professor of History at Wilfrid Laurier University in Waterloo, Ontario.

THE CANADIAN ARMY'S PSYCHIATRIC HOSPITAL at Basingstoke, England known popularly as "No. 1 Nuts," had dealt with hundreds of patients before the young officer arrived, and he was quickly absorbed into the routines established for such cases. The senior neuropsychiatrist, Dr. H.H. Hyland, was committed to the view that men of good basic personality could recover from episodes of acute anxiety with rest, reassurance and a "detailed discussion" of the factors "causing the immediate mental conflict and tension." Repeated talks with the patient, so that "repressed fears and conflicts" could be aired again and again, was Hyland's favoured method, though he was willing to try drugs and hypnosis or even electrical shock if psychotherapy failed.[1]

The officer was an especially challenging case. A tall, good-looking man with an open friendly face and an unblemished career had experienced a breakdown during routine training. The attacks of acute anxiety were accompanied by elements of "conversion hysteria," the term used to describe symptoms of physical impairment without apparent physical cause. Hyland was confident that psychotherapy would work with such a patient and gradually the mental and physical symptoms disappeared. The officer returned to his unit apparently one of Hyland's success stories. Unfortunately the symptoms returned and the officer was returned to Basingstoke.

A statistical study of men returned to duty from the hospital had demonstrated that fully three quarters failed to "remain well and efficient" and Hyland reluctantly had to agree that a second breakdown should mean a medical board, reclassification and return to Canada, but something about this young man led him to change his mind. After less than two weeks of further psychotherapy with Hyland and his colleague Dr. J.C. Richardson, Bert Hoffmeister returned to his regiment, took up his duties and embarked upon a military career which would see him become one of Canada's outstanding battalion, brigade and divisional commanders.[2]

Why would an individual find the experience of separation from his family and the routine of military life in wartime England more stressful than the exposure to combat and the responsibilities of command? Hoffmeister did not know and his psychiatrists thought such questions could not be answered with any precision or degree of certainty.

The two doctors who treated Hoffmeister were both trained as neurologists and approached such questions from the perspective of what was then called neuropsychiatry. In their experience emotional crises, described as acute anxiety neuroses, happened to individuals who were predisposed to neurosis as a consequence of their life experience, but also to men and women without such case histories. They believed that Hoffmeister's illness suggested he might be especially vulnerable when confronted with more stressful situations or that such situations might lead this sensitive, patriotic and intelligent officer to draw upon resources of strength and function at the highest levels. On balance both doctors decided Hoffmeister should be given another chance to serve his country.

The story of Bert Hoffmeister and his psychiatrists illustrates the main argument of this discussion of "Stress Casualties and the Role of the Commander." More than half a century after the Second World War we know very little about why some individuals are seriously affected by stress which others ignore, and we have an equally uncertain grasp of the reasons for the development of delayed reactions including Post Traumatic Stress Disorder. It is also evident that theories about the prevention and treatment of such casualties are just theories and must be treated with considerable caution.

What follows is a discussion of the history of the incidence and interpretation of combat stress reactions in the twentieth century. It is intended to offer an overview of a topic upon which expert opinion is deeply divided. Senior officers have a clear obligation to know as much as possible about issues which fall within their command responsibility and may benefit from a military historian's perspective on a topic which is usually dealt with by psychiatrists and psychologists who are directly involved in the issues and committed to specific explanatory models.

During the course of the First World War attitudes towards what came to be called "Shell Shock" changed dramatically. Initially the term shell shock was used to describe the effect of exploding shells upon individuals who exhibited symptoms of confusion, amnesia, paralysis, blindness and other effects that had no discernible physical cause. The assumption that the brain had been injured by shock waves from the explosion was challenged when it became evident that many individuals broke down in circumstances which had nothing to do with artillery bombardment. New explanations drawing upon existing ideas about the origins of "anxiety neuroses" and "conversion hysteria" were developed. The Dutch historian, Hans Binneveld[3] argues that three major divergent approaches dominated debate before war's end. The first theory accepted the centrality of the trauma that overwhelmed the emotional stability of the individual. A second approach insisted that the symptoms were the product of suggestibility, and claimed that the patient learned to play a role assigned to him by circumstance and the process of medical treatment. Finally the impact of Freudian ideas about neurosis were evident in the work of psychiatrists who insisted that only individuals pre-disposed to neurosis as a result of their early emotional life were likely to break down.

All three approaches had one thing in common: they were theories supported by subjective anecdotal evidence, the so-called case studies, which passed for research in psychiatry as well as many other branches of medicine.[4] Each theory required a different treatment regime. If the traumatic event was the cause, symptoms could be overcome by rest and reassurance provided as quickly and as close to the front line as possible. This evolved into a stalemate of the principles of proximity, immediacy and expectancy (of return to duty) which became the hallmarks of forward combat psychiatry after 1917.

The suggestibility theory demanded strict discipline and the de-medicalization of treatment for stress. This approach has had considerable appeal for combat leaders concerned with the impact the evacuation of stress casualties had on unit strengths and morale. During the later phases of the Second World War the German Army, as well as the SS, reversed their commitment to the trauma model and employed extraordinary disciplinary measures, including thousands of executions, solving the problem of combat stress at least as far as medical records are concerned.[5]

The proponents of pre-disposition advocated stricter selection criteria that would eliminate the vast majority of individuals likely to break down under the pressures of battle. This argument became especially popular after the Great War as thousands of veterans sought pensions on mental health grounds. Psychiatrists who dealt with these men were convinced that most of those who sought assistance had pre-enlistment records of nervous instability and argued that in a future war the new science of personnel selection, with its various psychological tests, would prevent such individuals from enlisting.

Between the wars the unresolved debates over shell shock and its aftermath attracted little attention. The Great War had been fought to end war, not to prepare for its resumption, and neither military nor medical authorities showed much interest in war-related illness. When the British Expeditionary Force sailed for France in 1939, there was general agreement that in a good, well-trained battalion breakdowns would only occur after prolonged combat. When they occurred, forward treatment by Regimental medical officers would serve to deal with most cases while others evacuated to a general hospital.

The battle of France and the retreat to Dunkirk punctured these illusions. Large numbers of soldiers showing all the classic signs of shell shock overwhelmed the Casualty Clearing Stations as hundreds of men cracked under the strain of a chaotic withdrawal under constant air attack. More than fifteen hundred men from Dunkirk were treated by Doctors William Sargant and Elliot Slater who initially shared the assumption that breakdowns would occur among men with a history of previous neurotic illness or the classic signs of pre-disposition. But many of their patients proved to be men of "reasonably sound personality" who were convinced that they could never endure combat again. Sargant and Slater recommended discharging such men to civilian life and urged the army to develop facilities for effective forward treatment which, they were convinced, would prevent the formation of the kind of deeply embedded neurosis common among the Dunkirk evacuees.[6]

The British Army at home showed little interest in these ideas preferring to concentrate on an elaborate program of personnel selection. British units in contact with the enemy were only marginally more interested. As late as the spring of 1942, casualties from shell shock, listed under the diagnostic label Not Yet Diagnosed (Nervous), did not appear to be significant. From an overall medical or manpower perspective, dysentery, hepatitis, malaria, sand fly fever and venereal disease were far more serious problems. In a theatre where injuries, not from enemy action, accounted for more hospital admissions than wounds, stress reactions were scarcely on the radar screen.

The Australians, defending the port of Tobruk, found that the stress of the siege produced a steady stream of psychiatric casualties and in May 1941, a war neurosis clinic was established to limit the necessity of evacuation. The Tobruk experience convinced the Australians that prompt forward treatment and "a certain hardness of heart" produced good results. In 1942, the 9th Australian Division required exhaustion casualties to contribute a pint of blood before receiving treatment. This voluntary sacrifice of blood was thought to give the soldier the feeling that he had "atoned for his breakdown" and remained a useful member of the group instead of an outcast. No follow-up studies of Australian soldiers returned to combat were carried out so it is impossible to say whether these measures had the desired effect.

The New Zealanders were far more matter-of-fact about exhaustion cases. They employed the techniques of forward psychiatry but found that the majority of patients had to be evacuated and reassigned duties out of combat. The Maori battalion pioneered a system of "battle friends" who lived and fought with new replacements or anxious veterans and credited this with lowering exhaustion rates, but the evidence was, as usual, anecdotal.[7]

After 2nd El Alamein Montgomery's 8th Army created additional forward psychiatric units where "aggressive forms of persuasion" were used and a strict military atmosphere maintained. The British kept patients for lengthy periods in the hope that most could be returned to unit but the only follow-up study noted that while eighty percent of a small sample were "on full duty" only a few had actually been in combat.[8]

The senior medical officers of the United States Army and Army Air Force had consciously rejected the validity of the lessons learned by the American Expeditionary Force in the First World War insisting that rigorous personnel selection would weed out the pre-disposed, making forward psychiatric units unnecessary. The Americans arrived in North Africa completely unprepared for the great numbers of acute anxiety states encountered in the combat zone.

The Surgeon-General responded to pleas for help by sending several psychiatrists to North Africa to treat American patients in British hospitals. One of the new arrivals, Roy R. Grinker, was introduced to the technique of assisting psychotherapy with sodium pentothal that encouraged patients to talk freely about their experiences. Grinker began experiments with army air force aircrew suffering from combat stress reporting his "conclusions" in the book *Men Under Stress* which became one of the early classics in the field.[9]

While Grinker worked with aircrew Lieutenant-Colonel Fred Hanson arrived to take control of US Army psychiatry. Hanson spent the first three years of the war with the Canadians at Basingstoke where he had absorbed the ideas about forward psychiatry advocated by William Sargant, a frequent visitor to the hospital. Hanson was able to institutionalize forward psychiatry in the army while serving under General George Patton's command.[10] This may seem ironic in the light of Patton's subsequent behaviour in the famous slapping incident in Sicily but forward psychiatry promised high rates of return to unit, not the accumulation of large numbers of patients in rear areas.

The Americans chose to call stress reactions "Combat Fatigue" while the term "exhaustion" or "battle exhaustion" was used in the Commonwealth armies. Whatever label was used it was soon evident that the nature of the fighting in Sicily and Italy produced thousands of stress casualties. By 1944, the Americans were committed to the virtues of forward treatment, appointing divisional psychiatrists and training medical officers to apply the principles of proximity, immediacy and expectancy in the hope of achieving a very high recovery rate. Military records suggest the American system, with its emphasis on sedation, abreaction and rapid return to duty worked, but it proved impossible to carry out reliable follow-up studies. Combat fatigue was largely an infantryman's problem and casualties in rifle companies were common and continuous. Attempts to trace the careers of those treated for combat fatigue were beyond the resources available in a theatre of war in a world without computers. Nor was it possible to evaluate the success of the British system that employed psychiatrists at the Corps level and continued the North African practice of longer periods of recovery and retraining.[11]

The Canadians in Italy took yet another approach to the diagnosis and treatment of stress casualties. Dr. Arthur Manning Doyle was assigned to 1st Canadian Division more or less by chance but his personal approach to battle exhaustion, which contrasted sharply with the views expressed by most of his British, American and Canadian colleagues, had a profound impact on the 1st Division during its service in Italy. Doyle was convinced that while situational factors, the intensity of combat and the quality of leadership and administration played a role in battle exhaustion, the crucial factor was the quality of the soldiers. After the costly battles of December 1943, including Ortona, Doyle reported that the majority of the five hundred and seventy cases he had treated "were really persons suffering from chronic psychiatric disorders" who should never have been in the army in the first place.[12]

After Ortona, Doyle seems to have *expected* large numbers of casualties who could not be returned to unit because they were, and always had been, inadequate for the task. Bill McAndrew, who has carried out the most detailed study of battle exhaustion in the Italian campaign, notes that some reinforcement drafts sent to Italy contained a large number of castoffs from units in England and suggests this may partially account for the very high number of battle exhaustion casualties and the low return to unit rate in 1st Division.[13] It is also likely that Doyle's commitment to a pre-disposition model led him towards a self-fulfilling prophecy.

The General Officer Commanding 1st Division, Major-General Chris Vokes, displayed a two-fisted, tough guy persona to officers and men of the division but both he and his senior medical officer accepted Doyle's approach to battle exhaustion. When Lieutenant-General Harry Crerar arrived in Italy to command the newly established 1 Canadian Corps he was taken aback by the high incidence of self-inflicted wounds, neuropsychiatric casualties and desertions. Crerar insisted that steps had to be taken to tighten discipline and convince soldiers that "any form of 'escapism' is a shameful thing." He accepted the reality of genuine "nervous breakdowns" but insisted that, "the mesh of the administrative sieve should be so close that the fake exhaustion case should be detected and held."[14]

When Crerar left Italy to assume command of First Canadian Army his successor, Lieutenant-General E.L.M. Burns, continued to emphasize disciplinary measures and insisted that exhaustion casualties varied directly with "the state of discipline, training and man management in the unit." The statistics from 1st Division regiments, which recorded wide variance between battalions, seemed to support this view. The policies advocated by both Corps Commanders were also advocated by the ADMS of 5th Armoured Division, Colonel Ken Hunter, a Permanent Force medical officer who agreed that "good pre-selection training" would eliminate many who might break down from battle stress, but once a campaign began strict discipline and man management were essential. "Major Doyle," he insisted, "emphasizes too greatly the importance of pre-selection and does not attach sufficient importance to the factor of unit discipline and RMO inflexibility."[15]

When the Corps battles in the Liri Valley began, the new, tougher approach to evacuating combat stress casualties was enforced in both divisions and it appeared to succeed. One battalion went even further requiring exhaustion casualties to work at the Regimental Aid Post (RAP) and return to their company lines for meals. "After 24 to 48 hours rest and duty at the RAP the great majority of these men returned to full duty with their companies."[16] The absence of good statistics on the incidence of battle exhaustion or its aftermath make it difficult to form any definite conclusions about these efforts but senior commanders were confident that their intervention had been effective.

If tighter discipline lowered the ratio of neuropsychiatric casualties in the battles of early 1944, it had less effect in the months that followed. By the end of 1944, the long-drawn-out campaign in Italy had produced chronic problems of physical and emotional exhaustion. Colonel Hunter's belief in the virtues of discipline and man management were unshaken but he acknowledged that the nature of the campaign inevitably produced large numbers of combat stress casualties. In December he reported:

> Neuropsychiatric casualties have been encountered in the same general proportions as we have come to expect. As a rule, these casualties appear among the most susceptible individuals very early in action. Following this initial influx, the incidence becomes gradually greater according to the length of time a unit or formation is in action, the weight of enemy shelling, the state of physical exhaustion of the personnel, the magnitude of the casualties suffered by the unit and the discomforts from bad weather conditions.[17]

There was little commanders could do about this given the strategic imperatives which called for continued pressure on the enemy to prevent transfer of his divisions to Northwest Europe.

The armies preparing for the invasion of France in 1944, were committed to the principles of forward psychiatry with particular emphasis on expectancy of return to unit. The senior Canadian medical officers adopted the American system of divisional psychiatry, appointing Dr. Robert Gregory as 3rd Division's psychiatrist. Gregory, along with medical officers from the three divisional Field Ambulance units, attended courses at a US Army hospital and absorbed the American view that while large numbers of "combat fatigue" cases were inevitable most could be returned to combat quickly if proper forward treatment was provided. Gregory was quite prepared to assist units in weeding out "neurotics" and "inadequates" who were "apt to give trouble in action" but in the three month period before D-Day just one hundred and twenty-seven men from a force of more than twenty thousand men were downgraded for psychiatric reasons. Gregory was confident that 3rd Division was in fine shape with excellent morale.[18]

Senior army officers had little reason to concern themselves with psychiatric policies which sought to provide forward treatment and prompt return to unit but less than a month after D-Day a battle exhaustion crisis challenged the pre-invasion optimism. Hundreds of men were breaking under the stress of combat and large numbers were being evacuated to England. Colonel M.C. Watson, the ADMS of 3rd Canadian Division, was not opposed to tighter discipline but his experience in Normandy led him to argue that in any formation under "severe battle strain" three main preventive measures must be implemented if high rates of battle exhaustion were to be avoided. First the "unstable soldier" must be removed from contact with the stable fighting soldier. "He is," Watson insisted, "a menace to the stability of a force even in rest periods." Second, troops must be confident that the operations are well-planned and all possible measures taken to ensure success. "Every effort should be made to minimize the possibility of surprise or uncertainty engaging the mind of the soldier during battle. If he is going to be bombed, shelled, mortared, sniped at, overrun, reinforced or not reinforced, tell him and he immediately becomes a better soldier."

Watson's third recommendation was to require rest periods and to protect against physical exhaustion especially through lack of sleep which in his view underlay much of the nervous tension which preceded a breakdown. Watson concluded his report with the comment that "a high incidence of exhaustion cases indicates deficient training, poor leadership with a low fighting ability in the force. Battles are won by causing exhaustion in the enemy's ranks. The battle of Normandy was won because the enemy were mild exhaustion cases towards the end."[19]

Watson's recommendations were, as he himself suggested, common sense, but after three months of close observation of 3rd Division he knew that there was a wide variation in exhaustion ratios between regiments and an equally wide variation between battles. Battalion leadership and administration made a difference, but so too did the luck of the draw, which placed some units in the centre of costly attritional battles. Watson also believed that prolonged service in contact with the enemy would eventually destroy the morale and effectiveness of all units and most soldiers.

The battle exhaustion crisis of July 1944, presented Lieutenant-General Guy Simonds with a significant challenge. During pre-invasion training

Simonds had concentrated his energies on questions of leadership. His experience in Sicily had convinced him that, "If well trained, directed and led, the Canadian soldier is unsurpassed by any in the world. Coupled with rugged courage, ready adaptability, initiative and amenability to sound discipline, the average standard of intelligence is very high indeed…" Simonds believed that those attributes, which could be a great asset to a commander, were also a challenge, for when such soldiers encountered "wavering and indecision in leadership" or detected a "badly planned or poorly organized operation" their confidence was more easily shaken than among "a more stolid soldiery."[20]

Simonds believed that acute stress reactions were a symptom of declining morale due to adverse fighting conditions such as those found in static warfare. He believed that firm disciplinary action was required to prevent malingering, straggling and absenteeism that he saw as part of a continuum which included battle exhaustion.[21] Simonds' biographer, Dominick Graham, insists that his tough approach was the correct posture for a corps commander. "Only success," Graham maintains, "would remove the cause of battle exhaustion" and Simonds' proper course was "to ensure success by every means within his power, even if it meant cautious plans and the use of overwhelming air and artillery support. It also meant removing officers whose performance did not contribute to success. In the meantime it was essential to take a hard line with those who could not stick it out…"[22]

Graham's views and Simonds' actions in 1944, may indeed be correct, the commander should oppose any suggestion that large numbers of battle exhaustion casualties are acceptable or expected. It is, however, important to note that directives on discipline had no impact on the incidence of acute stress reactions until the difficulty and costly battle conditions of July and August ended. Once the pursuit of the German army began in September morale soared and the "crisis" ended, to flare up again in operations to clear the Scheldt estuary and in the last great attritional battle of the war in the Rhineland.[23]

The development of high rates of battle exhaustion during periods of intense combat gradually came to be taken for granted in the Allied armies. It is, however, important to note that the rate continued to vary between units exposed to similar battle conditions, suggesting that leadership and administration played a significant role in maintaining morale and limiting individual breakdowns. It is also important to note that while it may be theoretically true that "every soldier has his breaking point"[24] the evidence from Northwest Europe suggests that even under conditions of intense and prolonged combat most men did not develop symptoms of acute stress reaction and were able to serve effectively so long as reasonable periods of rest were available.[25] It is apparent that commanders had a major role to play in limiting the number of battle exhaustion casualties.

The end of the Second World War led to a rapid and ill-considered demobilization of the Canadian forces with the attendant loss of most of the personnel with medical and psychiatric experience. When war broke out in Korea, the government chose to recruit a brigade using the regular force units as cadres. No provisions were made to deal with psychiatric issues and little in the way of screening of recruits was attempted.[26] The pattern of stress reaction casualties in Korea was similar to the one experienced in Northwest Europe. Initially such casualties reached crisis proportions among American troops and the system of divisional psychiatry based on the principles of proximity, immediacy and expectancy was reintroduced. Medical reports on "combat fatigue" cases suggested a rapid decline in rates per one thousand troops but it is evident that duration and intensity of combat remained the best indicator of overall rates subject to the previously observed differences between units.[27]

The end of the Korean War coincided with the publication of the first edition of the American Psychiatric Association's Diagnostic and Statistical Manual, known as DSM-I. This reference text for psychiatrists described a large number of psychiatric problems including "Gross Stress Reaction," a condition which could occur among soldiers in combat who had no previous history of mental problems. The editors of DSM-I, reflecting the experience of wartime psychiatrists, maintained that the reaction would normally disappear when the individual was no longer exposed to the stressful situation.[28] This was certainly the consensus among Canadian psychiatrists who had served in the armed forces. They argued that veterans who presented delayed or re-occurring symptoms of acute anxiety were chronic neurotics whose life histories indicated long term mental health problems which pre-dated the war and would post-date it.[29]

When the American armed forces began combat operations in Vietnam the military was confident that it had learned the lessons of previous wars. Combat Fatigue, now increasingly called combat stress, was expected to occur among a minority of men, but the incidence could be reduced by good leadership and a system of forward psychiatry which involved battalion-level medical personnel in the recognition and treatment of stress reactions. The emphasis was on expectancy, the prompt return of a soldier to his unit after brief rest and reassurance. Whether it was this regime or the 365-day limit to service in Vietnam the results were extraordinary. Rates of more than 50 per 1000 troops were common in the Second World War and Korea but less than 5 per 1000 entered the medical evacuation stream in Vietnam. No one thought the rate could be lowered much further and combat stress was seen as a minor component of an overall "manpower wastage" problem.[30]

The second edition of the APA manual, DSM-II, was published in 1968. Relying on reports from the war zone in Vietnam, especially the work of Peter Bourne,[31] the editors of DSM-II decided that "Gross Stress Reaction" no longer needed to be included on a list of psychiatric disorders. The pattern of anxiety symptoms, rather than the possible origin of the anxiety was thought to be a more useful way of categorizing such illnesses.[32]

The transformation of medical, social and military ideas about combat stress and its consequences began when a patient tentatively diagnosed as paranoid schizophrenic described his participation in the My Lai massacre to a social worker. Most psychiatrists working at the Veteran Affairs hospitals assumed that Vietnam veterans, like the veterans of previous wars, who presented symptoms of agitation, anxiety or depression were "suffering from a neurosis or psychosis whose dynamics lay outside the realm of combat." However, the My Lai story, which became public on 16 September 1969, galvanized opponents of the Vietnam war including the psychiatrist and author Robert Lifton.[33]

Lifton, who was already well known for his work on the victims of Hiroshima, began to focus his activism on the psychological effects of the war on Vietnam veterans. Together with Dr. Chaim Shatan, Lifton formed an association with Vietnam Veterans Against the War, a loose organization of local chapters of anti-war veterans and began to popularize the concept of a "Post-Vietnam Syndrome" which involved a delayed, massive trauma. The symptoms were said to be "guilt, rage, the feeling of being scapegoated, psychic numbing and alienation."[34]

By 1973, Lifton and his supporters had won a wide audience for their views among opponents of the war but the concept of a specific "Post-Vietnam Syndrome" had made little headway with psychiatrists. By early 1974, a full fledged campaign to persuade the profession to include such a diagnosis in DSM-III was underway and, despite opposition from those who believed that the process was driven by politics, a new classification to be called Post Traumatic Stress Disorder (PTSD) was included in DSM-III, published in 1980. PTSD was not the same as post-Vietnam syndrome because in the process of building support for their cause the proponents of the diagnosis had broadened the definition to include individuals traumatized by natural disasters and a broad range of man-made catastrophes.[35] Because the DSM was a reference manual designed to standardize diagnosis and justify insurance claims the "new" disorder was strictly defined.

Official recognition of PTSD was a turning-point in the history of psychiatry. Whereas previous explanations of chronic mental conditions had drawn upon biological or psychodynamic (life-history) theories, PTSD was thought to be the result of specific stressful events. Initially researchers assumed only major traumatic events "generally outside the range of usual human experience" could cause the illness and investigators concentrated on the veterans of Vietnam and other wars. One consequence of this was to blur or abolish the distinction between combat stress reaction and PTSD, as most writers assumed that PTSD was simply a delayed stress reaction, a variant of CSR.

In the early 1980s, PTSD was thought to be a reaction to combat or other equally intense external events and it was generally believed that apart from those who had served with the American forces in Vietnam few Canadians had been exposed to such stressors. By the end of the decade a growing body of reports on traumatic stress in groups of people other than Vietnam veterans led to a redefinition of the origins of PTSD. The diagnosis was increasingly applied to those who had suffered rape, physical abuse and physical injuries as well as those who had witnessed traumatic events or provided care and counseling to victims of trauma.[36] This broadened definition led to a massive increase in the number of patients said to be suffering from chronic PTSD and to the expectancy that large numbers of individuals would report such symptoms after exposure to stress. Psychiatrists believed that they were now treating an illness which had always existed but which had been unrecognized. Increasingly they argued that both Combat Stress Reaction (CSR) and PTSD were normal reactions to trauma.

The Canadian armed forces, as part of the larger society, began to respond to the evolving interpretations of CSR and PTSD when the transition from peacekeeping to peacemaking operations challenged previous assumptions about operational stress. The term "Critical Incident Stress" was selected to categorize, "events or circumstances outside the range of normal experience that disrupt one's sense of control and involves the perception of a life threat," and was incorporated into Canadian Forces training directives. CIS was simply a new name for CSR applied to soldiers who were not involved in traditional combat.

In March of 1994, the Directorate of Health Treatment Services issued a pamphlet on *Preparing For Critical Incident Stress*[37] which outlined the then current wisdom on the origins, prevention and treatment of CIS. The pamphlet begins with a statement which is echoed in other official National Defence publications; CIS is said to be "a normal reaction to an abnormal event." The author(s) go further insisting that "a strong reaction is a normal reaction" and few remain unaffected by a Critical Incident (CI), although reactions may differ. Some reactions are immediate and some may occur and/or recur days, even weeks later.[38] The pamphlet then offers a long list of symptoms characteristic of both immediate and delayed reactions and identifies PTSD as a medical diagnosis of chronic symptoms of CIS. Readers are informed that PTSD "occurs in only a small minority of people exposed to psychologically traumatic events and may be preventable by adequate management of CIS."[39]

Adequate management is said to consist of a variety of techniques to employ "both during and after the event" including stress management methods such as deep breathing, and talking about what happened and what you felt. The next step, described as CIS Defusing, involves a group meeting "to allow those involved to tell what happened and to talk about their reactions." The authors suggest that the next step is a CIS Debriefing which "ideally takes place 48-72 hours after the CI" and involves a structured intervention by specially trained members of a Critical Incident Stress Team.[40]

The Army Lessons Learned Centre offered a similar view of "Stress Management in Operations" in its 1996 *Dispatches*[41] emphasizing that no one is exempt from the possibility of CSR, which is the "normal" emotional and physical response of "normal" people. The Lessons Learned Centre, drawing upon examples from Operation Harmony, places considerable emphasis upon the Critical Incident Stress Debriefing Process (CISD) conducted by "specially trained members of the helping professions (i.e. social work officers, medical personnel, personnel selection officers and chaplains) and peer supporters belonging to the unit being debriefed.[42]

The approach to the stress casualties mandated by the Canadian Forces reflects the imprint of an analytical model derived from social psychology. The insistence upon educating soldiers to believe that CSR is a normal response to stress and that delayed stress reactions may also be expected has little empirical basis and is best understood as a treatment strategy. During the Second World War temporary evacuations for "battle exhaustion" reached levels of one in four non-fatal casualties during periods of intense and prolonged combat but the average over the duration of a campaign which involved high levels of fatal and non-fatal casualties was one in ten or less. If battle exhaustion were a normal reaction to combat most infantry battalions would have ceased to function before the end of the battle of Normandy. Is it possible that the type of deployments experienced by the Canadian soldier in the 1990s has proven to be more stressful than Italy or Normandy? It seems unlikely and it must be noted that despite the establishment of a military-medical model which *expects* CSR, and regards it as normal, only a small number of CF personnel report CSR or PTSD symptoms.

The current CF approach to operational stress has been criticized by Dr. Allan English, an historian who prepared studies for the Board of Inquiry—Croatia. English believes that the high incidence of in-theatre psychological problems and of "unexplained physical symptoms" reported by Canadian veterans of recent deployments may be due to the way in which the CF has employed "a model of stress as a disease" and the emphasis on "treatment over prevention." English writes:

> In both World Wars and in subsequent conflicts it has been found that the most effective way to decrease preventable stress-related casualties was through a comprehensive and integrated system designed to reduce the effects of the inevitable stress of operations on military personnel. The central principle for success in designing and running this type of system has always been that military commanders must bear the ultimate responsibility for the system. When they have delegated this responsibility to others, such as those in the health care professions, the result has inevitably been unnecessary operational stress casualties.
>
> We know that strength of leadership and unit cohesion are the only factors that have had a consistent impact on reducing operational stress casualties. These factors are the purview of commanders at all levels. Therefore, a new system for dealing with operational stress should be regulated by those in the operational chain of command.
>
> The most comprehensive model for dealing with operational stress is found in the Combat Stress Reaction (CSR) doctrine of the Israeli Defence Forces (IDF). Focusing on stress prevention by improving leadership practices and strengthening unit cohesion, this model has proven to be effective in reducing the effects of operational stress in the IDF over the past 20 years. It has many useful attributes, but

would require major modifications to be acceptable to the CF. Extensive research would be required to adapt existing CSR models for use by the CF.

Leadership, at all levels, is the key to reducing the effects of operational stress. There has been very little empirical research done in this area in the CF; however, the small number of studies that have been published indicate that there is a "definite association" between certain stress-related illnesses on deployments and the confidence that personnel had in unit leaders. This confirms the findings of other studies done on the effects of leadership in reducing preventable operational stress casualties.[43]

The suggestion that commanders must take responsibility for limiting stress casualties by reducing operational stress may seem simplistic, but recent studies of the incidence of such casualties suggests that a renewed emphasis on leadership, unit cohesion and rest may be the only effective means of reducing CSR and PTSD presently available. This is particularly important in the light of current research which challenges the social psychological model employed in the CF.

For example, Dr. L. Stephen O'Brien, who as a British Army psychiatrist was involved in the treatment of veterans of the Falkland War, now questions many of the underlying assumptions of military and civilian approaches to traumatic illness. O'Brien discovered that not all Falkland War veterans who responded positively to questionnaires about PTSD symptomology seemed actually to be ill. Some who reported experiencing classic PTSD symptoms were unaffected by it, living their lives successfully. What role, O'Brien wonders, does "investigator priming" have to play in the incidence of post-traumatic illness?[44]

O'Brien raises questions about the universality of stressful experiences: "If three men are in an armoured vehicle and the vehicle next to them bursts into flames, one may feel that witnessing the probable death of close peers is terrible. A second may see it as an indicator that they too will inevitably be killed, heightening his fear. The third may see it as a lucky escape and proof of personal invulnerability."[45] The stressor is the same but individuals respond differently. O'Brien notes that we simply do not know why some people suffer from CSR and/or PTSD and why others do not.

This uncertainty raises serious doubts about the value of psychological debriefing and CISD. Recent studies reported by O'Brien have posed the question "Early interventions are intuitively appealing but do they work?" Is it possible they may do harm? One of the few controlled studies of psychological debriefing found that no protective effect was obtained by such debriefing and that "neither previous experience nor longer training was predictive and the one identified predictive factor was a history of previous emotional problems."[46] Research on the effectiveness of early intervention with CSR casualties must also be examined carefully. Almost all writers draw upon the work of the Israeli Army in discussions of this question but the evidence is ambiguous. The major follow-up study of Israeli veterans of the Yom Kippur and Lebanon wars found the rate of PTSD was fifty-nine percent for those who had been "successfully" treated for CSR on the battlefield.[47] Since there is no information on the severity of the individual stress reactions it is possible that even a larger percentage of those who experienced an intense episode of CSR subsequently developed PTSD.

The current uncertainty about the causes and consequences of stress reactions is dramatically emphasized in a recent issue of the *Canadian Journal of Psychiatry* that begins with an editorial titled "Does Stress Cause PTSD?"[48] This serves as an introduction to two articles that challenge much of the current consensus. Dr. Laura Bowman reports that "greater distress arises from individual differences than from event characteristics" and argues that "evidence of the efficacy of current treatment procedures is fragile."[49] The second article investigates "Biological Factors Associated with Susceptibility to Post-Traumatic Stress Disorder" and introduces some "preliminary research on biological and genetic factors which may account for vulnerability to stress."[50]

The 1990s have been called the decade of the brain in medical research. The first decade of the new century will undoubtedly be marked by the results of the Human Genome Project. It seems likely that new diagnostic classification based on genetic paradigms will emerge rapidly and together with advances in neurobiology will transform the practice of psychiatry, including our understanding of why some individuals are especially vulnerable to stress.[51]

Few military commanders can be expected to stay abreast of psychiatric research but they should at a minimum be aware that current ideas on treatment and prevention are based on explanatory models that may lack empirical validity. Officers charged with the command of troops in stressful situations may find themselves required to work within an officially approved medical-administrative framework but they should resist those parts of the model which promote the view that CSR and PTSD are normal. They have the responsibility to ensure that the men and women under their command have confidence in the mission and in its leadership at all levels. They must strive to create an atmosphere in which expectancy means the expectation of courageous, disciplined, soldierly behaviour rather than potentially disabling physical, cognitive and emotional disturbance. In doing so they will not only contribute to the success of their mission but to the well-being of their soldiers.

NOTES

1. Terry Copp and Bill McAndrew, *Battle Exhaustion: Soldiers and Psychiatrists in the Canadian Army 1939-45* (Montréal: McGill-Queens, 1990), 19.
2. C.K. Russel Papers, Osler Library, McGill University and notes of an interview, T. Copp with Dr. J.C. Richardson, December 1982.
3. Hans Binneveld, *From Shell Shock to Combat Stress* (Amsterdam: 1997), 88-89.
4. See Joel Paris, "Canadian Psychiatry Across 5 Decades: From Clinical Inference to Evidence-Based Practice" in *Canadian Journal of Psychiatry* Vol.45 (Feb 2000), 34, for a recent discussion of the problems of research in psychiatry.
5. Manfred Messerschmidt, *Nazi Political Aims and German Military Law in World War II* (Royal Military College of Canada: 1981), 8-10.
6. William Sargant, *The Unquiet Mind* (London: 1967), 114.
7. Copp and McAndrew, 47-48.
8. Brigadier F.E. Barbour, "An Experimental Forward Psychiatry Unit" (December 1943). Public Records Office, UK WO 222/1492.
9. Roy R. Grinker, *Men Under Stress* (New York: 1948).
10. Copp and McAndrew, 50.
11. This issue is briefly discussed in Ibid, 133. Subsequent discussion with British Army psychiatrists reinforced the view that early estimates of successful attempts to return men to combat were based on wishful thinking.
12. Copp and McAndrew, 58.
13. Ibid, 60.
14. Ibid, 64.
15. Ibid, 85.
16. G.A. Sinclair ADMS 1 Cdn Inf Div "Exhaustion Cases May 26,44" National Archives of Canada (hereafter NAC) RG 24 Vol 16,657 Fldr. 55.
17. Copp and McAndrew, 83.
18. Ibid.
19. M.C. Watson, "Quarterly Report 1 July 44 to 1 Oct 44 ADMS 3rd Cdn Inf Div" 1 Oct 1944. NAC RG 24 Vol. 15,611.
20. G.G. Simonds, Lt. Gen comd. 2Cdn Corps To All Formation Commanders 2nd Canadian Corps 19 Feb 44. War Diary 2 Cdn Corps. NAC RG 24.
21. G.G. Simonds, "Fighting Strengths" 29 August 1944, Ibid.
22. Dominick Graham, *The Price of Command* (Toronto: Stoddart, 1993), 169.

23. Copp and McAndrew, Chapter 7. See also Terry Copp, "If This War Isn't Over..." in Paul Addison and Jeremy Craig (eds), *A Time to Kill* (London: 1996).
24. The phrase is usually associated with Lord Moran, *The Anatomy of Courage* (London: 1943).
25. Copp and McAndrew, 151fn.
26. H.F. Wood, *Strange Battleground* (Ottawa: 1966), 29-32.
27. A.J. Glass "Psychotherapy in the Combat Zone" in *American Journal of Psychiatry* 110 (1954), 217-220.
28. Wilbur J. Scott, "PTSD in DSM III: A Case in the Politics of Diagnosis and Disease" in *Social Problems* 37 (1980), 294-309. See also, Wilbur J. Scott, *The Politics of Readjustment: Vietnam Veterans Since the War* (New York: 1993).
29. Notes of an interview with Dr. Travis Dancey, Veterans Affairs Canada consultant psychiatrist, Montréal General Hospital, 1994.
30. Scott, 297.
31. See Peter Bourne, *Men, Stress and Vietnam* (Boston: 1970) for a full account of psychiatric services in Vietnam.
32. Scott, 297.
33. Ibid, 298-299.
34. Robert Lifton, *Home From the War—Vietnam Veterans: Neither Victims nor Executioners* (New York: 1985).
35. Scott, 303-307.
36. L. Stephen O'Brien, *Traumatic Events and Mental Health* (London: 1998), 6-17.
37. Canada, Department of National Defence, *Preparing For Critical Incident Stress* (Ottawa: DND, 1994).
38. Ibid, 2.
39. Ibid, 13.
40. Ibid, 9.
41. Canada, Department of National Defence (Army Lessons Learned Centre) *Dispatches* Vol. 3 No. 2, 1996, 17.
42. Ibid, 19. One "observation" drawn from reports on Operation Harmony does caution that "Soldiers of all ranks are extremely unreceptive to outside agencies/non-combat arms CIC debriefers and trainers" but this view is not reflected in the description of the ideal CISD team.
43. Allan D. English, "Creating a System for Dealing With Operational Stress in the Canadian Forces" (12 December 1999), 2-3. English refers to a study of Operation Harmony which indicates that 41% of unit personnel expressed low confidence in the leadership of junior officers while 38% expressed low confidence in senior officers and concludes that "this area requires immediate attention." Leadership always requires attention but such survey studies lacking control groups yield little useful information about leadership.
44. O'Brien, 282-283.
45. Ibid, 286.
46. Ibid, 273.
47. Ibid, 277.

48. Joel Paris, M.D., "Does Stress Cause Post-Traumatic Stress Disorder?" in *Canadian Journal of Psychiatry* Vol. 44, 1999, 20.
49. M.L. Bowman, "Individual Differences in Post-Traumatic Distress: Problems with the DSM-IV Model" in Ibid, 21-29.
50. R. Yehuda, "Biological Factors Associated with Susceptibility to Post-Traumatic Stress Disorder" in Ibid, 34-38.
52. Paris, 34-38.

IV

Civil-Military Relations

The Politics of Defence Decisions at Century's End

Joel J. Sokolsky

Dr. Joel Sokolsky is the Acting Dean of Arts and the Head of the Department of Politics and Economics at the Royal Military College of Canada and Senior Fellow at Queen's University Centre for International Relations.

INTRODUCTION: THE CONTINUING COMMITMENT-CAPABILITIES COMPLAINT[1]

AS IT WAS AT THE DAWN OF THE CENTURY, so it is at the end, Canada is dispatching forces "over there." In 1899, the Laurier government sent troops to fight with the British against the Boers in South Africa. In 1999, Ottawa has deployed air and then ground units to join the American-led allied effort against Yugoslavia over Kosovo. Later in the year, air, naval and ground units were sent to East Timor in Indonesia. As in the past, though, questions and criticisms are being expressed by Canada's allies, especially the United States about the state of the Department of National Defence (DND) and the Canadian Forces (CF). Do its capabilities match its commitments? In a speech last year on bilateral relations, the United States Ambassador to Canada urged Ottawa to continue to sustain "the world's most unique security partnership." One of the requirements for the continuation of these ties is, in the US view, increases in Canadian defence spending.[2] Noted American Canada watcher Joseph Jockel suggests that downsizing of Canadian Army units from brigades to battle groups will make them "unfit for combat" alongside American allies.[3] And from Britain, Richard Sharpe, editor of *Jane's Fighting Ships,* pointing to the twenty-three percent cut in defence spending over the last four years and the fact that Canada is now 133rd out of the 185 United Nations countries in defence spending as a share of gross domestic product, has declared that Canada's military is "losing its heart because of severe underfunding and the 'political myopia' of the federal government."[4] Newly appointed North Atlantic Treaty Organization (NATO) Secretary General Lord Robertson, used the occasion of meeting of allied defence ministers in Toronto to admonish Ottawa for its poor record on defence spending, advising it to use a portion of its budgetary surplus for the military.[5]

These are familiar complaints, ones heard throughout the century in hot wars and in cold. Indeed, for most of our history the apparent gap between capabilities and commitments has been the overriding concern of the professional military, especially in peacetime. And the blame is often put on the country's political leadership. Reflecting upon his experience in Canada in the 1860s when he was sent over to organize the Canadian militia against Fenian raids, Field Marshal Viscount Wolseley noted that while Canadians are a splendid race of men and they make first rate solders: "The Ottawa Ministers, so like our own in this respect make no effective preparation for a campaign that might never come off by the purchase of those stores and munitions without which not even the smallest fighting body can suddenly be placed in the field."[6]

It is, however, misleading to say that history is simply repeating itself, with Ottawa politicians again failing to appreciate strategic and military realities. The current situation is unique in a way that makes the present size and structure of the CF logical and dangerous at the same time.

In the past, for example the inter-war period, Canadian governments, while not wishing to spend a great deal on defence, also followed a policy of avoiding commitments abroad. To this extent, there was no so-called "commitment-capability" gap because while capabilities were few, so were the immediate commitments. In the Cold War, Canada assumed specific commitments and in the early years did build up the capabilities to meet them. As the Cold War progressed, the size and capabilities of the Canadian Forces (CF) declined and thus the gap emerged. But there was always a measure of subjectivity (indeed unreality) about this gap which made it easy and understandable for political leaders to largely ignore. This was because of the nature of the international strategic environment, specifically the centrality of nuclear weapons and the overall western goal of containment and deterrence. In the nuclear age who could say with certainty what was necessary to maintain the strategic balance let alone to "win" a war which few believed anyone would win. How important were conventional forces, especially those of middle powers like Canada, in the presence of the larger forces of allies and atomic weapons? If Canada had deployed double the number of Leopard tanks it did in the mid-1970s, would NATO have stood a better chance of holding back the Soviets? How many Canadian City-class frigates were needed to secure the Sea Lanes of Communication (SLOC) to Europe? If Canada had closed the gap, according to the *1987 White Paper* on defence, would the country have been any safer?

Of course, to the country's political leadership, the building and structuring of the forces were meant to serve a wide variety of significant national interests and purposes. By responding to allied strategies and needs, they were meant primarily as political symbols and played an important role in fostering Western solidarity, so crucial for containment and deterrence. The maintenance of the forces, especially their forward basing in Germany, was widely viewed as a means of securing Ottawa's seat at the table. Thus even incremental measures to narrow the gap, such as the mid 1970s equipment purchases, had some utility. And the CF had to be concerned with the operational effectiveness of the forces deployed to fulfill commitments. But overall, it did not really matter how the forces might have performed in combat because deep-down, few of Canada's political leaders expected the kind of protracted conventional war, on land, sea and air for which Canada raised and structured most of its forces in the Cold War.

In the present post Cold War era of peace, the CF is said to be facing yet another commitment-capability gap which needs to be addressed by the political leadership through force building, restructuring or both. But this gap is different. Similar to past eras, the capabilities of the CF are being reduced by budget cutbacks and personnel reductions. Yet unlike in a number of previous periods of peace, there is the widespread view, especially amongst the political élite, that not only does Canada have security interests at risk abroad, but that Ottawa needs to take an active international role in addressing them. This includes Foreign Minister Lloyd Axworthy's concept of "human security." Canadians and their government still have that "internationalist itch" which can sometimes only be scratched by dispatching the Canadian Forces abroad. Moreover, unlike the Cold War, this internationalist bent has resulted in the actual use of the CF in operations in which armed force, of varying degrees, had to be applied by the CF.

In other words, this is a real gap. The commitments are not to some theoretical never-to-be-implemented allied warfighting strategy in Europe or in the skies of North America, but to all-too-real conflicts in a host of dangerous places around the world. Moreover, increasingly over the post Cold War period, these operations have changed from blue to green helmets. When the CF is sent to dangerous places it will more than likely be as part of US-led multilateral operations designed to promote Western interests and/or values outside the North American/NATO/Europe area. Whether these operations are called "peacekeeping" or some other name, they are essentially forms of armed intervention and limited war, often followed by military occupation of the target region or country. When the CF is asked to go abroad, the decision will depend upon a combination of domestic and foreign considerations prevailing at the moment. The most important external factor will be the extent of the multilateral effort. If the operation is led by the US and involving most of our western allies (the countries that still really count for us) Canadian participation will be more likely. In this situation it really does matter if there is a gap between the ability of the CF to perform its roles, and thus support the foreign policy objectives of government, and the specific commitments the country's political leadership makes.

This chapter discusses the politics of defence decision making. It begins with a discussion of the nature of the strategic environment that Canada faces, arguing that while it may be a disorderly and dangerous world for some countries it is not for Canada. This has important implications for assessing the so-called commitment-capability gap and how political leaders respond. For if Canada does not really have solid and continuing commitments abroad, then the gap is not as wide, or as significant as some would argue. At the same time, Canada in collaboration with the United States and other Western countries has been venturing into dangerous places in this safe world for reasons unrelated to direct national interests and this is likely to continue. Because of this, the question of CF capability is important. The chapter therefore turns to the discussion of capabilities. Here it is suggested that if many commitments are, in a very profound sense, not commitments at all, but discretionary options, then the gap can be narrowed even further. Capabilities can be tailored in terms of size and structure to fulfill a limited number of roles in larger multilateral efforts.

More importantly, the chapter argues that it is not so much the commitment-capability gap that needs addressing by the political leadership, rather it is the commitment-credibility gap. That is to say given the reality of the present budget levels, what should most concern the government is that when it decides to commit the CF abroad in coalition efforts that the forces it sends have the capability to credibly perform the roles assigned by Ottawa in agreement with coalition partners and that these roles may well be limited.

PROMOTING CANADIAN VALUES IN DANGEROUS PLACES IN A SAFE WORLD

The *Defence Planning Guidance 2000* begins by noting that, "There is no direct or immediate conventional military threat to Canada and the risk of a global conflict, which could give rise to such a conflict is very low." It goes on to note that,

> there remain direct and indirect threats to our national security for which a military response may be required including drug smuggling, organized crime, illegal immigration, terrorism and the uncertainty caused by the growing proliferation of weapons missiles carrying weapons of mass destruction. In addition, general uncertainty and the likelihood of regional and local conflicts will pose serious challenges to the maintenance of international peace and security.[7]

While essential domestic concerns such as narcotics and illegal immigration may well require use of elements of the CF, it has been Canada's involvement in overseas regional and local conflicts that have highlighted the deficiencies of the forces, raised concern over the so-called commitment-capability gap and generated demands for greater defence expenditures.

A convincing case, however, cannot be made that current regional instabilities, ethnic conflicts, natural resource depletion or failing states constitute threats to Canadian security. A hard-nosed, pocketbook assessment of the foreign risks to Canadian security abroad and the impact on the CF could well support the view that the CF should simply be used at home for aid of the civil power and non-military sovereignty and not be trained for either operations other than war or combat.

It is the case that Canada, with so much of its economic well-being exposed to the foreign sector, is greatly dependent upon stable international financial and trading systems. In the broadest sense these can be adversely affected by general global instability. But arguments that Canada must send forces, particularly combat forces, abroad because it is dependent upon trade have no validity. The record of the 1990s shows that it is possible to have many cases of regional instability, including numerous wars, and still have a prosperous, expanding and stable international economic order for that part of the world most important to the Canadian economy, the wealthy northern west, especially North America. Indeed, given that over eighty percent of Canadian trade is with the United States and most of the rest with Europe and Japan, civil wars in Eastern Europe and Africa are of little economic consequence. Stability of the Persian Gulf region with its oil supplies is of concern to the West, yet since the Gulf War ended in 1991, and the waning of the Arab-Israeli conflict, the general threat to global economics from this area has been greatly reduced.

Not only do present day regional conflicts hold little threat to the economic wellbeing of Canadians, but there appears to be little relationship between western collective efforts to deal with these conflicts and the approach taken to trade disputes. As Michael Mastanduno has pointed out, the United States is pursuing an internationalist approach to military/strategic issues, but is increasingly adopting a confrontational and unilateral stand on trade disputes. "In relations with other major powers, the United States, in effect, has been trying simultaneously to play 'economic hardball' and 'security softball'."[8]

Indeed, in the midst of the campaign against Yugoslavia, wherein NATO and the West demonstrated remarkable unity of purpose and policy, trade disputes raged amongst the allies. Washington and Ottawa were at odds over Canada's policy on American magazines and Canada and the US squared off with the European Union over beef. While the Pentagon was coordinating the operations of allied weaponry, the Department of Defense, with Congressional backing, was taking steps to curtail trade in defence products.[9]

This is not to say that Canada and its traditional allies will never have to use force to protect its self-interest. The West may be required, or wish to, intervene in certain struggles, for the sake of its military or economic security. But the trend in the 1990s, though, has been one of intervention by the West, and thus Canada, for reasons other than vital interests but rather to impose what we regard as our values. Recent statements by the Minister of National Defence and the Foreign Minister indicate that Canada is going to be even more vigorous in the area of "human security," fighting for "just cause,"[10] intervening to "protect vulnerable civilians caught in savage conflict."[11]

It is easy to dismiss such statements as soft thinking about soft power. But values are important. As former US Assistant Secretary of State Joseph Nye has observed:

> In a democracy, the national interest is simply the set of shared priorities regarding relations with the rest of the world. It is broader than strategic interests, though they are part of it. It can include values such as human rights and democracy if the public feels that these values are so important to its identity that it is willing to pay a price to promote them. ...A democratic definition of the national interest does not accept the distinction between a morality-based and an interests-based foreign policy. Moral values are simply intangible interests. Leaders and experts may point out the costs of indulging these values. But if an informed public disagrees, experts cannot deny the legitimacy of public opinion.[12]

Thus the so-called "CNN factor" whereby governments may be compelled by public opinion to respond to humanitarian disasters witnessed on the television news, should not be disparaged. Nor should Mr. Axworthy's human security agenda. Behind them rests the real and noble humanitarian sentiments of Western populations. The media is effective in arousing public concern only because the public expects that the government will act in manner consistent with its values. All interventions need not and have not taken place for reasons of vital collective western interest. Genocide and humanitarian disasters are surely just grounds for Canada and other countries to intervene in foreign lands. For its faults, the "human security agenda" has struck a responsive chord amongst Canadians. Indeed, given the lack of threat, it may well be the best rationale the political leadership can give for overseas activities by the CF.

But humanitarian intervention whether to protect lives or promote democracy is not a neutral or non-military act, however much it must be accompanied by a range of non-military initiatives. Taken to its logical conclusion, the Axworthy "human security" agenda could entangle Canada in a never-ending series of "savage wars of peace" around the world, demanding greater and greater defence spending. Moreover, it must be made clear that Ottawa is sending forces abroad to save the lives of others, not to protect our security interests. Inevitably the lack of real interests in these tragedies leads to a cruel calculation in which Western states must decide how much blood and treasure they are prepared to risk for the sake of saving others and restoring democratic governance.

Despite what appears to be a lack of direct threat to Canadian vital interests abroad, the 1990s were years of involvement and military intervention. But it is unrealistic to believe that countries, especially middle powers like Canada, dispatch forces overseas and place them in near or actual combat situations only in cases of real threats to vital national interests. Canada will only go abroad as part of a coalition. The decisions will not be based on exacting calculations of the cost and benefits of sending forces assessed against the actual threat, but the cost and benefits both domestic and foreign of participating or not in this particular multilateral effort. Canada will dispatch forces overseas in coalition efforts simply because it wishes to remain active in global security affairs. From time to time, our major allies will get together under US leadership to apply Western pressure on behalf of Western interests and/or values. This will only occur providing that the application is consistent with the several national interests of our allies, especially the Americans. Ottawa will resent being left out and will set aside complex reasoning in order to participate in coalition efforts. Delicate weighing of the national interests will be forgotten and the national interest will be adjusted to rationalize participation, not the other way around. Everything will rest upon the international and domestic circumstances prevailing at the time and if they are favourable, the CF will participate. Will the public support the deployment? Can it be persuaded to support it? What will our allies do to us if we do not go? Who else is going? And, most important, if we go, how little can we get away with? To be sure, Ottawa may send as few as possible and it may send unprepared forces, but always some will be sent.

There is nothing wrong with these kinds of calculations. They are the reality of Canadian security policy-making. Nor should the Ottawa politicians be faulted for thinking in these terms; after all, is not war (or peace enforcement) simply the continuation of politics by other means? The approach was summed up by James Eayrs in 1965:

> the main and overriding motive for the maintenance of Canadian military establishment since the second world war has had little to do with our national security as such...it has had everything to do with underpinning our diplomatic and negotiating position vis-à-vis various international organizations and other countries.[13]

The fact that the CF is being deployed for political motives does not mean that it can neglect combat capability. Even if the original purpose and mandate of the multinational intervention is not to apply force, open conflict is possible. As Louis Nastro and Kim Nossal argued, the peacekeeping experience of the last few years, especially in Somalia, shows

> the ease with which low-intensity conflict can flare up if the local forces decide to resist outside intervention. This is why multi-purpose, combat-capable forces are needed to provide a back-up should peace-building require peacemaking. It is in situations like Somalia that we can see the linkage between collective security measures being employed to give cooperative security initiatives a chance to work. In such fluid and unstable circumstances, UN and coalition forces which are anything less than multipurpose and combat-capable will not only make foreign policy objectives harder to achieve, but will also put troops unnecessarily at risk.[14]

The question of how much influence our participation really secures Ottawa remains unclear and may vary from mission to mission. In the Cold War years Canada was able to participate in global strategic affairs at the highest levels with a small and declining contribution to collective defence. In the estimation of the political leadership this made good sense. After all, in the presence of strategic nuclear weapons and the large conventional forces of our allies and adversaries, what did it matter how many tanks, planes, or ships contributed, or how they would actually perform in war? Canada believed in the unquantifiable calculations of deterrence, not operational effectiveness in war. Moreover, there was always the unspoken assumption that war was not really possible and that if the impossible should happen then the level of Canadian defence spending could not forestall annihilation without representation. As a country, along with the rest of the world, we would enter the "thousand year night" of the day after Armageddon.

Moreover, during the Cold War Canada was able to secure our seat at the table with minimal contributions because while our allies, especially the United States, always requested greater Canadian contributions, we knew they knew that such increases would not be forthcoming and they were not going to do anything about it. Yet Canada did send forces and did support every major strategic and political decision of our allies. From the NATO, especially the American standpoint, Canada was not so much a "free rider" as an "easy rider." Canada was politically loyal and its alleged lack of contribution was of little significance.

However, given that Canada's allies, especially the US, have been engaged in increased actual intervention and warfare in the post Cold War era, with the possibility of more to come, the view that Ottawa can spend very little on defence and eschew capable forces and still keep its allies happy and maintain a seat at the table may be untenable. From the American view the "helmets may be blue but the blood's still red"[15] and more, not less, will be expected of those who join coalitions. Thus, "what we think keeps our allies happy is simply not enough: the kind of 'defence lite' that is pleasing to most Canadians (and their pocketbooks) may be enough to keep Canada at the table, but is not enough to generate high regard."[16]

At the same time, Canadian political leaders must be careful about how much a greater combat capability actually buys in terms of influence and regard. For indeed, in an era in which our allies are more likely to call upon the CF to actually engage in combat, we must be even more sure that the country's political leadership is not tempted to pay too high a price for the seat at the table, one doled out in blood as well as treasure, especially where our national interests are not involved. Canadians must avoid a Dieppe mentality where the government is anxious to please the allies and the military is eager to make a credible and honourable contribution to a collective western effort.

In making its case for combat-capable forces as the core rationale for the military, the CF leadership must not confuse operational compatibility and camaraderie with political and strategic coincidence of interests. The CF does need to be prepared to fight with the best against the best. And what this really means is fighting with the US where and whenever Washington has decided to build a coalition, or in the words of Sir Brian Urquhart, "round up the posse." In an otherwise safe world, the fact that American interests are at risk in some dangerous place, may not necessarily mean that Canadian interests or values are sufficiently at risk to warrant the dispatch of Canadian forces in large numbers.

At the same time, the willingness of the Americans to maintain a leadership role in international security affairs is absolutely essential to the preservation of global stability and with it, broad western and Canadian interests. It is right and proper that the CF should plan primarily to sustain its combat capability consistent with being able to operate alongside the US. In doing so, those who support a sustained combat role for the CF, must, however, be realistic about how the United States exercises its leadership and what it means for Canada. We must be likewise realistic about Ottawa's ability to exercise influence, especially when it chooses to place its forces in harm's way alongside our American allies. For the United States, multilateralism is a tool to be used to further American interests and/or ideals and values abroad. This applies especially to instances in which the US deploys forces abroad in combat roles. The United States must be encouraged to act multilaterally, but it also must be prepared to act unilaterally. It would be folly to criticize this approach because it is the only way to run a superpower and to ensure that American power will remain strong and available in the event of new major threats to Western interests and global stability.

There is also the consideration that a Canadian defence policy geared toward sustaining combat-capable forces on the basis of being able to support US-led coalitions will cause difficulties between the two countries. American expectations of automatic Canadian participation and commonality of policy and purpose may be unfulfilled, leading to a certain amount of acrimony—charges (so frequently heard during the Cold War) which accused Canada of not pulling its weight or doing enough for collective defence. If Ottawa tries too hard to please the Americans then Canada may run into the same kinds of public criticism which it faced throughout and to the very end of the Cold War. Repeatedly, the criticism arose that Canada was simply following orders and that we were again becoming powder monkeys on the American national security ship of state—partners to a behemoth. All of this would erode support for the CF in Canada.

There is also the view, argued in the American literature, that allies like Canada should take care of matters that do not require major combat forces, thus preserving the mighty American military for major challenges to US and western interests, a new international division of labour suited to American interests and American domestic politics.

This was captured in the title of John Hillen's article, "Superpowers Don't Do Windows." According to this view Canada and other countries should concentrate on low-intensity and even non-combat roles as its contribution to Western and American security interests. Hillen argues that, given the reductions in the US military, America can no longer afford not to be selective. Washington should therefore announce to its allies and partners situations in which it will use force "and by implication, the situations in which it will expect its partners to assume leadership. In other words, America proclaims that 'superpowers don't do windows,' so if you want your local windows washed you had better gear up to do them yourselves."

> ...the United States should focus its security policies on major threats such as other great powers or rogue regimes that can upset the balance of power in key regions. America's allies should take the lead in local crisis management, peacekeeping, and humanitarian relief operations.[17]

As argued below, niche roles for the CF may be the best approach; indeed, the approach that is already being implemented by the political leadership. There are, however, problems with this approach to Canadian multilateralism.

There is though, a difference between "burden sharing" and window washing. Burden sharing is where America's allies agree to assume an appropriate level of the cost in money and if necessary lives, in defence of common western interests, as in the case of NATO during the Cold War and the Gulf War. For much of the Cold War, Canada could rightly be accused of not assuming its proper share of the burden given its relative economic strength. In the post Cold War era the United States should not have to assume a disproportionate share of the costs for defending collective western interests.

But the situation is different when Washington asks Canada and other allies to intervene in places where it does not feel that American national interests or values are such that the US should place at risk the lives of its military or expend large sums of money. Nor should Ottawa be expected to deploy more ground forces or keep them in theatre longer because of Congressional pressure on the president to avoid US casualties in these situations. It could be argued that the international response to East Timor is an example of window washing. Here the United States is supplying vital logistical support and has backed up the operations with naval forces, including an aircraft carrier. But the dirty work on the ground is being carried out by other countries, Australia principally and by Canada whose small two hundred and fifty person force from the Van Doos (Royal 22nd Regiment) will spend several months in the jungles helping to establish order. Now it is certainly true that this is a worthy humanitarian undertaking, but it is not burden sharing, it is doing a job which Washington does not want to do, rather than one it wants others to help accomplish.

Window washing may be viewed by some as a humble task, but it takes skill and good equipment to operate twenty storeys up. Moreover, we must be careful that while we, and other smaller and medium powers, are doing the windows, the scaffolding does not suddenly collapse underneath us or is taken away. This could happen in a number of ways. At the time of deployment semi-dangerous situations may escalate into extremely dangerous ones. Without combat-capability the mission and the forces would be at risk. When the Canadians take over to wash the windows after the Americans have gone in to construct the building (restoring peace in an area of unrest) it may find that the situation will deteriorate and again the mission and our forces will be at risk unless they have adequate capabilities. Ottawa might deploy to a dangerous place at Washington's request, and then find that a new crisis, one more threatening to American interests could arise elsewhere. This problem would leave the Canadian forces in a possibly more dangerous and long-running commitment. In Bosnia, for example, the US has reduced its ground presence and hopes to do the same in Kosovo.

Finally Ottawa has to consider what the impact of this approach will be upon public opinion and upon the forces themselves. Any Canadian defence policy which is based upon serving as "window-washers" for Washington is unlikely to garner much public support. As for the CF, it is right that it prepare to fight with the best against the best, not prepare to go where the best do not think it worth going. There is a danger that sending the CF to do the dirty, dangerous and hopeless jobs the American military will not do will be corrosive on morale and further undermine confidence in the country's political leaders. Of course there is also the view heard in Canada that because of our non-superpower status and non-colonial history, we are more welcomed in some places than the Americans. This may well be true, but we must be careful that our own rhetoric on this matter is not used to send us where the Americans do not want to go.

This being said, and Hillen notwithstanding, the United States does sometimes wash windows and wants Canada and other allies to help it. Despite the constant reiteration that the purpose of the US military is to fight and win the nation's wars, the 1990s have seen American forces engaged in the full range of activities from the delivery of humanitarian assistance to the delivery of laser-guided weapons.

To this extent, the activities of the CF have not, in substantial measure, differed greatly from those of the US forces; both have been used across a wide spectrum of operations, especially small scale contingencies and Operations Other Than War (OOTWs). All of this must be taken into consideration when evaluating the decisions made by the political leadership. In the past few years there has been criticism and doubt surrounding the role of the Canadian forces. Much is justified and useful, but we do not have to apologize for not meeting our international responsibilities regarding security. That Canadians are willing to go to dangerous places in a world which for them is relatively safe, is a tribute to our commitment to global stability and humanitarianism. Nor should the relative scale of Canada's contributions be mocked. Given fallen numbers and budgets and in comparison with what other similar size countries sent, they were respectable. For example, there is the view that Canada should have sent ground forces to the Gulf War and that the lack of such forces undermined Ottawa's international standing, but Canada deployed nearly a quarter of its navy and almost as much of its front-line aircraft. This was not an insignificant contribution. In the Kosovo campaign Ottawa dispatched a significant proportion of its available front-line fighters and backed it up with a ground deployment of one thousand three hundred, along with capable armoured vehicles. Indeed, combined with the forces still in Bosnia, as well as ships rotating into the Adriatic, the

Canadian military presence in Europe in 1999, is about the same as at the end of the Cold War—and it is actively engaged in dangerous missions.

For many reasons, Canada will continue to send forces abroad. It will likely do so alongside the United States and other allies, although it might also go overseas to wash windows. Yet the foregoing also suggests caution in two respects. First, in the present international security environment, employing the CF abroad is more than likely going to be a matter of choice on the part of the country's political leadership. The decisions will be based upon shifting and transient priorities depending upon the nature of the issue at hand, domestic considerations and budgetary realities, rather than a set of enduring foreign commitments. Second, because such deployments may well be to dangerous places, capability counts. It is not just a matter of showing up, of being there for politically symbolic purposes. Allies will depend upon the CF to perform certain roles. A humanitarian mission which cannot protect itself, much less the people it is sent to protect, is a contradiction in terms. The two considerations are related and need to inform political decisions. If Canada does not have to go everywhere, it does not need a range of multipurpose combat capable forces. But if it wants to be effective when it decides to go, then the political leadership must make sure that the forces its sends can fulfill the roles.

COMMITMENTS AND COMPARISONS: THE POLITICAL CHOICES

On paper,[18] the Department of National Defence is still committed to maintaining the capability to deploy a Vanguard Contingency Force and a Main Contingency Force (MCF) anywhere in the world. The Vanguard force would have up to four thousand personnel and be ready to go within three weeks. It could be sustained indefinitely with troop rotations and logistic support. Contingencies would include the UN Standby or Standing High Readiness Brigade, or NATO Immediate Reaction Force. The MCF would have up to ten thousand personnel at any one time (including the Vanguard Force).

A *White Paper Staff Check and Mobilization Planning* study conducted by the Office of the Vice Chief of the Defence Staff a few years ago, noted that the Vanguard elements could be prepared to deploy within twenty-one days, while the MCF would take ninety days. The study looked at an initial deployment of six months, "including sixty days of 'combat' at average consumption/casualty rates with the remainder of the six months at 'operations other than war' rates." On this basis, the study concluded that the "CF is capable of generating the major combat equipments, material, and personnel for the MCF described in the White Paper," and that "Personnel requirements should be within the capability of the Regular Force." It further noted that the MCF could be sustained for a period of six months given existing stocks and personnel levels.[19]

Problems arise with regard to deployment. DND Planning does not specify a particular location, which complicated assessments of deployment. It was concluded, nevertheless that, "Assuming use of maximum available transport aircraft," the deployment of the Vanguard forces "might take up to 73 days," but the CF does not have the aircrews to sustain this usage. For the MCF deployment would take up to 95 days, "assuming the availability of charter ships and aircraft." Canada would have to rely upon allied nations or civil charter for deployment. Given a shortfall in deployment capabilities, "it could take up to six months from a decision to deploy to put the full MCF into a theatre. Also, it is not possible to deploy all the Vanguard or MCF elements simultaneously. These would have to be phased in an order of priority."

Given the uncertainties of deployment, and the unanswered questions of sustainment beyond six months, the study summarized the government's approach to the commitments of the *1994 White Paper* as a "policy that is squarely based in the traditions of the government party which sponsors it," which according to study was paraphrasing Mackenzie King; "If necessary a commitment to a military capability, but not necessarily a capability to make a military commitment."

The current policy is very much in the Canadian tradition of asking not, "How much is enough?" but "How much is just enough?" What is the minimal level of forces that need to be maintained that would still allow Canada to participate in multilateral operations overseas? From the government's perspective, the current level is probably just about right. To be sure, the CF is probably not able to deploy its presently maintained forces as quickly as the military would like to all parts of the world where the government might send them.

Yet, is this really a problem for the political leadership, one that needs to be rectified by significant increases in spending on air and sea lift capability? The answer surely is no. It may well be that some relations crises will require the rapid deployment of international forces from outside the region. However, in these instances Canada will simply have to say that it cannot get there quickly with its Vanguard and MCF units, but, given time, it can mount and deploy a useful contribution. There is no rule that says that the CF must "absolutely, positively have to get there overnight." The record of the 1990s suggests that it does take time for Western governments to make decisions on interventions, especially of ground troops. In the meantime, those states who are closer, or who can get there quickly, such as the US, and some European allies such as Britain,

France and now Germany, will have to employ their comparative advantages in deployment. The fact is, the contingencies that Ottawa will be asked to dispatch forces to are all overseas, and few countries in the world, even amongst the group of seven major industrial states, have the capabilities for rapid intercontinental intervention.

The political leadership is well aware of the fact that in comparison to NATO's other middle powers, such as Belgium and Spain, Canada has a higher percentage of its available forces outside its borders, six percent as opposed to an average of two percent.[20] In the Kosovo air campaign, "Canadian pilots flew 682 combat sorties, or nearly 10% of the missions against fixed targets—and they led half the strike packages they took part in," and were "among only five countries delivering precision guided munitions."[21]

The Kosovo operations also showed that given sufficient warning, the army can move quickly overseas with vehicles and integrated helicopter units. The Edmonton-based Lord Strathcona's Horse, was the second NATO force to enter Kosovo and the Pristina area after the British:

> Less than 72 hours after rolling hundreds of military vehicles and containers off a freighter in Greece, the Strathcona's were already spying on Russian peacekeepers and Serbian armoured units around Kosovo's only airport...Some 24 hours after that, a U.S. Marine Corps Expeditionary Brigade that is supposed to specialize in quick deployments arrived in the country.[22]

Nor should Ottawa apologize for not maintaining the capability to engage in protracted high intensity combat overseas. Parts of the CF, such as the CF-18s and the new frigates, can participate in such actions, while the army may be more limited. But, nearly all elements of the CF can, and have made a contribution to more frequent and more likely operations witnessed in the past few years. These are the combined NATO operations where mid-level combat capability is needed, and where prolonged high intensity combat against an adversary of equal capability is not likely. As noted above, it may well be that Canada will be unable to send its tanks overseas, either because they cannot get there in time or will be unable to be sustained in protracted armoured warfare. Here too, Canada is in a position similar to other nations of comparable size.

In this regard, some have noted the swiftness with which Australia, with a smaller military, was able to place several thousand troops in East Timor, and difficulties Canada has in trying to get its forces in theatre. This is a false and misleading comparison and in fact highlights reasons why Canada should not have dispatched forces at all in this instance and that what it did send was more than adequate. First of all, Indonesia is close to Australia and stability there is a vital Australian interest. Second, Australia does not have three thousand troops in the Balkans or any other far-off place. Third the Canadian contribution, of a ship, aircraft and ground forces is not inconsiderable and difficult enough to mount given the distance.

It is necessary to recognize the comparative perspective that the country's political leadership maintains. As Charlie Brown is wont to say about his dog Snoopy, "he's not much of a dog, but then again who is?" There are not many countries in the world who can today project power overseas, especially land power. Only the United States has such a global capability. Even with NATO, only France, Britain and perhaps Germany have the ability (and the willingness) to do so, and even then, it is mainly restricted to the European theatre. Compared to the rest of the Alliance, Canada's capabilities, and its willingness to use them as evidenced by the history of the first post Cold War decade, stand up rather well.

To be sure, as the Minister's Monitoring Committee has pointed out, there is a "disconnect," and "ends-means" gap between the requirements for further equipment improvements, including those related to the Revolution in Military Affairs (RMA) and the high tempo of operations which will make it difficult to function with the current "stable and predictable funding levels for DND and the CF."

> If operational tempo continues to increase, the effects of this disconnect could be far reaching and serious. The Committee therefore strongly urges the Department to be more proactive with the media and the public in communicating its perspective on the ends-means gap. Until the Government of Canada acknowledges this gap, and increasing funding to the military to meet its operations requirements, the gap will remain.[23]

It is hard to disagree with this. At the same time, realism in defence policy begins at home. Political decision-makers are acting in a logical and not in a myopic way. From Canada, the world looks safe. Deployments to dangerous places are never immediate enough to generate momentum in the government and the public to ensure a major long-term program of re-equipment. The recent federal budget did restore some funding to DND and improvements can and will be made. But continuing budgetary pressures, such as for further health care spending and tax cuts, and the absence of a major threat to Canadian security, strongly suggest that for the foreseeable future the posture and equipment of the CF is likely to be what it has today, minus attrition, plus the equipment currently ordered.

As real as the operational problems are for the members of the Armed Forces, from the perspective of the country's political leadership, Canada is doing more than its share and the CF is effectively supporting the foreign policy of the country.

This being the case, it will be all the more important for Ottawa to address the "operational tempo" side of the gap. Moreover, apart from equipment and supply shortages, the psychological and family strain on members of the CF as a result of the high operational tempo is also a major concern. There are high rates of divorce amongst the troops, especially at the lower ranks. Combined with the living conditions at some bases and the low rates of pay, the CF is facing a serious morale problem. The relatively large commitment now present in the Balkans, in both Bosnia and Kosovo, and the prospect that these operations will continue for several more years, provides ample justification for the government to reduce the number of missions it accepts or to contribute smaller units. In this regard the recent decision to pull Canadian forces from Kosovo in the new year and consolidate Balkan operations in Bosnia is a wise and welcomed move.[24] Communicated clearly, this is the kind of solution that the Canadian public, still anxious to see Canada continue to play an active role internationally yet concerned about the morale of the CF and unwilling to support major increases in defence spending, should understand and accept. It may well be that in the coming years funds will have diverted from capital to improve the quality of life for those whom Canada sends abroad to deal with "human security."

CONCLUSION

Are the Canadian forces stretched too thin? The answer is assuredly yes. But the problem cannot simply be attributed to the inability of the country's political leadership to understand the nature of the current international security environment. The leadership in fact has a fairly firm and clear grasp of international and especially domestic realities. Nor is it a question of money. With its new budget surpluses Ottawa does have the money to spend and defence is getting more of it. But the reality is, the current government will not spend significantly more on defence because it does not believe it has to, in order to secure vital Canadian interests, the security of the country and its prosperity. Nor given the experiences of the past decade can Ottawa expect that increases in defence spending in order to deploy more forces abroad in coalition operations will secure Canada enhanced influence in Washington or Brussels.

The real gap that needs to be narrowed, the one that should most concern the political leadership, is the commitment-credibility gap. This happens when politicians pledge Canadian forces to roles that they cannot perform and when the military goes along with such requests because it wants to appear useful or more moral. Mr. Axworthy's human security agenda must not be used to issue a blank cheque to the United Nations or other regional coalitions—a cheque that will bounce as Canada is unable to fulfill specific commitments. Here is the "disconnect" the Minister's Committee noted. The result is a force that at best serves neither the national or multilateral interests and at worst, places the men and women of the CF in needless danger. In part the commitment-credibility gap needs to be addressed in the debate over force structure and new capital. Some choices and trade-offs will have to be made especially between personnel and equipment. It may well be that overall personnel levels will have to come down to below fifty thousand in order to pay for new equipment and technology. It might also be suggested that the time is right for Canada to "come home" for a while, to ease the strain on the troops and their families, to enhance training, to attend to much needed repairs and refurbishing of equipment and in general to take a rest from the high tempo of global interventionism.

It is not, as Jockel indicates, a question of "soft-power and hard choices." The decisions facing the government are not that difficult. The Prime Minister and the Cabinet are aware that the public will not accept major increases in defence spending and that Canada's allies, including the US, will accept whatever contributions Ottawa can make. Thus far no Canadian contribution has been turned away. All that needs to be done is to maintain the existing capabilities with some modest improvements here and there and participate in coalitions with what you have. Given the multi-faceted nature of current operations, with their mixture of advanced weapons and lighter forces, there will likely be many roles which the CF can perform. Government decisions may only be hard on those who have to carry them out if too many missions are undertaken and if insufficient capabilities are deployed to specific commitments.

Thus when Canada does go forth again, the political leadership must be primarily concerned with wisely using the structure that exists, measuring individual specific commitments of the moment against what Canada can reasonably and effectively do to fulfill them. If this can be done then Canadian defence and foreign policy will be placed on a firmer, more realistic and ultimately more beneficial footing for Canada and for the world.

NOTES

1. Parts of this chapter will appear in, "Narrowing the Commitment-Credibility Gap: The Canadian Forces Structure Debate," forthcoming in an edited volume by Alan Sens, UBC Press and in "Du Partage Du Fardeau au 'Nettoyeage De Fenetres' La Cooperation militaire

canada-americaine a l'etranger," forthcoming in an edited volume by Paul Letourneau.
2. "The Challenges of Shared Security," remarks to the Canadian Club of Montréal, the Honorable Gordon Giffen, Montréal, January 11, 1999. (Text supplied by the Embassy of the United States, Ottawa).
3. Stewart Bell, "Military May Soon be Unfit for Combat," *National Post*, 18 October 1999, at www.nationpost.com.
4. As quoted in Peter McLaughin, "Funding Crunch Stealing Navy's Heart Report Says," *The Daily News*, 8 June, 1999 at www.hfxnews.southam.ca/story4.hmtl. See also, David Puglise, "Lightly Armed and Not So Dangerous," *The Kingston Whig Standard*, 10 May 1999, 8.
5. Jeff Salot, "NATO Head Hits Canada on Defence Spending," *The Globe and Mail*, 31 October, 1999, A3.
6. Field Marshall Viscount Wolseley, *The Story of a Soldier's Life* Vol. II. (London: Archibald, Constable & Co., 1930), 154.
7. Canada, *Defence Planning Guidance 2000*, (Ottawa, ON: Department of National Defence August 1999), 1-1.
8. Michael Mastanduno, "Preserving the Unipolar Moment: Realist Theories and U.S. Grand Strategy," *International Security* 21, Spring 1997, 52.
9. Stephen Handleman, "Defence Needs a Medic," *Time*, 3 May, 1999, 48-49.
10. Paul Koring, "Will Fight for 'Just' Cause, Eggleton Says," *Globe and Mail*, 9 October, 1999.
11. Robert Russo, "Axworthy Signals Support for Greater Armed Forces Spending," *Ottawa Citizen*, 24 September 1999 at southam.com/ottawacitizen.
12. Joseph Nye, "Redefining the National Interest," *Foreign Affairs*, 78, July/August 1999, 23-24.
13. James Eayrs, "Military Policy and Middle Power: The Canadian Experience," Gordon J. King ed., *Canada's Role as a Middle Power* (Toronto: Canadian Institute of International Affairs, 1965), 70.
14. Louis Nastro and Kim Richard Nossal, "The Commitment-Capability Gap and Canadian Foreign Policy," *Canadian Defence Quarterly* No. 27 Autumn 1997, 21.
15. Robert D. Warrington, "The Helmets May Be Blue, but the Blood's Still Red: The Dilemma of US Participation in UN Peace Operations," *Comparative Strategy* No. 14, 1995, 23-34.
16. Nastro and Nossal, "The Commitment-Capability Gap," 21-22.
17. John Hillen, "Superpowers Don't Do Windows," *Orbis* No. 41, Spring 1997, 257.
18. These figures and descriptions have been taken from various public briefings supplied by the Department of National Defence and from the document *White Paper Staff Check and Mobilization Planning* produced by the office of the Vice Chief of the Defence Staff, 4 September, 1998. Emphasis in originals.
19. DND *White Paper Staff Check and Mobilization Planning*, 4 September 1998.
20. David Haglund and Alen Sens, "Smaller NATO Members: Belgium, Canada, Portugal and Spain," unpublished paper.
21. Canada, DND, Speaking Notes for the Honourable Art Eggleton, Minister of National Defence, "Canadian Lessons from the Kosovo Crisis," Harvard University, 30 September 1999.
22. Fisher, "Allies in Kosovo," 16.
23. Minister's Monitoring Committee, Interim Report, 120.
24. Annie McIlroy and Graham Fraser, "Pulling Troops from Kosovo Will Ease Pressure Chretien Says," *The Globe and Mail*, 13 November, 1999, A8.

The Political Skills of a Canadian General Officer Corps

Desmond Morton

Dr. Desmond Morton is the Director of the McGill Institute for the Study of Canada.

EARLY IN SEPTEMBER 1954, I entered the third class of the Collège Militaire Royal de St-Jean (CMR). The family joked that I was destined to be Canada's first field marshal. Why not? An uncle was a major-general, and in 1921, an ancestor had become Canada's second general.[1] If I was short, flat-footed and unathletic, what about Napoleon Bonaparte in his cadet years? And who else entered CMR that autumn with his own copy of Clausewitz's *On War*, personally annotated?

Open assertion of such ambitions at CMR or anywhere else would have been both imprudent and un-Canadian. Yet, apart from those solely motivated by dreams of flying an F-86, or acquiring a free university education, or a few who had frankly hopped the wrong bus, was I unique? Who enters a profession in hope of resting on its lowest rungs? Commanding fleets or armies, determining the fate of entire nations was a reasonable expectation for someone raised on the novels of C.S. Forester or the now-insufferable George Alfred Henty. The indoctrination had indeed begun at cadet camp. All ten principles of war had been committed to memory. So were the four phases of an appreciation, the five stages of good instruction and all five parts of a proper operation order. With future lists to be absorbed on the path to high and faultless command, how could I fail?

THOUGHTS ABOUT ADMIRALSHIP AND GENERALSHIP

My life, of course, changed direction. The flat feet, ignored during my enlistment medical, gave me a nautical roll on the parade square that did not appeal to RMC's first naval commandant. They also marched me firmly from the Armour Corps to the Army Service Corps. Valued as a logistician might be, no Canadian with that background would be promoted past major-general until Bill Leach, who retired in 2000 as a Lieutenant-General and Commander of the Army. For a fatal second, as my eye looked elsewhere for advancement, concentration was lost. Meanwhile, good fortune and steady nerves kept the Cold War from turning hot, humanity survived the nuclear age, and by the time I graduated, Canadian defence had entered the retrenchment mode it has experienced ever since. Any temptation to appoint a Canadian five-star general would have to wait for a different millennium.

My ten-year military career became the overture of a life in politics, journalism and universities. Much that I learned as a young officer, including the principles of war and the sequence of instruction, was of immediate value in my next career, as the New Democratic Party's newest staff member. A range of experiences, from cleaning latrines, to thinking under stress, to dealing with high-ranking drunks, proved unexpectedly handy at other phases. When I have to do too much in a hurry, fragments of battle procedure filter usefully into my head. A naval inheritance of bounding up the stairs has helped me to keep fit. Some years ago, when I needed an administrator who would find reasons to say yes, not no, I turned to an ex-air force brigadier-general, and I was not disappointed. But I still rejoice at the circumstances that ensured that I would never become a general. So should you.

GENERALS AND ADMIRALS

Not that Canada has lacked generals and admirals. They have increased like the Gross National Product. In 1900, our 40,000 member militia borrowed its single general from Britain. By 1914, we had five major-generals of our own, plus an admiral. In August 1938, the Defence Forces List reported a rear admiral, eight major-generals (four in active postings), and an air vice marshal.[2] In 1990, when Canada maintained 80,000 citizens in uniform and another 20,000 in the reserves, the Canadian Forces needed 120 admirals and generals, more per capita than any NATO ally.[3] By 1997, intervention in the rank structure reduced the numbers in "star ranks" to 74, enough for one general or admiral per 723 other ranks in the shrunken Canadian Forces. In peacetime, when extraordinary demands and outstanding military achievements are uncommon, officers in their final years of service hope to achieve the top ranks and the flow-through tends to be more rapid than in the middle ranks. In a hierarchical institution, the competition for advancement is acute; the rewards of pay, pension, status and dignity are worth seeking.

Generals and admirals occupy the senior ranks of any naval or military force, the highest of three categories of commissioned officers, distinguished by richer arrays of gold lace and from one to four gilt maple leaves, analogous for purposes of identification, with the silver stars worn by their American counterparts. Their salaries are determined by negotiations with the Treasury Board: the arguments that count are based on personnel or financial responsibility, the rank of civil service or allied counterparts, by politics or tradition. Like other human resource categories, admiralship or generalship is subject to "classification creep." It is countered by multi-national comparisons: does Canada really have more generals than the Spanish?

OPERATIONAL COMMAND

Tradition dictates that generals and admirals are warriors-in-chief, leaders of fleets and armies doing battle for the sovereign or the state. The ribbons on their left chest symbolize valour and a lifetime of warlike experience.

Reality, in Canada's peaceable kingdom, is a little less dramatic. Service tradition dictates that an admiral cannot normally fly his flag in a ship smaller than a cruiser: since HMCS *Bonaventure* was scrapped, the only ships in the Canadian Navy large enough for the honour are firmly located on dry land. Having embraced the American principle that a brigadier is a general, Canada waited a generation to swallow the painful corollary that a colonel can command a brigade. Several of the army's most cherished vacancies dropped a rank, eliminating most of the operational commands for a brigadier-general. Only the 1st

Canadian Division Headquarters at Kingston, a somewhat theoretical organization, even looks like the traditional general's command. Like the navy, the air force commands its aircraft from the ground and far away, and generals resemble regional vice-presidents.

Yet it is the operational command role that has traditionally defined admiralship or generalship. The erect stature, the uniform with its splashes of gold and medals, the clipped voice and decisive manner portray an authority few ministers or chief executives can emulate. Generals and admirals send ships and regiments to victory or doom. They unleash mass destruction and, with a few curt words, reverse the tide of battle. We have visualized it with Sir John Hackett or John Keegan; we have even seen it happen at the movies or on the History Channel. Yet how many of Canada's twentieth-century admirals or generals have had the opportunity to perform this role?

GENERALS AND ADMIRALS IN WAR

Partly because of the modest scope of its forces and partly because of Canada's subordination to Imperial or allied command, only a select minority of admirals and generals filled operational commands in the two world wars. In 1917-18, Captain Walter Hose commanded the sole operational units of Canada's infant fleet, a collection of trawlers and yachts, from an office ashore. The Royal Canadian Navy's (RCN) lone front-line commander in the Second World War, Rear-Admiral L.W. Murray, flew his flag in St. John's or Halifax.

The Canadian Corps in the First World War offered significant scope to its successive commanders, notably Sir Julian Byng and Sir Arthur Currie, and somewhat less to the nine generals (including Currie) who commanded its four divisions in action. During the Second World War, Canadian generals were determined to have their own army, a dream threatened when 1 Canadian Corps was transferred to the Italian front.[4] General H.D.G. Crerar's First Canadian Army depended on British and allied divisions. In all, three Canadian generals commanded corps in the field, and thirteen (including the three future corps commanders) led divisions into battle. During the twentieth century, twenty-five generals, three of them British, commanded Canadian Army formations against an enemy.

The proportionate Canadian role in the air was much larger but the command presence was tiny. Canada provided a quarter of the flying personnel for the Royal Air Force (RAF) by 1918, but occupied no higher rank than Wing Commander that was held by R.H. Mulock. In 1942, after much pressure, 6 Bomber Group became Canada's only major air formation in the Second World War. Its two successive commanders, Air Vice Marshals G.M. Brookes and

C.M. McEwen, exercised distinctive operational command. Were there others of air rank?

HOW DID THEY DO?

The major study of Canada's wartime generals, J.L. Granatstein's *The Generals*, is a textbook for those who want Canada to have competent generals and admirals for a future major conflict. Apart from a chapter on Generals Pope and Stuart, he has little to say about the many generals who filled non-operational appointments in Canada and England. Most readers will be satisfied. Those who need to know what most generals (and admirals and air marshals) did for the war will keep on looking.

Of the two thousand or more Canadians who have borne the rank of admiral or general during the century, perhaps thirty—or a hundred and thirty, if the status is extended to commodore or brigadier—have played their stereotypical role against the enemy. None of them are currently in service. Indeed, no presently serving officer can have seen war service.

Gilles Lamontagne, a former Minister of National Defence recalled his sense of disillusionment when, during his term, he appointed the first Chief of the Defence Staff without wartime service. A survivor of flights over wartime Europe and of Nazi prison camps, Lamontagne had more fighting experience than Canada's newest top general, Ramsay Withers. Lamontagne was not necessarily justified. With the exception of General H.D.G. Crerar and Lieutenant-General E.L.M. Burns, neither of them stellar commanders, the common feature of Canada's Second World War operational commanders was that they had all been too young for the earlier war. Granatstein argues that the most successful of them, Lieutenant-General Guy Simonds and Major-Generals Bert Matthews, Chris Vokes and Bert Hoffmeister, had been junior officers at the outbreak of war in 1939. Matthews and Hoffmeister came from the Militia.

Nor have military or naval commanders received generous treatment from Canadians. At the time of General Jean Boyle's humiliation, it was apposite to recall the treatment of the victor of the North-West Campaign of 1885, Major-General Sir Fred Middleton. Denounced as a thief for some looting that occurred late in the campaign, Middleton and his French-Canadian wife were driven to live in England—where Queen Victoria did him the justice of making the old soldier Keeper of the Crown Jewels.[5] Sir Arthur Currie, commander of the Canadian Corps, returned in obscurity in 1919, until an unexpected vacancy allowed admirers at McGill University to install him as their Principal. In 1945, General Crerar was honoured by a national tour but lamented for the rest of his life that no appropriate appointment had come his way.[6] Rear-Admiral

Murray, who had turned Canada's corvette navy into an effective anti-submarine force, became the scapegoat for Halifax's V-E Day riots in April 1945, and retired with his modest pre-war pension to live in England.[7]

Generals Die in Bed, a 1928 novel by an American veteran of the Canadian Expeditionary (CEF), summed up a common feeling, though historian A.M.J. Hyatt insisted that the casualty rate for Canadian generals was about the same as that for privates.[8] No fewer than three biographers and a legal scholar have recorded a generally high opinion of Sir Arthur Currie, commander of the Canadian Corps in the First World War.[9] Two less substantial biographies celebrated Montgomery's favourite Canadian commander, Lieutenant-General Guy Simonds. A biography of the most admired Canadian divisional commander, Major-General B.M. Hoffmeister has long been promised. Montgomery's "good plain cook" of a general, Chris Vokes, tired of waiting for a biographer and contributed his own memoirs, a relative rarity among Canadian generals.[10] No one has yet tackled Canada's senior field commander, General Crerar, or Simond's rival, Lieutenant-General Charles Foulkes.

PLAYING THEIR ROLE IN OTTAWA

Foulkes and Crerar were not, on the whole, successful field commanders and both would have been replaced if they had not been Canadians. Both were brilliant at the bureaucratic games Canadian military and naval commanders must commonly play. As subordinates of a complex, contradictory and demanding political system, they prospered and, given the hostility to the army in the King government, perhaps the army prospered with them.

In war and in peace, Ottawa is where Canadian admirals and generals have faced their greatest challenges and the judgement of history has been passed. It has often been harsh. It has more often been obscure. While the conflicts of ministers and generals in the post-Confederation years, between the world wars, and in the era of unification, have been described, no one has looked at the war years in the Militia Department or in the Department of National Defence (Army).[11]

Revisionist history of the Battle of the Atlantic has, for example, been savage in its treatment of those who attempted to build an anti-submarine navy from the banks of the Ottawa River and the Rideau Canal. Disconnected from the relentless demands of both new technology and the old Atlantic, Naval Headquarters encouraged the corvette navy to grow too fast and to settle for equipment and training that crippled Canadian escorts in their battle with German U-boats. Perhaps Angus L. Macdonald, a powerful but short-sighted minister, would have been too much for them but it is not clear that the Chiefs of Naval Staff had either the will or the professional knowledge to challenge him.

The embarrassing tale, slowly dragged into the light by military historians Marc Milner and David Zimmerman, after most of those directly involved were dead, has become the sad central story of Canadian admiralship in war.[12]

In war or peace, the bulk of Canada's admirals and generals have not played operational roles. They are "Ottawa men" or their regional counterparts; they spend their days as managers, organizers, advisors. They approve memos, not fire-plans; they plot strategy for committees, not battle groups; they are judged by their influence on civil servants and, sometimes, on politicians. Most often they are judged on their skill in avoiding trouble, not causing it. Their acts of courage and opportunism are equally veiled in obscurity and indifference. Lieutenant-General Kenneth Stuart drove himself through sickness to serve his comrades and sacrificed his career to get conscripted reinforcements for the Canadian Army in Europe. He died in 1945, after 35 years' service, leaving his widow a pension of $180 a month.[13]

Admirals and generals wear uniforms and keep themselves fit. As part of the "ticket-punching" necessary for promotion, they have completed courses and even operational postings in ships, regiments and squadrons. They have attended Staff College, commanded ships or battalions or squadrons for a requisite term, and some have participated in allied courses. They will have to complete the courses devised as more practical substitutes for the former National Defence College. Many protest (with perhaps some self-conscious pride) that they were never really trained for their current job. Should we assume that they do it less well than those who have been doing it for much of their lives and who have conscientiously prepared themselves for it?

A PEACETIME TEST

One possible test of Canada's peacetime admirals and generals is how well they meet the needs of the Canadian Forces in the struggle for scarce resources.

According to the Minister of National Defence, eighty-eight percent of Canadians approve of the role and performance of the Canadian Forces. That is an impressive approval rating. Senior officers and the defence lobbies insist that Canada's forces are over-stretched and are constrained by outmoded, obsolete, "rusted-out" weapons and equipment. This is a claim that can only come from professionals, since they possess the required expertise. Yet only seventy percent of respondents in the same survey believe that more money should be spent to modernize the forces.

How does this measure the credibility of Canada's military leaders? Discussions with Ministers of Parliament suggest that military witnesses before parliamentary committees are not trusted nor are their opinions respected. The image of "the brass" as self-seeking and self-serving, purveyed by *Esprit de Corps* and echoed by *Frank*, has outlasted the departure of General Jean Boyle to the aerospace industry. This news, if believed, may inspire predictable outrage at politicians, journalists, academics and other Happy Hour witches and warlocks. Then senior commanders might assess the iota of truth that applies to them and where it might lead them or their successors.

UNDERSTANDING THE GROUND

Canadian admirals and generals will continue to be naval and military professionals but their performance in rank depends on understanding where they, like their predecessors, have done their work. They must study defence policy, not as an academic conceit but as the ground for their continuing campaign to allow Canada to be able to respond to what duly elected governments desire.

Defence policy-making has been a problem for a long time. Some of it is inherent. Canada faces few plausible threats. No peacetime defence organization can hope to have all that it needs, much less desires. Democratic politicians prefer commanders who solve their own problems. Other problems are structural. In most government departments, that advice comes formally from a single channel, the deputy. Since 1868, the Defence department has been a two-headed exception, with a civilian deputy and a military head.

Canada was eager to pioneer primarily because the problems of civil-military relations were continual and bitter. Between 1868 and 1904, only one militia commander completed a full term and departed with the government's appreciation. Relations with other commanders ranged from contemptuous to poisonous.[14] Sir Percy Lake proved skilful in handling his Liberal superiors, but he had gone before Colonel Sam Hughes became minister in 1911. Hughes fired his first Chief of General Staff (CGS) after less than a year, and only extraordinary ability and character allowed Sir Willoughby Gwatkin to survive the war years— that and Hughes's dismissal in 1916.[15] In 1922, when the new Liberal government created a single Department of National Defence, they hoped to get coherent advice; instead, army and navy simply fought each other at closer quarters. Despite the wartime brilliance of its senior officers, the army stagnated.[16] After 1922, the heads multiplied, with a full voice for the air force added in 1938. The long wait and well-founded suspicions that senior services looked after themselves, meant that each guarded access to the Minister as a lifeline. Twice, as the navy knew, the CGS had recommended its disbandment. The air force did not care that one of those episodes had been designed to preserve its existence; instead, it remembered the "Big Cut" of 1931. Experience taught any chief the folly of priorities or special efforts to reconcile differences. Any minister who believes that there must be a better solution than giving each service all or a similar fraction of what it wants faces frustration.

In any planning for the Second World War, Ottawa seemed determined to prevent army expansion and the slightest risk of conscription. Yet the Canadian Army overseas grew larger than it had been in the earlier war, and its casualties produced the unwanted conscription crisis. Opinions will differ on whether this was a national tragedy but it is hard to ignore the political abilities of some of the army's senior officers at NDHQ and overseas. General A.G.L. McNaughton might well have been a hopeless field commander and there was no reason to believe that Lieutenant-Generals Ken Stuart or Maurice Pope were better, but all three played a model role in serving the army's needs—probably all the more because all three understood the conscription issue and two of them—McNaughton and Pope—strongly believed that it would be unnecessary.

After 1945, Brooke Claxton restructured National Defence Headquarters and promoted Charles Foulkes to be Canada's first peacetime general in return for chairing the three chiefs of staff—but each chief could still meet the Minister alone. In the wake of a Cuban Missile crisis, in which service commanders had effectively ignored the Prime Minister—though not his defence minister—the Diefenbaker government collapsed. Its Liberal successor allowed Paul Hellyer to create a single Chief of Defence Staff and an integrated command structure and, in 1967, to impose a single uniform. Armed with its different functions and distinct alliance commitments, land, sea and air kept their distance and negotiated with a new Canadian Forces Headquarters, if necessary, through their allies. When Pierre Trudeau downgraded alliance commitments, defence chiefs fought back. Convinced of the rightness of their views, they exploited his ambiguities for the sake of policies they supported.

Vengeance arrived in 1970, with Donald S. MacDonald, the Management Review Group, "civilianization" of policy planning and a diarchy of deputy minister and Chief of the Defence Staff, with a civilian deputy in the most enhanced position ever held since Confederation. If defence policy was too important to leave to generals and admirals, MacDonald would involve civilians. Apart from a futile gambit by Alan Mackinnon in 1979, his successors, Liberal and Conservative, have not conspicuously altered the situation. Allied defence headquarters, from Oslo to Canberra, seem to have moved in a similar direction. Whatever their legal entitlement, Chiefs of Defence Staff have learned to accept that their moment of eminence will be shared with a deputy minister who, at least in defence analyst and former Lieutenant-Colonel Douglas Bland's view, has rather more power than responsibility.[17]

QUALITIES OF COMMAND

The job description for Canada's senior commanders should provide for much more political skill and experience than it ever has. This will not be popular with military traditionalists nor with liberal democrats. The former scorn "politics" as a complex and deceptive art—as though war was simple and straightforward. The latter also prefer their military subordinates to be predictable and, therefore, easily outmanoeuvred. Informal conversations with government backbenchers revealed an alarming mistrust of military commanders who had come before them. Whatever the issue, admirals and generals were assumed to be dishonest. The cost of this image, however unjust, is as incalculable as it is difficult to eradicate. In his parting advice to the US Army last year, General Dennis M. Reimer observed that "personal credibility is the coin of the realm with Congress" and cited a great predecessor, General George C. Marshall, whose unswerving reputation as a straight-shooter served him and the army in Congress.[18]

It may well be that the qualities of an ideal admiral or general combine apparently contradictory virtues—cunning and bravery, thought and decision, brutality and chivalry. Predictable simplicity is as common a recipe for failure as self-indulgent egoism. There are few mysteries and many compromises. And no size fits all.

Courage is the oldest quality—and the most enduring. Commanders need more than desperate bravery in a tight spot or valour as astonishing to the owner as anyone else. Courage must be physical and moral. War is brutal, sacrificial and exhausting. After watching courage during two wars, Lord Moran, a former medical officer concluded that it was a wasting asset. None of us have an unlimited supply. To be cool under fire—from their own side as well as the enemy's—commanders need a lot. Canadians expect commanders to share front-line dangers, and are scornful if they do not.

Commanders must also be durable. Operations used to cease in winter and seldom happened at night. Seasonal truces ended with the nineteenth century, and the advent of airpower in 1914 turned night into day. Operations in all three environments now ignore time and weather and front lines. The so-called "Revolution in Military Affairs" or RMA will expose commanders to physical and mental strain unimaginable to their predecessors. In the Second World War, several Canadian field commanders failed under pressure. Thanks to stamina, young officers became successful generals. Ageism and physical intolerance are politically incorrect. Is defeat preferable?

Courage and durability are prerequisites to effective command. Admirals and generals must be able to dominate the essentials of a complex operation. They must grasp a problem, conceive a solution, inspire subordinates, delegate successfully and find the reserves to respond to the inevitably unexpected. Command is a combination of intellect, knowledge and character. Of the three, character is by far the most important, particularly if it includes the capacity to exploit brains and information and bring them to a decisive conclusion.

The capacity for command depends on an impossible quality: mastery of the future. Generalship would be easy if we knew what was going to happen—or even what was happening now, on the other side of the hill. Military genius comes from the capacity to anticipate. Technology now presents commanders with vast arrays of information, much of it erroneous, some of it self-serving, all of it confusing. Wise leadership depends on foresight and the courage to use it.

Napoleon had a closely related requisite for his generals—luck. Very little in conflict is certain. Weather is always beyond any commander's control. So are a million unpredictable vagaries of nature, and seldom more than when science and technology have promised certainty. As countless biographers and historians have observed, fortune usually favours the brave, the tough and the decisive.

NOTES

1. In 1913, Sir William Otter had been forced to retire by the Conservatives with the rank of Brigadier-General but the Liberals, restored in 1921, gave him the post-retirement rank of general, just behind Sir Arthur Currie. See Desmond Morton, *The Canadian General* (Toronto: Hakkert, 1974), 311-313, 366.
2. Defence Forces List, (Ottawa, DND, August, 1938). For modern comparisons, there were one commodore, twelve temporary brigadiers and two air commodores.
3. As noted in a series of reports to the Minister of National Defence in 1997. Numbers were inflated when Canada's unified forces followed the American example and restored "star" or "flag" status to the rank of brigadier or commodore.
4. Canada could have had its own six-division Army in 1918, if Sir Arthur Currie had agreed to reorganize with three-battalion brigades. The new Army, Corps two divisions and six brigade headquarters could have made room for sixteen new generals and only six thousand more soldiers. Currie saw no benefit. See Morton, *A Peculiar Kind of Politics* (Toronto: University of Toronto Press, 1982), 152-156.
5. See Desmond Morton, *The Last War Drum* (Toronto: Hakkert, 1972), 168-9.
6. The late Colonel C.P. Stacey claimed that General Crerar had won discreet release from the Hull jail, where he had been booked on a drunk driving charge on his way home from a golf club. No confirmation has been found.
7. On the Halifax riots see Desmond Morton and J.L. Granatstein, *Victory, 1945: Canada From War to Peace* (Toronto: Harper Collings, 1995), 23-28.
8. Hyatt also found that hemorrhoids, presumably from long hours in a wet saddle, were a serious occupational hazard. See A.M.J. Hyatt, "Canadian Generals in the First World War and the Popular View of Military Leadership," *Social History*, XII, 24 November 1979.
9. Daniel G. Dancocks, *Sir Arthur Currie: A Biography* (Toronto: McClelland & Stewart, 1985); A.M.J. Hyatt, *General Sir Arthur Currie: A Military Biography* (Toronto: University of Toronto

Press, 1987); H.M. Urquhart, *Arthur Currie: The Biography of a Great Canadian* (Toronto: Macmillan, 1950) and, a study of the Port Hope libel trial, Robert Sharpe, *The Last Day, The Last Hour: The Currie Libel Trial* (Toronto: Osgoode Society, 1988).

10. See Dominick Graham, *The Price of Command: A Biography of General Guy Simonds* (Don Mills: Stoddart Publishing, 1993) and J.S. McMahon, *Professional Soldier: General Guy Simonds: A Memoir* (Winnipeg: McMahon Investments, 1985). A biography of Hoffmeister has been promised by Brereton Greenhous. On Vokes, see Chris Vokes, *Vokes: My Story* (Ottawa: Gallery Books, 1985).

11. See Desmond Morton, *Ministers and Generals: Politics and the Canadian Militia, 1868-1904* (Toronto, University of Toronto Press, 1970); James Eayrs, *In Defence of Canada: From the Great War to the Great Depression* (Toronto: University of Toronto Press, 1964*); In Defence of Canada: Appeasement and Rearmament* (Toronto: University of Toronto Press, 1965); and, as samples of a rich array, Douglas Bland, *Chiefs of Defence: Government and the Unified Command of the Canadian Armed Forces* (Toronto: s.n., 1995) R.B. Byers, "Canadian Civil-Military Relations and Reorganization of the Armed Forces: Whither Civilian Control?" in Hector Massey, *The Canadian Military: A Profile* (Toronto: Copp Clark, 1972). V.J., Kronenberg, *All Together Now: The Organization of National Defence in Canada, 1967-1972* (Toronto: Canadian Institute of International Affairs, 1973).

12. Marc Milner, "Royal Canadian Navy Participation in the Battle of the Atlantic Crisis of 1943" in James A. Boutilier, (ed.) *RCN in Retrospect, 1910-1968* (Vancouver: UBC Press, 1985); Ibid, *North Atlantic Run: The Royal Canadian Navy and the Battle for the Convoys* (Toronto: University of Toronto Press, 1985); Ibid, "The Implications of Technological Backwardness: The Royal Canadian Navy, 1939-1945," *CDQ*, XIX, 3, Winter, 1989*; The U-Boat Hunters: The Royal Canadian Navy and the Offensive Against Germany's Submarines* (Toronto: University of Toronto Press, 1994); David Zimmerman, "The Royal Canadian Navy and the National Research Council, 1939-45," *CHR*, LXII, 2, June, 1988; *The Great Naval Battle of Ottawa* (Toronto: University of Toronto Press, 1988).

13. Granatstein, *The Generals*, 235.

14. See Morton, *Ministers and Generals, passim*.

15. On Hughes and Mackenzie, see Ronald Haycock, *Sam Hughes: The Public Career of a Controversial Canadian, 1885-1916* (Waterloo: Wilfrid Laurier University Press, 1986), 155-172; and Desmond Morton, *A Peculiar Kind of Politics: The Overseas Ministry and the Canadian Expeditionary Force, 1914-1920* (Toronto: University of Toronto Press, 1982), 17. On Gwatkin: C.F. Hamilton, "Lieutenant-General Sir Willoughby Gwatkin," *Canadian Defence Quarterly* II, 3, April, 1925, 227 and Desmond Morton, "Sir Willoughby Gwatkin," *Dictionary of Canadian Biography* Vol. TBA.

16. Norman Hillmer and William McAndrew, "The Cunning of Restraint: General J.H. MacBrien and the Problems of Peacetime Soldiering," CDQ, VIII, 4, Spring, 1978.

17. Bland, *Chiefs of Defence*, 95-101 *et passim*.

18. General Dennis M. Reimer, "The Army and Congress: Thoughts from the Chief," *Military Review*, March-April 1999, 8.

Let Canadians Decide

Larry Gordon

Larry Gordon is the former Chief of Public Affairs Renewal at DND and is currently self-employed running the firm Gordon Communications.

ENOUGH TIME HAS ELAPSED, since I left the Department of National Defence and the Canadian Forces, to allow for some serious reflection on the role of public affairs and the associated responsibilities and obligations of military leaders, the generals and admirals. When I joined, in 1996, National Defence and the Canadian Forces had become the centre of a major controversy, having been hit by a tidal wave of justifiable public outrage. The controversy centred on the tragic murder of a young man in Somalia by Canadian Forces members and the perceived cover-up that followed. My views are a personal snapshot of a period of enormous turmoil and change.

When I was first approached by National Defence an inner voice advocating self-preservation whispered *refuse the assignment*. But an important national institution was at best in serious trouble and at worst at risk. My underlying faith in Canada's armed forces and the quality and commitment of the overwhelming majority of its members bid me to accept. That decision initiated a two-year period that remains one of the most rewarding of my career. The men and women of National Defence and the Canadian Forces represent some of the finest and most committed individuals that I have ever had the honour to work for or with.

Often solutions are not found until the right questions are asked. In this case the right question was whether what happened in Somalia was an unfortunate and isolated incident or an act that was indicative of a badly flawed institution, one out of sync with Canadian values and acceptable military standards. Understanding the nature and pervasiveness of the underlying issue, in order to undertake an appropriate response to the public demand for answers, was the challenge. As abhorrent as the murder itself was, I believed that what urgently needed to be addressed were the factors that created an environment that allowed the likelihood of such an action to move from unthinkable to possible. For me, Somalia became the trigger that blasted open an institution much in need of public scrutiny.

The incident in Somalia and the witches' brew within the Forces made public indifference impossible. Canadians wanted to know what was going on. What had happened to leadership, recruitment, training and values in the Forces that had allowed a murder to take place? Why was the institution not as outraged as they were? Canadians had questions about the institution's internal processes and procedures and how they may have been affected by major budget cuts, political indifference, and massive downsizing. They wanted explanations as to why the military was so far out of touch with their values and expectations. They needed answers as to why the "No People" within the institution were so dominant (no to women in combat roles, no to gays and lesbians) and why there was such resistance to change? I believed that Somalia was a symptom of an institution out of sync with Canadian values and expectations and that the institution, not comprehending the extent of the problem, initially pursued damage control as opposed to change and reform. It was the worst possible strategy at the worst possible time and the Forces suffered the consequences.

Reporting directly to the Deputy Minister (Louise Frechette) and the Chief of the Defence Staff (Jean Boyle, Larry Murray, and finally Maurice

Baril) I was asked to put in place a communications strategy to inform Canadians and re-build public confidence and to modernize public affairs in National Defence and the Canadian Forces. The view was that the extremely low levels of public confidence were undermining the ability of the institution to deliver its mandate, as put forward in the Defence White Paper, blocking funding and hurting morale. I was sure that Canadians wanted reform and a revitalized Canadian Forces. I was also certain that in the end, the Somalia crisis had the potential to launch the Department and the Forces on a program of reforms that, if successful, would give Canadians a better military. Too many people in the media, self-proclaimed military experts and some members of the Forces were prepared to destroy the institution. I felt certain that Canadians wanted a different outcome and it was going to be my job to give them the information they needed to decide on the fate and future of their armed forces for themselves.

At one point during the recruiting process I reversed my decision to accept the assignment; becoming convinced that leadership did not understand the nature and scope of the issue they faced. Initially, they appeared interested in a public relations solution as opposed to fundamental change. Some hoped that the right person with the right public relations skills could weave a veil behind which the department could carry on without change. They wanted the controversy to just go away. My view was that the department and the Forces should not manage controversy but tackle a complex problem urgently demanding change to strengthen the institution it had burrowed into. Shaken public confidence could not be restored if key players were not prepared to "think" differently and recognize the absolute necessity for reform. Rebuilding public confidence depended on communicating genuine reform activities back to Canadians. As discussions progressed it became apparent that as difficult as it would be there were many individuals in leadership roles who were prepared to move forward with change. The strongest supporters for reform, throughout my term at Defence, were the Deputy Minister Louise Frechette, Vice Admiral Larry Murray, the Chief of the Defense Staff, Maurice Baril, and the executive group composed of both senior military members and public servants. Senior leadership embraced reform and a communications approach based on change rather than public relations. It was the correct decision.

National Defence and the Canadian Forces were caught in a "circle of blame." A circle that overtook any search for solutions. The questions raised asked only what went wrong and who was responsible with little emphasis on corrective action. The circle was comprised of government, the media and the public. Unfortunately, our government encourages those who implement no-risk options and penalizes those who opt for creativity and innovation. Good performance is generally ignored and those who make mistakes, honest or otherwise, are punished. No action becomes the safest route. Add to that a media, particularly the national media, which seeks headlines and not necessarily accuracy or facts that might reduce a story's impact. Conflict and controversy are deemed to be more important than objectivity and public responsibility. The result is that the public is left to form opinion based on distorted, little, or no information. In addition, the military culture can be very difficult, especially for civilians. It is bound in tradition, focused on the past and generally resistant to change. There are individuals within the institution who I previously referred to as the "No People."

The No People exist in every institution and are fortunately a small minority within National Defence and the Canadian Forces. They are out of touch with Canada, mired in tactics and operations, and parochial beyond measure. Convincing them to behave and react more positively was not easy given the environment. The "circle of blame," with its inevitable finger-pointing and disregard for constructive criticism, made a bunker mentality extremely attractive. Encircled, as they were at National Defence, the No People felt justified in protecting their own, keeping the organization closed to outside scrutiny and policed internally. It was a self-imposed prison from which the department had to be released. At all costs and as long as it might take, the No People within the organization had to be won over. The external communications challenge could not be won without a corresponding win internally. It would then be necessary to reach out and communicate directly to Canadians and get beyond the superficial and corrosive Ottawa political and media environment. That was the job that lay ahead.

The confidence I had in National Defence and in Canadians and their faith in their Forces was the critical underpinning of the communications strategy. Its conceptual foundation was that strong public support would enable the department to advance the change agenda more quickly and effectively. It was premised on the belief that Canadians did fundamentally support their armed forces and that if the Forces were able to demonstrate a commitment to change, public confidence would be restored. The communications strategy could be summed up in one word, "Openness." And its implementation in the simplest form was to communicate "Direct" to Canadians with a "Human Face." But, the strategy could not be implemented without senior-level commitment. It is a tribute to them that they accepted a fundamentally different approach, one that defied conventional thinking in Ottawa. Change demanded innovation, innovation invited risk, and risk introduced the likelihood of error. Zero-tolerance for error within the public service and political leadership made reform at National Defence and the Canadian Forces that much more difficult.

But change did happen. It took shape in five main steps. Step number one, internally we had to turn those aforementioned No People around. They had to be convinced that if they did things right public support would result. Winning the Canada/United States fighter jet competition (Top Gun) resulted in major public recognition that sent a clear internal message that Canadians were still prepared to support their armed forces. Second, internal myths had to be exploded. For example, the military thought Canadians would not accept the combat capable role and warrior face of the military. To this end we revamped the recruitment-advertising program to portray, with considerable success, a more realistic picture of military activities. Canadians were not as naïve as many thought. They recognized that the military is an instrument of war. Third, we demonstrated that positive public response resulted from greater openness on issues and operations. We were more forthright, going public quickly and being more honest about failure. Wherever Canadian troops were deployed around the world we encouraged and supported direct media access to members of the Forces (this is discussed further in the following paragraph on public affairs policy). Fourth, we made a serious investment in internal communications, the *Maple Leaf,* to improve internal communications and give public recognition for a job well done. And fifth, we promoted the Canadian Forces as a single entity driving down but not out the intense cancer of parochialism that constantly undermined progress. As we struggled with reform and improved internally, much external communications work was needed. We began that work by rebuilding the communications capacity within the department and the Forces, equipping it with the tools (Internet, outreach programs, etc.) to get the job done.

Another vital ingredient of reform was the crafting of a modern public affairs policy. Again, the underlying principle that guided the formulation of the policy was "Openness." A key element gave staff and members the freedom to speak to the media, with no one being denied the opportunity to talk publicly about what they did in the Forces or the Department. The

Public Affairs Policy represented a complete reversal of the traditional approach. Members at all levels were finally able to communicate directly with fellow Canadians and share their experiences and accomplishments. It was a move greeted warmly as a welcome break from the past. And, it worked. Public confidence soared. National Defence is currently the only Federal Government department, of which I am aware, that has such a high standard of openness embedded in policy. As a strategy, it was a radical departure from the known, not an immediately popular reform or a "quick sell," but to their credit, it was embraced and endorsed by leadership. It remains both a personal and organizational accomplishment of which I am extremely proud, but there is always more that can and should be done. The policy was intended to be tied to an ongoing, fluid process that has the ability to respond to societal demands and environmental change.

To move forward it is sometimes necessary to leave the past behind. An important episode during my tenure was the shutting down of the Somalia Inquiry, or, as I like to refer to it, the "Blame Commission." As previously stated, I accepted the assignment because I believe the majority of the members of Canada's armed forces worthy of respect. I also believe that Canada needs its armed forces. The environment surrounding the Somalia Inquiry was focused on blame. As a Canadian, I did not, and still do not, accept that important national institutions must be destroyed by crusades designed purely to savage them and assign blame to individuals. Rather, we should invest in inquiries that identify problems and find solutions. I supported ending the inquiry because I believed it had become sidetracked. Its colossal failure and disservice to Canadians and to the Canadian Forces was to assume guilt and not address fundamental issues. The issues of recruitment, training, leadership and military values together had somehow failed Canada, the Canadian Forces and an innocent Somalian victim. Those issues are what the inquiry should have focused on, seeking the truth about how the system failed in such a fundamental way. In my opinion the direction of the inquiry was unproductive, damaging and of little merit. It simply did not do the job Canadians paid top dollar for.

The environment of the time was influenced by many factors. One was leadership style. Senior military leaders are highly skilled and dedicated operators. They work hard and are intensely loyal to the service and to Canada. Unfortunately, they do not generally accept that an investment in communicating with Canadians is a wise investment in their future. But, it must be the responsibility of the generals and admirals to communicate continuously with Canadians. To make sure Canadians know what their armed forces are doing on their behalf and, conversely, to ensure that the members of the Forces are keenly aware of the expectations of Canadians and ready and able to meet them. Military leaders must no longer argue against political influence and parliamentary interference. Parliament is duly elected and represents the democratic process that the Forces are sworn to protect.

Another factor affecting the environment surrounding National Defence and the Canadian Forces and its future was political leadership. It is the responsibility of Canada's politicians to develop appropriate policy and to give the military the tools to get the job they assign done. Policy that reflects Canadian society's expectations of their Forces. Politicians must also keep the public informed. They must stay current with the wishes of Canadians and communicate those wishes to the leadership within the Forces. They must make the decisions (monetary and otherwise) that enable the Forces to be all that Canadians want them to be. They must make the Forces understand that they are an expression of societal need and that they do not get to decide what they will be—Canadians do. It is the responsibility of both leadership groups to let Canadians decide on the future of their Forces based on open public dialogue and quality information.

The media equally contributed to a negative environment. The government has historically relied on the media to communicate with Canadians. The media was once viewed as society's watchdog, an important fifth estate in a healthy democratic society keeping governments honest and helping protect democracy and freedom. The unfortunate truth is that lately an attack dog has replaced the watchdog. The attack dog acts quickly. It doesn't need to be as knowledgeable or well trained as the watchdog that has to abide by the same societal rules, rights and freedoms it guards. The attack dog has no time to think, research or seek the truth. It just goes for the jugular and gets the headline. Deadlines, circulation targets, audience ratings and advertising revenues are infinitely more important than fact. Conflict and controversy, or negative news, is the only type of reporting that seems to matter. This attack dog mentality is not helpful to anyone. The facts get lost or misrepresented and everyone loses. There is increasing evidence that the media's influence on public opinion is in serious decline. Generally, the national media are always on the attack. Fortunately, the local and regional media tend to be more balanced. The media has an interesting modus operandi. It is free to criticize, and rightly so, but organizations cannot respond. Any effort to defend itself or any positive news from an institution is considered to be propaganda. And, the right of individuals to privacy is not accepted. If an institution withholds information it is automatically a cover-up, no other explanation is given any credence. But, if the media withholds information it is labeled editorial license. Canadians deserve better than that. They deserve a responsible media which serves at all times as their reliable and trusted watchdog. For all these reasons, the national media could not be, and were not, factored in as a key player in the process to rebuild public confidence in the Canadian Forces.

The final factor negatively affecting National Defence and the Canadian Forces was the relationship between the military and the public servants. It is sensitive and represents a "No Go Zone." It is not considered appropriate to challenge military/public servant integration. However, I must make some comment based on my experience. The military sees itself as different but so does the general public and this is reflected in how they are treated and reported on. In addition to periodic attack or criticism from outside, National Defence is sometimes at war with itself. Military members do not believe that public servants understand how things should work and vice versa. They do not always function as a team. They forget their goal is the same one. Public servants are not members of the club. Personally, I did not feel the need to be a member of their fraternity but simply committed to the end result. A critical ingredient in promoting a new culture is building higher levels of trust and communication between the two groups. The truth is the Military are different. Responsibilities should be divided based on differences. Civilians should not determine things like military strategy, tactics, rules of engagement and strength of the forces. But, recognition of their respective, unique responsibilities and contributions does not deny a single focus. Each must support the other in a unified effort to ensure that Canadian citizens are afforded the opportunity to dictate the institution's role. From a public affairs perspective the relationship and responsibilities of the military and public servant communicators needs reform. There is considerable overlap and duplication and the relationship between command public affairs and corporate public affairs is dysfunctional. All public affairs practitioners should work as a team and military / public service roles should be more clearly defined.

The spring of 1996, marked the beginning of my journey in an institution in serious turmoil. The spring of 1998, marked its end. My commitments to National Defence and the Canadian Forces were met and, according to the standard measures of today, met successfully. I believe that success came from focusing on change, addressing the negatives and nourishing the positives. We restored public confidence in the Canadian Forces to an all-time high and rebuilt the morale of the members, and pride in the Forces. To put names to the "we," they are the entire public affairs team and in particular Bob Quinn, Annie Tremblay, Scott Taymon, Colonel R. Coleman and Colonel Barry Frewer.

But, this is no time to sit back or drop the ball. A strong future for the Department of National Defence and the Canadian Forces depends on a continued commitment to promoting a new culture within the organization, to the ongoing engagement of Canadians through better communications and support of the new policy. Openness must not slip away. Old attitudes, such as resistance to change (women and gays in the military) and reluctance to air mistakes publicly, have to bend. But, Canada's Forces are not alone in their struggle with change; the struggle is evident throughout society. The institution must respond to it, think globally and work together (navy, army, air force, public servants) as a team with a shared goal. There is no room for the narrow-minded parochialism exhibited by some members within the Forces. A team approach is the only approach that can offer any hope of sustained success.

The challenge for National Defence and the Canadian Forces remains. I believe that their fate lies squarely on the shoulders of military leadership. One cannot expect the rank and file to change if there is no vision set forth by the leaders. Throughout history there are countless examples where the course of a war or the outcome of a battle has been altered by a leader with the ability to recognize the need for, and implement, change. It is leadership's responsibility to stay in tune and learn from Canadians, keeping pace with the public's expectations of a unique institution. They cannot rely on the media or anyone else. Our politicians of course guide military leadership; nevertheless, they should take their cue directly from Canadians, letting them decide and ultimately define the role of Canada's Forces. It is the duty of the senior leaders to then effectively communicate this role to the CF membership. By communicating directly with Canadian citizens the senior military leadership have the capability to defeat the No People within the organization, throughout the media and finally, the self-appointed experts—the military critics on the outside who offer no constructive criticism. National Defence and the Canadian Forces are at a turning point. Leadership has to continue to demonstrate to Canadians that they have changed, they are listening and they are willing to let Canadians decide what the institution will be. If they are unable to do so they will lapse into their old ways, lose public confidence, and their relevance as a national institution will be forever diminished.

The General/Admiral's Role in Public Affairs in International Operational Theatres

Colonel (retired) Ralph Coleman

Colonel (retired) Ralph Coleman is the Deputy Director of Communications Planning and Parliamentary Affairs Intergovernmental Affairs.

PUBLIC AFFAIRS IN AN INTERNATIONAL THEATRE OF OPERATIONS is a multi-faceted function that involves communicating with members of the Canadian Forces (CF) in theatre, as well as Canadians and international publics through the news media, even when no Canadian media is present. To do this it is vital that the public affairs function is properly planned, positioned, and resourced within any theatre of operation.

Public affairs is a command responsibility and CF general officers play a key role in the leadership and management of its execution during operations. On newsworthy international deployments, the dominant factor of necessity is relations with the media, including its capability to cover the activities of the Canadian Forces.

Canadian military and media come together on operations from very different backgrounds. Military commanders in international operational theatres, including generals and admirals, are likely to see themselves as defenders of Canadian democratic values, leading hierarchical, mission-focussed, team-oriented and disciplined forces adhering to common rules and regulations. Conversely, journalists are likely to see themselves as the guardians of free speech. They act as independent individuals, not as team players, and work in competition against each other, with very limited and self-imposed rules, in an arena of conflicting interests. The military commander's aim is to successfully accomplish the mission with minimum casualties. The journalist's aim is to be the first to tell the story.

These two worlds could hardly be more different or conflicting. Yet, in an operational theatre where the two must co-exist, each has the capability to dramatically affect the ability of the other to achieve their aim.

THE SYMBIOTIC RELATIONSHIP WITH THE MEDIA

Relations with the news media are of primary importance because of the immediate impact they can have on mission objectives. The relationship between them and the military on operations is a symbiotic one requiring the attention of senior commanders.

CENTRE OF GRAVITY

In a democracy, public support for an assigned military operation will almost always be one of our centres of gravity. Canadians have a right to know what their military members are doing on their behalf. The US experiences in Vietnam and Somalia illustrate the outcome when domestic public support is lost. The Gulf War success illustrates what can happen when governments and the military take active steps to win and maintain their citizen's support. The majority of the public form their opinion on an operation from what they see, hear and read in the news media. Consequently, the military needs the news media to communicate to the public, thus protecting its own centre of gravity.

NEWS MEDIA WILL ALWAYS BE THERE

Commanders must face the reality that news media will be in the theatre of operations and on the battlefield whether they like it or not. A CNN military affairs correspondent said after the Gulf War, "Wherever commanders go, they should plan for CNN. Like the weather, we'll always be there—just another feature on the battlefield terrain."[1]

In many cases, the media will already be in the area before the arrival of military forces. US Marines arriving on the beaches of Somalia near Mogadishu in 1992, in the pre-dawn darkness, were greeted by hordes of news media and television lights. When the NATO-led Peace Implementation Force (IFOR) began arriving in Bosnia in December 1995, and January 1996, it faced a contingent of several hundred reporters that had been covering the war in the former Yugoslavia for a number of years. Not surprisingly, they knew the ground and the belligerents better than the arriving military force. At the height of the Gulf War in 1991, there were some fifteen hundred news media present in the theatre of operations.

Even in places where the media have been excluded by a belligerent or in remote places like the Falkland Islands, which reporters cannot get to on their own, commanders must expect that the media, the public and the political leadership will insist that media representatives accompany the military force. For example, the British task force that sailed for the Falklands in 1982, to reverse the Argentinean invasion, included a press corps of about forty personnel. Similarly, after initially adopting a "no media" policy for the invasion of Grenada in 1983, the Pentagon quickly pressed US commanders to take reporters.[2]

Similarly, military leaders planning the invasion had considered only the operational aspects of the deployment and excluded public affairs personnel. As the operation was about to commence, six hundred news media descended on the neighbouring island of Barbados seeking to cover the impending conflict, catching commanders unprepared. Preoccupied with the details of the invasion, they reacted by denying the media access to Grenada for the first two days, stating that it was "too hard" to accommodate the needs of so many media in the heat of battle. The resultant public uproar eventually resulted in the media setting into Grenada. It also caused the U.S. Defence Department to revise its operational planning to include at least some news media in all operations from the beginning.[3]

The Grenada operation also illustrated why the military-media relationship is symbiotic. The media sometimes need the military to get access to the story, as well as to help get their stories out. News media could not have deployed to the Falklands nor filed their stories from there during the conflict without the full help and support of the British Forces. The media could have relatively easily made their own way to the Persian Gulf (subject only to visa requirements of the host countries); however, to cover the troops in the desert, to get on the ships in the Gulf, and to get their stories out from these remote places, they were dependent on the military. In general, they are far more dependent on the military in war situations, and far less so in operations other than war, where they can usually make their own arrangements. New technological developments such as the satellite-phone-in-a-briefcase will in future reduce or completely eliminate media dependence on military facilities to send their stories. But for the moment, dependency is still a powerful factor.

FIRST IMPRESSIONS ON THE PUBLIC BECOME LASTING ONES

In this television age of spontaneous gratification and instant results, the public is increasingly judging the success or failure of events within a shorter and shorter time frame. This is a phenomenon that military planners and commanders must recognize and plan for. It was not always so.

During the Second World War, in the Italian campaign of 1943, the Canadian Army's media relations and public affairs plans were in a terrible state. The Canadian government in Ottawa was under opposition attack and publicly embarrassed by newspaper stories complaining about poor press facilities, lack of transportation, accommodation and communications for journalists, no regular briefings in the field by army authorities and difficulties in getting accurate reports. The troops also complained that they wanted a Canadian Army newspaper like those of the American and British forces. Consequently, the Canadian Defence Minister of the time, the Honourable J.L. Ralston, appointed Lieutenant-Colonel Richard S. Malone, an infantry officer who had been a journalist before the war, to sort things out. Furthermore, he gave Malone the mandate and the resources to do it. By June 1944, the Canadian Army had one of the best, if not the best, public affairs organization in the Allied Expeditionary Force. Media relations were excellent and the troops had their newspaper—*The Maple Leaf*.[4]

But Malone had the entire Italian campaign to get things right and be ready for the invasion of Normandy and the campaign in North West Europe. With today's much shorter military operations, conducted under the scrutiny of live television coverage, we have no such luxury of using the first campaign to get it right for the subsequent ones. We must get it right the first time, because that is how we will be judged by the media and the public. First impressions count. Once the situation has stabilized, the mission will either end, as the Gulf War did, or become less "newsworthy," as happened in Bosnia, and the press will leave for greener pastures. It will then be too late to finally get the media relations plan working well.

Although the American military successfully rescued American hostages and secured the island of Grenada in a short campaign in 1983, much of the public's attention was diverted to the seeming "war" between the US military and the media, because of the total exclusion by the military of the press for the first two days of the campaign. This detracted from the positive message of the successful operation. In 1991, the Canadian Forces went to war as a formal belligerent for the first time since the Korean War.[5] Yet, the entire Gulf operation (Desert Shield, as well as Desert Storm) was shorter than the entire Italian campaign in the Second World War. Thus, there was little time to learn lessons and adapt, as the Canadian Army did in the Second World War. In the Gulf, the war was over and the news media gone by the time that process had even begun.

NEWS MEDIA AS STRATEGIC FACTOR

Media presence in an operational theatre is an important strategic factor for commanders to consider. Live television or rapidly transmitted video images by satellite can have dramatic and real time consequences. It has been widely postulated that the images of dead US servicemen being dragged through the streets of Mogadishu precipitated the US withdrawal from Somalia.[6] During the Gulf War, the airing of videos depicting coalition laser-guided munitions air strikes, during live-television media briefings in Riyadh, communicated a message to our centre of gravity, the public at home, that the coalition was doing everything to avoid civilian casualties. Conversely, Saddam Hussein used a highly controlled television media to send his messages to the same audience when coalition aircraft struck a bunker that contained civilians, causing many casualties.

NEWS MEDIA AS OPERATIONAL FACTOR

The only constant in planning operational public affairs is that every military deployment will be different, requiring distinct public affairs plans. The old cliché that generals use the last war's tactics to fight the next one can sometimes be applied to the news media. Many of the journalists in the Gulf War came to cover it expecting the same rules that had applied in the Vietnam War. They failed to recognize that the situations were not the same.

Vietnam consisted largely of widespread, small-unit, daytime actions in a tropical country. The American strategy was to move openly into areas, hoping to draw out the communist forces into combat situations where superior American firepower would inflict heavy casualties—the famous "body count." With such an open military strategy there was no need for secrecy. Consequently, media were free to cover whatever operations they wished, subject to the availability of helicopter transportation, then return to Saigon to file their stories and wait for the next operation. Their copy was not subjected to security review because it was not required.

The Gulf War, on the other hand, was a more conventional type of conflict with large-scale armoured coalition forces spread along a 300-mile front line in the desert, preparing to launch a surprise, fast-moving, left-flanking ground attack, at night, against an Iraqi army deployed in traditional, dug-in defensive positions. The only way that media could cover such an operation, and maintain its secrecy was through assignment in small numbers, to specific forces for the duration of the operation. Their copy was subjected to security review to prevent inadvertent release of information that might jeopardize operational surprise. This is what led to the successfully organized media pool system used by coalition force planners.

Those reporters who criticized this system during and subsequent to the conflict did not understand the fundamental difference between the Vietnam conditions that allowed for open, totally unfettered media access, and the situations in the Gulf that called for secrecy and surprise, and therefore, more restrictive arrangements.[7] The ground war in the Gulf was more conventional than Vietnam, but unlike the Second World War or Korea. It covered huge distances requiring great mobility. Media could not ride around in jeeps from one unit to another as in the Second World War, or hitch rides in helicopters as they did in Vietnam. The ground war simply moved too far and too fast, through barren desert terrain. Furthermore, ground units could not handle large numbers of media within the limited space of their combat vehicles. Only limited numbers were possible, hence the pools.

US and British military commanders had learned from Grenada, and the Falklands respectively. Although it was not possible to take all the media present onto the battlefield, with proper planning the military could accommodate some of them and still successfully accomplish the mission.

The NATO campaign against Yugoslavia in the spring of 1999, as a result of the Kosovo crisis, featured more than one type of media arrangement within the same campaign. During the air war phase, the Milosevic regime denied media access to Kosovo, thereby heightening the importance to the news media of the NATO and respective member country daily media briefings. The media were dependent on NATO forces for information about the air campaign, but the Alliance also relied on them to provide a conduit to the public. When the air campaign was suspended and ground forces began moving into Kosovo, the situation changed as media moved in on the ground with the NATO forces and they had direct access to events. They were capable of getting information to the Canadian public directly from the forces on the ground faster than the military could get that information back to national capitals. This, in turn, changed the nature of the daily media briefings in national capitals.

PUBLIC AFFAIRS AND POLITICAL REALITIES

Because the centre of gravity is public opinion, political and military leaders in Canada, as in other like-minded democracies, are keenly aware of media coverage of any operation and do not hesitate to give direction based on it. During the Gulf War, because of the success of the British and American live television briefings daily from Riyadh, Saudi Arabia, which were played around the world on the relatively new phenomenon of CNN, National Defence Headquarters (NDHQ) directed the Commander of the Canadian Forces serving in the Gulf, Commodore Ken Summers, to try to get more international visibility for CF activities in the Gulf via exposure on CNN.[8]

At the time, Summers conducted daily media briefings in Manama, Bahrain, where the Canadian Joint Headquarters was located. The commander of the Canadian CF-18 fighter jet task force located in Doha, Qatar did the same. While excerpts of these briefings were making the Canadian newscasts back home, they were not being carried live, nor were they getting much Canadian mention internationally. CNN was not in Manama or Doha. Canadian briefings in Ottawa were being carried live by Canadian television but were not picked up by CNN.

Among the non-Arab countries, Canada was the fourth largest contributor of forces to the 1991 Gulf War (after the Americans, British and French). It was also a very significant player in the air campaign against Yugoslavia in 1999, and in the initial ground force deployment into Kosovo. Against the public affairs campaigns and media coverage of our larger allies, Canada has always had to make a special effort to ensure our contribution was recognized internationally and at home. This is important not only so that Canadians know the role their forces play in the world, but also for the morale of those CF members involved.

This is not a new phenomenon, nor is it related to the size of the Canadian contribution. During the Second World War, despite the enormous Canadian military presence and role in the Normandy landings of 1944, the original draft communiqué for D-Day read, "General Eisenhower announces that British and American troops have effected a landing..." It was only through persistent efforts by the senior Canadian Army public affairs officer and a threat to make a political incident of it that the word "Canadian" was added to the final version of the communiqué.[9]

During the air campaign of the Gulf War, during every newscast CNN showed a scoreboard of allied aircraft losses. The Italians, who had half the number of aircraft deployed compared to the Canadians, lost one aircraft due to enemy action. As a result, Italy was always on the scoreboard. Canada, with no aircraft losses, was not. The resultant visibility given to the Italian contribution and not the larger Canadian contribution, together with the direction from Ottawa to get more visibility on CNN, gave rise to some black humour amongst the Canadians in the Gulf about finding a CF-18 pilot "volunteer" so that Canada could get on the CNN scoreboard.[10]

THE GENERAL AND ADMIRAL'S ROLE IN PUBLIC AFFAIRS

The Canadian general or admiral's role in public affairs in international operational theatres is a key one of leading by example, making sure that public affairs plans are appropriate to theatre conditions and ensuring that the mission is being communicated to Canadian and international publics. There are five key leadership and monitoring functions for the general officer in the following areas: (1) public affairs staffing and plans, (2) public affairs in the operational planning process, (3) public affairs logistics, (4) communicating to Canadians, and (5) internal information. These five functions are explained in more detail as follows.

1. Make sure there is an adequately sized public affairs staff under experienced leadership at the appropriate rank level, and that they develop a public affairs policy and plan appropriate for the theatre.

The American admiral in charge of the 1983 Grenada invasion admitted that his public affairs officer for the short pre-invasion planning period was an ensign straight out of journalism school because his normal naval commander public affairs adviser was on leave. Furthermore, he conceded that he did not pay any attention to press matters because of more "urgent operational matters." Consequently, the rather disastrous public affairs policy for Grenada, or the lack of any policy, "just happened."[11]

When Commodore Ken Summers first deployed to the Gulf during the Desert Shield pre-war period in 1990, he had a naval lieutenant-commander as his public affairs advisor, one other junior officer and a photographer. The air task force based at Doha was staffed identically. As war approached and he became Canadian theatre commander, Commodore Summers recognized that war operations would require more public affairs resources. As a result, in January 1991, he augmented his public affairs staff to ten (four in his own headquarters headed by a public affairs lieutenant-colonel, four with the air task force, one on the ships and one with the Canadian field hospital). He also added extra photographers. By the time the war started he had published a CF Public Affairs War Plan that was consistent with the other coalition forces, particularly with the Americans and British who had both benefited from their recent experiences.

When NATO first deployed to Bosnia in December 1995, there was a detailed public affairs plan as an annex to the NATO operational plan. In addition, there was a large NATO public affairs establishment of about eighty at the division, corps and theatre level. The public affairs plan was completely integrated with the operational plan, so that public affairs activities focussed on each major operational milestone in the Dayton Peace Plan as it approached.

2. Make sure that public affairs is properly positioned within the headquarters staff to provide input throughout the operational planning process, reflecting the strategic and operational factor that it is. Pay personal attention to it and provide direction to subordinate commanders.

The attitude the commander displays towards public affairs is a key factor. His views will quickly be picked up and followed by the senior officers who will, in turn, pass it on to their subordinates. Therefore, the commander must set the tone.

In the early days of NATO's IFOR deployment into Bosnia, the Allied Rapid Reaction Corps (ARRC) commander, a British Army lieutenant-general, conducted twice-daily secure radio conferences with his division commanders. Also on the radio conference was his public affairs officer because public affairs was a regular agenda item and the corps commander often gave public affairs direction to his divisions through this medium. Both he and the theatre commander, an American four-star admiral, included public affairs as a regular agenda item at their daily staff meetings.

During the air campaign against Yugoslavia, the Deputy Chief of the Defence Staff, Lieutenant-General Ray Hénault, (DCDS) not only had public affairs as an agenda item at his daily morning joint staff meetings, but he also had a small, separate morning meeting in his office exclusively on public affairs issues. In addition, he also conducted another meeting later in the day to prepare for the daily media briefing, as well as numerous conversations with his public affairs advisors in NDHQ throughout the day. This enabled him to provide daily public affairs guidance and direction to his Canadian operational commanders in the field and anticipate any public issues that might develop during a campaign that was under unprecedented public scrutiny through the medium of live television.

This is not to suggest that public affairs considerations must always be paramount; only that they be taken into account along with all the other factors a commander must consider when developing a campaign plan or making an operational decision. For example, very early in the air campaign against Yugoslavia, Lieutenant-General Hénault decided that CF-18 bombing videos would not be shown at the Ottawa daily news briefings. The paramount concern was security-related. With only a small number of CF-18 pilots in our air force coming from only two operational CF-18 air bases in Canada, regular showing of Canadian target videos would have made it relatively easy for the Yugoslavs to link specific targets with the Canadian units attacking them, thereby making it easier for them to target the home base of the pilots and their families with propaganda or threats. The United States, with a much larger air force and many bases, did not have this particular problem. They therefore showed their videos daily, without, of course, identifying the pilots or their units. NATO also showed videos at their daily briefings without naming countries or units.

At the crucial early stages of the air campaign, Hénault wanted to show the news media and the Canadian public that the Canadian Forces were going to be as open as possible. Not showing the Canadian bombing videos, when the United States and NATO were showing them, would run counter to this objective and the initial public affairs instinct was to show the film clips. However, after discussions with his staff in which public affairs fully participated, the DCDS decided that the safety of his pilots and their families outweighed the public affairs concerns. Because he was fully briefed on the implications of his decision, the DCDS was ready when the videos eventually did become an issue with the Canadian media. The media wanted to see the videos, and the issue was never far from the surface at the daily media briefings. Nonetheless, they eventually accepted the DCDS's explanation, especially when he promised to release film clips to the media when the air campaign was over and security was no longer an issue. As promised, Lieutenant-General Hénault did release a series of videos at one of the media briefings shortly after the campaign was terminated.[12]

3. Ensure there is a good public affairs logistics plan appropriate for the situation in-theatre that allows the media to cover CF operations and file their stories back to Canada. Where there are no Canadian media covering Canadian Forces operations ensure CF-produced information is available to the Canadian public. Adequate resources must be assigned this task.

There is an old rhetorical question, "If a tree falls in a forest and no one is there, does it make a noise?" Well, similarly, if the Canadian Forces are successfully completing a mission but the media are unable to get there and/or get their stories out, and the public whom we represent does not know it is happening, can the mission really be successful? In the public's mind, is it happening at all?

In US Army units during the Gulf War, there was an aversion to media coverage because of a perception that it could get commanders into trouble with General Schwarzkopf.[13] In addition, many senior army commanders still nursed old media wounds from the Vietnam War. Consequently, army units generally devoted little time or effort to accepting media with their units or getting media pool reports back from the desert to the media centre at Dhahran. Conversely, the US Marines, under General Walt Boomer, who had been a corps public affairs chief during his career, devoted more time and effort to the task. One journalist stated after the war, "The Marine pools got reports back in a timely fashion, but the army pools were never heard from until after the war."[14]

The result was that the key, spectacular flanking movement and role of the US Army's VII Corps in General Schwarzkopfs's "Hail Mary" plan received very little media coverage, while the Marines, in an important but lesser role, achieved exactly the opposite—lots of publicity. VII Corps was the proverbial tree falling in the empty forest. The difference can be attributed to the fact that the Marines have developed their combat training to include planning for the media. In a similar example of good public affairs forward planning, the British avoided the logistical problems of transporting media stories from the desert all the way back to Dhahran by establishing a satellite up-link station, run by BBC technicians, as an integral part of their armoured division headquarters. All the British had to do was get media stories back to division headquarters and from there they were sent directly to Britain by satellite.

Publicity can be important to unit morale. During the Second World War, Field Marshall Montgomery had a division pulled out of the line after a particularly hard week's fighting with heavy casualties, to rest for an upcoming, important battle. Noting that morale was low because their hard week's fighting had gone unreported in the media owing to his own army's censors, Montgomery called in a BBC reporter and the troops' daily newspaper. He gave them the story and ruled that it was to be passed by the censors, because he considered that in this case, division morale outweighed security considerations. While resting up for their next battle, the troops were able to see and hear glowing media reports about their recent action and morale picked up accordingly.[15]

There is also another old cliché, "A picture is worth a thousand words." With today's television and computer generation, if the public cannot see their military forces in action in a timely fashion, no amount of words will help. Modern technology can now supply live coverage of the battlefield and any other type of operation. This does not mean, however, that live television will always be there. Due to cost, logistical constraints, or the media's perception of a lack of "newsworthy" stories, the media may not come. Generally speaking, they will be there for combat deployments but not necessarily for all operations other than war. During the United Nations Protection Force (UNPROFOR) days in Bosnia and Croatia, Canadian media tended to show up to cover Canadian units when there was an incident or when NDHQ in Ottawa had organized a visit. But there were also long periods when no Canadian media were present.

Military forces have their own resources in the form of "combat camera" teams (both still and video) that can also be very useful in situations where no media are present. With satellite and digital camera technology, and a cash-strapped media willing to accept imagery from DND when they cannot get there themselves, any properly-resourced public affairs combat camera team can get the story visually to the media. This has been successfully done on a number of recent operations in 1998 and 1999, from HMCS *Toronto* deployed in the Gulf to troops deployed in Bosnia, Cambodia and East Timor. Another medium for communicating directly with Canadians is the internet. Where there is no Canadian media in an international theatre of operations, material (stories and photos) can be sent back to public affairs at NDHQ where it can be put on the DND website.

The military logistics required for media covering an air campaign are relatively modest and easy because air bases are static, access can be limited and controlled, media cannot fly in single-seat CF-18s aircraft, and the air bases tend to be near urban centres that provide commercial hotel accommodation and communications facilities. Naval logistics are similarly easy. The only limiting factor being bunk-space aboard and helicopter transport to and from the ship. But, unlike with the air force, where media can be put on and off the base at will, the media actually must live on the ship for a certain duration, increasing the chances during combat operations of inadvertently picking up operational information, and thus requiring a security review of their copy before it leaves via ship's communications.

The most complicated media logistics, however, are for army ground combat operations, where, as in the Gulf, the media must live with the troops under austere conditions. Furthermore, they must receive a limited amount of field training and indoctrination and must be equipped, housed, fed and transported by the military in order to keep up with the operation. In addition for the movement they also normally require the use of military facilities to file their stories. These operations therefore require the most extensive support.

Operations other than war do not normally require extensive logistics support to the media. In these situations, the media usually have their own transport, accommodation and communications. Also, most military movements are conducted in full view of the public and media. However, even in these situations, there will arise occasions when support to the media will be necessary and important. For example, in Bosnia in 1996, the IFOR commander's travel schedule within theatre was never announced publicly in advance for security reasons. When the commander was making a newsworthy visit to operational units, a media pool was organized. The pool was normally informed only a few hours prior to being required at the headquarters. At this time, they became an integral part of the commander's entourage for the duration of the trip, and only then were they informed of the destination.

In the spring of 1996, when the Serbs were vacating the designated suburbs of Sarajevo that were to be turned over to the Muslims under the terms of the Dayton Peace Agreement, they adopted a "scorched earth" policy of stripping or destroying their homes as they left. As the drama began to unfold, TV journalists had few images of IFOR troops in the suburbs and tended to do their "stand-ups" almost exclusively in front of burning houses, leaving the impression with the TV viewer that the entire suburbs were ablaze and in anarchy. Both the theatre and the ground force commanders became concerned that the nightly TV image of blazing suburbs might bring pressure on IFOR to take on a larger role in the suburbs than was necessary, which would take IFOR resources away from other critical tasks. The problem put to the public affairs staff was how to show the media and the public the real picture in the suburbs, which was bad, but manageable and not nearly as critical as the TV images might imply.

The media plan recommended taking news media up in helicopters to view the suburbs from the air where they could count the number of homes burning compared to the total number of dwellings. It also recommended taking media out on IFOR patrols into the streets to show that NATO forces were patrolling the areas. Finally, for those media who would not or could not go in the helicopters or on patrols, it was recommended that soldiers from the patrols come to the daily news briefing at the media centre in Sarajevo to explain firsthand their experiences in the suburbs. The plan also called for key interviews and background briefings for selected media by the theatre and corps commanders. They accepted the plan and ordered the necessary resources assigned to it, including helicopters.[16] The positive result for IFOR was a change in tone to the media stories and no change of mission for IFOR.

4. Monitor how your forces are communicating to the public and be prepared to make any adjustments to improve things, including becoming the briefer or spokesperson yourself.

At the outset of the Gulf War, the best media briefings were being given by the British, who, having learned from their experiences in the Falklands War, were using a public-speaking-trained, media-savvy senior military officer with an operational background who was well-plugged into the British operational planning. His backroom assistant was a Territorial Army lieutenant-colonel who in civilian life was a radio station manager. This accounts for the more lively tone of the British briefings.[17]

General Norman Schwarzkopf, the Coalition and also American Force Commander, quickly realized that US briefings were not getting the same attention as the British. He replaced the American briefers, who were low-ranking staff officers, with his director of operations, a two-star general, who took on the task as a full-time job. Knowledgeable in operational matters and with a strong on-air persona, he quickly became a media celebrity and established credibility and trust, thus achieving Schwarzkopf's aim of improving the US exposure.[18] General Schwarzkopf presented key briefs himself, making history with his now famous "Hail Mary" live-coverage media briefing at the end of the 100-hour ground war.

Putting commanders and operations officers up front as briefers is a long-established but often overlooked policy that lends itself to building credibility. The public and the media want to hear from "the guy in charge," or at the very least, from someone who is in a position to know.

5. Make sure the public affairs plan has a good internal information component so that the troops are well informed about the mission and how it is being communicated to the Canadian public.

The Chief of the Defence Staff, General Maurice Baril, has said that our soldiers are our best spokespersons.[19] Canadian Forces public affairs policy says that CF personnel can talk to the media without permission to discuss what they do. This means that on operational missions abroad it is incumbent upon commanders to make sure that the troops know as much about their mission as possible, as well as how the mission is being communicated back home to Canadians. Commanders must make sure that mechanisms are in place to do this.

We have seen that in the Second World War, the Canadian troops in Italy clamoured for a newspaper of their own, which they received, *The Maple Leaf*. Today, on multinational operations, there is more likely to be an in-theatre coalition forces newspaper such as SFOR has in Bosnia. Commanders will want to ensure that there are sufficient resources in place to provide a regular Canadian contribution to coalition internal information publications, and that the present-day version of *The Maple Leaf* receives regular information on international operations. There should also be good arrangements for the troops to know how their mission is being portrayed in the news both internationally and in Canada. This can take the form of newspapers, newspaper clippings, radio, videos, live satellite television, and news summaries produced in Canada or in-theatre.

Personal briefings from commanders remain a time-honoured way of passing information to the troops that has not been diminished by advances in technology. During the early days when Gulf War scud missile attacks were targeted against Coalition Forces, timely briefings by Commodore Summers over his Canadian joint headquarters public address system served the dual purpose of passing information and also reassuring people during a very stressful time.

CONCLUSION

Most public affairs problems in international theatres of operations in the past can usually be traced to public affairs not being part of the operational planning process, insufficient public affairs resources, including experienced public affairs staff, and lack of top-down communications and direction from the commander. This led to public affairs plans and actions not being appropriate for the situation. These are problems that the Canadian commanders in an international theatre of operations can usually avoid by following the five steps listed above, as well as making sure that public affairs is always an integral function of the commander's staff and fully integrated into the operational planning process. Canadians have a right to know as much as possible about what the CF is doing on their behalf on missions around the world. It is the duty of Canadian senior officers to make sure that this happens.

NOTES

1. Major Michael Galloucis, "The Military and the Media," *Army*, Vol 46, No.8, August 1996, 22.
2. Vice Admiral Joseph Metcalf III, US Navy (Ret'd), "The Mother of the Mother," US Naval Institute *Proceedings*, Vol. 117, No.8; and "Images of War," August 1991, 58.
3. Frank Aukofer and William P. Lawrence, *America's Team: The Odd Couple: A Report on the Relationship Between the Media and the Military*, (Nashville: Freedom Forum First Amendment Centre, 1995), 54.
4. Richard S. Malone, *A Portrait of War 1939-43* (Toronto: Collins, 1983), 209-213. As a lieutenant-colonel, Malone was in charge of Canadian Army field public relations in Italy and then North-West Europe, reaching the rank of brigadier by war's end. He then returned to a post-war career in journalism, culminating as publisher of the *Globe and Mail*.

5. The author recognizes that since the Korean War, CF members on peacekeeping or operations other than war have frequently found themselves in combat situations. Cyprus in 1974, and the Medak Pocket in Croatia in 1993 are but two examples. However, these occasions have been as so-called "neutral" UN peacekeepers. Since Korea, the Canadian Forces have been engaged in conflicts as formal belligerents on only two occasions: the Gulf War of 1991, and the NATO air campaign against Yugoslavia in 1999.
6. Galloucis, 21.
7. Aukofer and Lawrence, 9, 40, 43.
8. Recollections of the author, who was senior Canadian public affairs officer in-theatre at Canadian Joint Force Headquarters in Manama, Bahrain throughout the Gulf War.
9. Richard S. Malone, *A World in Flames 1944-45: A Portrait of War: Part II*, (Toronto: Collins, 1984), 21-22.
10. Recollections of the author from the Gulf War.
11. Metcalf, 56-57.
12. Recollections of the author who was the public affairs advisor to the DCDS for the air campaign against Yugoslavia.
13. Aukofer and Lawrence, 12.
14. Capt James B. Brown, "Media Access to the Battlefield," *Military Review*, Vol. 72, No.7, July 1992, 17-18.
15. Malone, 94-95.
16. Recollections of the author who helped work on the plan.
17. "How the War is Told," *Gulf Daily News*, Manama, Bahrain, February 15, 1991, 11.
18. Lieutenant-General (retired) W.A. Milroy and Lieutenant-Colonel (retired) J.D. Donoghue, "The Gulf War and the Media: a Canadian View," *Forum*, Vol.8, No.3, June 1993, 43.
19. General Baril's first news conference on becoming CDS, NDHQ, Ottawa, September, 1997.

The Media as a Tool of the Military Commander

Major-General (retired) Lewis W. MacKenzie

Major-General (retired) Lewis W. MacKenzie retired from the CF in 1993. He is currently a military analyst for the press, radio and television networks.

CNN'S CHRISTIANE AMANPOUR approached from the right. Her New Zealand camera woman, Mary, destined to be shot through the face some six months later, matched me step for step up the stairs leading to our makeshift headquarters in Sarajevo's PTT building. Christiane yelled out, " How did the negotiations go General MacKenzie—will there be a cease fire?"

The standard reply probably should have gone something like, "The UN has been negotiating with both the Bosnian government and the breakaway Bosnian Serbs led by Doctor Karadic for two days now. While the discussions have been honest, forthright and intense they have yet to produce any meaningful results." Instead I said, "Cease fire? I don't think the term exists in their vocabulary in this country!" The "proper" answer would not have made it out of the CNN editing suite set up in our underground parking lot. On the other hand the attractive sound bite was repeated ad nauseam on just about every news broadcast around the world over the next twenty-four hours and hopefully members of the Security Council understood the less than subtle message because they certainly were not responding to our normal means of communication with New York.

The title of this chapter, "The Media as a Tool," could very well be reworded to read, "The Media as a Weapon," depending on the circumstances and I suggest the circumstances will normally dictate the latter. I am certainly no expert in the subject and those that claim they are should be treated with a fair degree of skepticism. "The media" is such an all-encompassing term that no single person could hope, let alone aspire, to master the entire fifth estate. I did however, have the opportunity to learn some lessons the hard way during the early days of the Bosnian conflict. Martin Bell of the BBC shocked me during the summer of 1992 when he opined that I had been interviewed more than anyone else in history, over a one-month period, since the invention of television. I imagine O.J. Simpson's lawyers would ultimately have something to say about that, although I must admit that O.J. did not have the broad international representation or the cream of the crop that we had with us in Sarajevo. During the seven years following my retirement from the military in 1993, I have been under contract to both Canadian and American television networks and logged over a thousand television and radio interviews in addition to writing a multitude of articles for various newspapers including the *Washington Post*, the *Globe and Mail* and the *National Post*. If nothing else, you would probably concede that I have some experience dealing with the media, and with that as a somewhat questionable qualification I offer my own personal opinions on the subject at hand.

Off the top, it is important to stop using the term "media" when referring to anything less than the entire means of mass communications. The various sub-components of the profession covered by the term; print, television and radio, not forgetting photography, are as different as night and day and this includes their objectives, methods, style and degree of urgency. Consequently, your technique when dealing with each sub-component will be different.

The print folks see themselves as the purists of the news-gatherers. They were around a long time before the rest of their profession and they frequently benefit from the unrealistic deadlines or the demands of real time reporting endured by their colleagues, although they would never admit it. They frequently have time to research their pieces and their reporting usually includes context. If, for example, a television reporter was to include the amount of detail contained in an 800-word print column he or she would require at least thirty minutes on camera which would make the report more of a documentary than news. Print reporting does not have the same emotional impact on the public as TV and radio; however, it is extremely powerful as a tool to influence decision-makers. Staffers and assistants gather together the various print columns on a regular basis for their political bosses to review. On more than one enjoyable occasion, I have heard my printed words spoken by just the politician or leader I was trying to influence when I sat down to write a particular article. Coincidence, perhaps, but I doubt it was so in every case.

In order for the print journalists to do their job properly you will find their interviews with you last a good deal longer than those of their colleagues in TV and radio. As a result, you will have the opportunity to get to know them and more importantly, where they are coming from. Each and every journalist will swear that his or her attitude towards the interviewee has no bearing on the resulting article. Do not believe it, particularly in an operational theater. One Pulitzer Prize winner wore a pair of my pants around Sarajevo for over two months after his own self-destructed during an interview with me. I noticed a definite improvement in his attitude towards our mission in general, and me in particular, following the incident.

You do not have to wait to be approached for an interview to get your case across to the public. You will quickly discover which authors have the greatest influence with particular segments of the overall readership. Some are required reading for politicians while others will be slavishly read by the public at large. It was always a source of frustration for me when a public affairs assistant would try and brief me prior to an interview in Canada. The first point to be stressed was normally the alleged bias of the interviewer, frequently described as, "Friendly Forces" or "Enemy." What I really wanted to know was who read his or her column. Once *you* determine the most influential journalists in relation to your cause and message you can approach them directly or indirectly and make yourself available. Once you establish good relations with a number of print journalists you will find they frequently turn to you for both accredited and non-accredited comment. More importantly, you can turn to them to help publicize a particular issue. Believe me, many journalists go to bed every night wondering what they will write about tomorrow. As a rule, they appreciate being handed the basis for a good story.

Two aspects of print journalism will frustrate any commander's attempt to use the medium. Some newspapers are absolutely predictable in their political bias. If their preferred political ideology is running the government of the day you can rest assured that they will side with the government on all issues of substance.

That is not to suggest that you should avoid granting interviews to reporters from those papers. On the contrary, reporters are by nature a rebellious lot and frequently do not appreciate being coerced to toe a particular political line. As a result they are usually receptive to a reasonable and persuasive argument and their support should be cultivated. While the editorial page might hammer their reporter's position and by association your position on the same day the article featuring yourself appears, you will get your case in front of the public in an otherwise hostile publication, which is no mean achievement.

The second irritating aspect of dealing with print journalists is the phenomenal amount of time you frequently spend with a reporter for one measly quote. Do not be put off by this fact as there is a good chance that your input had an impact on the author throughout the preparation of the article. If reporting or writing opinions merely involved repeating quotes from interviewees a computer would be much more efficient. The author has to insert his or her own bias into the piece and you have a chance to impact on that bias during the interview. In other words, don't evaluate the success of the interview by how many times you were credited with a comment but rather by the content of the entire article.

Commanders do not have to wait to be interviewed. Presumably, generals and admirals can all write. Just about every major newspaper in the world has a comment page or equivalent for op ed commentary. There is always an editor for the page(s) and each and every one of them is receptive to articles of interest. In most cases they prefer opinion as opposed to researched articles so that makes it even easier and less time consuming for the author. There is a valuable hidden benefit to written comment. You will often be asked to elaborate on TV and radio following the publication of a written piece, which gives your opinions even greater exposure. Canadian commanders at home and abroad rarely take advantage of the opportunity to comment in writing, which represents missed opportunities.

Taking advantage of the long-term impact offered by the printed word is important. Two or three years after an event and your ensuing comments, you will rarely have anyone wave a cassette with a copy of your TV or radio interview in your face or refer to your opinions in an academic piece. On the other hand the written word is part of the easily accessible record and has a very long half-life indeed (not *always* an advantage!).

Radio has a massive audience world-wide and is wrongly assigned second place behind TV by those not familiar with its appeal. This was driven home to me when I was first approached by the US National Public Radio (NPR) for an interview in Sarajevo. At the time I had the three major American networks waiting for interviews and I was not inclined to insert a radio network into an already busy schedule. A casual happenstance conversation with an American officer enlightened me to the fact that the listening audience for NPR would be more than the three major TV networks combined. As I was in the process of discouraging misleading statements of US support to the Bosnian government, due to the negative impact such statements were having on our negotiations, I hastily inserted NPR into the schedule.

Because radio's recording and reporting equipment is relatively compact and inexpensive, the medium's reporters can and do pop up throughout an operational theater. Frequently they are on their own and have little if any support. If you take them in it is no guarantee of a positive story; however, providing their nationality or networks bias will not compromise your position such an act will certainly do your mission no harm. In addition you can get a message to a particular audience on what is, for all intents and purposes, a real time basis. Most radio reporters can and will send their reports by telephone. Satellite hook-ups permit them to broadcast live at the fraction of the cost of TV. In most cases they will be indirectly enlightening the staff at NDHQ before you have a chance to do so. You might as well make sure they get the story right.

In Canada, CBC's "As It Happens" and "Cross Canada Check Up" are valuable tools for getting out the word. They have very large national audiences and beam into the US on NPR and worldwide on short wave. In the absence of polling data they can provide a partial insight into the public's attitude on a particular issue—remembering of course that the program's call-screeners might be responding to their own biases or looking to stir up controversy where none exists. For credible worldwide coverage no one matches the BBC. You might get frustrated by all the departments that never seem to share anything: BBC 1, BBC 2, BBC International, BBC Wales, BBC Scotland, BBC Northern Ireland etc. However, the time invested is well worth the coverage providing you have a message that needs to get out.

In a nutshell, don't sell radio short. It has wide appeal and while it has less time than print to deal with a subject it has much more than TV.

Attempting to harness the power of television might be fraught with pitfalls but the risk is worth it. The overworked saying, "A picture is worth a thousand words," grossly underestimates the modern day power of a compelling image. Canada took the lead in mounting an ill-defined and predictably impossible mission in the Great Lakes Region of Africa strictly because the Prime Minister, by his own admission, was stirred to action by TV images on a quiet Sunday afternoon. Not exactly the best way to develop foreign policy, but it is reality nevertheless, and merely a reflection of the immense power of the medium to do both good and bad.

Before TV satellite digital communications and 24-hour news networks, TV reporters were like print reporters in a hurry. They had time to establish some context and when their piece arrived back at head office it was massaged and augmented by research and production staff that were not caught up in the emotion of the moment out in the field. What made the late news was, more often than not, balanced and informative. Martin Bell of the BBC covered eleven wars before succumbing to the lure of the British Parliament as an independent sitting member in 1997. In 1992, he explained to me that he reported on his first ten wars using the technique mentioned above. He went on to say, "Compare that, Lew, with what I'm doing here in Sarajevo—the "beast" has to be fed and I'm flinging off reports which are focusing on one-thousandth of one percent of what is happening in the rest of Bosnia and it's having an impact on what is being decided in the halls of power around the world." The potential for abuse by belligerents is huge and is not lost on the US-based public relations firms that are hired by any self-respecting rebel/terrorist faction before it crosses the line of departure.

Before tabloid journalism, news was news. In order to compete in today's market, news has to be entertaining. That means extreme views and avoiding the grey area where most stories reside. That means when you are interviewed you will probably be counter-balanced by an outspoken critic of the military or our country's foreign policy. Regrettably, your "opponent" will frequently be a retired senior officer whose only qualification is a reputation for criticizing the profession that fed him and his family for thirty plus years. Nevertheless, his or her presence is popular with the TV producers as it makes the sparks fly and wakes up the audience. It's not necessarily news or informative but it's entertaining. Avoiding such programs merely hands the stage to the anti-military pundits, which is a mistake. If they cannot be put in their place by the facts presumably there really is a problem that needs fixing.

There is very little time available on TV to present your case. Long-winded explanations will not see the light of day. I am frequently invited to TV studios to do an "in-depth interview on subject X." When I ask, "How long do we have?" the answer is usually, "Oh, about two to three minutes!" Consequently, TV loves the interviewee who can organize his or her response into short, sharp segments. If you get burned by a particular reporter or network you might have to limit yourself to live interviews only. Once they go "live to tape," your words can and will be edited at the discretion of the producer. The reality of TV permits a reporter to spend an hour or more with a subject for a mere ten-second sound bite. During the production of a major documentary on the United Nations I interviewed over a score of significant personalities from President Mitterrand to our Prime Minister. Each interview lasted well over an hour. It amazed me that after the first two or three interviews I could detect during the answers to my questions which ten- to fifteen-second sound bite the editor would ultimately use for our final production. It was always a statement reinforcing my own thesis or an outspoken contrary opinion. With that in mind you can't afford to score ninety-nine percent on an interview as the one percent you cock up will make the air. I will deal later with how to avoid that one percent.

Now that I have defined what I mean by the media, a few words on how to deal with the profession's employees. Contrary to some opinions, I have found reporters and journalists to be honest, trustworthy and likeable. Sure there are some exceptions but they are rare and other reporters will tell you who to distrust as they give their profession a bad name. The one reporter from a major international news agency who screwed up and defied the unwritten rules governing the media in Sarajevo was run out of town by the other media folks before I had a chance to evict him myself.

In an operational theater I tried to tell the media as much as possible for two reasons. First, it reinforced the perception of impartiality which was my mandate in both Central America and the former Yugoslavia. Second, it helped educate the reporters to the nuances and particularly the limitations of the UN mandates that governed our actions. I did not mind them criticizing the Security Council but I certainly did not want them criticizing my troops. Early on in the Sarajevo mission I called the media together including all of their support folks responsible for sound, camera work, production, editing etc and told them, "I'm going to tell you everything I can and that will be ninety-nine percent of what I know. I will tell you what you can attribute to me, what you can attribute to a senior UN official, and I'm the only one here, and what is off the record." In months of reporting I was not let down once. The media was part of the team helping to keep a miserable situation from getting worse and they knew it. The fact that they understood our limitations made them somewhat sympathetic with our dilemma and as a result they treated us fairly. The force grew much larger following my departure and the subsequent commanders, partly through necessity, stopped dealing directly with the media, opting instead to deal through official spokespersons. Almost immediately, the synergistic relationship between the media and the force deteriorated.

I firmly believe that the commander should treat the media's representatives as another element of "Friendly Forces." They will not always respond as expected or desired but the time invested in keeping them abreast of the current situation and long-term objectives is well worth the effort. Do not let your staff give them long military-style briefings. Use spokespersons as little as possible. Dedicate the majority of your time with reporters to responding to their questions and when you are not available designate a subordinate commander to fill in for you rather than a spokesman or a staff officer.

Whenever possible have your soldiers or junior ranks do the talking to the media once the more formal bits are over in your headquarters. The young privates, corporals and lieutenants tend to be a bit nervous on camera, which surprisingly, adds to their credibility with the viewing or listening audience. No one seems to trust a member of the establishment that has slick well-thought-out responses to each and every question. During these days of intense media monitoring by the

Department's senior leadership there is risk (for you!) involved with this approach; however, I remain convinced that it is worth it. Soldiers give the type of sound bites the media loves and they are the best advertisement for our profession and the country. I recall one heart-warming quote when a US reporter asked a Canadian corporal, "What were you thinking when you came under fire as you entered Sarajevo—you came to help these people and now they were trying to kill you?" His response, "No problem, that's what I'm paid for." Succinct!

These days with young ambitious freelancing journalists from all the media's components free to wander about the theater in search of that Pulitzer Prize winning photo or report, it has elevated the physical risk for the Establishment's media contingent. Whereas it frequently makes sense to send small teams of reporters out into the fray on a rotational basis with sharing of the stories at the end of the day (as suggested by the BBC and CNN in Sarajevo) this immensely sensible technique is usually rendered impractical by the freelancers. Once an Establishment reporter is scooped by a freelancer you can rest assured that the reporter's home office in London, Atlanta or elsewhere will be directing their personnel in your operational area to get back up to the sharp end. This modern day characteristic makes the media's job a very dangerous one. While deflection of resources to protect the media is a no-no for all the obvious reasons, you can and should ensure that the reporters always have the most up-to-date information that could enhance their security. As an example, before I would make a run to the Sarajevo airport I would advise any reporters tailing us which direction the sniper fire had come from over the previous few hours and tell them they were welcome to tuck up along the opposite side of my armoured car which would provide them with some protection. As they were in soft-skinned rental wrecks in those days it enhanced our relationship and saved at least two lives during the summer of 1992.

It is probably appropriate to say a few words about "off the record comments." I accept that my opinion is at variance with the popular wisdom regarding the subject; however, one is a prisoner of one's own experience. I have only been burnt a couple of times by a reporter publishing what I considered to be off the record or non-attributable comments. In every case I should have known better as we in the military are supposed to be pretty good judges of character and I placed trust in someone before I had made up my mind as to their trustworthiness. As far as the media is concerned all comments are on the record; however, once you get to know and trust a reporter, you can be pretty confident that he or she will respect your request for anonymity. If they let you down, cut them off.

If there is one key recommendation contained in this chapter that should assist the reader in making use of the media as a complement to the other operational tools it is—REMEMBER WHO YOUR AUDIENCE IS! In my opinion this rule, which should be chipped in stone above every commander's door, is all too often forgotten by senior officers, and the reputation of the Canadian Forces and the troops' morale suffer as a result. There was no better example of the abuse of this rule than the infamous performances of a number of senior officers at the Somalia Inquiry. In the case of the CDS of the day, when asked for his definition of leadership he gave the appearance of trying to respond to the three Commission members. At that unique moment in his career he forgot who his audience was. It was not the questioner but rather the men and women of the Canadian Forces, their families, their friends and veterans from service past who take pride from seeing the leader of their chosen profession come across as a strong, compassionate and confident leader. Here was an opportunity served up on a silver platter to tell the viewing audience and the assembled media what leadership was all about and to send a clear message to his command and at that precise moment he broke the (my) golden rule. Mind you he was not alone. A number of other officers followed his lead and spoke as if there was no viewing audience gathered together in every mess from coast to coast—waiting to be inspired by their leaders. Those that stood up for their subordinates, like the Acting CDS who took over from the individual referred to above, went some way to restoring confidence in the Force's leadership.

The rule does not only apply when you are hauled in front of a Commission of Inquiry! It applies each and every time you are interviewed. Even in the case of high profile interviewers like Tom Brokow, Larry King or a Dan Rather et al you are not speaking to them but rather their audience which includes your own target audience. In my case, during intense media scrutiny in Sarajevo, some of my responses were designed to reduce the level of concern on the part of families back home for the safety of their loved ones within my command, and that included some thirty countries other than Canada. On other occasions I would send a clear message to the UN in general and the Security Council in particular on a particular issue—usually an issue which they had failed to acknowledge through the official means of communication.

I strongly recommend that before any interview you close your eyes for a second and ask yourself, "Who is my audience?" Once you have the answer, do not forget what it was during the interview.

Related to the above golden rule is the necessity to talk to the media and your audience in civilian terms and forget the impressive vocabulary. Civilians do not even understand the most basic military terms including those that apply to ranks. The vast majority of folks still call me major because they think a major outranks a general, (I know a lot of majors who probably agree), so I've given up trying to explain. During the Kosovo campaign I wrote over fifty articles on all aspects of the conflict. One article received more favourable comment *than all the other articles put together*. It merely described how and why an army was organized in threes—three sections to a platoon, three platoons to a company etc, for the sake of maneuver. The article also described the ranks for each level of command. It was a sort of OCS Army Organization 101. "Thanks a lot, I never really understood how an army worked," was a typical comment. Assume that your audience knows next to nothing about the military. If your audience also includes soldiers they will understand why you have drifted into "civilianese."

"It's not the problem that gets you in trouble, it's how you handle it," may be an overworked cliché but it has been proven all too valid over the past decade. Having been accused of being on the Serb's payroll and raping and murdering a number of Bosnian teenagers, I guess you could say I have had some experience in dealing with potential disasters. The only way to avoid accusations of cover-up or guilt before all the facts are known is to tell everything you know and do not obscure the truth by omission or spin. You rarely need a lot of input from others to help you determine what is the right thing to do. While your staff is debating how the problem should be handled you would be better off using the time to address the issue head-on.

In conclusion, it is impossible to preclude missteps along the way in your dealings with the media—even if you are not the one stepping out of line. I recall a previous MND (closet separatist at the time) who tore a strip off me for recommending non-US intervention in the early days of the Bosnian war when I appeared as a witness in front of the US Senate. I responded, "Well Minister that happens to be your government's policy!" His retort, "I know that, but we might change our mind and then the Opposition will use you as an authority!" On another occasion the CDS was upset with me for something a national network reported that I had said in Saskatoon the night before his call. When I explained that I had never been in Saskatoon and had not made any statements the previous night the response was, "That doesn't matter, the CBC said you were there and that you made the quote." If you use the media it will occasionally bite you, but the benefits to your soldiers are worth it.

In my estimation the greatest satisfaction any military leader can earn (other than taking his command's objective without suffering any casualties) is the appreciation of his or her subordinates for supporting them, particularly when the going gets rough and it seems everyone is against them. There are many ways to send these messages of support and confidence to the soldiers and their families. Properly utilized, the media can be an invaluable tool in this regard. We can and should use all the Friendly Forces we can muster.

A Man (or Woman) for All Seasons: What the Canadian Public Expects from Canadian General Officers

David J. Bercuson

Dr. David J. Bercuson is a Professor of History and Director, of the Centre for Military and Strategic Studies at the University of Calgary.

CARL VON CLAUSEWITZ was a man of the early nineteenth century who spent his life as a professional soldier in the service of despots. This makes even more remarkable his observations in *On War* that war is a "paradoxical trinity" of the blind force of primordial violence provided by the people, the channelling of that violence into usable power by the army, and the application of that power for political ends by government. "A theory [of war] that ignores any of them," he wrote "or seeks to fix an arbitrary relationship between them would conflict with reality to such an extent that for this reason alone it would be totally useless."[1] Thus a military that is not "in synch" with the society that generates it cannot be effective.

It follows, then, that for a military to effectively serve a society which is dynamic and democratic, it must mirror the talent, creativity, ambition, drive, educational achievement, scientific and technological competence, even the humanitarianism of that society. If a military is properly organized, administered, and led, then the goal of keeping the armed forces and society united is achievable. From the recruitment process to the system of promotion to the highest ranks of general officers, selecting and educating leaders is the key to that objective because the higher a man or woman is in rank, the greater is his or her potential impact on the process of ensuring that the military evolves in parallel with society. War is ultimately the pursuit of policy by other means and, at the highest levels, commanders ultimately act in a grey area between politics and war. As the men and women who epitomize the military profession in a given country, it is their responsibility to create a national armed forces that will work in harmony with society to achieve its goals and reflect its strengths.

The most successful military leaders in history have understood the importance of building armies that mirror their societies. George C. Marshall, for example, the architect of the US Army that fought the Second World War, was a man in touch with the pulse of American society. Marshall spent so much time with civilians between 1927 and 1937 that, in the words of his official biographer, "he became familiar with the civilian point of view in a way rare for professional military men [and] regarded civilians and military as part of a whole."[2] One major result was that unlike some other major American military leaders of his day—George S. Patton comes immediately to mind—Marshall was a full participant in American society and his military philosophy reflected the unique characteristics of that society.

As a nation, the United States was a great and successful experiment in self-government; the United States Army in the Second World War reflected both the experimentalism and the success of American society because of Marshall and his protégés. They designed an army which replicated unique qualities of American society—mobility, mechanical know-how, democracy, and lack of rigid class division.[3] One historian of the US Army in the Second World War, Michael D. Doubler, specifically analyses what was, without doubt, *the* most important of those characteristics, the ability of Marshall's army to adapt. "If armies are a reflection of society," Doubler wrote, "the approach a military organization uses to effect change in wartime should reflect the major characteristics, attitudes and values of society at large." As a main theme of his book, he demonstrated how that took place. Put simply, the US Army showed itself to be extraordinarily good at changing tactical doctrine and either adapting or altering basic pattern equipment to meet the exigencies of field conditions.

Marshall prepared the US Army for a war of manoeuvre, for example, but when combat was eventually joined, the American forces often found themselves deficient in fire power. They found that movement alone was not enough to win against the Wehrmacht in many of the field conditions encountered in Northwest Europe. When the battle of the hedgerow country in Normandy "starkly exposed failures in training and leadership," in Geoffrey Perrett's words[4] the most important of American characteristics emerged—inventiveness. The ability to innovate quickly, from bottom to top and vice versa, was epitomized by Sergeant Curtis G. Culin Jr., of the 102nd Cavalry Squadron. It was he who field-modified the Sherman tank to re-establish movement in the hedgerow country. Seeing how tanks exposed their thin undersides to anti-tank fire when they rode up and over hedgerows, he thought of welding four large metal bars, or "tusks," to the front of a Sherman tank to enable the tank to plow through the hedgerows instead of riding over them. Within days Culin's idea took hold across the entire US front as dozens of tank repair units worked to adapt hundreds of tanks for hedgerow fighting.[5] The US Army succeeded in the Second World War because its general officers organized it to allow the talent, intelligence, and self-reliance of US society to emerge within all of its ranks. The US Army was in tune with the American people.

Despite some popular belief in the myth, nurtured by some very questionable scholarship,[6] that Canadians are not, in general, dynamic when compared to Americans, the earmarks of Canadian society show all the characteristics of a unique Canadian inventiveness. Without attempting to re-tell the entire history of Canada, it is axiomatic that "making do" began when the first settlers arrived from New France in the seventeenth century and found a climate very different from the one they had left, even though the latitudes of Québec and Normandy are about the same. "Making do" is still a major part of Canadian life.[7] Was it the case, then, that Canadian armies demonstrated that same adaptability when they went to war? Did Canadian general officers build military forces that allowed one of the unique strengths of Canadian society—the ability to "make do"—to emerge under the realities of the field? The answer is complex.

In the First World War, the Canadian Corps, led by Julian Byng and Arthur Currie, is acknowledged to have become one of the most innovative formations on the Western Front by mid-1917.[8] Very little historical research has been done on the question of how adaptable the Canadian Army of the Second World War was when faced with the inevitable gap between preparation for war and war itself, but one recent doctoral dissertation concludes that the Canadian Army was not as adaptable as it needed to be, at least in the Battle of

Normandy. Russell A. Hart concluded that the Canadian Army was so weak at the outbreak of war, and so unready, that it was forced "into an unhealthy dependence" on the British Army and became "an inferior clone of its British counterpart."[9] To some extent Hart's conclusions regarding the Canadian Army in Normandy add evidence for what military historian and former Lieutenant-Colonel John English has called a "failure in high command."[10] And yet in the first weeks of the Sicily campaign 1st Canadian Infantry Division showed a high degree of adaptability when forced to fight without much of its motor transport, field artillery, and command and control apparatus.[11]

Though there is no study that compares the composition, leadership, or adaptability of the Canadian Corps in the First World War to the Canadian Army of the Second World War, it is highly possible that the virtual non-existence of a professional Canadian Army in August 1914, allowed the Canadian Corps to evolve doctrine that reflected the inventiveness and the innovation of the country it grew out of. It is equally likely that in the inter-war period the straitjacket of British doctrine, inculcated into the minds of men such as Harry Crerar, Guy Simonds, and Charles Foulkes, made it difficult for that same inventiveness and innovation to emerge when war began.[12] Not until the fall of 1944, when the battalion commanders who had led the Canadian Army in Normandy were largely gone, their places taken by men who had been company or even platoon commanders on D-Day, that the Canadian Army really began to develop effective fighting power at the tactical level. The Canadian Army also developed an acceptable degree of competence at the highest formation level, demonstrated when it launched Operation Veritable in early February, 1945. In that battle—the opening phase of the Battle of the Rhineland—a Canadian Army headquarters barely able to function in early August 1944, showed sufficient staff proficiency to handle a major attack of some thirteen divisions, most of them British.

Military forces have only two reasons for existence: fighting wars and preparing to fight wars. A modern, post Cold War corollary to this rule might well be; to fight wars and enforce peace in near-war conditions, and to prepare for either. It is the primary task of the general officers to prepare militaries for war, or near-war, to build into those militaries the innovation such situations will demand, and to lead them. There are many ways to achieve those aims, but nothing will be successful that does not go *with* the grain of society. That is why the expectation Canadians must have of their general officers is that the Canadian Forces be trained, equipped, and prepared in ways consistent with the aims and characteristics of Canadian society, for whatever missions the government assigns.

This does not mean that Canadian Forces leaders should ignore the modern requirement of inter-operability. To the contrary. The Canadian experience of war (and near-war) has always been within a coalition context. Inter-operability is really the military equivalent of the institutional liberal internationalism that Canadian political leaders have sought for the past half-century via organizations such as the International Monetary Fund (IMF), World Bank, World Trade Organization, and others. Inter-operability, in other words, is as solidly within the Canadian tradition as was the adoption by Canada of the US standard rail gauge in the mid-nineteenth century.

As the new century dawns, Canadians are more secure in their identity as a people, and the world is more complex, than at anytime since the outbreak of the First World War. Thus the demand on the general officer corps to lead a military that is both effective and Canadian has never been greater. As recently as the 1950s, Canada was dominated by the two founding linguistic groups and was a Parliamentary constitutional monarchy which valued the "peace, order, and good government" of the community more than the rights of individual citizens. The past three decades have witnessed major change in the rules which govern this nation, in the composition of Canada's population, and in the way Canadians see themselves. What has emerged is a nation, which is quasi-republican in its constitution, raucous in the nature of its politics, and zealous in the protection of individual rights. The Canadian military is trying to change in response to these trends, but it has had many failures in the past decade. One major job at hand for Canadian Forces general officers is, therefore, to wrestle with the traditional conservatism that has characterized most militaries, most of the time, to ensure that there is not too great a lag between change in the nation and change in the armed forces. At the same time, of course, Canadian Forces general officers must struggle against the desire of some political leaders to use the armed forces as a captive instrument of social or political change at the expense of military effectiveness.

This task must be attempted alongside that of developing an advanced body of Canadian military thought to guide the Canadian Forces in these times of immense global change. With the destruction of the Berlin Wall, the old "balance of power" world created by the Great War of 1914-1918, the twenty-year cease-fire that followed, the 1939-45 war fought to finalize the outcome of the Great War, and the Cold War, rapidly disappeared. The emergence of American hegemony has drastically altered the political, economic, and social environments within which Canadian forces will be deployed. From 1914 to 1989, the Canadian government basically decided when its military would engage in war, or in war-like circumstances, largely in lock step with Great Britain or the United States. There was little need for original doctrinal thinking in the Canadian military because in the only truly important activity Canada's military engaged in—the defence of Western Europe—Canada's soldiers were expected to act in sync with Canada's allies or coalition partners.

Alliance or coalition military ties are still of immense importance to Canada, but events in Somalia, former Yugoslavia, Haiti, Rwanda, and Kosovo show that Canada's military must exercise a greater degree of independent judgement than at any time in Canadian history. A Canadian infantry brigade commander in the Battle of Normandy, for example—the lowest rank of general officer at that time—had to deal with a tenacious and skilful enemy. But he was essentially a coordinator ensuring that his battalions acted in concert on the battlefield and that the supporting arms, logistics, air support, etc., they would need to fight the battle were available and prepared.[13] The army determined that brigade commanders needed military staff school skills, but given the haste with which the Canadian Army grew in the Second World War, there was neither the time nor the opportunity to seek general officers who had demonstrated imagination and initiative either in a more formalized educational setting, or in the heat of combat itself. Some of those Canadian brigade commanders were as good as, or better than, any among the Allied forces. Others fell short. But the overall goals a brigadier needed to achieve—basically to advance the brigade to the objective assigned by the division commander—were elementary, though in war, as Clausewitz pointed out, the simplest things are hard to do.[14]

Although general officers in the Canadian Forces today see little opportunity to command in the field, and are not likely to in the near future, they must prepare the military for tasks that are much more complex, and which require quicker and more imaginative judgement, than at any time since the end of the Korean War. They must also do so in a national environment when more Canadians than ever are highly educated, aware of the world around them, and conscious of the "rights-driven" society they live in. Today's general officers must also prepare the Canadian Forces for a world of invasive news media coverage, in which "OOTW" (operations other than war) have become closer to real war than classic "Chapter VI" peacekeeping ever was, and in which one error at a roadblock in the Balkans can become a *causus belli*—and world headline—when CNN broadcasts its half-hourly summary of what is happening around the globe.[15] No case is being made here that anything a general officer does today is harder than ordering soldiers to die in combat. But ordering a soldier to do anything today is more complex than it ever was in peacetime, and may well prove more difficult in war, both in the giving of the order and in the manner of its execution.

What are some of the more significant characteristics of Canadian society today? The Canadian Charter of Rights and Freedoms has provided the basis for a strong belief that all Canadians have basic human rights that must be protected from possible abuse by government. Thus the courts play a greater role in the lives of Canadians than ever and governments must be mindful of the rights of citizens, landed immigrants, even potential refugees when acting. Soldiers have no fewer rights than other Canadians even though judges have upheld the special need for a system of military law to supplement civil and criminal law in regulating the actions of military personnel.[16]

Canada now draws its people from all over the world and the influx of immigrants to some of the larger cities has created a visible and dramatic change in the nature of the population. The full-time military is lagging badly in attracting visible minorities into the ranks of the armed forces, and both the militia and the cadets are more reflective of Canadian society today. Whether or not the Canadian Forces will ever come close to mirroring the multicultural nature of Canadian society, Canada's military leaders must always remember that the Canadian public pays the bills for the military and expects the military to be responsible to all the public including Canadians of ethnic extractions whose friends or family may be in conflict with Canadian troops in places such as the Balkans.

Canada is, today, a highly educated society. Almost five out of ten Canadians now go on to post-secondary educational institutions. In some areas, more than a third of the population possess university degrees. Graduate degrees are becoming commonplace in some occupations. This had led to a higher degree of technical competence, but also to greater knowledge of the world at large, the place of the citizen in the state, and the importance of maintaining international political and economic ties. It is inconceivable that Canada's general officers should not be the equal of other Canadians of advanced station in their education or in their ability to solve problems.

The Canadian Forces (CF) today must not only be able to fight and win in war, it must prepare itself for war by strengthening its links to the community, being sensitive to the rights of its members, displaying great media savvy, and reflecting the values and characteristics of Canadian society and the history and development of the nation. The Canadian public will not tolerate a CF leadership class that does not meet these high standards. Canada's general officers for the new century must be warriors, leaders, intellectuals, and organizers, who are aware of, and sensitive to, the CF's role in society and its links to it and the nature and history of the nation they serve—men and women for all seasons. But how to ensure that these high standards are met? Only through an interlinked system of selection, education, and training that will allow general officers to emerge who can fill these stringent requirements.

The process must begin with basic officer education. The government has already taken the first step by requiring that, with a small number of exceptions, a university degree be a prerequisite for a commission in the Canadian Forces.[17] But what sort of university education should be required? Aimed at what purpose? To train military professionals the way professional schools train physicians or engineers? Or to teach and nurture creative thinking and problem solving as a basis upon which to build the tenets of a military education? Surely it must be the latter and surely it must begin with a solid foundation in the liberal arts.

In the social sciences and the humanities—the core disciplines of the liberal arts—there are few clear answers. Learning comes not by amassing information but through the process of thinking and evaluating. That process helps to separate those men and women who can find the solutions to problems from those who can merely describe the components of problems. It helps to identify those minds that can adapt quickly to new knowledge, or respond quickly to new ideas, or facts, and which then create new conclusions. Debate, the challenge of ideas by other ideas, looking at old problems in new ways, sharpens minds and teaches lessons. The liberal arts teach process. They do not teach "stuff"; they teach "thinking about stuff."

The heart of a military liberal arts education must be military history. There can be no other. As the renowned American journalist Robert D. Kaplan observed in a recent article in *Atlantic Monthly:*

> Military campaigns, because they are fights for the sheer survival of nations and cultures, offer the most telling insights about the values, technologies, social relations, and intellectual life of historical periods. And because both death and defeat are undeniable, a military historian is forced to pierce the accumulated fog of philosophical abstractions and political agendas that frustrate other historical disciplines. Though rarely regarded as such, military history is as august a field as any in the liberal arts.[18]

How much more applicable are those observations to the military professional? And yet, although military history is taught to Canadian Forces personnel in a variety of ways, it is far behind technical studies and even managerial studies as a discipline favoured either by CF students or by the CF educational establishment. A Canadian general officer must have an education rich in Canadian, and Canadian *military*, history.

Other "liberal arts" disciplines are also vital to a modern general officer. Chief among them is the study of philosophy. Philosophy not only promotes precision in thought and language, it also teaches how human beings have tried for millennia to analyze the basic human condition. Philosophy is essential to the study of ethics, and a solid background in ethics is necessary for today's general officers because today's societies are founded on liberal principles such as individual rights, the rule of law, and the importance of safeguarding civil society. The public, which the military in a democracy serves, no longer countenances the wasting of human life, though the public has demonstrated as recently as the spring 1999 bombing of Serbia, that they are prepared to accept the destruction of some human life to achieve goals they believe central to their values. In other words, the public is prepared to accept ethically-sanctioned killing. This puts considerable onus on the military professional to understand just what ethically-sanctioned killing is, especially within the context of wars, or peace enforcement actions, that have limited political objectives. This is why the study of ethics is vital. It tempers the training of a profession that is, at bottom, dedicated to the taking of life.

Today's military leaders must have a comprehensive understanding about the human condition and the underlying sanctity of life and the lives they may be called upon to destroy. There is a parallel here to the practise in the Jewish religion of ritual slaughter to obtain kosher meat. The man whom the community designates as the ritual slaughterer is not simply trained in the technical points of how to kill quickly and painlessly. He must also know the basic texts of oral and written Jewish law and discourse. His education in the basic sources of Judaism is second only to that of the Rabbi. He must know and truly understand the ethical relationships that are at the heart of Judaism. He learns why he must sanctify his life with holiness in order to become a humane killer.

Democratic societies are increasingly insisting that their war fighters have a broad understanding of the human condition as preparation for undertaking the solemn responsibility of dealing death and destruction. As former Canadian Forces Chaplain Captain Eric T. Reynolds observed in an award-winning essay:

> Our military institutions must foster personal reflection, detachment and thought....The greatest challenge for military institutions is that they, like their personnel, must learn to question themselves, share their solutions with others, discuss life-sustaining and life-enhancing values, seek consensus in basic questions, and practise open dialogue.[19]

Political science is another discipline vital to the general officer. Clausewitz observed that "war is not merely an act of policy but a true political instrument, a continuation of political intercourse, carried on with other means." It is, therefore, incumbent on a modern officer corps to understand politics in all its institutional forms. And what else is required for today's officer corps? Many of the same elements that have traditionally formed core curricula in the western world's great institutions of advanced education: literature, the Great Books, or classics, of western civilization, basic experimental sciences such as physics or chemistry (to teach scientific method), even comparative religion. Only after that base has formed should military professionals begin to tackle whatever areas of technical expertise they are interested in—from psychology to geomatics engineering. From the establishment of the earliest universities in Western Europe at the time of the first millennium to now, a true advanced education always combined theoretical and practical learning—learning "stuff" and "learning about stuff"—in a symbiosis of examining both the "real world" and the human condition upon which it exists.

As Lieutenant-Colonel Jack English so recently argued, war is not a technological phenomenon but a social one; technology and technological innovation is not a precondition for war. Technological change will most assuredly enhance, sharpen, concentrate, make easier, or make bloodier, the enterprise of war, but it will not change the essence of it. War is decided upon, planned, fought, by human beings whose actions are not quantifiable and never fully explainable. War is not science, it is a terrible form of art. *Strategy* insisted English, is the art of war, *tactics* the art of battle, and *operations* the art of campaigning."[20] Thus, the preparation for it is best done by a basic education in the arts, not by an undergraduate education based on, or which emphasizes, science or engineering.

In a recent article in *Military Review,* Lieutenant-General Montgomery C. Meigs, PhD, Commandant of the US Army Command and General Staff College at Fort Leavenworth, and Colonel Edward J. Figzgerald, MS, Director, Centre for Army Lessons Learned, also at Fort Leavenworth, presented their vision of the next generation US Army. They foresee the evolution of a synthesis of instantly accessible advanced education knowledge from both civilian and military universities, and actual warfighting. They call the embodiment of this coming process University After Next (UAN), which will serve the Army After Next (AAN) through real-time, high-tech, rapid communication connections with virtually all the training, education, war preparation and warfighting elements of tomorrow's US Army.[21]

General Meigs and Colonel Fitzgerald are both imaginative and high-powered dreamers of what is to be. They may be correct, or, they may turn out to be very wide of the mark. We will find out soon enough. But regardless of the precise accuracy of their predictions, there are several important implications for the requirements for Canadian general officers which flow from their vision. First, Canadian general officers will be incapable of exercising the required sophistication of Command, Control and Communication that this vision projects without the highest educational qualifications consistent with their specializations. Second, if these educational qualifications are insufficient, it will be very difficult for the Canadian Forces to play a role of significance in coalition operations with the US. Third, in the future, a graduate level education may be as much a requirement for warfighting among high ranking CF officers as charisma, courage, an ability to think quickly and act decisively, or even a broad right shoulder.

The advanced education that tomorrow's general officers will require will supplement the more traditional leadership qualities already mentioned such as charisma, courage, and an ability to think quickly and act decisively, but it will never replace those characteristics. In future, an effective advanced military education will need to accomplish two inter-related goals: to impart advanced technical and professional training; to teach leaders about the larger world around them and how to think critically about that world as a prerequisite to understand the human context of war. This dual mission parallels the centuries-old dual, but integrated, mission of universities themselves; liberal arts-based education forming the foundation for vocational training.

In the mid-1980s, when the United States was just embarking on the massive transformation that changed the hapless military of the Vietnam War into the highly professional military of the late 1990s,[22] a book appeared written by a life-long civilian whose speciality was military education. Originally published in 1985, and widely used by the United States Marine Corps, *Manoeuver Warfare Handbook* was written by William S. Lind, to help the Marines grasp the concept of maneuver warfare. In the foreword to that book, retired marine Colonel John C. Studt wrote:

> Why [is this book] from a civilian instead of a professional soldier? In fact, the entire movement for military reform is driven largely by civilian intellectuals, not military officers...When you think about it, this is not surprising. We have never institutionalized a system that encourages innovative ideas or criticism from subordinates.[23]

On reading Lind's book, it is easy to see why he may not have been particularly popular with those who administered the US military academies of the last decade. In his section on educating and training the Marines for maneuver warfare he wrote:

> Education is more than the learning of skills or acquisition of facts. It includes acquiring a broad understanding of one's culture, its development and the principles upon which it is founded. Education develops the ability to put immediate situations into a larger context built of history, philosophy, and an understanding of the nature of man. Inherent in education is the ability to think logically, to approach problem solving methodically, but without a predetermined set of solutions….Military education requires much the same process of development. Thoroughly grounded in the art of war—the soldier's "culture"—an educated officer must understand the guiding concepts of his profession, why they are held to be true, and how they evolved. He must be able to put whatever military situation he faces into a larger context of military history, theory, and men's behavior in combat. The development of an ability to think logically, under the stress of battle, must always be a fundamental objective of military education.[24]

This is the same challenge that the Canadian general officer must meet today.

Formal education is not a sufficient condition for effective military leadership. Leaders are born, not made. Just as Bachelors in Commerce and MBAs do not make entrepreneurs, so Masters of War Studies or Masters of Strategic Studies do not make war fighters. All the leadership training in the world is of no use in instilling leadership qualities in men and women who are not natural decision-makers and who do not also have the personal charisma, the certainty of self, or the ability to evoke trust that are the essential ingredients for leadership of any sort. But once leaders have been identified and selected, then education is essential to reinforce their natural leadership abilities and to broaden their understanding of both the technological and the human contexts within which they must exercise that leadership.

The Canadian Forces do not have a long history of strategic thinking. The response to the public's demand that Canadian soldiers should be taught "ethics and values" to give but one example, is often to mount a course or two as if such programs can truly teach "ethics and values" any more than a lecture or two (and a movie on diversity training) can truly explain racism to soldiers.

Education is not a check list. A few hours discussing Canadian military history cannot expose a future general officer to how the nature of our civil society, the development of our economy, overcoming the challenges of climate and geography, our efforts to maintain an existence separate from Britain or the US, and the struggle of Francophones to survive the overwhelming English-speaking North American milieu, have shaped our military history as much as the invention of the machine gun.

The Canadian Forces cannot hope to achieve true military effectiveness in the twenty-first century without the development of an intellectual general officer corps. That development cannot take place until there is a strategic change in planning and in delivering military education in the CF. Military education must be an integral part of CF military training. The CF must recognize that a semester-long course in, say, Canadian military history, is *as necessary* for the development of a young officer as four weeks at Gagetown at the Combat Training Centre, and that much more is required for men and women at the general officer level. Education must not be an "add-on" to a list of qualifications that the CF demands before a member becomes an officer, or a general. CF members should never have to choose between education and training, between education and taskings, between education and six months in Bosnia. Career advancement in the CF officer corps should be dependent on education as much as any other factor. The CF must understand in its collective heart that education is process, that education is not training, that education is not about learning "stuff" but about "learning about stuff." When those conditions are fulfilled, the CF will have undergone a true Revolution in Military Education and when that happens, all Canadian Forces general officers will take their places at the front rank and alongside the best, most professional and most effective military leaders in the world. Only then will the Canadian public's high expectations of Canadian Forces general officers be met.

NOTES

1. Carl von Clausewitz, *On War* (Princeton, Princeton University Press, 1984), 89.
2. Quoted in Mark A. Stoler, *George C. Marshall: Soldier-Statesman of the American Century*, (New York: Twayne Publishers, 1989), 60.
3. See, for example: *Ibid*; Michael D. Doubler, *Closing with the Enemy: How GIs Fought the War in Europe, 1944-1945* (Lawrence: University Press of Kansas, 1994); Russell F. Weigley, *The American Way of War: A History of United States Military Strategy and Policy* (New York: Macmillan, 1973); Geoffrey Perrett, *There's a War to be Won: The United States Army in Worldm War II* (New York: Ivy Books, 1991); Joseph Balkoski, *Beyond the Beachhead: The 29th Division in Normandy* (Harrisburg: Stackpole Books, 1989).
4. Perret, 327.

5. Ibid, 333.
6. The most prominent recent representative of the genre is Martin Seymour Lipset, *Continental Divide: The Values and Institutions of the United States and Canada* (New York: Routledge, 1990).
7. One recent example is the emergence of a small, family-owned, snowmobile company—Bombardier—as one of the largest manufacturers of civil aircraft in the world. In part its success was built upon an expertise in building aircraft for northern bush flying that extends back more than half a century.
8. See, for example, Bill Rawling, *Surviving Trench Warfare: Technology and the Canadian Corps, 1914-1918* (Toronto: University of Toronto Press 1992); and Shane B. Schreiber, *The Shock Army of the British Empire: The Canadian Corps in the Last 100 Days of the Great War* (Westport: Praeger, 1997).
9. Russell A. Hart, "Learning Lessons: Military Adaptation and Innovation in the American, British, Canadian, and German Armies during the 1944 Normandy Campaign." Unpublished PhD Dissertation, Ohio State University, 1997, 547.
10. John A. English, *The Canadian Army and the Normandy Campaign: A Study of Failure in High Command* (Westport: Praeger, 1991).
11. David Bercuson, *Maple Leaf Against the Axis* (Toronto: Stoddart, 1995), 149-163.
12. In Simonds' case, he showed great flexibility in Sicily until he recovered his artillery and motor transport and reverted to "bite and hold" or "firepower over movement."
13. The best dedicated study of a Canadian infantry brigade in the Second World War is Terry Copp, *The Brigade: The Fifth Canadian Infantry Brigade, 1939-1945* (Stoney Creek: Fortress Publications, 1992).
14. Clausewitz, *On War*, 119.
15. Major General Lewis Mackenzie learned that quickly when in command of UN troops at Sarajevo airport. Lewis Mackenzie, *Peacekeeper: The Road to Sarajevo* (Toronto: Douglas and McIntrye, 1993).
16. Chris Madsen, *Another Kind of Justice: Canadian Military Law from Confederation to Somalia* (Vancouver: UBC Press, 1999).
17. Honourable Douglas Young, *Report to the Prime Minister on the Leadership and Management of the Canadian Forces*, http://www.dnd.ca/end/min/reports/pm/mndmilitary.html
18. Robert D. Kaplan, "Four-Star Generalists: Military history pierces the philosophical fog that often surrounds the other humanities," *Atlantic Monthly*, October 1999, 18-19.
19. Captain Eric T. Reynolds, "Ethical Competence and the Profession of Arms: A Contemporary Challenge to Military Institutions," *Canadian Defence Quarterly*, December 1993, 33.
20. John A. English, *Marching Through Chaos: The Descent of Armies in Theory and Practice* (Westport Conn: Praeger, 1996), 67.
21. Lt-General Montgomery, C. Meigs and Col. Edward J. Fitzgerald III, "University after Next," *Military Review*, March-April, 1998, 37-45.
22. James Kitfield, *Prodigal Soldiers: How the Generation of Officers Born of Vietnam Revolutionized the American Style of War* (New York: Simon and Schuster, 1995).
23. William S. Lind, *Maneuver Warfare Handbook* (Boulder: Westview Press, 1985), xi-xii.
24. Ibid, 41-42.

Public Expectations of the General Officer Corps

General (retired) Ramsey Withers

General (retired) Ramsey Withers is a former Canadian Forces Chief of the Defence Staff.

A WORD OF EXPLANATION

MY TREATMENT OF THIS SUBJECT, "public expectations of the general officer corps" is not a scholarly one based upon literature review, extensive interviews or specific polling; although all of these have played a minor role. Rather, it is an expression of one person's views distilled from more than fifty years of experience, encounters with a broad range of individuals and organizations, as well as observations that encompass the Second World War, the Korean Conflict, thirty-five years of regular service, six years of militia involvement and ten years in the private business sector. Mixed in are some twenty years spent in leadership positions in the volunteer and non-government organizations sector (NGO). This is, therefore, very much a personal appreciation.

THE PUBLIC

Who are, or is, the public? There is no simple answer. The "Canadian Public" covers a broad spectrum which can be divided into a multitude of categories: age, education, occupation, position in society, language, culture, location (urban or rural, regional), preoccupations, religion and economic well-being to name some. Given this range and the highly variable knowledge base in regard to the Canadian Forces, let alone their senior leadership, there is probably little value in attempting to define an across-the-board expression of the public's expectations other than in the most general terms; they expect them to be capable leaders. It is more useful to seek answers within a few key categories, specifically, the government and public service, business and industrial leadership sectors, educational and economic levels, experience, the media, and the impact of regional influence.

THE TIME (HISTORICAL) FACTOR

In a democracy the military is an integral part of, and a reflection of, the country's society. Society changes, and its expectations and views change over time. The military must adapt accordingly. Hence expectations of the general officer corps will also change; they have in the past and they will in the future. Looking back at the last half-century, Canada entered the Second World War as essentially an agricultural nation and emerged from that conflict as the fourth largest manufacturer on the Allied side, having had the highest per capita uniformed participation in the fighting, and returned hundreds of thousands of young Canadians to build a thriving peacetime industrial economy. Taking a much more prominent role on the world stage, Canada experienced an unprecedented increase in wealth, helped found the North Atlantic Alliance Treaty Organization (NATO) and broke fresh ground in United Nations peacekeeping. Then followed recession, recovery, the winning of the Cold War, explosion of communications and information technology, and widespread international regional conflicts. Society changed, the Canadian Forces changed and so did expectations. The historical factor is important in our examination of the ever-changing environment in which the CF operates. This brings us to the issue of the public's expectations of the military both today and tomorrow.

THE INTER-WAR YEARS TO 1945

Prior to the Second World War the military was popularly regarded as "freeloading parasites by good tax-paying citizens everywhere, scorned as strikebreakers by labour, and denounced by isolationist politicians, bureaucrats, and academics as imperial pawns."[1] Canadian military historian, Jack Granatstein's *The Generals—The Canadian Army's Senior Commanders in The Second World War,* is an outstanding study of senior Canadian military leaders up to and including the conduct of the Second World War. It also reveals much about the public's expectations. As the quotation illustrates, they were abysmally low until Canada took up arms in global struggle.

Commencing with mobilization in 1939, and throughout the course of the war, the public's expectations became much more positive. There was confidence in the capability of the senior leadership to achieve the expected victory. However, with the exception of the Canadian Army's generals, there was little public attention paid to the senior leadership of the other services. This was understandable in view of the fact that the Royal Canadian Navy (RCN) and the Royal Canadian Air Force (RCAF) had their identities obscured by subordination to British higher command. This is not to say that the public did not have high expectations for the valiant Canadians who served in their Navy, which was the third largest Allied naval force, or the quarter of a million courageous airmen who defended Great Britain and formed a significant part of Bomber Command. In contrast, First Canadian Army was an easily recognized entity as it fought its way in Fortress Europe and across North West Europe to liberate The Netherlands. For this reason Jack Granatstein's book is an excellent tool to understand the temper of the times.

Notwithstanding this temporary public support, our Second World War senior leaders were not long remembered. In the 1970s, I had occasion to address post-graduate military studies students at some Canadian universities. I normally began my presentations with a question to the class, "Name four Allied generals or admirals of the Second World War." I followed this by, "Name one Canadian." There was never a problem with the first question as the students called out, "Eisenhower, Montgomery, Mountbatten, Halsey, Trenchard, Harris." Sadly, there was never a single answer to the second question. No one could remember a Crerar, Nelles or Breadner.

ALLIANCE BUILDING AND PEACEKEEPING DEVELOPMENT: NATO, NORAD AND THE UN

In the fall of 1945, thousands of returning veterans entered our universities to gain the knowledge which, when coupled with their disciplined military experience and ambition, turned out a strong phalanx of leaders in business, industry and political life. The vast Canadian wartime industrial infrastructure was turned to the production of goods and services in worldwide demand. Canada entered an era of unprecedented economic growth as the balance shifted from agriculture and the production of raw materials to manufacturing. Not surprisingly, the society shifted from rural to urban. The Canadian Armed Forces were rapidly demobilized to a total regular strength of less than 50,000. Army Reserves returned to a Militia-dependent mobilization plan, the RCN to a few reserve divisions and the RCAF to a limited number of auxiliary squadrons. Although there was great pride in the accomplishments of Canada's men and women at arms, there was little interest in defence policy and certainly very little expression of public expectations of the senior leadership. But, with respect to defence policy itself, this was soon to change.

After five years of peace, growing concern with the global threat of the Soviet Union, the conquests of communism and the outbreak of war in Korea combined to create a substantial interest in defence policy. Canada was a founding member of NATO, joined the United States in the air defence of North America (NORAD) and became the fourth largest contributor to UN Forces in Korea. The regular services more than doubled their size in a very few years as an air division was formed and dispatched to Europe, an army division was committed to NATO's Central Front with one of its brigades permanently stationed in Germany and the Navy took on large responsibilities safeguarding the sea lines of communications.

The presence of many veterans in government, business, industry, the media and academia and their nation-wide distribution amongst the general public created a level of interest and experience which was unique in Canada. The public expected that the same quality of senior leadership which gave us victory in the Second World War would ensure that these new alliance commitments would be well and honourably led. Their support was unanimous. But, just as was the case during the Second World War, all the Canadian contributions to NATO were absorbed within forces commanded by the Allied "legends" of World War II, namely, Eisenhower, Montgomery, Norstad—but no Canadian in the limelight.

However, when Lester Pearson's initiative created the first peacekeeping force, following the Suez Crisis in 1954, a Canadian general, Lieutenant-General E.L.M. "Tommy" Burns, was appointed as the founding commander of the United Nations Emergency Force (UNEF) and became the first real focus for national public interest in a Canadian general officer in the post-war period. It is probably fair to say that his performance confirmed the public's expectations of the general officer corps; sound, effective, loyal leadership.

INTEGRATION AND UNIFICATION

The public's anodyne interest in the general officer corps changed with implementation of the Pearson government's policy of integration, in 1964, and unification, in 1968. Suddenly defence policy became a serious national issue and the general officer corps was front and centre. Bitter debate and strong public statements, particularly by flag officers, led to resignations, recriminations and wide public attention. For the first time in many years there was public concern about Canada's admirals and generals. At the end of the day, the public expected the general officer corps to be loyal to its political masters and to get on with the job. However, the interest of the political, business, industrial, media and academic sectors of the public in regards to the senior leadership of the Canadian Forces (CF) had been energized as never before. Critical consideration of expectations has continued ever since. In the academic world retrospective analysis of Canadian senior leadership in the Second World War went into high gear.[2]

AFTER THE END OF THE COLD WAR

The irony of the Information Age is that it has given new respectability to uninformed opinion.[3]

The last decade of the century has been witness to events, at home and abroad, which have cast dark shadows on the Canadian Forces and the general officer corps in particular. Its integrity has been called into question both officially in the Somalia Inquiry and unofficially in the media. That some of the damage had been done by uninformed opinion is true. However, especially at the start of this crisis of command, it must be admitted that efforts to inform and to present a reasoned, balanced picture were sorely lacking.

It has to be understood that we live in an age of institutional challenge and the challenge function is enhanced by the seemingly unquenchable thirst for information that will grab public attention in an exploding arena of media competition. Never before has there been such a drive to communicate information, not only as news per se but also as a form of entertainment. Never before has there been such competition among television, radio, print media and the Internet. An old friend, who is a much respected television journalist, told me that his network's research revealed that viewers will channel surf from twelve to forty times per minute, pausing only when there is an "arresting strike." The marketing department's deduction was that there must be as many "arresting strikes" as possible. They assess it rather like the judge in a boxing match; the more blows the higher the score. Thus, in news-oriented programming a preponderance of jobs are wanted—reporters must—go for the "grabbers." And, institutional challenge normally yields grabbers.

For the media, then, to challenge is to survive. Even "good" news reports must take on a hard edge. Thus the most heroic rescue story is likely to include some negative aspect such as a delay in reaction, inadequacy of training or equipment, some failure of the political leadership regardless of the jurisdiction level—federal, provincial or municipal; and if about the Canadian Forces, an inadequacy with the chain of command. Institutions are more than fair game in this sport, they are targets. Whether church, state, benevolent or charitable, none is exempt from the quest for a negative attribute. And none is without its dissident expert, enthusiastically courted by the media and ready to expound on the negatives of the organization from which he or she came. There is a difference between a dissident expert and a critic. A dissident expert typically is someone who feels aggrieved and has a personal ax to grind, while a critic is a person who has made an extensive study of the institution and the issue at hand. Furthermore, the institution cannot reveal facts about the dissident expert because that would be portrayed as a combination of invasion of privacy and continuing the same harassment that caused the individual to become a dissident in the first place. Counter-attack by the institution is out of the question.

Why go an at length about this? Because it is a key and continuing factor influencing public expectations. An oft-spoken, nasty little cliché is, "in Ottawa perception is reality;" unfortunately, it is true. Perceptions (which frequently are misperceptions) arise from failures in communication. The public expects general officers to be articulate, to communicate clearly, completely and truthfully. In the information age one must constantly strive to prevent uninformed opinion from achieving respectability. As will be seen later, the public has concerns.

TODAY

There are no specific indicators of the expectations held by the public about the general officer corps. However, there are fairly recent polling results concerning their opinions about the Canadian Forces and its leadership in general.[4] It is encouraging to see that 85% of Canadians agree that the Canadian Forces do a good job in the performance of their duties.[5] Sixty-five percent of Canadians believe that senior officers are accountable for their actions, 52% consider that the quality of leadership among senior officers is high, but only 35% think that they are honest when making statements to the public.[6] It is revealing that, in what might be called "the shakers and movers category," high-income earners (those who earn over $75,000) and university graduates give the lowest ratings to honesty in public and quality of leadership (30% and 45% respectively).[7] Finally, it is interesting to note that leadership achieves its highest ratings in the Atlantic provinces, probably influenced by the importance the Canadian Forces has in economic well-being, the praiseworthy performance of the Navy, the employment opportunities of military service, for young people, both regular and reserve, and, hopefully, because senior leaders are perceived as being a responsible, caring element of society.

In the fall of 1999, Dr. Douglas Bland, Chair of the Defence Management Studies Program, at Queen's University, conducted a survey of Senators and members of Parliament on their views on defence policy. His research provides valuable insights. Bland found that while 40.6% reported that they had spoken with the Chief of the Defence Staff on some occasion, only 34.4% had ever visited NDHQ. "This situation," he commented, "reflects more on the lack of attention that senior officers and defence officials pay politicians than any failing of the politicians themselves."[8]

In his concluding material, Bland wrote, "The immediate challenge facing the senior officer corps, therefore, is to establish within the Canadian Forces a set of ideas that will bring the officer corps into line with the way most Canadians think about national defence."[9] While he was making specific reference to the fact that military concepts and doctrine cannot substantially alter parliamentary ideas and attitudes about defence, the thought behind his words was clearly that the general officer corps must be in harmony with Canadian society, of which it is a vital, integral part.

SO—WHAT DO "MOST CANADIANS" EXPECT?

Unlike the time when veterans were found in all walks of life and when many university students took part in reserve officer training plans, individuals in government, the public service, business, industry and the media have very little knowledge of military matters. Their expectations, therefore, are most likely founded upon their own circumstances and experience and influenced by information received from various sources. When I retired as the CDS and became the Deputy Minister of Transport two days later, my peers' and subordinates' expectations were the same as if I had been in the public service for thirty-five years. My involvement with business and industry, both for five years in Transport Canada and subsequently for ten years in the private sector, taught me that chief and senior executives expected me to act along the lines of their positions. Most recently in work with academic leaders it was expected that I would be in tune with their thinking on higher education. In all of these experiences, I was expected to understand their cultures, the forces of change acting upon them and their respective niches in society. It is through their filters that they judge the actions of the senior military leadership.

In light of my experience dealing with these varied groups I have found that there are common trends which weave through and connect attitudes and philosophies that are important in understanding the root of public expectations. The first is a belief in your profession and a concomitant loyalty to your organization. Tied to this is integrity which is expected to be of the highest order, and conduct which must be entirely ethical. Furthermore, individuals are expected to be entirely accountable for their actions. Moreover, this is an expectation that you will be a part of the community in which you live, to accept its values and interests and to offer volunteer service for its benefit. In addition, there is an understanding that you can communicate effectively and be able "to sell your organization" honestly; that you understand that change is a fact of life and that adaptation is a continual necessity. Not surprisingly, much of this conforms closely with the published definition of the military ethos.[10]

One concept, however, which is a central theme of Canadian Forces leadership, but is not necessarily thought of by many in the public at large is "caring." Reduced to its simplest form, the military ethos is rooted in caring for subordinates. This issue is core to ethical leadership. It implies caring for troops before operations by training, equipping and supporting them to have a fair chance to fight, win and come home; caring for them during operations by professional leadership and support; and caring for them after operations by meeting their needs arising from that service, as well as honouring their deeds. Nowhere in the civilian sectors of our society is there such a comprehensive expectation. There is, for instance, no business or industrial enterprise which has total concern for its people and their families, twenty-four hours per day, three hundred and sixty-five days per year. It is not that the population at large does not expect senior officers to properly lead its sons and daughters in battle. Rather, it is a case where people need to be informed so that they understand this unique aspect of military leadership. One might say that it is a matter of explaining to the public what their expectation should be. This is an important issue because periodically, there seems to be the perception that the generals and admirals are primarily interested in looking after only themselves.[11]

For the media's part, their primary expectation is that generals tell the truth. It is my experience, having interacted with the media for thirty years, that there are virtually no dishonest journalists. There are, however, many cases of inarticulate or inaccurate interlocutors. If the truth is told it will be reported. Yes, a journalist may have a particular slant, preoccupation or lack of knowledge about the matter at hand. Thus the aim of the senior interlocutor must be to promote the journalist's understanding, to educate when needed and to find the linkages which will enable accurate work. Twenty years ago, on an official visit to the French Armed Forces, I learned of their inauguration of a two-week course of instruction in communications for all newly promoted general officers to achieve this aim.

Earlier, I wrote of the intense competition in the media, the urge to challenge and to search for the other side of the story. This is a reality which will continue and which is best served by telling the truth; completely and in a timely way. And since the public will receive most of the information which influence its expectations via the media, the importance is self-evident.

Finally, I have come to the expectation of the CF being in harmony with Canadian society. My previous quotation from Dr. Bland's survey[12] illustrates that there is serious concern in this regard. What should be appreciated is that Douglas Bland is more than a distinguished scholar who has made an extensive study of senior leadership and the development of defence policy and management in the post-Second World War era. Commissioned in the 8th Canadian Hussars in 1964, he served two decades as a regular officer and attained field rank. It might be said that he has viewed the matter comprehensively from both sides of the street.

What is the origin of this disconnection between the CF and society? It began in the late 1950s, when the Reserves were relegated to a minor role in the era of the nuclear battlefield, a scenario in which it was deemed that only forces-in-being could react in time. Despite Canada's success and battlefield victories being achieved by the mobilization of the reserves, seemingly the citizen-soldier was cast aside. Even in the early 1950s, in the response to the Korean War and in the creation of the first Canadian brigade to be assigned to NATO, the Militia was called upon to be an essential element of that limited mobilization. Then suddenly they were discarded along with our history. Consequently, we began to lose our military roots in Canadian society. Coupled with this, the fact that much of the army and air force were located in places rather remote from the increasingly urban population added to the sense of separation. Moreover, the general officer corps became increasingly involved in the NATO and NORAD alliance command structures and far less involved in operations at home. As for our military roots in society, they remained neglected for two decades as the top priority for limited resources went to building the fully ready forces to fight the Cold War.

The Cold War suddenly and unpredictably ended and the world changed. In the final decade of the century, regional conflicts caused the Canadian Forces to be placed in harm's way to an extent not seen since the Korean War, in 1953. The defence budget contracted quickly as the urge "to extract the peace dividend" became compelling. The concept of a Total Force, regular and reserve working classes together became a pillar of policy to deal with extensive troop requirements and severely limited funds. The Reserves were back in business and we regained the opportunity to restore our roots in Canadian society and to honour our military history. However, it was disappointing to see that the initiative was not grasped more firmly, certainly at first, and that it did not appear to take account of an important change that has taken place in the Canadian way of doing business; gone are the days of a lifetime spent working for a particular company. Current trends focus on part-time employment, re-education, retraining and continual employment if not employment change. Simply put, our society is functioning on a basis rather like the Reserves. To be in harmony with society, the senior leadership must appreciate its attitudes, philosophies and values. The public expects nothing less.

Yet another place where the public, especially "the movers and shakers," have expectations is in the education of the general officer corps. Canadian society has become knowledge-based. To be in sync with it requires extended academic pursuit. Accordingly, the senior leadership will be expected to achieve the same level of post-graduate qualifications that are now so much the norm in civilian life. An undergraduate degree will not be considered adequate for the top posts in a vital and integral institution of our country. It is most satisfying to see that this is being taken to heart.

CONCLUSION

Public expectations of the general officer corps have changed over the past half-century from traditional concerns associated with Canada's victories at arms to a more precise set based upon the values, education and experience of the various sectors that make up our society. All have been influenced in their views by the vast products of the information age. Many of their conclusions are similar or common and probably the most telling of these is the expectation that the senior leadership must reflect the values of, and be in harmony with, a constantly changing Canadian society.

The way ahead becomes clearer with every passing. "Canadians are fortunate," explained Douglas Bland, "...because Canadian Forces officers at this moment seem ready to meet the challenge, well armed with a fresh appraisal of their professional responsibilities and a willingness to be guided by the ethics of their profession and the interests of Canadians."[13]

NOTES

1. J. L. Granatstein, *The Generals – The Canadian Army's Senior Commanders in the Second World War* (Toronto: Stoddart, 1995), 261.
2. Douglas Bland, *Parliament, Defence Policy and the Canadian Armed Forces* (Kingston: School of Policy Studies, Queen's University in cooperation with the Université Laval, 1999), 13. Bland wrote, "...the travail of the post-Somalia deployment and the questionable performance of senior military and public service leaders excited discussion of Canadian civil-military relations, perhaps more than at any time since the end of World War II."
3. Veteran reporter John Lawton, age sixty-eight, speaking to the American Association of Broadcast Journalists, 1995. Quoted by Michael Crichton in his book *Airframe* (New York, 1996).
4. POLLARA Report, *Canadian Opinions on the Canadian Forces (CF) and Related Military Issues,* December, 1998, 77. The public considers the Chief of the Defence Staff to be a very credible or somewhat credible spokesperson for the CF (29% / 46%) and senior military to be very credible or somewhat credible (24% / 43%). Both are slightly higher than the figures for the Prime Minister and the Minister of National Defence. 77.
5. Ibid, 26.
6. Ibid, 63.
7. Ibid, 64.

8. Bland, 7.
9. Bland, 15.
10. Department of National Defence, *Officers' Professional Development Handbook*, 1997.
11. POLLARA, An indication of this can be seen in the polling on perceptions of salaries for CF personnel at sections 6.46 and 6.5 of the report (pages 66 and 67). It is also apparent in some editorial comments in the print media.
12. See note 9.
13. Bland, 16.

V
THE FUNCTIONAL ROLES
of
GENERALSHIP

GENERALSHIP AND DEFENCE PROGRAM MANAGEMENT

Major-General D.L. Dempster

Major-General D.L. Dempster is the current Deputy Commander of the Combined Land Staff at NDHQ, Ottawa.

Nor has there been adequate use of appropriate management techniques and policies to make the most economic use of available resources.
—Report of the Management Review Group to the Minister of National Defence, 7 July 1972

PART 1 INTRODUCTION
Context and Historical Background

DEFENCE IN CANADA is a large and complex enterprise consuming one percent of the gross domestic product and seven percent of the federal budget. Defence employs on a full- or part-time basis over one hundred thousand people. The resource magnitude is compounded by international and domestic political factors. Major inter- and intra-state conflicts in the world continue to propagate even as the memories of the two world wars grow fainter. Major defence acquisition decisions such as the Ross Rifle in 1916, the Avro Arrow in 1959 and the New Shipborne Helicopter in 1993 have temporarily dominated the political agenda and ultimately contributed to the demise of governments.

In all major Western democracies, and especially those with a Westminster parliamentary system, the post Second World War trend has been towards a single integrated defence services program. In Canada this began with the postwar defence management regime under the Minister of National Defence, Brooke Claxton. In tabling his estimates in 1947 he identified his first long-term objective as "progressively closer co-ordination of the armed services and unification of the Department so as to form a single defence force in which the three armed services work together as a team."

This was followed by the Glassco Commission of 1962, and the Hellyer Defence White Paper of 1964, both of which sought increased efficiencies in this expensive component of the public sector. The National Defence Headquarters integration and the subsequent unification of the Canadian Forces in the 1968-1972 period, continued the dual trends of increasing civilian control and increasing cost-consciousness. These changes, undertaken at times after acrimonious debate, took place nonetheless during an essentially stable international regime. The collective defence strategy of Soviet containment was led from Washington and tightly coordinated in Brussels. Throughout this time period combined operations at the single service level predominated in Canada. The notion of a single integrated Canadian Forces was seen by many senior military professionals as an administrative or legal construct driven from the political level rather than as a joint operational one supporting effective military performance.

The Decade of the 1990s

In the 1990s military professionalism in Canada began to mature along two separate axes. First, lessons learned during international and domestic operations produced a deepening understanding of the nature of conflict in the post Cold War world. These new operations began with the Iran-Iraq disengagement force in 1988, and moved through to the Persian Gulf in 1991, Somalia in 1992, Bosnia in 1993, Haiti in 1994, Rwanda in 1997, Zaire in 1998, and Kosovo and East Timor in 1999. Canadian military professionals learned about low-notice global coalition operations, as well as their command and control, information, logistics, public affairs and political interface issues. Within Canada, the Oka internal security operation of 1990, and four extensive domestic operations—the Saguenay flood of 1996, the central Canada ice-storm of 1997, the Manitoba flood of 1998 and the Year 2000 contingency operation—all contributed important operational lessons about jointness and inter-agency co-ordination. In short, the *1994 White Paper* policy articulating a capabilities-based force structure rather than a threat-based one was tested and validated.

Second, as tax resources available for program expenditure became scarce due to excessive public sector debt levels and the economic recession in the early 1990s, the government introduced the Expenditure Management System (EMS) together with Program Reviews 1 and 2. These top-down processes strictly rationed program funding, providing no recourse or appeal process. Within DND, the Management and Command and Control Re-engineering (MCCR) process unrolled and the Defence Management System was brought in to mirror the EMS. The importance of defence resource management was thereby brought into sharp focus. Baseline activities were examined for elimination, alternative service delivery and innovative change. Devolution of authorities to subordinate formations and bases provided new opportunities for streamlining and prioritization. Staff structures and processes began to evolve in response to the new resource environment. The role of the Environmental Chiefs of Staff, who relocated to Ottawa in 1998, became primarily focused upon the force generation process. This process is deeply intertwined with program management of not only operating budgets but also with the portions of corporate accounts over which they exercise an increasing degree of planning influence.

These two trends—operational lessons learned and resource constraints—are changing the nature of generalship in Canada. Generals (including flag officers for the purpose of this chapter) are now interfacing with sister services, allies, other government departments, non-governmental organizations, central agencies of government, parliamentary committees and the public. They are faced with complex resource allocation questions in a corporate context. Generals have to champion change while extolling core ethical and professional values and principles. The ultimate issue, therefore, is one of exercising individual and collective leadership of the overall defence enterprise so as to produce relevance, responsiveness and reputation.

Aim, Scope and Outline

Aim. The aim of this chapter is to describe the essence of strategic defence program leadership in Canada.

Scope and Limitations. This chapter will of necessity provide only an overview of a complex and multi-faceted subject in a country that is a self-professed middle power without military ambition or imperial pretensions. Canada has emerged from its history when important defence decisions were made elsewhere—in London until the 1940 Ogdensburg Agreement and subsequently in Washington. Generals now require increasingly sophisticated skill and knowledge sets to shape the future of defence in Canada. This chapter will highlight the key issues but cannot claim to be comprehensive in all respects.

Outline. Part 2 of this chapter will examine the defence program in its external public policy context, particularly in terms of alliance connections and competition from other policy portfolios. Relevant basic defence economic theory will be outlined. These factors lead to the program being both an open and closed system amenable to systems dynamics modelling. In Part 3, the operations or internal management aspects will be considered, especially various ways of viewing the program. Critical parameters such as the labour-capital ratio will be discussed and certain planning tools introduced. The underlying structures, processes and balances are highlighted. Capital program management is addressed in Part 4, describing the notions of horizons, asset allocation, and adoption rate for innovative doctrine and technology. The strategic capability planning process is introduced and political realities considered. Lastly, in Part 5, certain defence program management issues are identified for future development.

PART 2   DEFENCE IN A PUBLIC POLICY CONTEXT
The Nature of Defence

Defence is a public good. It benefits all Canadians by contributing to the nation's security, which in turn permits the exercise of sovereignty and the rule of law. Defence is primarily a form of national insurance against potentially catastrophic events. Defence policy is largely a question of setting the coverage required against the premiums that are affordable, and is therefore a risk management assessment. The current defence policy base developed through extensive public consultation has articulated the expected environment, capability requirements and financial resources to be allocated.

Kennedy has noted the universal relationship between national economic growth and the cost of national security. His research focussed upon the great powers in international competition and concluded that towards the end of a power cycle the "unproductive" security needs begin to erode the national economic base, thereby opening the way for a competitor which had concentrated more resources on economic growth. In the Canadian context, defence in strategic terms is often seen as discretionary given Canada's isolation in North America with but a single land neighbour, and the public policy issue is often expressed as the minimalist floor rather than the Kennedy ceiling. In this context, it is the NATO multilateral and Canada-US bilateral relationships which drive defence expenditures rather than the domestic threat perception. To have a North American economy, one needs a porous border. To have a porous border requires harmonized continental perimeter defence arrangements, be it for air or sea access, and this drives defence planning and expenditures in some form of partnership.

Defence also plays two important secondary roles in addition to the primary insurance role. Firstly, it assists in shaping the external geo-political environment through military diplomacy, peace-support operations and military exercises such as MARCOTs and NORAD forward deployments demonstrating political resolve. Secondly it supports national objectives such as industrial, technological, youth, aboriginal and regional development. These stakeholders all have a voice in the government, and see participation in the defence program as in their best interest.

The primary defence role is essentially one of potential capability at various degrees of readiness, while the two subordinate roles require active resource commitment on a continuous basis. Active operations may be seen, in the insurance analogy, as a claim with a deductible. Indeed, Defence has established an arrangement with the government that active operations beyond an established threshold or "deductible" will be separately reimbursed to the defence program.

In any given circumstance there is a fundamental need to balance the potential and active elements of the program. The cumulative budget reductions together with the high operational tempo of the 1990s can now be seen as overdrawing upon the potential side of the ledger, slowing modernization and often deferring higher-order collective training. The benefits, however, include new operational insights, a flexible and experienced force, and enhanced relationships with our allies. Without those experiences it might not have been possible to develop a long-term institutional strategy or to convince the central agencies to increase the resource allocation to Defence as occurred in the February 2000 Federal Budget.

THE ESSENCE OF DEFENCE PROGRAM MANAGEMENT

Defence program management lies at the nexus of several disciplines, including decision theory, economics, managerial accounting, political science, technology, organizational behaviour, operations research and strategic management.

Increasingly in-house professional expertise as represented on the National Security Studies and Defence Resource Management Courses is being complemented by post-graduate Public or Business Administration education. This chapter will link defence and military concepts to those of the business disciplines to provide new insights.

The term "program" may be generally defined as a "definite plan of intended proceedings." More specifically, the Defence Management System manual defines the Defence Services Program as "the total of all departmentally approved activities and projects which are deemed to be essential to the delivery of affordable and effective defence services to the Government and Canadians." Part of the program is baseline and ongoing while the rest is composed of one-time activities generically called projects. Projects may be capital investments, change initiatives or training exercises. The simplest definition of a project is "something that has a beginning and an end." The management of projects is also increasingly being professionalized, however, general officers will frequently be involved in leading, championing or supporting projects or portfolios of projects. The capital program and its project building blocks will be covered in more detail in Part 4. What differentiates program management from project management is its top-down, open-ended, holistic nature rather than one that is bottom-up, closed in terms of scope-cost-schedule and deterministic.

Key Defence Economics Concepts

Several defence economics concepts underlie the program, specifically the notions of value, elasticity and marginal utility. Of these, value is often the least well understood.

Value. Value is related to, but is not the same as, price and cost. Value is to effectiveness, as cost is to efficiency. Value is an output from a transaction or process while cost and price are inputs. The same block of ice that has no value when delivered into the hands of an Inuit in winter has tremendous value delivered into the hands of a man dying of thirst in the desert. In the defence program environment we attempt to minimize the price we pay for goods and services by concentrating our buying power to maximize discounts and by conducting fair competitions. Value is created, however, by acquiring the right thing at the right time in concert with the right training, logistics and doctrine. Within enterprises the value chain analysis tool is used to organize the internal handoffs to achieve maximum value-added for a given level of input costs. It is the consumer of the service or product who ultimately assesses the value. In the case of the defence program, it is the government and people of Canada receiving the defence good who assess its value. Defence must continuously strive to increase the value of its outputs, building upon its core competencies and producing synergy from its horizontal linkages.

Elasticity. Elasticity is the measure of the sensitivity of one variable to another. In Part 3, the elasticity of the labour and capital inputs will be analyzed. In general, elasticity depends on the availability of substitutes. Clearly where there are close substitutes, a price increase will cause the consumer to buy less of the good and more of the substitute. In this context, if defence costs and the price charged to the government climb, the government may choose to acquire substitute products, e.g., humanitarian relief from NGOs rather than via Defence. One of the key factors in assigning the counter-terrorist role from the RCMP to Defence was the availability of a close substitute in skill-set terms at a much lower input labour cost, given that Canadian Forces (CF) members do not receive payment for overtime. Elasticity issues come to the fore when setting transfer prices for providing services to other government departments.

Utility. The concept of marginal utility assists in explaining capability trade-offs. Utility is the level of satisfaction that a consumer gets from consuming a good or undertaking an activity. The principle of *diminishing marginal utility* explains that as more of a good is consumed, successive increments yield less and less satisfaction. For example, while one ice cream cone provides happiness, more than one at a time is of marginal utility because the need has been largely satisfied. In principle, balance among competing goods is maximized when their marginal utilities are equal. Individuals new to defence resource management are sometimes heard to say that if we could just eliminate one of the three services, there would be sufficient resources to do the remaining two well. This goes against the principle of marginal utility, however, as any environmental void would end up having the highest marginal utility and would therefore be resourced by any rational decision maker before allocating further resources to the other two environments.

The Dynamics Of Government Defence Resource Allocation

The Defence program has the attributes of both a closed and an open system. In the short term under the government Expenditure Management System resource allocations are fixed and the process is closed. This top-down resource allocation flows down annually through the business planning levels with successive sub-allocations, and then is rolled back up together with identification of tasks that cannot be completed as directed. The February 2000 Federal Budget emphasized that:

> Although additional funding is being provided for urgent operating and capital pressures, the Government will continue to operate in the

most efficient and cost-effective manner possible. Under the Expenditure Management System, departments will be required, to the greatest extent possible, to fund new cost pressures by internal reallocation and increased efficiencies.

During the later phase of the Cold War, defence received formula funding for real growth in order to meet commitments agreed to in the NATO Defence Planning Questionnaire (DPQ). A three percent real growth rate was achieved during the late 1980s, producing a stable but still largely closed system. The truth today is different, however, with defence resourcing being more volatile. The perturbations caused by the end of the Cold War concurrent with economic recession, excessive levels of national indebtedness and the Somalia Inquiry produced multiple budget cuts. The defence budget fell from a high of $12 billion in FY 93-94 by nearly twenty-three percent (thirty percent in real terms) before reductions ceased in 1998. A modest quality of life increase was provided in the 1999 budget. Defence continues to be one of only three departments receiving a prescribed level of automatic economic increase against inflation.

The government resource allocation system is now more open, although the rules are still being articulated. Ministers can submit memoranda to Cabinet for either new policy initiatives or for the integrity of existing policies. Departments can seek bump funding or loans for specific initiatives as occurred for Year 2000 computer remediation. The Treasury Board has introduced a program integrity process to buttress weaknesses in program delivery, usually across defined horizontal business areas such as infrastructure or information technology rust-out. As mentioned above, the department can access supplementary funding when operations surpass an agreed threshold. Success in obtaining required resources is a function of engaging the decision-makers at the bureaucratic, public, parliamentary, international and political levels in a coordinated and coherent fashion. It was this approach which resulted in the sustained budget increases in the 2000 Federal Budget, producing a stable long-term financial environment for defence planning.

A Strategy for Handling Unpredictability

A vital component of the success in obtaining a budget increase was the articulation by the senior leadership team of a long-term institutional strategy covering two decades. This had not even been contemplated previously in the stable Cold War environment. Within the public sector, as in the private, investors now respond to a strategic business vision with clear and measurable objectives. Together with success in global and domestic operations, *Defence Strategy 2020* transformed Defence from a cost centre to a centre for generating value. Decision-makers can clearly see the degree of fit between the strategic objectives and broad government policy. This congruence with government themes of innovation, national unity, human security and global trade should make allocation of scarce resources to Defence less problematic than in the past.

Clearly, the rate of change and unpredictability in the external defence environment are increasing. The change drivers are geo-politics, technology, national economic well-being and modern business practices. The many feedback loops and interfaces will allow defence performance to be modelled using system dynamics rather than by traditional static techniques. Regrettably Defence in Canada is still often perceived to be discretionary, especially when economic downturns force fiscal retrenchment. History tells us, however, that global or local economic depression is often followed by inter- or intra-state conflict.

Increasingly, Defence will likely have to compete effectively with other policy agendas, both within the foreign and defence policy envelope and across government overall. Concepts such as the human security agenda and the humanitarian relief exemplified by the Kosovo and East Timor operations are creating new and broader domestic constituencies for Defence.

Necessity is often the mother of invention. Austerity has forced defence organizational, capability and process change in Canada that has not yet been replicated by our major allies. For example, both the US and UK continue to support three distinct services with harmonization of expensive support services starting only in the past decade. Nonetheless Canada has made valuable contributions with its limited resources. In the Balkans, Canada's CF-18 Precision Guided Munitions capability and the new army Coyote vehicle provided high value in a complex coalition operation. Halifax Class frigates have been fully integrated into US carrier battlegroups, an accomplishment yet achieved by no other nation. The US Army is now actively paralleling Canada's initiative in creating a medium-weight digital army capable of rapid strategic deployment, albeit at a far greater scale. The *Defence Strategy 2020* military objectives of global deployability, interoperability and modernization are consistent with the NATO Defence Capabilities Initiative and resonate clearly with Canadians and our principal allies.

PART 3 DEFENCE PROGRAM STRUCTURE AND PROCESS
First Order Decisions On Defence Resource Allocation

Prior to unification and integration the primary disaggregation of defence resources was by service. Since that time the division by parliament has been by a vote structure of Personnel, Operations and Maintenance (O&M) (Vote 1), Capital (Vote 5) and Grants and Contributions (Vote 10). The theory of defence resource allocation is shown at Figure 3-1.

Making Defence - In Theory

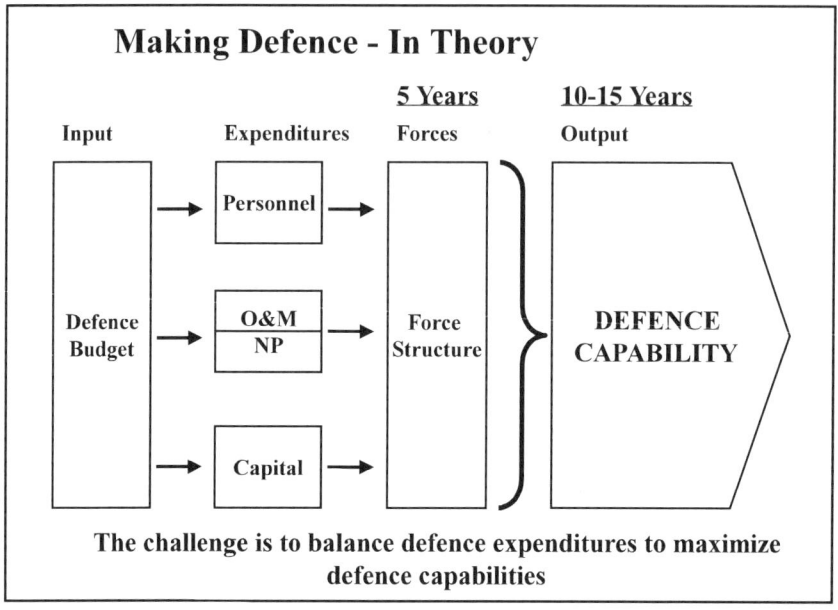

Input	Expenditures	**5 Years** Forces	**10-15 Years** Output
Defence Budget	Personnel O&M / NP Capital	Force Structure	DEFENCE CAPABILITY

The challenge is to balance defence expenditures to maximize defence capabilities

Figure 3-1 The Theory of Making Defence

Given a defence policy and resource envelope, the initial breakout of resources is into Personnel, O&M budgets and Capital. The Operating and Maintenance budgets are divided into two elements—National Procurement and Operating budgets. National Procurement (NP) is used to support activities, systems and equipments from the national level. Operating budgets are allocated to Level 1 managers and below for operating expenses such as fuel, civilian personnel, training and travel. There is a need to retain balance across program elements in several dimensions.

Personnel. During the budget reduction period in the mid-1990s most of the savings were achieved through personnel cuts and deferring of capital acquisition. Following a period when wages were frozen for both military and public servants, the cost of personnel has begun to rise. The driving factors for this increase are first, the need to improve the quality of life for the survivors of the reduction process and second, the need to accelerate professional learning and adjustment of the labour force to the information age. Both *Defence Strategy 2020* and the public sector Universal Classification System are designed to produce a multi-skilled workforce with fewer internal barriers to accelerating productivity through e-management.

If workforce quality increases without quantity trade-offs, the net effect will be that personnel will absorb an increasing percentage of the Defence envelope.

A key mitigating factor, however, may be that the government continue to compensate the Department separately for personnel-related economic increases. Note, however, that if the long-standing principle of comparability is upheld, any UCS-related increase in the cost of public servant wages will cause an equal increase in military pay, an account five times larger than all the Defence civilian salary wage envelopes combined. This is an area of critical concern to Defence resource planners.

National Procurement. The state of Defence capital stock drives the National Procurement in two important ways. Most obvious is that systems retained beyond their economic lifecycle become expensive to maintain as spare parts and technological expertise become scarce. Less obvious is the impact of new systems with complex software and electronics. These new systems change the concept of support, ultimately producing only two lines of support—one military located very close to the user and one industrial located distantly within the defence industry base. The affordability of the new systems can only be achieved if the requisite resource transfer occurs from the no longer required user and military support personnel to the NP account holding the industry in-service support contract.

NP demands rose inexorably throughout the 1990s as equipment aged and as new systems arrived. Lack of NP resources has led to deferred repair and overhaul activities for major systems, the acquisition of spare parts in less than economical ordering quantities and lessened operational availability of lower priority systems. Similar effects occurred in the infrastructure stock as rust-out proceeded, mitigated only marginally by the 1995 Infrastructure Reduction Program. The net effects of the personnel and NP pressures was to squeeze out capital funding, reducing capital spending to eighteen percent of the defence budget by 1999, with projections prior to the 2000 Federal Budget for further drops in the future.

Balancing Today and Tomorrow

Defence is a capital-intensive business. It has high fixed costs due not only to complex capital equipment but also to the nature of the training and support infrastructure required to train and operate. The marginal variable cost of adding or reducing one unit of operational capability is usually minimal due to these high fixed costs, which can only be adjusted slowly over a three- to five-year period as contracts are renewed or force structures adjusted. To achieve flexibility over time, it is important to find ways to convert these fixed costs to variable costs through different ways of providing the service.

A critical issue for general officer consideration is the balance between present and future capability. In the 1920s and 1930s the German General Staff assessed that the future would lie with mechanized forces that could restore mobility to the battlefield producing decisive action. They were correct. Their approach grew out of lessons learned on the First World War's eastern front, new concepts espoused by British thinkers such as J.F.C. Fuller and the realization that an approach based upon conventional heavy artillery was politically and economically unrealizable. As demonstrated by the Germans in the post First World War era and the Americans post Vietnam, being defeated in war accelerates the creative destruction of obsolescent doctrine and the experimentation with new and innovative concepts together with reinforcement of the enduring foundations of leadership and discipline.

From a Canadian perspective there are two broad choices—symmetry wherein we follow the best practices of our allies or asymmetry where we lead in areas of unique Canadian contribution and expertise. Examples of the latter in recent experience are armed boarding parties during the Persian Gulf operation and the Coyote reconnaissance vehicle and Electro-optic Reconnaissance Vehicle and Target Acquisition (ERSTA) Griffon helicopter in Kosovo. Ultimately a balanced combination of both approaches is required.

Balance Between Capital and Labour Inputs

Within Defence the pivotal long-term resource allocation issue is the balance between capital investment and labour. This is analogous to the private sector drive for increased productivity. This issue requires an appreciation of the rate of technological change, the likelihood of conflict and emerging concepts and doctrines. *Defence Strategy 2020* has posited the need for high-quality forces with the attrib-

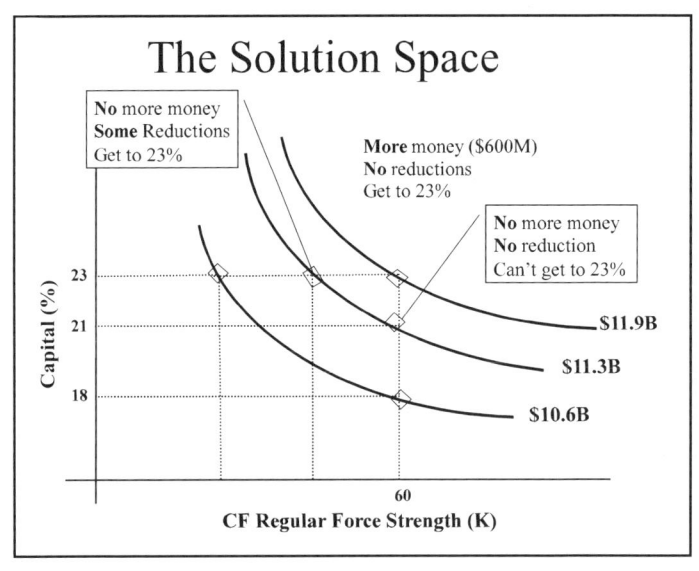

Figure 3-2 The Capital-Labour Trade-offs Post Budget 2000

utes of global deployability, interoperability and modernization. This in turn requires higher levels of capital investment than achieved in the 1990s. Execution of an ideal capital investment program is invariably frustrated by delays in political approval, policy or industrial issues, the impacts of periodic economic recessions, technological change, postings of project champions and federal elections. The principle of marginal utility needs to be consistently applied to determine the relative marginal value of one unit of personnel versus one unit of capital.

Figure 3-2 shows the current capital-labour trade-off curves before and after the 2000 Federal Budget. The effect of the budget was to permit twenty-one percent of the budget to be allocated to capital by 2003/04 with no further force structure adjustments. Defence has moved closer to an equilibrium, but is yet to achieve the twenty-three percent capital allocation selected by the senior leadership team. The solution space with the new funding requires less dramatic change than before and balance should be achievable over the next few years by a combination of new funding measures and force structure reductions.

Joint Capability Balances

Another important balance to be determined early is that between the single service and joint requirements. Historically each environment optimized its capability independently, usually in some form of benchmarking against major allies, and with minimal consideration of joint factors. This led to a primary focus on the fighter squadron, infantry battalion and frigate as the main elements of capability. Little inter-service coordination was essential in the Cold

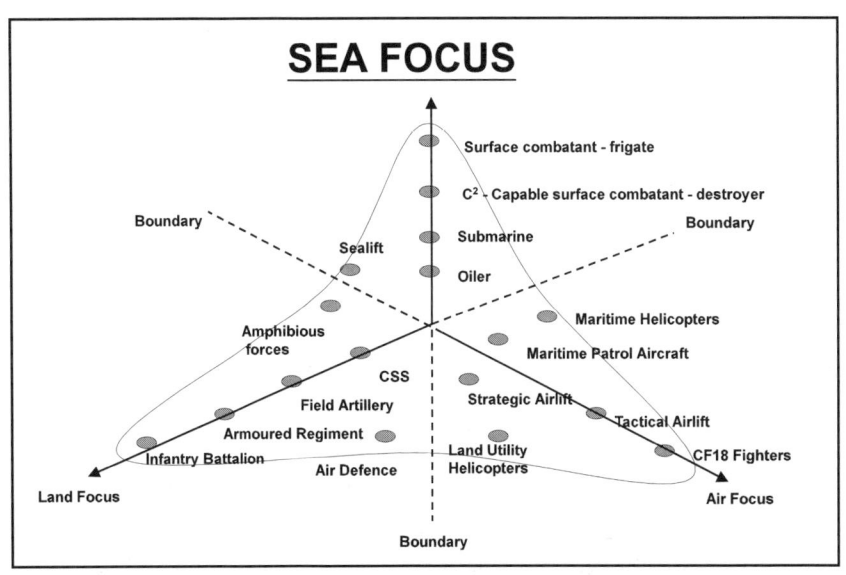

Figure 3-3 Environmental Focus and Capability Boundary Issues and Program Elements

war period as operations at the tactical level were combined, not joint. In this period, only the Low Level Air Defence (LLAD) project attempted to transcend the boundary between two services, however this LLAD consensus has not persisted following the departure of stationed forces from Europe, reductions in the air threat and major funding reductions.

Figure 3-3 describes the primary focus and boundary issues among the three services. During the Cold War when combined rather than joint operations were emphasized, the three environmental spaces were poorly connected. The legacy of this approach is solid tactical capability in the three services centred on the primary operating platforms. Joint and boundary issues are now increasingly important in order to generate the synergy and relevance demanded by the government.

This diagram can be logically extended from three to n-dimensions as space, support, reserve, allied and other issues are added. Issues at the boundaries such as reconnaissance UAVs, armed helicopters, strategic air and sealift, space-based sensors and communications capabilities were historically not well addressed. Defence introduced a process similar to the US Joint Requirements Oversight Committee in 1998, to harmonize the capability requirements. This process has been successfully used for Canadian Military Satellite Communications, the Maritime Helicopter, the Advanced Logistic Support Capability vessel, medical services and certain ASD activities. This joint capability requirements review process will continue to expand and deepen.

Process mapping assists in understanding the connection from inputs through to outputs. Defence has identified four core processes—corporate management, support services, force generation and force employment—as representing the business. The MCCRT made significant progress in defining the sub-elements and inter-relationships. Nonetheless there are still non-trivial issues associated with horizontal accountabilities as one process interacts and hands off to another.

A key element of the program is the first-order definition of program sub-components, or "service lines" as defined by the Treasury Board (TB). The TB requires that each department of government produce a mandate document called the Planning, Reporting and Accountability Structure, or PRAS. For a complex enterprise such as defence, this is a challenging construct as the ways we plan, report and account are different. Significant work has been performed to group defence activities into a more relevant set of sub-programs reflecting the needs of government, the internal Accountability-Responsibility-Authority (ARA) structure and the process view. Furthermore the structure must reflect program elements as embodied in the departmental financial (FMAS) and organizational (Enterprise, or HR) databases.

The TB has provided departments, and especially those such as Defence which are pilot departments in terms of modern comptrollership, flexibility in defining their business elements. Defence has chosen to emphasize the planning element of the PRAS with a single mission and seven program elements called service lines. These are as shown in Figure 3-4. Each program element has a significant resource content and reporting relevance in terms of outputs. For example, it is important to separate the capabilities into those that have higher readiness (Operational Forces) from those which represent potential capability (Reserves). Through the program view new insights can be gained upon the relative balances among the program sub-elements.

The government has placed particular emphasis on results orientation. Performance is a function of outcomes, that is, the degree to which change in the external environment is influenced by departmental actions. This is difficult to measure. Success in the battlespace is good performance. Deterring conflict is even better performance. Nonetheless, the CF is not always engaged in the battlespace. Moreover, many Defence activities are related to modernizing, preparing, training and supporting. For these reasons Defence needs a more complex construct for program management that starts with policy and strategy, conducts business planning, conducts activities and then tracks performance.

MANDATE

DEFENCE MISSION BUSINESS LINE
- To defend Canada and Canadian interests and values while contributing to international peace and security.

SERVICE LINES
- Corporate Policy, Strategy and Management
- Operational Forces
- Reserve Force
- Command, Control, Communications and Intelligence
- Human Resource Management and Training
- Supporting Infrastructure
- Logistic and Technical Support

DEFENCE OBJECTIVES
- Defence Advice and Information
- Surveillance and Control
- Aid of the Civil Power
- Bilateral and Multilateral Operations
- Assist Other Government Departments
- Support Government Programs
- Emergency and Humanitarian Relief
- Maximize defence capabilities

DEFENCE PLANNING GUIDANCE
- Directs Level One Implementation Activities

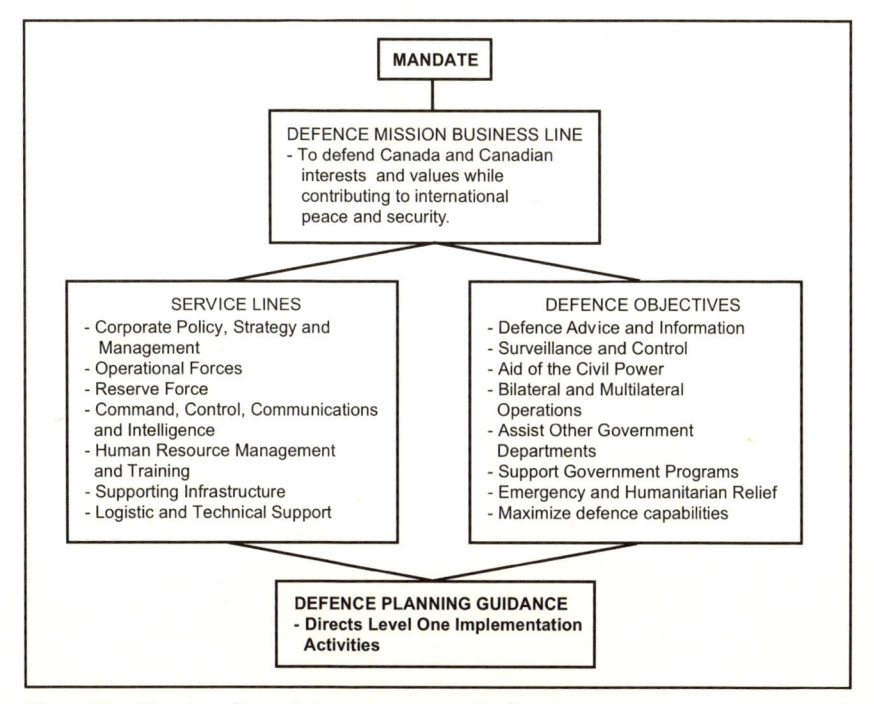

Figure 3-4 Planning, Reporting and Accountability Structure

Defence has been therefore one of the leading enterprises in the federal government to describe an end-to-end process from start to finish.

The singular Defence mission can be subdivided into defence objectives. These collectively reflect the mandate of the department. A recent conceptual breakthrough has been the notion that there are sustaining and change objectives, with the change objectives aiming to improve the delivery, efficiency or effectiveness of the sustaining objectives. In short, there is a need to define what has to be done ("sustaining agenda") and also how delivery will be improved ("change agenda"). Lastly, there is a need to delegate these agendas down through the organization. The annual Defence Planning Guidance is the vehicle for this process.

Interaction with Government Processes

The department interacts with government with two publicly accountable documents tabled by the Minister through the Part III estimates process. These documents are the *Report on Plans and Priorities* (RPP) tabled at the start of the fiscal year and the departmental performance report tabled six months after the end of the fiscal year. Defence starts the process off internally twelve months before the RPP with the DPG, beginning the internal planning cycle rolled down to the lowest organizational level and then integrated progressively up to the RPP. The cyclical process is shown in Figure 3-5.

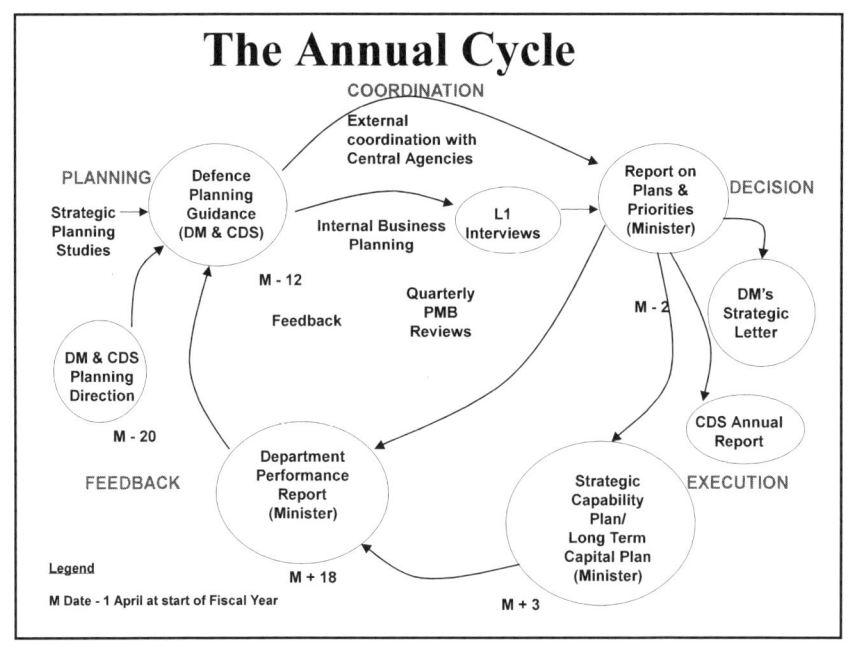

Figure 3-5 The Annual Program Cycle

Performance Management

Increasingly important is the feedback cycle that seeks to measure performance against the mandate and objectives. Feedback comes from several sources both external and internal to the department. An important element is the lessons learned from both operations and support activities. In addition, lessons learned by others are usually less painful than our own, although often not as well absorbed. Best practices, audit and evaluation and benchmarking are emerging as vital processes contributing to overall performance management.

As an example, Australia and New Zealand were early leaders in clarifying accountabilities, codifying resource allocation principles and being outcomes-oriented. Nonetheless both have recently faced significant resource challenges. The New Zealand Defence Force is facing severe rust-out and has decided not to acquire F-16's on a lease basis from the US. Australia reduced manpower significantly in order to acquire capital equipment; however, cost overruns on the Collins class submarine and other projects have largely negated their personnel savings. The recent operations in East Timor, in which Australia was strategically surprised by the unwillingness of the US to participate as coalition leader, will almost certainly lead to profound changes there. It is therefore vital to evaluate the experiences of others in our own context, to apply judgement, and to avoid the obvious pitfalls. Pilot projects, trials and experimentation of our own are essential to produce rational and enduring decisions.

Resource reserves are needed for the unpredictable. Because over-programming is used in the public sector environment to ensure that allocated resources are effectively used, reserves are usually situational, i.e., certain activities are stopped to do another, or provided from the central government fiscal framework when needed. Defence has chosen, following the Management, Command and Control Re-engineering review, to hold minimal reserves at the centre under the VCDS. The amount of reserves held is a function of the programmatic risk. Risk at the program level is a function of potential impact, probability and the ability to mitigate should the risk come to pass. Examples of risks endemic to the defence program are inflation, particularly for equipment, personnel salaries or fuel costs, increasing technological obsolescence leading to early replacement or accelerating support costs and the impact of implementing social change reflecting changes in societal values.

On a final note, it is noteworthy that *Defence Strategy 2020* contained only three quantitative five-year targets—to raise the portion of the defence budget allocated to capital expenditure to twenty-three percent, to reduce infrastructure by ten percent and to reduce the acquisition time of defence projects by thirty percent. Each of these represents a re-balancing to improve future effectiveness.

PART 4 CAPITAL PROGRAMMING
The State of the Capital Stock

Figure 4-1 displays a macro perspective of the defence capital equipment base, comparing relative operational effectiveness with the proportion of lifecycle expended. Clearly, there are some new systems and a group of systems, including four of the five major aircraft fleets, which are facing rust-out. This chart does not deal with the quality-quantity trade-offs or the rate of technological obsolescence that can produce premature ageing. Systems with complex electronics and software offer enhanced capability at the expense of more rapid depreciation. Nonetheless the chart provides a first-order, high-level perspective of the asset base. The introduction of accrual accounting in the department will provide a more systematic quantification of the rate of depreciation over time.

This chart does not indicate if the portfolio of systems held is what we actually need to meet the defence policy, nor in which priorities the department should invest first. It does not show how opportunities arising from new combinations of doctrine and technology should fit in to the capital plan. How should Defence make its investment decisions?

Innovation and Investment

During the Cold War the capital program was tightly tied to NATO needs. In certain cases, such as the Leopard tank, direct pressure from allied leaders at

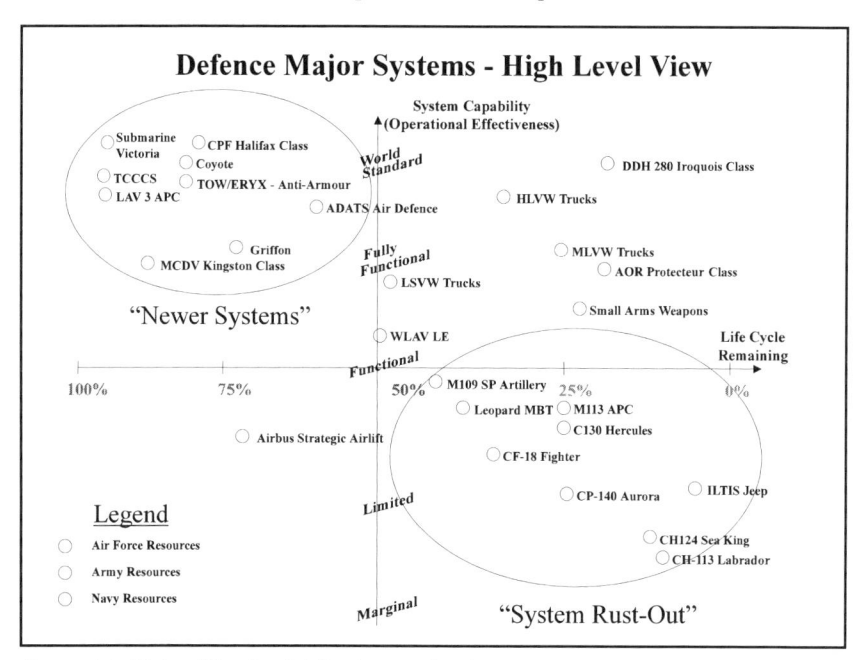

Figure 4-1 State of the Capital Equipment Stock

the top levels produced procurement actions by reluctant Canadian governments. One of the vital issues for strategic relevance and coherence is to connect the capital program to the institutional strategy as well as to the policy base.

Strategic Objectives 1 and 3 of *Defence Strategy 2020* are "Innovative path" and "Modernize." Canada has not been consistently strong in this regard and has yet to institutionalize experimentation. In both world wars Canadian soldiers proved adept at improvisation, but peacetime depression stringencies and lack of leadership stopped force development.

In the First World War the Canadian Army was renowned for its artillery, machine gun corps and field engineering acumen. On the other hand it acquired its first Bren Gun Carrier only in 1938. The inter-war force development void in Canada produced an officer corps with little expertise in modern warfare in the Second World War.[1] However, during Operation Totalize in August 1944, Lieutenant-General Simonds innovated tactically in several ways. For example, he quickly adapted self-propelled artillery pieces as armoured personnel carriers capable of keeping up with armoured forces.[2] There was no systematic approach to operations research or experimentation after the war, and most innovation during the Cold War was imported from allies. In 1999, however, Canadian land commanders in Kosovo had the Coyote, arguably the best reconnaissance vehicle in theatre. In short, while there are flashes of excellence, there has not been a consistent approach to the integration of new doctrines and technologies using the scientific method.

Similar parallels may be drawn for the navy and air force. The Canadian escort groups in the Second World War suffered from lack of effective radar, which, together with the rapid expansion of the navy, reduced their effectiveness. There was little time or energy during the war available for either collective training or experimentation. By the 1960s, however, the Canadian Navy led in the invention of the beartrap device for hauling down maritime helicopters onto a frigate deck and trialed a hydrofoil. The air force, unable to play an air-to-ground role during the Persian Gulf War of 1991, learned its lesson, acquired a limited laser targeting capability and was ready for the Kosovo air campaign, albeit with limited quantities of guidance pods and precision ammunition. A lesson from history is that the less money available for Defence in peacetime, the greater is the portion that should be used for experimentation, trial, and concept development, so that when crises and funding become available, the force is ready to adapt quickly.

The equivalent business notion is one of early or late adopters of new ideas. The art form for a middle power is to avoid being on the expensive bleeding edge of advanced Research and Development, but rather slightly behind the leader, ready to adopt once the initial problems are cracked.

Experimental capabilities in small quantities may have a disproportionate effect on the battlespace. When the German Army attacked the USSR in 1941, it did so with six million men, 650,000 horses and only 3,350 tanks.[3] Yet it was the small proportion of tanks, together with a relevant operational doctrine, ironically developed in peacetime using Russian training areas to avoid allied observation, which influenced the initial results more than any other. Equally, as the USSR mustered its economy and out-generated Germany in the production of mechanized forces, the student overcame the master.[4] As a more recent example of a small number of systems with excellent doctrine making a huge impact, the US deployed JSTARS aircraft from a Research and Development status into operations in the Persian Gulf campaign of 1991, providing an excellent common operating picture.

Planning Horizons

An important notion introduced in the *Defence Planning Guidance 2000* is that of horizons, shown in Figure 4-2. Horizon 3 (10-30 years) can be described only in conceptual terms using demographic trends, parametric forecasting techniques and alternate futures methods. Horizon 2 (5-15 years) has a strong conceptual base and should be planned out in some detail. Horizon 1 (1-5 years) is generally unambiguous and fully programmed in resource terms supported by a solid basis in concept and plan. While there is always the potential for discontinuities at the program level due to fiscal, geo-political or technological surprise, evolutionary program management approaches are more effective than revolutionary ones. Surprise is not a principle of administration.

Force Planning Horizons

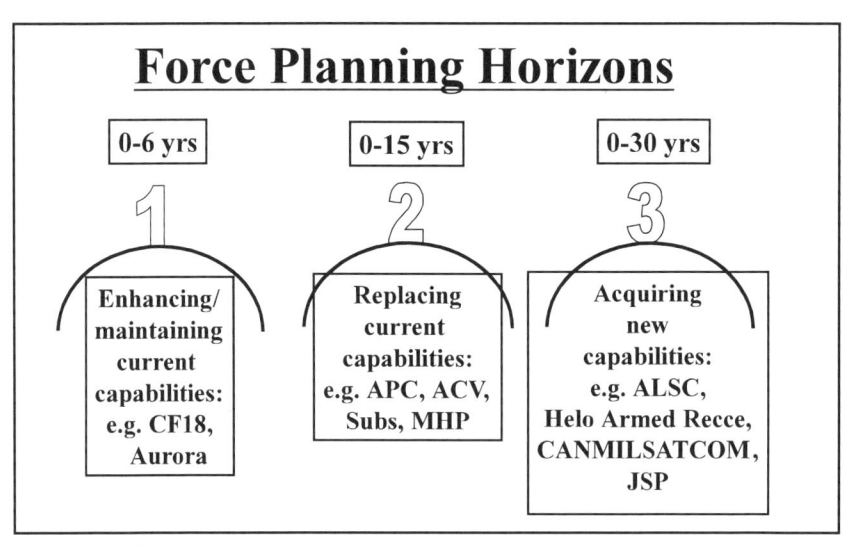

0-6 yrs	0-15 yrs	0-30 yrs
1	2	3
Enhancing/ maintaining current capabilities: e.g. CF18, Aurora	Replacing current capabilities: e.g. APC, ACV, Subs, MHP	Acquiring new capabilities: e.g. ALSC, Helo Armed Recce, CANMILSATCOM, JSP

Figure 4-2 Planning Horizons

Adoption flexibility in the short term is effectively limited to "Miscellaneous Requirements" and the non-strategic capital program. Horizon 2 from 5-15 years offers important opportunities for strategic investment while consideration of horizon 3 opportunities permits imagination unfettered by program resource realities. As technology accelerates, these time horizons will compress.

The use of horizons will allow defence planners to move from the highly programmed short-term perspective to the opportunities presented in the long-term future. Horizons 2 and 3 planning are amenable to the application of a range of business and defence planning tools including operations research techniques. There are significant choices to be made from the traditional to the transformational, as well as the spectrum in between.

The State of the Defence Capital Investment Process

Concept Development and Experimentation. Canada has begun to explore experimentation both at a single service and joint level. A set of initiatives under the rubric of Concept Development and Experimentation is now underway as part of a reborn force development process. This process also includes strategic capability planning, in turn linked to simulation and modeling activities, the Research and Development program and procurement reform to reduce the time of the acquisition cycle by thirty percent. There are further connections to the national joint training program, with the idea that at least fifteen to twenty percent of all major collective training exercises would be devoted to experimentation with new concepts, different ways of employing existing capabilities and trials of new equipment types, all in concert with our principal allies.

Rate of Adoption. As Canada engages increasingly in area control operations in all three environments, it is time to consider our adaptation rate for new capabilities. The attack helicopter and Unmanned Air Vehicle (UAV) proved to be pivotal in the US Army's Force XXI experimentation at Fort Irwin, California in 1998.[5] Are we late to need in adopting the armed helicopter as we were in adopting the Bren Gun Carrier in 1938? Space capabilities supporting navigation, telecommunications and surveillance are available to Canada either from our allies or from the commercial sector. What space-based capability choices will we make and in partnership with whom? What kinds of strategic lift capabilities are appropriate to Canada's isolation on the North American continent? At what point should Canada consider having these capabilities in the operational inventory, even in limited quantities? Is experimentation through loans, prototypes or combined exercises the most appropriate way to make informed decisions?

Long Term Capital Plan. The Long Term Capital Plan (LTCP) approved in June 2000, is the first effective plan produced since 1996. Since that time the ability to articulate a capital investment program has been stymied by three obstacles. First, there was no strategic vision beyond horizon 1. *Defence Strategy 2020* now provides a long-term context for force development and resource allocation. Second, there was insufficient funding to permit consideration of any course of action much more than patching up existing platforms. The government has now provided additional funding in the 2000 Federal Budget. Third, there was no conceptual framework such as the Canadian Joint Task List to allow a top-down program to be formulated in any balanced way across strategic, operational and tactical elements. The Strategic Capability Plan providing the necessary framework has now been exposed to academia and approved by senior management. The three obstacles have therefore been effectively removed. The resultant LTCP can now include elements permitting the CF to become modern, interoperable and globally deployable with modest and tailored exploitation of Revolution in Military Affairs (RMA) concepts.

Domestic Realities

In Canada there are important realities which require connecting the capability requirements to the domestic economic and political national interests. It has historically been easier given Canadian values to obtain approval for non-weapon systems projects than those with high lethality such as fighters or tanks. Not only the nature of the system but also domestic stakeholder inputs need consideration. Industrial, regional and aboriginal issues need to be integrated early at both the program and project levels. This is a particular issue in the aerospace industry, especially as Canada has little indigenous military aircraft industry at the system level.

Canadian-US bilateral issues need to be explored, recognizing that defence generally seeks a greater degree of bilateral integration and cooperation than the foreign policy desires to permit. Canada's defence industry cannot exist supporting the CF alone, and is effectively integrated in a North American industrial base supporting a global arms industry. Globalization of defence is proceeding apace as in all other industries. The historic Canada-US linkage is becoming more tenuous given changes to the government's defence industry support program controlled by Industry Canada and by US tightening up of the regulations on arms trading.[6] In summary, the classic Canadian middle power role supporting peacekeeping must however adapt to the more volatile world of ad hoc coalitions, continental and global industrial base realities and defence of national vital interests in partnership with major allies.

In terms of military capabilities, the Canadian public is generally more amenable to technological or national reputation arguments rather than to geo-political ones which it understands less well. Acquiring new capabilities requires careful consideration of the public policy arguments, Canadian values and the Canada-US dimension. As exemplified by the attempt to acquire nuclear-powered submarines following the 1987 White Paper and the more recent export permit debate on Radarsat 2, the American dimension should not be underestimated. In all cases a public information campaign is required to ensure that the issues are well understood and positioned.

PART 5 DEFENCE PROGRAM ISSUES

This section will review selected issues in defence program management beginning with the key feedback processes of performance and risk management. The issue of the changing direct threat to the homeland will be introduced. Six contemporary issues will then be explored, and conclusions drawn.

Performance Measurement

Within Defence the strategic resource allocation and business planning processes are reasonably mature. In horizon 1, however, it is performance management which provides immediate feedback from operations for force development. Metaphorically policy and strategy provide the central thrustlines while business planning provides a matrix of coordination. Performance measurement is then the mirror against which our efforts to provide defence can be seen. This is shown in Figure 5-1.

The government wants departments to manage for results.[7] Over the next five years it is essential to establish a self-assessing performance measurement

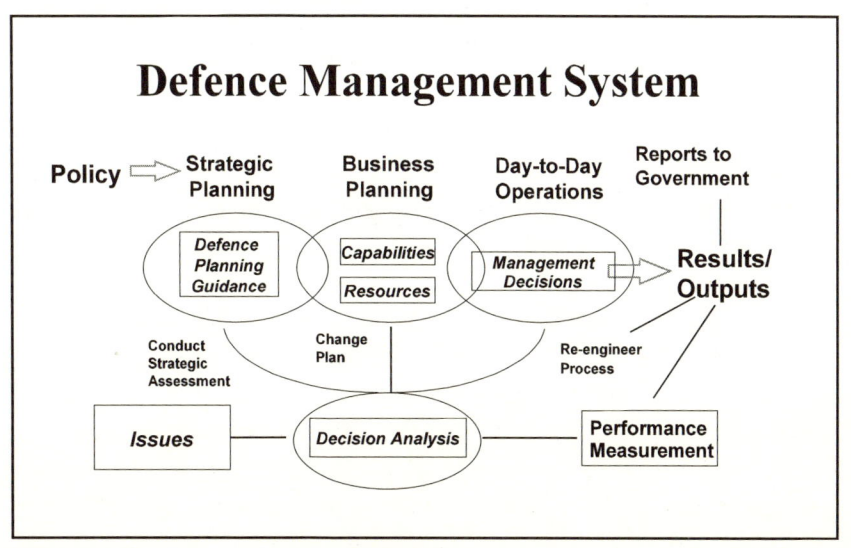

Figure 5-1 The Defence Management System

regime at all levels. This will require that we move from a reward/blame paradigm to one of continuous organizational learning leading to constant improvement. As industry has shown in their ISO 9000 processes, quality can be achieved only through constant attention to business fundamentals. To keep operations effective requires strong performance monitoring and rapid corrective action. This is in addition to audit and evaluation which continues to provide in-depth examination of the degree to which program elements are essential and objectives achieved.

Risk Management

Performance measurement at the operational level is, however, not enough. Defence needs to manage risk effectively at the strategic, operational and tactical levels. As an example, in 1995, Canadian Airlines International set out a strategy of exploiting the growing Asia Pacific routes and determined at the operational level to achieve zero variances on its scheduled aircraft push-off times. It had determined that each minute of delay cost $50 in lost customer satisfaction and aircraft utilization. It monitored its departure performance daily, and achieved a degree of excellence in terms of on-time departure consistency through electronic monitoring and rapid executive follow-up on unsatisfactory trends.[8] In spite of operational excellence the company's strategy was not robust when the Asian economy entered a prolonged recession in 1998. As a result CAI was absorbed by Air Canada in 1999. The moral of this example is that even with excellent operations, a flawed strategy ultimately produces failure.

From a strategic perspective the requirement is for comprehensive risk management supporting the corporate strategy. *Defence Strategy 2020*, although designed to be as robust as possible across alternative futures, could be marginalized through controllable or non-controllable factors. Examples of controllable factors could include another Somalia-type atrocity committed by Canadian soldiers or a major Crown project experiencing expensive and reputation-damaging cost overruns. Non-controllable factors also need to be forecast and mitigated. These could include, for example, election of a political party hostile to Defence, the end of peacekeeping as we know it, large casualties on an international operation leading to loss of support for international operations or a radical new technology fundamentally altering warfare. It is therefore vital to return to the assumptions underlying the strategy and to test them against experience coming from the real world. The risks implicit in the strategy must be managed proactively. Risk management is to strategy as performance measurement is to operations. Both are essential.

Direct Threat to the Nation's Homeland

The issue of strategic partnering addressed by *Defence Strategy 2020* needs additional emphasis. Historically, Canada has faced little direct threat in its homeland other than intercontinental ballistic missile attack. In a global economy, however, there are new vulnerabilities opened up by trade. Cyber-attack, biological or chemical attack and classic terrorism with or without weapons of mass destruction now potentially threaten the survival and sovereignty of the nation.

Canada lives next door to the world's only superpower. One potential US trend is the attempt to create the world's first gated community. As the US continues to play the role of the world's policeman, particularly in areas of its vital national interest such as in the Middle East, Europe and the Pacific, potential adversaries may choose to carry their conflicts into the US heartland. Cultural and economic disparities have the potential to create the motivation to find gaps in continental defences.[9] The open border provides little collateral damage protection against asymmetric threats directed to the US.

Asymmetric warfare requires profound shifts in the responsiveness and coordination of multiple domestic agencies across the federal-provincial-municipal spectrum and with the US federal and state governments. We are not ready or rehearsed as a nation for asymmetric attack catastrophe. There was an abortive attempt to deal with nuclear recovery operations in the early 1960s through the so-called "snakes and ladders" program. The Operation Abacus template is likely more realistic and needs to be both refined and exercised. The domestic response needs to have high reserve content with specialist skills, e.g., NBC attack diagnostic response, which can be rapidly engaged on a local basis through telecommunications connectivity. This response requirement is measured in minutes and hours rather than weeks and months, and needs a new paradigm not dissimilar to that provided by municipal emergency services, albeit on a national scale.

Emerging Issues

There are six emerging issues in program management of which general and flag officers should be conscious. Each of these issues requires further development across several posting cycles.

Costing. Resource management requires a solid understanding of the cost structures underlying the activities. What does it cost to commission a ship following refit? What is the true cost of qualifying an F-18 pilot to four-plane lead status? What is the relative cost of a Reserve versus a Regular Force member? Only through a program of activity-based costing can we understand the cost structures and business cases, producing appropriate trade-off decisions.

Understanding the real costs will lead to better organization, will support investment in innovation and will reduce the wastage of scarce resources into low value/high cost activities.

Capitalization of skills and knowledge. In the feudal age land was the primary resource and wealth was measured in terms of land owned. In the industrial age we valued capital stock such as machinery and described it as "assets" on a "balance sheet." Assets were depreciated for tax purposes. At the same time we expensed employees to the "income statement." As we move into the information age it is the skills and knowledge held corporately and individually which will become the real asset.[10] What is the capital value of the aforementioned four-plane lead CF-18 pilot whom we have trained for several years and over one thousand hours of flight time? How should we value the doctor whom we sponsored through five years of subsidized medical training? What is the real value of the Trade Qualification 6 naval electronic sensor operator? What is the value of our doctrine and all the information held in our data bases? While our real strength is based upon people, process, and information holdings, we fail to measure this at all well on any real accounting basis. We continue to provide training courses at a rate far beyond the private sector, yet fail entirely to identify the opportunity cost of early retirements and non re-engagement. Accrual accounting will bring in an industrial age accounting system. How will we handle the information age?

Management Integration. The Defence Management System (DMS) and its implicit devolution is designed for a defence management regime of limited transparency. Were transparency to improve, devolution could increase. As in industry, there is a need for full visibility and connectivity of management across the enterprise functions, geography and strategic business units. As the corporate applications (FMAS, Peoplesoft, MASIS, CFSSU, and CFCS) begin to converge into a single enterprise system, there is a fundamental need for an integrated business model and architecture to make sense of the relationships. Use of the Zachman architecture and object-oriented data bases may one day truly permit the full integration of departmental management functions. The definition phase of the Integrated Defence Management Framework project is now underway.

Human Resource Issues. The Canadian Forces continues to have an industrial age military occupation structure. There are one hundred and six classifications for officers and NCOs with overlaps and duplications. Great strides have been made in combining classifications, especially within single environments, however, there is significant distance to go, particularly for those occupations crossing environmental lines. We need increased flexibility and to better exploit the innate capabilities of our CF members. Is the relationship between officers and NCMs the same as it once was? Has the information age not changed the way we perceive our functions?

Organizational Issues. There is room for significant simplification of the CF organizational structure. If indeed joint operations are now the norm, could we not move to a single service functional structure for the CF, with three functional three-star commanders under the CDS for operational forces, support capabilities and training and doctrine activities? As we converge toward a single enterprise management system, could we not reduce to fewer ADMs for support services? If Ford can design and produce its cars on a global basis, can we not achieve true organizational integration with only a hundred thousand people in a single country? What is the right mix of flat organizational structures in the defence enterprise?

Marketing. Few parliamentarians or members of the national élite now have military experience. In order to have enlightened support, it is now essential to market defence actively in order that informed choices can be made. The UK now runs two-week orientation programs for its parliamentarians with extensive time with members of the force. It is likely time to extend the outreach program to more active but compressed training at the experiential level for the national public and private sector élites. As an example, a seven- to ten-day program could include time with some or all of an infantry battalion, on a ship or submarine, in fixed and rotary wing aircraft, deployment on an international operation and a counter-terrorist demonstration. Orientation such as this would pay great dividends in the case of national emergencies, international deployment decisions and defence policy reviews. In any event, Defence needs to market its capabilities and services in order to stay connected with the government, which may only infrequently face the option of using the CF in combat.

CONCLUSION

This chapter has examined the fundamentals of defence program management from an historical, public policy and internal management perspective. It has examined the structure and associated processes of the Defence program. The capital program was described. Key issues in defence resource management were identified. As the network of trained and experienced resource managers and business planners solidifies, we will move culturally closer to the ideal of obtaining maximum value from our resources.

The challenge for the general and flag officer is to retain operational currency as a military professional while simultaneously becoming expert in operational and strategic level resource allocation issues. Is it still acceptable that "One's stand depends upon where one sits"?[11] How do we achieve a collective vision amongst the General Officer Corps when most officers spend a relatively short portion of their career at the executive level?

The classic parochial single service views are increasingly being tempered and molded by a joint and corporate perspective. The Canadian Forces label is becoming more than just an administrative or legal construct, indeed, it is on track to become an integrated organization capable of managing complex global or domestic missions in a dynamic joint, combined and inter-agency construct. Horizontally—connected management of the corporate, support services, force generation and force employment processes are producing synergy and value. Equally the Department is becoming more closely connected with other horizontal and vertical government objectives and processes. In summary, executive military excellence demands comprehensive leadership and program management skills.

NOTES

1. J.A. English, *Failure in High Command-The Canadian Army and the Normandy Campaign.* (Don Mills, ON: Oxford University Press Canada, 1991), 262-267.
2. Ibid, 266.
3. Richard Overy, *Why the Aliens Won* (London: Pimico, 1996), 5.
4. Ibid, 212.
5. Visit by the author to Fort Monmouth, New York in 1998.
6. A.D. Edgar, and D.G. Haglund, *The Canadian Defence Industry in the New Global Environment* (Montréal: McGill University Press, 1995), 85.
7. Canada, *Managing for Results* (Ottawa, ON: Treasury Board, 2000).
8. Presentation by CAI at a symposium on performance measurement, Computing Devices (Calgary, Alberta: 1996).
9. S.P. Huntington, *The Clash of Civilizations and the Remaking of the World Order,* (New York: Touchstone, 1996), 212-217.
10. T.A. Stewart, *Intellectual Capital* (New York: Currency/Doubleday, 1999), 84.
11. Often quoted by Mr P. Lagueux, former Assistant Deputy Minister (Materiel), to explain the lack of a corporate perspective.

The Flag and General Officer as a Resource Manager

Vice-Admiral Gary L. Garnett

Vice-Admiral Gary L. Garnett is the current CF Vice Chief of the Defence Staff.

LEADERS ARE RESOURCE MANAGERS. This role is not new and is totally consistent with our military culture. Terminology and techniques may have changed over the years, but this does not in any way alter the fundamental responsibility of leaders at all levels for the judicious allocation and expenditure of resources.

The art and science of leadership has many facets, some of which are perhaps more evident than others. A flag or general officer must be capable—indeed, accomplished—in the employment of traditional military leadership techniques; that is to say, in inspiring his or her subordinates to accomplish their assigned objectives in the manner desired by the leader. In this sense, operational or combat command is and will always be the foundation upon which all military leadership is built.

Leadership comes in many shapes and forms, as varied and diverse as the almost infinite array of tasks that a leader may be called upon to fulfil. Capable leaders tailor their problem-solving approach and leadership styles to the needs of the moment. The role of the senior leader at the strategic and operational levels, at which the majority of Canada's general and flag officers work and operate in peace and war alike, often demands an "institutional" approach to leadership. Needless to say, the effective, efficient and imaginative management of resources is one of the most intricate and challenging aspects of institutional leadership.

The Department of National Defence (DND) and the Canadian Forces (CF) are large, complex organizations that are collectively charged with the gravest of responsibilities—the defence and support of the interests of Canadians and the policies of their government, both at home and abroad. In order to fulfil these duties, DND/CF is annually accorded a significant proportion of the national wealth, the judicious expenditure of which is an equally grave and challenging responsibility, particularly during periods of fiscal restraint such as were experienced during the 1990s. Additionally, heightened public interest in and scrutiny of the internal workings of public institutions has led Canadians to demand that government departments, DND/CF included, practice, and be seen to be practicing, logical, responsible, transparent and results-based resource management—in short, they want to see their tax dollars handled with the utmost in care and probity, and they want value for their money. In a decade characterized by declining manning levels and increasing operational tempos, the senior leadership of the Department and the Canadian Forces have had to learn to walk a tightrope, balancing resources against risk in order to achieve all assigned tasks within the scope of what has until recently been a constantly shrinking resource envelope.

Such an environment demands that leaders understand, practice and work to improve efficient, innovative and technically sound resource management practices, while at the same time working to evolve the institution in order to create an environment conducive to those practices taking hold. Leading and commanding effectively in the modern resource environment demands personnel capable of exercising foresight and initiative at the macro-level, keeping the core business of defence—combat capability—firmly in mind.

RESOURCE MANAGEMENT DEFINED

Every successful senior military commander in history has demonstrated, if not mastery of, at least competence in managing resources. Whether husbanding personnel, baggage animals, ammunition, fuel, food or forage and ensuring that these were provided at the right time and place, and in the right condition and quantity; the skilled application and employment of resources has always been an enduring characteristic of good generalship. Conflict between armed forces from peace support operations to war creates a massive demand for national resources, a demand that has increased exponentially over the past century as warfare has been successively and fundamentally altered by industrialization, mechanization and digitization. Our ability to generate, sustain and employ military forces depends upon how the senior leaders view and approach the management of resources.

Fundamentally, resource management is all about making the right resources available at the time and place necessary to accomplish military objectives. One school of thought advances a maximalist approach to the resource management side of leadership—making all possible resources available to their subordinates all the time. This approach is idealistic and has never worked, because it fails to recognize that resources are always finite and must be jealously husbanded. Failure to ensure the provision of resources has doomed scores of ambitious undertakings, including but not limited to the invasion of Russia by both Napoleon and Hitler. Commanders must apply resources as judiciously as one would apply firepower—with great care, great accuracy and in precisely the right quantity to ensure that the job gets done. Doing so demands not only ability, but also the courage to establish priorities, to make unpopular decisions for the greater good, and to husband resources such that the unit, formation or institution succeeds when and where it needs to succeed.

Every leader in the Canadian Forces has a tactical role, many have operational-level roles, and a small few have strategic roles. In much the same way that the commanding officer of an armoured regiment is expected to fight his own tank, all leaders have a measure of tactical-level resource management responsibility. Purely tactical leaders must allocate and expend resources—including human resources—wisely. Formation, area and environmental commanders work and manage resources at the operational level, assigning tactical-level objectives and the resources to enable subordinate organizations to meet them. This is arguably the most challenging resource management role, as the "flash-to-bang time" of the decision-making process is considerably shorter than at the strategic level, and the immediate impact of the decisions made can be further reaching and far more pervasive. Finally, commanders and group principles together act as a strategic body in support of the Chief of the Defence Staff (CDS) and Deputy Minister (DM)—who, supported by the Vice Chief of the Defence Staff (VCDS), are the senior strategic resource managers for DND and the CF.

Resource management is a military art that has its roots in business science. The fact that much of today's resource management terminology is derived from lessons learned by civilian enterprise has created a specialized vocabulary that tends to alienate military people because it somehow seems "un-soldier-like." This perception is ironic, given that the business schools responsible for the development of much of contemporary business management philosophy and techniques are themselves the offspring of the military staff colleges of the late nineteenth and early twentieth century, and that for the past decade, civilian executives have been feverishly studying classical military treatises such as Carl von Clausewitz's *On War*, Sun Tzu's *The Art of War*, and Miyamoto Musashi's *A Book of Five Rings* in an effort to improve their leadership and management techniques. The connection between military thought and resource management is firm and long-standing. Therefore, it is perhaps most appropriate to briefly examine the three levels of military command in order to discern their distinct roles in military resource management.

The Tactical Level—*Resource Consumption*

Both during operations, and in the course of day-to-day training, maintenance and administration, leaders at the tactical level—the "coal face"—expend resources. The tactical leader's role in resource management, therefore, is primarily the optimization of resource consumption—deriving the most benefit from the expenditure of assigned resources. At this level, commanders have complete flexibility in the use of assigned resources, but somewhat less flexibility in acquiring additional resources or in maintaining resource reserves. The business planning process is in part predicated on the fact that, given appropriate higher-level guidance (and in some cases, higher-level boundaries or constraints), the tactical leader is best placed to make an accurate estimate of probable future resource requirements. The tactical leader's role, therefore, must be to identify resource requirements clearly, usually through a careful analysis of historical activity levels and resource requirements, and conduct detailed planning to make use of assigned resources in the most efficient fashion possible. The true challenge to leadership at the tactical level emerges when resources become scarce—and they always do.

The Operational Level—*Resource Allocation*

The role of the operational level, in resource management as in war, is to exploit tactical activities to create the conditions for strategic success. The role of the operational level resource manager, therefore, is to ensure that resources are allocated judiciously so as to ensure that the right tactical level leaders have the right resources at the right time to enable them to produce the tactical successes needed to achieve strategic aims. Resource allocation at the operational level demands not only a detailed knowledge of tactical activities, but also a firm grasp of the overall strategic aims established by higher commanders, in order to permit the operational commander to allocate resources with full knowledge of the "cause and effect" relationship between support and activity. He requires not only the courage to choose where (and where not) to allocate scarce resources, but the courage (and foresight) to maintain a reserve.

The Strategic Level—*Resource Management*

True "resource management," in the modern sense of the phrase, occurs at the strategic level. The role of the strategic commander is to look well into the future and attempt to make accurate predictions of resource requirements in order to ensure that the resource base is appropriate to evolving needs. The strategic level macro-allocates resources, and in so doing determines the landscape of, and sets the conditions for, operational and tactical success. Shortsightedness at the strategic level means downstream problems for subordinate levels.

The strategic level seeks to maintain balance where balance is important, and attempts through careful historical and predictive analysis to determine whether the best interests of the institution will be served by a "steady as she goes" approach, or if in fact a change of course may be required. At the strategic level, resource management demands that leaders make choices, the impact of which may only be felt years or even decades down the road. For example, at the departmental level it takes ten to fifteen years to transform Program into Capability, a time lag that we are striving to shorten. The role of the resource manager, therefore, is ultimately about developing an institutional vision, and then using that vision as a guide to establish and enforce resource allocation priorities. Long-range targets are flexible and may be adjusted to respond to changing circumstances. As a result, the impact of priority setting at the strategic level is rarely as immediate or dramatic as at the tactical or operational levels. Strategic priorities are, however, fundamental to the long-term viability of the institution.

HISTORICAL BACKGROUND

Prior to integration of the Department of National Defence and the Canadian Forces in the 1960s, the senior civilian personnel in the Deputy Minister's office had primary responsibility for resource management at the strategic level. Canadian Forces officers were rarely involved.

At the operational level, senior CF officers were primarily concerned with providing direction to their assigned military forces, and they worked within strict resource management rules and guidelines. Generally they had little flexibility or scope for initiative in resource management issues. Indeed, there was little if any awareness of the costs generated or resources consumed by defence activity. Rules were generally followed and someone else, usually in National Defence Headquarters (NDHQ), paid the bill.

At the tactical level, officers did the best they could with the resources they were provided, again within strict rules and procedures established by higher authority. There was little if any flexibility in assigning resources. There was even less ability to influence the allocation of resources as given by higher headquarters.

With the establishment of an integrated NDHQ, flag and general level officers worked alongside their civilian counterparts within DND and the government. However, only a few officers became intimately involved in resource management at the strategic level, and these were mainly in the non-operational side of NDHQ. The majority of flag and general officers within the military sections of the national headquarters had little if any involvement in resource management (with the exception of those in the personnel branch who were responsible for the control of military human resources). At the operational and tactical levels, the situation with respect to resource management remained basically the same as prior to integration.

With the evolution of NDHQ, and the strengthening of the Vice-Chief of the Defence Staff position in the 1970s and 1980s, a limited number of flag and general officers became increasingly involved in strategic resource management. However, it was not until the late 1980s and early 1990s—the era of consecutive budget cuts and, most importantly, the need to fund the *1994 Defence White Paper*—that senior military officers began to be expected to become much more expert in all aspects of resource management. With the implementation of the White Paper Program Review (1 and 2), this expectation evolved from a need to an absolute necessity.

TRENDS IN DEFENCE RESOURCE MANAGEMENT

The 1990s bore witness to the greatest evolution to date, in terms of resource management, in the history of DND and the CF. Prior to the Base Delegation of Authority and Accountability Trial (DelegAAT) and the adoption of the principle of devolution in business planning, resource management was often considered a mere accounting exercise. However, this evolution unleashed the power of resource management, conducted by leaders and managers at all levels—and matched it to an equally awesome responsibility.

Devolution

Born in the era of downsizing and severe resource reduction, devolution, along with the concomitant allocation of accountability and responsibility, has simultaneously emancipated and empowered leaders and managers. For those who understood the imperatives and were prepared to take risks and meet challenges head-on, the rewards were great. For those who chose to ignore the possibilities or were insulated from the process by the chain of command, the results were disappointing, and led to the uneven success and slow implementation of business planning in some commands. Nevertheless, the complimentary devolution of authority and responsibility for resource management for the first time gave leaders at all levels a voice in how and where resources were assigned. This is a fundamental principle of resource management.

DelegAAT

DelegAAT was an early experiment conducted in 1994 by the Assistant Deputy Minister (Finance) and his staff. Its goal was to demonstrate, to all who cared to look, the type and range of innovations and savings that could be achieved through devolution due to the removal of the myriad of centrally controlled processes and the elimination of what has been referred to as a "risk-adverse rule set." The timing could not have been better, as this was a key to the success of meeting the resource reductions of Defence Expenditure Review (DER) 94, and Program Reviews 1 and 2 whilst in the main, preserving the efficacy of the "sharp end" of the Canadian Forces.

D2000

Called by different names by different groups, the principles of Defence 2000 have proved to be powerful tools in involving all institutional leaders, managers and stakeholders in the business of managing resources, making savings and having the authority to invest some of those monies back into the institution. Those on the "shop floor" and those involved in customer service were given the opportunity to identify inherent inefficiencies, and demonstrate how to overcome them. Participants needed to be motivated to join in and accept responsibility for their portion of the enterprise, however small. D2000 demonstrated to all participants how small investments could, and did, lead to significant baseline savings. One of the underlying principles was that employees must have a stake in success—the individual or individuals initiating the savings must benefit from them. This principle was put to work by numerous leaders and managers, often with surprising results.

The Strategic Level

At the strategic level in NDHQ, flag and general officers were heavily involved in establishing DelegAAT, the business planning process, D2000 and the Management, Command and Control Re-engineering Team (MCCRT).

Resource management expanded from those officers within the domain of Associate Deputy Minister (Materiel) (ADM(Mat)), Associate Deputy Minister (Infrastructure and Environment) (ADM (IE)) and Associate Deputy Minister (Finance) (ADM(Fin)) to include flag and general officers throughout NDHQ, eventually growing to include the VCDS, Deputy Chief of the Defence Staff (DCDS), and Associate Deputy Minister (Personnel).

At the operational level, commanders were delegated full authority over their operating budgets, flexibility in their allocations and the ability to carry over a portion of their funds. This had a tremendous impact on the roles played by flag and general officers. They now needed to understand their resource bases, establish priorities, see the opportunities for trade-offs, approve initiatives to exploit opportunities, and make one-and two-year investments.

At the tactical level, commanders empowered by the business planning process and establishment of single operating budgets had a significant increase in flexibility to assign resources to activities. Every item and activity was recognized as having a dollar value. At this level commanders become the fundamental business planners of the Canadian Forces, a distinct and important—and unprecedented—responsibility.

Throughout, as resource management rules and regulations gradually became more flexible, there was a greater need for senior officers to provide subordinates with clear direction, and hold them accountable for the effective and efficient use of the resources they had been allocated. Flag and general officers in turn became increasingly responsible for ensuring that national-level systems were established to achieve and maintain control throughout the resource management domain, and exercise ongoing responsibility for the effective operation of such systems.

RESOURCES DEFINED

The realm and scope of resource management extends well beyond the world of finance, budgets, dollars and cents. It is therefore necessary to define precisely what we mean by "resources." The Defence resource base is made up of human resources—our people; capital resources—our equipment and infrastructure; financial resources—the Defence Budget; and, intellectual capital—our knowledge and ethos.

An added dimension that must always be taken into consideration when determining limitations to our resource base is time, because it is the one resource that is always beyond our control. Management of the resource base cannot be limited to today's terms. We must consider, particularly at the strategic level, the management of our future resource base—how to define it, how to build it, how to sustain it and how to improve it. Indeed, even where change and reform are demanded, how to institutionalize it. Often considered an implacable enemy in military operations, time can even be turned to our advantage through careful planning and foresight.

Human Resources

Our people and their families are not only our most important asset; they are a precious national resource that we manage on behalf of the country. The human part of our resource base is an extended family comprising more than half a million Canadians, made up of 60,000 Regular Force personnel in more than a hundred military occupations; 30,000 Primary Reserves; 65,000 Supplementary Reserves; 20,000 civilian employees; 60,000 cadets with a further 6,000 Cadet Instructor Cadre and 8,000 Civilian Instructors; 5,000 Canadian Rangers and (800) Junior Rangers; 150,000 veterans and annuitants, and 130,000 family members. Management of human resources is designed to do one thing—to put the right person with the right skills in the right place at the right time, now and in the future. To do this we must create an environment that attracts and retains highly skilled and motivated people. The creation of such an environment depends on the ability of senior management to balance the needs of the service against the needs of the individual.

Financial Resources

The Defence Budget or annual reference level is a vital, and perhaps the best known, element of our resource base. Since the inception of the government's Expenditure Management System, budget planning has become far more predictable, allowing for the evolution of a true strategic planning capability. The current annual financial resource base consists of slightly over $10 billion, divided as follows: 32.5% into operating budgets and various corporate accounts; 31.5% in CF personnel; 14% in capital (a cumulative 19% once parts of other budget areas are factored in); 13% in national procurement; 7% in statutory payments; and 2% in grants and contributions. Strategic resource management in this area focuses on achieving the best possible balance among the various allocations and between the Level 1 managers. With a substantially reduced budget since 1994, the challenge of maintaining an appropriate balance has been enormous. Our force structure is directly affected by the balance we maintain. We must continually ask ourselves questions, such as "how much do we balance the requirement to spend on equipment against the need to spend on personnel?" Is it worth having more people with obsolete equipment, or fewer people with the best equipment? And, how do we invest in the future when nearly every penny is being consumed by present requirements?

The only way to ensure that the correct balance is found is to develop a vision—one that has been derived through rigorous analytical methodology, and one that can be regularly measured, revisited and tested. The development of such a vision is the fundamental purpose of the DND keystone strategic guidance document, *Shaping the Future of Canadian Defence: A Strategy for 2020* (*Strategy 2020*).

Equipment

Due to the aging state of the military inventory of the Canadian Forces, capital investment has been assigned a relatively high priority over recent years, and we need to invest even more to ensure that the CF will remain relevant in the increasingly complex and lethal battlespace of the future. Our major systems can be roughly divided into three categories in terms of system life. Our newer systems, including the Light Armoured Vehicle (LAV III), the Coyote, the Victoria Class submarines, the Halifax Class frigates, and the Griffon helicopter are in their initial years of service with well over fifty percent of useful life remaining. Approximately $1.5 billion of approved program remains to complete the acquisition of our newer systems. The next category contains those systems approaching "life-out" or those with considerably less than fifty percent of their useful life remaining. These systems include our fleets of trucks, our small arms, the Tribal Class Destroyers (DDH 280s), and the Auxiliary Oiler Replenishment ships (AORs). The replacement cost for the systems is in the order of $11 billion, of which $2 billion is approved in the program. The last category contains those systems facing or already in "rust-out," either with very little useful life remaining or well beyond projected retirement date. These systems include the M109 Self-Propelled Gun, the Leopard Main Battle Tank (MBT), the M113 Armoured Personnel Carrier (APC), and the majority of our airframes. Replacement cost for these systems is on the order of $15 billion, with some $2.5 billion in the approved program.

Managing our capital, however, is more than finding ways to replace old equipment. Senior leadership must shape how we will fight and operate in the future and, using a top-down approach, determine acquisition priorities within the context of our defence objectives and strategic goals. Again the tough questions are; how will we fight in the future, and what will we need to succeed? What capabilities do we start changing and developing now so that we can excel later? Long term capability planning is being built around our vision of the future—and *Strategy 2020* is the document that provides shape and guidance to the exercise.

Infrastructure

As the single largest government department and one of the largest institutions in the country, we are also responsible for the management of almost half of the entire infrastructure holdings of government. We lease or have custodial responsibility for more than 900 sites, and manage some 2 million hectares of land, approximately 24,000 buildings, and some 20,000 married quarters. We service 5900 kilometers (km) of roads, 1750 km of fencing, and 3000 km of underground piping. Forty-four percent of our infrastructure is more than forty years old, and only fifteen percent is less than ten years old. In sum, our infrastructure assets are worth on the order of $23 billion.

Managing such an enormous and diverse array of infrastructure is a constant challenge. It is difficult to divest the Department of infrastructure assets in any meaningful way without the issue becoming political. Re-investment must be considered in the context of our vision for the future, not as a one-for-one replacement exercise. Currently our infrastructure is, on average, in fair to poor condition because we have not invested enough in it. Yet arguably, we have the wrong mix of infrastructure to meet current Defence Support Program delivery, let alone to meet our *Strategy 2020* vision. We are experiencing a simple maintenance backlog worth over $1 billion. If we do not improve our position we could face a situation where, in ten years, fifty percent of our realty assets will be unusable. Another challenge indeed.

Intellectual Capital

The final element of our manageable resource base that must be considered is knowledge. As we move into ever more integrated methods of warfighting, supported by rapidly developing information technology, and applied through increasingly complex weapon systems, the knowledge held by our service personnel and civilian employees will become a source of power unto itself. Futurist authors Alvin and Heidi Toffler had written about Third Wave warfare, and the Drucker Foundation sponsors the notion of "knowledge workers." These concepts are upon us now. Job descriptions are becoming more difficult to write and adhere to, particularly in a headquarters environment, because it is becoming increasingly difficult to categorize what we do into a simple job description.

Because knowledge is most useful in team environments where it may be exploited to maximum advantage, the informal team is becoming a powerful knowledge-based tool. Managing this resource demands that senior leaders avoid the pitfall of trying to "know everything." Instead, we must create an environment where knowledge is cultivated and shared through education and integrated interaction. We must seek to generate desired results, allowing for some maneuvering room in our organizations in order to let our knowledge workers get on with the job of producing results. In such an environment, senior leaders are often best employed in managing the knowledge worker, rather than the knowledge itself.

PLANNING FOR RESOURCE MANAGEMENT
Business Planning

Trying to simultaneously "run the business" and "change the business" requires an integrated, adaptable and flexible planning mechanism—the business planning process. The viability of the process is predicated on a number of key elements, including hierarchical agreements between managers on the prioritization of their piece of the business; the acceptance that a new tasking, when it comes, will supplant the agreed deliverables; and the existence of a tool for measuring results against commitments in order to generate feedback to support the self-correcting nature of the process.

Performance Measurement

Performance measurement is an indispensable element of modern resource management. Through the business planning process, one is able to link resources to activities. Performance measurement then gives the leader an objective view of how effectively resources are being expended, and how necessary the activities are to the overall success of the enterprise. Performance measurement means many things to many people, and its character often depends upon the level at which one is operating. Tactical commanders need feedback on how well they conduct their tasks in relation to activities and standards. For example, a ship or naval squadron will measure their performance in air defence combat to determine whether work-up training was sufficient to enable them to achieve established standards.

Operational level leaders need both hard feedback in relation to standards, and a certain amount of feedback and data from subordinates to generate a higher-level view of success or failure in relation to less tangible questions or issues. The goal of this process is to enable the commander to reallocate resources as necessary, and to make the most efficient use of resource reserves to reinforce success or change course as necessary to ensure tactical success.

The strategic level is probably the most difficult area in which to conduct performance measurement, but it is also the most important. Strategic performance measurement seeks to gain knowledge about the institution as a whole so that long-term decisions can be made to most effectively influence the operational and tactical levels. This is the level where resources must be linked to institutional results. This precludes a simple examination of task by task feedback, for the tasks assigned to lower levels may be achieved, but if they are not the right tasks, then resources have not been allocated appropriately. Feedback at this level must consist of data processed into information, which is then transformed into institutional lessons or knowledge. With knowledge, senior leaders can make the best decisions. It must be remembered that everything has a cost. Therefore, the results must be known in order to enable commanders to manage resources in the best interests of the institution.

EXECUTION OF RESOURCE MANAGEMENT PLANS
Working at NDHQ

Flag and general officers work with DND public servants of equivalent rank. Due to the exigencies of military life, CF personnel are often newly appointed to their positions, and are focussed primarily on the CF. Furthermore, they have limited resource management experience outside of a purely military environment. Conversely, DND public servants are often long-term, experienced personnel who have been in their position or worked in a similar domain for a relatively long period. They tend to be focussed not only on DND, but also on government as a whole, and have often been involved in resource management for many years. They also invariably have an extensive network of colleagues throughout government, from whom advice and assistance may be sought. These differences create a very steep learning curve that senior military officers must negotiate in order to develop the skills and knowledge necessary to be as effective as their civilian counterparts in the area of resource management. That said, flag and general officers have the advantage of having considerably more experience in evaluating and understanding the implications and impact of resource allocation decisions, both on operations in the near term, and on capability in the long term. This mix of knowledge, skills and experience makes for a formidable Defence Team.

In the execution of resource management plans, flag and general officers are expected to work in an environment that requires the development of consensus, the exploitation of innovative approaches, and the exercise of top down direction, while allowing and encouraging bottom-up initiatives. Again, for flag officers and generals that have not had the opportunity to work extensively at a senior level in this type of environment, there is a need to quickly develop new skills to become effective strategic resource managers and "Ottawa interlocutors."

Within National Defence Headquarters, these leaders quickly find that they must interface with organizations and agencies external to defence, such as the Treasury Board, the Department of Finance, the Auditor General and the Privy Council Office. They may also be called upon to appear before the Standing Committee on National Defence and Veterans Affairs (SCONDVA) and, on occasion, before Cabinet. Once again, generals and flag officers are required to develop the confident demeanor and expertise to act effectively in such milieu.

Accountability

The public, and therefore the Department and the CF, are demanding far more financial accountability from our chain of command. This is a result of the devolution of resources to the lowest possible level, while accounting for results at the highest levels. Leaders and commanders must therefore audit themselves. The leadership is ultimately responsible for resource management. This responsibility cannot be delegated to functional specialists. Comptrollers and financial specialists advise, provide scrutiny and ensure technical compliance, but the leader makes the final decision.

As an advisor to commanders, comptrollers play a key role in fostering understanding and application of modern comptrollership and resource management principles. Comptroller support is also key to assisting commanders in understanding the financial implications of decisions before they are taken. Comptrollers are charged with presenting commanders with options and assisting in monitoring compliance. They can also assist commanders with risk management, performance measurement, ensuring the existence of sound internal controls and financial integrity, and objective commentary and independent advice. However, it cannot be over-stressed that comptrollers only provide commanders with specialist support. It is the commanders who are financially accountable.

LEVERAGING

In closing this chapter on the general or flag officer as a resource manager, there are a few areas outside DND/CF that must always be kept in mind as good avenues for leveraging resources. The business community has emerged as an outstanding partner in many initiatives that provide the services needed by defence more cheaply than could be provided within the defence establishment. Moreover, with concepts of innovative financing gaining increasing acceptance, partnering with industry to achieve capital equipment or research and development goals is a must.

Academia is another exceptional area that may be drawn upon to leverage resources. Canadian universities offer excellent middle- to executive-level resource management and strategic thinking courses that can be of enormous benefit to the CF. Through partnerships with leading authorities and academic figures, the CF can learn about the world in which we live, explain our case, and benefit from critique. Our important symposia, such as the Revolution in Military Affairs (RMA) Symposium and Policy Forums, benefit tremendously from interaction with academia.

Finally, we must not ignore past generations of serving military and former DND civilian employees. Their experience and perspective are enormously valuable, more so if they are willing to speak out on important defence topics. It is essential to "keep in touch" and use the old networks to best effect.

THE FUTURE

The adoption of the new government Expenditure Management System and its integration into the Department and the CF has meant that conducting the business of defence like a civilian corporate enterprise is the order of the day. This new approach has been brought about by revolutionary developments in a number of important areas.

Financial Information Strategy

As we move into the future, we must also capitalize on those initiatives that have the potential to further enhance our resource management and performance measurement frameworks. The government's Financial Information Strategy, which encompasses the introduction of accrual accounting, is one such initiative. With this strategy, we will finally be focussing upon the rate at which we consume resources in delivering defence outputs, as opposed to simply the rate at which we spend actual dollars. This will force DND and the CF to look as closely at managing our physical assets as we now do at managing our financial assets. If government goes the additional step of introducing accrual-based appropriations, which consensus suggests it will, then we will enjoy the added benefit of multi-year commitment authority for capital acquisitions. Imagine the flexibility of being allowed to spend perhaps $15 billion in a given year, notwithstanding a limitation of maybe $12 billion in terms of the resources we are actually budgeted to consume in delivering the defence program. The future promises to be very different from today's world.

Integrated Defence Management Framework (IDMF)

The IDMF will further develop modern management practices within DND by providing integrated linkages between business rules, resources, outputs and performance measurement. Inspired by the Zachmann Framework methodology, IDMF will first seek to fully define the business rules within DND, and then link strategic guidance and resource allocations to outputs. The Modern Comptrollership Capacity Check and the Strategic Review of NDHQ Resource Planning and Management Systems both referred to the need for NDHQ to improve planning, structures and processes. They emphasized the importance of developing meaningful connections between resource planning and defence policy, to business planning and outputs. The IDMF will provide the rigorous mechanisms needed to enable the leadership to make tough decisions in the larger interests of the CF. When complete, the IDMF will define the management framework that will support senior management in making decisions, based on timely, accurate and complete information providing a set of common tools. This will be accomplished by conducting a high level review of the current DMS with the aim of achieving full integration.

FINISHED WITH MAIN ENGINES!

For the uninitiated, it is perhaps a bit of a stretch to ponder resource management in the same vein as the heady business of leadership at the flag and general officer level. Nonetheless, it is important to realize that sound leadership at the highest levels demands expertise in resource management. Resource management is a military art. It is one we are all familiar with because at its root lie all of the principles and fundamentals of good combat leadership. All levels of command have a role to play. After all, it is a commander's responsibility.

DND and the CF has undergone tremendous change in the past decade. Everything from our force structure and operational roles to our equipment and corporate obligations have been affected in one way or another. Dealing with this change has been the most significant institutional challenge that the defence establishment has faced in a very long time. Part of the change process has been determining how we must evolve the manner in which we manage the full spectrum of our resources. We have met with considerable success, and have persevered to maintain core capabilities. The success, in large part, has been the result of a change in attitudes about how we run the business of defence.

There should be no doubt in anyone's mind that we are expected to conduct defence more like a business. The Standing Committee on Public Accounts (SCOPA), expects the deputy minister to be able to explain in significant detail where Defence is gaining in efficiency. The auditor general insists that, *inter alia*, materiel acquisition be a logical, integrated, top-down process that generates the proper equipment to perform defence missions. And clearly, the Treasury Board demands that DND and the CF operate as good corporate entities in Ottawa, utilizing modern management practices and getting the most for the defence dollar. In the end, only by taking a logical, structured, transparent and accountable approach to the management of defence resources can we expect to remain capable of fielding the highest quality combat forces for operations.

Contemporary Canadian Generalship and the Art of the Admiral: The Importance of Intellectualism in the General Officer Corps

Lieutenant-General (retired) Robert Morton

Lieutenant-General (retired) Robert Morton is a graduate of the Royal Military College who spent much of his thirty-seven-year career in air operations in Europe and North America, retiring as NORAD Deputy Commander in 1992. He chaired the Officer Development Review Board in 1994-5.

INTRODUCTION

THE PURPOSE OF THIS CHAPTER is to discuss and inform both the internal military audience and the general public on the need to develop officers and prepare them intellectually to serve Canadian society at the most senior levels of military command and experience. The audience has a wide spectrum of knowledge about the profession of arms. Some have years of experience in the Canadian Forces (CF), while others have little or no familiarity at all about military affairs. The concept of professionalism is, therefore, a good place to start. A historical sketch will show how, within the military itself, attitudes and processes on the best way to prepare qualified professionals have been neither homogeneous or smooth; indeed, there were serious stumbles along the way. Finally, some thoughts on the enormous challenge for contemporary military leaders who are faced by a complex and dangerous world and obliged to meet the altering currents of social change in the society they serve. It is a tough time to be a leader.

THE CONCEPT OF PROFESSIONALISM

The word "professional" is often used to mean the opposite of "amateur." The more specific meaning, though, applies to those who work in a social context to perform an essential service to society. In that sense of the word a professional is an expert in his field, having acquired knowledge by long study and practical experience. The knowledge is intellectual in nature. The history of the knowledge is recorded as part of the culture of the society from which it evolved. Within each profession are institutes of education and research that develop, impart, and extend that knowledge throughout its community of practitioners: by in-house study, seminars, the internet, professional journals, and other means. These are characteristics of all professions, including the profession of arms. The means whereby this knowledge is achieved in the military, and why it is so important to the General Officer Corps is the purpose of this chapter.

TRAINING

Training is synonymous with military service. Preparing recruits for the armed forces, either for commissioned or non-commissioned service, requires that each member be trained until proficient or qualified for whatever tasks are associated with the initial service employment. Job-specific training is supplemented by an introduction to the twin notions of professionalism and group ethos to impart a sense of the history of the organization and an exposure to its customs, traditions, and obligations. These are extremely important factors, indeed essential for membership in the profession of arms. The desired output from the training is a set of universally shared ethical values, along with the principal hallmarks of military service—teamwork, trust, respect, and loyalty. When trained for the job and indoctrinated as a team member, the newcomer is prepared for his or her first employment. Periodically, additional training will follow, in line with the individual's experience, skill level, and aptitude for advancement.

The word "training" in the above context means imparting knowledge and skill, individually and as a group, with drill and practice as required, to prepare the candidate to perform familiar tasks, repeatedly, in a competent manner and to a set of standards. Training and its purpose applies equally to commissioned and to non-commissioned members.

Education for military service has traditionally focused on commissioned personnel—although that is quickly changing, along with most aspects of military life. The complexity of modern weapon systems is putting new demands on non-commissioned members and their responsibilities are increasing. The altered nature of duties in recent years—generally a trend to greater responsibilities at a lower rank—signals a likely need for higher academic achievement and training for both commissioned and non-commissioned members. In any event, many in both groups are pursuing educational upgrading: the officer, as a condition of employment; and other ranks, often as a matter of choice, much to their personal credit and value to the CF.

THE MEANING OF EDUCATION

Education differs from training; a distinction that is probably crystal clear to educators but less so to the layman. The dictionary gives us a hint: education is "the process of (training) and developing the knowledge, skill, mind, and character for some desired purpose, especially by formal schooling. The product of education is knowledge and ability."[1]

The distinguishing feature of education, setting it apart from training, appears to be more focus on development of mind and character. One might infer from the definition that education occurs more often through a formal process of structured learning, as occurs in an institution—a university or college setting—rather than in one of many places that training takes place: in an aircraft, a ship, a tank, or a computer lab as examples. Educators speak of the output of education as an ability to think critically. Thus, whereas the process of training prepares one for repeatable and practiced tasks, education prepares for new, unfamiliar or unexpected tasks. Clearly, some of each is needed by everyone, in proportions that depend on the job. But in general terms, at lower ranks, training is key, education is secondary; while at higher ranks, these are reversed.

For years, this distinction tripped some military leaders. The two words, training and education, are almost always used together as if they are inseparable or at least hopelessly intertwined. That was an unfortunate mistake. It resulted in a view, strongly held by some senior officers, that formal education beyond the secondary school level was not universally required for commissioned officers. The corollary, implicit in the view, is that in-service training alone, with staff skills added when needed, and wide experience in the field, would together impart all the necessary talent needed by an officer.

Adherents to the view had examples of exemplary service by accomplished individuals who, for one reason or another, had not acquired formal post-secondary education, yet performed superbly, probably through a blend of native ability, wide experience, and frequent opportunity. For some people, and for part of our recent history, they were probably right.

LEARNING ON THE JOB

The early decades of the Cold War did provide fertile development opportunities for Canadians serving in NATO. But conditions changed along the way, which seriously reduced opportunities to learn on the job. For the last quarter of the century, roughly from the early 1970s onwards, the experiential learning opportunities that had earlier been widely available, mostly in NATO Europe but in NORAD and UN Peace Operations as well, were simply insufficient to meet the demand. This was due to Canada's dramatically reduced force levels in Europe (a fifty percent cut), and proportionally fewer positions within the NATO structure. At home, no shift to alternative learning opportunities was enacted to adequately pick up the slack.

REDUCED OPPORTUNITY

The decline in Canadian Forces presence in the Alliance meant fewer opportunities to work closely with officers of other NATO nations. The Cold War had assembled an enormous concentration of conventional forces in Europe, and maintaining their credibility and proficiency required high military skill levels. Many CF members had experience in agencies charged with developing joint doctrine, exercising in large troop formations, air exercises, and naval fleets, and participating in theater-wide command post exercises. These demanded well developed staff skills as well. All of these opportunities declined sharply in number, removing an extremely valuable learning source for the officer corps. That imposed a new need for an alternate way to develop the skills at home.

These events, as noted above, occurred in the early 1970s. In retrospect, steps should have been taken then, in spite of stretched budgets, and extended for as long as necessary, to improve substantially the professional development system. It would have required tough personnel policy decisions; it would have shifted badly needed funds from other worthy programs; it would have occurred in a period of slashed budgets; and it coincided with a national and international disinterest, even a dislike, for things military. In all, it would have been an extremely tough thing to do in the circumstances of the day. But it was needed.

A DEVELOPMENT ALTERNATIVE—THE ROWLEY REPORT

Not by coincidence but rather by design, a solution to the problem was available in the form of a major study called the *Report of the Officer Development Board*, commonly known as the Rowley Report. Work had begun in 1967, on the direction of General J.V. Allard, then Chief of the Defence Staff. It was completed in 1969, by Major-General R. Rowley and his fifteen-person team. It was a superb piece of work! It identified deficiencies in professional development, highlighted the diminished learning opportunities in Europe, and exposed the impacts that unification had on officer development, as the former independent Services were brought together. The study identified the problems throughout the professional development system and presented solutions to improve them.[2]

OPPORTUNITY MISSED

But only some of the recommendations of this exceptional study were implemented. One contentious action that was recommended, for example, that all officers must have at least a baccalaureate degree, did not take effect for thirty years. Even then the standard was not adopted by the CF, as Rowley and his team had recommended, rather it was imposed on the CF by ministerial direction as one of many follow-up actions to the Somalia Inquiry. In the thirty years after Rowley's report, numerous other studies followed and gave similar advice, repeatedly, to that contained in the 1969 report.

DEFICIENCIES IDENTIFIED

Rowley's team had researched analyses that were done on the Canadian officer corps prior to the Second World War. Many officers, they discovered, particularly the most senior, were deemed to be short on higher level military abilities and also lacked strategic vision and political awareness.[3] The comprehensive professional development system which was put in place after the war was meant to remedy such deficiencies. Actions, such as creation of the National Defence College in 1947, the reopening of the Royal Military College of Canada (RMC), and the creation of the Canadian Military College (CMC) system comprising three institutions, were each intended to contribute to the redress of identified shortfalls in officer development.

Rowley concentrated his recommendations on changes to structure and process on the assumption that if these were corrected, officer professional development would improve. If any criticism of the Rowley Report could be offered, it might be directed at his concentration on structure and process, to the exclusion of a conceptual framework for an improved professional development system, a philosophy, and an implementation process.

A WARNING BY THE CHIEF OF THE DEFENCE STAFF

With admirable prescience, and not a little foreboding, the Chief of the Defence Staff (CDS), General Allard, recorded his thoughts about needed changes in the professional development system for officers in a foreword to the Rowley Report. He placed the needed changes to the system in a context of serious departmental financial limitations and manpower shortages, but he still gave priority to Rowley's recommendations on professional development. His conclusions, written in March 1969, warrant repeating. He wrote, "A sound system for the production of effective professional officers is vital to the success of the newly unified Canadian Forces. It matters little whether the Forces have their present manpower strength and financial budget, or half of them, or double them; without a properly educated, effectively trained, professional officer corps the Forces would, in the future, be doomed to, at the best, mediocrity; at the worst, disaster."[4]

Additional studies and analyses that followed the Rowley Report, identified many of the same weaknesses. Three reports, one by Major-General G.C. Kitchen in 1985; a second by Colonel D.L. Lightburn in 1986; and a third by Major-General R.J. Evraire in 1988, concentrated mainly on general and senior officer development. Those three, plus the auditor general's annual report to Parliament in 1990, highlighted, in particular, deficiencies in the education of senior officers. All recommended more education at the graduate level for senior and general officers, specifically in strategic and national security studies. All pointed to the absence of an underpinning philosophy and conceptual framework for professional development beyond the issues of military tactics.[5] If one phrase were needed to describe the common thread of weakness in the professional development system over the years it would be "adequate and largely unsystematic."

Sometimes it takes time, as well as a crisis, for new ideas to be tried. As Rowley's ideas gathered dust, the crisis eventually arrived—roughly twenty-five years after his report. It arrived in a series of onslaughts, many budget driven but not all, but taken together diminished the professional development system to totally unacceptable levels. The Staff School was closed. Then two of the Canadian Military Colleges were shut down. The senior development course was eliminated by closing the National Defence College and no alternate was put in place. These actions left only remnants of the earlier system, isolated in uncoordinated pockets of activity. The mid-1990s was the low point in the long saga of inadequate CF professional development.[6] Fortunately the system has greatly improved since then. Indeed, much of what Rowley recommended and others endorsed is either now in place or under departmental review for consideration under the title Officer Professional Development 2020. It gives every encouragement that the resolve now exists to remedy all remaining deficiencies.

THE MILITARY ROLE IN NATIONAL AFFAIRS

In the professional military view, only the statesman can furnish the principal elements of national policy. The civil power is supreme and at the highest level the military can only advise on military aspects of national policy. For example, the CDS would be expected to warn of the possibility of over-committing the nation beyond its military strength and capability, if such circumstance were to arise. In our democracy the people choose their defence policy, normally in a package deal as one of many topics of a national platform of policy options, offered by each political party. The traditional military ethic holds that politics were outside the scope of military authority and competence, and the military's role therefore is limited to providing advice on military preparedness as one component of national security, while maintaining a clear understanding of the other determinants of security.

In Canada, defence rarely has influenced, in a decisive way, the outcome of an election, although it did in 1963.[7] When the people choose their government, the defence arrangement so chosen brings with it the means whereby national security will be provided. In Canada this normally identifies partners in defence, alliance affiliations, and the military capabilities that the people desire the nation to possess, and are willing to pay for.

Implicit in their selection, the people establish their desired security apparatus—such as a regional or a continental defence arrangement like NATO and NORAD, or the United Nations—and within one or other forum they expect the nation to make its contribution to the collective defence effort should one come along, or to a peace operation, or to a humanitarian mission. This has been the security format of the last half century. It is likely to continue. It requires the constant production of educated, skilled, and experienced officers to advise, lead, and manage the effort.

THE ROLE OF GENERALS AND ADMIRALS

When the people make their choice of security arrangements, they assume that all resulting military commitments, missions, and tasks that ensue will be carried out efficiently, with impeccable leadership, unblemished ethical and professional standards, and with measurable performance goals—all enforced by generals and admirals who have been appointed to their billets because they have learned how to do those things, and can lead and manage the forces accordingly. These things the people expect will be done without undue strain on the treasury, with minimal risk of injury or death to Canadians, and with minimal damage done anywhere, or to anyone—even those, it seems, with whom we might, from time to time, be in conflict.

Military leaders must be able to explain what the defence options are—along with assessments of the merits and risks of each. Governments normally reserve the communication of options to the people unto themselves, but seek input and advice from the military as a matter of routine. Periodically, major parliamentary reviews of defence policy allow for more thorough and fundamental public examinations of trends and capabilities, such as occurred in 1994.

LINKS TO SOCIETY

It can be argued that the military profession has an additional obligation. As a profession, with a strict code of conduct, and with an obligation to society for security, the military should help the public understand defence issues by making available information that is relevant to the subject. This can be done in the same way that other professions stay linked to the communities they serve: by professional journal articles, public seminars and service club speeches. Institutes of learning, such as the Royal Military College, the Command and Staff College with its expanded mandate, also provide excellent forums for this kind of intellectual interchange—from the professionals engaged in and committed to national defence on a day to day basis—to those seeking assurance that the art and science of defence is in capable hands. An observation from years of personal bewilderment over the public apathy about defence is that while the public seldom ever ask, they are always eager to listen.

A DEARTH OF PUBLIC UNDERSTANDING

Military leaders need reminding that the vast majority of Canada's population has had little or no contact ever with the military and views the military as a closed society. Generally they show their interest in it only when a crisis erupts. Breaking down those barriers was always difficult, but the task now is more difficult. The reasons are the complexity and confusion about security and defence needs in the post Cold War era and the explosion of information available to the public—the so-called Information Age, much of it in the defence and technology fields, and much of it uninformed or speculative.

The profession of arms finds itself confronted by the characteristic apathy about national security affairs, but this is now complicated by the unstable global environment characterized by danger, dynamism, and unpredictability. In contrast, the Cold War period, while dangerous, was an era of amazing stability. In such new and uncertain circumstances it is problematic that anyone could confidently forecast dangers to Canada's peace and security, and offer tailored military solutions to show how these can be mitigated. So, the notion of "general purpose, combat-capable land, sea, and air forces" continues to make eminently good sense in this environment. It is up to military professionals, who understand by their knowledge and experience what that means, to give form and substance to the notion for public understanding and clarity.

BROAD SECURITY ISSUES

While the issues of art and science of defence are complex in their own right, generals and admirals need a thorough grasp of the wider determinants of the state's security—the social, economic, political, trade, religious, and cultural circumstances that pertain, at home and abroad. Those, too, must be acquired over the preparatory years of formal and self-education. They must also understand Canada's place in the community of nations, the values she holds dear and projects, and her many interests abroad. These additional factors in the security equation bring a perspective on defence that is wholly at variance with the first motives for a military career such as flying jets, maneuvering armour, sailing frigates, delivering goods, or repairing the machines of war.

LEADER IN THE MAKING

Somewhere along the line from recruit to admiral—perhaps everywhere along the spectrum—some naval practitioners, and some of their army and air force counterparts, are undergoing a metamorphosis from operator and tactician, to leader and strategist. Not every young officer wants that change. Not everyone can make that change; but some must and do, so the profession can function and the society be served. The steps to get there are steep; the off-ramps, frequent. The system that makes possible this transition in responsibilities must be nurtured with greater attention and higher priority in the future than it has in the past; the selection process must be fair and efficient; and the magic of new learning technologies must be harnessed and used. The output is a steady flow of educated, skilled and experienced experts in the profession of arms, from which selections for senior appointment can be made with confidence.

THE PRODUCT

What can result is a General Officer Corps. Not a corporate élite, but an aggregate of leaders who are educated and experienced military professionals, agile of mind and quick to learn, especially in new or unforeseen situations; a filter of trivia and a trap for essentials; a capacity and willingness for quick adjustment in behavior and the communications skills to make it happen. In short, an intellectualism of individuals and of the group that thinks and reasons its way to a correct military, ethical, and moral action for each and every event.

That is why intellectualism is important in the General Officer Corps and that is what society expects!

NOTES

1. Webster's Dictionary, Second Edition.
2. Canada, *Report of the Officer Development Board* (Ottawa: Department of National Defence, 1969).
3. Ibid, 10. "The high price paid in blood by Canadians during the First World War did not enhance the image of the military profession in the eyes of Canadian society. The cessation of hostilities was naturally followed by a period of anti-militarism and isolation."
4. Ibid, iv.
5. Canada, *Final Report of the Officer Professional Development Review Board* (Ottawa: Department of National Defence, 1995), 16.
6. While those steps were not quite enough to crush morale, the following actions were: the defence budget was cut, a major downsizing undertaken, a reorganization implemented, record setting deployments abroad ordered, and the final blow: the Somalia Inquiry …unleashed its vile condemnation of the profession of arms, showing uncomprehending bitterness towards the Canadian Forces in front of the nation. That the armed forces continued to function at all in these circumstances is a tribute to every member then serving.
7. Diefenbaker government was defeated in April 1963, in part over the issue of nuclear armament.
8. The Joint Parliamentary Review of Defence Policy, 1994, preceded the *White Paper on Defence*.

Intellectualism in the General Officer Corps

Brigadier-General (retired) W. Don Macnamara

> *Brigadier-General W. Don Macnamara retired from the Canadian Forces in 1988 after thirty-seven years' service. He joined the faculty of the Queen's University School of Business until his second retirement in 1999.*

INTRODUCTION

IT IS DOUBTLESS TRITE to say that advancing technology and changing world conditions will challenge the leadership of tomorrow's Canadian Forces, demanding more and better education. This has been a theme through reports on officer development since the end of the Second World War, and probably for decades before. One could argue that evidence of the need for intellectual generalship dates back to the days of Sun Tzu (500 BCE) and *The Art of War*, the basic thesis of which "is to try to overcome the enemy by wisdom, not by force alone."[1] In Biblical, Greek and Roman times, while there was little formal "military education," as such, many of those societies' leaders (*strategos*) did study with the great philosophers such as Plato, Socrates and Aristotle.

Formal "military education" was a much more recent (sixteenth century) phenomenon, and was largely a response to advances in military technology, mainly in artillery and engineering fortifications. In the eighteenth century, military schools developed in Paris, St. Petersburg, Munich, Wiener Neustadt and Woolwich, also in response to technological advancements, while Fredrick the Great established the first "staff college"—L'Academie des Nobles—in 1763. Formal education as a prerequisite to commissioning came late in the nineteenth century, as did the proliferation of staff and war colleges at various levels.[2]

Officer Professional Development in the Canadian Forces has been the subject of numerous reports, especially since unification in 1968. The first, and most comprehensive, of these was the 1969 *Report of the Officer Development Board*, popularly known as the Rowley Report, after the chair of the Board, Major-General Roger Rowley. The importance of the subject is emphasized in an oft-quoted excerpt from the foreword to that report, signed by the then Chief of the Defence Staff, General J.V. Allard. "It matters little," he wrote, "whether the Forces have their present … strength and … budget, or half of them, or double them; without a properly educated, effectively trained, professional officer corps, the Forces would, in the future, be doomed to, at the best mediocrity, at worst, disaster."[3]

That report remains today the touchstone because, in spite of many valuable recommendations from subsequent reports, the basic philosophy, research and analysis of the Rowley Report have remained amazingly relevant.

Given the importance of the responsibility to be prepared to defend the nation, its assets and its values, to have persons of superior intellect as the senior military leaders would be evidently very much in the nation's interest. Given the complexity of military technology, on the one hand, and the daunting challenge of understanding the changing international environment and its impact on the nation's interests on the other, to have persons in senior leadership positions engaged in intellectual activity addressing these issues should also be seen, logically, to be in the nation's interests. Furthermore, at the political-military interface, where the understanding by politicians and officials of the utility and management of military force cannot be assumed, a capacity for rational discourse at an appropriate intellectual level on the part of the senior military leadership should be seen to be a self-evident need.

WHAT IS MEANT BY INTELLECTUALISM?

The terms "intellectual" or "intellectualism" may be frequently used in a negative or derogatory sense reflecting some disdain for those who are seen to be perhaps too thoughtful or rational. The *Oxford Canadian Dictionary* defines intellectual as "a person of superior intelligence; a person interested in intellectual matters; a person professionally engaged in intellectual activity." Intellectualism is then "devotion to intellectual pursuits; the exercise, especially when excessive, of the intellect at the expense of emotions; (philosophy) the theory that knowledge is wholly or mainly derived from pure reason."[4]

It is not the intention to become bogged down in a philosophical discussion of intellectualism, as such, or to address a spectrum of philosophical positions from rationalism to empiricism. Intellectualism, for the purposes of the following discussion, may be better considered as rigorous analysis as opposed to opinion; reason over "gut feel" or intuition; judgment based in wisdom and understanding as opposed to "impression."

Intellectualism does not just happen, neither is it simply a matter of education, although education is exceptionally important. In certain quarters of the Canadian Forces over the last half of the twentieth century, at least, it would be fair to say that there has been a frank anti-intellectual attitude, actively discouraging some officers from pursuing post-graduate education and, for those who persist, appearing to stagnate their careers.[5] Innovators appeared to threaten tradition and stability in organizations, and were therefore discouraged.

For an organization to seek intellectualism in its leadership will require the creation of an environment which will foster intellectual pursuits, value those who seek to combine their professional experience and skills with their education, and encourage further education and development throughout a career. It will be an organization that seeks improvement through innovation and change.

THE NEED FOR INTELLECTUALISM IN THE GENERAL OFFICER CORPS

The Rowley Report stated that, traditionally, officers in the Canadian Forces have been drawn from the top fifteen percent, intellectually, of the population of Canada. Figure 1, taken from that report, shows the anticipated growth of university education in Canada, indicating that virtually *all* officers should be drawn from university graduates to ensure an appropriate level of intellectual ability, not only for generals, but also throughout the officer corps. Intellectual ability and development, although important, is not the only, or most important quality for generalship. The Rowley Report listed eight qualities of officers requiring fostering and development—soldierly virtues, command ability, branch and specialty skill, list competence (i.e. land, sea or air operations), military expertise, intellectual capability, executive ability and military-executive

Figure 1

FIGURE 1 - INTELLECTUAL CAPACITY

% of Male Population of Military Age (Approx)

NOTE:
▨ Projection of Historical Source of Officers

▨ University Attendance

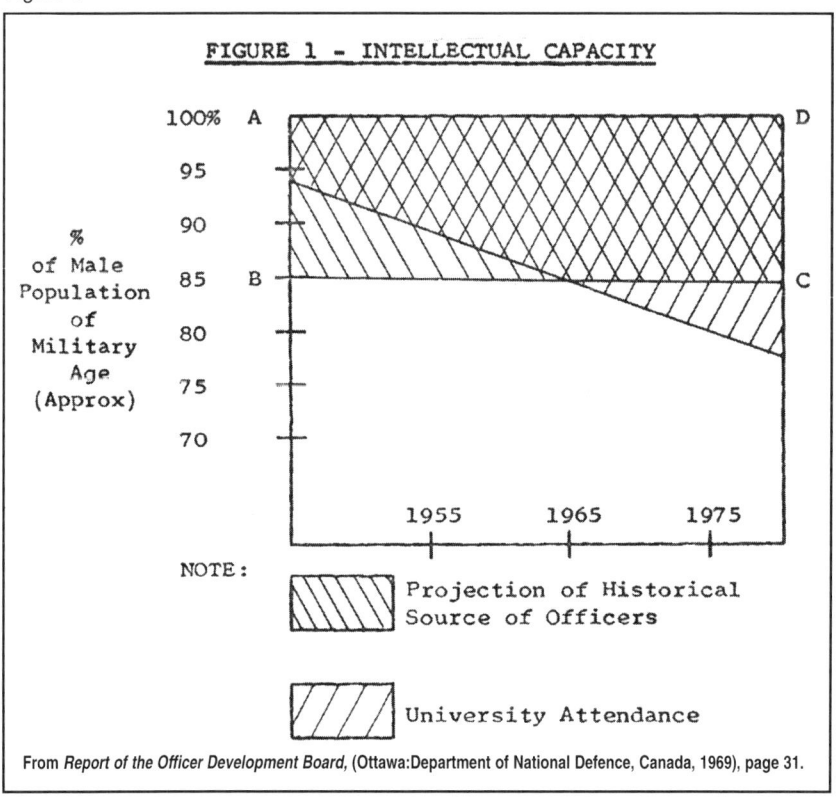

From *Report of the Officer Development Board,* (Ottawa:Department of National Defence, Canada, 1969), page 31.

Figure 2

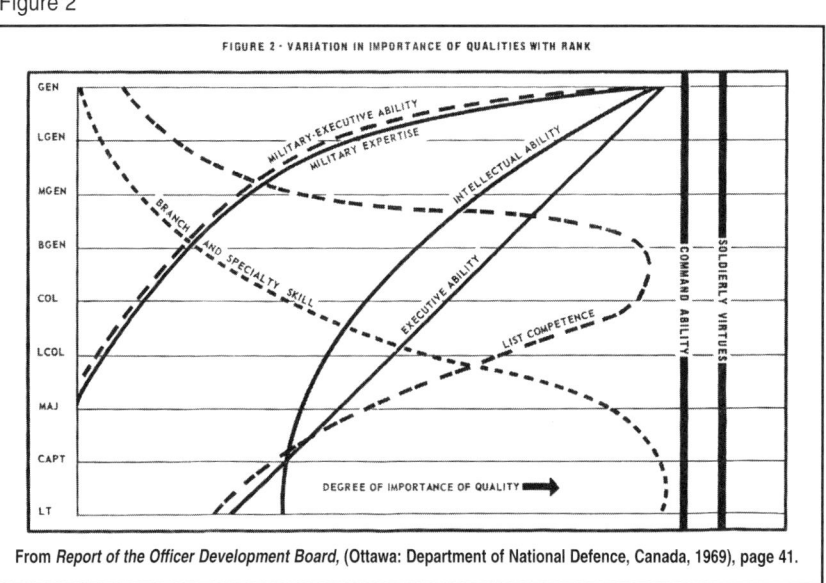

FIGURE 2 - VARIATION IN IMPORTANCE OF QUALITIES WITH RANK

From *Report of the Officer Development Board,* (Ottawa: Department of National Defence, Canada, 1969), page 41.

ability.[6] These qualities are not required evenly through a career or any given rank, and the variations in importance were described in that report using a model-type diagram (Figure 2). It is clear from this model that the importance of intellectual ability increased dramatically with rank beyond that of colonel, reaching a coincidental peak at general with military-executive ability, military expertise and executive ability.

In addressing leadership development, the Banff Centre for Management recently developed a similar model for executive intellectual development and application (Figure 3), which bears out many of the factors mentioned by Rowley.[7] In Figure 3, the stages of intellectual development start with data, which when placed in context through analysis become information. The information, through experience and meaning—understanding—leads to knowledge. Through the exercise of practice and judgment based in that knowledge, wisdom develops. Innovation, the final phase, is the product of wisdom exercised by thoughtful action and feedback, which further builds wisdom. The important feature of this model is that experience and practice are required to make the most of the early education stages.

Notwithstanding the somewhat artificial differentiation between training and education, the definition of education as "the development of a reasoned response to unpredictable situation" would more clearly define a general officer's

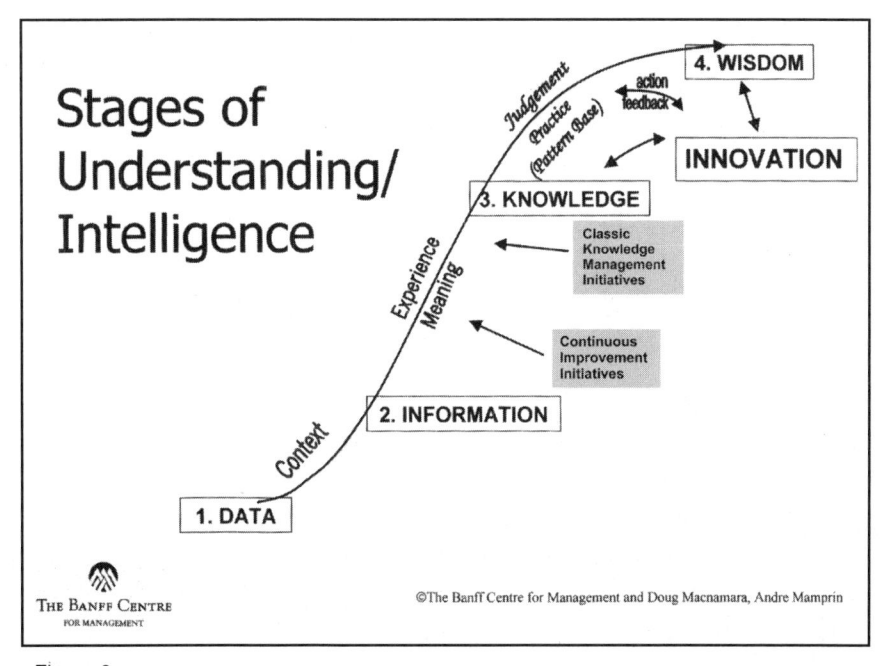

Figure 3

developmental need, as opposed to training to "develop a predictable response to a predictable situation."[8] Indeed, decisions to commit the nation's most precious resource—its young men and women—to potential combat, and thereby possible loss of their lives, cannot be capricious. Such decisions must be the product of rigorous analysis of the circumstances, the assurance that the nation's interests—values and / or assets—are indeed at risk, and that all measures possible through appropriate training, equipment and planning, have been undertaken to minimize the vulnerability of those so committed. The advice to the nation's political leadership on these risks is the purview of the most senior levels of military leadership. Only those with the intellectual capacity, essential education, experiential development and demonstrated leadership capability should be entrusted with such awesome responsibilities. Intellectualism in the General Officer Corps must therefore be fostered.

EDUCATION AND GENERALSHIP

Recognizing the need for education is one matter, but fostering its presence in the General Officer Corps is another. During the First World War, at least half of Canadian Army general officers (major-general and above) had a university degree or Royal Military College (RMC) diploma—and less than half came from the pre-war regular force. During the Second World War, of the sixty-eight major-generals and above in the Canadian Army, twenty-one had university degrees and twenty-one held RMC diplomas—fully sixty-two percent of the General Officer Corps, and over half of the general officers came from the pre-war Permanent Force.[9] (Similar data for the RCN and RFC/RCAF are apparently not available.)

Although the desirable requirement for a university degree (or equivalent, i.e. Royal Military College) as a prerequisite for commissioning was recognized during the inter-war years, and was the only route to an automatic permanent commission on entry to the Canadian Armed Forces in the post Second World War period, the principles and the practices were at odds.

Since that time, and notwithstanding this wartime record and the several studies on officer professional development, the number of university graduates in the General Officer Corps failed to keep pace with the changes in Canadian society, and indeed, the recommendations of the Rowley Report in particular.

In 1997, following the Somalia Inquiry, the then Minister of National Defence, the Honourable Doug Young, commissioned a number of papers by Canadian academics to address some of the perceived problems in the Canadian Officer Corps. One author, Dr. J.L. Granatstein, pointed out that for well over a decade, the Canadian Forces had intended that officers have a degree, but failed to meet the aim. Only about half the officers at that time achieved the standard. He attributed the failure to "a large number of senior officers (who) believe that education is *not* a necessary qualification for officers."[10] In a climate best described as anti-intellectual, it is not surprising that the growth in graduates in the General Officer Corps has been relatively slow. Development of the intellect of officers at all levels appears not to have been accepted.

Recent data indicates that within the Canadian population (25-64 year olds) 18.6 % have a university degree—the fourth highest level in the world (after the United States, Netherlands and Norway).[11] Of these, about 20% have a formal graduate degree—34% if graduate diplomas and MDs are included.[12] Table 1 shows the progress made within the General Officer Corps over the last thirty-two years.

Table 1

Canadian General Officer Corps Education Level, 1968-2000

Year	Number of General Officers	Number with Degree (% Total)	Number with Graduate Degree (% Total)
1968	113	49 (43.4%)	10 (8.8%) 8 MBA, 4MA, 4MS, 2 PhD
1972	109	25 (22.9%)	10 (9.2%) 1 MBA/MPA, 5MA, 4MS
1975	23	49 (39.8%)	16 (13.0%) 7 MBA/MPA, 5MA, 4MS
1980	122	68 (55.7%)	13 (10.6%) 3 MBA/MPA, 6MA, 4MS
1985	134	81 (60.4%)	17 (12.7%) 6 MBA/MPA, 3MA, 8MS
1990	148	107 (72.3%)	16 (10.8%) 9 MBA/MPA, 6MA, 1MS
1995	116	86 (74.1%)	20 (17.2%) 8 MBA/MPA, 4MA, 8MS
2000	70	59 (84.3%)	15 (21.4%) 4 MBA/MPA, 5MA, 5MS, 1PhD

Calculated from 1968 data in *Report of the Officer Development Board* (1969) and data provided by Director of Human Resource Information Management, 2000.

For the Canadian Forces at large, only 53% of officers in 1997 had a bachelor's degree and 6.8% had graduate degrees. For the General Officer Corps, the situation is somewhat better. Currently over 84% of general officers have a bachelor's degree and 21% have a graduate degree—well below the desired 100% for both. Notwithstanding the progress—doubling both the bachelor's and graduate degree rates—the situation remains that Canada has probably the most poorly educated officer corps in the Anglo-Saxon community. This certainly does not reflect the expectation of drawing officers from the top 15% of the population. Vis-à-vis the United States, where virtually every officer has a bachelor's degree and most officers above the rank of major have one or more graduate degrees, with over 90% of general officers holding advanced degrees, Canadian officers are not among their academic, or indeed intellectual, peers. As Granatstein reported, "The result, one officer who had served with the US forces put it, is that the US general officer corps is 'a collegial intelligentsia.' No one could say this of the CF senior leaders."[13]

The Canadian Armed Forces are expected to be capable of "fighting alongside the best against the best." As such, the need for an intellectually competent general officer corps in Canada is self-evident. The Rowley objective of 100% with a university degree has not been achieved, although the goal of 20% with graduate degrees has been achieved. The current state of undergraduate and graduate qualification within the Officer Corps in general, and General Officer Corps in particular, is clearly less than ideal. Improvement in this field at the same rate as the last thirty years is definitely not in the national interest. The situation must be addressed with some priority and urgency.

EDUCATION AND INTELLECTUALISM

It is beyond the scope of this discussion to delve into educational theory. The general assumption that an undergraduate education develops a "critical analytical" intellect, is certainly subject to scrutiny, especially in the generalization of the success of the aim. Then, the academic content of the degree taken may also have a bearing on the extent to which the critical analysis capability has been developed, as well as the level of achievement of the individual. Long arguments can also be held over whether a science or engineering degree is better than / as good as / not as good as a humanities degree in fostering such intellectual development, or whether an arts and humanities degree without any numeracy competence fits a graduate for today's high-technology environment. The assumption that an undergraduate degree *should* be, at minimum, an indicator of a critical analysis capability as well as some broad understanding of what the world is and how it works, may reasonably be the basis for certain *selection* procedures, among other testable criteria for officership. The content and military relevance of various undergraduate degrees was discussed in the Rowley Report[14] and will not be repeated here. Suffice it to say that, without an officer corps with a minimum of a first degree, any aspirations for an intellectual general officer corps would be seriously self-limiting. The changing needs of an officer's knowledge and skills will demand a more general education, emphasizing science and technology as well as arts and humanities, along with modern management science. This is a tall order, but is being addressed to a significant degree at least within the curriculum changes now underway at the Royal Military College.[15] However, if the RMC is to be the source of only about a quarter of Canadian Forces officers, then the curricula pursued by other subsidized and direct entry officers will deserve greater scrutiny to avoid making undue assumptions about their intellectual skills. As one Chief of the Defence Staff said, "I am the CDS, with a degree in math and physics, and my son with a degree in history is a combat systems officer on a frigate. I need his degree and he needs mine." The reality is that both need both—and the demand for the capacity for broad understanding will only increase rather than decrease.

GRADUATE DEGREES

An undergraduate degree as a pre-requisite for commissioning—even if not yet generally achieved—is no longer seen to be enough, especially for senior officers, and for general officers in particular. A graduate degree at the Master's level is seen to be most desirable, and there is some discussion that there should be more PhD degrees among general officers.

The starting point for the discussion of graduate degrees must be, "What is the purpose?" Rowley argued that advances in technology and management sciences would demand that the senior leadership be schooled in these areas, that the instructional needs of the staff and military colleges would require graduate-degree-holding officers, and that there would be a need to maintain parity with other professions.

Graduate degree needs for the Canadian Forces may be classified in three areas:

Specialist education to meet a civilian professional standard as well as a service requirement, e.g. specialty training / education for doctors (surgeons, internists etc), lawyers and chaplains;

Technical education to ensure that the Canadian Forces is knowledgeable at the leading edge of critical technologies, (e.g., aeronautical engineering, materials technology, information technology, nuclear technology etc); and for which specific positions in design, test or procurement areas can be identified, and for which individuals may be educated / trained and then employed in those positions;

Formative education to develop the general intellect of selected officers in areas of *general professional* interest to the Canadian Forces.

The numerical requirement for the first two of these categories should be clearly identifiable through processes such as the "special personnel qualification requirement" (SPQR), which should lead to the annotation of positions and the appropriate longer-term planning to select, educate and employ candidates accordingly. The third category is, however, much more difficult to quantify due to the variety of degrees, individual interests, and the means by which they may be achieved.

Let it first be said that the maximal benefit will be derived by an individual who has decided that he/she is interested in pursuing a graduate degree in a particular area. Unlike the first two categories, the interests of the service may well be best served by any graduate degree, as long as the individual does achieve appropriate intellectual development. But, all Master's degrees, like people, are not created equal. Those pursuing their own interests, in common with the interests of the Canadian Forces, should be aware of differences in content and outcome for various Master's programs.

The Ontario Council on Graduate Studies published its most recent guidelines for graduate programs in October, 1998, in a document entitled "Terms of Reference for Appraisal Consultants."[16] The following several excerpts are taken from that document to set the stage for the subsequent examination and discussion. (Italics are my emphasis.)

> Basis of Appraisal: *Because of the variety in type of graduate programs offered in Ontario, the judgment of quality cannot be tied rigidly to an examination of a common list of specific characteristics that all programs must share.* There are different formats and models of graduate education and, therefore, the Appraisal Committee is not looking for a particular pattern of research, course work, general examinations, language requirements, size, etc., against which all programs must be evaluated. Rather, each program is assessed against its own stated objectives.
>
> *Nevertheless, a graduate degree must ensure that the holder has achieved an appropriate level of intellectual development beyond that acquired*

during the undergraduate program. For those programs that also serve the purpose of professional or vocational training, it is essential that the intellectual and professional objectives and content be more advanced than those of the undergraduate degree.

Despite this variety, master's degrees and graduate diplomas must include a component whereby research and analytical/interpretive skills are developed. This component may take the form of a thesis, a major research paper or short research papers within the courses required for the degree, a comprehensive examination, or other specified activity appropriate for the discipline and designed to test the analytical/interpretive skills. ......"

In all cases, it is important that graduate programs be demonstrated to be more focused, advanced and scholarly than is the case for undergraduate programs. Some of the more general criteria that are sought by the appraisal Committee in its evaluation of graduate programs are listed below:

Master's Degree & graduate diplomas—Graduate study at the master's and graduate diploma levels are offered through a diverse range of programs:

The research-oriented master's program in an academic discipline offered to the graduate with an honours degree in that discipline is the most traditional sequence. Advanced courses and the challenge of doing intensive research, usually resulting in a thesis, major research paper or cognate essay, are provided as means of developing the skills and intellectual curiosity required for doctoral studies and/or a leadership role in society.

The *course-based* master's program offers advanced training to a similar clientele. While this type of program does not require the performance resulting in a thesis, it must contain elements that ensure the development of analytical/interpretive skills.

The *professional* master's or graduate diploma program offers to the graduate of any one of several honours or more general undergraduate programs a coordinated selection of courses in a range of disciplines and their application or related skills, in preparation for entry into a profession or as an extension of the knowledge base required of practicing professionals. Such programs also need to develop analytical/interpretive skills relevant to the profession.

While all three types of program may assure that "the holder has achieved an appropriate level of intellectual development beyond that acquired during the undergraduate program," the outcome and expectations may be quite different. Note that it is only the research-oriented master's program that forms the basis for subsequent doctoral studies "or a leadership role in society." Clearly, candidates who have serious academic interests and intellectual bent should be encouraged to participate in such programs. Also, a research-oriented master's program is normally undertaken in the field in which the candidate already holds an honours bachelor's degree. Although switching fields is not unknown, it usually requires extensive make-up course work, thereby extending the time required for master's degree completion.

The second type of program, the course-based master's degree, is particularly suited to candidates who wish to complete a graduate degree on a part-time basis. It too is suitable for those already possessing a solid major in an honours program, which would permit some advanced study and, perhaps, an area of specialization. Although not normally intended to be a precursor to doctoral studies, the course-based master's degree can certainly provide the intellectual development needed at the senior level.

The *professional* master's program represents an area of significant importance to the Rowley development model, that is, managerial and analytical skills, including such areas as strategic and policy planning. The Master of Business Administration and Master of Public Administration are the predominant degrees in this area. These are very much practical programs, not intended to lead to any doctoral studies. At the same time, they represent real value to military and public service organizations by developing and honing the kinds of analytical and planning skills that are the lifeblood of such organizations. A further advantage of the professional master's program is that entry may be achieved from a range of undergraduate degree programs, plus appropriate experience in the subject area. One could argue that the military staff colleges, developed in the nineteenth century, in fact served as models for such professional programs, and continue to be very close in content. Indeed, in a recent analysis, the Canadian Forces Command and Staff Course effectively not only meets but also exceeds most of the usual requirements for a typical Master of Public Administration degree.

The above programs normally are completed in one or two academic years, depending on the discipline and the undergraduate degree of the candidate, and whether undertaken on a full- or part-time basis. In the professional category, there are a number of executive and in-service programs that are designed specifically for the part-time candidate holding a full-time position. In addition, these programs have been developed to take advantage of a variety of distance learning techniques so that being located in a university town or city is not necessary to pursue a graduate degree.

Not to be ignored in discussing graduate-level education are the courses delivered by the Canadian Forces, which may provide substantial credit toward all of the above categories of master's programs. The Command and Staff course offered by the Canadian Forces College has already been accredited for certain undergraduate and graduate courses, and the new Advanced Military Studies Course (three months) and National Security Studies Course (six months) have been specifically designed to be conducted at a graduate level, and have received some accreditation towards a RMC War Studies graduate degree. A continuing issue in accreditation, however, is the academic qualification of the military instructional staff. Again, failure to meet the undergraduate and graduate degree goals over the last thirty years also failed to provide sufficient senior staff qualified to teach at a graduate level, and now stands to complicate the accreditation of the courses, notwithstanding their quality.

The critical factor continues to be, however, time. The urgency to achieve the required graduate level intellectual development for the General Officer Corps cannot be ignored. Neither, however, can the severe constraints placed on personnel resources by the cutbacks of the 1990s, which have left many senior officers at such an operational tempo that graduate-level study is not only unrealistic, it is patently unfair. However, the goal of an intellectually competent general officer corps can no longer be compromised, and cannot ethically be achieved by exploiting the professional dedication of senior officers. Identifying the candidates, identifying their graduate study interests and facilitating their full or part-time studies must be seen to be an operational priority—a vital interest for the Canadian Forces.

HOW MANY PHDS ARE NEEDED IN THE GENERAL OFFICER CORPS?

Although a quick answer to that question may be "none," it spawns another question, "Where does the PhD degree fit into the military intellectual requirement?" A research doctorate (as opposed to practice-based doctorate, e.g. DEd) represents independent *original* research and the preparation of a thesis, in addition to a demonstrated comprehensive knowledge of one or more 'fields.' Although primarily a degree pursued by those seeking a career in an academic environment, it is not exclusively so. In the sciences, doctoral level research is the stuff of the leading edge of science, and may indeed represent a real service need. On the other hand, in arts and humanities it may merely represent pursuit of an intellectual challenge to achieve a significant body of research for publication for personal satisfaction. The real *military* requirement for doctorates would normally be in military universities and senior schools, particularly at the war college level. This requirement would achieve both the academic credibility necessary for such institutions, as well as ensuring a supervisory rigour for the research conducted by the military students. Because of the intensity of doctoral programs, candidates normally select themselves to pursue the program, and may do so with or without direct service support. In addition, there could be graduate prize-winning scholars from military undergraduate programs who could be given the opportunity to complete a doctorate immediately after the first degree.

Would the possession of a doctorate make a senior officer a better general? The quick and obvious answer is "not necessarily." Recalling the various qualities indicated in Figure 2, there is simply no guarantee that a PhD, as opposed to a research-based Master's degree, would make any real difference in the quality of the performance of an individual except perhaps, and only perhaps, in the intellectual ability component.

In the United States forces, doctoral degrees are obtained either on individual initiative or with service sponsorship to meet service needs. Individual initiative is not necessarily supported, although study leaves or credit for specialized employment may enhance the opportunity for those so motivated. Sponsorship is provided for those normally selected early in their careers to ensure leading-edge knowledge in specific areas e.g. critical technologies, behavioural sciences, where supervising research or development activities or contracts would require knowledge and skills to protect the interests of the forces. Later in careers, senior officers with demonstrated academic and professional attributes are invited to apply for sponsored doctoral programs which would lead to employment as professors at the military academies, the senior schools (War Colleges) and perhaps ultimately in certain sensitive areas, e.g. the National Security Council. In return for such limited employment and career opportunities, retirement in the rank of colonel is virtually assured, and in a few cases, brigadier-general.

The most critical issue in providing opportunities for doctoral-level studies is the time requirement. While a research-based Master's degree can be obtained within two years, or less, a doctoral program is at least two, and perhaps three years beyond the Master's, in most Canadian universities. Requirements in US and UK universities may be somewhat less time-consuming, depending upon the area of study and the experience of the candidate.

CONCLUSION

It is clear that the Rowley Report goals for the intellectual ability needs of the General Officer Corps, as represented by both undergraduate and graduate degree achievement, have not been met over the thirty years since their adoption. It is equally clear that the Canadian Officer Corps in general and the General Officer Corps in particular, do not reflect the intellectual component of Canadian society consistent with the academic levels of the general population, its corporate and government executives, nor indeed comparable with their military peers in allied nations, the United States in particular.

The intellectual challenge and demands of the domestic and international political, economic, social and technological environments will test the best-educated and experientially-prepared general officers. Because the quality of the advice on the use of military force and the "management of violence" provided to politicians and officials have a direct bearing on Canada's interests and position in the world, as well as on the very well-being of the young Canadian men and women serving Canada in the Canadian Forces, anything less than the sharpest intellects in the Canadian General Officer Corps is unaffordable. Understanding the needs for intellectual development, the means by which it can be achieved and providing the resources to achieve it is a professional, moral and national responsibility. It is ultimately up to the Canadian General Officer Corps to meet that intellectual responsibility as well.

NOTES

1. Han-chang T'ao, *Sun Tzu's Art of War* (New York: Sterling, 1990), 13.
2. Martin Van Creveld, *The Training of Officers* (New York: The Free Press, 1990).
3. Canada, *Report of the Officer Development Board* (Ottawa: Department of National Defence, 1969).
4. Katherine Barber, *The Canadian Oxford Dictionary* (London: Oxford University Press, 1998).
5. This statement arises from personal experience and observation, also sharing the experience of a number of other officers. The observation is also included in J.L. Granatstein's report.
6. *Report of the Officer Development Board*, 1969, 39-40.
7. Doug Macnamara and André Mamprin, The Banff Centre for Management, Banff, Alberta, 2000.
8. Canada, *Final Report of the Officer Professional Development Review Board* (Ottawa: Department of National Defence, 1995), xiv.
9. J.L. Granatstein, *The Generals* (Toronto: Stoddart, 1995), 6.
10. J.L. Granatstein, *For Efficient and Effective Armed Forces: A Paper Prepared for the Minister of National Defence* (Canada: Department of National Defence, 1995), 20.
11. Statistics Canada, 1996 Census – Nation Tables.
12. Organization for Economic Co-operation and Development, *The OECD in Figures* –

Education Performance, 66, OECD (Paris: June, 2000).
13. J.L.Granatstein, *For Efficient and Effective Armed Forces*, 19.
14. *Report of the Officer Development Board*, 1969, 35-37.
15. Council of Ontario Universities, Ontario Council on Graduate Studies Terms of Reference for Appraisal Consultants (Toronto: October, 1998), 6.
16. W.D. Macnamara, *Report on the Command and Staff Course as a Professional Graduate Program*, Royal Military College, May 2000.

Stragegic Thinking General/Flag Officers: The Role of Education

Brigadier-General Ken C. Hague

Brigadier-General Ken Hague retired from the Canadian Forces in the summer of 2000. His last appointment was that of Commandant of the Royal Military College of Canada

---

It matters little whether the Forces have their present...strength and...budget, or half of them, or double them; without a properly educated, effectively trained professional officer corps, the Forces would, in the future, be doomed to, at the best, mediocrity; at the worst, disaster.
—General J.V. Allard, former Chief of Defence Staff[1]

INTRODUCTION

SOME CRITICS WOULD ARGUE that the Canadian Forces (CF) reached the "future" that General Allard referred to in his quotation in the 1990s. I, however, would not. The requirement for an educated officer corps became readily apparent during this period and is now more critical than ever as we prepare our vision for 2020 and beyond.

The last decade has seen the Canadian Forces embark on a series of diverse, complex and dangerous peace support operations which have taxed military personnel to the limits of their experience, knowledge and leadership abilities. At the same time, the expectations of the Armed Forces stemming from the Canadian government, the media and society have changed dramatically. Transparency in every facet of our operations is not just expected but demanded, with the results receiving media attention to a degree unknown in the history of our military. If change has been the byword of the 1990s, then accountability was its constant companion. From the Somalia scandal, to the *Macleans* magazine's sexual assault investigations, to the Croatia contaminated soil allegations, to business plans and empowerment, the senior leadership of the Canadian Forces has been under constant pressure to accept responsibility for their actions and hold members accountable for their transgressions, alleged or proven.

We, the general and flag officers, are that senior leadership—the buck must stop with us. We are responsible for the stewardship of the Canadian Forces which includes all aspects of responsibility and accountability for the actions of every one of our members, both military and civilian. We must answer to our political masters, the media and ultimately the Canadian people for the effectiveness of our troops in action. Yet upon analysing the events, activities, operations and incidents that have traumatized us the most, it is evident they were primarily ones for which we, the leadership, receive little if any formal education or training.

To illustrate this modern day challenge in an operational scenario, I wish to use an example from my own experience with UNPROFOR in Croatia. In February 1993, I was appointed Deputy Commander of Sector West which was commanded by a brigadier-general from Jordan. My only preparation was a five-day generic peacekeeping training package delivered by the Directorate of Peacekeeping Operations at NDHQ. Nothing in the package developed my understanding of the tasks awaiting me in Croatia.

Once on the ground, I quickly discovered that no terms of reference (TOR) existed for the position, as the incumbent had been virtually ignored in the Sector HQ routine. When the senior political advisor for Sector West decided to leave UNPROFOR without any prospects in the long term, or even short term, for a replacement, he convinced the sector commander my TOR should include his former duties, at least temporarily. Thus, I found myself within five days of arriving in the Sector with responsibility for negotiations between the Serbs and the Croats regarding enforcement of the peace accord, cease fire violations, nation building tasks, and refugee control. Within a month, I also volunteered (for lack of a better term for "no one else stepped forward") to organize at least a dozen non-governmental organizations (NGO) who had been working in the Sector without co-ordination or control. I executed these tasks for approximately three months before a professional UN civilian political advisor was posted to Sector West.

To say I had no professional preparation for these types of complex, politically sensitive tasks is a gross understatement. Assuming responsibility for the delicate, volatile, and totally foreign role imposed upon me without the benefit of even a familiarization period was the most daunting challenge I have ever faced in my career to date. To succeed required leadership qualities, knowledge and interpersonal skills that were previously never utilised.

I could similarly illustrate the challenge of twenty-first century command using a domestic non-operational example. What preparation does an officer receive when he/she becomes the de facto "president" of a modern, progressive, vibrant Canadian university? As Commandant of the Royal Military College, the appointee is confronted with the unfamiliar intellectual demands of his/her academic responsibilities in addition to the more familiar yet increasingly complicated duties of commanding a somewhat non-traditional military unit.

When you have no formal preparation for a particular assignment and consequently find yourself in uncharted territory from an experience and knowledge perspective, how do leaders succeed in these situations? The answer lies in an educated officer corps. This chapter therefore, is to demonstrate the value of education in developing the qualities that general and flag officers require to execute their responsibilities in the future strategic environment.

THE STRATEGIC ENVIRONMENT

> Officers now need a much more sophisticated understanding of the relationships between society and violence, because they cannot count on compartmentalising their experience and relying on doctrine and training. In short, flexibility of mind that arises from a broad education must compensate for our ability to predict the circumstances under which forces will be employed.[2]

No proof is required to validate this quote by Major David Last given our operational deployments in the 1990s. To say that our sudden commitment to Zaire as the lead nation of a coalition humanitarian operation was unpredicted would be an unparalleled understatement. Shocking would be a better description. Moreover, the situation will not change in the new millennium. The international strategic environment facing Canada and her allies in the next twenty years is vividly described in *Canadian Officership in the 21st Century*, the Officer Professional Development (OPD) Statement of Operational Requirement:

> Predicting the world of, say 2010, is fool's play. Yet 2010's major powers are tolerably clear. So are the global processes that will shape 2010, if not how these processes will play out.
>
> *Global military power.* In aggregate military terms, the United States is indeed the sole superpower. That state of affairs will change, if at all, only close to 2010, conceivably by a Russian resurgence but more probably by the emergence of an Asian peer, most probably China.
>
> *Political and economic power.* The United States, Japan, Europe, Russia and China will shape 2010's world. There is uncertainty about the last two, and room for arguments about whether, say, India or Brazil, might reach the list.
>
> *Dispersion of power.* If the nation state is not about to go away, beneath states, power is dispersing. Bankers, terrorists and drug traffickers all act around and through states, challenging state power from beneath. National leaders are thus held accountable yet their control of events is fading.[3]

Colonel Howie Marsh predicts a very different world evolving over the twenty-year period encompassed by the CF's Vision 2020:

- the quantity of innovation in the next 20 years is likely to exceed all innovation discovered in the 20th century.
- Future Canadian societies are likely to be more isolationist and less intrusive in international affairs.
- Global warming will pose even greater problems for future generations.
- The United States will create new, revolutionary security and command relationships to counter the future national security environment.[4]

Most intelligence agencies provide a three-option scenario for the world of the early twenty-first century. The first option is the status quo of today—continued regional instability based on religious, racial and ethnic conflicts, deterioration of the nation state, and economic disparity between East and West. The other two options are either an improvement from the status quo based on the New World Order theory or a considerable negative deviation from the status quo with increased chaos and instability. Although many analysts would not agree with Robert S. Kaplan's extreme prediction for the future security environment facing us,[5] most strategic thinkers conclude the world will continue to slide towards increased instability. Military leaders will therefore continue to face challenging, complex operations with ambiguous mandates, ill-defined combatants, intense media scrutiny, and "third rail"[6] ethical dilemmas.

In addition to the international parameters making up the future strategic environment, there are two other national factors that will exert significant influence on general and flag officers, resource management and technology/information management.

Treasury Board, our Minister and by consequence our senior departmental leadership will continue to demand strict accountability for the stewardship of our allocated resources. There will be increased pressure to adopt best business practices in all management activities. This goal will be attained with leading edge technology that provides vast quantities of information to decision-makers. These three factors will generate levels of stress that our senior leadership must accept and harness to be effective. The climate confronting our generals and flag officers is summed up well by William J. Crowe, Jr in his address to the US Naval War College in Spring 1997:

> Perhaps more than any other period, we will need officers who are versatile, innovative and independent thinkers. Certainly the ability to face the unexpected and unplanned challenges will be highly prized. In this environment, military officers are increasingly called upon to be all things to all people. You will be expected to be sensitive to the nation's political problems, social strains, and international role. You will be called upon to act as negotiators, advocates, public educators, and counsellors. In essence, the minefields of the mind will require as much attention as the more traditional variety.[7]

This new strategic environment has lead analysts to declare that the "industrial age is waning rapidly and the information age is upon us."[8] Terms such as a Revolution in Military Affairs (RMA) are used to describe the exponential changes to warfighting, primarily in equipment, that militaries must make to cope with advances in technology. But University of Calgary Professor David Bercuson, in an address to the Conference on Educating Canada's Military at RMC in December 1998, stated the following:

But while Canadian military leaders have spent decades casting covetous eyes on the first line, first rate, advanced kit of our principal allies, they have virtually ignored the real revolution that has transformed the fighting forces of those allies, principally the United States. That revolution is not an RMA, but an RME—a revolution in military education—and it is harder to understand, harder to replicate, harder to get excited about, and not nearly as sexy.[9]

EDUCATION VERSUS TRAINING

Military personnel often use the terms education and training almost synonymously. They are far from being synonyms. Therefore, to ensure we have the same understanding of the interpretation of training versus education, let me offer these two definitions.

Training enables a soldier to respond in a predictable manner to a predictable situation.[10] Simply stated, training provides the battlefield skills needed by military personnel to react decisively, appropriately, and without direction to a combat scenario envisioned by their leaders. The best example from my experience is the drills learned by paratroopers. The reaction to any parachute malfunction is automatic, almost instinctive.

Education on the other hand, is "a reasoned response to an unpredictable situation—that is critical thinking in the face of the unknown."[11] As general and flag officers, we will more likely face the unknown in our daily activities than situations that require a predictable response. We will also be challenged by increasingly complex scenarios that demand better ethical judgement than needed in the past. Education represents the key enabling mechanism for developing this essential senior leadership trait.

QUALITIES OF GENERAL/FLAG OFFICERS

Given the above future environment, it is safe to state that leadership at the senior levels in the Canadian Forces will be challenging, complex, fraught with pitfalls, not terribly fun, but extremely rewarding. As a result, general and flag officers must have a unique set of qualities in their database of personal traits and attributes to succeed in such a diverse, unstable, and unpredictable set of parameters. What are these traits and attributes?

The Public Service Commission has attempted to identify these "competencies"[12] required by Associate Deputy Ministers (ADMs) and senior executives. They include Intellectual Competencies (cognitive capacity, creativity), Future Building Competencies (visioning), Management Competencies (action management, organizational awareness, teamwork, partnering), Relationship

Competencies (interpersonal relationships, communications) and Personal Competencies (stamina/stress resistance, ethics and values, personality, behavioural flexibility, self-confidence).

Of these competencies, most can be developed almost exclusively by experience in command and staff positions at various levels in the Canadian Forces. Maturity, job variety, training, and experience all contribute to their acquisition throughout an officer's career (Figure 1). There are a few, however, that do not fall into this category. They include cognitive capacity, creativity, and visioning.

Figure 1 Senior Officer Development

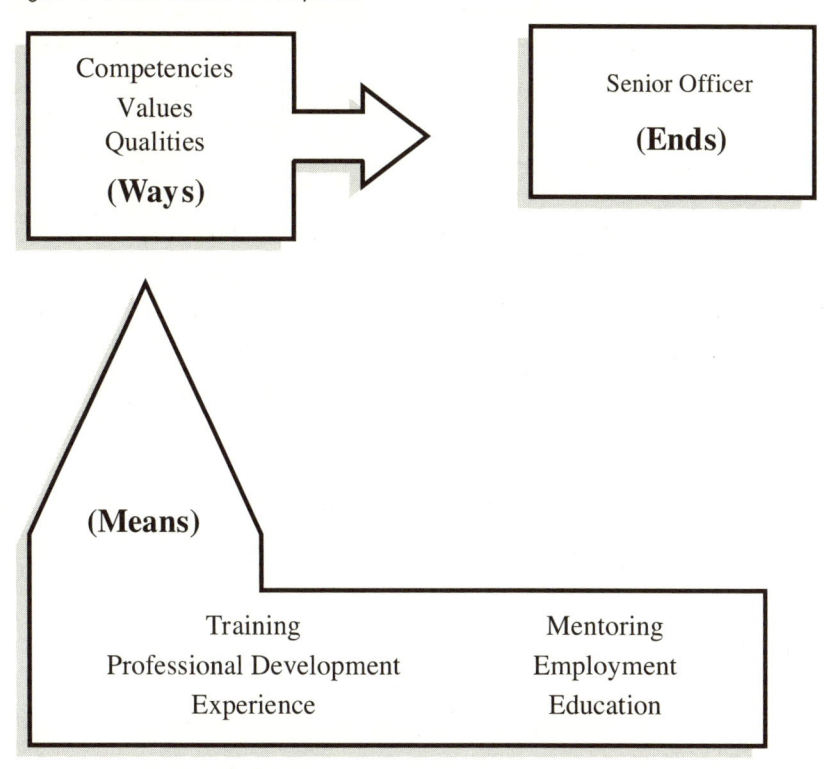

```
Competencies                       Senior Officer
Values         ⟹
Qualities                              (Ends)
(Ways)

(Means)

Training                Mentoring
Professional Development   Employment
Experience              Education
```

Cognitive capacity means understanding and responding strategically to the complex challenges and scenarios faced by the senior leadership of the Canadian Forces and the Department. It allows a leader to perceive parallel and divergent issues within these challenges and scenarios and to interpret key messages and trends. Leaders "use their cognitive capacity to protect the public interest, create order out of chaos, and develop long and short term strategies that will prevent as well as solve problems."[13] Concomitant with this philosophy is the necessity for our senior leadership to remain focused on the strategic aspects of their duties rather than the daily rigours of routine staff work. Lieutenant-General Dallaire, during his tour as ADM (Human Resources Military (HR-Mil)) and later as the Special Advisor to the Chief of the Defence Staff (CDS) on Professional Development, espoused creating a corps of "Iron Colonels" in NDHQ to handle the "tactical mindset and quagmire of the day-to-day emphasis of the in-basket."[14] The aim of such a concept is to leave the general/flag officers time for strategic thinking and long-term planning.

Creativity permits leaders to respond to challenges and ambiguity with innovative solutions and policies by using intuition, non-linear thinking, fresh perspectives, and information from non-traditional sources. The goal is to create new and imaginative ways to succeed. Promoting a continuous learning environment in the workplace enhances creativity. Risk taking and experimentation in the pursuit of unique and effective solutions are encouraged and rewarded.

Creating, promoting and implementing the vision of the future Canadian Forces must emanate from the General and Flag Officer Corps. We must commit to the vision, thereby sending the message to all military personnel that change is positive, sought, and necessary. But why is a vision necessary? "Vision is a sense of the future…providing an intellectual bridge from today to tomorrow. It gives leaders a basis for positive action, growth and transformation. Leaders use vision to mobilize people, to facilitate change and growth, to create a future for their organizations."[15] Vision is what achieves the "organization after next."[16]

The Role of Education

> Two sorts of knowledge are fundamental to the military profession. The first concerns the conduct of fighting (training). The second deals with the military force's purpose in society (education). It is this that allows an army to adapt to change and continue to be useful. It provides the environmental awareness that allows a force to be a "learning organization." Of these two types of knowledge, the second is more important because it sets the conditions for use of the first.[17]

Both the Minister and the CDS in their addresses to the Conference of Defence Associations Annual General Meeting in January 1999 confirmed DND and the CF's commitment to an educated officer corps. I cannot agree more for one fundamental reason. We cannot hope to have general and flag officers with the prerequisite qualities if we do not start developing those qualities in our junior officers from the Development Phase (DP) 1 level.[18] I am not totally confident, however, that any particular undergraduate degree will produce the results we are seeking. We need to guide the educational content of our officer-cadets via a process similar to the one currently underway at the Royal Military College (RMC), that is a "structured" approach to achieve a specific objective.

The RMC core curriculum is being developed and implemented to ensure each student receives a well-rounded education in the humanities, sciences and mathematics, but with a particular emphasis on the military profession. The content of the core curriculum must be carefully selected by RMC in conjunction with the Environmental Commands (ECs) and must be validated by the Officer Professional Development Council, and it must be subsequently refined. For non-RMC undergraduates, the core curriculum subjects must be the focus of OPD programs as determined by individual Commands. Why? "While we must develop every part of the national defence establishment intelligently, nothing exceeds getting the education of our soldiers right. Today we are educating the leaders who will devise and carry out the campaigns of the future."[19]

Core curriculum subjects will set the tone for future professional development. They will be the building block for personal study and subsequent formal education at the Canadian Forces College at the DP 3 and 4 levels. The education must focus on those skills required, over the period of an officer's career, to develop the qualities in our senior officers needed for success at the operational and strategic levels of conflict, and in the executive boardrooms of the Department of National Defence (DND). These include facilitation and mediation, group dynamics, team building, negotiation, and conflict resolution among others.

Other nations are realising that investing in educating senior officers in these twenty-first-century core leadership competencies is essential. For example, the US Army War College and the Industrial College of the Armed Forces have introduced changes to their core curriculum that focus on thinking skills. They will monitor the content of research papers, promote the analysis of prevailing procedures and doctrine, and encourage the creation in the classroom of a sceptical, if respectful, mindset to foster cognitive capacity and innovative thought.[20]

The War College is on the right track. Thinking is the key element in the skill set possessed by a successful general/flag officer. "Today's leaders must widen their perspectives and lengthen the focal point of their thinking. Leaders today have to learn how to thread and weave together disparate parts and move beyond analytical to integrative thinking. Indispensable to a leader is a sense of breadth, the intellectual capacity to handle complex mental tasks, to see relationships between apparently unrelated objects, to see patterns in incomplete information, to draw accurate conclusions from inchoate data."[21] The end result must be an officer capable of strategic thinking, the one quality that distinguishes a senior officer from a junior officer.[22]

Developing the ability to think creatively and strategically, to have a flexible mind, to respond to the vague and uncertain situations of higher command requires education. But the concept of education should not be limited to the confines of the schoolhouse, whether that schoolhouse is RMC, the Canadian Forces College (CFC), civilian institutions or continuing studies programs. We can, and need to, learn from the experiences of our colleagues, both Canadian and foreign. The general/flag officer symposiums on Ethics, for example, have been invaluable for senior officers in preparing one another to successfully meet the pitfalls and challenges of complex peace operations and modern business practices. Another idea is to establish an informal mentoring program for newly promoted brigadier-generals and commodores so valuable lessons and experience are shared on a more personal basis. Major-General C.G. Kitchen even recommended that Armed Forces Council members act as personal mentors and sponsors of one Defence fellow as he/she undertakes a post graduate (PG) program.[23] Other ideas have also been proposed for selected officers with the potential to reach senior leadership positions:

- Increased use of foreign command and staff appointments to provide exposure to other military organizations and strategic leadership appointments, both civilian and military.
- Introduce sabbatical leave with industry, independent think tanks, research centres and civilian universities.[24]
- Secondment to other government departments that play a role in developing strategic national security, defence and foreign policy.
- Post them as professors/teachers at our educational institutions.[25]

CONCLUSION

Generalship brings together the two concepts of strategic thinking and leadership. Strategic vision combined with strong leadership is required if the CF is to successfully meet the challenges of the future. This is one reason that makes ongoing officer education and professional development so important. No one can accurately forecast the future. Therefore we cannot train or educate our personnel with specific skills to meet the requirement of 2020 with any precision. But we can prepare them intellectually to be able to cope with ambiguity and complexity.[26]

Developing officers with the rare competencies of cognitive capacity, creativity and visioning is not an easy task. The current emphasis on educating the Officer Corps is a step in the right direction. The War College courses at CFC, particularly with their emphasis on academic rigour, are forcing senior officers to produce intellectual thought based on serious research and in-depth analysis. Yet the CF bureaucracy has not responded to this cry for educational reform in our Armed Forces:

- the War College courses are under-subscribed;
- the War Studies program at RMC is suffering from a dearth of sponsored candidates, particularly from the Combat Arms;
- many senior officers still view PG programs as self-serving and of no help to the CF;
- current PG students are still subject to negative sanctions from Merit Boards for volunteering to increase their potential effectiveness as a senior officer.

Such negativism to higher education will only be eradicated by imbedding the absolute necessity for an educated officer corps into our culture by translating the Minister's policy into accepted practice among the leadership of the CF. What is required to achieve this objective? Dr. Ron Haycock summed up the solution in these words: the CF requires a "unified policy on education that is clearly defined, promulgated, administered and executed from the centre which guarantees that there will be a flow of senior officers toward the universities." We also require "a long-term management policy for higher education as a vital part in selecting our general officers."[27] On this particular issue, the senior leadership must lead the way. We must demonstrate with clear policy statements in combination with action at the coalface that education is the number one professional development priority of the CF. A structured approach to the educational requirements is necessary, however, to ensure degree programs meet the specific professional development needs of the officer corps, and thereby avoid the creation of a "ticket punching" mentality with the sole purpose of adding letters behind one's name.

Let's not let history repeat itself. Although we were highly regarded during the two great wars of the last century as master tacticians, we were the only Dominion in the Commonwealth that did not produce a Field Marshall despite the significant contribution made by our country in human resources.

According to Dr. Haycock, Canadian generals have defaulted to the Department of External Affairs in the development of a unique Canadian foreign policy, much of which revolves around defence issues. Why? We lack the professional and intellectual capacity to enter into the debate with the diplomats. We are instead mired in Department related issues that preoccupy our daily routines. "To get out of this fix, the generals need an appropriate liberal education—and the time to pursue it…Such an education will give them the agility to recognise the problem and the knowledge to do something about it."[28]

The CF Command Inspector, Colonel Howie Marsh goes so far as to challenge the pool of officers from which our generals and flag officers are selected.[29] He alludes that officers who excel at the tactical level are selected for grooming as our next senior officers. These officers are most likely to have the Myers-Briggs personality type ISTJ (Introverted, Sensor, Thinker, and Judge). Such a person (an introverted thinker) seeks answers to ambiguous situations from internal resources or past experiences (gut feel). Therefore he/she is unlikely to produce an innovative solution to a new situation. Of the Myers-Briggs sixteen personality types, the ISTJ personality is the strongest at resisting change. They excel at maintaining the status quo. If the CF wishes, therefore, to have innovative, strategic thinkers in their stable of general/flag officers, it may be necessary in some instances to eliminate the command requirement in the selection process.

The principal of RMC appropriately expressed the absolute requirement for education in these words during his investiture in October 1999:

> Today, when a young officer may be called upon to be a skilled leader, a technical expert, a diplomat, a warrior and even an interpreter and aid expert, there is no question that good training is not enough. Skills are not enough. The job calls for judgement, that odd distillate of education, the thing which is left when the memorised facts have either fled or been smoothed into a point of view, the thing that cannot be taught directly, but which must be learned. Without the mature judgement that flows from education, we fall back on reflexes, which are damned fine things for handling known challenges, but which are manifestly unreliable when faced with new ones. And there will be new ones.[30]

If this message is applicable to junior officers graduating from RMC, and it most definitely is, then it is even more applicable to us, the senior leadership of the CF. Only one question remains to be answered, "How to sustain the warrior spirit while enhancing those aspects of leader personality that will embrace change, agility, creativity and self awareness when the need for these attributes is paramount."[31] The answer is a balanced approach to officer development, placing emphasis on education at appropriate stages in an officer's career, identifying those officers with general/flag officer core competencies, then focusing their employment into positions and assignments that promote the development of strategic thinking abilities.

> *The officer corps of the future must be less dependent on software and hardware, and far more dependent on grayware—their own minds.*
> —Lieutenant-General R.A. Dallaire[32]

NOTES

1. Included in the Foreword to the Rowley Report, March 1969.
2. Major D.M. Last, CD, PhD, "Educating Officers: Post-Modern Professionals to Control and Prevent Violence," in Bernd Horn, ed., *Contemporary Issues in Officership: A Canadian Perspective* (Toronto: CISS, 2000) Chapter 1.
3. Gregory F. Treverton, *The Changing Agenda* (RAND, Santa Monica, Calfornia, 1995), 5.
4. See Colonel Howie J. Marsh's contribution in this volume, "Command Challenges in the 21st Century."
5. Robert S. Kaplan, "The Coming Anarchy," *The Atlantic Monthly*, February 1944.
6. Term used at the US Army War College in 1994-1995 to describe issues that produced lose-lose outcomes for politicians. "Third rail" refers to the inner rail of a subway system that transmits electricity as the source of power. Hence the connotation, "you touch it, you die!"
7. William J. Crowe, Jr., US Ambassador to the Court of St James. Address to the Naval War College. Spring 1997, 69-78.
8. DND, *Canadian Officership in the 21st Century: OPD 2020 Statement of Operational Requirement,* January 2000, 8.
9. David J. Bercuson, "Defence Education for 2000…and Beyond," Royal Military College, Kingston, 5 December 1998.
10. Ronald G. Haycock, Presentation to the Canadian Club of Kingston, "Clio and Mars in Canada: The Need for Military Education," 11 November 1999.
11. Ibid.
12. Public Service Executive Programs, "Leadership Competencies for ADMs and Senior Executives," Public Service Commission of Canada.
13. Ibid
14. Lieutenant-Colonel Bernd Horn, "Wrestling with an Enigma – Executive Leadership," in *Contemporary Issues in Officership: A Canadian Perspective,* Chapter 5.
15. Gordon R. Sullivan, *Hope is not a Method* (Toronto: Random House, 1996), 79.
16. Ibid, 80.
17. Last, Chapter 1.
18. The DP levels correlate to the following rank levels. DP 1 – Officer Cadet to Second Lieutenant; DP 2—Lieutenant to Captain; DP 3—Major to Lieutenant-Colonel and DP 4 – Colonel and above.

19. Lieutenant-General (retired) D. Holder, Conference on Military Education for the 21st Century Warrior sponsored by the Naval Postgraduate School and Office of Naval Research, Texas A&M University, 15-16 January 1998.
20. John W. Brinsfield, "Army Values and Ethics: A Search for Consistency and Relevance." *Parameters, US Army War College Quarterly*, Autumn 1998, 13.
21. Thomas E. Cronin, "Thinking and Learning about Leadership," *Presidential Studies Quarterly*, 14:1 (Winter 1984), 33.
22. See General M. Baril's contribution in this volume, "Officership: A Personal Reflection."
23. Major-General C.G. Kitchen, "Out Service Training for Officers," March 1985.
24. Colonel John E. Greenwood, "Editorial: Educating for Tomorrow," *Marine Corps Gazette*, September 1999, 4.
25. Lieutenant-General Romeo Dallaire. In his presentation to CSC 24, he stated, "the streamers must not go from command to staff and back to command as a way of broadening their experience. No, they must go from command to teaching and possibly some staff time before their next command tour. This will ensure their intellectual development, their growing awareness of conflict and war, their links to the next generation, and the honing of their warfighting competencies."
26. Ibid.
27. Dr. Ronald G. Haycock, "The Art of Generalship and its Canadian Context," Briefing to the Newly Promoted Brigadier-General and Commodore's Symposium, Canadian Forces College, Toronto, Ontario, 22 November 1999.
28. Ibid.
29. Marsh. The selection theory for senior officers in this paragraph comes from Colonel Marsh's Chapter. I will not indicate direct quotes.
30. Dr. John S. Cowan, Installation Address of the Principal, Royal Military College of Canada, Kingston, Ontario, 4 October 1999.
31. John W. Brinsfield, "Army Values and Ethics: A Search for Consistency and Relevance." Parameters, *US Army War College Quarterly*, Autumn 1998, 11.
32. Lieutenant-General Romeo A. Dallaire, "Future War and the Development of Agile Leadership," Notes for Presentation to CSC 24, 24 October 1997.

The General as a Trainer

Brigadier-General (retired) Ernest B. Beno

Brigadier-General (retired) Ernest Beno served the Guns and the Army for over 37 years. He is currently a consultant in training, contingency planning and human resource management.

The armed forces should primarily be trained and equipped for the possibility of conflict with a first-class power—the most severe testing they may have to face. It has been proven over and over again, that well trained and well disciplined military forces, trained primarily for major warfare, can very easily and effectively adapt to lesser roles of aid to civil power or peace keeping. The reverse is not the case.

—General Guy Simonds, 1972[1]

BACKGROUND

IT IS MY BELIEF THAT TRAINING is what makes the army capable of accomplishing its mission on operations. People, equipment and resources are certainly key components, but the army only achieves its operational capability through the focus of energy in a seamless fashion, and it is through training that all the critical components are brought together. Effective training brings about cohesion, standardization, individual and team confidence, and intelligent, disciplined and innovative approaches to achieving military objectives. There is nothing more important to the army than training. Training must therefore be acknowledged as the paramount command responsibility. If he is to command troops effectively, the general must understand training and be particularly adept in all related aspects; i.e., training philosophy, training concepts, the training process and the practical aspects of training. Collective training is the main purview of generals and commanders, but they must also understand individual training, if only to ensure that their subordinates get the resources and guidance they need to prepare for collective training.

ARMY TRAINING VERSUS NAVY AND AIR FORCE TRAINING

This chapter is about army training, because that is what I know best. I believe that the principles and fundamentals expressed in this chapter apply equally to the navy and the air force, but since their focus is more equipment-oriented the practicalities of the way they train is different from the army. With a greater emphasis on joint operations in the future and with a need for general and flag officers to be able to command joint forces, or indeed to fill positions such as Deputy Chief of the Defence Staff, an understanding of army training is vitally important to senior naval and air force officers—they may well be responsible for conducting army training and may be held accountable for its results.

RESPONSIBILITIES OF GENERALS
AND FORMATION COMMANDERS

In peacetime, training for war is the primary responsibility, perhaps the only true responsibility of an officer. Everything else needs to be tied back to that basic principle. The peacetime officer who does not feel that way about training and fails to conduct his life accordingly is being negligent.

—Major-General (Retired) H.R. Wheatley, 1999[2]

Commanders at all levels have profound responsibilities for training, whether to meet the anticipated requirements of the immediate future or to ensure the continuation of the military's viability and effectiveness in an unknown future. The steps in army training appear simple, but in reality the thought that must go into training calls for extensive knowledge and wisdom, and a feel for soldiering. Generals and formation commanders do not need to know all the right answers, but they do need to ask the right questions, and then seek out the right answers. They must set the tone for the proper training climate.

In short, the general must create an environment that encourages continuous learning—a learning environment that is robust and perpetual—which will influence not only immediate subordinates, but the whole command, and will continue on its own momentum. The training environment established must not only serve his tenure, but must continue on to that of successors. If there were to be only one responsibility for generals and formation commanders it would be to create a healthy and vibrant learning environment.

CHALLENGES OF THE NEW ENVIRONMENT

Events since 1988 demonstrate clearly that the armed forces are facing a new environment that has a major impact on training. No longer is war a theoretical exercise for Canadian soldiers, played out in "war games" on the farms and forests of western Germany, or in the map exercises at staff colleges—with powerful and elaborate fictitious "enemy" organizations taken out of staff officers' handbooks. Since the fall of the Soviet Union the likelihood of being engaged in a world war on short notice has greatly diminished, and many would argue that perhaps there is more time to prepare for any major mobilization situation. Paradoxically, for units in the Regular Force the likelihood of going from a peacetime setting to being in a war has actually greatly increased. The time available to prepare for operations allows less of a buffer than was previously the case. Units are regularly and repeatedly sent into war zones with what they have or with whatever can be cobbled together. However, in the final analysis it is the warfighting capability that gives the Canadian Army its peacekeeping credibility. It is this capability that will permit Canadian soldiers to deal with belligerents as a credible force and with her allies as an equal partner. That credibility comes from training.

THE DEMANDS OF PEACE SUPPORT OPERATIONS

We are in an era of frontier soldiering. This means that generals (must) sort through the crap and decide on what is important.
—Lieutenant-Colonel BA Reid, 2000[3]

The peace support operations of the post Cold War era are very different from those of the 1960s, 70s and 80s. The Gulf War, Bosnia, Somalia, Kosovo and East Timor provide clear examples of peace support environments very different from those of the Golan Heights, the Sinai, Vietnam, and Cyprus. These more recent operations have called for formed, operational and tactically robust units (battle groups and formations) operating with wartime organizations, establishments, capabilities and training. It is not well appreciated how important the army's warfighting doctrine, training and equipment has been in enabling Canadians to so effectively play a role in these situations. Even in the absence of numbers, firepower or modern equipment, Canadian officers and soldiers have demonstrated professional military competence that is equal to the best of our allies. This capability has been the result of our constant focus on warfighting.

But, peacekeeping is not war, and the generals and formation commanders must find the right ways to prepare leaders and to train units to withstand the different challenges of modern peace support operations. Brigadier-General Joe Sharpe's findings on the Operation (OP) Harmony 2 deployment to the Former Yugoslavia give some insight into the difficulty that units face in preparing for and serving on peace support operations:

> The second key factor relates to the dichotomy between achieving the mission assigned to the unit and ensuring the safety of troops in the unit—what is often referred to as force protection. In conventional combat operations it is accepted doctrine that the priority in descending order is mission, own troops, self....The difficulty is that during the types of operations to which the CF was committed in the 1990s missions were virtually never clear cut, the chain of command was not uniquely Canadian, Rules of Engagement were ambiguous and Canadian endorsement of the mission, either formally through the Government or in terms of Canadian public opinion, was often tenuous. In these circumstances dogmatic adherence to warfighting doctrine remains inappropriate and unlikely to receive sustained support by subordinates....It is possible that some portion of the leadership...during their tour in Croatia either could not resolve this dilemma or proceeded on the grounds that the mission must take precedence irrespective of the risk. The final answer in any given situation is by no means self-evident nor are the leadership approach or training methods necessary to prepare future leaders.[4]

He also provided the following recommendation:

> ...leadership for peacekeeping training be developed for all rank levels that will give guidance about when and where it is appropriate to modify the normal 'warfighting' approach to peacekeeping-oriented training when appropriate.[5]

Clearly, training for peace support operations must cause units to transition from a warfighting mode to a mission-specific state. General officers and formation commanders have to work this through, as it cannot be left to individual commanding officers to resolve such dilemma in their own individual ways.

WHAT HAS CHANGED REGARDING TRAINING

What is different for the general or formation commander as a trainer? Given the increased operational tempo, even though it is peace support and not warfighting, there should be a much greater emphasis on realism than may have been the case in the past. For example, mine warfare, first aid, rules of engagement and the Laws of Armed Conflict were virtually ignored in the past—but all are critically important today. One could also argue that officers and non commissioned officers (NCOs) will be expected to think things through much more thoroughly than simply doing a combat estimate. Even in training for warfighting they should be trained to think—not just to react to orders from above. These are factors that have changed the focus of army training and have made it more realistic than the traditional approach used to re-fight the "Fantasians."

Other dramatic changes have also affected the manner in which the army trains. For example some of the major changes in the past decade are:

- Brigades are no longer commanded by brigadier-generals who would have had four to six more years' experience than the Colonels who now command these formations;
- There is no longer a division headquarters to tie two or more brigades together in training, nor to establish and enforce common doctrine;
- Canada no longer has troops deployed in Germany working alongside our US, British, German, French and other allies; and
- Canada no longer periodically deploys a brigade to work with NATO forces in the North Flank area.

All of those conditions permitted and/or encouraged training for operations in a high-risk environment with other major players. The benefits we derived from the training and operational environment of a decade ago no longer exist.

Perhaps some issues that seemed self-evident in the past are not so clear today. For example, Generals and formation commanders will have to explain the need and fight for equipment, resources and training opportunities, that may have previously been forthcoming. Clearly opportunities to train with allies in large formations no longer exist, and the experiential and psychological impact of warfighting training and deterrence operations are absent.

Add to these changes the changing focus, shape and roles of the Canadian Forces, such as:

- Joint operations on short notice, typically in peace support missions, will be the immediate concern and heavy demand for the foreseeable future; and
- Information technology and sophisticated training technology will create new opportunities which must be exploited.

Generals and formation commanders must ask themselves how these new circumstances can best be accommodated, and how the army can maintain its professional edge in face of the new situation. In my view, the difference must be made up with training that is much more effective than we have at the moment.

THE MODERN GENERATION IN THE ARMY

The people in the army today are very different from those of the past. The army is now made up of better educated, computer literate, technologically agile young men and women. Their standards, ethics, interests and aspirations are very different from when the generals and formation commanders enrolled twenty or more years earlier. The young people in the army continue to improve their education, even while on operations. For example, in teaching a correspondence course for the Royal Military College I have frequently had students at the corporal level serving in Bosnia, Central Africa Republic and Kosovo. Two infantry corporals serving as Section 2 ICs in battalions in the former Yugoslavia send e-mail from the front lines on a regular basis.

As the individuals charged with the responsibility for training the army, general officers will have to keep attuned to the changing people in the army—and anticipate such changes so that future training motivates and stimulates their subordinates, while preparing them for the circumstances and responsibilities they will encounter later. Today's young men and women will not be motivated by needless repetition nor wasted time and energy in training. They want and deserve to develop to their full potential. The doctrine, philosophy and guidance on training which emanates from the senior leaders must take this into account.

TRANSPARENCY AND PUBLIC SCRUTINY

Thankfully transparency in all activities has changed significantly. Troops and the public now know, or can easily find out, what training is being conducted and the degree of success being achieved. The results of this are, or should be, broadly disseminated. Such transparency can be a motivator for individuals and units, given that they and others are able to see continuous improvement. In the past there was little or no transparency, and leaders conducted the training they wanted using whatever resources they could obtain. The real outcomes were never visible other than to a small group. This new transparency means that commanders cannot hide behind the cloak of being the "Exercise Director," and therefore able to call the shots on what was done, what was reported on and what was learned. Instead, they must be active participants in the learning and team building experience.

WHAT HAS NOT CHANGED

In spite of significant advances in technology over the past generation there have been precious few changes in training. Yes, information is passed faster and training programs are more capable, advancing for instance from the overhead projector to videos, to power point and the CD-Rom, to web-based training. However, information is not instruction. Too often it has been mistaken for training, but it is not. It is merely the passage of information or the repetition of already mastered knowledge and skills. It is vitally important to create the conditions for people to want to learn, and then provide such an opportunity. That is not different from the past.

The objectives of specific training today may have changed, but overall the training must be aimed at maintaining a high degree of professional competence in warfighting. The challenge for the generals, formation commanders and commanding officers is to determine the right balance to meet today's commitments and to prepare for tomorrow's challenges.

THE WAYS AND MEANS OF DELIVERING TRAINING

Generals and formation commanders have the responsibility to develop the desire to learn and then provide the resources to get the job done. Only then will training become meaningful and productive. Units will learn if offered the opportunities and challenges. But they also need constructive feedback, the outcome of effective evaluation. It comes down to challenges and opportunities. There is no "silver bullet." Focus on the output, i.e., a measurable performance capability, rather than the input, which is the training process. This philosophy and approach to training must be understood, embraced, nurtured and managed by commanders; not left to the staff to organize and oversee.

THE TRAINING PHILOSOPHY

The training philosophy is not just the product of establishing a vision and then aligning people. That is a commonly accepted, but bankrupt approach to re-engineering. It is an approach that suggests that senior leaders are all-knowing and that putting their bright ideas into practice merely entails issuing the appropriate directives and guidelines to a willing followership, or selling their ideas to a reluctant followership. That approach will not work any more, if in fact it ever did. Generals and formation commanders must instead invest their time and energy in understanding the basic issues, and then guide the team through a continuous transition. The solutions to achieving and maintaining an operationally capable army will not be found at the top, but the senior leaders can define the challenges and the issues to be overcome through various means, including training. When training solutions are found they can be disseminated and adopted, building on strengths and overcoming limitations. Generals and formation commanders can put a continuous process of learning in place within a disciplined development environment, and perhaps that should be the extent of "philosophy." From that point forward a momentum and sense of direction will emerge, carrying the army through progressive stages of improvement.

Army generals and formation commanders must establish and demonstrate through their own actions the importance of training in the grand scheme of things. Training is not just one more activity to be performed. When not engaged in operations it is *the fundamental activity*. It is the raison d'etre of an army in peacetime and the most important activity in preparing for operations and war. Even if assigned frequent taskings in para-military roles and non-warfighting missions and even if the support in terms of money, equipment and other resources is not at the optimum, officers and non-commissioned officers must keep the profession of arms alive through training. And training is the responsibility of the leadership of the army. Training is the means by which the character, soul, spirit and muscle of the army is moulded, exercised and developed.

THE OBJECT OF TRAINING

Good formations and units practice their purpose—how to fight—at every opportunity: what works and what doesn't, or more precisely, what is likeliest to work in war, is the most important lesson learned weekly, monthly, yearly.

—Brigadier-General (Retired) C. de L. Kirby, 2000[6]

Within the training philosophy, the army generals and formation commanders have to establish what they intend to achieve. Is it a general-purpose capability to meet the demands of a conventional mechanized war? Is it a multipurpose capability to meet para-military as well as general-purpose operations? Is it to be a high-tech capability with limited demand for a physical presence? If all members of the army are to play their role in achieving the desired end-state they must at least have a broad understanding of the capabilities required in the army of the future.

In the words of General Vuono, former Chief of Staff of the US Army, "The Army must be trained and ready in peacetime to deter war, to fight and control wars that do start, and to terminate wars on terms favorable to US and allied interests."[7] He goes on to say, "This requires that all leaders in the Army understand, attain, sustain and enforce high standards of combat readiness through tough, realistic multi-echelon combined arms training designed to challenge and develop individuals, leaders and units."[8]

These are clear statements of purpose and focus that have prepared the US Army for the many varied, and tremendously challenging, missions they have encountered since the end of the Cold War. Not only has their purpose been clearly articulated, but the way it is to be achieved, i.e., through sound training, has been reinforced with vigourous and determined action.

I cannot emphasize enough the need for a focus. Without such, the training will most certainly stray from what the Canadian Forces wants and needs. One very good unit, the Canadian Airborne Regiment, lacked a clear and well-articulated purpose, which caused it to stray from that which Canada needed. Training varied from raids, to operations in North Norway, to jungle operations. Good people did the best they could with what they had—but with no clear and widely accepted raison d'etre it could not possibly survive in the long run. Many units today, both Regular Force and Militia face a crisis in role or purpose.

When units are assigned a specific situation, such as an operational mission, the training obviously becomes more focussed on the operational requirement, and the necessary steps or stages become more clear. A known, desired end-state sets the parameters for the required capability, and this drives the training concepts, plans and processes.

Specific-to-mission or specific-to-theatre operations (such as operations other than war and domestic operations) require special attention to the training and the evaluation of committed units. I can emphasize from personal experience the need to ensure that guidance and intelligence received from higher headquarters is translated into specific training requirements and objectives and the necessity to clearly outline conditions by which the unit will be evaluated as being prepared for deployment.

The army is being tasked very heavily to provide units on peace support operations. Although commanders and commanding officers continue to do the best they can with ad hoc units and ad hoc training, it is just a matter of time before significant difficulties occur. Relying almost entirely on "general-purpose/multi-purpose combat training" as the principal way to train for any operation has worked reasonably well to date. From a broad perspective and under most conditions this concept suffices. But, it is becoming clearer that more specific-to-theatre and specific-to-mission training is *also* required. The army should create standardized training plans with appropriate scenarios and make these essential for unit preparation. Additionally, expert training teams should be constituted to assist in developing, conducting and evaluating specific-to-mission training and in-theatre analysis of training. Such measures would undoubtedly assist in ensuring common doctrine and common practices while improving our ability to learn from others.

There has been a tendency for training to stop when the troops enter the deployment phase. There are numerous historical examples of continuing training of troops in-theatre in war. It was noted in the Second World War, "When German units were not in the line, they trained long and hard." There must be continuous learning, adaptation, modification, adjustment and re-training during deployment and on arrival in theatre. Other training, even non-mission related activities, should also continue whenever opportunities permit; e.g., trade/MOC courses. It can not be overstated that commanders at all levels must ensure the creation of a continuous learning atmosphere, even in operational theatres.

THE DESIRED END-STATE

Whether units and formations are training for war, peace support operations, domestic operations or humanitarian assistance, commanders will have to decide on what they believe are the key indicators of a well-trained unit, hence what they should be looking for. What is the desired end-state after a defined period of training and preparation? Indicators of a well-trained unit or formation are listed below, and these are the objectives which generals should look for:
- Sound leadership;
- Effective command and control;
- Cohesion;

- Standardized ways of doing things;
- Sound discipline and a disciplined way of doing things; and
- The use of good battle procedure whether the task at hand is operational or administrative in nature.

Although I have listed some indicators of the desired end-state, commanders have to decide what they believe is important, within the concept of their superior intent. They must identify the indicators of the key qualities; e.g., what are the key signs or ways of determining unit cohesion? Examples might include how orders are passed, how sub-components respond, how the unit survives in the absence of a few key individuals, and how the unit reacts to changing circumstances.

PRINCIPLES OF TRAINING

Training is a great art; there are principles of training just as there are principles of war.

—Field Marshall Bernard Montgomery[9]

In Canadian doctrine there are ten Principles of War. These are easily translatable into "Principles of Training." For example, "Selection and Maintenance of the Aim" is very clear, "Economy of Effort" implies the wise use of resources in training, and "Concentration of Force" translates into applying the critical resources to the most likely avenue of success. Principles of Training are less clearly enunciated in Canadian doctrine. The applicable Canadian Forces manuals may list principles for training delivery, but not broad strategic principles of training.

It would be appropriate for senior army officers to articulate what they see as the principles of training, and then establish these as the foundation for training practices in all army formations and units. I will offer a few, and acknowledge readily that some of these have been borrowed from United Kingdom and United States doctrine.[10] These are only suggestions. Those in command must articulate where they stand on basic principles. If they do not agree or would like a different emphasis, then they should so state, and if it becomes unrealistic to follow through on a principle, then there needs to be a rationalization—either the principle is wrong or the ongoing practices are wrong.

The suggested fundamental principles of training are:

Training is a Function of Command. British doctrine rightfully lists this as the first principle of training. It states, "Though responsibility for the detail of training can be delegated, the overall responsibility for the state of training of individuals, sub-units, units and formations rests always with the commander. It is therefore important that commanders become involved in, and place their authority on, training." In the United States doctrine the principle is similar:

> Make Commanders the Primary Trainers. The leaders in the chain of command are responsible for the training and performance of their soldiers and units. They are the primary training managers and trainers for their organizations.

Training Must Have an Aim, Focus and Objectives. All ranks need to know the purpose of their training and understand why it is being conducted the way it is. They all contribute to the outcome and should have a vested interest in success. With a clear vision of the commanders' intent all subordinates can progress toward the goal in their own manner and at a rhythm and pace best suited to local circumstances. Establishing this intent also implies setting priorities. General Bruce C. Clarke, US Army, said:

> Do essential things first. There is not enough time for the commander to do everything. Each commander will have to determine wisely what is essential, and assign responsibilities for accomplishment. He should spend the remaining time on the near essentials. This is especially true of training. It is the responsibility of the general officers, not the staff, to set the aim and priorities, as only then will they be reflected in action.[11]

Train as You Will Fight. Troops will respond in operations as they have been trained—so it is vital that they be trained as they will have to fight. I would add to this—trained as they will have to function in operations, such as peace support missions and aid of the civil power/assistance. Train them for the worst case first, and for the specific operation before committing them.

Disciplined Initiative Must Be Practiced and Inculcated in Training. As with mission-oriented tactics, if subordinates are aware of the purpose and are provided adequate resources, they can achieve the aim in a manner best suited to their situation. Retired Canadian Brigadier-General Kip Kirby would refer to this as disciplined initiative, which is not possible without a clear understanding of the object. British Colonel G.F.R.Henderson wrote at the turn of the last century: "Intelligent discipline, [is] best illustrated, perhaps, by a pack of well-trained hounds, running in no sort of order, but without a straggler, each making good use of his instinct and following the same object with the same relentless perseverance."[12]

Commanders Must Go For the Centre of Gravity. Major-General Alderson wrote in 1908, "Tis said that, the Army hangs on the Company; hence the nation does. What a responsibility rests on the company commander!"[13] Commanders at all levels must determine what the real centre of gravity is for their units or formations, the centre of gravity being as Clauswitz says, "the hub of all power and movement, on which everything depends." Might this be the Combat Team for the Canadian Army? Some might argue yes, in most circumstances, but it is the Battle Groups that we commit to operations, and these Battle Groups that are the building blocks for the Canadian Army of today—and brigades/divisions if we anticipated major operations of war. Some might argue that platoons would be the appropriate level for the militia, but through exploiting modern technology I believe that companies should be the training centre of gravity. What is important is that the army generals and formation commanders determine the army's training centre of gravity and concentrate on training that component well. The army cannot and will not be able to do all things well on a continuing and sustainable basis, so, generals must decide on what is the centre of gravity to meet immediate needs, while at the same time providing a foundation to meet the long-term needs.

The Army Should Train Individuals "Two Up". Budget conscious staff officers may not like it, but it has to be said. "Training-to-need" and training to the lowest common standard are simply not acceptable. In training and in peace support operations there have been frequent situations in which officers and NCOs have to do the jobs of their immediate superiors and often the one two levels up. Whether it is the result of individuals being pulled out of the line or merely exercising the leave policy, filling in for higher positions is common practice. In war, training two up is critical. My point is, that although some may see this as superfluous training, the fact of the matter is that in the army training two up is essential. An army that has not achieved training two up cannot sustain itself and is therefore not ready to be committed to operations.

Training Must Be Permissive of Error. Again, British doctrine states, "Training should allow people to learn from the experience of their mistakes. It is not a selection process. It should be clear, however, that not all errors (such as those which breach the law or safety regulations) are permissible. Nor are repeated mistakes acceptable." The United States Army essentially believes in the same philosophy, that making mistakes is by nature a part of the learning process and it is through the after-action review and lessons-learned process that training improves individual and team performance.

One Should Never Pass Up The Chance To Learn Lessons. This was inculcated in us as junior officers at the tactical level, and still applies to generals and formation commanders at the operational and strategic levels. It is widely accepted that Bismark stated that "Fools say that you can only gain experience at your own expense. I have always contrived to gain my experience at the expense of others." Generals and other senior officers should encourage all ranks to continuously take notes and learn lessons. Create the environment of a learning organization no matter the task at hand or the opportunity that presents itself. As General Sullivan and Colonel Harper argued in *Hope Is Not A Method*: "The only real failure is the failure to learn."[14] As an example of recording lessons, Major-General Alderson's book *Lessons From 100 Notes Made in Peace and War*, is chock full of wonderful gems which apply today, and it was published in 1908! He said:

> I have for some years been in the habit of jotting down, in a note book, or on any available scrap of paper, notes of things that I saw, and heard, and read, that struck me as likely to be useful in the future. These notes have been made in war, at peace manoeuvres, and at sport. As I glanced over them the other day it seemed to me that many applied, not only to the good and bad things we see done in war, but also to the good and bad things we see done during peace exercises and manoeuvres, and it occurred to me that to reproduce some of these notes might help us all to avoid the bad and increase the good. I cannot add to this, except to say that this thinking should be inculcated in all leaders, from Section Commander up.

One Must be as Meticulous in Planning Training as in Planning Operations. We have estimates and the operations planning process for planning operations, and then we have a very clear and methodical battle procedure for following through on operations, but all too often the planning for training is given less attention. Orientation, Mission Analysis, Desired End-State, Intent, Synchronization, Rhythm and Pace, Courses of Action, Testing Courses Of Action, Risk Analysis, Branch and Sequel Planning are all familiar terms in planning for and engaging in operations. Planning for and engaging in training deserves equal attention. This is covered in considerable detail in my booklet "Training to Fight and Win: Training in the Canadian Army."[15]

Training Must Reflect Operational Doctrine. Both American and British training doctrine emphasize the point, and both discuss the need to train as you fight. Generals and formation commanders must know the doctrine and when they visit training they should see to it that doctrine is either being followed or that initiatives are being taken to modify doctrine if there are better ways to fight. In following doctrine there must be a high degree of realism, and to achieve this generals must ensure that units and formations have the right mix of weapons simulation and live fire. Unrealistic training wastes time. When one puts this all together one must conclude that the doctrine should reflect reality (i.e., linking doctrine to Canada's real roles and real equipments/weapons, and realistic settings) and the training should be conducted to ensure units can meet the worst-case demands of reality.

Training Must Be Objectively Evaluated. Later in this chapter I will deal with evaluation and the technology to permit it. Suffice it to say, if training is not evaluated then chances are it is, or will soon become meaningless. General officers and formation commanders must use all the means at their disposal to evaluate training, and then put the results to good use in providing feedback and incorporating lessons learned. Dispatching units on operations without effective evaluation is like firing a weapon blindfolded and hoping you hit somewhere in the target area.

Technology Should be Exploited to the Fullest. This philosophy needs to be inculcated in all ranks, and it will only be so if the general officers and formation commanders insist on it. Not only can resources be husbanded, but the quality of training can improve exponentially if modern technology is exploited. This is especially important in the process of preparing and declaring units operationally ready for overseas deployments. It is also critical for Reserve units who are typically long distances away from their training facilities. There is no doubt that the Weapons Effects Simulation (WES) system is no longer a nice-to-have; it is essential to maintain a degree of combat readiness. Additionally, inter-connected virtual simulators are vital to preparing units so that the benefits of WES can be realized.

PROGRESSIVE STEPS OF TRAINING

At all levels (platoon, company, battalion, battle group, brigade and higher) it must be confirmed that all training objectives have been achieved before pushing on. This requires the personal attention of sub-unit, unit and formation commanders. Commanding officers must not be allowed to begin unit level exercises until they have clearly established that sub-units are ready to progress to advanced training. This requires a measure of evaluation. The most reliable method commanders have to do this is to see for themselves the level of competence achieved by actively getting involved in the concluding stages of unit training. Only after formation commanders have confirmed that units and battle groups have achieved the desired level of training should the formation attempt to progress to the next stage. Although this appears self-evident, units and formations often launch into higher level training before the sub-components are fully prepared. The results are predictable—a broad, but shallow level of training wherein the organization will not be able to withstand the pressures of sustained operations.

PACE AND RHYTHM OF TRAINING

Training should have a pace and rhythm, which is orchestrated to build one step after the other. Effective evaluation at each level is critical, to determine the optimum pace and rhythm of the subsequent step. The different means of training, such as constructive simulation, field exercises, virtual simulation and field simulation should be woven into a progressive training program to exploit the best qualities of the training medium.

CREATING A LEARNING ENVIRONMENT

All commanders and leaders must consistently work at creating a learning environment, no matter what task is at hand. Encouraging this philosophy must start at the top and once it catches on, it must be part of the thinking and action at every level—be it the section, the counter in the quartermaster stores, the transport platoon, the commanding officer's "O" Group or the higher headquarters.

General Sullivan and his colleague, Colonel Harper, have said it all in their book, *Hope Is Not A Method*. That book is well worth the read. The learning organization philosophy they espouse is based primarily on Peter Senge's concepts as set out in his book, *The Fifth Discipline: The Art and Practice of the Learning Organization*, also well worth reading. These books make for a good study and should stimulate a change in attitude and actions. Canada's Army can learn much from the US Army experiences of the seventies to the nineties, and it must learn to become a learning organization.

SUPPORT TO TRAINING

Dealing with resource issues is a major responsibility of general officers and formation commanders, and training is a major resource-consuming activity. Training should not just be assigned the residual after all other demands are allocated resources. The right amount and proper nature of training must be determined first, and appropriate time, ammunition, people, equipment and consumables assigned to achieve the desired end-state.

HOW MUCH IS ENOUGH?

General officers and formation commanders are the judges of "How much is enough?" or the reverse, "How much is too little?" With all the operational taskings, ceremonial taskings, and other, often unforeseen demands, there comes a time when the general officers and formation commanders just have to say "No!" A scale of annual or periodic training has to be developed and it must remain sacrosanct so that army units are assured the minimum necessary training. On the other hand, there have been cases of units spending over two hundred days per year in the field on "training" with virtually no measure of effectiveness other than gut feel. All this to say that general officers must ensure that units get sufficient training, in the right concentration, in those areas of greatest importance—and that training resources not be frittered away.

TRAINING OVERSIGHT

Commanders should visit units and formations in training whenever the opportunities arise—which should be often. This is part of every commander's job and responsibility and should be considered a normal component of the training evaluation process. In addition to the planned visits, casual visits should occur frequently. Visits should never be without purpose, even the most casual of visit, and there may well be times when a commander is looking for something very specific—such as the standard achieved at a particular point in time, especially when units are training for a particular mission.

Whenever possible, commanders should be included in the training, but *not* as a VIP. Army generals and formation commanders should enjoy soldiering and should not mind getting cold, wet and tired. Spending a day with a section, in a tank, in a gun detachment or on a delivery point (DP) can reveal a lot about a unit.

During their visits general officers and formation commanders should demand good briefings from NCOs and junior officers, to include:
- Where they are in the training cycle and the rationale behind the training;
- Christening of the ground and outline of the specific activity;
- The aim and scope of the training;
- The conduct of the training;
- Safety measures;
- Lessons learned to that point in the training; and
- Remedial or additional training required.[16]

Commanders at all levels have the right, necessity and obligation to know what is going on throughout their organization. Field Marshall Montgomery was noted for his "phantom system" of staff officers strategically placed at subordinate levels, reporting directly back to him—in his words, "You will not have time to visit sub-units in the front line; if you want a line on how they are working, send some other officer to get that information for you." Wellington, Napoleon and Patton were all noted for similar ways of learning what was really going on. The extreme, however, were the "chateau generals" of the First War, who were completely out of touch with the front, or those commanders under Westmoreland in Vietnam who went overboard, constantly looking over the shoulders of, and interfering with the authority of, subordinate commanders.

Each commander must find the best way to become and remain informed, in a way that fits his personality and the climate of his organization. Informal channels, like "gathering information by walking about," keeping attuned to the regimental sergeant majors' or second-in-commands' networks, asking the right questions of medical officers and padres, are some of the ways of assuring oneself that the formal feedback one is receiving really does coincide with reality.

I remember, as a young captain in Germany, the visit of the Commander Corps Artillery, the Commander Division Artillery and my own Commanding Officer—all visiting when I was in the middle of a fire plan. On a nearby knoll the three of them leaned back on their shooting sticks chatting away and occasionally lifting their binoculars. Meanwhile my armpits were getting sweaty under the pressure of the British Instructor-in-Gunnery (IG) and my own Battery Commander. As H-hour pressed down upon me and I still had a few more targets to sort out, I was getting ever more nervous and agitated. Beads of sweat formed on my brow. Just then my Tech, a Newfoundlander said, "Lard Jesus Sir, take it easy. If you think you got problems look at them guys over there—with the sticks stuck up their arses." Well, that was their way of learning what was going on at the front—but no doubt the IG reported back what a splendid fire plan I pulled off, once I relaxed.

Commanders must learn about the effectiveness of the training of their subordinate organizations to determine their effectiveness as a whole, and they need to direct their telescope to assure themselves of the reality.

THE GENERAL TRAINING HIMSELF

> *... if the General is not trained to command a formation in the field, then he will not be a good trainer."*
>
> —Brigadier-General (retired) S.V. Radley-Walters, 1999[17]

Service in the profession of arms must entail lifelong learning. Generals and formation commanders need to learn continuously. This can be achieved through reading, studying operation, and keeping abreast of doctrine and international developments. Walking the ground and discussing tactics, such as Tactical Exercises Without Troops (TEWTS) in Norway and Germany, as well as battlefield studies of Normandy and Italy of the Second World War are examples of relating current doctrine to ground and also learning from our history. Immediately after the Second World War, the British Imperial Defence College did battlefield tours of major Canadian battles of the war, yet we did not do the same until several generations later. The Gulf War, Oka and even Bosnia and Somalia have yet to be studied in detail by army generals, and the voluminous after-action reports produced for operations such as these are not particularly instructive as they tend to contain too much detail, with several different opinions, and often miss the important points. They typically miss the main points. It is tremendously important that the senior officers of the army take time to reflect on their profession, thereby maintaining a body of knowledge of operations at the higher level. It is equally important that they pass on their thoughts to the next generation in a free exchange of ideas.

Participating in major operational studies, battlefield tours, field exercises and Command Post Exercises (CPXs) of our allies would also be instructive if approached with the positive attitude of maintaining professional knowledge, which would entail documenting and bringing back lessons to include in doctrine and/or in writing professional papers which can be widely disseminated and discussed.

As difficult as it may be, general officers and formation commanders must keep abreast of technology and be prepared to work with training simulation equipment. Do not just ask for an aide-memoire and try to memorize what you do not know. The troops will see through this very quickly and will not forget. However, if you give it an honest effort and stumble in doing so, the troops will forgive your clumsiness. It never hurt to do sword drill under the tutelage of the RSM and out of sight of the soldiers, as long as you got it right when on parade, but today one can no longer prepare oneself out of sight. Generals must get some personal time on the technology so that they can understand the basics. They then must work at it so that they can work with it intelligently—then they will not have to "act."[18] With the technology being introduced with the Land Force Command, Control and Information System general officers and formation commanders will have no option but to be technologically agile.

As already stated, general officers must also personally involve themselves in training—including the planning, execution, personal participation and assessment of the training. Once so committed they automatically prevent the proverbial distracters (e.g., taskings, other opportunities, resource re-allocation) from interfering with the focus, purpose and momentum of the training. Not only must they oversee what the staff are doing, but they should personally go through the planning process as they would in operations and they should play their operational role to the fullest. They must get right in there, allow themselves to be trained and tested, and allow themselves to be critiqued. It's only embarrassing the *first* time you make a mistake—after that you do not make the mistake. Without such a degree of personal commitment general officers and formation commanders cannot keep abreast of (and better yet ahead of) doctrine. Furthermore, without their personal example the subordinates will surely lack interest and commitment.

COACHING

It is the business of the teacher not to cram his pupils, but to teach them to think; and how to read, and think, and act for themselves.

–Major-General E.A.H. Alderson[19]

Not talked about much in the past, and a relatively new concept in civilian training, coaching can have a significant and lasting impact on subordinates. Coaching can be achieved by engaging in professional dialogue and debate at study groups or during Tactical Exercises Without Troops (TEWTs). It can be done through personal contact (of course being alert to perceptions of favouritism), and it can be done via correspondence, videoconference and personal example. In my own case, since retiring, I have found it extremely instructive to teach correspondence courses for the Royal Military College and remain in regular contact with dozens of serving members at all rank levels. I only wish that I had done such a thing while serving. For a serving general officer to offer a university level course while continuing with other responsibilities would be extremely refreshing and enlightening. They would be more aware of the concerns, aspirations and capabilities of the soldiers, and would be able to coach them through with personal examples and pass on the years of experience. For example, coaching officers through running a distance learning course on leadership, military history, peacekeeping or operations planning would keep the general current while at the same time passing on what they have to offer. This can be done without rupturing the chain of command if a "coaching" mentality were adopted. The impact of coaching through putting pen to paper can be significant. Very few general officers have articulated their thoughts on training, leadership, the impact of technology on operations or the future of warfare/conflict. These are examples of subjects of fundamental concern to the army, and the leadership of the army should be provoking new thought from the future generation. Example can be a powerful tool. The British *Army Field Manual, Training For Operations* states:

> Coaching is one of the most important functions of command and leadership at any level, and also one of the most neglected. Good coaching requires techniques which can and should be consciously developed....confidence on the part of the coach, a sensitivity to the individual development needs of the subordinates, and an acceptance that he or she has a role to play in meeting those needs, and the building of relationships conducive to coaching.[20]

DEVELOPING, NURTURING AND LEVERAGING THE TRAINERS

Not all officers or senior NCOs were meant to be leaders and commanders. The same would apply to trainers. Some are naturally good at it. The best of these individuals should be singled out and further developed, nurtured and exploited to gain maximum advantage of their particular talents. I am not referring to "Training Development Officers," who as their name suggests, are technical experts in developing training and advising on technical aspects. I am referring to proven leaders whose natural talent is training. They should be employed as such rather than being rotated through staff and command positions. Montgomery observed, on the state of troop training in the Canadian Army in England prior to the invasion of Normandy, "little time was spent in teaching officers how to train troops." Company commanders who had "never been taught how to train companies" thus employed "old fashioned training methods that were in use 30 years ago, with the result that much time was wasted and many men bored." [21]

To avoid repeating the mistakes of the past, general officers and formation commanders should be selecting, encouraging and employing the really skilled and talented trainers. Create an effective training cadre, perhaps as a secondary military classification, develop a training philosophy within which they can manoeuver, and use their talents and skills for the maximum benefit of all.

Commanders should employ teams of training experts to bring back lessons from the field and especially from ongoing operations. Similarly they should deploy training teams to operations involving other nations, either during or immediately after the military operation. Their observations, findings and recommendations should be incorporated into Canadian doctrine and the training process. These same trainers could be responsible for national joint and combined exercises for Chief of Land Staff and/or Deputy Chief of Defence Staff. Three specific roles would be:

- An "Operational Review" capability, deployed immediately to new mission areas to gather doctrinal and training observations;
- An "Operational Evaluation" capability, charged with reporting back to senior commanders on the operational capability of units in training and/or assess the results of training on operations;
- An operational level "Lessons Learned" capability, beyond the existing tactical level staff but working in close conjunction with them, to provide and coordinate doctrinal lessons for the development of joint and combined doctrine and training; and
- An operational level exercise and simulation staff to organize, develop and run multi-formation, joint and combined training exercises.

LEADERSHIP TRAINING AND DEVELOPMENT

If there was one area of individual training where the generals and formation commanders must take an interest it is in leadership training. The army leadership environment is significantly different from that of the navy and air force, yet there is only one CF doctrinal base, and it is woefully out of date. There is no subject more highly studied in the business community than leadership, a fact that can be readily seen when looking through the titles of the most current literature. Of the top twenty books regularly advertised, fully eighty percent will have the word "leader" or "leadership" in it. One university has recently offered a degree in leadership, and Corrections Canada is creating an individualized lifelong leadership program for all employees and developing a multi-million dollar leadership institute. Regrettably, leadership development takes place only in brief courses at the commencement of careers, and as pointed out, is based on twenty-five-year-old doctrine on transactional leadership models. Hardly appropriate when business concerns itself with human resource management issues like transformational leadership, emotional intelligence and intellectual audits.

This chapter is not about leadership, but it is abundantly clear that the operational effectiveness of units is dependent upon it. The quality of training is magnified greatly by good leadership. No matter how good the training plan, process or activities happen to be, without sound leadership the effectiveness of army units to fulfill operational missions will be significantly reduced.

Leadership in its entirety: selection, training, development, evaluation, research, and doctrine need to be re-thought in the Canadian Forces and particularly in the army. We do not place enough emphasis on this core matter—from training section commanders through to developing generals. We don't even have an "owner" or "patron" for leadership, but there are several "management" gurus and much money is spent on promulgating management materials.

In our training at all levels, section to brigade, especially in a resource constrained army, the emphasis in training should always be on developing leaders. We need to create operationally effective units to meet specific tasks and we must train in operations of war to develop and maintain a capability in current doctrine—but it is through the development of sound leaders that we will be ready to meet the tasks of today and prepare for the unknowns of the future. Therefore even as we train we must realize that developing leaders is of greater importance in the long term. Likewise, even if we do not have the resources to train at the level we would like—by emphasizing thinking leaders, intellectual agility and robustness, a common sense approach, and ethical conduct, we will at least ensure that we can effectively and professionally employ all the available resources in any emergency or war. Perhaps large armies can do things differently and rely on a "come as you are" philosophy, but history has shown that the Canadian Army should capitalize on people, especially leaders.

CREATING A LEARNING ENVIRONMENT

Remember the more that education permeates down to the private soldier the better.

—Lord Wolseley

Invest in education, professional development, intellectual capital before, and if necessary at the expense of equipment purchases. The professional-intellectual capacity of the army and its people is worth so much more in international security than is the technical capacity. Technical training is a must, but Canada's greatest contribution to world peace and security can be through people—its soldiers.

Perhaps it's time to concentrate energies on "learning in the army" rather than "training in the army." Training implies the delivery of information and the teaching of skills, but a different philosophy might emphasize continuous learning from available information and the acquisition and practice of skills. Might this mean calling the "Combat Training Centre" the "Combat Learning Centre," or the "Land Force Doctrine and Training System" being re-named the "Land Force Doctrine and Learning System?" Such changes would indicate a significant shift from the delivery of training to an emphasis on the receipt and absorption of knowledge and skills. It might be worth thinking about!

EVALUATION

I have always taken this as a lesson that we must judge all men, and all units, by practical results, and not by words.
—Major-General E.A.H. Alderson, 1908[22]

Over the past decade and a half, in the absence of effective evaluation, the Canadian Army has been sending units into conflict and hoping for the best. Hope is no longer an option. Periodic evaluation exercises are required at all levels. Battle Task Standards can assist in setting the goals and outside trainers/evaluators can help confirm the degree to which battle task standards have been achieved. In the final analysis the training needs to be evaluated to confirm that the desired objectives have been achieved and the resources applied have been appropriate.

All training needs to be evaluated by those in command. Commanders must assess the standards achieved by subordinate units against specific training objectives. A "contractual agreement" between the brigade commander and the CO concerned, or the CO and his subordinate commanders, is a good starting point for these assessments. The superior provides the time, money and resources for their subordinates to expend in training and has a right to expect an agreed deliverable—and the means by which the deliverable can be judged is through effective evaluation.

By going through the following step-by-step overview one can clearly see that evaluation is the critical component of the training process. We have traditionally approached evaluation in an ad hoc manner and built resistance to change rather than embracing positive change. Consider the following observations with a view to determining the value and importance of objective evaluation of observed performance in relevant training situations:

> The Centre of Gravity for achieving a healthy, vibrant, professional and effective army is achieved through training. Pay is a satisfier, equipment an enabler, people provide the heart, soul and spirit—but it is through good training that an army learns how to learn, and then learns.

> The key to learning, and continuous learning, is feedback. Useful feedback comes from thorough and objective observation as well as from self-critique (team-critique in the case of units and sub-units). Useful feedback is the result of having sound evaluation.

Evaluation is the key to useful feedback. One can achieve sound evaluation through the objective and focused collection, collation and analysis of observations. Assuming that the training is well designed and a thorough and professional evaluation process is in place, the feedback can help a learning organization continuously raise its standards and improve its operational capability.

Once an objective, focused and professional evaluation process is in place the standards become more clearly defined and broadly accepted. Those standards then become the benchmark to measure subsequent performance. Good leaders naturally strive first to achieve and surpass the standards that are set, and to set new and higher standards for themselves and their team. Even in the absence of clear and high standards set by some higher authority, a good evaluation process will soon generate suitable standards as a bi-product of the evaluation process. Those standards provide the yardstick by which success or failure in performance should be measured.

Another benefit, and some would say the primary benefit, is that effective evaluation causes commanders at all levels to be accountable for using resources wisely to meet the expectations of the army. In the absence of an evaluation process there is no means by which units and their leaders can be held accountable to achieve a desired end-state.

The after-action review is the process by which effective evaluation is turned into constructive lessons learned. Effective after-action review takes place when there is frank, perceptive, organized and open dialogue between the trainers and those being trained, and within the teams in a 360-degree sense. Good commanders use the lessons learned to improve doctrine, practices, equipments, skills, knowledge, team composition, training techniques, etc.

From a broader perspective, with a good evaluation process in place it is only a matter of time before:
- Open and frank dialogue and thorough analysis become commonplace;
- Individuals learn their strengths and limitations and improve their proficiency;
- Leaders personally grow and then develop the next generation of leaders;
- Cohesive teams become proficient and continue to improve;
- Drills, tactics and SOPs continuously and progressively evolve;
- Doctrine (i.e., the desired end-state) is tested, modified and improved;

- Standards (i.e., the criteria for success) become more clearly defined, more realistic and more professionally demanding;
- Evaluation becomes more sophisticated, and therefore more useful;
- Confidence, morale, esprit de corps, pride and professionalism develop; and
- Units become evermore operationally capable.

Training needs analysis, training plan development, tactical doctrine, resource allocation, the conduct of training, standards, evaluation and the after-action review are all inter-connected and inter-dependant. The evaluation concept must be in harmony with all other aspects of training. Although good evaluation is the key to useful feedback, it is just one part of a complete training process and philosophy that has to be embraced.

With effective evaluation commanders at all levels, and the Canadian Forces as a whole, will have a better sense of unit capability and viability. Training evaluation should be part of the annual or ongoing unit capability profile. A measure of operational effectiveness and value for each training dollar invested would be the outcome, which in turn will help explain and validate the need for the resources consumed and the energies expended.

The above discussion illustrates that having an effective evaluation process is critical to achieving high standards of operational capability in the army. It also makes the whole system accountable for the effective and efficient use of resources. If one accepts that good training is the key to creating and developing operationally capable units then one must conclude that a sound evaluation process is a vital component of that training. The challenge then is to find the right evaluation tools. That will be discussed under simulation and training technology. It is now possible to evaluate the training of units realistically and effectively by using simulation and associated technology.

THE AFTER ACTION REVIEW

Evaluation of training is only productive if the After Action Review (AAR) is conducted in a deliberate, professional, frank and open manner. The aim of the AAR is to review the training with the primary training audience to identify key events, critical moments, weaknesses in training and corrective actions required. The after action reports we have all seen in the past typically entailed great reams of paper but were relatively ineffective. The AAR to which I am referring is something quite different. General officers should ensure that appropriate AARs are conducted and that they are followed through to improve both near-term and long-term operational capability.

The AAR is an essential and integral part of all training. It will be of value only if orchestrated with great care, if it is properly focused and if it is conducted in a timely manner. The purpose cannot be to embarrass or criticize people, but to gain objective insights into how teams performed against clearly articulated standards. Ideally, because of the transparency and the way the AAR is conducted, the lessons will come from the primary training audience, and not necessarily from the exercise director or control staff—although the latter will have noted the lessons so that they can ask the right questions of the players.

General officers and formation commanders should be aware of the importance of conducting the AAR professionally, hence the following steps are offered as a possible format. The exercise director will have carefully planned the atmosphere of the AAR, to include the format, appropriate seating, training aids (maps, charts, diagrams, etc), supporting information (audio, video, written, etc) and take-home material. The following was borrowed from Colonel (Retired) John Joly[23]:

What Was Planned. This is a review of what was planned in order to identify the intent before events leading to success or failure occurred.

What Actually Happened. This describes the events that led to success or failure. This is best accomplished through a chronological review of the activities, and through the identification of key events that influenced the result.

What Was Done Well. This reinforces what was done well to drive home the benefits of the event. The identification of what was done well is often related to the effective application of principles, functions or activities.

What Was Not Done Well. This identifies what should have been done differently to achieve greater efficiency, or to improve the overall results. The objective analysis of what actually happened will identify the violation of principles, functions or activities that may have reduced the success that was achieved, or more seriously; triggered the conditions that led to failure.

What Should Be Done Differently Next Time. The criteria for success in evaluation is the identification of action that should be taken to perform the activity better next time in order to achieve the required operational standard of efficiency.

The outcome of an effective AAR is a primary training audience motivated to improve their performance, and a training system motivated to improve processes, doctrine, equipment, drills and procedures that will improve the operational effectiveness of the army.

SIMULATION AND TRAINING TECHNOLOGY

For many reasons the army has not been particularly adept at buying all of the required simulation and training technology when it makes major capital purchases. In the exploitation of simulation the Canadian Army is more than a decade behind the US, British and other armies such as Israel, Norway and Sweden. The acquisition of WES (Weapons Effects Simulation) will be a major breakthrough. For once the army will be able to prepare units for operations under simulated warlike (or peace support operations) conditions. WES will permit effective evaluation at all levels and will build unit cohesion, battle acuity and combat readiness. WES will permit commanders to design exercises that can be as stressful, demanding, challenging and realistic as the soldiers would encounter in peace support operations or war. Effectively employed, WES will bring about a noticeable shift in professionalism and operational capability. Why? Because it provides the situations described above and enables effective evaluation of teams operating in these realistic settings. Through effective training with WES systems individuals, teams and the Army training system will learn lessons that will improve operational effectiveness and enhance the likelihood of success in operations.

WES is not the be-all and end-all of training. It is but one part, and one could argue the most important part, of an essential continuum from individual, to team, to higher-level command and staff simulation, to virtual simulation at the team level, then WES, and then live field fire and manoeuver training. Inter-connected virtual training is still several years away for the Canadian Army, but it is an important prerequisite in preparation for WES training. Even though it is essential, live field fire and manoeuver is becoming increasingly problematic for the army because of cost, time available and resource constraints. The limited opportunities which will exist will have to be exploited to their fullest. This necessitates that simulation be used extensively and wisely to maximize the benefits of live fire training.

ACCOUNTABILITY

Accountability is a fundamental part of officership at every level and increases in importance with higher rank.

—Major-General H.R. Wheatley, 1999[24]

In my opinion the bottom line is accountability. Accountability has been sadly lacking in the training process in the Canadian Army and must be reintroduced in a deliberate and methodical manner. A comprehensive evaluation process will assist with many aspects of accountability, but still there must be a higher degree of accountability to demonstrate the wise expenditure of resources. For example, the system must be able to identify the cost savings when new simulation technology is introduced. Commanders must be able to justify the ammunition, and other, expenditures in support of multi-purpose and mission-specific training. They must also be able to explain to the government how much training is enough, and conversely how much training is inadequate. Then the generals and formation commanders must be held accountable to deliver the right amount of training to the right audience at the right time. A great deal of guesswork has gone into such factors in the past

To ensure accountability for achieving the training standard expected, clear responsibilities must be articulated. The quality of operational capability must be evaluated and the commander at the appropriate level must be held accountable. Civilian companies do this all the time. The only difference is that the bottom line in the military is difficult to define because it is not just profit that counts. Other armies are able to do so without going to the extreme of a "bean counter" approach. Surely Canada's generals can determine the appropriate yardsticks to hold commanders accountable for the results of their training efforts and resource consumption.

THE FUTURE

Recruiting high quality talent will be a major challenge. The best and brightest are not likely to want to serve in the army at a time when the army will be becoming more and more dependent upon technology. Those who do join will be capable of far greater responsibility than in the past, by virtue of their enhanced education and experience, but they will probably not be looking toward a full career in the Army. The so called "sovereign individuals" who are used to instant gratification will not feel comfortable with the training environment and methods which most general officers grew up in. Recruits skilled in the trades will be hard to find, and what remains of the militia will not be able to fill the vacuum.

The effects on training will be significant. Self-paced training, distance learning, virtual experiences, and instantaneous communication from commanders in mission areas will help prepare soldiers for operations more effectively than is possible today. The soldiers will be absorbing the information and seeking out greater authority and responsibility.

Army generals will have to determine the appropriate balance of trades and skills to meet tomorrow's requirements, and will have to determine the separation of responsibilities between officers and non-commissioned officers.

Simulation capabilities will be greatly enhanced with many parts of training being conducted in a virtual reality setting.

SUMMARY OF TRAINING RESPONSIBILITIES OF GENERALS AND FORMATION COMMANDERS

The above discussion clearly points out the importance of training and the role of the general officers and formation commanders in regards to creating the right conditions for effective training, and following through to conduct effective training. In summary, from my observations, study and experience, I have concluded that the responsibilities of generals and formation commanders in training are:

- Create and promulgate the philosophical and doctrinal base for training, i.e., establish the strategic intent and the broad lines of operation to achieve that objective;
- Orient the units and formations by making the desired end-state, both immediate and long-term, absolutely clear;
- Clearly identify, in discussion with subordinates, the center of gravity in training, i.e., that training which is essential to success;
- Articulate the principles of training, i.e., the fundamental thoughts and beliefs. Set out the sequential steps through which the training should progress. Set guidelines concerning the pace and rhythm of the training;
- Develop branch plans for parallel training and sequel plans for the subsequent training or re-training, just in case conditions change;
- Provide the resources, facilities and technology essential to achieving the desired capability, for without the people, time, ammunition, gas, etc., the training will be inadequate;
- Monitor the vital training from the most effective vantage, looking particularly for the indicators of success or failure;
- Stimulate initiative, leader development and teamwork—the three keys to continuous improvement;
- Allow for responsible risk taking, but demand safe practices;
- Have the training evaluated against clear, objective and meaningful standards;

- Insist on accountability for producing results;
- Ensure that there is feedback, at all levels, in the form of after-action reviews and collated lessons learned;
- Acknowledge success and encourage continuous improvement; and
- Ensure that lessons learned are embraced and incorporated, especially with a view toward long-term improvement of all teams.

CONCLUSION

Training is the most important function of an army that is not actively involved in operations. We all have opinions on training because we have all experienced it, yet unless there is one seamless, over-arching and all-inclusive philosophy and a clear strategic plan for the future, then training will be treated as a residual activity—a nice-to-have after all the other commitments are met and after the resources have gone to other activities. Clearly that is not acceptable, and training must be assigned the priority it deserves. Our young men and women who serve in operations and who will be the leaders of tomorrow deserve quality training.

Effective training is the key to success for the future army—no matter what the challenges may be, and that is the responsibility of the generals and formation commanders.

NOTES

1. Lieutenant-General G.G. Simonds, "Commentary and Observations," in Hector J. Massey, ed., *The Canadian Military: A Profile* (Toronto: Copp Clark, 1972), 268.
2. Major-General (retired) H.R. Wheatley, personal correspondence with author, 1999.
3. Lieutenant-Colonel (retired) B.A. Reid, personal correspondence with author, 2000.
4. *Report of Special Review Group Operation Harmony (Rotation Two), Part 3 Recommendations,* httm://www.dnd.ca/menu/press/Reports/harmony_2/index-e.htm.
5. Ibid.
6. Brigadier-General (retired) K. de L. Kirby, "Toward a Systematic Vocational Dialectic/Dialogue/Educational/Training On Ways and Means of Defending Canada By Land," 2000, (Unpublished), 6.
7. *FM 25-100, Training the Force,* Preface, by General Carl E. Vuono, Chief of Staff, United States Army, 15 November, 1988, i.
8. Ibid.
9. John A. English, *The Canadian Army and the Normandy Campaign: A Study of Failure in High Command* (New York: Praeger 1991), 315.
10. *FM 25-100,* and English, 317.
11. *FM 25-100,* British Army Code Number 71630, *The Army Field Manual, Volume 1 Combined Arms Operations, Part 7 Training for Operations,* 1997.
12. Major-General E.A.H. Alderson, *Lessons From 100 Notes Made in Peace and War* (London: Gale and Polden, Ltd., 1908), 31.

13. Ibid, 27.
14. General G.R. Sullivan and Colonel M.V. Harper, *Hope Is Not A Method* (New York: Random House, 1996), 143.
15. Brigadier-General (retired) Ernest B. Beno, "Training to Fight and Win: Training in the Canadian Army", Private printing, Kingston, 1999.
16. English, 315. I strongly recommend the study of Montgomery's aid-memoire, "Some General Notes on What to Look for When Visiting a Unit," which can be found at Appendix A to *The Canadian Army and the Normandy Campaign: Failure in High Command*. I would suggest that those are the very things commanders should be looking for.
17. Brigadier-General (retired) S.V. Radley-Walters, personal correspondence with author, 1999.
18. General Alderson, "Upton Letters": "As I go on in life the thing I desire is simplicity and reality, pose is the one fatal thing." As to say, "A soldier who poses is no better than a ninepin in a skittle alley, and he is as easily knocked over!"
19. Ibid, 27.
20. *The Army Field Manual, Volume 1 Combined Arms Operations, Part 7 Training For Operations*, 1997.
21. English, 130.
22. Alderson, *Lessons Learned from 100 Notes*, 28.
23. Colonel (retired) John Joly, "Coordinating and Managing The Conduct of Exercises," July 2000, unpublished.
24. Major-General (retired) H.R. Wheatley, personal correspondence with author, 1999.

INDEX

A
AAN (Army After Next), 418
AAR (After Action Review), 546–548
Adams, Michael, 203
AIDS, 260
Air Canada, 460
Airborne Regiment, 157
aircraft, 28–29
Alanbrooke, General Chief of the Imperial General Staff (CIGS), 71
Alderson, Major-General E.A.H., 533–534, 540, 544
Alexander the Great, 22–23, 26–27, 34
Allard, General Jean Victor, 146, 486, 492, 508
Alliance Strategic Concept Rome 1991, 224
Allies. *See* coalition warfare
Amanpour, Christiane, 399
Anatomy of Courage. see Moran, Lord
Anderson, Vice-Admiral John, 245–246
Andrews, Commander Stu, 247
Annan, Kofi, 251
AOR (Auxiliary-Oiler-Replenishment) ships, 245
Aristotle, 491
Armilla Patrols (UK), 234
Army Chief of the General Staff, 49
Army Examiners, 43
Army Field Manual, Training for Operations, 541
Art of War. See Machiavelli; Sun-Tzu
artillery, 24, 27
As It Happens. *See* CBC
Atlantic Monthly, 416
Australia, 31
 Collins class submarine, 453
Aviano, Italy, 277
AWACS Canadian air crew, 277
Axis. *See* coalition warfare
Axworthy, Lloyd, 344, 347, 359

B
Bahrain, 235
Balkans, 123, 133, 292, 415, 445
Banff Centre for Management, 495
Barbarossa, 25
Baril, General Maurice, 172, 375, 396
Bass, B.M., 115
Battle of the Atlantic, 366

Battle of the Rhineland, 412
BBC (British Broadcasting Corporation), 403
Belgium, 250
  pull out from Rwanda, 258
Bell, Martin
  BBC reporter, 400
  member of British Parliament, 404
Bennis, W., 112
Bercuson, Professor David, 511
Berlin Wall, 224, 413
Bidwell, Shelford, 44
Binneveld, Hans, 321
Bion, Major W.R., 44
Bland, Douglas, 369
  professor at Queen's University, 429, 433
blitzkrieg, 27
Boer War, 28, 31, 342
Bomber Command, 425
Book of Five Rings. See Musashi, Miyamoto
Boomer, General Walter US Marine Corps, 393
Bosnia Herzegovina, 217, 219, 226–227, 229, 352, 439
Bourne, Peter, 330
Bowman, Dr. Laura, 335
Boyle, General Jean, 365, 368, 374
Breakwell, Glynis
  description of stress, 302, 304
British Commonwealth, 30, 32
British Commonwealth Air Training Plan, 42
British Empire, 32, 123
British Imperial Defence College, 539
British Staff College (Camberley), 197
Brokow, Tom, 407
Brookes, Air Vice Marshal G.M., 364
Burns, Lieutenant-General E.L.M., 71–73, 131, 325, 365, 426
  as Lieutenant-Colonel, 72
Burns, J.M., 115
Burundi, 250
  coup d'état, 26
Bush, President George, 229
Byng, Sir Julian, 364, 411

C
Cadieux, Leo, 221–222
Canadian Airlines International, 460
Canadian Armed Forces integration, 191

Canadian Army Journal, 49
Canadian Charter of Rights and Freedoms, 415
Canadian Defence Quarterly, 76
Canadian Forces College, 503, 515, 516
Canadian Forces Command and Staff College, 190, 488
Canadian Forces Publication, 106–109, 115, 118, 216
Canadian Institute for Security Studies, 233
Canadian Joint Staff, 278
Canadian Journal of Psychiatry. see PTSD
Canadian Officership in the 21st Century, 510
CANFORGEN (Canadian Forces General), 152
CAR structure
  Competency, Authority and Responsibility (CAR), 83
  emotional competency, 84–85
  extrinsic responsibility, 86
  intellectual competency, 84
  interpersonal competency, 85
  intrinsic responsibility, 87
  legal authority, 85
  personal authority, 85
  physical competency, 84
Carolingian wars, 23
Caron, Brigadier-General J.H.P.M., 291
Carthage, 23
Cavalry, 27
CBC (Canadian Broadcasting Corporation), 403
CDS (Chief of Defence Staff), 152, 180, 281
  intent, 287
CEF (Canadian Expeditionary Force), 40–41, 366
CFB Suffield, 193
CFB Trenton, 237
Charles XIII, 19
China, 32
Churchill, Winston, 19, 96
CIC (Citizenship and Immigration Canada), 281
CIS (Critical Incident Stress), 331
CISD (Critical Incident Stress Debriefing Process), 332
Clarke, General Bruce C.
  US Army, 532
Clausewitz, Carl Von, 17–20, 25–27, 32, 35, 361, 409, 414, 418, 468, 533

553

Claxton, Brooke, 140, 369, 438
CLDO (Chief of Land Doctrine and Operation), 191
CMC (Canadian Military College system), 485
CMR (Collège Militaire Royal de St-Jean), 361
CNN, 389–390, 414
coalition warfare, 30–32
Cold War, 33, 58, 123, 129, 133–137, 148, 168–169, 172, 198, 283, 343–344, 349, 412, 432, 444, 450–455, 484
　increased multidimensional missions since, 272
　post-war environment, 275–276
Coleman, Colonel Ralph, 381
Combat Fatigue, 324
Combat Logistics Force, 235
　multi-language communications, 237
Command and Control (C2), 80, 287
　as chain of command, 80
　communications technology, 246–247
Communist, 29
conflict resolution
　as alternative to warfare, 253
　monitor, assist, create and investigate, 259
　moral accountability, 261
conscription, 21, 22, 27, 367–369
　as a divisive force, 58
Cornet, Annie, 192
Crerar, General H.D.C., 44–45, 52–53, 71–75, 325, 364–366, 412
crimes against humanity, 250
Croatia, 292
　contaminated soil allegations, 508
Cross Country Check Up. *See* CBC
Crowe, William J., Jr., 511
Crusades, 23
CSR (Combat Stress Reaction), 331
Cuban Missile Crisis, 134, 369
Culin, Sergeant Curtis G., Jr.
　modified Sherman tank, 411
Currie, Sir Arthur, 364–366, 411
Cyprus, 132, 277

D
D-Day, 327
Dallaire, Lieutenant-General Romeo A., 89, 99–102, 514, 519
　Commander United Nations Assistance Mission for Rwanda, 250

Dark Ages, 23
Dayton Peace Accord, 292–293, 391, 395
DCDS (Deputy Chief of the Defence Staff), 277
　media spokesman, 281, 283, 287
de Chastelain, General John, 244
　Chief of Defence Staff, 233
De Re Militari. *See* Vegetius
debt
　effect of public & personal, 204
Defence Economic Review (1994), 198
Defence Management Committee, 170
Defence Planning Guidance 2000, 345, 456
Defence Stategy 2020, 444–448, 453, 455, 458, 460–461, 474–475, 510
DelegAAT (Delegation of Authority and Accountability Trial), 470, 471
Démocratie oblige, 28
Desert Shield. *See* Gulf War
Desert Storm. *See* Gulf War
Dextraze, General Jacques, 108, 153
　as Chief of Defence Staff, 143–144
　on the Art of Leadership, 149
DFAIT (Department of Foreign Affairs and International Trade)
　participation with media, 281
Diefenbaker, Prime Minister John, 134
　collapse of government, 369
Dieppe, 72, 125
Dill, Howard, 240
Director of Military Training, 48
Directorate of Health Treatment Services, 332
Dixon, Dr. Norman, 195
DLCIS (Directorate Land Communications Information Systems), 191
DMS (Defence Management System), 462
DND (Department of National Defence), 115, 138, 151, 160, 170, 180, 192–199, 204, 275–276, 342, 466, 515
　creation of, 368
　media campaign, 282
　personnel sustainment, 280
Dominican Republic, 31
Doubler, Michael D., 410
Douhet, Giulio, 29
DPC (Defence Planning Committee), 216–218, 226

DPKO (Directorate of Peacekeeping Operations), 310, 508
Drapeau, Michel, 171
DREV (Defence Research Establish Valcartier), 191
Drucker Foundation, 475
Drucker, Peter, 174
DSM-l (American Psychiatric Associations' Diagnostic and Statistical Manual), 329
DSM-ll (American Psychiatric Associations' Diagnostic and Statistical Manual)
　second edition, 329
DSM-lll (American Psychiatric Associations' Diagnostic and Statistical Manual)
　third edition, 330
Dubai, 233
Dunkirk, 322

E
Earle, Edward Mead, 215
East Timor, 276, 342, 352, 356, 439, 445, 456
Eayrs, James, 348
ECS (Environmental Chiefs of Staff), 278, 279
El Cid, 24
EMS (Expenditure Management System), 439, 443, 473, 479
English, Dr. Allan, 333
English, Lieutenant-Colonel Jack, 412, 418
Environmental Chiefs of Staff, 169
ethnic cleansing, 283
EU (European Union), 295
　recognition of Federal Republic of Yugoslavia, 292
Everts, Colonel P.L.E.M., 89
Evraire, Major-General R.J., 486

F
Falklands War, 20, 31, 385
　treatment of veterans, 334
Farley, K.M.
　Canadian Forces Personnel Applied Research Unit, 303
Fenian Raids, 342
FEPP (Force Employment Planning Process), 278, 279
Fifth Discipline: The Art and Practice of the Learning Organization, 536
First World War, 28–30, 40, 42, 125, 364, 411
　shell shock, 321
　Western Front, 29
Fitzgerald, Colonel Edward J., 418–419

Fleet School and Warfare Centre, 235
FMAS (Financial Management and Accounting System), 192
Force Employer
Deputy Chief of the Defence Staff, 277
Force Generators
Environmental Commanders, army, navy, air force, 277
Foster, Harry, 71, 74
Foulkes, Lieutenant-General Charles, 74, 366, 369, 412
France, 31, 33, 39, 216, 227
Operation Turquoise, 251
Franco-Prussian War, 27, 31
Frechette, Louise, 374–375
Frederick the Great, 19, 25, 58, 79
established first staff college, 492
French Imperial regiments, 38
French Revolution, 26–27
Frewer, Colonel Barry, 381
Frost, David, 144
FRY (Former Republic of Yugoslavia), 291
security for KVM, 293
fuel cell technology, 201
Fuller, Major-General J.F.C., 448
FYROM (Former Yugoslav Republic of Macedonia), 291

G
Gal, Reuven, 308
Israeli military psychologist, 303
Ganong, General, 71
Gardner, Brigadier Jim, 221
Geilenkirchen, Germany, 277
General Officer Corps, 168, 172, 482, 490, 497
intellectualism in, 496
Generals. see J.L. Granatstein
Generals Die in Bed, 366
Geneva Convention, 263, 284
intervention for humanitarian reasons, 270
German General Staff (1920/1930)
future as mechanized force, 447–448
Gibb, C.A., 114–115
Glassco Commission, 438
global warming, 202
Gorbachev, Mikhail, 224
Graham, Dominick
biographer of Lieutenant-General Guy Simonds, 328
Graham, Major-General Howard, 49
Granatstein, J.L., 365, 425, 496–498

Great War. *See* First World War
Greco Pizza, 241
Greek, 23
armies of city-states, 22
Gregory, Dr. Robert, 326
Grenada, 31, 385
Grinker, Roy R., 324
Guderion, General, 29
Gulf War, 134, 169, 224, 233–248, 253, 346, 384–385
"Persian Excursion," 233
live television briefings, 389
media coverage, 388
Gustavus Adolphus, 25
Gwatkin, Sir Willoughby, 368

H
Habyarimana, Juvénal, 261
president of Rwanda pre April 1994, 255
Hackett, Sir John, 56
Haiti, 31, 276, 278, 439
Halifax, 233
Naval Dockyard, 234
Hamilton, 96
Hammond, Major J.W., 118
Hanson, Lieutenant-Colonel Fred, 324
Haque, Brigadier-General Ken C.
Deputy Commander of Sector West (Croatia), 508
Harper, Colonel M.V., 534, 536
Harris, Stephen, 41
Hart, Russell A., 412
Haycock, Dr. Ron, 517–518
Hayes, Lieutenant-Commander Jim, 234
Health Canada, 281
Hellyer, Paul, 124–125, 134, 369
Henault, Lieutenant-General Ray
DCDS public affairs briefings, 391, 392
Henderson, Colonel G.F.R.
British Army, 532
Hillen, John, 351, 353
Hitler, 53
HMCS *Athabaskan*, 233, 236, 238, 242, 245, 247–248
as Command Ship, 237
HMCS *Bonaventure*, 363
HMCS *Iroquois*, 236
HMCS *Preserver*
as command ship, 244
HMCS *Protecteur*, 233, 240, 245–248
as destroyer and alternate command ship, 242
HMCS *Provider*, 245

HMCS *Terra Nova*, 233, 245, 247–248
HMCS *Toronto*, 394
Hoffmeister, Major-General Bert, 71–75, 320, 365–366
Holbrooke, Richard, 293
Holloman, C.R., 114
Holocaust, 53
Holy Grail, 44
Homer, 21, 44
Hong Kong, 72, 125
Hope Is Not A Method, 534, 536
Hose, Captain Walter, 364
Howard, Sir Michael, 38, 60, 190
Hughes, Colonel Sam, 50, 70
became minister in 1911, 368
Minister of Militia, 40
Human Genome Project, 335
Hunter, Colonel Ken, 325
Huntington, Samuel, 296
Hussein, Saddam, 387
Hutu, 250
Hyatt, A.M.J., 366
Hyland, Dr. H.H., 319, 320

I
IBM
nanotechnology, 201
ice storm (1997), 439
shortcomings of NDOC, 279
ice-storm (1997), 276
ICRC (International Committee of the Red Cross), 262
ICTR (International Criminal Tribunal for Rwanda), 251, 261–262
ICTY (International Criminal Tribunal for the Former Yugoslavia), 262
IDMF (integrated Defence Management Framework), 479, 480
Ignateiff, Michael, 203
Iliad. See Homer
IM/IT (Management and Information Technology), 191–199, 204
PeopleSoft, 192
IMF (International Monetary Fund), 413
Industrial Revolution, 28
infantry, 22
Internet
media use, 394
Iran, 243
Iran-Iraq disengagement force (1988), 438
Iraq, 235, 237, 246
Izetbegovic, President, 292

J
J-Staff. *See* Canadian Joint Staff
Jacobs, Jane, 194
Jane's Fighting Ships. *See* Richard Sharpe
Japan, 32
　assault on Hong Kong, 72
Jashari, Adem
　massacre of family, 293
Jervis, 25
Jockel, Joseph, 342
Joly, Colonel John, 547
Jomini, Antoine de, 17, 19–20, 25–27
Judd, Deputy Minister (DND) James, 172

K
Kagame, General Paul, 258
　commander RPF, 254–255
Kahn, R.L., 110, 115
Kanungo, 115
Kaplan, Robert D., 416, 511
Katz, D, 110, 115
KDOM (Kosovo Observation Diplomatic Mission), 295
King's Regulations and Orders for the Canadian Militia, 39
King, Larry, 407
King, Prime Minister Mackenzie, 70, 75, 123–124, 355, 366
Kirby, Brigadier-General C. de L. "Kip," 528, 532
Kitchen, Major-General G.C., 486, 516
Kitching, Lieutenant-Colonel George, 54
KLA (Kosovo Liberation Army), 292, 293
Korean War, 31, 47–48, 125, 277, 329, 414, 426, 432
Kosovo, 31, 219, 275–290, 283, 342, 352, 439, 445, 455
　Air Campaign, 276, 279, 284, 285, 356
　Democratic League of Kosovo, 292
　expulsion of Albanians, 283
　refugees cared for in Canada, 277
　refugees, involvement of officials, 281
Kotter, J.P., 111–112
KVM (Kosovo Verification Mission), 277, 291–294, 299
　a civilian operation, 297

L
L'Academie des Nobles. *See* Frederick the Great

Lahr, Germany, 221
Lake, Sir Percy, 368
Lamontagne, Gilles
　Minister of National Defence, 365
Last, Major David, 510
Laws of Armed Conflict, 285
Leach, Lieutenant-General Bill, 362
Leaderless Group Test. *See* Bion, Major W.R.
Lessons From 100 Notes Made in Peace and War. *See* Major-General E.A.H. Alderson
LFCCIS (Land Force Command Control Information System), 191
Liddell-Hart, B.H., 19
Lifton, Robert, 330
Lightburn, Colonel D.L., 486
Lind, William S., 419, 420
Link trainer, 42
LLAD (Low Level Air Defence), 450
LPK *(Leizja Popullore e Kosoves)*
　Popular Movement for Kosovo, 292
Luxembourg, 19

M
MacArthur, General Douglas, 96
Macdonald, Angus L., 366
MacDonald, Donald S., 369
Machiavelli, 19, 24, 58
MacKenzie, Major-General Lewis W., 399
MacKinnon, Alan, 369
Maclean's
　sexual assault investigation, 508
Mahan, Admiral, 26
Mai Lai massacre, 330
Maillet, Colonel Paul
　Director of Defence Ethics, 156
Malone, Lieutenant-Colonel Richard S., 386
Mamelukes, 27
Maneuver Warfare Handbook. *See* William S. Lind
Manitoba Floods (1998), 276, 439
Manning Doyle, Dr. Arthur, 324–325
Manske, F.A., Jr., 112
Maple Leaf, 377, 386, 396–397
MARCOT, 441
MARLANT HQ, 197
Marlborough, 19, 25
Marsh, Colonel Howie, 510, 518
Marshall, General George C., 410, 411
　US Army, 370
Massey, Vincent
　Canadian High Commissioner, 73

Mastanduno, Michael, 346
Mathews, Bruce, 71, 74
Matthews, Major-General Bert, 365
McAndrews, Bill, 325
McCafferty, Master-Corporal Pat "Rat," 240
McClean, Captain Doug, 240, 247–248
MCCRT (Management Command and Control Reengineering Team), 169–170, 175, 192, 439, 450, 471
McDermott, Major J., 113, 119
McEwan, Air Vice-Marshal C.M., 364
MCF (Main Contingency Force), 354, 355
McLuhan, Marshall, 191
McNaughton, Major-General Andrew G.L., 73, 369
　command of 1st Canadian Infantry Division, 70–71
McWha, Lieutenant-Colonel, 240
　Task Group Air Commander, 245
media, 262, 279, 311–312, 379, 383–397, 427, 428, 431
　CNN immediate updates, 266
　demand for information, 280, 281, 282
　information age, 276
　information operations, 286
　Second Front, 238
　ships' company interviews, 241
　to spur international participation, 271
Meigs, Lieutenant-General Montgomery C., PhD., 418, 419
Members of Parliament
　demand for information, 282–283
Men Under Stress. *See* Roy R. Grinker
Mendonca, 115
merchant marine, 29
Metallurgy, 24
Microprocessor
　future effects of, 200
Middleton, Major-General Sir Fred, 365
military schools, 492
Militia Staff Course (MSC), 70
Miller, Rear-Admiral D.E., 247
Milner, Marc, 367
Milosevic, President, 283, 292, 293
　denied media access, 388
MINCON (Supply System), 192
Mintzberg, Henry, 192
Montcalm, 25
Montecuccoli, 19, 25

Montgomery, Field Marshall Bernard, 30, 73, 366, 393, 531, 538
  as Lieutenant-General, 71–72
  forward psychiatric units, 323
Moran, Lord, 35, 370
Morton, Desmond, 41
MR (Miscellaneous Requirement), 191–192, 201
Mulock, Wing Commander R.H., 364
Murchie, Lieutenant-General J.C., 75
Murphy, Commandant Michael, 51
Murray, Rear-Admiral L.W., 364, 366, 374, 375
Musashi, Miyamoto, 468
Myers Briggs personality test, 196, 518

N
NAC (North Atlantic Council), 216–218, 225–227
NAC C (North Atlantic Cooperation Council), 224
Nanus, B., 112
Napoleon, 26–27, 34, 58
  revolutionary or evolutionary, 57
National Defence College, 485, 487
NATO (North Atlantic Treaty Organization), 33, 47–48, 125–134, 169, 214–222, 228, 235, 246, 271, 277–281, 311, 342, 349, 424–426, 432, 441, 454, 484
  bombing campaign in Kosovo, 294
  civilian International Staff (IS), 219
  defence capability, 445
  first peace implemented in Bosnia Herzegovina, 229
  IFOR (Implementaion Force Bosnia), 385
  Immediate Reaction Force, 354–356
  International Military Staff (IMF), 219
  media access, 388
  public affairs plan, 391
  Standing Naval Force Atlantic, 236
  Supreme Allied Commander Atlantic (SACLANT), 219
  Supreme Allied Commander in Europe (SACEUR), 219
  target assignment, 285
NBC (nuclear-biological-chemical) defence capability, 243

NDCC (National Defence Command Centre, 279, 288
NDHQ (National Defence Headquarters), 134, 277–279, 287, 369, 429, 470, 477
NDOC (National Defence Operations Centre), 279
Nelson, Admiral Horatio, 25, 28, 34
New France, 39, 411
New Zealand, 31
  Defence Force, 456
  Maori battalion, 323
NGOs (non-governmental organizations), 253, 258, 264–265, 305, 423, 443, 509
Nobel Prize for Peace, 125
Non Permanent Active Militia (NPAM), 69–70
NORAD (North American Air Defence Command), 125, 127, 130–132, 235, 426, 432, 441, 484
Normandy, 46, 74
Northwest Passage
  sovereignty of, 203
NP (National Procurement), 446, 447
NPR (National Public Radio), 402–403
nuclear weapons, 29, 31
Nye, Joseph, 347

O
O'Brien, Dr. L. Stephen, 334–335
OCS (Officer Candidate School), 49
Odlum, Major-General Victor, 70
Officer Professional Development 2020, 487
Ogdensburg Agreement 1940, 440
Oka insurrection, 252, 278, 439
On War. See Clausewitz
Ontario Hydro, 201–202
OOTW (Operations Other Than War), 132, 353, 414
OPDC (Officer Professional Development Council), 515
Operation (OP) Bandit, 278
Operation Friction, 233, 234
Operation Totalize, 455
Operation Turquoise, 254
Operational Art, 214
Order-in-Council (27 June 1946) created brigade group structure, 190
Organization of American States, 31
OSCE (Organization for Security and Co-operation in Europe), 226, 277, 291–294
  all members fluent in english, 298
Ottawa, 133

P
Panama, 31
Patton, General George S., 30, 324, 410
Pax Britannica, 28
PDD 25 (US Presidential Decision Directive 25), 254
Peacekeeping Stress, 304
Pearkes, General George
  Victoria Cross winner, 71
Pearson Peacekeeping Centre Press, 233
Pearson, Prime Minister Lester B., 125, 426
Pentagon, 346
Permanent Force (PF), 69–70
Persian Excursion. See Canadian Institute for Security Studies
Persian Gulf War, 31, 233, 276, 278, 285, 439
  global conflict as spectator sport, 280
  harassment of families in Canada, 282
Personnel Selection history, 46
Personnel Selection Officers. *See* Army Examiners
Peter the Great, 25
PGM (Precision Guided Munitions). *See* weapons
phantom forces 201
Philip of Macedon, 22, 26
Pickford, Commander John, 247
Plato, 19, 491
Plutarch, 22
Poland, 32
Polish Lancers, 27
political/military interface, 214
Pope, Lieutenant-General Maurice, 369
Potts, General, 71
Praetorian Guard, 59
Preparing for Critical Incident Stress. See Directorate of Health Treatment Services
Price, Major-General Basil, 70–71
professional officers, 22–26
propaganda, 26
psychologists, 42
PTSD (post-traumatic stress disorder), 321, 330–332
  as an injury, 268
  Israeli veterans, experience, 335
  more prevalent in conflict resolution, 267

Q
Quinn, Bob, 381

R
Radley-Walters, Brigadier-General S.V., 538
RAF (Royal Air Force), 42, 364
Ralston, Colonel J.L., 75, 386
RAP (Regimental Aid Post), 326
Rather, Dan, 407
Raymond, Corporal Dixon, 38
RCAF (Royal Canadian Air Force), 42, 425–426
RCN (Royal Canadian Navy), 364, 425–426
  weapons innovation, 455
Red Cross, 281
Reid, Lieutenant-Colonel B.A., 523
Reimer, General Dennis M., 370
Renaissance, 23, 24, 33
Report of the Officer Development Board. See Major-General Roger Rowley
Report on Plans and Priorities, 452
Republic. See Plato
research & development, 199–200
Reynolds, Captain Eric T., 417
Richardson, Dr. J.C., 320
RMA (Revolution in Military Affairs), 57, 276, 357, 370, 458, 478, 511
RMC (Royal Military College), 39, 48, 54–55, 70, 72, 162, 192, 194, 205, 362, 485, 488, 496, 499, 509, 511–518
  correspondence courses, 526, 540
  War Studies graduate degree, 503
Roberts, Major-General J.H.
  scapegoat for Dieppe, 72
Robertson, General Lord, 342
Rockingham, Major-General J.M., 48
ROE (Rules of Engagement), 251–252, 270, 285, 287
Rogers, General Bernard
  SACEUR, 222
Roman legion, 23
Rose, General Sir Michael, 296
Rost, J.C., 111, 114–115
Rowley Report (1969). *See* Major-General Roger Rowley
Rowley, Major-General Roger, 145–146, 485–487, 492
Royal Military Academy, 156
Royal Navy, 29
RPF (Rwandan Patriotic Front), 250–254
Rugova, Ibrahim, 292
Russo-Japanese War, 28, 32
Rwanda, 89, 99–102, 133, 254, 439
  government of, 250
  massacre of Belgian soldiers, 250
  massacre of civilians, 250

S
Saguenay Flood (1996), 439
Saigon, 31
Salmon, Major-General, 72
Sandhurst. *See* Royal Military Academy
Sarajevo, 395
Sargant, Dr. William, 322, 324
Scherber, Commander Frank, 247
Schwartzkopf, General Norman, 144, 393, 396
SCONDVA (Standing Committee on National Defence and Veterans Affairs), 477
SCOPA (Standing Committee on Public Accounts), 480
SCUD missiles, 235
Sea Control, 243–244
Sea King helicopters, 240, 245
Sea Sparrow Anti-Aircraft Missile, 236
Second World War, 30–42, 125–128, 235, 320, 364, 369, 424
  Battle of Normandy, 411
  Canadian army general officers, 69
  D-Day media coverage, 389
  German unit training, 530
  Italian Campaign media, 386
  United States Army, 410
Senge, Peter, 536
Sex in the Snow. See Adams, Michael
Shalikashvili, General John
  Partnership for Peace (PfP), 224–225
Sharp, Mitchell, 221
Sharpe, Brigadier-General Joe, 524–525
Sharpe, Richard, 342
Shatan, Dr. Chaim, 330
Simonds, Major-General Guy, 71–73, 327–328, 365–366, 412, 455, 521
  in Sicily, 72
Slater, Dr. Elliot, 322
Slim, Field Marshal Sir William, 51, 119
Socrates, 38, 491
Somalia, 94, 125, 132–134, 157, 165, 276, 375, 384, 439, 508
  Inquiry, 378, 427, 485
  murder of civilians, 373
  naval command support, 244
  US pull out, 258
South Africa, 39
Spacie, Keith
  description of stress, 302, 304

SPQR (Special personnel qualification requirement), 500
Spry, Dan, 71, 74
Srebrenica, 89
  fall of, 229
Stacey, Colonel Charles, 46
STANAVFORLANT, 277, 279
stealth technology, 285
Stokesbury, James, 54
strategos, 18
  as societies leaders, 491
strategy, 18, 20
Strategy for 2020, 151
Stuart, Lieutenant-General Kenneth, 75, 367, 369
Studt, Colonel John C., 419
submarines, 29–30, 243
Suez Crisis, 31, 426
Sullivan, General Gordon R., 534, 536
  Chief of Staff (US Army), 184
Summers, Commodore Ken, 389
  public affairs plan, 390
Sun-Tzu, 19–20, 34, 468
Superpowers Don't Do Windows. See John Hillen

T
Tadjman, President, 292
Tanker War, 234
Taymon, Scott, 381
TCCCS (Tactical Command Control Communications System), 191
Telegraph, 28
TEWTS (Tactical Exercises Without Troops), 539–540
Thirty Years' War, 25
Thucydides, 19, 20
Tobruk
  Australian forces, 323
Toffler, Alvin and Heidi, 475
Top Gun
  Canada/United States Fighter Jet Competition, 377
Tourville, 25
Transformation of War. See van Creveld, Martin
Tremblay, Anne, 381
trench warfare, 28–29
Troy, 24. *See also* Homer
Trudeau, Prime Minister Pierre Elliot, 124, 369
  decision to reduce European forces, 221, 222
Turenne, 19, 25
Twagiramunga, Prime Minister Faustin, 99, 256

U

UAN (University After Next), 418
UCK (Ushtria Clirimtare e Kosoves). *See* KLA
UN (United Nations), 31, 123, 126–133, 224–228, 270–271, 277, 306–307, 426
  peace operations, 484
  peacekeeping, 424
  Security Council, 217, 250, 400
  Security Council mandate for Rwanda, 260
  Standby or Standing High Readiness Brigade, 354
UNAMIR (United Nations Mission for Rwanda), 99, 250, 254–255, 258, 262, 265
UNAMIR ll (United Nations Mission for Rwanda) post massacre, 251
UNEF (United Nations Emergency Force), 427
Union of Soviet Socialist Republics, 30–31, 32, 137, 169
  ceases to exist, 224
  German invasion 1941, 456
United Kingdom, 33
United States Army and Army Air Force
  approach to psychiatric units, 323–324
United States of America, 30–33, 42, 48
  Civil War, 27, 58
  leading technological development, 286
  Permanent Joint Board on Defence, 76
University of Syracuse, 200
University of Texas
  synthetic life forms, 202
UNMIK (United Nations Mission in Kosovo) replaced KVM, 294
UNPROFOR (United Nations Protection Force), 217, 302, 308–310, 394, 508–509
Urquhart, Sir Brian, 350
USA National Security Act of 1947, 204
  modification to, 203
Uwiliyingimana, Agathe Prime Minister of Rwanda, 255

V

V-1 rocket, 30
van Creveld, Martin, 21
  doctrine for conflict resolution, 253

VCF (Vanguard Contingency Force), 354, 355
Vegetius, 24
Victoria Cross, 71
Victoria, Queen, 365
Vietnam Veterans Against the War, 330
Vietnam War, 31–33, 215, 329–330, 384, 419
  media coverage, 387
Vision 97, 169–170
Vokes, Major-General Chris, 72–73, 325, 365–366
Voltaire, 59
Vuono, General Carl E., 529

W

Walker, Ambassador William, 294, 297
Wallenstein, 25
War of 1812, 39
Warrior's Honour. See Ignateiff, Michael
Warsaw Pact, 137
Washington D.C., 31
Watson, Colonel M.C., 327
weapons of war, 28
  Armoured Personnel Carrier (APC), 474
  Avro Arrow, 438
  Bren Gun Carrier, 455
  CF-18 fighter aircraft, 277, 284
  contributing to the demise of governments, 438
  Coyote reconnaissance vehicle, 445, 448, 455, 474
  Electro-optic reconnaissance vehicle, 448
  F-86, 362
  Halifax Class frigates, 445, 474
  Harpoon missile, 242
  Leopard Tank, 343, 454, 474
  Light Armoured Vehicle (LAV lll), 4474
  PGM (Precision Guided Munitions), 284–285, 287, 445
  Phalanx Close-in System, 242
  Ross Rifle, 438
  Self-propelled Gun M109, 474
  shipborne helicopters, 438
  Target Acquisition Griffon Helicopter, 448, 474
Wehrmacht, 42, 74, 411
Welsh, Jack
  General Electric CEO, 199
WES (Weapons Effect Simulation), 535, 548

WEU (Western European Union), 228
  as European security and defence identity, 225
Wheatly, Major-General H.R., 522, 548
White Paper, 375
  1986, 148
  1987, 49, 343
  1994, 169, 231, 355, 439, 470
  Hellyer on defence 1964, 438
Withers, General Ramsay, 365, 430
Wittgenstein, l., 87
Wolseley, Field Marshal Viscount, 342, 543
women
  in combat role, 242
  in military role, 32
  in the labour force, 29
World Bank, 413
World Trade Organization, 413

Y

Year 2000 contingency operation, 439
Young, Doug, 496
Yugoslavia
  accountability for actions of armed forces, 261
  campaign against, 346
Yukl, G., 114

Z

Zaire, 133, 439, 510
Zaleznik, A, 110
Zimmerman, David, 367

ABOUT THE EDITORS

LIEUTENANT-COLONEL BERND HORN received his Honours BA in Political Science from the University of Waterloo and his MA and PhD in War Studies from the Royal Military College, Kingston. He joined the Canadian Forces in 1983 as an infantry officer in the Royal Canadian Regiment. His regimental service included operational tours to both Cyprus and Bosnia. He has also served in the Canadian Airborne Regiment, as well as a variety of staff positions at National Defence Headquarters in Ottawa. He currently teaches military history at the Royal Military College, and lives in Kingston, Ontario.

STEVE HARRIS was born in Toronto in 1948, and educated in Burlington, Ontario. He received his MA in history from McMaster University in 1970, and then spent four years teaching military history at the Canadian Forces College Extension School, Toronto. He began his doctoral studies at Duke University, Durham, North Carolina in 1975, and completed them in 1979. Dr. Harris joined the staff of the then Directorate of History (now History and Heritage), National Defence Headquarters, in 1978. He is currently the chief historian at the Directorate and lives in Ottawa, Ontario.